Contemporary Movements
and Ideologies

Contemporary Movements and Ideologies

Roberta Garner

DePaul University, Chicago

McGraw-Hill, Inc.

New York   St. Louis   San Francisco   Auckland   Bogotá   Caracas   Lisbon
London   Madrid   Mexico City   Milan   Montreal   New Delhi
San Juan   Singapore   Sydney   Tokyo   Toronto

This book was set in Palatino by York Graphic Services, Inc.
The editors were Jill S. Gordon and Larry Goldberg;
the production supervisor was Denise L. Puryear.
The cover was designed by Delgado Design.
R. R. Donnelley & Sons Company was printer and binder.

Photo Credits

Pages 2 and 9: Bettmann   *Page 10:* AP/Wide World   *Page 37:* Bettman   *Page 40:* AP/Wide World   *Pages 65 and 68:* Bettmann   *Pages 81 and 84:* AP/Wide World   *Pages 103, 108, 128, 130, 152, 154, and 191:* Bettmann   *Pages 194 and 229:* AP/Wide World   *Pages 232, 267, and 270:* Bettmann   *Page 301:* Stern/Black Star   *Page 304:* Black Star   *Page 336:* Bettmann   *Pages 338, 360, 364, and 398:* AP/Wide World

CONTEMPORARY MOVEMENTS AND IDEOLOGIES

This book is printed on acid-free paper.

1 2 3 4 5 6 7 8 9 0   DOC   DOC   9 0 9 8 7 6 5

ISBN 0-07-022900-7

Library of Congress Cataloging-in-Publication Data

Garner, Roberta.
    Contemporary movements and ideologies / Roberta Garner.
        p.   cm.
    Includes bibliographical references and index.
    ISBN 0-07-022900-7
    1. Social movements.   2. Ideology.   3. Social change.
    4. Collective behavior.   I. Title.
    HN17.5.G364   1996
    303.48′4—dc20   95-16727

About the Author

Roberta Garner is a professor of sociology at DePaul University. She teaches in the international studies and women's studies programs and has served as faculty director of the university's foreign study programs in Hungary, Mexico, and Italy. She received her A.B., A.M., and Ph.D. degrees from the University of Chicago. Her areas of interest include social movements, sociological theory, and comparative political sociology. She is the author of two books, *Social Movements in America* (Markham, 1972; Rand-McNally, 1972 and 1977) and *Social Change* (Rand-McNally, 1977). Among her articles on social movements are two with Mayer Zald, "Social Movement Organizations" (1966), which contributed to a major theoretical shift in the social movement field, and "The Political Economy of Social Movement Sectors" (1985). The Italian Communist Party and European sociopolitical systems are the topics of several articles she published with Larry Garner. In 1994, her article "Transnational Movements in Postmodern Society" appeared in the *Peace Review*.

For Henry and Morris,
in memory.

Contents

Part Two
THE MOVEMENTS

Chapter Thirteen   Green Warriors, Green Lobbyists   339

Part Three
CONCLUSIONS

Chapter Fourteen   Making History   365

Preface

I have written this book in the hope that it will "open the conversation" for readers interested in contemporary political and social movements. It is an introduction to the topic—it is not meant to be the definitive statement about any of these movements, but is offered to stimulate further exploration. The topic is timely: Many of these movements are given daily coverage in the media, often in stereotyped slogans—"the failure of socialism," "Islamic terrorists," "militant feminists." I would like readers to question these labels and to seek out more in-depth information for themselves; my book is designed to start the process of inquiry.

I have selected movements that fit three criteria. They have a role in contemporary history, in the events of the twentieth century and, especially, its last decades, and there is reason to believe that they will continue to have an impact. They have a vision of a transformed society and are not merely aimed at a limited and pragmatic goal. They are international and transcultural in scope, spanning several nations and cultures.

For each type of movement, I have combined major variants, since movements have different forms in different times and places. This "lumping" may disturb some readers; it is designed as a starting point for discussion, not as a fixed and undebatable set of categories.

I have summed up the essentials of each ideology and emphasized its coherence as a vision of an alternative society. I have provided short discussions of the historical circumstances in which each movement emerged and developed, since I believe historical analyses are crucial to understanding movements. In summarizing the ideologies I have often taken the viewpoint of the "insider," or participant. In analyzing the historical conditions I have taken the viewpoint of the "outsider," the objective observer. I think both perspectives are important for understanding a movement; yet I realize that in an age of deconstruction, some readers will question whether such a dual discourse is possible at all and will deny that the ideologue's "inside" can be distinguished from the objective observer's "outside." I welcome this line of questioning and hope you will keep it in mind as you read. Questioning the text is in accord with my aim to make this book the beginning and not the end to engagement with the topic of movements and ideologies.

I briefly analyze characteristics of movements such as organization, resource mobilization, and strategy; these characteristics have been covered in more detail for each movement in other sources, listed in the Bibliography. These are the means that movements use to mobilize support and accomplish their ends, the transformation of society. In my view, it is their ends—their visions of society—that differentiate them and give each movement a unique character. Once again, I am aware that this statement will disturb some readers, and once again I welcome the challenge.

Writing a book is an act of magic. The author places words in a rigidly linear order—like pearls on a string—and puts the string in a small container, the physical book; this object then purports to show reality to the reader who opens it and looks into it. Writing about ideologies is a particularly flamboyant act of illusion; the book does not purport to contain reality, but irreality, visions of alternatives to the here and now, images of what is not and perhaps cannot be. Keep your imagination with you as you enter this world.

The recommendation to keep your imagination on hand is especially important for the pictures and chapter opening quotations. Selecting and captioning the pictures was an intense and disturbing experience for me; each picture seemed to require a thousand words of explanation. Edward Said comments: "When photographs or texts are used merely to establish identity and presence—to give us merely representative images of *the* Woman, or *the* Indian— they enter . . . a control system." I have tried to make the pictures function in the opposite way—to be looked at "against the text" as sources of ambiguity and tension that suggest the possibility of multiple interpretations. I hope that the chapter opening quotes will also lead the reader to look at some familiar words in new ways within new contexts; sometimes I have even used the quotation to create challenges to the chapter contents. All this material is not to be seen as simple illustration or confirmation of the text, nor as reaffirmation of conventional wisdom, but as openings into many ways of looking at movements.

ACKNOWLEDGMENTS

I would like to thank all the students in my international movements and nationalism classes at DePaul University in 1990, 1991, 1993, and 1994. They not only had to contend with reading early drafts of this material but made major contributions to it. I would like to recognize two individuals in this lively and hard-working group: Angel DeJuan, who single-handedly put together an outline for liberation theology and Greg Schelonka who took the lead in organizing the report on the Christian Democrats.

Special thanks go to colleagues at DePaul: Ted Manley, who led me to see the compatibility of conflict and interactionist perspectives; Chuck Suchar, John Koval, and Noel Barker for just being there; Bob Rotenberg, who offered me the opportunity to teach the course; Ken Fidel for explaining bazookas and rocket launchers; Beth Kelly for knowing so much and sharing it with me; Deena Weinstein for saving my Bibliography from becoming roadkill on the information superhighway; Glovenia Gilton and Latricia S. Runles for helping me turn ideas into hard copy. Like so many of us at DePaul, I remember Joe Baker's generosity with time and energy—you are still with us, in our hearts.

This project would not have been possible without Jill Gordon, sponsoring editor at McGraw-Hill. Becky Kohn guided me in improving the book's reader-friendliness, and Terry Baker encouraged me to "keep revising." The patience, acuity, and responsiveness of Larry Goldberg and Gretlyn Cline made the production process exciting and rewarding. Special thanks go to my mother, Renée, who cheerfully shared my task of proofreading. Anne Manning, the photo editor, came up with a wonderful set of pictures—I wish there were room for all of them. The following reviewers for McGraw-Hill made enormously valuable suggestions for revisions: Patricia Atchison, Colorado State University; Jeff Haydu, University of California–San Diego; Ken Kusterer, The American University; Jill Quadagno, The Florida State University; David R. Simon, University of California–Berkeley; Randy Stoecker, University of Toledo; Ronald Weitzer, George Washington University; and Mayer Zald, University of Michigan. As always, Mayer Zald made me feel that writing about social movements is like coming home.

And, of course, thanks to Larry, Michael, and Julia.

Roberta Garner

Contemporary Movements
and Ideologies

PART ONE

Understanding Movements

Founding Fathers: The signing of the
Declaration of Independence.
Philadelphia, July 4, 1776.

CHAPTER 1

Introduction

Entering the Conversation

Since we will be together for many pages, maybe you should know a little about me and about how I came to write on social movements.

I am a child of the Battle of Stalingrad, born 9 months after the Soviet victory over Nazi Germany, the turning point of the Second World War, when it became clear to the whole world that the Allies would win. I grew up in a Big Ten college town where my father was a professor of modern languages and linguistics. He came of age in Germany during World War I, the revolution at the end of the war, the turmoil of the Weimar Republic, and Hitler's rise to power; he had his fill of movements and conveyed to his family an attitude of skepticism toward political enthusiasms. This attitude was reinforced by my mother's gentle conservatism, perhaps reflecting her traditional childhood as a Greek landowner's daughter.

In high school, I decided that I was a member of the Beat Generation: I wore black and hung out in the darkest, smokiest part of the university student center. In 1960, at the age of 16, I set off for the University of Chicago—a good place for a rebellious girl! My adolescent world expanded at the same moment that the larger political world opened up to Jack Kennedy and the Civil Rights Movement. Federal money flowed to math, science, and the social sciences. My new boyfriend—a mathematician—and I saw a secure future unfolding for us in graduate school and university careers. My wedding picture in 1962 shows me as an 18-year-old bride in a stiff white dress and white pumps, my Jackie Kennedy-style bouffant hairdo carefully sprayed into place.

From then on I was on the roller coaster ride of the Baby-Boom Generation from Kennedy's assassination in 1963 to the fall of Saigon in 1975. Growing up, with all of its normal uncertainty, coincided with a war, political uncertainty, cultural vertigo, and collective mood swings that soared and plunged among euphoria, despair, imagination, hope, rage, and paranoia. We made choices about sex, marriage, children, and occupations in a climate of unpredictable change, amid the accelerating freakiness of the counterculture. I was present at two of the major campus revolts, at Columbia University in New York in 1968 and at the University of Chicago in 1970; I was already a junior faculty member, and this role, along with my own disposition—studious, skeptical, ironic, cautious—kept me at the sidelines of these events, although I was stirred by the utopian visions of the activists. I was involved in the movement against the war in Vietnam and participated in a number of the enormous marches in New York and Washington. I believe the movement contributed to the United States' disengagement from a pointless war, unfortunately not soon enough to save 58,000 Americans and three million Vietnamese, Cambodians, and Laotians. Contrary to misrepresentations that were later circulated, the vast majority of the antiwar movement was not indifferent or hostile to the fate of those in the United States services; my brother's best friend died in Vietnam, and I believe this was a typical and not an unusual situation. Other people I knew at this time died under different circumstances—of overdoses or in explosions of clumsily assembled homemade bombs that claimed the vulnerable, the innocent, and the impulsive. "Dreams die hard."

Even so, those years were usually lively and carefree. My house in Chicago became a hangout for a crowd of blues piano players, rock vocalists, artists, mathematicians, computer scientists, anarchists, dreamers, and idlers. We had many projects, one of which was "Computers for the People"—a collective devoted to turning esoteric technology into a mass convenience—which certainly happened in the following 20 years, but not in the political way in which we had envisioned it. The house swarmed with activity and seemed to us to be the future in microcosm, a world of racial harmony, creativity, and imagination, in which everybody had a strange and wonderful story.

In the spring of 1975, the last helicopters left the roof of the American Embassy in Saigon, and the war in Vietnam ended. A few weeks later, I left the house on Webster Street. The nation settled down to the Ford administration, and I settled down to a university career and a family; but a more conservative way of life did not have to mean being frozen by the big chill of yuppiedom.

Throughout the 1980s I was active in the Organization in Solidarity with the People of Guatemala. The organization is part of the larger movement to support human rights and democracy in Central America; it draws attention to the magnitude of repression in Guatemala, where the military is responsible for over 40,000 "disappeared," the bombing of Maya villages in the early 1980s, and the destruction of unions, peasant cooperatives, and Christian base communities. My university, with its commitment to social justice and human rights, supported and sustained my involvement.

Amid the political turmoil of the 1960s and 1970s, I began to write about social movements. My first article grew out of an essay exam question that I had opted to write in graduate school. My professor, Mayer Zald, liked what he saw in the blue book, and together we published an article that contributed to a shift in the field of social movements. This article led to a contract to write a book; it was a history of social movements in the United States, influenced by my growing interest in marxist thought. Later, Larry Garner and I wrote a number of articles about Italian politics and the dilemmas faced by the Italian Communist Party; we lived for extended periods of time in Italy (at the height of Red Brigade terrorism), Mexico, and Hungary as it began its transition toward a market economy.

This is only a capsule autobiography, but I think it gives a sense of how I am involved in movements and, yet, somewhat detached from them, an activist and an observer at the same time. It also gives you a sense of how the personal and the political intertwine, how biography and history connect to each other, how each person's life is lived out within specific historical moments—"the times"—that are shaped by movements, geopolitics, and cultural trends (Katz, 1992).

INTRODUCTION

The purpose of this book is to present an outline for the study of social movements and familiarize the reader with a number of movements that have had a role in contemporary history. The book provides a basic vocabulary for "entering a conversation" about movements and ideologies. By this phrase I mean that the reader will know enough about specific contemporary movements and ideologies to be prepared for critical reading and viewing of news media; for upper-level college courses in political science, political sociology, and international studies; and for the informed dialogue and debate that are part of being a citizen. The topic of movements and ideologies is necessarily a contentious one; movements challenge existing institutions and are in conflict and competition with one another. Often fine distinctions of wording hide great differences in goals. Ideologies with names that sound similar (for instance, "liberation theology" and "libertarians") may be totally different, even diametrically opposed to each other. For this reason, a guidebook is helpful; think of it as a traveler's guide to the world of movements and ideologies. It is an introduction to the topic; it provides an overview and a general orientation so that you can read and discuss more detailed and complicated texts with confidence.

FORMAT AND BASIC PREMISES

The format is quite simple. Part One presents a framework that can be used to discuss all social and political movements. The terms are widely used in sociology and political science. The framework points to the different dimensions of movements—the different kinds of characteristics that can be used to describe a movement and to distinguish one movement from another. Chapter 2 introduces the basic terms and definitions.

Chapter 3 summarizes the major current theories of social movements, ways of explaining the rise and actions of social movements. Frankly, I am rather eclectic in my use of theories as both useful and limited. Movements are understood more clearly if several theories are considered together to explain the origins, forms, and outcomes of each movement. So, in chapters on individual movements, a number of theories are brought together.

Chapter 4 looks at the complex relationship among movements, societies, and states. Many movements try to use the state (or government) to change societies. Chapter 4 draws attention to these efforts and discusses some of the difficulties movements experience in trying to change societies.

Chapter 5 presents some background on modern societies; it defines the term modern, discusses how the major transnational movements are responses to modern society, and concludes by asking whether we have moved into a postmodern historical period that is giving rise to new forms of social movements.

Having established this analytical framework, I define and describe each movement in terms of the framework and the following goals:

Fair and Coherent Summaries of Ideologies. I want to be as fair and neutral as possible in my wording. I try to avoid being an advocate for some movements and an opponent of others, and to present a coherent and intelligent summary of each movement's ideas. There are two movements and ideologies to which I feel close: Liberalism in its many varieties, including movements for civil rights, human rights, and democracy; and socialism, especially through the perspective of marxism. Feminism has influenced my outlook on societal issues, and so has conservative thought, especially the conservative organicism of Edmund Burke. There are movements and ideologies that I find repulsive—fascism, Nazism, and all forms of ethno-racism—or very different from my own way of thinking—religious funda-mentalism, for instance. I think a coherent rendering of an ideology is use-ful. Most of these movements have or had millions of followers and have persisted for some time, so it is necessary to understand the depth and com-plexity of their appeal.

Current Terminology. Current terminology in mainstream sociology and political science is used. I do not always agree with these perspectives, but I think the reader is served by a fairly standard vocabulary. When I see a great discrepancy between the terminology of the disciplines and what I consider to be the best formulation of a concept, I explain why there is dis-agreement over usage.

Recognition of Differing Perspectives. Differences in the definition and inter-pretation of movements are indicated. There is controversy about the defi-nitions and history of movements among sociologists, political scientists, historians, journalists, and activists themselves. I try to familiarize the reader with such controversies; in some cases, the controversy is much too large and complex to be fully explored in an introduction to the field. Ref-erences are provided that develop the issues in more detail.

Movements are contentious, and almost everything that can be said about movements is also contentious. In writing an introductory book there is always a temptation to present conclusions in a simple, one-dimensional way; I have tried to do the opposite, to present controversies and multiple points of view, even if this approach sometimes leaves ques-tions unsettled.

"Lumping" rather than "Splitting." Since movements are concerned with ideas and words, they often make fine distinctions in their conceptualiza-tions and split organizationally over these fine points. *What is* is single and simple; *what could be* or *what should be* is almost infinite in its possibilities. Since movements are attuned to the *could* and *should* in the world, they look toward multiple competing possibilities that easily fragment the unity of the movement. To the outsider, these controversies look like "hairsplitting."

As a person keenly interested in ideas, I appreciate the tendency to fight over words; small shades of meaning in a text point to vast differences in visions and practices—as an intellectual, I am inherently a "splitter." But as the writer of an introduction to the subject of movements, I have to "lump," identifying broad categories of related movements and then treating these movements together for the purpose of brevity and simplicity. So I empha-size similarities within large categories of movements rather than differ-ences among them, even at the risk of oversimplifying. The reader is en-couraged to look at the bibliographical suggestions for much more nuanced and differentiated treatment of movements within each category.

The Choice of Movements

Sociopolitical Movements   Which movements have I selected for this volume? I have tended to choose movements that are societal and/or political in nature. By these terms I mean the following: The movements in this book have as their goal the *transformation of a whole society* and many of them use *political means* to bring about such a transformation. That is, they seek to influence, capture, or dismantle the state—the political system—in order to bring about changes in social relationships.

Less attention is given to movements that are primarily about individual redemption, about changing the actions and beliefs of individuals on a personal and one-to-one basis. These redemptive movements are also very important. The boundaries between the political movements and the redemptive movements are not always clear-cut. Individual conversion is often one important strategy for a movement that seeks societal change, a prerequisite for gaining political weight. Furthermore, many movements believe individual change is a necessary outcome of political change. Movements shift back and forth from political goals to individual-redemptive goals depending on circumstances. For example, in the Roman Empire, Christianity shifted from being a movement of persecuted individual converts to a movement that had the support of the emperor himself; but even in its political form, it placed emphasis on inner change. In our own times, the environmental movement is highly political, but also seeks to change individual behavior to encourage less waste and more recycling. Both feminism and Christian fundamentalism have a great deal to say about the personal and the political, which they see as inevitably interconnected. I try to remain sensitive to the interconnections of the political and the personal, the societal and the individual-redemptive, but in the interest of conciseness I am focusing on the societal-political movements.

Contemporary Movements: Actors in Twentieth-Century History   A second criterion for my selection of movements is their role in contemporary history. I have tried to put together a list of movements that were major "actors" in this century, to help us gain an overview of "what happened." Transnational social and political movements had and continue to have a major role in geopolitics and in the histories of individual nations. What we call "twentieth-century history" is, in large part, the story of movements, the states they formed and influenced, and the conflicts among movements like nationalism, liberalism, communism and socialism, fascism and Nazism, Islamic revolution, and so on.

I believe that most of these movements will continue to have a impact in the next century as well; some may be reborn in new forms. When a movement has a compelling ideology and speaks to the dreams of millions of people, it rarely disappears completely. The form changes, the strategies and organization are updated, the ideology is revised; the movement mutates but does not vanish.

Thus, for instance, liberalism has mutated so often that it is often difficult to recognize it as the ideology of the French and American Revolutions. Nationalism has undergone a number of transformations since its origins as a modern ideology in the eighteenth century. Present-day Christian and Islamic fundamentalism draw on centuries of tradition, but are not hesitant to use electronic media or computerized mailing lists.

Transnational Movements   A third criterion is that the movements span several cultures and/or nations. Their claims are global, their vision is transnational. Nationalism is, of course, something of an exception here in its specific forms, but the goal in general—self-determination as a right of all peoples—is international.

Movements and the Flow of History

A major goal of this book is to develop an understanding of the role of movements and ideologies in historical change. Therefore, I devote attention to the historical conditions in which movements arose and to their role in the social changes we call "history."

Movements and Modern Societies   The book begins with the clash of conservatism and classical liberalism. Liberalism is the oldest of the modern movements. In many ways, it defines the modern age. It has become the prevailing way of thought in the market democracies and an insurgent force in other nations in the form of civil rights, human rights, and prodemocracy movements. The following chapters examine movements that challenged liberalism. Some of these movements like religious fundamentalism have ancient roots, but their contemporary forms emerged after the rise of liberal democracy and capitalism. They attack what they consider the negative side of modernity, the secularism, individualism, and separation of spheres that liberal ideology advocates. Other movements—nationalism and fascism—accept the nation-states that liberalism helped make the globe's dominant political form, but they reject or question liberalism's universalistic message of *inalienable rights of all human beings* and liberalism's *critical stand* toward many institutions. Movements like socialism and feminism want to preserve some of the changes liberalism brought about—like juridical equality—but assert that these changes alone are insufficient to emancipate human beings. The last movement discussed is the environmental movement, which questions the whole modern mentality of growth. Thus, much of the book looks at the establishment of modern society by movements like liberalism and nationalism and subsequent challenges to this type of society by other movements.

Movements in the Postmodern World   While nation-states and markets continue to exist at the end of the twentieth century, in recent decades there have been some dramatic changes in their forms and in their cultures. These changes have sometimes been labeled "postmodern." Characteristics of the postmodern involve changes that have been caused by movements and also have made an impact on movements. The major transnational movements considered here are likely to persist but in different organizational forms and probably with substantial changes in their ideas as well.

Movement Interconnections   Discussed are the movements' relationships to each other and to the types of societies and states that they help bring into ex-

Civil rights activists sit in at a Woolworth lunch counter where African Americans had been refused service. Greensboro, North Carolina, February 3, 1960.

istence. Movements have to be understood as responding to each other. Movements are not separate, compartmentalized "things," but human beings engaging in thoughts and actions that are interconnected. These interconnections are a major part of the story, even if the chapters of the book are focused on one movement at a time. The responses of movements to each other and to preestablished states, the dynamic of movement and countermovement, give shape to the organization of the book.

The Emergence of Market Democracies   It is useful to begin this discussion with the late eighteenth century, with the French and American Revolutions, the formation of the liberal state, and the impact of capitalist industrialization. Other movements can then be seen as engaged in debate—and often, open conflict—with the ideologies of this formative period. In this age of deconstruction, this beginning may well look arbitrary or Eurocentric: Once upon a time . . . in 1776, the settlers in the North American colonies revolted against the English king, and Adam Smith published *The Wealth of Nations*. . . .

This is more than an arbitrary narrative device, however. We live in a global capitalist economy, and the United States and other market democracies still have an overwhelming economic, cultural, and military weight. The world of our lifetimes is still, in large part, the world made by the explosion of Europe, of technology, of capitalism, and of the modern nation-state. Movements initiated this state of affairs, movements gave shape to its global expansion, and movements continue to challenge it.

The Congress of South African Trade
Unions (COSATU), with over 1,250,000
members, is an important part of the
alliance that supports the African National
Congress. March by COSATU members
against the labor policies of the apartheid
regime. Johannesburg, South Africa,
October 14, 1989.

CHAPTER 2

Concepts and Definitions

The Boston Tea Party . . . the Committees of Correspondence . . . the Fourth of July and the Declaration of Independence . . . Thomas Jefferson's words: "We hold these truths to be self-evident, that all men are created equal, that they are endowed by their Creator with certain inalienable rights and that among these are life, liberty and the pursuit of happiness" . . . the shot heard round the world . . . the Continental Congress . . . the winter at Valley Forge . . . George Washington and the Marquis de Lafayette . . . the Constitution and the Bill of Rights.

Every schoolchild in the United States has heard these names and phrases, so familiar and timeworn that it is difficult to think about them with surprise and curiosity. But repeat them to yourself slowly and ask yourself about the story behind each one. Why did a group of Bostonians dress up as Indians and dump tea in the harbor? What was in the letters of the Committees of Correspondence? Why would a wealthy slaveowner like Thomas Jefferson write such stirring words about equality? Who fired the "shot heard round the world" and why did the conflict between England and the colonists become violent—could it have been otherwise? Why did the French king send help to antiroyalist insurgents? What values, interests, and compromises are packaged into the Constitution?

As we try to answer these questions, we discover that the simple stories of our elementary school days are events and incidents of a complex process—the making of a revolution and the establishment of a nation based on the ideals of the revolutionaries. As we think about these questions, we begin to look at all the elements of a movement—its ideas, its supporters, its organization and strategies. We begin to see the powerful opposition that movements face and the way movement activists attempt to beat the odds to change the reality that everyone else believes is unchangeable.

INTRODUCTION

In this chapter, I will define **movement** and introduce terms that social scientists use to analyze the ideas, organization, and strategies of movements. These terms refer to parts or elements of movements and to the processes in which movements are involved. The terms are shared by most of the theories discussed in the next chapter.

MOVEMENTS

Noninstitutionalized Discourses and Practices of Change

What is a movement? A movement is constituted by human beings engaged in discourses and practices designed to challenge and change society as they define it. It is formed by people who, over the course of time, are involved in non-institutionalized discourses and practices of change.

It is important to recognize that, like many terms in the social sciences, "movement" is an abstraction from reality. A movement is not really a "thing"—a physical object like a desk or a loaf of bread. All that really exists in society are human beings engaged in **practices and discourses.** To put it a little differently, what we call society, institutions, and movements are always human beings engaged in actions, interacting with each other, and using the human capacity for language and symbol (Blumer, 1951).

Practices means *doing;* this doing includes talking, writing, engaging in physical violence, and many other kinds of interactions. Practices can also involve physical objects—flags, guns, desks, books.

Discourses means *saying* something, so a discourse is really one specific type of practice. Discourses can be written, spoken, or electronically recorded. Discourse is usually taken to mean a cluster of statements, not just isolated utterances of everyday life (like "please pass the biscuits"); a discourse puts together statements about what is construed to be reality. A discourse often includes an explicit or implicit rule about what can or cannot be said.

Discourses and Practices of Change   A movement is really a number of people engaged in specific practices and discourses. The discourses are about changing society and/or individuals, about bringing into being a state of affairs that is in some way different from the existing one. The discourse of a movement always says something negative about the existing situation as it is defined by the movement. Even a movement that seeks to preserve the status quo is reacting to fears of impending change. The practices of a movement are those actions that the actors believe will bring about the changes considered desirable.

Noninstitutionalized Practices and Discourses   A movement is people engaged in activities that are not institutionalized. *Institution* is another social sciences term that appears to refer to a thing but really refers to human beings engaged in practices and discourses. To say that practices and discourses are institutionalized means that they recur on a regular basis, persist over time, are to be found throughout a society, and encounter relatively few social controls to prevent them from taking place. Institutions are supported by **legitimating discourses,** discourses that support the institution by saying it is legal, moral, good for society, and so on; for example, one could say that, in the United States in the 1990s, in capitalism—private enterprise and free markets—is pretty well institutionalized. Its practices are recurrent and found everywhere; a discourse of opposition to it is not widely found. Other established practices, like the legal system, support it.

Other practices are widely found, but not institutionalized. Acts like rape and robbery may take place frequently, but there are strong discourses and practices opposed to such acts. In the United States, the practices of the law treat robbery and rape as crimes, while they do not treat capitalist property claims as a crime or as a problem.

These examples highlight some of the meaning of **institutionalized and noninstitutionalized practices,** although the reader can see that this definition is not a simple matter, since many practices fall in the middle. These practices are the subject of ongoing negotiations between those who want to institutionalize them and those who oppose their institutionalization. Movements are involved in conflict over what is or is not institutionalized and legitimated. This conflict and negotiation over institutionalization applies both to the goals of movements and to the means they use.

Movement goals are often focused precisely on these practices in the middle, like the formation of churches by cult groups, the legalization of marijuana by libertarians, the establishment of domestic partnership benefits for gays and lesbians, or the extension of rights to publish and circulate information in a society with government censorship of the media.

Although movements are not themselves institutionalized, they often use institutionalized means for attaining their goals; for example, forming political parties or winning court cases. These examples show that institutionalized or noninstitutionalized is not a sharp distinction, but a difference that is itself the subject of dispute and negotiation.

Movements are noninstitutionalized in several ways. Not all movements share all of the following characteristics, which merely suggest some of the ways in which movements fall outside institutions—the routine, time-tested, widespread, and fully legitimated activities of a society.

First, movement discourses and practices may *not be widely shared.* Thus, there is little that is widely diffused or commonplace about them. Compared to the number of people engaged in jobs and families, the number of people engaged in social movements is rather small. Movements range in size from mass movements involving millions of people who may actually form a majority of a country's population—like some of the mass socialist parties in Europe—to small sectlike groups numbering in the hundreds—like the Branch Davidians. But even the mass movements do not include everyone.

Second, movement discourses and practices may be *generally opposed or opposed by people in power,* groups that sociologists call **agents of social control.** Such groups have the ability to restrict movement activity through a set of practices, for instance through the legal system. These opposing forces are often, but not always, concentrated in the institution of the state, in the political system. For example, in the spring of 1993, the FBI and other agencies of the federal government decided to put an end to the activities of the Branch Davidian cult, which had retreated to a bunker near Waco, Texas, and stockpiled arms. The government's siege of the bunker is an example of social control, of efforts to limit or halt movement actions and define such actions as dangerous or disruptive.

Third, insofar as their discourses refer to bringing about a situation that does not exist, the movement ideologies are *not well embedded in the practices of everyday life*. They thus have something ethereal or unrealistic about them. They are disconnected from practices that people have to engage in to survive on a daily basis and to satisfy physical needs. It is usually much more difficult to "live" one's movement attachment than to "live" one's occupation or conventional gender roles. This difficulty is also inherent in institutionalized religious discourse, but organized religion has developed rituals and relationships that connect teachings to everyday life. Being a physician or a practicing Catholic are identities that are guided by existing rules, roles, and relationships. Living as a socialist in the United States or preparing for the Rapture as a Christian fundamentalist are identities and practices that have to be invented in opposition to prevailing discourses and practices.

Fourth, movement practices and discourses are often newly invented or are new reformulations of other discourses; they are *not yet recurrent and seem not to have "stood the test of time."*

It is important to realize that the distinction between institutionalized and noninstitutionalized is not clear-cut and rigid. The lines are constantly renegotiated among movement adherents, social control agents, sympathizers, the media, and so on. Many movements exist in a disputed area between institutionalized and noninstitutionalized behavior.

Within a movement, some organizations may engage in institutionalized actions, while others do not. For example, some organizations in the environmental movement in the United States lobby Congress, an institutionalized practice. Others (like Greenpeace or local antinuclear power groups) use sit-ins and other forms of direct action, which are usually considered noninstitutionalized.

Movements themselves may be quite conflicted about whether they want to become more institutionalized or not. If they do become institutionalized, they probably expand their resources and their support bases and become more likely to accomplish some reforms. But institutionalization may also make them too routinized or inclined to compromise, and thereby reduce their ability to challenge the status quo.

For example, for many years the NAACP had been seen as rather institutionalized by the media, much of its support base among African Americans and white supporters of civil rights, and the public at large. Its primary focus was on civil rights court cases, which were generally handled by professional staffers and attorneys. In the early 1990s, the organization organized more meetings with radical black groups like the Nation of Islam ("Black Muslims") and participated in gang summits in some cities. These new activities reduced its perceived institutionalization and led to the disaffection of some of its previous supporters, but perhaps gained it new supporters and expanded its challenge to the racial status quo in the United States (Muwakkil, 1994).

In other words, institutionalized and noninstitutionalized are terms whose meanings are negotiated by movements, media, movement organizations, and external supporters and opponents. They involve constant shifts and redefinitions of actions, rather than fixed characteristics. Let me reformulate my definition. A key characteristic of social movements is that they blur and challenge the distinction between institutionalized and noninstitutionalized practices.

Reform and Revolution   At this point, many texts on movements proceed to classify movements, often distinguishing revolutionary movements that seek total change from reform movements that seek only partial changes in society. Reform movements also tend to use institutionalized means, while revolutionary movements do not and are more inclined toward violence and other extralegal strategies. I am going to be cautious about classifying movements in this way or any other, because these differences are often quite fluid. Movement participants themselves are usually too shrewd to treat the difference between reform and revolution as permanent. All the societal-political movements look toward a major transformation of society and in this sense are revolutionary; reform is often seen more as a cautious first step or an expedient strategy than a final outcome.

Having defined movements as people engaged in noninstitutionalized discourses and practices aimed at changing society, I am now going to define elements of movement practice.

IDEOLOGY

Discourse

Ideology refers to the discourses of the movement, to what people think and say. The ideology is the ideas held by people who see themselves as connected to the movement. A little more specifically, the ideology is the set of ideas expressed by the most active participants (Greene, 1990).

Usually, an ideology has some degree of coherence; the ideas hang together in some way. The discourses are interconnected. The discourses specify some way of looking at reality. They specify what is *really important*. They are a way of making sense of life experiences and situations. The discourses spell out what the current situation is and why it should be changed. They identify some preferable state of affairs that becomes the goal of the movement. For example, Operation Rescue identifies conception as the starting point of life and specifies the overriding importance of protecting the fetus; this goal is central to the movement's understanding of what *really matters* and brings with it the practice of stopping abortion by a large variety of legal and illegal means.

Notice how ideologies carry with them a certain language, a set of rules about how to talk, about how to say things, and about what can and cannot be said. For Operation Rescue, the fetus is an unborn child. Of course, this concern for words is an essential feature of all discourses, not just movement discourses. The choice of words is inherent in the human capacity for language. In this respect, movements are not different from institutionalized discourses. Many institutionalized discourses also carefully specify ways of talking: The use of a Latin- and Greek-based vocabulary in medicine or of a special terminology in law are good examples of very structured and specialized institutional discourses that participants learn and use in highly self-conscious ways. But, in movements, the participants underline the tension in the difference between their discourse and that of others.

Let's look in a little more detail at ideological discourses. We can say that attention is focused on representations of reality. A discourse presents a certain view of what "reality" is. It attempts to capture the nearly infinite complexity of the world in a number of key images and key terms. It highlights some aspects of reality and ignores or specifically dismisses others.

For example, Operation Rescue focuses attention on the first 9 months of human life and on the relationship of women to their children; fetuses are represented as unborn children and women are represented largely as actual or potential mothers. Pregnancies are represented as unexpected rather than as unwanted. In contrast, the movement to keep abortion legal represents itself as standing for *choice;* women are represented as people with a range of roles. The unborn child of Operation Rescue is a fetus to those who participate in the movement to keep abortions legal. Both movements tend to highlight the issue of the first weeks or months of human life and fetal development. Both recognize that the quality of life of (born) children and adults is an important issue, yet the problems of child care, education, health care, and so on, are not the primary focus of either movement's discourse. Operation Rescue gives little—and largely negative—attention to contraception.

Movement discourses speak about some elements of reality, not others, and this selection of a sphere of discourse contains the *why* of the movement.

Symbols

Differences in representation are easily concentrated and compressed into **symbols** and slogans: *Life* and *choice* have become dramatic shorthand ways of referring to the legality of abortion. Some current movement theorists prefer to use the term **framing** for the way in which movements organize their discourses and align them with the values, ideas, and discourses they believe to be prevalent in society; I will return to this concept in the next chapter (Snow and Benford, 1988).

Sometimes, institutionalized discourses set limits to movement representations and a movement ideology has to use "code words." For instance, when former Ku Klux Klan leader David Duke ran for public office in Louisiana, he used words like "welfare" to appeal to some white voters' sentiment against poor black people, since direct racial remarks have become off-limits in U.S. electoral campaigns.

Representations are also translated from words to visual images and symbols. A swastika refers to the Nazis and is a way of calling up all they stood for—the Führer, ethnic genocide, anti-semitism, the "Aryan race" and racialist ideas, and so on. The Virgin of Guadalupe—the Madonna represented as an Indian woman—was a powerful symbol in Cesar Chavez' organization of Catholic Mexican American farmworkers. Her image as a dark-complexioned woman in a blue cloak lined with roses refers to a Mexican tradition that dates back to the sixteenth century, when her apparition gave value to the hopes of the oppressed and conquered Native Americans who had been recently and forcibly converted to the Christian faith. The gay rights movement has used a pink triangle as its symbol, in an ironic gesture; the Nazis imprisoned homosexuals, and just as they made Jews wear a yellow star, they made homosexuals wear a pink triangle. The gay rights movement adopted this symbol, turning its negative meaning into an affirming symbol of solidarity and defiance. An "X" is associated with Malcolm X, who selected this letter to replace the English surname (Little) that linked his family to slave owners; the letter X stands for a break with Eurocentrism and the burden of having been someone else's property.

Some symbols are **condensation symbols** that stand for everything that the movement is "about"; they are a shorthand for its discourses and practices, ideas and goals. Sometimes a leader, an individual, may serve as such a symbol. Martin Luther King was not only an actual leader and organizer of the Civil Rights Movement, but also a symbol of nonviolent opposition to injustice. The Ayatollah Khomeini became a symbol of the Islamic revolution in Iran; millions of people came to his funeral to express not only their reverence for him as an individual but also their unity with all the goals and hopes of the movement.

In some cases, the leader as a condensation symbol can be said to become the object of a **cult of personality** or cult of the individual. The term was first used in communist and socialist movements to refer to a worshipful attitude toward Joseph Stalin and, later, Mao Zedong. Socialism in the Soviet Union and China was distorted by an uncritical obedience to powerful party leaders (Deutscher, 1966). This expression always has a negative connotation and implies that movement participants have lost sight of the distinction between the values of the movement and the accomplishments of any individual human being, no matter how talented or important to the organization. It implies that the movement participants have come to worship the individual leader.

Negative Symbols: Scapegoats and Folk Devils

Movements also deal extensively in **negative symbols.** Some movements **scapegoat** specific groups in society, identifying them as the source of all evil and calling for their suppression, expulsion, or even extermination in order to begin cleansing and revitalizing the society. When a movement comes to power it may begin its program of change by attacking such groups. Ethnoracist movements like the Nazis and neo-Nazis point to ethnic groups (for example, Jews and Gypsies) in this way.

Scapegoating is also closely related to identifying **folk devils,** groups that are defined as a threat to vital values and interests (Cohen, 1973). Movements may use folk devils to frame their definition of the current condition of society as one that is evil, threatening, or inadequate. The schools are being taken over by secular humanists, according to parts of the New Christian Right. Jews run

Wall Street or Washington, according to the neo-Nazis. Some populist movements may talk about shadowy "elites" whose machinations threaten ordinary citizens.

Not surprisingly, movements engage in scapegoating and identifying folk devils and are often stereotyped and targeted as folk devils by nonmembers, social control agents, the media, and countermovements. "Islamic terrorists," for instance, are folk devils in the United States, probably out of proportion to their actual operations in the west. The "femi-Nazi" is a folk devil that conveniently blends two rather different movements; it is a folk devil used to create loathing for feminism by linking it with a movement that most Americans find repugnant (Nazism). The New Christian Right, on the one hand, and left and libertarian groups, on the other, portray each other as threats to core American values. We will return to some of these processes when we look at movements and countermovements.

Sometimes movements are largely invented, especially by local media, in order to provide folk devils and scapegoats who can be blamed for youthful misconduct, alienation among teens, and other social problems—satanic cults are a prime example (Gaines, 1992).

Practices

An ideology is not only a set of words or visual images. It is also lived in practices. Rituals and routines embody the ideas of the movement. Going to demonstrations, selling movement newspapers, and dressing in a certain style all convey to oneself and others a solidarity with the ideas of the movement. Engagement in these activities is not just "going through the motions." It is an affirmation that the movement is meaningful.

Before leaving the topic of ideologies and symbols, let us note that many movements are not totally consistent in their ideologies. They recognize that their discourses need to be nuanced for different actual and potential supporters. Some theorists use the term **constituencies** for these different categories of supporters. For example, when the Nazis were trying to gain influence with conservative German political and industrial elites, they represented themselves as anti-Communist and pro law and order. When they addressed crowds of young, unemployed, and uprooted followers they highlighted their "action" orientation, their street fighting ways, and their opposition to the institutions of capitalism.

Movements also shift their ideologies in order to respond to changing environments or correct mistakes in their earlier "line." For example, the Comintern (an international network of Communist parties and movements) realized in the mid-1930s that the policy of opposition to moderate socialists and centrist democratic parties had inadvertently made it easier for the Nazis to come to power; the Comintern shifted to a "popular front" discourse that emphasized common interests among socialist, communist, and centrist forces and laid the groundwork for a Soviet-western alliance against the Axis (Germany, Japan, and Italy) in World War II (Abendroth, 1972).

Ideologies as Universalizing Discourses

Ideologies often make claims that their discourse is good for everyone (or at the very least, for a wide range of people); this claim is what is meant by **universalizing the discourse** of the movement. Within the ideology there may be goals that reflect the self-interest of some category of people. For example the value of free enterprise may be greater for a business owner than for a worker. The value that feminism places on expanded rights for women is more immediately in the interest of women than of men. But, ideologies have to package these narrower goals in terms that make the ideology appealing to a broad range of people. Historically, free enterprise has been packaged together with freedom in general, which may appeal as strongly to the worker as the business owner. Feminism offers more than an end to male domination; it offers everyone—men as well as women—a society with less hierarchy and less violence.

As specific ideologies are discussed, ways in which appeals to a core support base are broadened and universalized to attract a larger range of participants will be indicated. Only movements with broad-based appeals can put together a **bloc** of diverse supporters (Gramsci, 1971; Garner and Garner, 1981).

Ideologies and Lies

The term ideology is often used to mean a *false* representation of reality, a false consciousness that is distinct from a scientific one. In addition, it is used to mean a false consciousness that is propagated by the classes that dominate a society economically, culturally, and politically. Here I am not using the term this way; when I speak of a movement's ideology I am not implying that its ideas are false, only that they are coherent and interconnected. A movement that is not in power can be said to have an ideology, just as the ruling classes of a society propagate an ideology that supports their dominance. Here I am using *ideology* in the most general way as a system of discourses, without reference to truth or falsity. Be aware that the term has several different meanings to social scientists.

Can Movement Ideologies Be Classified?

Fluidity in discourse, over time or for different audiences, makes it difficult to classify movements into rigid typologies. Two major typologies are commonly used, however.

Reform or Revolution   One typology distinguishes reform movements from revolutionary movements. The former seek to change some aspect of society, some specific institution; in other words, some specific set of practices. The latter seek to change the totality of practices; their goal is to change all institutions, and in their discourse they view "society" as a system that has to be changed completely if it is to be changed at all. Some scholars prefer to use terms like **reformative** to refer to movements with a limited scope and **transformative** for movements with the goal of changing the whole social order (Aberle, 1966).

For instance, the Chicago Recycling Coalition is a reform movement; it seeks to change the way individual citizens dispose of trash and the way the city of Chicago handles waste disposal. Its goals are fairly limited, not only in its geographic scope, but also in the set of practices it targets for change. In contrast, revolutionary socialism or Islamic integralism have broad goals of change; in the view of their ideologies, everything in a society should be different—law, politics, the economy, the family. Most important, not only should each of these institutions be changed, but the way in which the institutions are put together—the very form of the whole society—should change.

Sometimes it is not so easy to tell reform movements from revolutionary movements. A movement may appear to target a specific set of practices for change, when, in fact, its goal is a much larger vision of change. For instance, Operation Rescue appears to be a single-issue movement focused on abolishing legal abortions. Is that really all there is to it? Or is that goal only part of a larger goal of transforming family life, gender relations, and the relationship between church and state in American life (Luker, 1984)? Some individual participants might talk about a specific concern—abortion—but others, including leaders, might refer to a vision of society that challenges the individualism and secularism they believe currently prevails. Thus, we will use the reform/revolution dichotomy very cautiously, keeping in mind that a movement may have elements of both, shifting back and forth in different situations or for different types of supporters.

Left and Right?   A second major typology that is often used in the study of political movements is the distinction between the **left** and the **right.** This spatial metaphor derived from seating in the Assembly, a parliamentary body that was part of the government of France during the period of the French Revolution. The further left a person sat the more he favored radical measures of redistributing property to poorer people and undoing the power of the monarchy and the nobility. The right was the area of the conservatives, who favored protecting existing property rights and undertaking only limited changes in the political system.

Since then, the core of the left has come to be associated with socialist and communist movements; more generally, it stands for an emphasis on human equality and takes the view that rights to survival and physical well-being supersede property rights. The left is more inclined to make systemic changes. The right is more conservative, less inclined to challenge existing institutions, more convinced that hierarchy and continuity of traditions, rather than equality, are essential in human society, and more sympathetic toward property rights.

Rather than think about left-right as a dichotomy, it is more useful to think of it as a spectrum. Socialists and communists are clearly left; Reagan and Thatcher conservatives (and their successors) are fairly clearly right. There is also a center, somewhere between these two positions. Movements, parties, and points of view can be placed along the spectrum. For example, in the United States, the Democratic Party is left of the Republicans, but not very far left on the spectrum as a whole.

This distinction breaks down at times, however. Left/right really covers several dimensions: One is the attitude toward economic equality—the left is more strongly for it, the right does not give it high priority. So far, the distinction is fairly clear, but the spectrum becomes more complicated when we add other dimensions of ideology to the issue of economic equality. The second dimension is government control over individual behavior. The third dimension is the attitude toward the power of the state in general. Once we add these last two dimensions the spectrum becomes less clear.

The left includes forces that would strengthen state power, especially in the economic sphere, and forces that would reduce it, especially in the sphere of personal liberties. Traditionally, the left has been willing to use the power of the state to promote more economic equality. However, there are substantial parts of the left that would like to reduce the power of the state, and especially the power of the state to regulate personal behavior. This libertarian left, which was quite a strong current in the New Left of the 1960s, would like to eliminate or reduce laws like antisodomy laws or harsh penalties for drug use.

The right is generally opposed to having the state do things like regulate business or redistribute tax revenues to equalize economic standing; but some parts of the right are not opposed to having the state regulate personal behavior, so it cannot really be said that all of the right is consistently for less government. Examples of the right's willingness to use government to regulate personal behavior include the Reagan-Bush war on drugs and the passing of laws restricting access to abortions, a policy supported by the right wing of the Republican Party.

In Latin America, right-wing military dictatorships have intervened deeply in their societies, restricting civil rights and using the power of the state to suppress dissent and prevent political organization. Movements and regimes described as "far right"—like the Italian Fascists and the Nazis—*were active* in regulating and directing the economy. They left enterprises in private ownership but did not shy away from interfering with the market mechanism.

As you can see, the left/right distinction holds up fairly well in the middle of the spectrum. For example, in the United States, we might place Reagan conservatives on the right; next are moderate Republicans and conservative Democrats; then, a bit further to the left, liberal Democrats; and leftmost, moderate socialists. In the middle of the spectrum the terms *progressive* and *conservative* are often used to refer to the left and right positions. Progressives see themselves as working for progress toward more social and economic equality and a more democratic political system. Conservatives see themselves as preserving a more laissez-faire type of economy and more traditional forms of family life.

The problems of the left/right distinction are more serious near the ends of the spectrum. Both ends tend to split over questions of state power; the split separates libertarians from proponents of the strong state, on *both* the left and the right. At the far left, we can find anarchists and left-wing libertarians (pro-economic equality, anti-state power) as well as supporters of centralized redistribution (extensive state involvement in society in the name of a vision of social equality in the future) (Polanyi, 1957). At the far right, we can find right-wing libertarians (pro-free market, anti-state power) as well as fascists and right-wing authoritarians (extensive state involvement in society and economy, support for a strong state, little concern for socioeconomic equality, and explicit opposition to equality), and right-wing anarchists.

Alliances and coalitions can form at each end of the spectrum, but these alliances may be unstable or unable to agree on policies. For example, in the elections in the spring of 1994 in Italy, the neofascist sectors of the right that supported a strong centralized state and extensive state enterprise entered into an electoral alliance with right-wing political groups that called for a weaker state, cuts in spending, extensive tax cuts, privatization of state-run services and enterprises, and a federal structure in place of a centralized one. Although all the forces in this electoral alliance are considered right wing, they had difficulty in agreeing on a single program for a governing coalition (Leonardi, 1994).

"Post" Left and Right?   Theorists of the postmodern often imply that part of postmodernity is that the left/right distinction no longer makes much sense. The left/right dimension has run into problems with the collapse of the political systems headed by Communist parties in eastern Europe and the former Soviet Union. The disappearance of such a powerfully institutionalized left position has made it more difficult to define "leftness."

Surveying the scene in Moscow or Warsaw, journalists and social scientists have trouble deciding who is left or right, and find it easier to use the terms liberal and conservative. Liberals favor more market mechanisms and western-style democracy; conservatives favor a return to central planning and a stronger state. This usage of terms is quite different from the standard U.S. usage, but closer to the original meaning of liberal and conservative in the nineteenth century. It is difficult to match the liberals and conservatives with a left or right position in this case.

Movements like religious fundamentalism and ethnic nationalism that have emerged with great vigor after the end of the cold war often do not seem to fall very neatly on the left/right spectrum. Therefore, the left/right typology has to be used with great caution and precision, and with full recognition of shifting ideologies in the post-cold war world. I believe it is still useful in many contexts.

THE SUPPORT BASE

A second major characteristic of a movement is the support base; this term refers to categories of people likely to agree with the movement's ideology and participate in its practices. Usually, social scientists identify the support base in terms of certain demographic characteristics: social class, ethnicity, religion, gender, age, occupation, region of residence, and so on. Of course, these characterizations of the support base do not apply to every single individual. They are just statements about relatively higher rates of involvement. For example, historians studying the composition of the Nazi Party in the 1930s found that proportionately more lower-middle-class than working-class people were members. Artisans, small businesspeople, independent farmers, and white-collar workers joined at higher rates than those of factory workers. Thus, one might say that it had a lower-middle-class support base. It also tended to have more support in the Protestant regions of Germany than the Catholic ones.

Some movements draw support from diverse kinds of social bases; this diversity may influence the ideology, which cannot focus exclusively on the concerns of a single group. In this case the movement either has to universalize its ideology, speaking to general concerns or a diffuse "public interest"—or it has to put forth different kinds of appeals to its different types of supporters, hoping that no one will "compare notes." I have already mentioned that the Nazis had a conservative message for industrialists and big business and an action-oriented and vaguely anticapitalist message for unemployed youth.

Other movements may have a precise and narrow support base. For example, in contemporary France there are farmers' movements that favor policies to protect farmers against global competition; these movements have a sharply defined and relatively limited support base.

It is historically accurate to say that movements of the left tend to have a support base among poorer people and/or those who own little or no property. Left-wing ideologies of economic equality, public ownership of enterprises, and redistribution of wealth obviously appeal more to those without property than those with a great deal of it. Mass movements of the right—like fascism and Nazism—have tended to appeal to small property owners; on the one hand, this stratum is afraid of losing what it has, but on the other hand, it feels under pressure from big business, banks, and "capital"—thus it looks for a movement that promises to stand for the "little guy."

Theorists use terms like **adherents, constituents,** and **beneficiaries** to refer to different relationships among movements and support bases. Adherents share movement ideologies, constituents provide resources for movements, and beneficiaries stand to gain from movement's attainment of goals (Zald and McCarthy, 1987:23).

Sometimes a distinction is also made between *conscience* constituencies and adherents on the one hand and those supporters who have more immediate self-interest at stake (Zald and McCarthy, 1987:23). For example, in the United States in the 1980s, a Central America solidarity movement opposed Reagan administration policies in the region (especially the contra war against the Sandinista government in Nicaragua), although few adherents had any immediate stake in the outcomes. In contrast, the farmers' movement in contemporary France is engaged in a defense of fairly clearly defined economic interests. In many instances, the differences between conscience and self-interest may be blurred, however.

Intellectuals

Intellectuals have a special role in almost all movements. Since movements deal so extensively in ideologies—in discourses about what should be or could be—they depend on persons who are skillful at inventing discourses, whose specialization is ideas and words. Or to put it another way, intellectuals are particularly likely to start movements. Almost regardless of the contents of a move-ment ideology, a movement has a core of intellectuals. Movement intellectuals are often drawn from among students, lawyers, clergy, and professors—partic-ularly those "idea workers" who cannot easily be absorbed into stable employ-ment in a weak economy. For this reason, many movements include individu-als of the middle class or lower middle class, especially within the leadership, since these social groups are more likely to be both educated and dissatisfied (Greene, 1990; Lasswell and Lerner, 1966).

Specialists in Violence

Some movements also include **specialists in violence.** Movements that define themselves as revolutionary, insurgent, or "engaged in armed struggle" need such specialists. In some cases, they are recruited from the ranks of the institu-tionalized military. For example, the core of the revolutionary forces in the Por-tuguese revolution of the early 1970s were young officers who had been radi-calized by their experience fighting anticolonial guerrillas in Africa. The first insurgents against the right-wing Guatemalan military regime in the early 1960s were young officers (Black et al., 1984). In other cases, a movement may develop its own specialists in violence (Lasswell and Lerner, 1966).

Mobilization

A movement may try to **mobilize** and involve as participants a large pro-portion of its support base in one or more organizations. Mass movements are, in part, movements that succeed in doing so. Mass mobilization was an impor-tant goal for the European socialist parties that emerged around the turn of the century, for example. Mobilization is especially important when a movement plans to make changes by taking part in electoral politics.

Some movements may give less attention to this project of mobilization, preferring to maintain only small organizations. These small organizations are prepared to penetrate major institutions like the army and swing them around to support for the movement at a moment of crisis when the state is weak. Small organizations can also try to launch guerrilla offensives that may destabilize a government, disorganize its police and military apparatus, and lead to its col-lapse. This was the strategy of the *foco* in Latin America, based on Fidel Castro's revolutionary movement in Cuba; elsewhere and later in Latin America, in Guatemala and Bolivia in the 1960s, this small movement strategy did not suc-ceed (Black et al., 1984).

ORGANIZATION, STRATEGY, AND TACTICS

Organization

Movement participants arrange their activities, their practices, in a way that they believe will make it possible to attain their goals, the outcomes indicated by their ideology. A large variety of terms designate different aspects of these arrangements. By **organization** social scientists mean a relatively stable patterning of relationships within the movement. To say that a movement is organized or has an organization also implies that it has boundaries, that a discourse and a set of practices distinguish people in it from those who are not in it, even if the latter are sympathetic to its goals. These boundary-maintenance mechanisms can include practices like paying dues, signing a pledge, or taking an oath of secrecy.

Movements and Movement Organizations   The organization differentiates between people who agree with the movement's discourse—the movement in a broad sense—and those who are mobilized to engage in a specific set of relationships and practices. We can thus distinguish between movements and **movement organizations** (Zald and Ash, 1966). Some movements remain largely unorganized, taking the form of currents of opinion rather than mobilizing people into one or more specific organizations. For example, the number of people in the United States who are Protestant fundamentalists in their beliefs far exceeds the number of people who are participants in nationwide organizations that represent this viewpoint. These individuals may be mobilized to vote in a specific way or to give money, but they are not members of organizations.

Movements also differ in the extent to which their movement organizations are multiple and competing or single and unified. For example, the Civil Rights Movement in the 1960s included a number of organizations: the Southern Christian Leadership Conference, the Student Non-Violent Coordinating Committee, the Congress of Racial Equality, to name a few. Movements that compete as political parties make an effort to unify potential supporters to vote for that party; for example, socialists in Germany are probably more inclined to vote for the SPD (the Socialist Party of Germany, a large mass party), whatever their differences in viewpoint, whereas in a country without a strong socialist party they might be more inclined to form multiple smaller groups. Once in power, a **movement organization** has access to concrete rewards like patronage jobs or government contracts that strengthen its relationship to the support base.

In short, the relationship among the support base (those categories of people that are disproportionately likely to participate in the movement in some form), the movement (those who share the ideology and occasionally take part in specific actions), and the movement organizations is a complicated one that has to be examined carefully in specific cases. There are marked differences among movements in the extent to which the movement attempts to mobilize its support base into distinct organizations. In most movements the relationship between the movement and the movement organizations is quite fluid; many movement organizations do not have clear boundaries or firm definitions of membership, and adherents "drift" in and out. This tendency toward fluidity has probably increased in recent decades, as many movements take on the form of loose networks, rather than clearly defined organizations (Klandermans, in Morris and Mueller, 1992).

Organizational Structure and Authority   Within the boundaries of movement organizations, relationships are patterned by the people seen as belonging together. One important patterning of relationships is defined by the distribution of power.

Centralized Power   In some movement organizations power is **centralized**, concentrated in the hands of relatively few people who make decisions that all participants in the movement are expected to follow. Centralized power may reside in an executive committee or an individual.

The large Communist parties that were major global political forces from the 1920s to the 1980s typically were quite centralized, with decision-making power vested in a central committee. The committee discussed policies, but once a decision was reached, it was binding on members and implemented through a hierarchical structure.

Decentralized, Acephalous, and Segmented Power Structures   Power can be **decentralized**, diffused throughout the organization. Some movements have a **segmented**, acephalous (headless), or polycephalous (many-headed), form (Gerlach, 1983). Instead of having a clear center, authority resides in local branches or cells that can act independently of each other; the movement is held together by its shared ideology, rather than by a central authority. For example, the pentecostal movement within the Christian religion tends to have a segmented, decentralized structure. These segmented, polycephalous, networklike movements may be becoming the prevalent form of movement, displacing the more structured, centralized, and clearly defined organization.

Hierarchy and Alternative Structures of Authority   Another element of movement organization is the presence or absence of hierarchy. A hierarchy is a structure of authority that has many levels or ranks of subordination and superordination with power flowing downward. The Nazi Party—in part—was organized hierarchically.

There are a number of alternatives to hierarchy. One is a relatively egalitarian organization that permits decentralized decision making. Sometimes an apparently structureless or decentralized organization may have a de facto power structure composed of the most active or committed members. It may then exclude decision making by others as completely as the formally centralized organization does, as Jo Freeman found in some of the collectives in the more radical part the women's movement in the United States (Freeman, 1973).

Another alternative is the concentration of power in the hands of a single leader who exercises direct authority over the followers, unmediated by a hierarchy of officials; this pattern is sometimes found in small, cultlike groups, like the Branch Davidians under the leadership of David Koresh.

The Bases of Authority   What is the source of **authority** in movements? The German sociologist Max Weber identified three major types of authority: **traditional** authority, based on a discourse of custom, an appeal to long-standing practices; **rational-legal** authority, based on a discourse of matching means to ends in an efficient manner, and often structured into a bureaucracy; and **charismatic** authority, based on a discourse about the extraordinary nature of an individual. Authority in movements is less often traditional or customary than in institutionalized organizations (Weber, 1958).

Many movements have charismatic leaders, individuals who are believed to have extraordinary powers that allow them to "make the rules" rather than follow customary or bureaucratic procedures. Movements that have a religious ideology but have broken away from major institutionalized religions—cultlike movements—often have a charismatic leader. Sometimes movements with a charismatic leader seem to lose touch with the realities of everyday life. The leader interprets "reality" for his followers in a way that makes them susceptible to mistaken perceptions of society that lead to the end rather than the success of the movement. For example, Jim Jones led his followers from the United States to Guyana, where they were eventually forced to commit mass suicide by drinking poisoned Kool-Aid; more recently, the Branch Davidians under David Koresh came to a fiery end in their compound after a long holdout against the FBI.

Movements with charismatic authority are not only likely to get mired in the fantasy world of the leader, but also apt to have difficulty surviving the leader's death or discrediting. While many major religions began with a charismatic leader, the ones that survived were generally those that were able to transform charismatic authority into more stable forms of authority. They solved the problem of succession of leaders and **routinized charisma** into traditional and/or rational-legal structures. In the history of Christianity, for example, Peter and Paul were among those who initiated these kinds of structures; Paul's letters and travels linked together communities of Christians in the Roman Empire, while Peter became the founder of the papacy, an institutionalized pattern of religious leadership.

Some movements assume a rational-legal system of authority from the start, trying to create a structure that makes possible the most efficient pursuit of the goals of the movement. Such movements tend to become **bureaucratized,** especially once they reach a certain size. They develop a hierarchy, move people into key positions on the basis of specific skills, and operate according to formal and impersonal rules. Far from the popular stereotype that equates bureaucracy with inefficiency, bureaucratic organization is actually an effective way to mobilize people and resources on a large scale. The large socialist parties of Europe, especially that of Germany, used this type of structure effectively.

Internal Division of Labor   An important element of movement organization is the **internal division of labor**. Some movement organizations develop specialized roles; for example, specialists in violence or in communications and public relations or in formulating ideology. The organization recruits people who have these skills or trains members for these specializations. Other movements prefer members who are generalists, who are committed to the movement and prepared to take on any of these roles as the movement's needs change. Movements that take on a rational-legal or bureaucratic form early in their history are especially likely to rely on specialists and have a large staff of movement professionals, individuals who may draw a salary from the organization and see it as a full-time commitment. For example, the socialist parties in many western European countries were and continue to be large, bureaucratized formal organizations. Some of the newer social movements in the United States in the areas of civil rights, women's issues, and environmentalism, that use strategies of lobbying for legislative change or legal action also rely heavily on movement professionals (McCarthy and Zald, 1987).

Strategies and Tactics

Movement organization is closely related to movement **strategies,** the plans that the movement has for making its goals become a reality. Political movements plan to use the political system in some way; the precise plan depends on the nature of the society and the political system as well as the movements' ideologies. Other movements focus more on building a mass base and changing the views and actions of many individuals. A strategy is not a fixed method; a movement's strategies can change as the society and the historical circumstances change.

Political movements aim at influencing the state—or government—in some way. The state is an institution that can use coercive power to induce people to act in a certain way; it has at its disposal police, courts, the correctional system, and—in some situations—the military. Thus, if a movement can capture the state, or at least influence it, it gains a powerful means for making people change their actions. Revolutionary movements attempt to capture the state as a whole and then use it to transform the society. For example, in the October Revolution in Russia in 1917, the Bolsheviks succeeded in taking over the institutions of the state; they changed some of these institutions and used their state power to transform Russian society (Carr, 1972; Gurley, 1975).

Reform movements do not focus on capturing the state as a whole; they influence the existing state to pass and enforce laws that promote the goals of the movement. For example, the antiabortion movement has influenced state legislators to restrict access to abortions by instituting waiting periods or requiring parental consent for minors. The environmental movement has succeeded in getting state and federal governments to set clean air standards and prohibit the dumping of toxic wastes.

Strategies and Political Systems   The nature of a nation's political system is a major factor in shaping a movement's political strategy. I will discuss **political opportunity structures** in more detail in the next chapter, so the following discussion is focused on the effects of political structures on movement organization and strategy.

Clandestine Organizations   A nation that has single-party rule and a repressive political system allows little "space" for movements to organize openly. In these systems, movements may have to operate "underground," as clandestine organizations.

This environment may force them to assume an organization that can protect its secrets, perhaps by having a compartmentalized **cell structure** so that the capture, interrogation, and torture of members will not lay bare the entire structure of the organization. For much of the twentieth century, Communist-led parties and movements operated effectively in repressive political systems; the Bolsheviks in tsarist Russia, the Vietnamese National Liberation Front, and the anti-Nazi Communist-led resistance movements in France and Italy are examples.

Forming Parties or Pressure Groups   More open political systems permit the formation of mass parties and mass movements. Where the constitutional framework encourages smaller parties and gives them a potential role in coalitions, movements may form parties. This development typically occurs in political systems that have some measure of proportional representation and low threshholds for parliamentary representation; in these systems even a small party can have a role in parliament. The Greens—an environmentally oriented party—in Italy, Germany, and other Western European countries exemplify the transformation of a movement into a party under these conditions.

On the other hand, two-party systems like that of the United States tend to force movements to become pressure groups within the major parties; third parties have little chance of election victories, so a movement makes better use of its resources in working within the two-party structure. It can take over the local party organization and get its members nominated or it can pressure other candidates. In the United States, the two major parties are not difficult to influence by movements. Local party organizations involve few people; the national party platform committee is not difficult to capture; primaries have low voter turnout; candidates are not subject to uniform party discipline (the agreement that all party representatives must take the same stand on an issue or risk expulsion from the party), but can make deals with pressure groups on specific issues. These circumstances provide opportunities for energetic and well-organized movements. For instance, the Christian right had a strong input in writing the 1992 Republican platform and has consistently influenced a number of legislators.

Armed Insurgencies   Movements also confront the state apparatus head on, in strategies of **armed insurgency**. Movements do this when the state is too repressive to permit them to form parties or pressure groups. "Todas las puertas cerradas, Solo un camino nos dejan" [All the doors are closed; they leave us only one way]. So sang the Quiche Maya as they joined a guerilla movement against the military dictatorship in Guatemala (cited in Black, 1984:61).

Such a strategy is also used when the movement decides that the state appears weak enough to "crack" under a military confrontation. A successful frontal assault may give the movement more opportunity for restructuring the state than an institutionalized accession to power.

Movements sometimes create mass armies, such as the large armed force organized by the Chinese Communists, by means of which they took power in 1949. In other cases, smaller guerrilla forces can show up the weakness of the state; the regular army is demoralized by its inability to control the guerrilla fighters and falls apart as its soldiers eventually refuse to fight. This strategy worked well for the Cuban insurgents led by Fidel Castro; a small band of armed insurgents was able to precipitate the fall of the Batista regime in 1959 (Wolf, 1969; Zeitlin, 1967).

Destabilization   Another important strategy for the seizure of power is **destabilization**. The movement takes actions that polarize the society, weaken support for the incumbent government, and suggest to the public that the state is no longer in control. The movement that has helped to create this situation of crisis then steps in to offer its services as a force for law and order. This strategy was used very effectively by fascist movements in Europe in the 1920s and 1930s; both the Nazis and the Italian Fascists came to power through the invitation of incumbent elites, after their paramilitary wings had spread violence and created a sense of crisis.

Terrorism is often used as part of the strategy of destabilization. The targeting of victims, the sense of insecurity it brings about, and the polarization it encourages all weaken the state. If the state does little to stop terror it appears ineffective and unable to protect its citizens; if the state takes strong action, resorting to repressive measures, it accelerates social polarization. The Red Brigades in Italy in the 1970s used terror in this fashion—assassinating labor leaders, journalists, and politicians. Although their tactics failed to destabilize the Italian state, the Red Brigades did succeed in preventing a coalition between the Christian Democrats and the Communist party.

Expanding the Movement   Other movements may give less attention to the political system and put their energy into the recruiting of new members and the diffusion of discourse in the society that is favorable to them. Their primary strategy may be to build up a large support base and a favorable climate of opinion before they turn to the use of state power. Political strategies do not preclude strategies of **mass persuasion**; on the contrary, they often occur together. For example, the Christian right in the United States has combined strategies of building a mass base with strategies of influencing the political parties, running candidates, and supporting specific legislation.

How do movements go about the strategy of mass persuasion? They can develop their own media. The Christian right in the United States owns TV stations and magazines that diffuse messages of Christian fundamentalism and social and political conservatism (Hadden 1993). Movements can put pressure on existing media to represent them in a favorable way. They can engage in events like demonstrations to draw attention to the movement, hoping thereby to promote an image of efficacy, commitment, and solidarity. For instance, the Gay and Lesbian Rights March on Washington, DC, in April of 1993 was organized, in part, with the goal of showing the nation the strength and solidarity of the movement.

Often **direct action** is used more as a means of recruiting for a movement or projecting its image, than as a direct means of change. Movements have to use the media, in part, and this reliance creates complex problems in **framing movement discourse** in such a way that movements will get adequate coverage (Gamson and Wolfsfeld, in *Annals,* 1993; Gitlin, 1980; Ryan, 1991). For example, when Operation Rescue activists block the entrances to abortion clinics, their goal is not primarily to stop abortions on that particular day as much as it is to draw attention to the movement.

Movements can use means like direct-mail solicitation to target a potential support base. Both antiabortion groups and the Central American solidarity movement used these methods of reaching potential constituencies. Development of networks and personal relationships to recruit new members is also an important element of the strategy of mass persuasion (McCarthy, in Zald and McCarthy, 1987; Snow et al., 1986).

Matching Organization to Strategy

A movement has to make decisions about connecting its strategy to its organization. If the main strategy for realizing goals is electing people to office and changing legislation, members must organize the movement as a mass party. If the main strategy is capturing the state in armed struggle, they must include or train specialists in violence, develop clandestine operations for all or some of the movement, and prepare either for protracted guerrilla warfare or for bringing parts of the existing military institutions over to the side of the movement. If the main strategy is influencing existing elites, they must organize as a pressure group, project an air of responsibility and "mainstreamness" and develop some media support. If the main strategy for change is individual redemption—changes in the ideology and practices of individuals—they must develop ways of converting and recruiting masses of followers.

These strategic and organizational decisions only make sense if we keep in mind the ideology of the movement, its set of goals for social change. A movement has to be flexible in its organization and strategy, matching its operations to the realities of the social and political environment.

For example, in western Europe, the Communist movement went through phases of being a mass party (in Germany in the 1920s, in Italy and France after World War II) as well as a clandestine resistance organization (in France and Italy during the Nazi occupation). Sometimes it engaged in coalition building and sometimes it did not, depending on its assessment of the political climate.

Similarly, Islamic fundamentalist movements organize as mass parties (currently in Algeria), mass movements (as in Hamas, a fundamentalist Palestinian organization), small terrorist groups (as in Lebanon), broad-based insurgent armies (as in the Afghan mujahideen movement against the Soviet invasion), sectlike groups with charismatic leaders (as in the organization of the Iranian Islamic movement in exile before the 1979 revolution), and intellectual currents. The ideology and goals remain basically the same—the formation of Islamic states—but the organization and strategies vary with circumstances.

Vanguard Parties, Fronts, and Coalitions   Historically, several terms have appeared frequently in discussions of movement organization and strategy. One such term is **vanguard party.** It derives from the practice of Communist parties, especially those operating in political systems in which they were illegal (Healey and Isserman, 1990). The vanguard party is relatively small compared to the movement as a whole. It is relatively "professionalized," in that its members have a complete and full-time commitment to the movement. Sometimes the term "professional" implies that money is an important incentive for full-time commitment to movement work; but not in this case—the vanguard party is supposed to be motivated primarily by commitment to the ideology of the movement. It is composed of people who are particularly clear about the movement's ideology and goals; while the movement as a whole may include people who share these ideals to some extent, many of these peripheral participants may not fully grasp the ideology.

The distinction between the vanguard party and the support base is expressed in the term **spontaneity.** The mass support base, left to its own devices, might spontaneously engage in direct action and in the formation of unions; by itself, however, it cannot formulate or carry out a strategy for capturing and transforming the state apparatus. The vanguard party is small enough and has a sufficiently centralized decision-making process to allow flexibility in its relationship to the mass support base which it guides toward capturing the state apparatus.

Movements that have a vanguard party organization also often have a **front** structure; the front is a broad coalition of groups that share some of the ideology of the movement and are prepared to cooperate with it. In some cases, the vanguard party itself may organize the front groups, using this structure to reach categories of potential supporters. Sometimes these groups support the goals of the party, as in Vietnam, where the Communist Party formed the core of the National Liberation Front, which brought together many groups that sought independence. In other instances, the front is composed of groups that are seen as having "special interests" within the movement. For example, the Communist Party might be supported by women's or students' groups in a larger front.

Although this terminology of vanguard party and front derives from the communist movements of twentieth century, it is a framework that is visible in many other movements as well. Highly committed and ideologically coherent cadres formed into a small, centralized organization lead a larger movement of people who have a less sophisticated understanding of the political system and less of an overview of the goals and strategy of the movement.

Most movements include in their strategies the effort to form **coalitions** or **alliances** with other movements. These alliances may be formed through a united front, as described above, or through an **umbrella organization** that brings together two or more movements on a relatively equal basis. Movements also form looser alliances around common goals. These alliances may form around specific goals that movements share.

When distinct social groups, especially classes, are brought together in such a front or alliance, social scientists sometimes speak of a **bloc.** For instance, in the Nicaraguan revolution of 1979, the Sandinista movement represented a wide range of groups and a broad and diverse support base; poor peasants joined middle-class reformers who detested the Somoza dictatorship. During the Resistance in Italy against the Nazis and the Fascists, Christian Democrats, Communists, and radical intellectuals joined forces, although their ideologies and social support bases were substantially different.

Let me summarize the terminology: A front implies organization of groups under the leadership of a vanguard party or other cohesive movement organization; coalition and alliance refer to looser cooperative ventures among relatively equal movement organizations; and bloc refers to a joining together of diverse support bases into a large, powerful force in society.

Tactics

The last term to be defined in this section is **tactics.** This term means the methods of accomplishing a precisely defined intermediate or short-term goal. A strategy is the overall plan; tactics are specific techniques for attaining specific goals. Strategies change when there are major shifts in society to which the movement must respond. Tactics are more flexible, and are somewhat more likely to be decided locally or in a decentralized way, even in a centralized movement. These terms are not always used in a precise or consistent way, however, and there is considerable overlap in strategy and tactics.

TRANSNATIONAL MOVEMENTS AND EXTERNAL SUPPORT

Movements throughout the twentieth century have operated across national borders, and in our increasingly globalized world, there is every indication that they will continue to do so. All the movements identified in this book are transnational. We have already discussed how movements adjust their strategies and forms of organization to adapt to different types of societies and political systems. Nation-states also have a direct impact on movements. They are a major source of resources for movements. They can offer economic aid, arms, and territorial bases or "sanctuaries." For example, the Soviets (and at times, also China) provided arms for the Vietnamese revolutionaries. The United States provided arms and economic assistance to the anti-Soviet Afghan insurgents. South Africa provided support to guerrillas against the governments of Angola and Mozambique.

Who used whom, in these innumerable instances of **external support?** Did a large power—in recent decades, often one of the Cold War superpowers—use a movement as a pawn in its own global strategy? Or did a movement skillfully manipulate the fears or ambitions of existing nations in order to obtain support? In any case, such external support has become a crucial factor in twentieth-century movement outcomes.

In addition to direct support for a movement, nations can involve themselves in movement outcomes in more subtle ways. Once a movement comes to power in a society, even by legal means, a hostile nation can block access to credit and can stimulate disinvestment. A well-documented example is the action that the United States took after a socialist government was elected in Chile; the United States blocked loans for Chile in international credit agencies. Similarly, the long-term U.S. trade embargo against Cuba has contributed to a difficult economic situation there and weakened Cuba's ability to achieve the goals of the revolution.

External resources can be used to influence the outcome of elections. The United States channeled money into Nicaragua in the 1990 elections to help shift support from the Sandinistas to the National Opposition Union (UNO) coalition and its candidate, Violetta Chamorro; while this money did not go directly to a party, it created a climate of opinion that was more favorable toward UNO.

The withdrawal of investment from South Africa and international trade sanctions helped to bring the de Klerk government into negotiations with the African National Congress (ANC). South Africa's worsening economic situation was a factor in the government's decision to end the illegal status of the ANC and to open the way for a reorganization of the political system.

Once a movement comes to power in one country, it has a territorial and resource base to help affiliated movements in other nations. For example, the Islamic revolution in Iran has aided other Islamic movements. Even without state power, a strong base in one country can provide support for a movement worldwide; for example, the wealthy and powerful Mormon community in the United States supports the propagation of Mormonism in many other countries.

During the Vietnamese war, United States policy makers coined the term "domino effect" to describe this potential spread of a movement; the term specifically referred to fears that a Communist victory in one nation in Southeast Asia (i.e., Vietnam) would spread to other nations in the region (like the Philippines, Malaysia, or Indonesia). Similar fears were expressed in Washington that the Cuban revolution would be "exported" to other nations in Latin America. These fears were probably exaggerated, but transnational support is a reality in movement success.

Some theorists distinguish **relational** from **nonrelational** diffusion of movement ideas across national boundaries (McAdam and Rucht, in *Annals*, 1993). For instance, New Left ideas spread from the United States to Germany through both direct personal contacts and similarities in the conditions and cultures of the two nations.

MULTIORGANIZATIONAL FIELDS

A movement rarely exists by itself in a society. Usually a society has a number of movements active within it simultaneously. All movement activity taken together is often termed the **social movement sector** of the society. The size, complexity, and volatility of this sector is markedly different from society to society, varying with the political system, current strains, and cultural traditions. The United States, for example, has a long-standing tradition of a high level of movement activity (Garner and Zald, 1985).

Some of the simultaneously existing movements may be in support of each other, in alliances or fronts that have overlapping or similar goals, or simply in parallel and compatible actions and ideologies. For instance, the animal rights movement is part of a larger environmental movement (Jasper and Nelkin, 1993). Within each movement may also be multiple organizations. Some movements may operate largely independently of other movements. And some movements may be locked into combat with other movements; for example, sectors of the women's movement and the antiabortion movement in the 1980s, or the Civil Rights Movement and white supremacist groups like the White Citizen's Council in the 1960s. When movements have directly opposed goals, we can use the term **movement and countermovement** (Mottl, 1980; Zald and McCarthy, 1987).

Social Control Agents

Movements also are in relationships with **social control agents,** institutions designed to eliminate movements and/or integrate them into the political mainstream. Social control agents can repress movements—especially movement organizations—by charging their members with criminal actions or raiding their offices, as police departments did to the Black Panthers in the 1960s and 1970s (Brown, 1994). In some instances, social control agents use illegal violence, such as death squad activity by units of the military against peasant organizers in Guatemala (Smith-Ayala, 1991).

Social control agents can also co-opt movement members, offering them a chance to pursue careers or work toward a limited set of reforms within the existing institutions. For example, the Mexican ruling party, the (Institutional Revolutionary Party) (PRI), has often drawn peasant, worker, and student leaders into the party structure, providing them with career lines and an opportunity to accomplish some small improvements in return for leaving insurgent movements (Riding, 1984).

Social control agents can limit the effectiveness of movements by encouraging countermovements to form or by supporting those countermovements that come into existence on their own. In some cases, such countermovements may be largely sham, simply paid-off thugs or government agents; but in other cases, they may have a genuine social base and an independent ideology and purpose. For example, in northern Italy in the early 1920s, one of the most important points of growth of the Fascist movement were the *squadre,* groups of Fascist activists who formed a countermovement against left-wing organizations that had mobilized rural workers. The Fascist squads attacked members of left-wing groups, broke up meetings and strikes, and intimidated individuals. While the large landowners of the region supported the Fascists, the Fascists were not simply "hired guns" of the landowners, but formed a movement with an ideology and a strategy for eventually coming to power (Cardoza, 1982).

Social control agents are often part of a government that would like to suppress the movement, and may be government agencies designed specifically for this purpose. For example, the antiterrorism division of the FBI concerns itself with identifying and bringing to trial groups and individuals engaged in terrorist activities within the United States.

In some cases, social control agents may be divided in their attitude toward social movements. The role of the FBI during the Civil Rights Movement illustrates these complexities. Some parts of the agency were investigating murders in civil rights workers by members of white supremacist groups; other parts of the agency were investigating civil rights activists (Garrow, 1987). These actions did not just reflect concerns about both types of movements; they also reflected divisions within the national government and the agency over government support for the Civil Rights Movement.

In a federal system like the United States, the interaction of movement-countermovement-social control agents is even further complicated by different levels of government. For example, local sheriffs and police departments were sometimes openly harassing civil rights activists or even supporting white supremacist countermovements.

When a movement comes to power, like the 1979 Islamic revolution in Iran, the Cuban revolution in 1959, or the American Revolution in the 1770s, the revolutionary regime has to act as a social control agent against **counterrevolutionaries,** forces that would like to overthrow the revolution, curb its influence, or prevent it from accomplishing its goals. For example, in the American Revolution, the Loyalists initially formed a countermovement against the revolutionary movement in the colonies; as the revolutionaries came to power, they repressed and harassed the Loyalists, forcing them to either accept independence or go into exile in Canada. These actions were carried out at the local level, through harassment and intimidation. Committees for the Defense of the Revolution organized at the local level had a similar social control function after the success of the Cuban revolution.

In summary, social movement sector, countermovement, and social control agents are terms that draw attention to the complexity of relationships, including antagonistic ones, among different kinds of movements and organizations. Like the concept external support, these terms are ways of referring to the environment within which social movements act. They draw attention to the **multiorganizational fields** in which movements operate, environments in which the major "players" are other movements and movement organizations that are possible allies and/or competitors, countermovements, and organized social control agents (Curtis and Zurcher, 1973; Klandermans, 1992).

HISTORICAL CONDITIONS

Social scientists give a great deal of attention to the question of what preconditions lead a movement to emerge, grow, and succeed. Ideologies that may have been "floating around" for a long time suddenly seem to be translated into action and organization. Movements that have existed in a **becalmed** or **dormant** state suddenly become active again (Taylor, 1989). New ideologies and movements emerge, sometimes in surprising ways. People who have "accepted" poverty and repression for generations suddenly and unpredictably rebel. States that have had an iron grip on their societies fall apart, sometimes for no clear reason.

For example, the Portuguese were for decades written off as passive and accepting of a dictatorship that had been imposed in the early 1930s. Suddenly in the 1970s, a mass revolution swept Portugal, dismantled the repressive government, and brought Portugal into the liberal democratic framework of western Europe. What were the specific conditions that precipitated this revolution? Similarly, the supposed monolith of Communist Party regimes in eastern Europe and the Soviet Union collapsed within a few years, under the impact of a large but weakly organized and unarmed mass movement.

In the same surprising way, powerful movements may disappear as circumstances change. Students for a Democratic Society and other movement organizations of the New Left of the 1960s shrank and faded after the United States withdrew from Vietnam.

What causes these shifts? We cannot answer this question in general or in the abstract. The answers lie in a careful examination of historical circumstances. The specific, concrete circumstances of a nation's history contain part of the answer. So does the historical **conjuncture**—the configuration at any given moment of the global economic and political balance of power. The col-

Movement and countermovement: Vigil in front of the United States Supreme Court. Washington, DC, June 29, 1989.

lapse of the Communist parties in eastern Europe became possible as the Soviet Union decided not to control the region anymore because of the pressure of its own economic crisis and the arms race. Portugal exploded in 1974 because it was fighting the last colonial war in Africa, a war for which it received no support from other European powers.

In the next chapter, I will review a number of theories that dissect these historical conditions in a more detailed way. As I discuss movements, I will try to give some indication of the historical factors that account for the specific course of the movement.

SUMMARY

In this chapter, I have introduced a series of terms relevant to discussion about movements: ideology; support base and constituencies; organization, strategies, and tactics; external support; movement sector, social control agents, and countermovements; and historical conditions. These are terms that are widely used by sociologists and political scientists (Greene, 1990). I have tried to give the reader a picture of what movements *do* within each of these categories— how they go about stating their ideologies, how they reach out to their support base or bases, how they make choices about organizational forms and strategies, and how they receive help from existing states. These concepts allow us to compare movements—we can compare their ideologies, their support bases, their organization and strategies, their sources of external support, and the circumstances in which they emerged.

In the next chapter, on social movement theory, I will review different explanations of movements that use more detailed and finely nuanced versions of each of these concepts in order to explain the emergence, forms, and outcomes of movements. In later chapters, in which I discuss specific contemporary movements, I will use these concepts as a framework for organizing the chapters.

One of the most important concepts is *ideology*—the ideas and discourses of the movement. These are the *ends* of the movements; organization, strategies, and the mobilization of support are the *means* a movement uses to accomplish its ends or goals. It is the ideology—the ends—that most clearly distinguishes movements from each other, since there can be a considerable overlap in the means they use. One way to understand a movement is to comprehend its ideology, to assume the insider's perspective, at least temporarily. The ideology is one answer—the insider's answer—to the question, Why has this movement emerged?

Another way to understand a movement is to examine the historical conditions in which it emerged and continues to operate. Looking at historical conditions is an outsider's way of understanding a movement; implied in this perspective is the view that a movement can be explained objectively and scientifically. Sometimes movement activists and social scientists agree in their interpretations and point to the same reasons or causes for the existence of a movement, but generally movement ideologies and the analysis of historical conditions do not offer the same answers to the question, Why has this movement emerged?

KEY TERMS AND CONCEPTS

the definition of a movement
movement
practices and discourses
legitimating discourses
institutionalized and
   noninstitutionalized practices
agents of social control
reform and revolution

ideology and related terms
ideology
symbols
framing
condensation symbols
cult of personality
negative symbols: scapegoats and
   folk devils
constituencies
universalizing discourses
bloc
reformative and transformative
   movements
left and right

support base
adherents, constituencies, and
   beneficiaries
intellectuals
specialists in violence
mobilization

organization
organization
movement organization
organizational structure

centralization, decentralization,
   segmentation
authority: traditional, rational-legal,
   charismatic
routinization of charisma
bureaucratization
internal division of labor

strategies and tactics
strategies
political opportunity structure
cell structure
parties or pressure groups
armed insurgencies
destabilization
terrorism
mass persuasion
direct action
framing movement discourse
vanguard parties
fronts
coalitions and alliances; blocs
tactics

movement environments
external support
social movement sectors
movement and countermovement
social control agents
counterrevolution
multiorganizational fields

historical conditions
conjuncture

Opposing mobilizations: Harassment of civil
rights activists sitting in at a lunch counter.
Jackson, Mississippi, June 12, 1963.

CHAPTER 3

Social Movement Theories

Danger, disquiet, anxiety attend the unknown—the first instinct is to eliminate these distracting states. First principle: Any explanation is better than none.
—Friedrich Nietzche
Twilight of the Idols.

At a major intersection in Saigon, on June 11, 1963, a Buddhist monk, Thich Quang Duc, undertakes a protest against the anti-Buddhist policies of the ruling Catholic oligarchy in South Vietnam, against the general repression practiced by the government, and against the war itself. With help from other monks, he douses himself with a flammable liquid and sets himself on fire. He sits still as the flames flare up; his face and body blacken; he crumples to the pavement, still burning.

Millions of viewers saw this suicide on film, television, and in newspaper photographs. Most viewers probably asked the same questions: What cause is worth dying for? Is there any ideal in which I believe so strongly that I would set myself on fire? Even if I were sure my suicide would bring about a change, would I be prepared to die in this way?

This chapter will look at ways in which social scientists have tried to answer the question: Why do people form movements? Why do they undertake acts of courage, desperation, and cruelty in order to change the world? These theories can explain some of the reasons why movements emerge, but for many, Thich Quang Duc's suicide will remain a disturbing mystery.

Source: Based on T. E. Vadney, *The World since 1945*, Penguin, New York, 1987, p. 313.

INTRODUCTION

In the preceding chapter, I defined a number of terms that most sociologists and political scientists use to discuss social movements. There is considerable agreement about these concepts, most of which refer to parts or aspects of movements. In this chapter, I will introduce a number of theories that social scientists use to explain movements and here we will see more differences and disagreements. A theory in any type of science is an effort to answer a question

41

Why? A theory points to causes of phenomena or tries to account for differences among phenomena.

New theories emerge in response to both internal and external pressures. Some new theories are proposed to solve problems or fill gaps in the existing theories—to explain something that the existing theories do not explain very well. Others emerge as the social environment itself changes. For example, after the rise of fascism and nazism, many social scientists looked for the explanation of social movements in terms of the irrational psychological characteristics of movement adherents. After the Civil Rights Movement and opposition to the war in Vietnam in the 1960s—movements that held the sympathies of many sociologists and political scientists—social movement theory shifted to emphasis on the rational side of movement organization and mobilization.

Changes in theories in response to both internal and external pressure take place frequently. Theory in the social sciences is not a single fixed way of understanding the world, but competing and shifting types of explanation (Kuhn, 1962).

What Is Theory?

An example from biology can illustrate the purposes of theory. Imagine different teams of researchers investigating the causes of cancers. They would probably all use the same terms to refer to the organs of the body and processes in cells, just as social scientists would have considerable consensus on the terms used to refer to elements of movements. The teams of researchers are in major disagreement about the causes of cancers: One team is examining genetic predispositions; a second team is looking for environmental causes, like air and water pollution; a third team is studying the personal habits of individuals, like smoking or dietary factors. These explanations or identifications of causes constitute different theories.

Theories are not necessarily mutually exclusive; some researchers may, in fact, be trying to combine these different theories into one larger value-added theory that identifies the relative weights of all these factors in explaining the outcome—the presence of a specific type of cancer.

The example of cancer research is not used to imply that theorists explain only problems, situations they would like to reduce or eliminate. Theorists also try to explain favorable situations; for instance, why some individuals have strong immune systems. In this case, too, they might look for the *why* in genetic predispositions, in environmental conditions, and/or in personal habits.

Two examples of theories in the social sciences are discussed below. In the social sciences, there is often not only disagreement about explanations but also on exactly what is to be explained. The examples are drawn from psychology and criminology; they illustrate how theories use different definitions of *what is to be explained* as well as provide different explanations.

Two Examples of Psychological Theories   Psychologists seek to explain the actions of individuals, their ways of behaving and being. Behaviorist theories concern the cumulative, complex processes of conditioning, ways in which behaviors are rewarded or punished, reinforced or extinguished. Of course, in the case of human beings these patterns of reward and punishment are themselves complicated, not just food pellets or electric shocks.

Psychoanalytic theories point to the formation of the personality in unconscious processes that result from the impact of external reality on the drives of the infant, child, and adult; the sexual drives are a key element because they are powerful but also malleable (in a way that hunger, for example, is not) and variable from individual to individual.

Not only are these two theories different in their way of explaining what individuals do, they also disagree about exactly what it is they want to explain: Behaviorists seek to explain behavior—observable and measurable actions—while psychoanalytic theorists are more interested in interior and even unconscious processes that constitute the personality.

Sociological Theories of Crime   In criminology, there are many theories to account for crime. First of all, crime can be defined differently, either as an individual act or as a rate for a given society or community. The why question can be, Why does this community or society have a high crime rate? or Why has this individual committed crimes, when others in the same community have not?

We can explain differences in crime rates in terms of the cultures of the communities or the levels of economic or social stress they are under. At the level of the individual, we can explain criminal actions in terms of personality characteristics, childhood and family experiences, exposure to economic and social stress, a cumulative labeling process in schools and other institutions, differential association with people who already are involved in crime, the absence of legal opportunities for success and the presence of illegal ones, or a breakdown in formal and informal social control. Each of these explanatory theories has come to have a name (differential association, opportunity structure, labeling, control, and so on) and many are associated with specific theorists. It is hard to *prove* or *disprove* any one of these theories or even test them directly against each other. Each theory is basically a different way of thinking about why—they may point to different questions as well as to different ways of answering them.

SOCIAL MOVEMENT THEORIES

Different theories point to different *why* questions and to the answers to these questions. The basic definition of a social movement is a group of people who are engaged in an ideologically coherent and noninstitutionalized way of changing the present state and trajectory of their society. This definition points to a lot of possible *why's* for theories to focus on.

Why are there people dissatisfied with the current state of society and the direction in which it appears to be headed?

Why are they engaged in a social movement rather than coping with these problems on an individual basis or through institutionalized channels?

statement that divert our attention to causes of phenomenon

Why do they believe that this kind of change is possible and desirable?

Why do some individuals join movements and others, subjected to the same stresses, do not?

Why do some societies or types of societies have higher rates of movement activity than others?

Why do movements within the same society (or type of society) differ in form and in ideological contents?

Why are some movements successful in accomplishing their goals and others are not?

Since the theories reviewed in this chapter focus on several aspects of movements and use different types of explanations, they are not mutually exclusive. For this reason, theories can be combined with each other to give a more complete understanding of the phenomenon.

Changes in Social Movement Theory

Social movement theories have changed over the last couple of decades. Some of these changes have causes that are *internal* to the field. Existing theories did not seem to cover some aspects of movements, so new theories were proposed to fill these gaps.

Some of the changes in theories have *external* causes, because theories in the social sciences respond to changes in society. For example, by the 1960s, movements like Nazism and Stalinist forms of communism were no longer "center stage" for European and North American researchers. The New Left and guerrilla insurgencies in places like Vietnam and Latin America began to draw the attention of movement theorists. In the 1970s and 1980s, feminism and new decentralized social movements in Europe as well as Islamic movements seemed to require new types of theories.

Finally, social movement theories respond to changes in the *cultural and intellectual climate,* to ideas that are fashionable and popular among intellectuals. For example, in the 1940s and 1950s, social movement theory was influenced by psychoanalysis which intrigued American intellectuals and even influenced American pop culture. In the 1960s and 1970s, a rekindled interest in marxism in western Europe (and to a lesser extent, the United States) led to the introduction of marxist perspectives into social movement theory. Then, in the 1980s, and now, 1990s, deconstructionist and postmodern philosophy and cultural studies have emphasized discourse in movement theory.

One way to approach this chapter would be to write the history of social movement theory from the 1940s to the present, tracing the various shifts in theory as social scientists respond to existing theories, to external social and political changes, and to intellectual fashions. Instead, I have organized the theories in terms of the scope of the analysis, from those that are very broad and sociohistorical, to middle-range theories that focus on specific societies, and to the micro theories that look at individual mobilization. From time to time, I will indicate why some theories became popular at a certain time while others faded away.

MACROHISTORICAL AND SOCIOHISTORICAL THEORIES

Types of Societies and Social Movements

Theories are referred to as *macro* theories because they cover a very large scope of time and place; their time frame is in centuries and their scope is global. They try to answer the question, Why does a type of society generate certain types of social movement? These theories tend to fall into two categories: **Marxist theories,** which point to capitalism as the determining force of movements, and theories of modern or mass and postmodern society, which point to a wider array of social and cultural factors that generate movements.

Marxist Theories   Marxist theories focus on the characteristics of capitalism as a global system that creates certain contradictions. The basic contradiction is that between human creativity and the constraints on this creativity, constraints that arise out of the unequal social relations of production. The class structure of capitalism, its **social relations of production,** vests power over resources in privately owned firms and gives employers control over the labor power and products of employees, hence, over their very conditions of survival in a market economy. At the same time, capitalists (the owner/employers) are in heated competition with each other in national and global markets, a situation that puts them under enormous pressure to lower labor costs. They can do this by reducing their work force, speeding up production, moving their operations to lower-wage economies, or by introducing machinery; these are overlapping and not mutually exclusive strategies (Mandel, 1975).

These economic imperatives generate social strains experienced in different ways by different groups. The antagonistic relationship between workers and owners produces class-based movements. Workers may join unions or socialist parties, while owners will develop movements to block these efforts (Gurley, 1975).

Alternatively, capitalists and workers in each nation may decide to band together as nationalists, agreeing to limit their antagonism with each other in order to reduce the impact of global capitalist competition; thus, the global competition inherent in the capitalist system generates nationalist movements as well as class movements. Different regions of the world experience the impact of capitalism differently; thus, regional and national movements arise that propose specific solutions to these varied strains (Chaliand, 1989; Hobsbawm, 1989).

Some insurgents focus on the effects of capitalism, rather than its defining social relationships; for example, they see stress on families or the dissolution of traditional communities and religious institutions, and may engage in efforts to reconstitute these ties, giving rise to conservative movements.

In short, a marxist analysis does *not* point only to the economic motivation of individuals—class interest in the narrowest sense; rather, it indicates that a wide range of responses can arise out of the stresses created by the **capitalist mode of production.** Accounting for the full range of movements requires attention to the specific circumstances of each society within the global capitalist system. Marxist theories sometimes do not give enough attention to the way capitalism brings about movements that are not class conscious—movements like religious fundamentalism or nationalism.

Finally, marxist theories point to the political and ideological relationships associated with capitalism as forces that shape movements (Aronowitz, 1973; Donald and Hall, 1986; Gramsci, 1971; Miliband, 1969). Representative democracy and individualistic ideals create opportunities for movements and a sense that people can shape their own destinies; at the same time, though, individualism can diminish the commitment to the collective solutions offered by social movements.

Mass/Modern Society Theories   Mass/modern society theory has a global scope and long-term time frame similar to marxist theories, but points to a larger array of causal elements, less clearly grouped around the mode of production. It tends to emphasize strains that grow out of a cluster of related processes: Capitalism is one of these processes but not necessarily the "master process," since industrialization, urbanization, bureaucratization, culture contact on a global scale, global communications and the emergence of an electronic "global village," secularization, the formation of representative democracies as well as strongly centralized repressive states, and many other transformations are also at work.

The sum total of these processes is to create societies in which many people experience the stress of social change at the same time that traditional controls have broken down. This condition produces the mixture of dissatisfaction and sense of possibility that are the necessary elements for the rise of movements (Arendt, 1965; Berman, 1982; Kornhauser, 1959). The immediate result of the modernization processes is **anomie**—a sense of normative breakdown. The breakdown in traditional communities and controls leaves many people open to social movements. Traditional answers to life questions no longer make sense; people have to look for new answers, answers that also point to the possibility of a change for the better. This ongoing sense of crisis in modern society is both a source of stress and of opportunity (Lerner, 1958). Traditional hierarchies of landowners and peasants, men and women, the elders and the young, and rulers and ruled are collapsing everywhere—indeed have collapsed already in the west and in the Communist and post-Communist societies. The condition of modern society has led individuals everywhere to see that human beings can shape society and influence their own destiny (Zeitlin, 1994).

But there are no obvious new answers: Some people turn to conservative movements that attempt to reconstitute traditional institutions like religion, stretching and redefining these values and institutions to respond to the new strains. Others look to the creation of new bases of solidarity—race, nation, gender, class. New "imagined communities" of this sort take the place of the older, face-to-face village communities (Anderson, 1991). All of these movements, even the apparently conservative ones, are modern: They have to address the anomie and disruption of modern life whether they do this by revitalizing traditional institutions or inventing new bases of solidarity.

Postmodern Society   Modern and mass society theories have been updated by a variety of theories of **postmodern society.** These theories emphasize one or another characteristic of societies that appeared after the Second World War. Some theories point to economic change, new electronic and biogenetic technologies, the globalization of markets and media systems, and the growth of the service and information sectors (Reich, 1992). Some of these theories specifically use the term postindustrial to identify this new type of society (Bell, 1973). Some theorists point to the shrinkage of the industrial working class in the developed capitalist nations and the blurring of class boundaries (Gorz, 1982; Touraine, 1971). Other theories of the postmodern emphasize challenges to western, modern, and/or Eurocentric culture (Wallerstein, 1990).

Because these changes are still under way, there are many disagreements about their nature, magnitude, and likely outcomes. Marxist and nonmarxist theorists disagree over whether these changes become comprehensible by extension and elaboration of the categories and concepts used to analyze capitalism in general, or whether they require some new "postmarxist" theoretical framework (Anderson, 1984; Mandel, 1975).

Whatever the postmodern changes may be, they are likely to amplify rather than end the anomie and unsettled feelings associated with modern society. Theorists are looking at the impact of these changes on social movements (Scott, 1990). We will return to these discussions at the end of Chapter 5, "From Modern to Postmodern: Movements in History."

MIDRANGE THEORIES

Marxist and modern/mass/postmodern society theories offer answers to the questions concerning social movements on a very large scale, pointing to a type of society (capitalist, modern, and/or postmodern) and a historical epoch. Many theorists prefer to look at specific societies and at shorter time frames—years or decades rather than centuries. Their question is, Why has this movement emerged in this society at this point in time? They also look at structural strains that affect specific categories of people within a society: Why has this movement emerged among this category of persons, distinguished by class, ethnicity, region, gender, and so on? And finally, they ask, How has this movement organized and mobilized supporters and resources to accomplish its goals?

I will cover three different types of midrange theory: structural strain, resource mobilization, and political opportunity structure. These theories were generally first proposed in the 1960s and 1970s. Their appearance reflects a changing attitude in the social sciences toward movements during that period. Psychological theories that looked at irrational motives for joining movements gave way to theories that looked at movements as largely rational responses to real stresses in the society. This theoretical shift was probably due, in part, to the emergence of the Civil Rights Movement in the United States with which most movement theorists were in sympathy.

I will use two movements to illustrate these midrange theories: the Civil Rights Movement in the United States and the Chinese Communist Revolution of 1949.

Structural Strain Theories

Structural strain theories point to the heightening of strains or contradictions at certain moments; these strains are both objectively present in the institutions of society and subjectively experienced as such by individuals. However, individuals may "read" the strain in different ways, in many cases preferring to deal with it in a more individual or institutionalized way. Once the strain is present and recognized as a condition that can be changed, individuals come together to alter the situation.

There are a number of ways to conceptualize strain as an objectively present condition. For instance, it can be as a **disequilibrium** in society, a state of tension between different parts of the social system, especially between economic institutions and cultural values (Johnson, 1964). Some parts may change more rapidly than others, causing these strains. Strain can be thought of in more marxist terms, with an emphasis on tensions between the class system (the social relations of production) and the human capacity for creativity. Strain can come from specific historical processes like the conquest or enslavement of one ethnic group by another.

The subjective recognition of strain is the *why* of two important strain theories: Relative deprivation theory and the J-curve theory of changing expectations. These theories try to answer the question of why a category of people who are in a condition of strain eventually define themselves as a group with common interests in fundamental social change.

Relative deprivation theory suggests that objectively present strains become subjectively experienced dissatisfaction when people are able to compare themselves to others, to a **reference group** of people who seem better off. As long as people live in closed situations, cut off from other communities and the larger society, they are more likely to "suffer in silence." As their horizons broaden, they are more likely to make comparisons and feel discontented. The Civil Rights Movement, for example, came into being as a new generation of African Americans, who had served in World War II and lived or traveled in the north, were able to see that the oppressed condition of black people in the south was unusual and intolerable by these larger standards.

The **J-curve theory** proposed by James Davies (1962) points to one way in which strain is recognized. When an intolerable situation has improved, but threatens to revert suddenly to its original oppressive condition, people are more likely to engage in collective action to prevent this outcome. When hopes are raised, disappointment is likely to set in if change seems to be slowing down or reversing. For this reason, it often appears that the initial efforts of elites to reduce strain actually precipitate movement activity rather than lessen it. **Rising expectations** and concern about a return to an oppressive status quo ante can bring people together into a movement.

Structural strain theories also look at how different groups are affected differently by strains. Racism, for example, is a condition of the whole society but it affects the minority far more than the dominant racial group. The strains are different in their objective impact on different parts of the population and in the way they are defined subjectively by different categories of people. Racism is a top priority for social change for most African Americans in the United States, while it is overlooked or denied as a strain by many European Americans. Societies clearly vary in the amount of strains present within them, the extent to which categories of people perceive the same strains or different strains, and the clarity and immediacy of these perceptions of strains.

Resource Mobilization Theories

Resource mobilization theories put less emphasis on the objective presence or subjective recognition of structural stress and more emphasis on how individuals and groups create opportunities to change their condition. The structural problems may exist on a long-term basis as do the discontents and, therefore, don't explain very well why a movement arises at a given moment; what needs to be explained is how a collectivity forms to change the existing state of affairs. The resource mobilization perspective developed in North American sociology and political science in the 1960s and has continued to be influential in the social movements field; Mayer Zald and John McCarthy's work on movement organizations and movement professionals (1979), Anthony Oberschall's comparative analysis of political movements (1973), and Jo Freeman's studies of the women's movement in the United States (1975, 1979, 1983) are examples of the growth of this perspective.

Resource mobilization theories put a strong emphasis on **movement organizations,** rather than on movements as currents of opinion among dissatisfied people (Zald and Ash, 1966). They see movement organizations as **institutional actors,** groups in the political system that are capable of making decisions and allocating time and money to achieve their ends. Resource mobilization theory tends to see movement organizations as rational, if not in their ends, at least in their means. Even a movement whose ends we might judge to be irrational—for example, the Nazis—can be quite rational in its choice of means. As researchers, we must not let our feelings about the contents of movement ideologies overwhelm our analysis of how movements organize themselves and accomplish their goals.

Movement organizations identify strategic tasks and reach out to potential supporters. Support comes not only from reaching new members but also from turning elites into sympathizers and building coalitions with other institutional actors like other movements, parties, religious organizations, and so on. Movements often form around preexisting networks and institutions, which constitute the framework for new kinds of activities, as Jo Freeman showed in her analysis of the origins of the second-wave-feminist women's movement in the United States in the 1960s (Freeman, 1983). Movement organizations select incentives to encourage participation and muster external support. Movement professionals have a key part in movement organizations (Zald and McCarthy, 1987). They turn a movement from a current of opinion or belief into an organization that can be an effective institutional actor in the political system, competing and cooperating with other organizations like parties and pressure groups.

The why question that resource mobilization theories answer is, Given a certain level of structural strain and dissatisfaction, why are some groups able to mobilize supporters and organize time and money effectively to make changes?

Political Opportunity Structure Theories

Political opportunity structure theories put emphasis on political institutions as the key to whether structural problems can be successfully challenged. As long as political institutions are themselves firm, unyielding, and coherent, dissatisfied people will have to resort to individual coping mechanisms or whatever institutionalized channels there are for a redress of grievances. But at certain times, the political system may open up intentionally or unintentionally and create opportunities for movements (*Annals*, 1993).

An intentional opening up of the political system may occur when **elites** decide to **co-opt** or **support** movements (Berry, in *Annals*, 1993; Hershey, in *Annals*, 1993; Kitschelt, in *Annals*, 1993; McCarthy and Wolfson, in Morris and Mueller, 1992). For example, the Reagan administration accepted electoral support from Christian fundamentalist constituencies and movement organizations, in return making some efforts to limit abortion access and appoint judges who opposed legal abortions; these reforms encouraged the pro-life movement. In the 1930s, the Roosevelt administration entered into a reciprocal relationship with the labor movement that was organizing industrial unions in heavy industries like automobiles and steel. Changes in legislation improved the climate for union organizing, and organized labor became a major supporting force for the New Deal. In the 1960s, the Kennedy administration created a favorable climate for the Civil Rights Movement. Under pressure from countries that placed economic sanctions on South Africa as well as in response to internal pressures, the white apartheid government of South Africa had to open up the political process to the African National Congress, a movement organization that supports a one-person, one-vote policy and a multiracial society.

All these examples show the complex relationships among fully institutionalized political actors, especially governments and parties, and social movements.

An unintentional opening in the political system occurs when **states collapse** or are weakened. Weakening or collapse is often associated with war.

Both the Russian and Chinese Communist revolutions occurred because the states had become weak—practically nonexistent—during a prolonged international war. The tsarist state collapsed during World War I, a military debacle for the regime with devastating consequences for Russian civilians and soldiers. In February of 1917, sections of the armed forces no longer obeyed orders to suppress demonstrations against the war, a situation that led to the abdication of the tsar. The succeeding months were a period of competing efforts to form a new political system, power struggles that enabled the Bolsheviks to capture what was left of the state apparatus and reorganize it. The Chinese nationalist state, already weakened during the warlord period in the 1920s (when regional military and paramilitary leaders were in effective control of the territory), was further disorganized during World War II and the Japanese occupation. The French and American Revolutions at the end of the eighteenth century were made possible by the weak financial situation of the French and English kings; and this **fiscal crisis** was, in large part, the result of the wars between Britain and France (which North Americans refer to as the French and Indian War) (Skocpol, 1979; Trotsky, 1959).

So, one why question that political opportunity structure theories answer is, Given a level of strain and dissatisfaction as well as some propensity to form movements and mobilize resources, why are these movements able to succeed at certain crucial points in time? What changes in their **political environment** make it possible for them to bring about changes or even to seize power?

Another type of question that political opportunity structure theorists answer is about *the effects of political structure on the organization and strategies of movements*. The answers focus on variables like the ease of forming new parties, the level of repression, the degree of centralization, and the weight of different branches of government (*Annals*, 1993; especially articles by Berry and Hershey). These variables include both characteristics of the **constitutional framework** (for example, multiparty electoral systems, the role of the judiciary) and the actual **behavior of political elites.**

In some societies, it is easy to form parties and, therefore, movements do so in order to participate in politics. Multiparty parliamentary systems are especially conducive to this strategy. For example, in several western European countries, the environmentalist Greens were able to form parties to run for seats in parliaments. In the two-party system of the United States, movements would be more likely to operate as pressure groups within the major parties.

Political systems that are *repressive* shape movement characteristics in a different way. They may succeed in preventing large movements from appearing, but those that do survive may be more likely to form a guerrilla army, or terrorist organizations, and to seek external support. For example, over a period of several decades the government of Guatemala has repressed movements that seek to organize farmers and workers, and the consequence is an ongoing armed resistance movement in the highlands (Black, 1984; Smith-Ayala, 1991).

The level of *centralization* of a political system is also a factor in movement strategies. Some democracies like the United States have a federal structure. Laws and policies vary from state to state. Movements that act in the political arena can and must operate in many states at the same time; for example, those parts of the antiabortion movement that sought legislative changes began to do so in each state. Other representative democracies, for example, Italy and France, are much more centralized. Movements operating in the political arena can and must focus on decisions made by the national government. These differences in structure lead to differences in strategy, leadership styles, and resource mobilization.

A final example of the effect of political structure is based on the *relative weight and independence of judicial, legislative, and executive branches in governments*. The United States is a society with a strong, active, and relatively independent judiciary; in such a political system, it makes sense for movements to focus their strategies and resources on winning court cases. For example, in recent decades, the Civil Rights Movement, the women's movement, and the environmental movement have all used this means of changing society. The role of constitutional courts is much less prominent in England and Japan, and here social movements are likely to use other strategies to bring about change.

Political structure is not static or unchanging. States respond to movements, often by attempting to co-op them or make reforms. These interactions of movements and authorities produce waves or **cycles** of protests and movement activities. After a certain point, the state may have exhausted the resources it needs to make reforms, so it begins to ignore or even repress movements; and the movement sector of the society becomes too clogged with claimants. Protest, change, and reform slow down. Recent theory has focused on charting and explaining the outcomes of such cycles; for example, the cycle of left-wing protest movements in Europe in the late 1960s and 1970s (Garner and Zald, 1985; Tarrow, 1991).

Theorists often use political opportunity structure theory in conjunction with strain and/or mobilization perspectives. Some examples of these approaches include Theda Skocpol's analysis of a wide range of revolutions (1979), Charles Tilly's work on uprisings in modern European history (1978), Sidney Tarrow's studies of the Italian Communists and other groups on the left in Italy (Blackmer and Tarrow, 1975; Tarrow, 1989; 1991), and Jenkins and Perrow's analysis of the farmworker movement in the United States (1973).

In summary, a variety of midrange theories focus on the rise and success or failure of specific movements, explaining them in terms of structural stresses, resource mobilization, and/or political opportunity structures.

Conjunctural Theories

Midrange theories are sometimes linked to **conjunctural theories,** theories that look at a given historical moment for clues about the rise of social movements. Global situations like the Great Depression, World War II, or the long economic boom from 1945 to 1960 create special conditions for the formation, success, and/or failure of movements. These particular historical periods or moments—conjunctures—create strains, open (or close) political opportunities, and influence the level of resources that can be mobilized.

The Great Depression, for example, gave considerable impetus both to Communist parties and to the Nazis, as people in the developed capitalist countries were in desperate economic conditions and ready to look for new answers to the problem of unemployment and the collapse of industries. The Great Depression could be termed a structural strain, but its exact form is unlikely to be repeated. During World War II, when the Japanese occupied the colonies of European nations in Southeast Asia such as Vietnam and the Dutch East Indies (now Indonesia), they inadvertently created opportunities for nationalist insurgencies against the European powers. Anticolonial nationalist movements were also made possible by the fighting in Europe itself. These were not ongoing opportunities, but opportunities created by a specific historical situation. Similarly, the long economic boom in the 1950s and 1960s created many of the conditions for the New Left, specifically the massing of affluent young people on university campuses in many different countries. Historical causes include both structural conditions and unique conjunctures.

Using Midrange Theories to Explain Movements

Examples of two distinct movements illustrate how midrange approaches explain social movements, how they include the role of conjunctural factors, and how these theories often work well together.

The Civil Rights Movement   In the Civil Rights Movement, the *strain* was racial inequality, especially its manifestations in discriminatory laws and practices in public facilities, schools, and electoral politics. This strain had been present for a long time (since slavery, and more specifically, since the introduction of segregation in the years following Reconstruction, after the withdrawal of federal troops from the south in 1877). But, by the 1940s, the structural strain existed side by side with structural changes that allowed people to recognize the strain and come together to remove it. During World War II, defense industries moved to the south and the region began to experience more urbanization and industrialization; practices and values from other, less segregated parts of the nation began to make an impact. African Americans who had served in the armed forces and/or who had lived in the north were deeply dissatisfied with southern segregation. A long-term structural stress came increasingly to be seen as a situation to be challenged.

From the resource mobilization perspective, from the 1940s on, it became easier for people who opposed segregation to challenge it. More African Americans lived outside the southern small towns and rural areas where they were at the mercy of white landowners and white power holders. As they moved to cities, developed networks in the north, and entered colleges in increasing numbers, young African Americans felt they could challenge the entire structure of segregation. A desegregated society without lynching, humiliating Jim Crow laws, and voting restrictions had been a dream in the earlier part of the century; now, more education, more communication, and more contacts with national elites opened resources and opportunities (McAdam, 1982; Morris, 1984).

Segregation became an embarrassment to the United States in an era of international decolonization and the formation of new nations in Africa; national elites—especially forces within the Kennedy administration and many national media—became supporters of change in the south.

The Chinese Communist Revolution of 1949   A similar combination of strain, resource mobilization, and political opportunity theories can be used to explain the Chinese revolution. Poverty and inequality had existed for a long time in China, but by the end of the nineteenth century, landowners became more attuned to national and international markets; peasant-landowner relationships became less personal, less contained within the clan structure, and more openly exploitive. Foreign commercial ventures were also seen as exploitive and disruptive. These kinds of changes heightened structural strain in Chinese society. To some extent, these strains had an effect on all Chinese, but the impact was most intensely felt by peasants (Wolf, 1969).

The warlord period of the 1920s and the Japanese occupation during World War II created openings in the political opportunity structure, as the central state under control of nationalist forces was weakened. The Communist Party had a major role in resistance to the Japanese; it built up support among poor and middle-level peasants for this resistance movement and continued to win followers by land redistribution in areas that it controlled. In the process, it formed a large army that was eventually capable of defeating the Nationalists.

Note how our explanation here encompasses several kinds of theories: Marxist theories point to new strains in landowner-peasant relations as modern capitalism penetrated Chinese society. Resource mobilization theories emphasize the strategies of the Communist Party as a movement organization. Political opportunity structure theories point to the weakness and outright collapse of the Nationalist regime, especially after its defeat in the Japanese invasion. Conjunctural theories emphasize how all these forces came together at a particular point in history; the unique situation as well as the general factors influence the outcome. All of these theories together give considerable insight into the revolution.

COLLECTIVE BEHAVIOR THEORIES OF MOVEMENTS

Another major social movement theory ties the study of social movements into the field of **collective behavior,** which encompasses the study of fads, crowds, audiences, riots, and panics—the full range of sudden, spontaneous, short-lived, and often irrational behavior of groups of people who are caught up in a whirlwind of "contagious" actions and mob hysteria. In fact, historically, the field of social movements grew out of the collective behavior field within North American sociology, so this approach predates the resource mobilization perspective based on the rationality of movement organizations, which emerged in the 1960s and 1970s (Turner and Killian, 1987).

The questions that collective behavior theory answers are: Under what conditions does a series of spontaneous incidents "gel" into a movement and movement organizations? What kinds of experiences and dissatisfactions precipitate riots and demonstrations? Under what conditions does an instance of collective behavior (e.g., a riot or demonstration) precipitate a series of reforms or even a revolutionary upheaval?

Collective behavior theories see social movements as a "swelling and gelling" of other collective phenomena like riots, fads, and crowds. In this perspective, events like lynchings, hysterias, lootings, riots, and demonstrations are steps toward the formation of more stable and organized movements, perhaps "early warning signs" that structural strains are being experienced and dissatisfaction is growing. They bring people together physically, create an awareness of common grievances, and form the basis for more organized action. For example, the LA riot of 1992, following the Rodney King verdict, was an outpouring of spontaneous anger about police behavior and economic conditions; social movements and community organizations may slowly emerge from the ashes in order to work for change. It might be difficult to explain the LA riot in terms of resource mobilization theory, since there was no organized movement that set it in motion.

From the resource mobilization point of view, such events are more likely to be deliberately planned incidents that a movement uses in a calculated way to gain followers, frighten the opposition, draw attention to itself, or force elites to undertake reforms. For example, to use the case of the Civil Rights Movement, a resource mobilization theorist might point out that Rosa Parks' refusal to give up her seat to a white bus rider was not a "spontaneous gesture" but a planned decision, based on years of involvement in the NAACP and other civil rights groups and carried out with an acute sense of timing given the changing political climate in the nation, especially in the south in the mid-1950s (Parks, 1992).

It would be a little more difficult to use a collective behavior model to explain the Civil Rights Movement; such an explanation might focus on the way in which freedom rides and lunch counter sit-ins took place almost simultaneously across the south, the way in which the actions spread so quickly, and the extent to which the participants were "ahead" of more organized constituencies, like the black churches.

I would have to advise caution in choosing between resource mobilization and collective behavior theories: Look carefully at the events, the existing organizations, and the outcomes before deciding on one or another theory as the best way of understanding what took place. *Resource mobilization theory emphasizes the continuity and similarity between social movements and institutionalized political actors. Collective behavior theory emphasizes the discontinuity between movements and institutions.*

MOVEMENTS, DISCOURSES, AND CULTURES

Many social movement theories put an emphasis on the ideas and contents of movements and try to understand these ideas in terms of the cultures and discourses within which they arise and which they try to challenge. Movements are necessarily limited by the fact that they cannot suggest ideas that are "totally outlandish" to potential participants; they have to talk within one or more discourses that already exist and have a hold on the society, yet, at the same time, break the hold of these discourses.

How do people who are subject to structural strains come to define these strains, how do they "see" and "talk about" these common problems, and how do they eventually "see" that they can do something about the problem? The strains have to be **framed** in a discourse that asserts that they can be alleviated by collective social action. If this framing does not take place, people will continue to cope with stress in individual ways or through institutionalized channels. The process of framing is itself a contested process. Movements frame certain events as part of a strain and subject to change through collective action, while authorities frame such events as normal, routine, or impossible to do anything about. Movements and countermovements have diametrically opposed frames.

Once again, the theorist can emphasize the continuities between movement discourses and prevailing discourses, or discontinuities—the radical break that a movement ideology claims to be making with the culture from which it emerges. Some theorists, in fact, define movements as new intellectual projects, as offering a **new cognitive praxis**—new ways of thinking, new issues for the historical agenda, new definitions of problems, and new answers. These theorists emphasize the creativity and novelty of social movements (Eyerman and Jamison, 1991:161).

The nature of these prevailing discourses and their effect on movement ideologies and practices is the topic of a number of theories. The fundamental questions here are: Why and how can movements simultaneously *make sense* to followers who share a given culture and *break with* the discourses of that culture to move their adherents to see their condition in a radically new way? How do movements seek to give meaning to the situation of their potential supporters or constituencies?

These broad questions have been given a variety of different answers and theorists have developed distinct terminology to talk about these issues. Some (mostly theorists influenced by marxism) use the term **hegemony;** others use terms like discourse and discursive framing, collective action frames, and collective identity.

Cultural Continuities

Some theorists emphasize the role of culture in shaping movements, especially in the formation of ideologies. The specific contents of ideology vary widely depending on the preexisting culture. Similar structural strains may be experienced and understood in different ways in societies with different cultures. The ideology of a movement has to fit in some way with the prevailing culture.

For example, growing strains in landowner-peasant relations were present in Iran in the 1970s as well as China at midcentury; but in a deeply Islamic nation like Iran the revolution took the form of an Islamic republic, not a secular Communist-led transformation (Riesebrodt, 1993). In this perspective, even the Communist ideology of the Chinese revolutionaries has to be viewed with some reservations; this ideology was perhaps far more congruent with traditional Chinese notions about justice and order than it was with European communism.

Cultural theories of ideology and social movements point to *continuities between movement ideologies and existing cultures.* The ideologies may extend or modify these existing cultural themes, but it is unlikely that they can break with them entirely. Some theorists use the term **frame alignment** to describe the process in which movements make their own assignment of meanings fit the meaning and discourses that people already have. Usually, a movement has to link its frames—its assignment of meaning—to existing frames; only rarely does a movement venture to **transform frames.** For example, the Bolshevik revolutionaries in Russia used the slogan "Land, bread, peace"—three deeply held values of the Russian people; the revolutionaries also put forth more radical frame transformations linked to the meanings of socialism and communism (Snow and Benford, 1988).

Other theorists use the language of discursive frames, but include concepts like **mentalities** to refer to the ongoing and very slowly changing popularly held ways of thinking and feeling. Popularly held beliefs, values, and ways of looking at the world do not change rapidly. Neither does **political culture,** ideas about the nature of politics and political action in a society (Tarrow, 1992). Movement discourses must be somewhat congruent with mentalities and political culture to "make sense" to potential supporters. For example, in the United States, movements must show respect for the value of individualism, which most Americans claim is important. So the theme of individualism shows up in some form in movements as different as the New Left and the Christian right.

These theories of frame alignment, cultural continuities, and mentalities have implications for the transnational movements we are examining in this book. The theories point to the fact that transnational movements have to develop ideological themes (or framing practices) that are specific to national cultures. Socialist movements in Germany, for example, have to appeal to different values and mentalities than socialist movements in Guatemala. Islamic movements in Sudan cannot be identical in discourse to Islamic movements in Algeria.

Theorists can emphasize the continuity between a movement and the culture in which it arises or they can emphasize the movement's innovative and radical features. Let's take a movement like the Branch Davidians, the cultists who died in a confrontation with the United States government in Waco, Texas. Should we see them as a group that had broken with reality and lived in a "world of its own" based on the teachings of David Koresh? Or should we look at the continuities among these teachings and much more widely diffused activities, institutions, and discourses in the culture of the United States? These crucial cultural influences include the Seventh Day Adventist Church from which the Branch Davidians emerged as well as long-standing traditions of utopian and millenarian religious thought in the United States (Boyer, 1992). Indeed, these utopian and apocalyptic themes have appeared repeatedly in Christian thought, especially since the Protestant Reformation. The continuity perspective would tend to place the Branch Davidians into a long history of radical cults and sectarian movements within the Protestant tradition, beginning in sixteenth-century Europe and amplified in the utopian climate of the United States.

One of the purposes of framing is to construct collective identities that will mobilize the potential support base in the direction of the movement. Every person has potentially many identities (along the lines of gender, class, ethnicity, occupation, region, nationality, and so on). The movement leadership frames discourse in such a way as to bring out the identity that will dispose individuals to support the movement and weld together different support bases. For example, the Islamic revolution in Iran used religious discourses rather than class-oriented discourses to rally people against the Shah; a religious framing brought together a bloc of merchants and peasants, where a class-oriented framing might have failed to unite them.

Hegemony and Discursive Framing

Cultural theories and frame alignment theories can be linked to marxist and structural strain theories via the concept **hegemony.**

Cultural and marxist theories together make use of hegemony, which refers to a process or condition in which subordinate classes accept the right of the economically dominant class to rule. Hegemony implies the consent of the subordinate groups to their own subordination. It may include some specific ideologies, but it also includes a process that creates a general inability to even imagine a different state of affairs; subordination becomes equated with "common sense." As long as this condition is unchallenged, movements remain limited, and structural strains are coped with on an individual or institutionalized basis.

The concept hegemony originated with Antonio Gramsci, an Italian Marxist, and referred, especially, to a process of cultural dominance by a social class; since then, it has been used in a more general sense and could include other kinds of cultural control, for instance, in gender or ethnic stratification (Gramsci, 1971).

Intellectuals play a key role in both sustaining and challenging hegemony. Intellectuals are broadly defined as people who create and propagate ideas, define discourses, and "frame" issues in the media, education, religious institutions, and other cultural institutions. Some intellectuals intentionally or unintentionally confirm hegemony; others, often those associated with movements, challenge it.

Framing and the Media

Theorists who look at framing and hegemony are especially interested in the role of the media. The media are one of the channels through which potential supporters learn of a movement. Thus, each movement wants to influence the **media framing** of information about itself or events related to the movement. For example, North Americans who were sympathetic to the Sandinista movement and government in Nicaragua tried to discourage the media from framing Nicaraguan coverage in terms that defined the Sandinistas as Communist, the contras as anti-Communists, and the conflict as one of freedom fighters on the United States side versus Communists aligned with the Soviet Union (Ryan, 1991).

Generally, movements need the media more than the media need movements (Gamson and Wolfsfeld, in *Annals,* 1993). The media usually have many resources available to them, and movements tend to find it difficult to change media framing practices. The media often focus on sensationalistic elements of movements, usually put movements in a bad light, and promote certain movement activists as "leaders" and "spokespersons" regardless of their real role in the movement. These processes were particularly evident in media coverage of the antiwar in Vietnam movement (Gitlin, 1980). Some theorists hypothesize that the larger and more transformative the goals of the movement, the more likely it is to be given negative coverage or treated as bizarre, while movements with narrower, single-issue or limited reform goals are given more serious coverage (Gamson and Wolfsfeld, in *Annals,* 1993).

Discourse and Power

Social Movement Theory after Feminism and Foucault   Interests in discourses have become particularly important in social movement theory under the impact of feminism and the "poststructural" radical thought of Michel Foucault. Both of these theories in the social sciences and humanities focus on how social control is exercised in discourses and relationships.

For instance, feminist theorists are looking at how gender stratification takes place in language and in intimate relationships. "Gender" is not an attribute of an individual but an "accomplishment" or process that is carried out in interactions. Thus, gender hierarchy is not simply embodied in laws or religious teachings, but is constantly recreated in our interactions. Social movement theorists can expand this idea to suggest that all forms of power and all structural strains are really embedded in discourses and relationships. Also, no one will respond to structural strain by joining or starting a movement unless a process of discursive framing creates meanings and constructs collective identities that support movement activism.

The most recent twist on this notion of discursive framing derives from the work of Michel Foucault, a French philosopher. Foucault pictured power as a process that goes on everywhere and is built into different types of **discourses** that limit and define human nature. The exercise of **power** through discourse is especially acute in contemporary society; after the French Revolution, as part of "modernization," social control is no longer exercised primarily through corporal and capital punishment (torture, dismemberment, executions), but through an ongoing process of discipline, surveillance, and above all, self-discipline. It is not only exercised by the state, but also diffused throughout modern institutions like schools, psychotherapy, the corporation, the "welfare system," and so on. No specific class controls this process and Foucault would not accept the idea that capitalists or a political elite is its prime beneficiary.

Foucault points toward resistance as a process that is also diffused and pervasive. "Where there is power, there is resistance." Movements that are aimed primarily at the state or at corporations may thus miss the most important sites of control, the discourses that are imposed throughout society. An overthrow of a state or economic system does not alleviate the domination that is embedded in all institutions and discourses (Foucault, 1979, 1982; Sawicki, 1991; Weinstein and Weinstein, 1993).

This line of thought, combined with the growth of many decentralized movements, has contributed to new-social-movement theory, a perspective that emphasizes these decentralized, ongoing, diffuse, and discursively focused conflicts. We will return to these postmodern conceptions of movements in Chapter 5, "From Modern to Postmodern: Movements in History," and in Part Three, "Conclusions."

Cultures of Resistance   Foucault's ideas about the diffusion of resistance also converge with some recent developments in cultural marxist theory, most notably the work of Paul Willis (Willis, 1990). Studying young people in England, Willis found that resistance to capitalism is no longer found primarily on the shop floor, let alone the barricades. Deindustrialization, youth unemployment, and the restructuring of the English economy during the Thatcher period left many young people completely excluded from workplaces—and, in fact, also increasingly reluctant to work. Willis (and other observers of English youth culture like Hebdige, 1982) found that resistance took cultural forms without any organized or centralized structure—music, clothing styles, the recycling and patching together of clothing, and the use of punk and Third World styles to express alienation from conventional or dominant (or hegemonic) English culture. For orthodox marxists, it was a bit zany to think that young people who spent their days smoking marijuana, making fun of the "telly," and shopping in flea markets were engaged in class struggle. The value of Willis' research is that it points to the overlap and mutual influence of cultural trends and political movements, including the way movements can exist in a dormant or latent form as diffuse practices that challenge hegemony.

The Construction of Identities   Foucault and deconstructionist philosophers emphasize that there are no simple, "natural," or straightforward identities. Identity is always socially constructed. So, to understand why one individual joins a nationalist movement, a second becomes a feminist, another becomes a socialist, and yet a fourth remains indifferent to movements, we have to look at the way in which each was *constituted to have* an identity that supports a particular choice of action. Deconstructionist philosophers point out that every identity is the suppression of an alternative identity (Handler, 1992:699).

These various theories of movement discourses, new social movements, and collective identities are currently a "hot" area in social movement theory. There are efforts underway to bring them together with resource mobilization and political opportunity structure theories (Zald, Morris, in Morris and Mueller, 1992).

PSYCHOLOGICAL THEORIES OF SOCIAL MOVEMENTS

A large and distinct body of social movement theory is influenced by social psychology and even psychoanalysis. It emphasizes the individual bases of movement participation. Given uniform levels of structural strain and available resources, why do some individuals become activists and others do not? Are some societies especially prone to one or another form of movement activism because of the kinds of personalities found among their members?

Like collective behavior theory, social-psychological theories have often stressed the irrational side of social movements; they tend to see social movements as unusual phenomena rather than fairly routine and rational organizational responses to structural strains. The influence of psychoanalysis led to inquiries into unconscious mechanisms like **projection** in the formation of movement belief systems. In the view of psychoanalytic theories of movements, unconscious desires and hostilities that emerged from individuals' psychosexual development were projected onto groups or institutions that were then seen as threatening. These explanations of social movements in terms of the unconscious and/or irrational motivations of participants tended to give little attention to the objective reality of structural strain and to the rational organizational side of movements.

In the history of social movement theory, social psychological theories developed especially in the period from the 1930s to the 1950s to explain Nazism, fascism, and, to a lesser extent, Stalinist communism. Therefore, the theorists placed a heavy emphasis on studying anti-semitism, paranoid conspiracy theories, and authoritarian personality structures in the adherents of these movements.

One of the most influential theories was referred to as the theory of the **authoritarian personality;** it made use of a personality inventory known as the F scale (for fascism) that probed tendencies toward homophobia and other sexual fears, exaggerated deference toward authority, rigidity, and a tendency to see the world in terms of conspiracies. The phenomena of Nazism and fascism were thus explained, in part, in terms of the personalities of movement supporters (Adorno, 1993). In a popular but not carefully researched version of psychological theories, the concept of the "true believer" was used to lump together Communists and Fascists, as well as other movement activists, and emphasize their irrationality and fanaticism.

When the 1960s came along, and more researchers felt positively toward participants in the Civil Rights Movements, the antiwar movement, and the New Left, social psychological theories lost some of their popularity. Movement participants were more likely to be seen in positive terms as people who take an active role in their society, concern themselves with social justice, and are willing to be leaders. Psychological theories often had a debunking tone toward the movements they analyzed; they seemed to imply that social movement participants were "abnormal" in some way, and so they lost ground as social scientists came to emphasize positive or, at least, rational motivations for joining movements. The resurgence of Nazism and ethnoracism in central and eastern Europe may once again turn theorists' attention to irrational bases of movement activity.

There is continuing interest, however, in the socialization of movement activists; for instance, some participants in the New Left had parents who had been union organizers and left activists in the 1930s (Flacks, 1988). The midlife left-democratic commitment of former New Left student activists also pointed to continuities in dispositions and values (Fendrich and Lovoy, 1988).

In the 1990s, there has been a reawakening of interest in social psychological approaches to social movements. These do not use the previous types of psychoanalytical or "abnormal psych" concepts, but rather look at the formation of **collective identities.** They often are a synthesis of social psychological perspectives and discourse-oriented theories that focus on the social construction of identities. Also, they may use a **micromobilization** approach to understand how individuals are recruited. For example, Taylor and Whittier look at how lesbian identity is formed and politicized (Gamson, in Morris and Mueller, 1992; Taylor and Whittier, in Morris and Mueller, 1992).

PUTTING IT ALL TOGETHER

The astute reader will probably have decided by now that each of these theories has something to offer to an overall understanding of movements. In fact, one sociologist has proposed a **value-added theory** of social movements; Neil Smelser suggests that movements can be explained as the result of processes involving six contributing elements (Smelser, 1963). I will use the Civil Rights Movement that ended legal racial segregation in the United States to illustrate each element.

The first of these elements is structural conduciveness. By this term Smelser means the general conditions in a society, as well as more specific factors like the political opportunity structure (to use the current term) and the presence of channels of communication. For instance, in the United States, in the late 1950s and early 1960s, we can see a society that was generally fairly open to social movements and pressure groups and provided good channels of communication and opportunities for political organization.

The second element is structural strain, which is the specific problem, tension, or condition of inequality, largely viewed here as an objective condition. In the case of the Civil Rights Movement, the strain was the problem of persistent legal segregation in the south as well as informal and formal barriers to voting by African Americans in the region.

The third element is a system of generalized beliefs, the spread of discourses and ideas focused on the stress that is subjectively experienced because of the structural strain. Usually, these ideas have to be somewhat congruent with other beliefs or values in the society, while at the same time calling for change. By the 1960s, virtually all African Americans and many other citizens of the United States had come to feel that legal segregation was morally wrong and a breach of such American values as political equality and equal opportunity. This is the element of social movements on which discourse and framing theorists now focus.

The fourth element is precipitating incidents, events that galvanize potential movement participants. The Montgomery bus boycott in the mid-1950s was such an incident, and demonstrated to a large public that collective action was effective. The intervention of the federal government to enforce school desegregation in Little Rock and elsewhere was also a signal that the federal government would no longer tolerate local resistance to desegregation, if such resistance was visible and open, especially in the form of harassment of children entering school buildings. (Resistance to desegregation later became quiet and much less visible, through the establishment of private, segregated academies; but that is another story, the story of countermovement strategies.) This is the element of social movements that collective behavior theorists emphasize.

Leadership and communication are the fifth element; as activists like Martin Luther King emerged and the African American churches were drawn into the movement, it became stronger and developed a larger institutional base. The shift from civil rights organizations like the NAACP to the churches drew in extensive grass roots support in African American communities. College campuses in the south became another important node for leadership, organization, and communication. This element is one part of what resource mobilization theorists emphasize. Resource mobilization theory published after Smelser's work contributed to a much stronger understanding of this element of social movements.

The final element is the response of social control agents. Groups in power can respond by co-optation, repression, an effort to redress grievances, or some combination of all of these. In some ways, this element is the *intentional* aspect of the political opportunity structure discussed on p. 50. In the case of the Civil Rights Movement, national elites—specifically the Kennedy administration and the national media—gave some support to the movement, even though state and local power holders often tried to repress it. The motives of national elites were perhaps not solely altruistic; considerations of the global image of the United States and the Democratic Party's search for a southern African American voter base were probably also involved, but whatever the mix of motives, the outcome was the success of the movement.

Smelser suggested that each stage or element is a condition for the following one, and that all must be present in order for a movement to emerge as a major social or political force. This model is useful if we do not consider it a rigid or mechanical statement about chronological sequence; in practice, all these elements are processes that can go on simultaneously. The importance of the model is that Smelser is encouraging us to bring different theories together into a unified explanation that recognizes the complexity of social movements.

In recent years, theorists are again seeking to build bridges between different theories. The most recent essays in social movement theory call for pulling together all the current perspectives: resource mobilization; discursive framing and collective identity; and structural theories, especially those focused on political opportunity structures (Zald, in Morris and Mueller, 1992; Morris, in Morris and Mueller, 1992). There is even a resurgence of the term "social psychology," although it now focuses more on collective identity (Gamson, in Morris and Mueller, 1992; Taylor and Whittier, in Morris and Mueller, 1992).

USING THEORY

In summation, theories are like tools; once we understand the uses of each, we can make an appropriate selection from the toolbox. For most projects we will probably need to use several of the tools. We should never be too reverent or too rigid in our choice of theories, but should give careful attention to what we want to explain.

Insofar as this book deals with transnational movements, it has to look at strains, organization, and discourse framing that cut across national boundaries (McAdam and Rucht, in *Annals*, 1993). For that reason, I give considerable attention to marxist and modernization/postmodern theories that point to large-scale, transnational processes. At the same time, we need to realize that specific national instances of movements have to be understood in terms of the specific strains in each society, the cultural context, and the national political structure and resources available for mobilization. Sometimes this level of detail cannot fit into the space of an introductory book, but the omission does not mean that I consider it unimportant.

For these reasons, I have tended to use the term **historical conditions** as a blanket concept that allows me to discuss transnational processes, structural strains, political opportunity structures, cultural contexts and discursive frames, possibilities for resource mobilization, patterns of collective behavior, and prevalent "character types" as an interconnected package of causes. It would be difficult to go over every one of these separately for each transnational movement, let alone for each movement organization and national case of transnational movements. I hope, however, to give some indication in each substantive chapter of how these different explanatory models can help us understand movements.

In the final analysis, I think we have to make our own judgments on the basis of a movement's ideology. It is ideology—ideas and goals—that distinguishes Nazis from the human rights movement, to choose a particularly clear example. Theories may differ as to whether these movements use rational means, the extent to which they break with the prevailing culture, the "abnormality" of their adherents, the importance of political opportunities and con-

An example of discursive framing: Poster at a pro-life demonstration. Washington, DC, April 28, 1990.

junctural factors in their formation, the nature of the structural strains to which they claim to be responding—all important to us as social scientists for understanding their emergence and actions. But our own actions as citizens and human beings ultimately have to be a response to these movements' ideas and goals. Neo-Nazis and human rights movements may be responses to the same strain in the same society and may even use similar *means* of organization, strategy, discourse framing, and resource mobilization; what makes them different is their *ideas, values, and goals.*

SUMMARY

The outsider's perspective is built into social movement theories. These are social scientists' explanations for why movements emerge; why they take on a specific form; and why they succeed, fail, succeed partially, or become "becalmed" or dormant. I have reviewed a number of these theories in this chapter. Many of them are actually more detailed ways of referring to the historical conditions under which movements emerge. The theories can often be "mixed and matched"; several of them can be brought together into value-added explanations of movements.

Looking Ahead

The next two chapters return to the themes of ideology and historical conditions. In Chapter 4, we will try to understand what contemporary movements are seeking to accomplish. We will look at their ideologies as visions of what society is and should be. I will suggest that, although their discourses appear very different, it is possible to compare them.

In Chapter 5, we will look more closely at the long-term, global historical circumstances in which all of these movements emerged. (The chapters on specific movements will explore the particular historical conditions for each movement.) The large-scale historical circumstances that I discuss in Chapter 5 can be summed up as "the modern world," but this term needs a more careful explanation. At the end of Chapter 5, we will see that the modern is not a static type of society, but one that changes constantly, perhaps now mutating into the postmodern. Movements within this type of society also constantly change and mutate.

One more introductory note is necessary. As you read the chapters on specific movements, you will see that they are not identical in either length or format. These differences reflect differences in the movements themselves. Movements with a longer history require longer chapters. Some movements have a very complex ideology with many variants that require careful attention. Because I do not think all these movements can be accommodated by a single uniform format for each chapter, I use the concepts and theories introduced in Chapters 2 and 3, but not always with identical emphasis. The chapters have to reflect the diversity and complexity of movements.

KEY TERMS AND CONCEPTS

macrohistorical and sociohistorical theories
marxist theories
social relations of production
capitalist mode of production
mass/modern society theories
anomie
postmodern society

middle-range structural theories
structural strain
reference group
J-curve theory
relative deprivation
rising expectations
resource mobilization
institutional actors
movement organizations
political opportunity structure
elite co-optation and/or elite support

state collapse
fiscal crisis of the state
political environment
constitutional framework
behavior of political elites
cycles of movement activism
conjunctural theories

collective behavior theories

cultural and discourse theories
framing
new cognitive praxis
hegemony
cultural continuities
frame alignment and frame transformation
mentalities
political culture
media framing practices
discourses and power

cultures of resistance

**social psychological theories of
  social movements**
projection
authoritarian personality

collective identity
micromobilization

value-added theory

historical conditions

During early phases of revolutionary state formation, supporters of the Islamic republic carry a picture of Ayatollah Ruhallah Khomeini. The Islamic movement succeeded in consolidating a new regime. Tehran, Iran, February 6, 1979.

CHAPTER 4

Movements, Societies, and States

And the devil took Jesus up on a high mountain and showed him all the kingdoms of the world in a moment of time. And the devil said to him, "All of this power will I give to you, and their glory; for it has been delivered to me, and I will give it to whom I will. If you, then, will worship me, it shall all be yours." And Jesus answered, "Begone, Satan! For it is written, you shall worship the Lord your God, and only him shall you serve."

—Luke: 4:5–8.

You are a revolutionary in a small Latin American nation. The revolutionary alliance has come to power through a long insurgency against the dictator and his vicious national guard—a war that has cost the nation 50,000 lives (2 percent of the population) and the destruction of its industries, bombed by the national guard to punish opposition forces in the business community. Equally daunting are the longer-term effects of dictatorship and dependency: rural poverty, reliance on export crops like cotton and coffee with variable prices on world markets, chronic underemployment and settlements of the poor on the edges of the cities, almost no history and tradition of democratic institutions and democratic participation in politics, and a 55 percent illiteracy rate.

Your ideals: A mixture of socialist and Catholic values of social justice and popular democracy. Your task: To preserve an alliance of poor peasants, unionized workers, some wealthy industrialists, some parts of the small middle class, and students—an alliance that has to take unified action to move the country forward. Your known opponents: the dictator and his cronies, now in exile; the national guard; and most of the agro-export-oriented landowning classes. Uncertain forces: much of the country's upper and middle classes; its major media, which opposed the dictator, but now consistently attack any further reforms; the nation's African American and Native American minorities, concentrated along the seacoast and unsure what the revolution means for them; and the United States, which let your revolution happen in "its backyard," but may soon have second thoughts.

What can you accomplish? Will your alliance hold together? Once you have distributed the vast land holdings and businesses of the dictator and his family, will you undertake further measures of economic redistribution? What kind of government will you form and how will you establish democratic political institutions? How will you solve the problems of dependency in world commodity markets? How can you distinguish critical supporters from enemies? How can you build organizations that will lead the country and also respect democratic rights and the reality of multiple, competing interests?

Imagine yourself in these circumstances and try to answer questions like these.

Source: Based on Henri Weber, *Nicaragua: The Sandinist* [sic] *Revolution*, Verso, London, 1983.

INTRODUCTION

This chapter discusses movement ideologies as visions of what a society is and should be. Movements differ in their discourses, often to the point that comparisons appear impossible. For example, civil libertarians defend individual rights; socialists attack capitalism; fundamentalists speak in "God talk"; feminists identify male domination and patriarchy as the basic form of inequality. Are these ideologies talking right by each other? In this chapter, I suggest that their visions of society are in fact comparable, even if worded in different types of discourse.

A discussion about the relationship between movements and states follows. Movements seek to capture or influence the state, a centralized institution with coercive powers, in order to change societies.

MOVEMENT IDEOLOGIES AND THE
STRUCTURE OF SOCIETIES

Societies can be thought of as constituted by four practices and sets of relationships. The **economy** or the **mode of production:** practices and relationships that contribute to physical survival and the production of material objects. The **political system** or the **state:** practices and relationships of power, including coercion; the only sphere that is capable of making and enforcing decisions about the society as a whole. The **cultural sphere:** practices and relationships that create and propagate discourses about reality, which includes religious institutions, the media, and education. The sphere of **social reproduction:** practices and relationships associated with gender, sex, and societal as well as physical reproduction.

Keep in mind that these "spheres" are abstractions from reality. They are concepts social scientists use to group together practices and relationships. All individuals participate to some extent in all spheres: Each person makes a living, is influenced by government and politics, holds values and beliefs, and has personal relationships.

Some social scientists (functionalist sociologists and anthropologists) suggest that each of these four spheres of practices is necessary for societal stability and viability (Parsons and Smelser, 1956). Other social scientists see one or the other of these spheres as the determining one, the one that causes the form of the society as a whole. For example, many social theorists influenced by the work of Karl Marx see the mode of production as the determining element (Althusser, 1969). In any case, the form of each of these spheres can be quite different from society to society; even more important, the *way the spheres are connected to each other differs from society to society.*

In small societies, without a state and without class differentiation, all these spheres are connected through the web of kinship. All activities and practices are embedded in kinship obligations. But in larger societies, with more productive economies, more complex social organization, and a growing number of nonkinship relationships, a wider range of possibilities for social structure is evident. How the society is and should be organized become matters for reflection, negotiation, and conflict.

Movement ideologies are, in large part, discourses about how a society should be put together. They are discourses about *the form that each institutional sphere should take* and about *how the totality should be constituted.* In the second part of the book, in the chapters on individual movements and ideologies, the views of each movement will be explained in more detail and I will discuss specific examples of the movements and the changes they try to bring about in society. The purpose of this chapter is to establish a common framework for comparing and contrasting ideologies. The major types of ideologies are distinguished by their contrasting ideas about the organization of society. They disagree about how societies are, can be, and should be organized.

Liberals and the Separation of Spheres

Liberals, civil libertarians, and human rights activists agree that all these spheres should be as separate and disconnected as possible and that the state (the sphere of coercion) should be as limited as possible. Liberals want to keep church and state separate. Liberals (in the original, classical sense of the term) want to keep government out of the capitalist economy. And liberals and libertarians want to keep the government from involving itself in family life, sexual activities, and other personal habits of individuals. The state should not limit or restrict what the media can say or what organizations people can join—in other words, individuals should enjoy freedom of speech and assembly.

Liberals single out the state as a sphere of coercion and try to keep it from interfering in **civil society**—all the other relationships and practices people engage in, which liberals believe should be *voluntary and consensual.* Liberals' basic reference point is the *individual;* his or her freedom should be maximized, as summarized in the phrase "life, liberty and the pursuit of happiness."

Socialists and the Primacy of the Mode of Production

Socialists also prize the individual, but they have quite a different view of what the society is and should be. From the viewpoint of socialist ideology, the lib-

eral "separation of spheres" is something of a sham. In this view, such separation has never existed in the past and cannot exist in the present, because the
economic sphere (the mode of production) shapes all the other spheres. Socialists argue that in **capitalism** the sphere of economic relationships—the mode of
production—is fundamentally split between those who own the means of
production and those who do not, between investor/owner/employers on the
one hand, and workers on the other hand. Socialists believe that this fundamental inequality in the economic sphere carries over into all other practices
and relationships of capitalist society, rendering it unequal, exploitive, and
unjust.

In socialist ideology, the political system is the only institution that is large
enough and powerful enough to alter the capitalist system; thus, in some way,
the socialist movement has to capture and use the state apparatus to transform
private ownership of the means of production, used for profit, into public ownership, used to satisfy human needs and wants. In the view of socialists, only
then can individuals be truly free to develop their unique talents and creative
powers.

There are other movements on the left that share the socialist analysis of
capitalism but are not as convinced that the state can ever be a bridge to a more
cooperative and egalitarian society. These ideas are held by movements like the
New Left of the 1960s, left anarchists and left libertarians, and the "new social
movements" in contemporary Europe, comprised of left-wing feminists, environmentalists, and peace activists.

Movements of Faith

Religious movements have yet a third discourse about society; it is framed in
religious terms, but it is not irrelevant to the question of how society should be
constituted (Zald and McCarthy, 1987). For religious movements, the sphere of
religious values should be the ascendant one. Strange as it may sound, movements of faith seek to end "religion"—in their view, religion should not be
thought of as a separate institution that has to compete with other discourses
and activities. Religion needs to be replaced with *faith expressed as a totality of
practice, discourse, and belief that permeates society as a whole.* Religion should not
be in competition with other cultural discourses; to participants in many religious movements, only one religion can be the true faith. The state should devote itself to implementing and promoting the values of a specific religion. The
family and gender system should be structured in accordance with religious
teachings.

In this respect, then, religious ideologies are different from liberal ones. Liberals want to separate spheres; religious ideologies want to integrate them
around the teachings of a specific faith. For religious movements, the separation of religious institutions, the state, and the family/gender system is not the
hallmark of individual freedom (as it is for the liberals), but the abandonment
of precisely those essential values that make human beings human. Thus, reli-

gious movements tend to be **integralist;** that is, committed to the connection of all spheres of practice.

In contrast to socialism, many religious ideologies imply that the capitalist economic sphere can be left largely intact as most religions provide for charity, tithing, and teachings of social justice to lessen the gap between rich and poor, rather than look for a total transformation of class relations.

Feminism and Movements of Sexual Orientation: The Centrality of Gender and Sexuality

Feminist movements are similar to socialist movements in that they point to a state of inequality in one sphere as the source of inequality and injustice throughout society. But, in feminist ideology, it is the gender system that is the sphere from which injustice emanates. As long as all societies are characterized by male domination and one form or another of patriarchy, all other practices—economic, cultural, and political—are likely to be characterized by violence, inequality, injustice, and exploitation. Gay and lesbian movements also point to practices of domination and violence associated with the imposition of heterosexuality. Feminism and movements of sexual orientation tend to be more suspicious than socialists of the possible uses of the state to change conditions of inequality.

For these movements, then, it is the sphere of social reproduction and the gender system (what liberals tend to term the sphere of "personal life") that must be changed.

Fascism and Nationalism: Maintaining Societal Boundaries

Fascist and nationalist ideologies are less concerned with the substance of practices and discourses in a society; these movements are primarily concerned with **maintaining strong boundaries** in preserving or establishing the ethnic unity and homogeneity of a society. They assume that ethnic homogeneity will, in and of itself, take care of problems of injustice or internal tensions. The goal of homogeneity may mean killing or expelling "foreigners" or "inferior races" and bringing into the nation scattered groups of coethnics, of the "race" or "Volk." Movements with this way of implementing the goal of homogeneity can be termed **ethnoracist.** National homogeneity can also mean the forced assimilation of groups that are different from the core ethnic group of the movement.

Most fascist and nationalist movements see the state as an important institution for accomplishing these ends; in this respect, they tend to give a good deal of weight to the state. Cultural institutions and the family should also be aligned with the overall aim of national-ethnic unity. On the other hand, from the viewpoint of most nationalist ideologies, no total restructuring of capitalism is necessary; ethnic unity outweighs class divisions, which are entirely secondary to ethnic differentiation. It may, however, be deemed important to improve the nation's position within the global economy.

Nationalist and fascist movements tend to be rather indifferent or even opposed to the ideology of individual rights; in their perspective, the individual attains humanity in unity with a specific ethnic group, or more inclusively, the people of a nation.

Environmental Movements: Opening the System

Environmental movements seek to "open the circle," by including all of nature within an ethic of care. A good society is not one in which relationships are confined to human beings, but a system that encompasses nature as a whole. For human beings to live in harmony and cooperation, we have to recognize not only our interdependence with each other but also the interconnection of everything on the planet, living and nonliving. States, nations, national economies, and the economic systems of both capitalism and Communism (socialism as it was practiced in the Soviet Union, eastern Europe, China, and so on) prevent us from seeing and respecting these interconnections. Barriers and rivalries among different existing societies need to be broken down along with a fading of boundaries between "humanity" and "nature."

Conservative Ideology

Conservatism is a term with many meanings, some of which I will explore in a later chapter. Here I would like to include what I believe to be the most important and original strand of conservative ideology, **conservative organicism** (often associated with the writings of Edmund Burke). I have saved it for last in my discussion of movement visions, because it questions and denies the value of these visions; its own vision is an antivision, an antitotalization, a denial of both the value of transformative movement goals and the possibility of their realization.

Conservatives who hold this position believe that the only desirable and indeed the only feasible change in human societies emerges from a gradual and ongoing process of small shifts in existing institutions. "Organicism" refers to an analogy of societies with living, growing beings (like plants or animals) that develop slowly, naturally, with a functional and interdependent harmony of their parts. Revolutionary social change—large, sudden, planned changes that use the state to bring about a transformation in the structure of society—are usually destructive. Social revolutions are almost inherently incapable of realizing their goals, of bringing forth a decent and functioning new society. Conservative organicism is suspicious of all totalizing visions and projects. Of course, this position is itself a totalizing vision. In practice it often celebrates the status quo, even if in theory it admits the value of gradual change (Burke, 1961).

Movements as Discourses about the Form of Society

We have seen that many elements of movement ideology can be summarized in the framework of thinking about each society as a system of interconnected spheres of practices with a boundary around the whole. We can thus examine how movements resolve to reorganize the system by providing insight into and comparison of movement ideologies. Far from being bizarre rantings or crazy ideas, movement ideologies are quite coherent statements about how society is currently structured, what is wrong with society, and how it should be reorganized. We may disagree with one or another of these ideologies or all of them, but we need to recognize them as speaking to a single basic set of questions about the form of the good society. Although they may use dissimilar types of discourse, the core issues addressed by movements are the same:

- What is the good society?
- What is wrong with currently existing societies?
- What set of social practices is and should be at the core of society?
- Which sphere, if any, is the "master sphere"—the one whose form shapes the whole society?
- What must be done to change this sphere and to change its relationship to the other spheres of practice?
- What form does the social order—the totality of social practices—take at present, and how should it be changed?
- How can we change society to make it correspond to our vision of the good society?
- Can the state be used to redirect all practices into closer accord with our vision of the good society?

STATES AND MOVEMENTS

Movements in Power: Regime Formation

Most of the movements in this book are movements that are political and *totalizing* in that they have a comprehensive vision of a good society. They realize that the state is a powerful means of bringing this vision into being. The state in all complex societies is an institution for reaching decisions that affect all members of the society and for enforcing these decisions, using coercion and violence in the case of opposition. Thus, movements are always inclined to capture or at least influence the state in order to attain their ends.

Many movements claim that, in the long run, they would like to reduce the sphere of coercion. Liberalism makes this reduction an immediate goal. Socialism and communism look ahead to "the withering away of the state." Religious movements hope to build a community of faith, regulated by shared beliefs and not coercive practices. Feminism would like to reduce the role of domination, hierarchy, and violence in society. Environmental movements express hope for a community based on cooperation, not coercion. Yet, all movements are tempted by the strategy of capturing and using the state to attain their ends, by the dialectical concept that the state must become stronger in order to establish conditions under which it can wither away.

There is a basic division in the book between those movements that have come to state power and those that have not. Movements with liberal, conservative, socialist, populist, fascist, nationalist, and religious ideologies (or some combination of these) have at one time or another held or influenced state power, with more or less complete control in some societies. There has been considerable variation in the amount of power they were able to exercise. Some have formed governments but accepted the presence of competing opposition forces within a framework of liberal democratic politics, like the socialists in Sweden, who were occasionally voted out of office. Other movements have been in complete control of the state apparatus, ruling through a single party and forming a movement-state, like the Nazis in Germany (1933–1945). These movements have given some indication of how they use the state to transform society, and have already encountered the difficulties inherent in this project.

On the other hand, feminist and environmentalist movements have not held state power. The more radical feminists and environmentalists, as well as a whole cluster of related **left-libertarian** and **new social movements,** claim that state power is not a goal. In fact, they would like to erode state power by creating communities and networks that operate in indifference or opposition to governments. Whether this project is capable of realization remains to be seen. Meanwhile, less radical feminists and environmentalists seek to influence states and the process of forming and implementing government policy; they realize, however, that they are still a long way from being in power.

The Movement-State   Those movements that have come to state power discover two closely connected issues. Using the state to change society is very difficult, far more difficult than most adherents of ideologies recognize (Fagen, Deere, and Coraggio, 1986; Gurley, 1975; Schoenbaum, 1966). It is also a long-term project; the state cannot be permitted to wither away before its work of transformation is accomplished. Movements in power tend to be frustrated by the limits of state power and often respond to these frustrations by expanding rather than diminishing the sphere of the state.

When movements aimed at influencing or controlling the state attain their goal they are confronted with the problem of converting their vision of society into a reality within the circumstances they have inherited from the past. Many of their policies cannot be realized, given the constraints of reality itself. Thus, they are forced into making compromises, but if they compromise too much they run the risk of losing legitimacy with their supporters and eventually faith in themselves. The constraints inherent in reality can take many forms.

Opposition Forces   One form of constraint is opposition from well-organized social forces that are in a position to launch countermovements. For example, the revolutionary Sandinista government in Nicaragua faced a **counterinsurgency**, the contras, that was supported by the Reagan administration as well as by Nicaraguan exiles in the United States and some key sectors within Nicaragua (Burbach, in Fagen, Deere, and Coraggio, 1986). These kinds of insurgencies against reformist, populist, and socialist governments were not new to Latin America. In 1954, the reformist government of Jacobo Arbenz was overthrown by a military coup in Guatemala; and in Chile, in 1973, the elected socialist government of Salvador Allende was similarly overthrown by the military under General Augusto Pinochet (Petras and Morley, 1975; Schlesinger and Kinzer, 1983).

In the context of geopolitics, opposition forces to a movement that has come to power in one country are often able to find external allies. The opposition can form a countermovement and seek aid, arms, advisers, and effective media coverage abroad. This process was especially notable during the cold war, as the example of the Nicaraguan contras illustrates (Halliday, 1989). With the end of the cold war, external support for opposition forces has diminished somewhat, but regional politics may produce similar patterns in which contending regional powers support contending forces within a smaller third nation.

These patterns of **external support for opposition forces** amplify revolutionaries' fears of **counterrevolutionary** efforts to scuttle their revolution, and they sometimes contribute to a climate of paranoia and growing repression. It may become impossible for the movement in power to distinguish internal, friendly criticism from externally supported counterrevolution. The revolutionary state may launch a purge or "reign of terror" that eliminates critical friends as well as foes. This outcome can be seen in the French Revolution's Reign of Terror, in Stalinist trials of former Bolshevik revolutionaries accused of being Fascists and Trotskyists (supporters of Stalin's rival Leon Trotsky), and in the violence that followed the revolution in Ethiopia (Deutscher, 1966; Halliday and Molyneux, 1982; Skocpol, 1979).

The Economy   Another constraint on movements in power may come from the economy itself. Abstract promises about more equality and justice must be translated into concrete policies such as more evenly distributed incomes, more public services, and, especially (in the case of socialist movements and some forms of populism), conversion to public ownership of businesses (Fagen, Deere, and Coraggio, 1986).

These concrete policies may turn out to be very difficult to implement. Nationalizing enterprises sets off resistance from their owners even if the owners are compensated. Expanding public services often has an inflationary effect. Using taxation to redistribute income or carrying out land reform meets with opposition.

These kinds of problems are exacerbated in the case of a small nation with an economy that is weak and dependent on larger economies. Nationalizing foreign companies creates a risk of intervention. International credit agencies cut off loans to nations they define as poor credit risks. In this way, movements that have socialist programs or even vaguely populist aims are likely to face a worsening economic climate as they attempt to carry out reforms, let alone revolutions (Payer, 1982).

Chile, in the early 1970s, and Nicaragua, in the 1980s, are examples of countries in which socialist-oriented movements attempted to make major economic reforms that did not succeed within the given national and global economic structures. Some analysts would point to the inherent difficulties of moving toward socialism within countries that have export-led economies and major social class cleavages. Others might emphasize the opposition to such reforms from powerful nations (especially the United States) and from international lending and development agencies (Baumeister and Cuadra, in Fagen, Deere, and Coraggio, 1986; Petras and Morley, 1975; Spalding, 1994).

Cultural Forces   Efforts to change a nation's culture also meet opposition both within and without; whatever the specific content of these efforts—secularizing the society or promoting religious values, emancipating women or restricting their rights, celebrating indigenous culture or encouraging westernization—some forces in complex modern societies are likely to oppose them.

For example, when socialist forces came to power in Afghanistan they moved forward rapidly with land expropriations and land redistribution, the expansion of women's education and legal rights, and efforts to curb the power of *mullahs* (local Islamic leaders). In a deeply conservative Islamic country, in which landowners and peasants were often linked together in extended families, these projects soon faced widespread opposition at the grassroots (Halliday, 1989:42–43).

In addition to the opposition of specific key actors to economic and cultural change, there is also the inertia inherent in social structure and civil society. Social change is generally more difficult and more time-consuming than movement adherents recognize. Social and cultural change means changing the practices and routines in the everyday life of millions of people. It means changing family life; it means changing interactions among people who have followed certain patterns of behavior all their lives; it means changing how people make a living, and how they eat, dress, and think. This type of transformation does not take place readily.

Coping with Constraint: Compromises, Coercion, and Factionalism   The movement that has come to state power faces difficult choices. It can abandon most of its projects and promises, perhaps concentrating on only a few that seem most important and most feasible. For example, a socialist movement might nationalize a few large, foreign-owned enterprises that produce key natural resources and earn hard currency (freely convertible currency that can be used to pay external debts and purchase imports), but abandon other projects like changing the condition of women, reducing the role of religious institutions, or converting all enterprises to public ownership. **Goal shrinkage** is a term that could be used to describe this reduction in the scope of movement goals.

For example, goal shrinkage can be said to have taken place in a number of African countries that, at the time of their independence, defined themselves as socialist as well as nationalist. Many of the states formed by nationalist movements or even national revolts (like that of the Mau-Mau in Kenya) carried out only limited parts of their socialist program (Hanlon, 1990; Hyden, 1980; Walton, 1983).

Alternatively, a movement in power can try to pursue the full range of original goals, but in a gradual and tentative manner. **Gradualism** may be associated with a loss of ideological commitment. The movement in power easily slides into a stance of preserving its hold on the state at all costs, giving up its program and concentrating on remaining in office. The National Liberation Front in Algeria seems to have slipped into this position after it came to power in 1962; it became highly authoritarian and bureaucratized, and pursued neither its socialist nor its Islamic ideals with much vigor (Howe, 1992). In this way, many nationalist postcolonial regimes disappointed their followers and citizens, setting the stage for a new wave of movements, for example, Islamicist movements in North Africa and western Asia.

The movement in power has another choice: It can push through all of its programs, becoming **coercive** if it meets with opposition. It builds barriers against global political and economic pressures to give up its charted course. For example, the Soviet Union under Stalin took this route, attempting to build "socialism in one country" in the 1920s and 1930s, in the face of international isolation (Gurley, 1975). This choice often leads to an increasingly paranoid stand among the party leadership; old allies leave or are pushed out of the ruling bloc. The regime may attempt to create an **autarkic** political economy, based on self-reliance—a possibility only for nations with a large and diversified resource base.

As the movement in power considers the range of options, it may split into radical and realistic wings. The former pushes for a "hard line," for a self-reliant break with the global economy, for more consistent commitment to its original ideals. Ironically, the more a movement strives to attain the vision of solidarity and justice that most movements share, the more intransigent and repressive it must become to withstand opposition.

On the other hand, if the realistic faction comes to power, it abandons movement goals and returns to policies and structures that are more similar to the institutionalized status quo ante. These processes can be seen at work in the Islamic revolution in Iran. After the death of Ayatollah Khomeini, there was a marked shift in a pragmatic direction of accommodation with international trading partners and foreign media and less tampering with the market economy within Iran. Nationalization of enterprises and land reform were not pursued further. Support for Islamic insurgencies abroad was softened (Abrahamian, 1991).

Movement Ideologies and the Outcomes of State Power   The problems of institutionalizing revolution vary with the goals of the movement and with the circumstances in which it comes to power.

A liberal movement that promises a small role for government and a large sphere of free enterprise clearly is in a better position once it is in power than movements that seek specific changes in all the spheres and their interrelationships. Liberal ideology has made primarily formal and not substantive promises—free enterprise, free markets, checks and balances, civil liberties—that are relatively easy to keep because they involve a disengagement of the state from civil society. This relatively limited set of goals may be one of the reasons that liberalism has been successful as a movement in power in many nations. It promises an enlarged sphere of civil society but does not specify the nature of that society, so it is easier to implement the goal. Liberal movements promise to limit the use of state power and let social and economic arrangements "take their course." Therefore, once they come to power they are under less pressure to produce specific institutional changes.

Nationalist movements have a similarly limited range of goals. Since their initial goals are self-determination and an end to foreign rule or indirect control, they are less likely to be held accountable by adherents and the public at large for transforming social relationships or changing the economy once they are in power.

Movements that promise social justice, economic equality, and/or cultural revitalization face considerably greater challenges; they have, in effect, promised to transform society by the application of state power, a goal that is harder to deliver than the shrinkage of state power. These issues are particularly acute for socialist and religiously oriented movements that promise more justice and solidarity, goals that require extensive changes in values and relationships.

Historical Circumstances and the Outcomes of State Power   Specific economic, historical, and geographic conditions are factors in the outcome. We can think of these conditions in terms of both political opportunity structures and conjunctural factors.

The examples of the Portuguese revolution in 1974 and the Sandinista revolution in Nicaragua in 1979 highlight the importance of such conditions for the outcomes of revolutions. Both revolutionary movements combined revolutionary socialist goals with more general goals of democracy and social justice; both revolutions overthrew authoritarian regimes that dated from the 1930s. In neither case did revolutionary socialists prevail; both revolutionary movements lost their hold on the state.

In Nicaragua, the Sandinistas were defeated and forced out of governing positions only after the long contra war, which divided the nation and destroyed the economy. A socialist-oriented revolution within the U.S. sphere of interest in Latin America, during the Reagan era, was confronted with an internal opposition that had powerful external support. Neither the place nor the time was conducive to the success of socialist reforms carried out by a revolutionary state, and the end of the Sandinista government came about primarily through violent means, even if it formally took place through elections. (Halliday, 1989; Hamilton, Frieden, Fuller, and Pastor, 1988; Marchetti, in Fagen, Deere, and Coraggio, 1986).

In Portugal, the revolutionary socialist forces were isolated and eased from positions of power in the armed forces within a year and a half. Electoral support shifted toward the center of the political spectrum. There was no long-term war with counterrevolutionaries. The proximity of the European Community and the promise of economic integration into western Europe shifted public opinion toward a liberal market democracy and away from support for the revolutionaries.

In both cases, revolutionary socialists lost their hold on state power; but in one case (Nicaragua) it was only after a prolonged war that left the country impoverished and divided, while in the other case (Portugal) it was the "carrot" of integration into the European economy that quickly undercut support for the more radical aims of the revolution. Geography and historical conjunctures destined a limited lifetime for both revolutions, but in rather different ways.

To conclude: Political movements use the state to develop their vision of society. This project is fraught with difficulties of organized opposition as well as general problems inherent in changing cultures and economies. A case-by-case historical analysis is required to understand the possibilities for success and failure for each movement in a specific country or region.

Emiliano Zapata (1883–1919): Armies of poor and landless Mexicans under the leadership of Zapata and Pancho Villa captured the capital in 1914 but were unable to consolidate state power and form a revolutionary regime.

Overall, it appears that liberalism with its goals of a reduced state and a large sphere of civil society (including a free-market economy) may be somewhat easier to implement than other forms of ideology. In this model of society, the state is required to do less; that is an easier goal for the movement in power to accomplish than using the state to bring about changes in cultural and economic practices.

SUMMARY

I have sketched out how major ideological movements have differing visions of how to rebuild society, of how to connect social institutions to each other, and of which values should guide the whole: discourses about both what is and what should be. These visions are generally coherent; we may disagree with the goals and/or believe that they are inherently impossible to realize, but we need to recognize that they are internally consistent. The major movement ideologies are also, in large part, mutually exclusive, although later we will examine some examples of cooperation, overlap, or convergence among movements.

Once a movement comes to power it attempts to implement its vision, which is difficult given the weight of circumstances. Movements in power and movement-states face organized opposition forces; in some cases, armed counterinsurgencies. They also face problems in transforming their economies and in changing the institutions of culture and social reproduction. Some movements may become more pragmatic and accept goal shrinkage or gradualism in implementing their plans. Others may become more coercive, hoping to suppress or eliminate opposition forces, especially countermovements that are (accurately or inaccurately) believed to be receiving external support.

All current movements must contend with the weight of past history, including the successes of past movements—most notably liberalism and nationalism. This historical configuration is the subject of the next chapter.

KEY TERMS AND CONCEPTS

elements of society
the economy; mode of production
political system; the state
culture and ideology
social reproduction

movements as totalizing visions of society
liberals and the separation of spheres
civil society
socialism
capitalism

religious fundamentalism and integralism
feminism and the gender system
fascism
nationalism
boundary maintenance
ethnoracism
environmental movements
conservative organicism
left libertarians and the new social movements

**movements in power; movement-
    states**
regime formation
counterinsurgency
external support for opposition
    forces
counterrevolution

goal shrinkage
gradualism
coercion
autarchy
movement ideologies and the
    exercise of state power

The workplace as a site of class struggle:
Sit-down strikes contributed to the success of
industrial union organizing in the late 1930s.
Production workers hold the auto plant,
while managers and office workers stand at
the gate. Detroit, Michigan, March 9, 1937.

CHAPTER 5

From Modern to Postmodern

Movements in History

Human beings make their own history, but they do not make it just as they please;
they do not make it under circumstances of their own choosing, but under
circumstances directly encountered, given and transmitted from the past.
  —Karl Marx, *The Eighteenth Brumaire of Louis Bonaparte,*
    International Publishers, New York, 1963, p. 15.

A person born in the United States in 1900 began life in a world without television, air-planes, antibiotics, and computers. A majority of the population was still rural. Women were not allowed to vote, and few had good jobs. African Americans, Native Americans, and Asian Americans were legally discriminated against and violently pushed to the margins of society.

On the surface, the world of 1900 seems totally different from the world we experience at the end of the twentieth century. Technology and fashion, ads and fads, a cornucopia of new products, the rise and fall of leaders and celebrities, and a growing public commitment to equality and diversity all give a sense of rushing along in the fast lane, leaving the sleepy past behind us.

Yet—we still live in a world of global markets. The world is still divided into a small number of rich industrial nations engaged in fierce competition; a semiperiphery of "in-between" countries; and the poor regions, now independent states rather than colonies. The gap between the lives of ordinary people in these different regions is as great as a century ago, maybe greater. The list of the world's twenty richest nations on a per capita basis changed very little between the late nineteenth century and the late twentieth century (Thurow, 1993:204). The great experiment of building revolutionary socialism in the Soviet Union has come to an unsuccessful end.

In the United States as well as globally, continuity may be a stronger force than change. A majority of adults in the United States continue to marry and raise children, although divorce is easier and families are smaller. The institutions of property have not changed dramatically. Small businesses continue to exist and gigantic ones continue to dominate some sectors of the economy; a large part of the population continue to be employees who go to work for wages and salaries in offices, stores, and factories. For better or for worse, our political institutions have not changed a great deal. Women and ethnic minorities have experienced major improvements in their positions in society, but these have come about through a series of reforms rather than a sudden upheaval. The

United States continues to be a nation of immigrants and a layered casserole of many cultures (not as fused as a melting pot, but neither as crisply distinct nor as egalitarian as vegetables in a salad bowl).

Change or continuity? This chapter challenges you to think about both. Participants in social movements claim to be agents of change. How much change has really taken place? How much of that change can be attributed to the actions of movements?

INTRODUCTION

Movement ideologies are not only about society in the abstract; they are about the specific, concrete forms of societies that exist when the movement emerges. All major contemporary movements have to take into account the structure of the societies in which they operate—the very structure that they seek to change in some way. Movements over the past 200 years have had to address the problems of "modern society," a form of society with certain key characteristics. We will see shortly that movement ideologies are not in exact agreement as to what these characteristics are; they are in great disagreement as to *what is to be done* about this society.

However, we can point to a number of features of modern society that social scientists usually consider to be essential elements of the "modern." Movement ideologies address these features, evaluating elements of *the modern* separately as well as in their sum total. Movement ideologies do not always use the language of the social sciences (although some do), but they generally recognize the same characteristics.

In many respects, the key characteristics of modern society continue to exist into the present. In the last few decades, however, some striking changes have taken place—changes that some choose to call "the postmodern." Other theorists see these new forms of society as extensions of the modern. The characteristics in question include the *globalization of markets, the restructuring of national economies and corporations, new technologies, and challenges to western culture and values. The collapse of Communist states in the Soviet Union and eastern Europe* also appears to be a part of this emerging postmodern world. These new patterns have implications for social movements which we will examine at the end of the chapter.

THE MODERN WORLD

Characteristics of Modern Societies

Modern society is characterized by **industrial capitalism** in the economic sphere, the **liberal state** and the **expansion of civil society** in the political sphere, the **compartmentalization of religious discourse** and the rise of competing world views in the sphere of culture, and a high degree of **individualism** in the sphere of personal life. These characteristics are not evenly or fully developed globally; modernity in some regions is characterized only by inclusion in global markets rather than by any of the key features of modernity.

Industrial Capitalism   The first important characteristic of modern societies is industrial capitalism (Hobsbawm, 1962). This term refers primarily to practices in the economic sphere, in the mode of production. By capitalism we mean an economy in which *the means of production are privately owned* and goods are made and distributed in response to *the market*, to perceptions of demand and supply. In capitalism, wealth is used to produce more wealth, rather than consumed. Thus, capitalism is characterized by accumulation, by investment and expansion.

While commerce and markets have existed since prehistoric times, capitalism as a distinct economic system is relatively recent in human history; we can point to the period from 1500 to 1800 in western Europe as a takeoff phase of capitalism as a system (Heilbroner, 1989). During this period, capital began to be invested, institutions of banking and credit were established, and labor became "free," which means that the laborer sold his or her labor power in a market rather than being coerced into working as a slave or serf or obligated to do so within a system of family and kinship (Polanyi, 1957). The laborer was also separated from ownership of the means of production, which was concentrated in the hands of the capitalist in the form of factories, buildings, and above all, machinery.

By 1800, not only was capitalism established in Europe and rapidly expanding, the **industrial revolution** was under way. It was a change in the methods of production. Production shifted from agriculture and crafts to mass production of goods in factories using machinery (Hobsbawm, 1962). This shift first took place in the textile industry in England, but rapidly spread to other countries and industries.

Workers ceased being guild members or subcontractors working with their own tools in their own cottages; they became *wage workers* hired to work for a certain number of hours in a factory using machinery that belonged to the factory owner. Industrialization developed in association with modern capitalism, an economic system based on the hiring of wage and salaried workers by an employer who is also the owner of the means of production (tools, machines, factory buildings, office space, etc.).

The Liberal State and the Growth of Democracy   Another major change of the late eighteenth century was the **political revolution** that happened in several different places, most notably in the American colonies in 1776 and in France from 1789 to 1793. These revolutions were the most dramatic points of a shift in European institutions from rule by the nobility and an absolute monarch to a political system usually referred to as liberal democracy. In the **American and French Revolutions,** people joined together to gain control of the nation and its political system (Hobsbawm, 1962; Moore, 1965). Henceforth, they saw themselves as citizens, not subjects of a king, and claimed the right to create and alter their political institutions. The main mechanism for doing so was representative democracy.

It took a long time before universal suffrage was attained in countries that claimed to be democratic (Therborn, 1977). With the end of the absolute monarchies came civil rights and liberties for citizens: the right to petition and organize, the right to a free press and free circulation of ideas; the right to a trial by a jury of one's peers; full citizenship status for religious and ethnic minorities (although at first these rights were only imperfectly realized, especially in the United States, which continued to allow slavery); protection against torture and forced self-incrimination; freedom of religion and the disestablishment of religious institutions, that is, their uncoupling from the state and their relegation to a private sphere.

At the same time, the feudal rights of a small landowning nobility were swept away. The titles and special privileges of the nobility as well as feudal land rights were abolished. Citizens became formally equal before the law. Land became fully a **commodity**—that is, it circulated freely in a market rather being passed down in a system of primogeniture or feudal obligations.

The Diversification of Discourse   Associated with these economic and political changes were changes in culture, discourses, values, and systems of beliefs. The Protestant Reformation of the early sixteenth century had already opened the door to highly individualistic interpretations of religion. Sects and new denominations flourished. It became increasingly difficult for holders of political power to control religion; that is, established churches discovered that their support from the state was weakening. Sometimes there were unintended consequences in this process; for example, the Puritans and pilgrims came to the American colonies to establish a theocratic society, but their very act of separation from the Church of England set the precedent of "religious freedom and toleration" in the New World.

Change in culture accelerated with the growth of science throughout the sixteenth, seventeenth, and eighteenth centuries. More and more areas of human thought were opened up to **scientific inquiry.** Some of the scientists saw themselves as devout believers whose respect for God was demonstrated in their effort to understand Creation; but in the long run, religious systems of thought were probably net losers in this development. Religious institutions had to compete with other cultural institutions. It became increasingly difficult for religious institutions to prevent the dissemination of new ways of thinking about the physical world, as the Roman Catholic Church had tried to do with Galileo's sun-centered Copernican model of the solar system. The prerogative to teach about the physical world was shifted from religious institutions to secular scientific and educational institutions.

This shift culminated in the **Enlightenment,** an intellectual current that emphasized critical inquiry not merely into the physical world but also into human institutions and societies (Zeitlin, 1994). The discourse of science and the Enlightenment was one of progress and reason; continued inquiry into nature and human society would (it was believed) lead to improvement in the human condition. Faith as a shared and unquestioned practice gave way to "religion," an identifiable cultural institution that had to compete with other systems of belief for individual allegiances.

Individualization in Family and Gender Systems   Less well documented are the changes in the gender system and families that accompanied this shift into modernity. What seems to have happened is that by the end of the eighteenth century, the institution of the **nuclear family** became more clearly established, especially among the upper and middle classes in western Europe and North America. Historians of the family are now beginning to point to the early roots of the "modern family"; in England, already by the sixteenth century, much of the population lived in nuclear families, married late in life (midtwenties), and selected their own spouses (Laslett, 1984). In fact, some historians would argue that in northern Europe, the large patriarchal family of the Mediterranean world had never taken hold.

Whatever its origins, the nuclear family began to prevail not only in terms of the practices of everyday life, but also as a discourse, an **ideology of domesticity.** This ideology emphasized monogamous, romantic love between the spouses, an intense commitment to motherhood as a self-conscious practice by women, and a sharp household division of labor between a father-breadwinner and a mother-homemaker (Fairchilds, 1984). This pattern spread to most of the middle class in western Europe and among European settlers in the nineteenth century and somewhat later, to other groups as well—to the European/European-origin working class and to some parts of the urbanized middle classes of many different ethnic backgrounds. The term *neotraditional family* can be used to refer to this pattern, distinguishing it from extended family households, polygamy, arranged marriages, and other family arrangements that are presumed to be more traditional.

On the one hand, this form might appear male-dominated and unequal; on the other hand, its ideology emphasizes individual choice. It contains the idea that relationships are voluntarily entered into and can be dissolved with the consent of individuals; marriage and the family were becoming individual arrangements. The family of Benjamin Franklin provides a good example of this growing individualism and independence; in Franklin's correspondence he complains that his daughter is about to marry someone of whom he does not approve but that there is nothing he can do about it.

As more production took place in factories, the family lost its functions as a unit of economic production; it became specialized for consumption, raising children, and fulfilling emotional needs.

The Uneven Spread of "Modernity": Global Inequalities   Modern forms of society expanded globally throughout the nineteenth century and through most of the twentieth century. The expansion of capitalism, European colonialism, and modernization was largely a process of subordinating other societies and cultures to the modern world as defined by western Europeans and North Americans. The modern social order was not exported from western Europe and North America as an intact whole. Its expansion was uneven. Other regions were brought into the industrial capitalist system in an exploited and dependent form, as a **periphery** and **semiperiphery** of the developed capitalist nations, the **core** regions which were located in western Europe, North America, and (later) Japan (Wallerstein, 1974).

Subordination consisted of several parallel processes: economic exploitation, the establishment of political institutions without democracy and civil rights, and a partial and uninvited importation of modern institutions and cultures. Economic exploitation meant that the peripheral areas became **colonies** or dependent regions that provided cheap raw materials and cheap labor. For example, rubber was imported to Europe from colonies in Africa and Southeast Asia, where the tappers lived in great poverty and conditions of near slavery (Gide, 1994; Wolf, 1969).

Even when the colonial empires ended after World War II, much of the globe remained economically dependent on the developed capitalist nations. The prices of commodities like coffee, sugar, and copper were directly or indirectly set by the developed buying nations, not by the producing ones (Sharpe, 1977). Transnational corporations were usually owned and headquartered in the developed nations (Rhodes, 1970).

With this uneven economic development came the absence of liberal-democratic institutions. The indigenous institutions of regions that became colonies had ranged from relatively egalitarian tribal societies to class-stratified kingdoms and empires. Whatever the indigenous forms were, the colonial powers imposed decidedly undemocratic regimes on the colonies. Nations like England, France, and the Netherlands that were liberal and increasingly democratic "at home" did not export these institutions to the colonies. In the colonies, the population was ruled by European administrators with few or no representative institutions. Political and economic opportunities were extended or denied on the basis of racial criteria. Institutions like forced labor in lieu of money taxes, and the use of corporal punishment (e.g., floggings) persisted, although they had been abolished in the colonial powers in western Europe and North America.

After decolonization (which generally took place in the 15 years following the end of the Second World War in 1945), many of the former colonial powers and the other developed nations supported or tacitly accepted authoritarian governments in areas of dependency. Such governments were believed to keep labor costs low, discourage an independent union movement, and maintain a stable climate for investment (Frank, 1981). For instance, in the Philippines, the Marcos regime and its imposition of martial law was tacitly accepted by the United States (Anderson, 1988). The United States also supported the Shah in Iran and military dictators in Guatemala (Schlesinger and Kinzer, 1983). The French government did little or nothing to democratize regimes in its former colonies.

Given these global economic and political inequalities, the cultural values and practices of modern society seemed rather hypocritical to populations of former colonies and economically dependent regions. The process of cultural modernization had been carried out by colonial regimes, and was experienced by indigenous populations as the imposition of western institutions. Institutions like Christianity, formal schooling modeled on the educational systems of the colonial powers, European legal systems and judicial practices, European property law and the transformation of communal lands into alienable individual property, and monogamy and western European forms of the family were experienced as foreign impositions. These cultural changes took place within a framework of political and economic inequality and frequently on the basis of racist assumptions. Westerners asserted that the "modern" way of life was best—in some sense, "higher" or more advanced than that of other societies, an assumption that was offensive and unacceptable to the growing numbers of educated people in the former colonies.

Modern came to be identified with *western,* with the global power of western Europe and North America. As new nations asserted their political independence and tried to extricate their economies from dependent development, they also began to question western/modern cultural institutions.

Movements as Responses to the Modern Condition

Now I want to return to the view that contemporary movements began as responses to the characteristics of modern societies and to the way in which these characteristics had spread throughout the globe.

Liberalism and the Perfection of the Present   Some movements wanted to perfect and propagate the modern form of society. These movements—loosely speaking, liberal and liberal-democratic movements—favored capitalism, the liberal nation-state, citizen rights and representative government, and individualism. While not always antireligious, liberal movements called for the confinement of religion to a private sphere. They celebrated the separation of religion, government, the economy, and personal life from each other.

This liberal point of view was held by some ideologues as a defense of the status quo in the developed capitalist nations; there the ideology became institutionalized and was often used to oppose social movements. But, for other liberal ideologues, liberalism still needed to be perfected and realized. The positive side of the modern was not a reality as long as repressive governments existed, religions were imposed by the state, and individuals did not enjoy personal liberties and citizen rights. Thus, liberal-democratic movements formed around the goal of fulfilling this vision and expanding it globally. Other movements questioned the modern social order, but they questioned it from different vantage points.

Conservative Movements: Looking to the Past   Conservative movements wanted to go back, to a status quo ante. They wanted to keep some features of modernization, especially technology and the nation-state. For some conservative movements, capitalism was acceptable, but often not in its unregulated free-market forms.

Conservative movements were usually opposed to modern forms of belief, culture, and family structure accompanied by individualism and secularization. It was especially in these areas that they wanted to preserve or revive older institutions. In any case, they wanted to "unbundle" the package of the modern, accepting only some of its characteristics and rejecting many others.

This type of conservatism was a particularly powerful impulse in those regions where modernization was imposed by western imperialism. Nationalist movements in these regions wanted to preserve only a few selected features of western modernity—especially its technological and economic dynamism—but jettison much of the cultural and political baggage.

Movements of religious integralism and fundamentalism also wanted to reconstitute a social order in which religion was a central institution that permeated political decisions, family life, and gender roles.

Socialism and Feminism: Looking to the Future   Other movements, especially socialism, thought that modernization was a change in the right direction, but had not gone far enough; capitalism was seen as the roadblock to the realization of the promises of equality, individualism, and freedom that are offered—but not fulfilled—in modern societies.

Feminism also accepted some of the changes promised by modernization—specifically, greater juridical equality and the weakening of patriarchal authority; but like socialists, feminists felt that it was necessary to go further.

To summarize: In the 200 years that followed the political and industrial revolutions, movements generally fell into several categories: Movements to perfect and expand the modern social order; movements to extricate a nation or region from western domination, in the process preserving only selected features of the modern social order; movements to reconstitute tradition—primarily the ascendancy of religion; and movements to bring about an end to capitalism, replacing it with socialism and/or transformed family and gender institutions.

Movement ideologies not only are visions of the good society, the best possible organization of the economy, political system, culture, and social reproduction, but also have located the good society in *time*, in history. Some called for the perfection of institutions that exist in the present, others located the good society in a revitalization of the past, and yet others believed that it was only a potential in the future. Movement ideologies use ideas about time and history to express their challenge to the institutional status quo.

These movements—even the ones that appear to want to "go back"—were a product of the shift to modern society. In one way or another—sometimes in highly metaphorical language—movements take a stand on capitalism, industrialization, the modern nation-state, the compartmentalization of religion and the rise of competing systems of discourse, and growing individualism in the sphere of family and sexuality. Above all, they take a stand on the structure of the modern *totality*, the form of society defined by the following features: the separation of the spheres of religion, state, economy, and personal life; markets as the leading element of the economy; a high level of secularization; and private, individual choice as the criterion of the good life and the basis of all action.

FROM MODERN TO POSTMODERN?

At the end of the twentieth century, after two centuries of development and expansion of modern societies, we appear to be at a breakpoint that is summarized by the term *postmodern*. It may no longer be appropriate to use the term *modern* to describe the types of societies that are forming today. Modern implies continuity with the societies that formed from the end of the eighteenth century to the middle of the twentieth century, and perhaps that continuity is now coming to an end. Observers who believe that we are definitely moving into a new form of society use the term postmodern. Others prefer the term advanced capitalist or late capitalist (Jameson, 1984; Mandel, 1975). To others, modern implies continual change; thus, the changes currently underway are just part of the ongoing process of modernity within a capitalist economic framework (Berman, 1982).

Yet, these different theorists point to a similar set of social, economic, and cultural changes that are currently under way. The economy is more completely globalized than ever before. There are **global markets** in labor and skills, investments, technology, the media, and culture and information (Appadurai, 1990; Reich, 1992). The Communist states' challenge to capitalism has collapsed (Przeworski, 1991). Cultural diversity has increased as movements and peoples challenge Eurocentrism or western cultural dominance and reassert their own cultural traditions (Wallerstein, 1990). At the same time, a global culture is emerging, in large part because of transnational media; transnational systems of communications; and transnational markets for labor, capital, and products.

Some of the changes seem contradictory, and we remain uncertain about the nature of the changes in the global system. That uncertainty—perhaps more than any specific change—is what is implied in the term postmodern. For example, apparently contradictory trends in the contemporary situation are that markets and media systems have definitely become global, and yet many people are trying to revive diverse local traditions that existed before modernization and westernization (Wallerstein, 1990).

More and more people participate in transnational markets and transnational culture. Whole populations move around in enormous streams of refugees and labor migrants. A fifth of the population of El Salvador lives in the United States. Transnational families connect Lagos and London, Chicago and Guatemala City. Processes of production stretch from New York to Bombay, as corporations separate and globalize not only manufacturing but management and information systems (Reich, 1992). Blue jeans and afro-pop, pizza and martial arts, soccer and the icon of Michael Jordan, Brazilian soap operas and Japanese cartoons are the signs that we are participating in a world culture, a global village united by images carried over satellite links and optical fibers. At the same time, groups seem to be closing themselves off into hostile ethnonation-alist movements and enclaves.

This part of the chapter concerns some of the changes that may be taking place in societies on a global scale and the ways in which movements them-selves are changing. Movements are, in part, causes of these postmodern changes and are also affected by them. I will return to these themes at the end of the book, in Part Three, "Conclusions," after we have examined some spe-cific movements.

Here I would like to indicate several themes of postmodern movements and the world in which they are emerging. One theme I will explore is the global preeminence of the market economy. This development is both an economic process involving globalized markets and a political process involving the de-feat of the Communist states and a partial disengagement of liberal states from economic functions. A second theme is the emergence of identity politics and the reassertion of cultural traditions against the ideology of western/modern culture. A third theme is the fragmentation of movement structure, though not necessarily of movement visions; this fragmentation helps movements become more transnational and adapt themselves to a larger variety of political envi-ronments.

The Global Preeminence of the Market Economy

Berlin Wall/Mexican Border   At the end of the twentieth century the entire globe is involved in a market economy. Markets in labor, technology, ideas, in-formation, and investments have been partially global for a long time, but we are now in a phase of accelerated globalization (Appadurai, 1990). There is a po-litical as well as an economic side to this globalization, because the controls of the nation-state over markets have weakened in recent decades.

The most dramatic instance of the expansion of markets at the expense of states is the collapse or defeat of the Communist states that followed the Soviet model. This collapse has major implications for movements. Leadership by a vanguard party, the single-party state, the centrally planned economy, and the emphasis on rapid industrial development appear not to have been viable. Whatever its successes may have been in overcoming an initial condition of poverty and underdevelopment, socialists can no longer offer this model either to the developed capitalist nations or to the poor capitalist nations. This failure is a great disappointment to those who had seen it as a viable alternative to cap-italism and had hoped that it would make possible a better quality of life in the peripheral capitalist world.

The implications for movements are complex and multiple. All movements have to think about the implications for movement organization and strategies and for the concepts of "revolution" and "state power." Socialism has to come up with new models if it is to survive as a movement and not merely turn into an academic and theoretical critique of capitalism. The global preeminence of market economies also focuses concern on the problems of capitalism itself, es-pecially the problems of its uneven global development. The issues are twofold.

The first issue is that there remain enormous problems of poverty and in-equality, left over from the days of colonialism and not solved by the current globalization of markets. Only about one-quarter of the world's population lives in material comfort, with high levels of health and education and strong purchasing power in world markets. This fortunate fourth includes a large part of the population of North America, western Europe, Japan, Australia, and New Zealand as well as smaller well-to-do strata in other countries.

About half the global population lives in moderate or meager circum-stances. They are not in immediate danger of starvation, but their purchasing power is limited, their housing is inadequate by the standards of the wealthy nations, and they are only spottily served by health-care systems, public trans-portation, and infrastructures like water supplies and electricity. Though gen-erally literate, they rarely have access to schooling beyond the primary grades. Their possessions are few—a bicycle, household utensils, a little furniture, clothing, a watch, a radio, and perhaps a television. Daily life is a struggle to make ends meet and usually requires the effort of a whole family. High national unemployment rates, insecure jobs, and fluctuating markets create an uncertain long-term outlook. Many rural and urban people in Asia (including China) and Latin America live in these conditions. Despite historically strong levels of ed-ucation and health care under communism, many people in eastern Europe and the former Soviet Union in the post-cold war world also find themselves in a situation of insecurity at middle levels of material prosperity (Przeworski, 1991).

About one-quarter of the world's population lives in absolute poverty, and the percentage increased during the 1980s. They are disproportionately located in Africa south of the Sahara, in some parts of southern Asia, and in Haiti and the northeast of Brazil, but there are very poor populations throughout the world, especially among marginalized ethnic groups, unemployed urban mi-grants, and the landless rural poor. Daily life is a struggle for physical survival. The very poor face malnutrition, possible starvation, high rates of infant mor-tality, and low life expectancy; many are illiterate and, in urban areas, some are homeless (Durning, 1990; Scheper-Hughes, 1992).

Many movements in what used to be called the Third World, in peripheral capitalist regions, seek to end this poverty and inequality; the adherents of these movements believe that global markets will not operate to level out these enor-mous gaps but, rather, will exacerbate them. Some of these movements claim to be socialist, like the Shining Path guerrillas in Peru. Others are within religious traditions, like Islamic movements, or seek solutions in nationalism. Some movements, like the African National Congress in South Africa or the Guatemalan opposition, work for democracy, civil rights, and human rights; these intermediate goals are seen as necessary conditions for a longer struggle for a more just and egalitarian society. As much of the former Communist world faces a future on the middle or lower rungs of the global economy, this spec-trum of movements emerges in the post-Communist states as well as in the for-mer Third World (Przeworski, 1991).

The postmodern condition is signaled by the fate of two great barriers. The fall of the wall in Berlin signals the end of Soviet-style Communist models. The ever more desperate efforts by Mexicans to cross the fence along the U.S.-Mexican border signals the ongoing problems of the market economies in peripheral regions.

Decline of the Fordist Accumulation Model   The second issue that emerges from these new conditions is that even the developed nations face considerable uncertainty in the global economy. Political and economic arrangements that protected workers and businesses in these nations in the past are in decline. Some economists summarize these problems as **the decline of the Fordist accumulation model.** By the term Fordist accumulation model they mean that the developed market economies had boomed in the twentieth century on the basis of a social and economic system in which mass production and mass consumption functioned together in domestic markets (Hounshell, 1984). The workers who produced the Ford motor car also bought it. Workers' wages were high enough to fuel the mass market for the products made by industrial workers. Despite manufacturers' initial opposition to unions, by the 1950s, in Europe and the United States (and somewhat less so, Japan), organized labor had an important part in maintaining this system. It accepted the prerogatives of management to organize the process of production and, in return, received high wages and good benefits. It accepted a somewhat secondary role within the political system as a whole. Capital benefited from the cooperation of workers and the assurance that products would be bought within the domestic market (Aronowitz, 1973; Geoghegan, 1991, 1994).

The Fordist model both included and excluded ethnic minorities in the United States and Europe. Insofar as they found jobs in the major core industries and belonged to unions, ethnic minorities were integrated into the more prosperous parts of the working class. But many were excluded from the start, forced into the lower half of a dual economy, and relegated to a peripheral sector of low-wage work in small firms.

By the 1970s and 1980s, the Fordist model was in decline. New technologies and areas of production—especially in electronics and computerization—changed industrial processes and reduced the need for skilled and semiskilled factory workers. The labor force became increasingly divided between professional and managerial workers, on the one hand, and low-skill service workers, on the other. The Fordist model was based on high-wage economies in Europe and North America, and some companies preferred to shift to lower-wage regions, especially in Asia and Latin America. New technologies made it much easier to globalize production, shifting parts of manufacturing processes into lower-wage economies (Reich, 1992). The role of unions weakened, partly because of the changing nature of the labor force and the structure of occupations, partly because of political shifts. Industrial regions like the northeast in the United States and the north in England experienced extensive deindustrialization (Bluestone and Harrison, 1982; Harrison and Bluestone, 1988; Reich, 1992).

Together, all these changes produced the crisis of the Fordist model of accumulation and development, which contributed to the creation of the postmodern world. The signs of the crisis include rising unemployment rates over the last two decades in most developed market economies (apart from shorter-term fluctuations in the business cycle), deindustrialization or declines in heavy industry in some regions, and a growing discontent among young people who are no longer easily absorbed by the labor market unless they have specialized skills or a high level of education (and sometimes, not even then). Social problems like crime and the "underclass" are, in part, reflections of the developed economies' difficulties in absorbing people without specialized skills or higher education. Ethnic groups marginal to or excluded from the Fordist core sector to begin with are now among the most vulnerable to these kinds of economic and social dislocations (Wilson, 1987).

The miniborders of gates, armed security guards, and cul-de-sacs erected by prosperous communities within the United States suggest that large gaps in living standards and accompanying high crime rates are no longer problems that are confined to the global south, but have spilled over into the heartland of capitalist democracy (Davis, 1990; Soja, 1993).

The rise of neo-Nazis in western Europe and of anti-immigration parties and movements in both the United States and Europe may be responses to the economic and social dislocations caused by the decline of the Fordist model. Faced with unemployment, the disappearance of high-wage jobs, and economic competition within multicultural societies, some people turn to racism and various forms of nationalism to protect their position. These responses are part of what observers call **identity politics,** an increasing focus of movements on cultural differences rather than shared class interests.

The Second World of Communist nations has disappeared. The Third World is appearing within the First World in the forms of cultural diversity, labor migration, and Third World problems of poverty and marginality. First World manufacturing processes and even sophisticated high-tech industries are relocating to the former Third World. This rearrangement of our sense of geography is part of what we mean by postmodern.

Observers seem confused whether these developments are on the whole positive, a move toward functioning markets and liberal democracy in ever larger regions of the globe, or negative, the beginnings of global anarchy and barbarism (Fukuyama, 1992; Kaplan, 1994).

Goodbye to the Enlightenment?

Revitalizing the Past and the Rise of Identity Politics   If the forms of social order associated with industrial capitalism, the Enlightenment, individualism, and liberal democracy are in flux, and if communism has failed as a real alternative, maybe some features of the status quo ante can and must be revived. Status quo ante here refers to the forms of society that existed before the Enlightenment and the industrial and liberal-democratic political revolutions. This effort to revive traditions and challenge western forms of the modern is one theme of postmodern movements.

Postmodern discourse is sometimes seen as a challenge to the Enlightenment. In this view, the social order and forms of practice and discourse that emerged from the Enlightenment, the rise of science, and the liberal state are *on their way out* in many regions of the world. In this sense, modernity has come to an end as a global system; its claim to offer a universal set of values is no longer accepted (Wallerstein, 1990).

Movements that opposed the modern have thus become successful, if not globally, then at least locally in **revitalizing "premodern" traditions**. It turned out that religion and tradition were far more powerful than liberals and socialists believed. Phenomena like the Islamic revolution in Iran, the rise of Islamic movements throughout the Muslim world, the success of Christian evangelicals and Mormons in Latin America, and the wide diffusion of Christian fundamentalism in the United States are evidence for the vitality of religion (Marty and Appleby, 1992; Riesebrodt, 1993). East Asian societies have successfully blended capitalist economies with their own social structures and cultural traditions like Shinto, Buddhism, and the Confucian ethic. The cultures of indigenous peoples—from the Kayapo in the Amazon to the Inuit in the Arctic—are forming the basis for movements that challenge industrial development and the misuses of modern technology. Increasingly, we have to turn to movements of indigenous people, "keepers of the forest," to help us undo the environmental degradation that the modern misuses of science, technology, and industrial development have brought about.

Such resurgent local, particularistic, and neotraditional movements can also be violent and racist; the ethnonationalist conflicts in Rwanda and some post-Communist territories like Yugoslavia, Transcaucasia and central Asia, as well as western European neo-Nazis suggest a large potential for brutality and bloodshed in particularist mobilizations.

Meanwhile, postcolonial societies have not "bought into" the liberal democratic state. Family structure in much of the world has not followed the patterns of nuclear households and falling birth rates set by the west. Individualism has not been an ideology that most cultures find acceptable. While media have become technologically modernized, their content is by no means only western or secular or liberal democratic. Science has turned out to be disappointing, bringing only limited progress to many people and, in some cases, legitimating environmental destruction.

Theorists who hold this view of postmodernity generally admit that capitalism is a global system and that industrialization is taking place in many contexts; but they deny that these economic changes automatically bring about a transformation toward a modern social order. They sometimes point to places like Japan and other East Asian nations as successful societies that have only adopted the technological and economic elements of the modern, while preserving a good deal of their traditional culture, gender system, family life, and social relationships (Van Wolferen, 1990). The concept postmodern implies the recognition that the societies of the future will not be clones of the modern European and North American societies, but much more complex mixes of several traditions, formed in a clash of western/modern ideologies and revitalized indigenous cultures.

Of course, one can't ever "go home again." Neither the preservation of tradition in East Asia, nor the upsurge of fundamentalism in the Christian and Islamic worlds, nor the movements of indigenous peoples to reclaim their territory and their culture, produce exact replicas of societies that existed prior to the explosion of modernity from western Europe. These reconstituted traditional ideologies, movements, and societies are deeply influenced by the intervening impact of the modern. They certainly have to come to terms with capitalism as a global economic system. They are quite prepared to use modern technologies in organizing their movements. In their discourse they can be *antimodern* and *postmodern*, but hardly *premodern*.

Sometimes these efforts to revive national, ethnic, and religious traditions and form movements that challenge the claims of modern and western culture are considered forms of identity politics, a term often used to suggest a shift away from class politics. During the period of Communist movements and states and the successful functioning of the Fordist model, political action rested on a class-based collective identity. With the collapse of Communism and the decline of Fordism, there is a search for a new basis of political action. Identity politics combines a sense of uncertainty with the tendency to look for a basis of action in religion, ethnicity, nation, and the reconstitution of cultural traditions that were under siege from modern ideologies. (Some authors also include gender and sexual orientation in the category of identity politics, but these two bases of collective identity are less clearly challenges to modern values.)

Postmodern Movements

New Social Movements   The postindustrial shifts in the economy, the globalization of markets, the decline of a large industrial working class in the core capitalist nations, and the questioning of modern forms of culture all set the stage for new types of social movements.

Some social movement researchers in Europe believe that the **new social movements** that emerged there in the 1970s and 1980s were prototypes of such movements. These movements addressed issues of the environment, gender issues, the restructuring of cities, and the arms race. They included mass peace demonstrations, squatter takeovers of buildings to protest housing shortages and gentrification, the formation of feminist collectives, experiments in media and the arts including cultural protests like Punk, and many local actions against nuclear power plants and industrial pollution (Mayer, 1991).

These movements were different from the movements that had characterized European politics through much of the late nineteenth and twentieth centuries. They did not have a clear-cut class base, as had the large working-class socialist movements. They organized in the name of the public or consumers or the marginalized, as well as women and youth (Scott, 1990). In terms of social origins, activists included educated middle-class young people as well as more marginal people. The children of the traditional working class could no longer find jobs in industry. Young educated people rejected work in corporate hierarchies and government bureaucracies. Together they provided a support base for some of the new social movements and the increasingly **decentralized forms of cultural resistance** (Hebdige, 1982; Willis, 1990).

In the climate of economic restructuring and the decline of the Fordist model, class lines were becoming blurred (Gorz, 1982). Incidentally, this kind of blurring had always been a feature of society in the United States. Indeed, many of the characteristics of the new social movements in Europe, such as the lack of a distinct class base, a lack of enthusiasm about the benefits of government initiatives, and a decentralized structure were not so new in the United States (Mayer, 1991).

The new social movements did not seek to capture the state or use it to carry out reforms; rather, they harassed it, sniped at it with local actions, worked around it, and showed their contempt for it. Even in rather culturally and politically centralized nations, the new movements were self-consciously local, decentralized, antibureaucratic, and antihierarchical. These attitudes can be interpreted as an attempt to once again enlarge the sphere of civil society, a sphere that had become constricted by the increasing role of the state, even when its motives were benign, as in the case of western European welfare states.

Scholars studying these movements emphasized their challenge to all institutional claims of rationality, whether by corporations or governments. The movements opposed these claims of rationality (Habermas, 1987; Touraine, 1981). They challenged the role of experts and technocrats in making decisions for other people, such as the siting of nuclear power plants, the deployment of NATO missiles, or the urban renewal of city centers (Castells, 1983).

It is now by no means certain that these new left-libertarian social movements in Europe are the only prototypes of postmodern movements. In Europe, they may now find themselves confronted by movements that have similar forms but with racist and nationalist ideologies, like neo-Nazis and neo-Fascists. New movements in other regions have ideologies like religious fundamentalism. The new social movements in Europe do, however, perhaps contain some elements that we can expect to find elsewhere and with increasing frequency: blurring of class identity in the support base of movements and, with it, a search for new agents of history; and more localized and decentralized forms of organization.

The Search for New Agents of History   Both capitalist democracy and socialism were identified as movements of social classes—the first with the European bourgeoisie and the second with the working class. In each case, the movement ideology universalized the concerns and interests of the class that presented itself as the **agent of history,** the social force that could bring about a better society.

The ideologues of postmodern movements are asking themselves whether class-identified movements have reached the end of the line. They look for alternative core support groups. The revival of ethnonationalism represents one such search: A good society can only be established where there is ethnic and cultural homogeneity and consensus. Here the movement ideologues give up on the search for a universal historical agent. The successes of many varieties of religious fundamentalism represent another answer: Only the community of believers can form a good society, united by faith. And feminism points to yet another new agent: The new agent is constituted by women and those men who are prepared to unite with women to transform society away from male domination and hierarchy that lie at the heart of all injustice and inequality. Environmental movements and the new social movements in Europe claim to be representing categories like "humanity in general" or "the public." Of course, these movements do not deny that there are also class issues involved; but they emphasize that classes as historical agents have not produced satisfactory social orders.

Shifts in Vision   This brings us to the final postmodern concern of movements: The shift from the vision of a sudden and total transformation of the social order to the hope that partial, local, and continuous changes will add up to a transformation as profound as a revolution. The major types of movements that contended on the terrain of modernity represented large blueprints for change and hoped to reconstitute the entire configuration of society in a single process usually involving the state: capitalism, progress, socialism, democracy, liberalism, revolution. Movements that used these large terms had a fairly clear idea of how society should finally be structured and looked to the state as the lever of change.

Partial and Total   Part of the postmodern climate is a withdrawal from totalizing visions realized through the state. The hope is that change can be local, piecemeal, gradual, partial; the totality should indeed change in the long run, but it cannot change all at once in a process planned and implemented through the state. This is a view that a particular school of conservatives (associated with the legacy of Edmund Burke) has had all along; in this respect postmodern thought returns to some themes in **conservative organicism**. To say that local, gradual, and organically evolving change is the only change that is possible or desirable is itself a bit of a totalization; that is, an ideology with a coherent view of society and social change.

Many postmodern movements use this conservative, organicist view of change in a strategy of total subversion—yet another irony of postmodernism. "Wherever there is power, there is resistance," say the postmodernists; so resistance is diffused into all interactions, into all contestations of discourse. Decentralized piecemeal change can add up to total collapse of the system. But, perhaps an invisible collapse, because if resistance is everywhere, it may turn out to be nowhere; in other words, the centers of power like modern states and transnational companies will not be dissolved by these interactive and cultural resistances (Handler, 1992).

Theorists have attempted to capture some of these contradictory changes in movements with terms like *new social movements* and *postmodern movements*. As I noted above, the former term was first used by European theorists to describe movements that emerged in the 1970s and 1980s. The peace movement, the women's movement, environmental movements, movements of squatters protesting against the gentrification of neighborhoods all formed part of a larger movement that was directed against the rationalization of life, top-down planning in the welfare state, the post-Fordist restructuring of corporations and capitalism as a whole, and other processes of control. Power and control had to be opposed continously and everywhere.

Local and Global   The new social movements did not take the form of large party organizations. They deliberately remained local and unclearly defined, with a **fragmented movement structure**. Activists shifted from one protest, tactic, or issue to another in a pattern of overlapping participation; individuals were active as feminists, in the peace movement, as protestors against nuclear power plants, without making long-term commitments to national organizations. One year the activists organized a day-care co-op; another year a different, but overlapping group ran a feminist bookstore; then they shifted to sitting-in at a NATO missile site; and, yet again, redirected their energies to guerrilla theater, to squatter collectives in vacant buildings, or to graffiti art on the Berlin Wall (Beccalli, 1994; Scott, 1990).

The activists saw themselves as parts of networks, collectives, communities—not as members of a single stable party or movement organization. They were linked across national boundaries, yet their actions were often local. Their identity was seen as constructed in these shifting struggles, rather than as given by class position. They opposed using the state to achieve their goals; the state was part of the problem, not part of the solution.

New Social Movements and Postmodernism as Subversion   Surprised to see the difference between these new social movements and the more stable, organizationally coherent and class-based movement activity that had characterized western Europe in most of the twentieth century, theorists felt the need to develop a new social movement theory. As Margit Mayer points out, these shifting, networked, nonparty, and non-class-based movements had always existed in the United States (Mayer, 1991). Perhaps their appearance in Europe was a result of Americanization of European political and cultural life. The cultural diffusion of unstable, pervasive, and decentralized social activism without a strong sense of class identity is itself, perhaps, part of the postmodern.

But, even in the United States, analysts noted more unstable, more decentralized, and less predictable forms of movement activity. One of them remarks that the postmodern means subversion (Handler, 1992). In philosophy books, it means the deconstruction of texts; in the streets, it means movements that arise and disappear suddenly, have little national organization other than networks, are local and decentralized but linked to each other, and distrust the state rather than seek to capture or use it.

It was disturbing that these kinds of movement forms, which originated on the left, also appeared on the right and among violent forces with little ideology of any kind. Nazi skinheads and the paramilitary right, though far more violent than the new social movement activists, shared the decentralized, structureless, and networked organizational forms of the left activists. Conflicts in Eastern Europe, central Asia, and regions in Africa suggest that anarchic mobilizations among angry, unemployed youth are likely to produce murder, banditry, ethnic conflict, genocide, and primitive, protracted warfare—not the cooperative communal societies envisioned by the new social movements (Denitch, 1994; Kaplan, 1994).

It is a little odd that this emphasis on the local and partial should crop up at the very moment that cultural, economic, and technological globalization is nearly complete, when we can talk of a total global system. When capital and populations move at dizzying speeds, when the electronic media have turned the world into a "global village," where every hamlet can be linked into computer networks, when transnational corporations and international investment make national economic policies difficult to sustain, when production can be carried out on a global assembly line using factory workers in Mexico and computer programmers in Bombay—is it disingenuous, naive, or very smart to think of localizing movements (Reich, 1992)? When the global village has been connected by optical fibers, satellite links, and transnational assembly lines, the local *is* the global.

Can movements succeed in "opting out" of this global system? Can they undermine it from within and transform it by a continuous, protracted, multiform, and localized creation of alternatives? Does resistance in all interactions and institutions add up to change nowhere (Handler, 1992)? Can movements ignore the state and realize their visions without influencing or controlling it?

Members of the Zapatista Army of National Liberation (EZLN) near Huixtan, Chiapas, Mexico, January 3, 1994. The movement's goals are land rights and improved conditions for poor and indigenous people as well as democratization of Mexican politics.

If identity politics proliferates, which collective identities will win out as the basis of action—class, nation, ethnicity, "race," gender, religion, sexual orientation? If movements do indeed undermine global markets and nation-states, in the name of what values, if any, will this insurgency be carried out? Is this vision of decentralized movements a position of the right or the left? Are such movements and insurgencies likely to produce protracted violence and little else? Being able to ask but not to answer these questions is itself a sign of the postmodern condition.

SUMMARY

This chapter looked at movements in history. It began by examining the emergence of modern society and some of its key features: industrial capitalism, the nation-state, multiple discourses, individualism and the weakening of kinship ties. These features appeared under different conditions in different regions; a periphery and semiperiphery experienced them as externally imposed rather than as indigenous developments, so there was more opposition to them than in the core regions. Movements took a stand on the "modern"—seeking to expand and perfect it, to undo it in some way, or to go beyond it. This orientation to history, to time, is an important element of movement ideologies.

Some theorists believe that a postmodern form of society has emerged in recent decades. It is characterized by global markets and cultures, by the decline of the Fordist model of economic development and a shrinkage of the industrial working class in the core regions, and by a questioning of modern and western culture. The new forms of society may be accompanied by identity politics and new types of social movements. Class is not the major basis of identity and action for participants in these movements; religion, ethnicity and "race," gender, sexual orientation, nation, and issues (like peace and the environment) form the basis for collective identity and action. The new organizational forms seem to be more decentralized and network-based and less oriented toward influencing or controlling the state than were movements in the modern period.

KEY TERMS AND CONCEPTS

modern societies
industrial capitalism
liberal state
expansion of civil society
compartmentalization of religious
    discourse
individualism
industrial revolution
political revolutions: the American
    and French Revolutions

commodity
scientific inquiry
the Enlightenment
nuclear family
ideology of domesticity
core, periphery, and semiperiphery
colonialism

postmodern societies
the global market economy;
    globalization of markets

the decline of the Fordist
  accumulation model
identity politics
revitalizing "premodern" traditions
new social movements

decentralized cultural resistance
agents of history
conservative organicism
fragmented movement structure

PART TWO

The Movements

Edmund Burke (1729–1797): Writer, member of the House of Commons, and pioneer of modern conservative thought.

CHAPTER 6

Conservative Movements and Ideologies

Fragmentation and Recombination

It is one of the excellencies of a method in which time is amongst the assistants, that its operation is slow, and in some cases almost imperceptible. If circumspection and caution are a part of wisdom, when we work only upon inanimate matter, surely they become a part of duty too, when the subject of our demolition and construction is not brick and timber, but sentient beings, by the sudden alteration of whose state, condition and habits, multitudes may be rendered miserable.
—Edmund Burke, *Reflections on the Revolution in France,* Doubleday/Anchor,
Garden City, NY, 1961, p. 184.

Picture yourself as a French aristocrat during the French Revolution: Your land has been taken away from you by the very peasants who had once seemed so respectful. Your friends have been imprisoned, dragged through the streets by the mob, and guillotined. Even people who supported the Revolution and never plotted against it have been executed. When you close your eyes at night, you can picture the blood spurting from their severed necks. You have been driven from your beloved France and live in an unhappy exile. The Parisian mob has wrecked your town house and stolen your furniture and your treasures. The churches in which you worshiped, where you were baptized and married, have been looted and desecrated. Has any of this murder and destruction improved anyone's life? No! To you it seems only like wanton cruelty. A world that had order, meaning, and beauty was wrecked; the new society is treacherous, insecure, and valueless. It is still a society of rich and poor, powerful and powerless. But the new rulers seem to have no traditions to restrain them; neither custom nor religion limit their actions.

This is the frame of mind that you have to share in order to understand the ideology of the **conservative reaction,** as social scientists and historians term the opposition to the Revolution. While it is no longer directly part of the ideology of movements of our own times, it has had a powerful impact on social thought. Many of its ideas continue to influence contemporary conservatives, the right in a broad sense of the term, and religious movements. As an ideology, it was born at the same moment as liberalism; therefore, it is a good starting place for our discussion of movements.

CONSERVATIVE IDEOLOGY

Origins

Before the French Revolution and the industrial revolution, the values and discourse of the landed aristocracy were hegemonic. They formed the ideology of the ruling classes throughout Europe, the landed interests and the nobility.

Like any hegemonic ideology, these values did not have to be constantly discussed and elaborated; they were "lived," embodied in the routines and practices of everyday life. Insofar as they were made explicit, these values were propagated primarily by religious institutions; especially in Catholic countries, the church was established as the religion that had the support of the state. Life was difficult for people who had other faiths (like Jews or Protestants) or who were not believers. In the political system, the absolute monarchy represented the interests of the nobility, although it began to be increasingly influenced by the class of merchants, manufacturers, professionals, and intellectuals—the bourgeoisie. Rich and poor were highly visible; most people were poor. The majority of the poor lived on the land and worked as peasants and tenant farmers on large estates and a smaller number lived in cities, working as artisans and laborers.

When industrialization and the French Revolution ripped this social order apart, conservatives came forward to call for a return to the status quo ante, the state of affairs that had existed *before* the upheaval. They tried to reconstruct the legitimacy of the prerevolutionary ways of doing things by pointing to the social and human values of the world that had been lost. The French Revolution, after all, had brought with it war and the Reign of Terror, the execution of thousands of people who were neither nobles nor traitors to the Revolution. The industrial revolution brought with it the unemployment and pauperization of handicraft workers, terrible conditions in factories and mines, a pace of work far more frenzied than that of farm labor and cottage industry, 12- to 14-hour workdays, alcoholism and epidemics in the new industrial cities, child labor at an intensity heretofore unknown, and a general brutalization of people's lives. The new "ideal of domesticity" functioned for the upper and middle classes, but for the poor woman there was only factory labor or the orphanage for her babies. This grim view was how the new social order looked to conservatives. Most of all, conservatives were troubled by what seemed to be a society that had turned its back on tradition, custom, and religion.

Fundamentals of Conservative Social Thought   The lessons the conservatives drew from the industrial and political revolutions were warnings (Zeitlin, 1994:55–67):

> *Stability and order in social institutions, not individual rights, are the basis of a good society.* The individual needs **authority, tradition, community,** and **hierarchy** to make sense out of life. Human beings exist only as members of a society; the "individual" is a fiction, because language, tradition, values, and family always shape each person and precede his or her existence. Therefore, society cannot be based on an ideology of individualism.

A good society is based on stable hierarchies and reciprocal rights and duties, not individualistic competition. Since there will always be differences in wealth and power, it is best if these are regulated and limited within traditional frameworks of reciprocal rights and duties, especially through religious institutions. The alternative to traditional hierarchies is, unfortunately, not freedom, but only new, crueler, and more rapacious inequalities.

Society and social institutions cannot be changed rapidly. Most long-standing institutions have **functions** that can be disrupted only at great cost to human beings and society. Loyalty to existing institutions is almost always preferable to change. Even well-intentioned changes usually turn out to have unintended and unanticipated costs. All institutions are interrelated, and apparently progressive reforms of one institution may have terrible unintended consequences for others; for instance, the factory system increased the availability of consumer goods but at the cost of destroying the health of the workers, the livelihood of those left unemployed, and the integrity of the family.

Order *and* **stability** *are necessary for the survival of human society; they cannot be imposed by the state, however, but must be sustained by all the institutions of society—especially the family and religion.* To the conservatives, the French Revolution had eroded these institutions of the social order. In place of the traditional limits placed on individual action by these institutions, the revolutionaries had made the state the limiting and coercing force in society. Thus, the Revolution had not really freed individuals at all—it had just substituted the power of the state for the traditional web of obligations, duties, and rights that once permeated society. After the Revolution, there were no longer effective intermediary institutions between the all-powerful state and the isolated individual.

Property *is a source of order and stability.* Conservatives whose social origins were in the landed gentry and nobility or among mercantile commercial interests saw private property as a major element of social order. Property represented the continuity of family interests, a commitment to social order, and protection against sudden changes, especially those initiated by the state. Conservatives of the time did not equate property with open competition and the free market, however. On the contrary, property was associated with family inheritance of land and with the protected interests of the mercantile trading companies (Sibley, 1970:510).

As the French Revolution challenged the existing social order and the industrial revolution undermined it, the ideologues of prerevolutionary landed classes began to articulate a coherent ideology in defense of that order, with several major themes: order, authority, hierarchy, and opposition to free thought; respect for traditions, especially religious traditions and traditional forms of the family; the importance of property as a source of stability; the importance of community and shared values, in contrast and opposition to free-market capitalist themes of individualism, economic self-interest, and contractual relations.

Note that, as an ideology of the **ancien régime** and its landed classes, these themes form a logical and coherent "package" of values and ideals.

Edmund Burke and Organic Change   Many conservatives came from the ranks of the displaced nobility, especially in France. Of course, they would have preferred a return to the status quo ante, the condition of society before the Revolution. But, increasingly, conservatives saw that such a return was unlikely. Instead, they focused their attention on slowing down change and preserving or reconstituting the essential features of the old social order. To return to the ancien régime (the old regime) or the "world we have lost" was not possible for every detail of that way of life; but what could be kept was a slow pace of change and respect for tradition. Society, of course, did change, but it was best if that change was organic—a slow, natural process rather than the result of a sudden imposition of abstractly conceived plans. Conservatives believe that the accumulation of many small, slow, unplanned changes is a more natural process than rapid, totalizing, and purposive change guided by theories. The outcome of an **organic process** preserves the best institutions of the past and ensures that all institutions continue to function together.

The most eloquent spokesperson for this updated conservatism was Edmund Burke, an Irish social theorist and politician. Burke had favored the Revolution in the American colonies, but he was appalled by the French Revolution a few years later. In his *Reflections on the Revolution in France,* Burke advanced his thesis that positive change can only come about gradually, in a piecemeal fashion, incrementally, and organically—without sudden, totalizing, revolutionary, top-down blueprints. As long as change "moves along" in this slow, evolutionary way it can incorporate all the positive features of the past. Sudden change, imposed by intellectuals with a total vision of a better society, is likely to fail and lead to disruption, misery, and loss. Abstract intellectual plans are especially likely to be imposed through the state and, hence, conservatives should be suspicious of such state involvement in a society (Burke, 1961).

Fragmentation and Recombination

Ideological themes that merged coherently and logically became separated and fragmented when their support base lost political and economic power in most regions of the world. As the landed and mercantile groups that had expressed this ideology declined in political and economic power, ideologues of other social groups picked themes out of the original unity of conservative thought and adapted them to express their own world views. In this way, the original unity and coherence of conservative thought fragmented and was "recombined" with the ideologies of new, modern movements. Sometimes the fragments contradicted each other. Conservative thought continued to have a powerful influence on ideologies, even in these fragmented, recombined, and sometimes contradictory forms.

The Changing Support Base   In the years after the French Revolution, the support base for conservative ideology altered dramatically. The original support base for the conservative reaction had been the landed aristocracy and the **landed gentry.** Until the industrial revolution, they had formed the most powerful social class in many regions of the globe. They controlled the key re-source—land—in western, eastern, and southern Europe, Russia, Latin Amer-ica, China, and Japan. The land of the gentry (and other kinds of **landed elites**) was worked by peasants or by unfree labor like serfs, slaves, and peons.

As political forces at the beginning of the nineteenth century in Europe and Latin America, the landed elites stood for the continued privileges of the landed nobility or gentry and for an established religion (especially the Catholic Church in southern Europe and Latin America). They wanted to make or keep society as much as possible as it had been before the Enlightenment, the French and American Revolutions, and the industrial revolution. They were generally hostile to industrialization, the growing economic power of manufacturers, the rising demands of factory workers and the middle class, and institutions like freedom of speech and universal suffrage. They used the state to suppress lib-eral movements that represented freedom of conscience, the interests of the middle classes and their allies in the working class, and the end of the power of landed interests. A mercantile commercial class was allied with landed inter-ests in many parts of the world up to the end of the eighteenth century, espe-cially in western Europe and the colonies in North America. This class derived its wealth from monopolistic trading companies that were usually chartered by the monarchy or the state (in France, England, the Netherlands, and so on). The companies did not engage in a free-market competition with each other, but had clearly defined and protected territories and products (for example, fur trading) (Wolf, 1982).

As industrialization grew, land ceased being the major source of wealth and the landed classes began to lose their economic power. Mercantile capitalism gave way to a more competitive and less regulated laissez-faire capitalism. In-dustrial production, rather than commerce in raw materials and handicrafts, formed the basis for the new economy.

The French Revolution was a decisive turning point in the loss of political power of the landed classes. The economic power of traditional landowners and mercantile interests was eroded by the industrial revolution and the rise of free-market capitalism. Much of the first part of the nineteenth century saw the con-frontation of conservative landed classes (sometimes allied with **mercantile commercial interests**) with a wide range of insurgent forces that formed a bloc of opposition to the conservatives.

This insurgent bloc included manufacturers, commercial and professional interests in a growing middle class, and their allies among an increasingly restive population of urban and rural poor people. For example, in the United States, the Jeffersonian and Jacksonian revolutions (the sweeping electoral vic-tories of these candidates and the subsequent major shifts in policy) marked the defeat of the mercantile interests in the Federalist Party at the hands of a bloc of commercial farmers, rising entrepreneurs and speculators, and urban working classes (Schlesinger, 1988).

By the middle of the nineteenth century, these insurgent forces had gained state power in many places and pushed the landed interests out of power or into a secondary position in which they controlled only one region or one sector of the economy. In the United States, for example, the Union, representing north-ern industrialists and free labor, decisively defeated the southern slave-owning planter class (Moore, 1965; Genovese, 1969). In Mexico, in the presidency of Benito Juarez, *La Reforma* emancipated Indian communities and expropriated church lands, two measures opposed by the landed oligarchy (Wolf, 1969). In Russia, the serfs were emancipated as first step toward modernizing the na-tion. The unification of Italy marked the defeat of the papacy and conservative forces (Clark, 1984; Mack Smith, 1969). In Japan, the Meiji restoration was an elite revolution in which modernizing forces interested in industrialization pushed aside feudal lords (Trimberger, 1978; Moore, 1965).

Conservatives could continue to exercise power in all these regions only if they were prepared to be allies of the new industrial capitalist classes and/or themselves shifted to a more modern economic outlook as large-scale commer-cial farmers or agro-exporters. For example, in Germany, the Junkers—the landed aristocracy in the eastern parts of Germany—were able to remain a pow-erful force in German society (Abraham, 1986). In Mexico, the old landed inter-ests became part of a new agro-export class that produced crops like sugar and henequen fiber for the world market. In the United States, the southern cotton growers could no longer contend with Yankee manufacturers as equals, but they still held regional power.

The weakening of the landed interests and virtual disappearance of mer-cantilism meant that the *original forms of conservatism lost their social base.* By the middle of the nineteenth century, the conservatives had lost political power throughout western Europe and in much of Latin America. They became an op-position force that challenged the new liberal states and, generally, had to form alliances with other movements and groups in order to make this challenge pos-sible. A return to a preindustrial status quo ante became increasingly unlikely.

By the twentieth century, conservativism faced the fragmentation of its originally coherent ideology. If conservatism meant conserving or preserving institutions, *which institutions* were to be preserved? If it meant keeping all that was valuable from the past, *which historical moment of the past* was the defining one?

Different answers to these two questions defined differences in conserva-tive ideology. Different forms of conservative movements were supported by a range of new social groups. Conservative ideology blended with other ideolo-gies that addressed the new realities of industrial capitalism. Elements of the original coherent core of conservative thought combined with other ideologies to form powerful new challenges to many features of modern society. The orig-inal core remained a powerful but fragmented memory; different elements con-tinued to exist within the ideologies of other social movements and institution-alized sectors of society.

Reactionary Conservatives   Conservative thought was most nearly kept in its initial, complete form by key social groups in many societies throughout Eu-rope and Latin America—especially the military and the upper levels of the hi-erarchy of the Catholic Church. The elements of original conservative thought that these groups preserved was the emphasis on **hierarchy, authority,** and **tradition.** They were strongly opposed to secularism, individualism, and increased social equality, as well as any form of revolution. They protected property rights, but maintained an ambivalent attitude toward the free market (Mayer, 1971).

In many countries, the upper ranks of the officer corps of the armed forces retained a reactionary type of conservative and hierarchical worldview. Frequently, military officers were drawn from the ranks of the old landed elites; even in the United States, well into the twentieth century, military officers were often young men whose social origins were in the plantation-owning classes of the south. Officers who did not share these social origins also came to hold ideologies that stressed hierarchy, order, authority, and tradition.

These conservative forces within the military establishments of many nations generally did not form social movements on their own. However, they did enter into alliances with movements of the **radical right** (fascism, for example), especially in a number of European countries during the period between the First and Second World Wars. Nationalist and fascist movements sometimes included supporters of the old forms of reactionary conservatism, although, in these movements, traditional conservatives had a difficult relationship with more radical and populist currents in the movement. For example, parts of the German officer corps were originally sympathetic to programs of the Nazis, but by 1939 found that they were replaced in leading positions by new officers who were closer to Hitler and the Nazi Party. By the later years of the war, a distinct conservative position was no longer identifiable or tenable in the armed forces of the Nazi state (Müller, 1987:35–41).

Conservatives in the military took action on their own, leading counterrevolutionary military coups, when they believed that the nation was under threat from socialists, communists, anarchists, and other left-wing forces. Some notable instances of such military counterrevolutions were General Francisco Franco's attack on and defeat of the Spanish republic in the late 1930s, the military coup against the left-reformist government of Jacobo Arbenz in Guatemala in 1954, and the coup led by General Augusto Pinochet against the elected socialist government of Chile in 1973. While these coups were not social movements in the usual sense of the term, they did have some social support (usually in the upper and middle classes who were opposed to the left). In any case, the conservative military became key players in the political arena.

Parts of the hierarchy of the Catholic Church offered an institutional basis for conservative ideologies. As in the case of the military, the narrow class interests of the upper parts of the hierarchy, who were recruited from landed families, were often universalized within the church into a conservative viewpoint that was accepted even by those who came from more humble origins. The church opposed the individualism and secularization that liberal states and movements promoted. As we will see in later chapters, the church was not unified in this reactionary conservatism (Crahan, 1988). By the early part of the twentieth century, it began to search for new allies, beyond the landed oligarchy, and this shift became more marked after World War II and in the 1960s.

The Radical Right   Conservative ideologues increasingly detached themselves from the old landed interests like the European aristocracy, the landed oligarchy in southern Europe and Latin America, and southern plantation owners in the United States. The landed elite support base seemed to have little future in a world that was industrializing. Conservative ideas could best survive in revitalized and recombined forms, forms that made compromises with modernity. One major recombined fragment entered the ideologies of radical right-wing movements like fascism, Nazism, and ultranationalism. This fragment preserved the themes of **order, hierarchy,** authority, and the opposition to free thought and recombined them with an emphasis on **the strong state.**

Some conservative ideologues began to take a leading part in right-wing movements like fascism. These movements tended to have a much more middle-class base than the original forms of conservatism. Small property owners and white-collar workers were involved in such movements, which became particularly powerful in Europe between the First and Second World Wars, culminating in the rise to state power of the Italian Fascists and the Nazis in Germany (Carsten, 1967; Gerth, 1940; Mayer, 1971; Sohn-Rethel, 1987).

The right-wing ideologies retained some key ideas of opposition to modernity, but they combined these antimodern ideas with new, decidedly modern themes. The ideologues of the radical right agreed with the reactionary conservative opposition to individual freedom. Like the reactionary conservatives, the radical right preferred hierarchical relationships, but they shifted the location of these relationships from traditional institutions like religion, the patriarchal family, and peasant-landowner relationships to new grounds—the party and the state. They supported a strong state, far stronger and more interventionist than the preindustrial state. They embraced modern technology. When in power, as in Italy and Germany in the 1930s, the radical right (Fascists and Nazis) intervened extensively in the economy; they continued the original conservative opposition to the unregulated market. In the United States, however, movements that were termed radical right or right-wing extremists have been less consistently statist (Bell, 1964; Lipset and Raab, 1978).

The radical right are not supporters of traditional established religious institutions, although they were prepared to make alliances with them, like the Lateran pact between the Italian Fascists and the Catholic Church (Clark, 1984).

Nationalism and Anticommunism   The radical right and large sectors of more moderate conservatives preserve two other key features of original conservative thought: patriotism and nationalism, and an anticosmopolitan outlook. In original conservative thought, attachment to a nation was one of the social anchors that kept a society stable. To many conservatives, "nation" appeared to be a primordial source of loyalty, identity, and order, while too much concern with "humanity" seemed whimsical and unrealistic. The radical right and moderate conservatives agreed (Sibley, 1970). Conservatism was increasingly combined with nationalist ideology.

Both the radical right and moderate conservatives continue to support property rights and are strongly opposed to communism, socialism, and any left-wing movement that challenges these rights. As moderate conservatives made their peace with modern capitalism and liberal-democratic political systems, they saw themselves increasingly as allies of liberals against communism and socialism.

Religious Fundamentalism   **Conservatism** lives on in the ideologies of **religious fundamentalism** and integralism, especially in Christian and Islamic societies (Capps, 1990). In this new form of conservatism, the elements that are retained are the emphasis on *traditional religion and the traditional family as the building blocks of society*. The meaning of the term *traditional* is, however, complicated and by no means a simple reference to age-old practices (Cohen, 1990).

In the United States, where Christian fundamentalism is strong, traditional family values are defined more in terms of nineteenth-century patterns than older preindustrial traditions. Traditional religion is defined by its interpretation of the Bible that emerged in the late nineteenth century as a reaction to new historical and antiliteralist explanations. In these respects, Christian fundamentalist conservatism does not preserve a preindustrial past, but is itself a modern movement (Wills, 1990).

In both Christian and Islamic conservatism, some themes of hostility to individualism and secularism are preserved. These traditional themes are combined with a new militancy, a spirit of conversion, and a high level of political activism. However, the social base of these fundamentalist movements is not a landed elite, but the lower middle classes and parts of the urban working and lower classes. This combination of conservatism, revitalized religious traditionalism, and political activism will be explored in more detail in Chapter 9, "Movements of Faith" (Wilcox, 1992; Hadden, 1993).

Free-Market Ideology   A rather different "fragment" of the original conservative package was adopted by ideologues who favor the market as the guiding institution of society. This theme retains some key elements of original conservative thought—respect for property as a social institution, acceptance of social and economic inequality as natural and inevitable, and the Burkean distrust of state-initiated efforts to change society (Gilder, 1981). These elements are combined with support for a free-market economy, decidedly not part of the original ideology. The "moment of the past" that free-market conservatives selected to preserve is not the long-ago past of the feudal nobility or of mercantilism, but the relatively recent past when governments intervened less in the economy—basically the period before Roosevelt's New Deal or before the European welfare states were established after the Second World War.

The social support base of free-market conservatism are property owners who believe that a more **laissez-faire** economy would be in their interest and would lead to faster economic growth. They typically include many small business owners as well as some large enterprises. They oppose a large state sector, high levels of taxation, and government regulation (Lo, 1990).

At most, free-market conservatism puts secondary emphasis on segments of the original conservative package like hierarchy or religious traditionalism, and sometimes rejects them altogether. Stability is a major theme of conservative thought, but it does not combine well with the key characteristics of market societies: rapid change, innovation, individualism, and mobility. Free-market conservatives are not entirely comfortable with allies who are religious fundamentalists or who favor a strong state. The difficulties in these alliances can be seen within the Republican Party in the United States, where the Reagan revolution encompassed both right-wing Christian fundamentalists and free-market forces who did not share the social agenda of the Christian right. The Conservative Party in Britain, the party of Margaret Thatcher in the 1980s, also tilted more toward a free-market conservatism, with themes like order, hierarchy, and authority being secondary and somewhat muted (Edgar, 1986).

In many respects, free-market conservatives are actually very close to classical liberals or "negative liberals" and we will encounter them again in more detail in Chapter 7, "The Expansion of Civil Society: The Varieties of Liberalism" (Friedman and Friedman, 1980; Goldwater, 1960; von Hayek, 1944).

Conservative Social Thought and the Preservation of Community   Another fragment of conservative ideology survives within ideologies that are diametrically opposed to free-market constructs. It emphasizes *community*, with its associated themes of opposition to the market and to individualism. These ideologies appear in some movements on the left, for example, in the critique of capitalism voiced by liberation theology. These movements seek to halt or slow down what they see as the corrosive effects of the market on communities and on social cohesion.

For example, communities of Maya Indians in Guatemala and Mexico or peasants in the Brazilian northeast are under extreme stress from the expansion of agro-export industries like cattle ranching or sugar cane, the loss of traditional lands for subsistence crops, and the destruction of the web of social ties. In these cases, the basis of a **communitarian conservatism** is not the landed rich but the landed poor, seeking to preserve a way of life and, at least, a "limited good" against the impact of global markets (Scheper-Hughes, 1992).

Some left-wing movements and socialist revolutions have actually begun as masses of people mobilize to preserve rights or a way of life against the rapid changes brought about by capitalism. For example, in the Mexican revolution and the Vietnamese revolution, the demands of peasants were first voiced as a desire to preserve rights to land that were being undermined by the expansion of plantations producing for the export market (Wolf, 1969; Womack, 1971). The Zapatista insurgency currently under way in Chiapas, Mexico, also uses a conservative discourse of the *preservation* of Indian communities' land rights against encroachment by cattle ranchers and agro-business.

In Summary   Original forms of conservative ideology lost their social base in the landed and mercantile classes throughout Europe and Latin America (and in somewhat different forms in Asia as well). Ideologues of other movements picked up strands from conservative thought and wove them into their own ideologies. Conservative ideology continues to influence movements, but in a less coherent and unified way.

Some of the recombined forms are in many ways contradictory to each other. For example, the strand that emphasized property rights has become intertwined with free-market or laissez-faire ideology that justifies rapid, market-oriented social change; it is no longer easily consistent with the strands of conservatism that have become intertwined with fascism and the radical right or with the defense of tradition.

THE NEW RIGHT

Consolidating Free-Market and Cultural Conservatism

The term **New Right** was used as early as the 1950s, and then more vigorously in the 1970s and 1980s, to refer to a new form of conservative movement that appeared most clearly in the United States and Britain and combined **free-market ideology and neotraditional culture** (Levitas, 1986).

Ideology   New Right ideology combines a free-market position with support for neotraditional family, gender, and religious institutions—positions that could be termed *cultural conservatism*. Neotraditional means a modified version of nineteenth-century European and Anglo-American institutions. What the right means by traditional family values is a strong nuclear family, the authority of parents over children, and breadwinner-father/homemaker-mother gender roles (David, 1986)—not what sociologists and anthropologists mean by traditional—some kind of premodern family structure with extended family households. The cultural conservative side of New Right ideology also includes the preservation or reawakening of values like the work ethic, community, and self-reliance rather than reliance on government (Levitas, 1986).

Indeed, there is some consistency in the New Right's selection of time period and social milieu that symbolizes a more harmonious state of affairs than the present: the European middle classes in the nineteenth century (in the United States and Europe). This period was probably characterized by less government intervention in the economy than in the later part of the twentieth century and by more authority and hierarchy within middle-class households, although historians are not in agreement on these conclusions (Coontz, 1988; Lasch, 1979). New Right ideologues recognize that many people were left out of this model of a good society, but they imply that market forces would have gradually expanded prosperity, and that union movements, socialist movements, and the expansion of the welfare state were not necessary conditions for an improved standard of living in North America and Europe.

In the United States, the New Right also hearkens back to the 1950s, seen as a period when nuclear families were stronger, the work ethic was more widely believed in, and crime and social disintegration were less apparent. Social historians have disputed some of these images, but the position of the New Right has effectively aligned with many Americans' memories of the 1950s as a period of prosperity, low crime rates, more social order, and less turmoil (Coontz, 1993). Some New Right analyses blame government efforts to redistribute income, provide more subsidized and public sector services, and mobilize poor communities as the cause of current problems like the welfare system; high crime rates; drug abuse; and violence in schools, homes, and on the street. For example, former Vice President Quayle blamed the Great Society government programs implemented during the Lyndon Johnson presidency for having set in motion a disruption of inner-city communities; he suggested it was this government involvement in society, rather than Reagan-era economic restructuring, that was responsible for unemployment, crime, and social disorganization in cities like Los Angeles.

The New Right also acted as a countermovement to some of the new social movements. It opposed policies of affirmative action for ethnic minorities and the goals of feminism and gay and lesbian movements, especially when these movements called for policies that legitimated a wider range of family patterns and lifestyles, like family leave for working mothers, adoptions by same-sex couples, or domestic partner benefits. It questioned the value of environmental regulation.

The New Right's position should be distinguished from a radical right or fascist ideology, although organizations like the John Birch Society may have included individuals inclined in either direction (Bell, 1964; Lipset and Raab, 1978). During the last decade in Europe, there has been a degree of overlap between racist and antiimmigrant currents and some culturally conservative wings of the New Right that emphasize the European, white, and/or Christian nature of the national culture and the need to protect it from "alien influences"; for example, Muslims, Jews, Asians, Africans, and West Indians (Seidel, 1986).

The New Right is not identical to conservative religious forces, although there is also some overlap here, and it successfully mobilized support among some Christian fundamentalists (Capps, 1990; Wilcox, 1992).

Emergence of Organizations   A number of organizations formed to disseminate the ideological themes of free markets and cultural conservatism in order to influence the major parties and shape government economic and social policy. One forerunner of the New Right was Young Americans for Freedom, a largely campus-based organization whose emphasis was the free-market ideology and an antileft position, rather than cultural conservatism. Goldwater's 1964 presidential campaign was a period of movement formation, although Goldwater himself consistently kept his distance from the cultural conservatives and the social issues side of the movement.

In the 1960s, a number of conservative activists (among them Paul Weyrich, Adolph Coors, and Richard Viguerie) formed the Committee for the Survival of a Free Congress and began to bring together a broad spectrum of conservative groups into an electoral alliance (Davis, 1981:38). Viguerie contributed his skills at direct-mail techniques of mobilizing supporters for fund raising and voting.

The important characteristic of the New Right was that its direct-mail and networking methods allowed it to assemble groups that had originally defined themselves as single-issue movements and did not always have compatible positions or a coherently conservative vision. Throughout the 1970s, a relatively small number of activists who did have this vision combined taxpayer leagues, antibusing groups like BUSSTOP in Los Angeles, the Right to Life antiabortion movement, groups committed to neotraditional family and gender values like the Eagle Forum which opposed the ERA, politicized Christian fundamentalist groups, and some National Rifle Association members (Davis, 1981:38).

In some respects, this New Right coalition was much like the vanguard party/front structure that the Communist movement had used earlier in the century; an ideologically coherent core group mobilized a large and ideologically heterogeneous spectrum of support groups and single-issue constituencies. The decisive new ingredient, however, was the effective use of electronic technologies to pinpoint, reach, and connect potential supporters. The ability to focus financial support and voting strength gave the movement a role in the Republican Party and in Reagan's election in 1980.

The New Right was similar to the old left in its use of an organizational model much like the vanguard party/front structure to consolidate and focus diverse, narrow, and weakly conceptualized interests into a more ideologically coherent movement. There are also similarities in social bases, mobilization strategies, and organizational forms between the New Right and the new social movements discussed in Chapters 3 and 5.

Structural Changes   The first of these similarities is that both can be interpreted as responses to the same structural strain, the **decline of the Fordist accumulation model**. The end of the long economic boom around 1970 and growing economic problems constituted a strain; stagflation in the 1970s—a mixture of high inflation rates and rising unemployment—made many people anxious about the economy, the ability of government to restore high growth and prosperity, and the general quality of life.

The end of the Fordist model also meant an end to the cooperation (or truce) among labor, business, and government. In the 1950s, Charlie Wilson (head of General Motors and later secretary of defense) could say, "What is good for GM is good for the U.S."; some listeners were offended, but many agreed—growth in consumer durables industries and labor-management cooperation spelled prosperity for the nation. By the 1970s, this cooperation was breaking down, but not always in predictable ways, like more strikes. Rather, a fragmentation seemed to take place within the ranks of both labor and business. Competition within classes as well as increased tension between classes became visible (Edsall, 1984). For example, business interests began to split increasingly along regional and sectoral lines—sunbelt against snowbelt (or rustbelt), the service sector against manufacturing firms, defense contractors against unprotected sectors (Davis, 1981:40).

At the same time, the industrial working class declined both as a percentage of the labor force and in political strength. The working class as a whole—in the sense of wage earners—did not disappear, but it fragmented along lines of sectors, gender, generational experiences, region, ethnicity, and even lifestyles. "When relative prosperity or impoverishment may hang on the timing of a house purchase or the fact of working in (say) aerospace rather than the auto industry or having been born in 1940 rather than in 1950, the sense of commonality of experience and needs disintegrates" (Currie, Dunn, and Fogarty, quoted in Davis, 1981:45).

The fragmentation of the class basis of political action and the blurring of class identity were not, however, symmetrical processes that affected all classes equally and in similar ways. On the contrary, the waning of organized labor as a result of this fragmentation and blurring left a large sector of the U.S. population (and the British one) without an organizational force for "pressing the interests of the working and lower-middle classes. . . . There exists in no Western democracy any other major organization cutting across racial and ethnic lines that can defend progressive distributional policies of both taxation and spending" (Edsall, 1984:142).

These patterns of fragmentation produced new social movements, left and right, that no longer had clear-cut class bases, contributing to movement volatility and instability. Organizers and activists were forced to find ways of mobilizing support without forming large stable face-to-face organizations. Conservatives discovered new opportunities to mobilize blue-collar constituencies along social issue lines like opposition to busing to achieve integration, opposition to abortion, and support for school prayer; these social issues were disconnected from economic interest issues (Phillips, 1970).

The Changing Political Opportunity Structure   The structural strains underlying the New Right and New Left movements were filtered *through changes in the political system and the media.* The political structure itself was changing, shrinking the opportunities for some kinds of movements but expanding them for other types. In the United States, the New Deal coalition was disintegrating. The Roosevelt administration, in the 1930s, had brought together a support base consisting of organized labor, white southern interests, African Americans, the European-ethnic working class in northern cities, and strata of educated people and business interests with a commitment to an expanded role for government ("liberals" as the term is used in the United States). This coalition began to fall apart after the 1960s for a variety of reasons. Some white southerners blamed the Democrats for the Civil Rights Movement's successes. The affluence of the 1950s and 1960s enabled the white working class to suburbanize and increasingly form collective identities as taxpayers and Republicans (Ladd and Wilson, 1983; Lo, 1990; Whyte, 1956). Organized labor lost some of its strength in a changing economy (Edsall, 1984; Geoghegan, 1991; Harrison and Bluestone, 1988).

A major result of these political shifts was a disillusionment with the role of government, a central tenet of the New Deal. Some of this disenchantment with government was expressed by the left, in the New Left and the new social movements. Probably, however, the net winners in this shift in sentiment were the new conservatives. In their view, government had been able to solve some problems, but only by creating new ones—an increasing tax burden on home owners, intrusive actions in desegregation by school busing and affirmative action policies, and transfer payments to people who were no longer defined as workers in temporary distress but as "welfare dependents" (Murray, 1984; Rieder, 1985). In Britain, similar shifts in opinion reflected strains in the welfare state and fueled movements to alter the role of government. In the United States, the war in Vietnam also contributed to anger at the federal government on both the left and right.

The *media* are an additional factor in the political opportunity structure that accelerated the formation of both the new social movements on the left and the

New Right. The shift from newspapers to television as the major medium of news coverage may have contributed to a climate of alienation, disenchantment with government and other institutions, and a floating resentment toward elites (Robinson, 1981). The public formed opinions as a result of direct exposure to television, replacing older patterns of opinion formation that had been mediated through social relationships and organizational memberships (especially unions). The net result was a high degree of volatility, quick shifts from one issue to another, a detachment of opinions on issues from stabler economic bases of identity (like class and occupation), and shift in trust from institutions to individuals (including media stars, news anchors, and politicians who used the media effectively). [David Riesman (1961), a sociologist, had already predicted some of these patterns in his analysis of the emergence of the "other-directed" character structure.] These shifts in the formation of mass opinion contributed to new social movement patterns of instability, support-base fragmentation, and volatility; probably the New Right benefited more than the New Left movements from these media changes.

New Forms of Organization   Both sets of movements were similar in that they experimented with *new patterns of organization and mobilization*. They moved away from the goal of bringing large numbers of supporters into stable organizations with well-defined boundaries. [The John Birch Society on the right and Students for a Democratic Society (SDS) on the left might almost be considered the last effort to build more traditional movement organizations with defined boundaries and members.] Instead, they shifted to networking local and/or single-issue movements with overlapping goals in order to aggregate resources and votes for local and national goals. The right was, on the whole, considerably more skillful and purposive at this sort of aggregation. No doubt, the greater success of the right was based on its access to support from certain sectors of the business community, generally single-family-owned, labor-intensive, antiunion, and sunbelt enterprises (and specifically not defense contractors and high-tech firms) (Davis, 1981:40). It may have been because the right was less intent on ideological coherence or purity among its supporters, more accepting of the fact that most individuals in mass publics rarely have a coherent ideology (Converse, 1964).

Finally, the new social movements and the New Right were also connected as movements and countermovements. The New Right was able to reach potential supporters who saw the Civil Rights Movement, the black power and black nationalist movements, feminism ("women's lib") and the pro-ERA forces, and other new social movements as causes of the disintegration of American society. In a similar, but less successful way, the Thatcher government tried to rally parts of the English public to its side against the "folk devil" of the new social movements (McRobbie, 1994).

The New Right and Government: Accomplishments and Limitations

In both the United States and Great Britain, the New Right had an influential role in the Reagan and Thatcher governments (Blumenthal, 1986; Desai, 1994).

The perspectives from Chapter 4, "Movements, Societies, and States," may help us understand the extent to which the New Right was able to accomplish its goals through electoral victories. The New Right in the Reagan and Thatcher governments faced many of the same problems that any ideological movement encounters when it is able to influence state policies. In Chapter 4, we saw that movements that come to power through a revolution face many constraints; those that come to power through electoral processes are even more limited in their capacity to change society.

Multiorganizational Field Opposition   The New Right in a position of power during the 1980s faced at least three major problems: One was the *environment of organizations and institutions that opposed or limited it or supported only its economic policies.* Among these was the civil service (or government bureaucracy) that had to implement its policies, often in a spirit of indifference or opposition. As one writer says of the British civil service, its "status, size, and salaries" could be shrunk, but it was hardly eliminated and, in most essentials, continued to operate as before (Desai, 1994). Other forces *within* the governing parties (Conservatives in Great Britain, Republicans in the United States) did not share a New Right ideology, and these moderates opposed New Right proposals and policies. The most obvious opposition came from the parties that were out of national office (Labour and Liberals in Britain, the Democrats in the United Sates) and other movements and pressure groups. In the United States, for example, the American Civil Liberties Union and a new organization, People for the American Way, opposed the policies favored by some cultural conservatives.

Even the media did not accept a totally supportive role. While they supported many of the market-oriented reforms that were taking place and the more assertive foreign policy stands (like the Falklands-Malvinas War, the Grenada invasion, the expansion of defense spending), they were less enthusiastic about cultural conservatism (Desai, 1994; Hertsgaard, 1989).

Meanwhile, the New Right received support from forces within the business community for its market-oriented economic policies. These programs could bring together the New Right with more established constituencies of the Republican Party (or the Conservatives, in the case of Britain). The New Right, a large part of the Republican mainstream, and many business owners could agree on tax cuts and reductions in government spending on social programs, while they continued to disagree on subjects like prayer in schools or abortions (Edsall, 1984). A bloc of powerful allies formed around the economic policies but did not support the social issues.

Structural Limits   A second limitation emerged from a *structural* problem: *it is easier for an administration to change economic policy than to change social policy.* This structural constraint imposed goal shrinkage on the New Right within both the Thatcher and Reagan governments; economic policies were implemented, social policies had to be limited or entirely dropped.

Governments in modern nation-states have, at their disposal, powerful levers of economic policy. These include fiscal policy (raising or lowering the levels of taxing and spending) as well as monetary policy (regulating the money supply and interest rates). In addition, governments can regulate or deregulate business, raise or lower protectionist measures like tariffs and import quotas, and privatize public sector enterprises or move private enterprises into the public domain.

Although the administration in office does not have complete control over these decisions, it has considerable room for maneuver. Both the Thatcher and Reagan administrations made some substantial changes in these areas, in large part along the lines of expanding market mechanisms and shrinking the role of government in the economy. The Thatcher government privatized many enterprises that had been in the public sector, and in the United States, the price structure of industries like trucking and the airlines was deregulated. Social service programs were cut. Taxes were cut for that sector of the population that was most involved in investment, in hopes that these **supply-side policies** would stimulate the economy more effectively than policies of government spending designed to stimulate aggregate demand. Monetary policies based on high interest rates and the strengthening of the dollar and the pound were pursued, especially in the early stages of the administrations. Inflation was curbed, but with the trade-off of higher unemployment rates. There is considerable debate among economists whether these measures were good for the economies, and it is outside the scope of this book to evaluate the long-term effects of economic policies. The point is that these policies, based on the free-market side of New Right ideology, *were put into effect to a considerable extent.* [There is some debate even on this conclusion; one of the main ideologues of supply-side policies, David Stockman, believes that these policies were not really tried at all (Stockman, 1986; Roberts, 1984).]

The cultural conservatism side of New Right ideology was not easy to implement at the federal level. As noted in Chapter 4, changing people's family life, personal behavior, gender roles, values, and religious beliefs and practices is not easy. The project would require extensive intrusion by government into what is defined as private life in most modern societies. If undertaken, it is likely to meet with resistance; for example, in the United States, from groups like the American Civil Liberties Union, feminists, and gay and lesbian organizations. This resistance was particularly strong at the national level, which has a long history of liberal activism (Davis, 1991).

In addition to organized resistance, the design and implementation of a program of reform targeted at the values and behavior of millions of individuals and households, particularly in an open and heterogeneous society like that in the United States would be difficult. In Britain, the Thatcher administration did not pursue this side of New Right ideology consistently or effectively, although restrictions were placed on minors' access to contraceptives. Insofar as neotraditional, Victorian gender roles were reinstituted at all, it was probably more through an indirect mechanism than a program of reform, as high rates of unemployment frustrated women's efforts to enter the labor force and kept them at home (David, 1986). Local councils and other decentralized decision-making bodies lost their powers to the central government, illustrating the New

Right's somewhat contradictory stand on the question of government authority and centralization (Wolfe, 1981).

In the United States, the New Right did not gain the support of the federal government for any major redirection of social behavior and cultural institutions. Little was done beyond some efforts to limit the availability of abortions, a process in which the federal courts accepted state regulation. The ERA was halted because it failed to obtain ratification in state legislatures, but it is questionable whether that made any practical difference in everyday life. In any case, the process suggested that it is easier for conservatives to exercise influence at state and local levels. Spending cuts reduced the levels of government transfer programs like Aid to Families of Dependent Children ("welfare") (Piven and Cloward, 1982). Generally, busing passed from the scene as a way of implementing racial integration; affirmative action policies in hiring and contractor set-asides were less vigorously pursued than they might have been. Yet, despite some New Right successes in legislation, budget decisions, and the courts, there is little evidence of major changes in family structure, behavior, or personal values of the population as a whole along lines advocated by cultural conservatives. For example, sexual behavior did not shift markedly into more conservative or traditional patterns (Michael et al., 1994).

The New Right and cultural conservatives are now refocusing their efforts at the local level, in more grassroots movements, to influence school curricula, school board elections, local library policy, and state abortion regulation, having recognized that the federal government is a difficult instrument to use to change social institutions. Change has to begin at the grass roots level, in locations where the public feels some affinity for New Right ideas. A successful electoral alliance at the federal level does not translate easily into changed social behavior or values.

Activities of the Christian right and cultural conservatives at the local level, especially efforts to control local committees and caucuses of the Republican Party in states such as Texas, have led to opposition from Goldwater Republicans, who remain committed to individual privacy rights as well as free markets. The grass roots activism within the Republican Party has put strains on the already tenuous connection between the two elements of conservatism.

Contradictory Effects of Policies   The third reason for the relatively limited character of changes brought about by New Right participation in the Reagan and Thatcher administrations was inherent in the recombined nature of New Right programs. The free-market policies actually were contradictory to the cultural conservatism of the movement; *the consequences of the expansion of market forces in a modern society tended to undermine the social institutions favored by cultural conservatives.* This expansion affected both values and social institutions. The market brings with it innovation, change, and the erosion of traditional loyalties and communities. It is based on and heightens individualism, economically motivated choices, and contractual relations. In a market-based society, individuals accept few values as sacred and show little respect for customary authority. The values and mentalities that go with a market economy, at least in the west, are inherently opposed to conservative concerns for authority, stable hierarchy, natural respect for one's "betters," and a static social order.

Some readers might object that these two value systems are not inherently incompatible, since Japan and other East Asian nations represent successful blends of conservative and market values. I would suggest that this combination works only with careful controls on the market, and perhaps is easier to sustain in a Confucian or Shinto/Buddhist moral order. In North America and western Europe, conservative or neotraditional values hearken back to an eighteenth- or nineteenth-century postfeudal social order, often associated with the Protestant ethic, and carry a heavy charge of individualism.

The expansion of the market in the 1980s not only amplified values of individualism and change, but also had social consequences that undermined the effort to restore neotraditional families (Harrison and Bluestone, 1988). A fast pace of economic change, geographic shifts in industries, deregulation of industries like the airlines, decreasing company loyalty on the part of both employers and employees, and less union-based job security disrupted neotraditional families and propelled women into the labor force (Moberg, 1993). Job stress and the possibility of downward mobility carried economic tensions into domestic relations (Newman, 1988). The formation of edge cities—suburban commercial and industrial developments—transformed and weakened community life in both the cities and the suburbs (Gaines, 1992, Garreau, 1992). Shifts in the location of industries eroded traditional blue-collar communities, both in Britain and in the United States.

Since the Second World War, the America of neotraditional imagery has been under cultural and economic stress: Edge cities of suburbanizing business activity and impoverished inner-city neighborhoods replaced stable urban villages (working-class ethnic enclaves) and suburban bedroom communities; shopping malls replaced mom-and-pop stores and local department stores; impersonal and tracked high schools replaced not only the little rural schoolhouse, but also the neighborhood school; and televangelism threatened "the little brown church in the vale." With the restructuring of the 1980s, even the neotraditional family, presumably the last institution to hold out against individualism and commodity relations, was transformed (Harrison and Bluestone, 1988:131). Neoconservatives sensed that the neotraditional home as "haven in a heartless world" was being blown away in the gale of creative destruction inherent in the expansion of market forces, as all its members, including women and teens, went into the labor force to maintain middle-class living standards (Lasch, 1979; Schumpeter, 1983/1942). The two sides of New Right ideology offered visions that were contradictory; an economic program to expand the market led to an accelerated erosion of neotraditional social institutions and stable communities.

This contradiction was perhaps insoluble. If the New Right's combined vision of free markets and neotraditional culture were possible, it could happen only through long-term, patient, one-on-one transformation of values and family life. Cultural conservatives had to build institutions of gender, family, media, and religious life that brought conservative values of order and authority

Margaret Thatcher: Former British prime minister and leader of the Conservative Party. Under her direction, the party combined free-market ideology and themes of cultural conservatism.

together with adaptation to the rapid change inherent in the expansion of markets. These institutions already existed among Mormons and some Protestant fundamentalists; the question was whether they could be expanded to a larger social base.

The contradictions could only be reconciled at the grass roots level (if they were indeed reconcilable), not by electoral alliances oriented at federal policy. In its original form, the New Right had experienced success at the level of national politics too quickly; it had mobilized resources and votes, but had not devoted itself sufficiently to the transformation of people and values. At least some of its component currents returned to this task; for example, Christian fundamentalists began to assemble families and communities in which neotraditional gender and family roles could exist side by side with successful adjustment to market forces, including practices like mothers working outside the home (Stacey, 1991).

SUMMARY

The original ideology of conservatism included the following themes: order, hierarchy, and authority; the value of traditional forms of religious and family institutions; property as a foundation for social stability; community; opposition to both individualism and the market; and a belief that change can and should come about slowly and organically. As the social support base of this ideology declined when the landed gentry and nobility lost economic and political power, these themes were split apart and separately recombined with the ideologies of modern movements.

Conservative ideology has influenced a current within liberalism itself, as conservative concern for property rights is combined with liberal support for the free market. Conservative themes of order, hierarchy, and authority have been adopted by the fascist, nazi and ultranationalist right. Conservatism has influenced religious fundamentalism, especially Christian fundamentalism. And, although movements like socialism and feminism explicitly reject conservative ideology, they have been forced to seriously consider many conservative criticisms of capitalism, individualism, and market institutions.

The most coherent recent effort to reconstitute a unified conservative ideology has been associated with the New Right, especially in the United States and Britain. The New Right combines support for free-market policies with neo-traditional cultural conservatism. This movement had a role in the Thatcher and Reagan administrations. It was easier to realize some of its economic than its cultural goals, given the structural constraints in the political system. In many respects, the New Right's successful expansion of market forces even undermined the efforts to revitalize neotraditional social institutions.

KEY TERMS AND CONCEPTS

the origins of conservative ideology
conservative reaction
authority, tradition, community, and
   hierarchy
order and stability
the functions of institutions
property
ancien régime
Edmund Burke
organic process

fragmentation and recombination
the social bases of conservatism
landed gentry, landed elites
mercantile commercial interests
reactionary conservatives: hierarchy,
   authority, tradition

the radical right: order, hierarchy, the
   strong state
nationalism and anticommunism
conservatism and religious
   fundamentalism
conservatives and free-market
   ideologies; laissez-faire
communitarian conservatives

the New Right
free-market ideology and
   neotraditional culture
decline of the Fordist accumulation
   model
supply-side economic policies

Revolutions against monarchies in France
and America were part of the process of
forming states based on ideals of citizenship.
Execution of Louis XVI, Paris, 1793.

CHAPTER 7

The Expansion of Civil Society

The Varieties of Liberalism

We hold these Truths to be self-evident, that all Men are created equal, that they are endowed by their Creator with certain inalienable Rights, that among these are Life, Liberty and the Pursuit of Happiness—That to secure these Rights, Governments are instituted among Men, deriving their just Powers from the Consent of the Governed, that whenever any Form of Government becomes destructive of these Ends, it is the Right of the People to alter or abolish it, and to institute new Government, laying its Foundations on such Principles and organizing its Powers in such Form, as to them shall seem most likely to effect their Safety and Happiness.
    —Thomas Jefferson, Declaration of Independence, 1776.

You're a French businessman in the eighteenth century, enraged by the special privileges of the nobility and the arbitrary powers of the king. You're an African American in Mississippi in 1950: You are barred from voting, you have to use the "colored" drinking fountain and washroom in the local bus station, and your children have to attend underfunded segregated schools. You are a woman in Argentina in the early 1980s, whose son is among the disappeared by action of the military regime; you fear that he has been tortured and murdered—and so, you and other mothers stand silently in front of the presidential palace every day to draw the attention of the world to what has happened. You are a Chinese student in 1989, demonstrating in Tiananmen Square, in the heart of Beijing, for a free press and the right to form political associations. . . . Does a single ideology encompass all these feelings? Do the movements that these individuals are forming sum up to a single movement? This chapter proposes a yes to both these questions.

LIBERAL IDEOLOGY

Basic Ideas

The French playwright Molière has one of his characters—an ignorant fellow—express surprise when he is told he has been "speaking prose all his life." A similar surprise grips many Americans when they are informed that they are liberals! In the last few decades, in American political discourse, the word "lib-

eral" has been used in a narrow and historically inaccurate sense to mean someone who favors a lot of government intervention in the economy and, especially, is keen on "taxing and spending." Young people often use the word to
mean people who are permissive about sexual matters, perhaps even libertines
themselves. This discussion suggests a larger and more complicated set of
meanings for liberal that will encompass these current connotations and give
them historical perspective.

Classical Liberalism   Classical liberalism is an ideology that emerged around
the beginning of the nineteenth century. The discussion is based on many
sources (de Tocqueville, 1990; Hartz, 1955; Hofstadter, 1948; Laski, 1936; Lowi,
1969; Macpherson, 1965, 1973; McCoy, 1982; Mill, 1978/1859; Przeworski, 1991;
Wills, 1981). Basically, classical liberals supported what had happened in the
French Revolution and were in favor of the new course of capitalism, which was
freeing itself from the mercantilist system. Mercantilism was an early form of
modern capitalism in which the state maintained control over trade. Classical
liberals believed in three interrelated premises.

   *The first was that the state should be limited in its right to intervene in **civil society.*** The state is a sphere of coercion; **civil society** is the entire set of other practices and relationships. Civil society, by definition, is based on private, voluntary, and consensual relationships. Liberals favor a small sphere for the state
and a large, separate sphere for civil society. More specifically, the state should
be separate from religion. Religion is a private matter; the state should not support or establish any specific religion or even promote religion in general.

   Furthermore, the state should not intervene in the economy. In sharp contrast
to the mercantilist model of development, liberals stood for free trade. The state
should not give out monopoly charters to favored companies (as the English
crown had done for the East India Company and the Hudson's Bay Company).
Entrepreneurs should be able to enter any sector of industry or trade freely. Governments should make little or no attempt to regulate trade or industry.

   *The second major premise of classical liberalism was that the state is established vol-
untarily and operates with the consent of its citizens.* Although the established state
has coercive power over its citizens, it should reflect a **social contract** among
free individuals. These individuals are **citizens,** not subjects. In practice, this
premise usually implies a representative democracy, with two or more parties.
In turn, democracy implies the right to form autonomous organizations and associations, independent of the state and political parties. These organizations
represent the interests of individuals and can represent citizens in dealings with
the state (Lipset, 1960).

   A very important concept for liberals is that the power of the state should
always be carefully circumscribed by law. No party or individual should have
total or arbitrary power. Officeholders, whether elected or appointed, must always follow the law. Thus, liberals reject the notion of an absolute monarch or
a charismatic leader who stands above the law. Social scientists sometimes use
the German word **Rechtsstaat** to describe this type of state, which implies the
elaboration of a code of **civil rights.** Such rights include the right to organize,

petition, speak and write freely, and be protected from torture and forced self-incrimination. Some of these rights protect the individual from the power of the state; others ensure the right to organize in order to influence the political process. The Bill of Rights—the first ten amendments to the U.S. Constitution—is a good example of this type of code.

The third major premise of classical liberal ideology is that the free development of individuals should be the aim of society. Society and the state exist to serve, protect, and nurture the individual, not the other way around.

In terms of the framework elaborated in Chapter 4, "Movements, Societies, and States," classical liberalism calls for a small, confined sphere for the state and a large sphere for civil society. Furthermore, it calls for a separation of spheres, particularly a separation of the state from civil society, from all the spheres of voluntary and private practices and relationships. And finally, it uses the criterion of individual choice and individual freedom as the standard of a good society.

Perhaps, you can see why I think most Americans—Reagan Republicans as well as left-wing Democrats—are really liberals, and why columnist George Will said that Ronald Reagan is a liberal. In his brilliant book, *The Liberal Tradition in America,* Louis Hartz (1955) argued that the United Sates was a liberal society from its very beginning. Although citizens of the United States differed in the extent to which they favored some expansion of the functions of the state, these disagreements were about matters of degree; in the final analysis they all agreed that individualism was a guiding value, that the state should not run the economy, and that a good society has a large sphere of private voluntary relationships, which the state respects. The practice of the slave owners was a glaring exception to this idea of free and equal citizens engaged in voluntary, contractual relations with each other; the slave owners and their ideologues even tried to use liberal concepts—the state's obligation not to interfere in the property rights of citizens—to justify their system (Hartz, 1955).

From Revolution to Institution   The initial support base for classical liberalism in the United States and western Europe included capitalist entrepreneurs, professionals, and middle-class intellectuals at the core of the revolutionary bloc, along with allies among the poor, the peasants, and a few of the more progressive nobles and gentry. The ideology of classical liberalism is a powerful package that contains free-market ideas as well as the concept of **civil liberties.** It reflects the self-interest of entrepreneurial classes as well as a universal vision of human freedom. The rising bourgeoisie and associated middle strata could originate liberal ideology and consider it a seamless web, a coherent view of what society should be like (Macpherson, 1965, 1973).

If we look at classical liberalism from the point of view of other social groups, it tends to look incomplete and highly self-interested. For example, from the viewpoint of the mercantile classes, liberalism is an attack on the role of government in organizing trade; the merchants who held royal monopoly charters that gave their companies exclusive trading rights were not likely to be keen on free markets. From the point of view of the clergy of an established church, freedom of religion was both an attack on their power and a foolish invitation to disorder. From the point of view of poor people, civil rights were difficult to put into effect as long as a society contained great disparities of wealth.

Classical liberalism had a great advantage in the fact that that "men of ideas" were part of its social base (Coser, 1965). Middle-class intellectuals and professionals—lawyers, writers, journalists—were eloquent specialists in disseminating ideas.

The social groups that were actually or potentially in opposition to liberalism were not as good at creating and disseminating a universalistic ideology. The ruling strata of the old order had "lived" their ideas and had difficulty in presenting them in an explicit, universalizing, and attractive new package. The poor produced few political *theorists* (as distinct from activists and radical preachers) from their ranks. They had little access to printing presses to give a permanent form to their voice. In the short run, they supported some liberal goals, forming part of a bloc against the old regime and the landed elites. It was only later, in the nineteenth century, that their differences with liberalism took the form of a systematic alternative vision—socialism (Thompson, 1963).

The hold of liberalism in the United States is particularly strong and reflects the early and extensive power of entrepreneurs and middle-class intellectuals. The liberalism of the United States is associated with the weakness of two other kinds of ideology that were important in Europe (Hartz, 1955).

One ideology that did not exist in the United States is conservative reaction. Lacking a feudal aristocracy, the United States provided little support base for a European-style conservatism that celebrated feudal hierarchies, the absolutist monarchy, and an established religion. There were mercantile interests in New England; they formed the social base of the Federalist Party. But, within a few decades of the Revolution, they lost their political and economic power; the presidencies of Jefferson and Jackson wiped out their access to government. So, in the United States, conservatism has consistently been liberal—that is, it has focused on a discourse of free markets and individual freedom.

The other ideology is socialism. There certainly was a working-class base for socialism in the United States and, in fact, there were socialists, but they were not able to form the type of mass party that appeared throughout western Europe by the end of the nineteenth century (Laslett and Lipset, 1974). Liberalism continued to be the ideology of most North Americans; the tendency of many Americans to identify themselves as "middle class" is associated with the power of liberal ideology.

But, in the course of the next 200 years, liberalism underwent a series of changes. One might say it mutated into diverse forms that embodied different responses to changes in society. Liberal ideology developed many variants, corresponding to different movements and social support bases. The forms that will be discussed in the following pages are liberalism as hegemonic ideology, liberal democracy and the expansion of political participation, negative liberalism and laissez-faire ideology, and positive liberalism and the expansion of state functions.

Hegemonic Ideology   In much of western Europe and North America, liberalism lost its radical and revolutionary fervor. It was the ideology of the new classes that rose to power after the landed nobility were defeated and diminished. Large capitalists and their allies among professionals (like doctors and lawyers), government officials, small businesspersons, and commercial farmers were not keen on additional revolutions which would have threatened their new power and prosperity. Therefore, they tended to ignore or tone down the revolutionary themes in liberal ideology. Thomas Jefferson had written of watering the tree of liberty with the blood of tyrants; this sort of rhetoric came to seem a bit violent and reckless.

Liberalism changed from a revolutionary ideology into a defense of the new status quo in much of Europe and the Americas. It may be useful in this context to remember that, in the United States, a substantial portion of the population were property owners, especially farmers, merchants, and self-employed artisans. Rural property owners were also numerous in France, since a stratum of small farmers was formed when peasants seized nobles' estates during the Revolution. In Latin America and southern and eastern Europe, the social support base of liberalism was much narrower; most people were still peasants, living at a subsistence level, and often involved in sharecropping or even serfdom and peonage.

In the process of becoming the ideology of states, liberalism began to pick up some of the ideas of the conservative reaction. Liberals did not support mercantilism, the rule of the landed nobility, or a reestablishment of the king and the church—but some of them did come to like Burke's idea that change should be slow and organic, not sudden and revolutionary. As long as the bourgeoisie and its allies were a revolutionary class, they put forth a stirring and universal call to revolution against the monarchy, the nobility, and the mercantile interests. Once they became a new ruling class, these social forces had to emphasize the universal benefits of the new status quo.

The new hegemonic ideology still upheld the universal value of liberalism and insisted that the benefits were now available to all. In the new social order, citizens were juridically equal and could participate in politics, and the free market provided opportunities for anyone with ambition and initiative. From the viewpoint of liberals in power, these conditions meant the fulfillment of the goals of liberalism as a revolutionary movement. They ignored two issues that engaged new movements: one was that many people remained excluded from political life, chiefly women, people of color, and (in many nations) white males who owned no property; the other issue was that large economic disparities—class inequality—persisted. The first of these issues was addressed by movements for **liberal democracy.** The second was taken up by socialists.

Liberal Democracy: Political Participation   Only gradually and under great pressure did liberal states become *liberal democratic* states, states that had institutions of representative democracy and universal suffrage (Dahl, 1963, 1983). In the United States, white males had voting rights in most states by the 1840s, but racial and gender barriers persisted into the twentieth century. In western Europe, property qualifications were gradually reduced during the nineteenth century, but women did not gain the vote in some countries of Europe and Japan until after the Second World War. With the gradual expansion of voting came an increase in the number of offices that were directly elected. Of course, liberal democratic institutions like universal suffrage and regular, fair, and competitive elections did not guarantee genuine democratic involvement on a mass basis, but most liberals came to see these institutions as forming a necessary foundation for democracy (DuBois, 1991; Therborn, 1977).

The pressures that transformed liberal institutions into liberal democratic ones often came from movements that looked upon expanded civil rights as a first step toward other movement goals. For example, socialists in the nineteenth century formed mass parties in many countries of western Europe; insofar as the socialist movement could expand voting rights, the parties had an increased chance of gaining seats in the national parliaments and eventually forming a government. Similarly, first-wave feminism in the early twentieth century made suffrage a major goal of the movement, seeking the vote for women as a means toward achieving more far-reaching reforms in the gender system and society as a whole.

Negative Liberalism and Laissez-Faire Ideology   Some ideologues emphasized more and more strongly that the state was not to interfere in the economy. Originally, this theme had been part of a general "package" of opposition to the repressive practices of the absolutist monarchy; opposition to mercantilism existed alongside opposition to torture, royal decrees, and established churches. As these other issues lost their immediacy in western Europe and North America, one important wing of liberal ideology concentrated on the separation of government and economy. Its main theme came to be the virtues of *laissez-faire* capitalism, a capitalist system in which state intervention is minimized. This new focus of liberalism (**neoliberalism**) was favored by businesspeople and entrepreneurs who did not want their enterprises limited or regulated.

This wing of liberal thought has sometimes been referred to as "negative liberalism"; its emphasis is on limiting the role of the state in the economy, confining it to the role of a **night watchman** who prevents violence and guarantees contracts but does not guide the economy (Berlin, 1958; McCoy, 1982). Its guiding images are the free market and free enterprise.

The core support base of negative liberalism is the business community. This support base does not include all capitalists, since many eventually came to benefit directly from government involvement in the economy and/or to see the important stabilizing function that government provided. But, despite these exceptions, the business community has been at the center of opposition to the expansion of government functions from the nineteenth century on. The Reagan administration illustrates the application of some principles of negative liberalism; for instance, cutbacks in regulation generally, the deregulation of industry price structure in airlines and trucking, and withdrawal of government support for unions (as in Reagan's firing of the striking members of PATCO, the air traffic controllers' union, early in his first term).

Positive Liberalism   The influence of socialism and mass pressures from the working class was creating another change in liberal ideology. A new wing of liberal thought emerged that considered the goals of individual development and citizen participation more weighty than the standard of no government intervention in the economy. This wing has been referred to as "positive liberalism" in that it believes that the state should take a positive or proactive role in guiding the economy (Berlin, 1958; McCoy, 1982).

Positive liberals believe that there is some tension between the capitalist economy, on the one hand, and the ideals of democracy and the equality of citizens, on the other hand. Like socialists, they see that the economy contains a great deal of inequality, which "spills over" into the political system that is supposed to be a sphere of formal equality. It is difficult to sustain the equality of the political system as long as there are great wealth differences in the economy. Campaign spending is a concrete example of such a spillover; billionaires can draw media attention to themselves and muster support in a way that ordinary people cannot. Large corporations can influence policy making. Furthermore, positive liberals believe there is evidence that economic growth and development are slowed by the persistence of poverty and large income differentials among citizens, which cannot be reduced by market mechanisms alone (Heilbroner, 1989). Finally, humanitarian and environmental concerns seem to point toward the need for social programs and government regulation. All these reasons add up to support for a more active state than the night watchman state of the negative liberals, though still far from a socialist one. Unlike socialists, positive liberals support private ownership of enterprises and look to the market as the major guiding mechanism of the economy.

The split between negative and positive liberalism began to take shape during the nineteenth century and in the **Progressive Era** in the United States at the turn of the century, but it was greatly accelerated by the **New Deal** in the United States and by center left governments in Europe that expanded the **welfare state** after World War II.

Positive liberalism was both a top-down development launched by governments to cope with social and economic problems and a bottom-up movement backed by liberal reformers, labor unions, and socialist parties. The relative weight of these forces in each nation influenced the policies that were implemented and produced different outcomes for different nations. For example, in Sweden, from the 1930s to the 1970s, unions and the socialist movement had a great role in shaping the political economy; the resulting policies are more tilted toward the working class than in the United States where socialism remained weak.

Governments undertook measures of economic intervention, not to replace capitalism by socialism, but to make capitalism function more smoothly and equitably. The **guided capitalist economy** had to carry out a host of new functions that an entirely free-market economy appeared unable to accomplish (Heilbroner, 1989). Already in the later nineteenth century and the Progressive Era, government in the United States abolished child labor, regulated utilities, created national parks in response to the conservation movement, regulated the quality of food and drugs, and established the Federal Reserve System for implementing monetary policies (Hofstadter, 1955). In the New Deal, these government functions were expanded to include programs such as Social Security, the regulation of financial markets and banking, the legalization and formalization of union organizing, farm subsidies to preserve the family farm, and many other areas of life (Heilbroner, 1989).

Government had a major impact on society by defense spending, highway construction, and urban renewal, even during the relatively laissez-faire administrations following World War II. Increasingly, these programs were carried out not only for their stated purposes, but also as a **countercyclical fiscal policy** designed to keep recessions from plunging into depressions. (Unfortunately, it was politically unpopular to implement tax increases that would cool off an overheating inflationary economy and reduce government deficits. And so, countercyclical taxing and spending worked better in theory than in the real world of politics.) Similar processes, but with more extensive pressure from unions and socialist parties, formed the western European welfare states. They generally provided national health-care programs and other systems of social rights; in some of these nations, much of the national energy and transportation infrastructure was nationalized. All these societies remained capitalist. Even in Sweden, 90 percent of companies are privately owned. As systems, these societies remained liberal democratic, even if reforms were being pushed by socialist parties that had been voted into office; in this regard, they remained within the framework of liberalism in the broadest sense of the ideology (Heilbroner, 1989).

The support base for positive liberalism included middle strata and parts of the working class. A self-interested core support base for positive liberalism was the expanding sector of government employees. Unionized workers who had benefited from the New Deal (and equivalent programs in western Europe) were a constituency of positive liberalism. Major sectors of the capitalist class preferred positive liberalism to negative liberalism; expansion of government functions stimulated their businesses and, in some cases, provided contracts and other immediate benefits. The great economic boom in the developed capitalist countries in the quarter century after World War II both consolidated a support base for positive liberalism and demonstrated its benefits.

One of the consequences of positive liberalism was that it accomplished the **integration of the working class** into the capitalist system in the developed capitalist nations. In the nineteenth century and the early decades of the twentieth century, workers had supported a variety of socialist movements. But, as the post-World War II boom and its skillful management by governments with a positive liberal ideology raised living standards, large segments of the working class became firmly integrated into the prevailing social and economic institutions.

In summary, liberalism continues as the dominant ideology of the developed, democratic capitalist nations. It has split into two variants that are in agreement about basic tenets but in disagreement about the most desirable extent of the role of the state in the economy. These two variants have different (though overlapping) support bases. Negative liberalism is strong in the business community, especially among small- and medium-sized businesses that want "government off our backs." The negative liberal position is similar to the free-market conservative position described in the preceding chapter.

Positive liberalism draws support from employed middle strata, organized labor, and poor people; individuals and businesses that benefit from the government sector of the economy; and ideological supporters of liberal democracy who believe that democratic participation requires a relatively equal and high standard of living. While they do not call for the socialization of property, they favor widespread benefits and relatively level incomes.

Both negative and positive liberalism in the developed market democracies are no longer clearly social movements, in the sense of people mobilized to change the status quo; in large part, these ideologies are two competing positions within the status quo. There is, however, some overlap in support for positive liberalism and socialist, social democratic, left feminist, and left environmentalist mobilizations, and (as we saw in the preceding chapter) an uneasy overlap between laissez-faire negative liberalism and conservative movements. These overlaps exist both at the level of ideas and discourses and in activities of the support bases; for example, the formation of pressure groups within the Democratic and Republican parties in the United States.

Civil Libertarians   Negative liberalism (in the sense of limiting the role of government in society) is not only an ideology of a business community that opposes government regulation, but also the core of an ideology of movements and organizations that defend civil liberties, protect the individual against the state, and preserve the separation of church and state. Civil libertarian principles form the ideology of organizations whose first priority is the preservation of civil liberties and the separation of government from religious institutions and private behavior. The American Civil Liberties Union is the strongest and most noted organization of this type in the United States. Primarily, it uses strategies of initiating court cases to defend civil liberties, especially free speech and the separation of government and religion. The defense of civil liberties is becoming an important mobilization on a global scale and constitutes part of the human rights movement.

Differences and Agreements among Liberals   Negative liberals stand for free enterprise and the free market, for a minimum of government involvement in the economy. In Europe and Latin America this position is termed liberalism and sometimes neoliberalism. In the United States, this position might be identified as pro-free enterprise or pro-free market and could even be called conservative. A strong free enterprise position is particularly widespread within the Republican Party in the United States and among some of the center right parties in Europe; for example, the Thatcherite wing of the Conservative Party in Great Britain.

Positive liberals stand for some measure of government involvement in the economy in the interests of diminishing class inequality in the society, enhancing democratic participation, and/or making the capitalist economy function more smoothly. In the United States the term liberal usually refers to positive liberalism. It is a position that is usually associated with the Democrats more than the Republicans, although there is considerable overlap between the parties. In western Europe this position might be associated with the term welfare state and appears at the center left of the party spectrum; for example, in some portions of the British Labour Party.

It is important to see that both negative and positive liberals are *liberals;* the differences that seem so important at election time are maybe not really that great when they are put on the scale of all contemporary ideologies. Negative and positive liberals agree that the state should remain separate from civil society; every society should have a large, autonomous sphere of private and voluntary relationships; the state's sphere should be limited; individualism is a beneficial ideology; capitalism (defined as an economic system of markets and private ownership of the means of production) is and should be the prevailing economic system; states should operate only by the rule of law; individuals have extensive rights concerning their person, their property, and their political actions; some form of representative democracy is desirable; and freedom or liberty is a central value.

The Post-Communist States   Politics in the post-Communist states underlines many of the fundamental agreements among liberals, agreements that in the west have been obscured by the split into positive and negative liberalism. In the post-Communist states, liberalism has become a fairly unified position, as it was in the nineteenth century in western Europe and North America. In the transition from Communism to capitalism, liberals stand for free-market reforms *and* a democratized state with the right to form independent parties and organizations. Even if these goals mean short-term (or medium-term) economic dislocations like high unemployment or failing enterprises, these problems seem like a necessary cost of bringing about more individual freedom. This position is very close to the original meaning of liberal. The new liberals generally look to western European experiences for models of a free-market economy and a liberal state.

Conservatives in the post-Communist states want to keep a strong central state and go slow on privatization of enterprises and market-oriented reforms; they are more inclined to turn to their own traditions—national and ethnic—for answers to questions about what the new society should look like. As in other parts of the world, the names of parties can be misleading; for example, the Russian Liberal Democrats are really nationalists with little commitment to market reforms, extended civil rights, or democratic participation.

Before discussing strategies of liberal movements, it might be useful to consider two distinct kinds of ideologies that emerge from a classical liberal core ideology: libertarians, and conservatives.

Libertarians   Libertarians are the most radical negative liberals. Libertarians reject state intervention in civil society in every form, except the enforcement of contracts, national defense, and the prevention of violence in private relationships. They are totally laissez-faire in economics, opposing any regulation of economic activity by the state. They even oppose measures like health and safety regulation or the licensing of physicians, which most other free-market advocates accept. In the sphere of personal behavior, they are also opposed to any state intervention; for instance, they favor the decriminalization of drugs. Libertarians believe that each individual can and should judge for himself or herself what behavior to engage in; it is not the business of the state to prevent people from doing foolish or self-destructive things. On the contrary, when the state passes laws of this type it merely contributes to the infantilization and continued irresponsibility of individuals who are rendered unable to think for themselves. Any behavior that is not violent or coercive should be decriminalized. The state should not involve itself in any welfare activities; services can be provided within the private sector as business enterprises or nonprofit organizations. In the view of libertarians, public welfare systems create dependency and undermine self-reliance—withdrawing these state services will, in the long run, contribute to creativity and mutual aid among citizens as they wean themselves from dependence.

Most libertarians in the United States tend to see themselves as aligned with laissez-faire ideologies and are on the right end of the political spectrum. A left libertarian position emphasizes a reduction of state functions and the expansion of voluntary, cooperative relationships in society; left libertarians would not put much value on business enterprise or the profit motive, but would encourage small-scale nonprofit community ventures. Their position is close to the ideology of left-wing anarchism and their views influenced the goals of many of the new social movements in Europe, like women's movements, the peace movement, and some environmental mobilizations.

Conservatives   It may seem strange to include conservatives in a chapter on liberals, but there is actually a considerable amount of overlap in their positions. Historically, conservatism has developed in market democracies in opposition to liberalism, but with many points of convergence. Conservatives within the liberal tradition in the broadest sense of the term liberal are an important reality on the North American scene. Some conservatives are really negative liberals, combining laissez-faire economic ideas with strong support for civil liberties and privacy rights of individuals; in the United States, this position is sometimes associated with Senator Barry Goldwater (1960).

Other conservatives, as we saw in Chapter 6, combine the free-market/free-enterprise ideology of the negative liberals with nonliberal ideas about restraints on individual freedom and the need for government regulation of personal behavior. This position is sometimes referred to as cultural conservatism. For instance, cultural conservatives typically want to crack down on drugs, restrict abortion, institute prayer in schools, and *limit* the regulatory or welfare functions of the state. Conservatives would like government to take more action to safeguard family values—that is, support a neotraditional type of family.

However, the contemporary conservative tendency to support a laissez-faire economy makes their appearance in a chapter on liberalism appropriate; like classical liberals, they support a separation between the state and the economy. They do recognize the validity of the state–civil society distinction, even though they would like the state to have a role in shaping values. Conservatives are sometimes influenced by religious ideologies; they are often inclined to question the rigid separation of church and state that is called for by classical liberalism.

Organizationally and strategically, conservatives in the United States have formed a large number of coalitions and networks (described in Chapter 6) and have been active within the Republican Party as well.

THE INSTITUTIONALIZATION OF LIBERALISM IN GLOBAL PERSPECTIVE

At the beginning of the nineteenth century, liberalism was still a revolutionary ideology in Europe. In much of central, southern, and eastern Europe as well as colonial Latin America, the forces of reaction—monarchies, established churches, quasi-feudal landholding classes—were still in power. Liberals went underground, forming clandestine secret societies and illegal movements. The imperial ambitions of Napoleon gave some support to liberal ideals, but at the cost of linking them to invasions by a foreign power (France); and Napoleon was by no means much of a liberal himself.

It was not until the second half of the nineteenth century that liberal movements triumphed in much of western Europe and in some parts of Latin America. For instance, the state that was formed in the unification of Italy was referred to as the liberal state. The presidency of Benito Juarez in Mexico was associated with *La Reforma*—liberal reforms that took away the property and political power of the Catholic Church and awarded civil rights to the Indian population. In many regions, liberalism was not fully institutionalized. For example, in Russia, in the 1860s, serfdom was ended as a small step toward liberal ideals, yet little extension of political rights took place. In some parts of Latin America (like Colombia and Guatemala), liberals and conservatives continued to battle each other; when liberals came to power, they often used liberal rights merely as a cover under which plantation owners could gain access to the land of Indian communities (Handy, 1984).

In the nations that are referred to as market democracies, one or another form of liberalism has become institutionalized. The constitutional framework institutionalizes liberal principles: the separation of state and religion, private property rights, civil rights and civil liberties, the separation of powers or "checks and balances" to limit state actions, representative democracy. In these nations the party system usually reflects the spectrum of positions within liberalism from negative liberals at the center right to positive liberals at the center left; sometimes these nations have one or more socialist parties at the left end of the spectrum as well as right-wing parties that call for a stronger state and a reduction of democratic rights.

In many of these nations, competition is mostly among parties that represent different forms of liberalism; competition is carried out in the electoral system, and different ideological positions are embodied in party positions and in the formation of pressure groups within the parties. Once the framework of liberal democracy is established, parties and interest groups with a liberal ideology are assured "political space." Thus, they are satisfied to accept the rules of the game and lean toward strategies of electoral campaigns and persuasion.

Liberal Democracy and Capitalism

Why is there an affinity between capitalism and liberal democracy? This affinity makes good sense at the level of ideology; we have already seen that, historically, they formed part of the same package of ideas—the separation of state and economy and a general limitation of the powers of the state. Different explanations offer reasons why they continue to be connected to each other.

Proponents of liberalism—particularly negative liberalism—argue that freedom and capitalism are associated with each other because only the free market creates a sphere that is free of state power, a sphere in which individual liberty is preserved. In this view, capitalism protects and makes possible individual freedom. This view has been most succinctly presented by Milton Friedman, a monetarist economist and strong negative liberal (Friedman, 1962; Friedman and Friedman, 1980).

Marxists give a different twist to the explanation. In a liberal democratic capitalist society, production and distribution decisions are made through the market mechanism. Government is spared the need to make tough decisions, economic decisions that affect everyone every day. Therefore, government and the political system are less likely to become the site of explosive conflicts—class conflicts over property and income. This insulation from class conflicts makes it easier for government to refrain from coercion and repression and to sustain civil rights and democratic participation.

Furthermore, say the marxists, market democracies (capitalist systems with liberal democratic political institutions) also provide a sense of political equality and political participation; thus, liberal democratic political institutions are mechanisms for establishing the legitimacy of capitalist dominance in the economy and society.

Note that liberal and marxist explanations are not that different—both focus on the separation of spheres and the limited powers of the state vis-à-vis the economy, the characteristics that are at the heart of liberalism.

NEW FORMS OF LIBERALISM

Liberalism has not come to an end as a movement. Although institutionalized in the market democracies, its vision is not yet fulfilled everywhere, either within these countries or on a global scale. In the second half of the twentieth century are two significant areas of movement activity. One is the **Civil Rights Movement** in the United States in the post-World War II period, culminating in the 1960s. The discussion is based on many sources (Brown, 1994; Carson, 1981, 1991; Eagles, 1986; Garrow, 1987; Graham, 1990; Harris, 1983; Lincoln, 1984; Malcolm X, 1965; Marable, 1985, 1991; McAdam, 1990; McMillen, 1991; Morris, 1984; Morrison, 1987; Parks, 1992; Zinn, 1964). The other major recent mobilization is the formation of ongoing movements for human rights and civil liberties in countries that are not liberal democracies.

The Civil Rights Movement

In all the nations that became market democracies, political rights were only gradually extended, often through the efforts of movements. For example, in western Europe, voting rights for men were won through movements like Chartism in England in the nineteenth century; women won the right to vote much later and only through the struggles of the suffrage movement in many countries, including the United States and England (Dubois, 1991; Therborn, 1977).

But a glaring exception to the extension of political rights and juridical equality persisted in the United States to the middle of the twentieth century. African Americans remained segregated by law throughout the south, being restricted in the use of public spaces; they were subjected to barriers to voting like poll taxes and literacy tests; they were forced to attend separate schools; intermarriage between whites and blacks was prohibited in many states. These conditions were most severe in the states of the former Confederacy, but they were also present—through law as well as force of custom—in many other states. African Americans were supposed to have come into the full rights of citizenship under the Fourteenth Amendment (equal rights, 1868) and Fifteenth Amendment (voting rights, 1870), but these amendments were weakened by court decisions. The situation deteriorated further after federal troops were withdrawn from the south in 1877; whites organized into groups like the Ku Klux Klan and used violent means to segregate blacks and to keep them from exercising political rights. In 1896, in the *Plessy v. Ferguson* decision, the Supreme Court upheld the constitutionality of segregated facilities (in this case, railroads; but by extension, virtually any business or public sector institution).

Change came very slowly until World War II. Even the armed forces were not fully desegregated until 1950. The federal government seemed primarily responsive to white voters in the south who showed no inclination to change. But, beneath this surface of racism, movements were beginning to take shape. By the 1940s and early 1950s a variety of forces in U.S. society focused their energy on ending legal segregation: The National Association for the Advancement of Colored People, an organization formed during the Progressive Era—and during the height of lynchings and the imposition of "Jim Crow" laws; unions with African American membership like the Brotherhood of Sleeping Car Porters; parts of the left, especially the Communist Party; and some Protestant churches (such as the Quakers). Particularly, the NAACP took the lead in pressing court cases to desegregate educational institutions. Training sessions for organizers were formed, and a few tentative freedom rides began as early as the late 1940s.

Society itself was changing. Returning African American veterans could not stand to see the segregation and humiliation that African Americans were subjected to in their own country, so different from their welcome in the countries they had liberated from the Nazis. More and more African Americans were moving to urban areas and/or the north, leaving behind the closed systems of southern small towns and entering into a larger world. The south itself was changing; New Deal policies of regional development and the defense boom during and after the war expanded the economy from cotton production based on sharecropping to a more diversified economy with a large role for federal defense contractors. And finally, the decolonization movements and the cold war provided the international backdrop; the United States could hardly afford to look racist in an era when it was competing with the Soviet Union for allies in the Third World.

In the mid-fifties two events touched off the movement: the 1954 ***Brown v. Topeka Board of Education*** unanimous Supreme Court decision that ended the "separate but equal" doctrine in education and the **Montgomery bus boycott,** initiated by Rosa Parks' refusal to give up her seat to a white bus rider. Parks was a seamstress—and she was not just a tired woman on a bus who suddenly "snapped" into a spontaneous gesture of resistance. The decision to confront the racist practices of the bus company had been thought through, and Parks was acting as a member of a movement. She was active in the NAACP and had worked with both the Quakers and the left in developing skills as an organizer; both her family and her husband's had a history of movement commitment (Parks, 1992). The bus boycott was crucial because it brought the black churches into the Civil Rights Movement, thereby connecting organizations like the NAACP with a broader mass base; Martin Luther King was a leader in expanding the movement (Parks, 1992).

The movement gained momentum after the success in Montgomery. By the early 1960s, African American college students became an important force in the movement, especially in lunch counter **sit-ins** throughout the south. These sit-ins began the desegregation of public places of business. **Freedom rides** engaged both African Americans and sympathetic European Americans in the integration of bus terminals and other public facilities. They met violent counter-movements, club-wielding racist crowds, often organized by the Klan or by White Citizens' Councils (Carson, 1981, 1991).

The tactics of public sit-ins, freedom rides, and **nonviolent civil disobedience** were excellent ways of drawing the attention of national media, especially the new medium of television. The climate of the Kennedy years was favorable to a new wave of liberal movements to extend civil rights and political participation to a group that had been segregated and disenfranchised.

Yet, despite considerable support from the executive branch, the Civil Rights Movement's achievements were hard fought. Southern white opposition remained adamant. The movement could not be won on television; it had to win "on the ground," in the small towns of the south. **Voter registration drives** in the deep south became the cutting edge of the movement, the point where organizers risked their lives to bring new people into the movement (Harris, 1983). Identity formation was not the problem faced by the movement; an African American identity and community existed already, formed by both internal forces like cultural traditions and the black churches and by the external forces of white racism. The challenge was mobilizing people who already had a clearly defined collective identity to take *actions*—especially registering as voters—that might lead to a loss of jobs and access to land, beatings, and even their murder.

By the mid-1960s the immediate goals of the movement were essentially won. The **1964 Civil Rights Act** banned discrimination in public places of business involved in any way in interstate commerce, as well as in employment. The **1965 Voting Rights Act** abolished literacy tests, barred changes in state voting laws that reduced black voting power regardless of the intent of the law, and permitted the U.S. attorney general to monitor registration procedures. The liberal goals of civil rights, juridical equality, and enfranchisement had been accomplished.

Now African Americans and the antiracist movement faced the challenge of ending racism in other U.S. institutions—the economy, the residence patterns of cities, the practices of schools, and the informal habits of everyday life. In many ways, this would prove a harder and slower process; and it was less clear what type of movements would be most effective.

Positive liberal ideologies could play some part; pressure could be put on government to redress the historical disadvantage of African Americans in employment or to intervene in real estate markets and school districting. Organizations like the NAACP and the Urban League continued to bring court cases to make civil rights laws a reality, end **de facto** as well as **de jure** school and residential segregation, develop affirmative action policies, and work on federal programs that would alleviate poverty and isolation among African Americans.

Ethnonationalism became important in mobilizing African Americans; **cultural nationalist** movements expanded, including some with a religious discourse, like the Nation of Islam. The activists in these movements were doubtful about integration; to them, integration was a process in which people lost their culture, in which they were forced to assimilate in a unilateral and unequal encounter with a white or Eurocentric culture that was associated with control of the economy and the political system (Malcolm X, 1965). By the 1980s, some of these ideas were also developed in Afrocentric ideology that emphasized African Americans' African cultural heritage. One area in which the ideology has made an impact is school curriculum.

Themes from socialist movements and anticolonial movements were adopted by groups like the Black Panthers; African Americans were seen as an **internal colony** that shared many of the characteristics of colonized peoples in the Third World. Some of the organizations that had been in the forefront of the voter registration drives also took a turn toward **black power** ideology. Self-defense, community organizing, and identity formation were important elements of this strategy (Brown, 1994). Both the FBI and local police departments monitored these groups closely, in some cases infiltrating them, provoking them into illegal actions, and even attacking them with little provocation (as in the killing of Fred Hampton, a Black Panther, by Chicago police officers). Martin Luther King, like other leaders of the Civil Rights Movement, became openly critical of U.S. involvement in the war in Vietnam; and in 1968, he was assassinated as he began support work for the municipal sanitation workers in Memphis. In other words, in the last years of his life, he shifted attention from civil rights issues to economic inequalities in the United States.

The movement divided, becoming many different movements that pursued a variety of strategies once the goals of its liberal phase were won. Some of these goals brought the successor movements into confrontation rather than cooperation with the existing political structures. As the movements turned from winning **political and juridical equality** to the more intractable issues of **economic equality** and **cultural autonomy,** it became more difficult to contain them within the existing liberal framework.

The Human Rights Movement: A Global Ideology

As mentioned above, even within the core regions of the globe, liberal and liberal democratic institutions were, at first, fully established in only a handful of nations, located mostly in western Europe, North America, and the settler states of Australia and New Zealand; after World War II, Japan, Germany, and Italy also formed liberal democratic states; by the seventies, they were joined by Spain and Portugal. Other regions—like Latin America, India, and parts of eastern Europe—had more fragile traditions of liberal democracy. There, liberal democracy could not be taken for granted, but had to be defended and even restored by movements after periods of authoritarian rule.

On a global scale, a variety of systems confronted intellectuals and activists who were committed to liberal democracy. Each of these systems presented different problems to movements. They were characterized by different political opportunity structures as well as different historical political cultures. In some regions, the issue was one of restoring liberal democracy (Uruguay in the 1980s, Greece in the 1970s), in others, the problem was establishing it in the first place.

Structural Strains

Maintaining or Restoring Liberal Democracies in Nations with Structural Inequalities   In some regions, there were liberal democratic traditions, and even long stretches of liberal democratic governments, *but economic inequality made these political institutions fragile and tenuous.* Democratic institutions were difficult to manage and sustain, as long as societies were polarized along class lines, sometimes with superimposed ethnic cleavages. In some countries, democratic governments were overthrown by military regimes. For example, a number of South American nations have liberal democratic traditions, but with interruptions by military dictatorships—among them, Brazil, Chile, and Uruguay (Wiarda and Kline, 1990).

The fragility of liberal democratic governments was often caused by polarized class situations, in which a large, militant working class faced intransigent business interests. Electoral victories by socialist or liberal reformist parties representing the working class led to social and economic policies that were unacceptable to middle- and upper-class groups. Growing social and economic tension created a situation in which the military intervened to oust the socialist or reformist government. This scenario unfolded in Chile in the 1970s. Chile was a nation with a long history of liberal democracy, but also one with major class cleavages. The electoral victory of **Unidad Popular,** a socialist coalition headed by Salvador Allende, set in motion a process of reform and reaction. Efforts to implement economic and social reforms created further polarization, disinvestment by businesses, and inflation. In 1973, a military coup led by Augusto Pinochet resulted in the murder of Allende and tens of thousands of Chileans and a prolonged period of military dictatorship (Petras and Morley, 1975; Przeworski, 1991).

In these societies, class conflicts were difficult to contain within the liberal democratic system. The stakes in elections became too high and the policy differences between right-wing and left-wing parties too large. After the military coups, movements for democracy worked to restore the democratic institutions that had been overthrown by the military.

Establishing Liberal Democracies   Other nations have not had an extensive history of democracy. They have a long history of repressive state institutions, and so the issue for activists is not one of defending or restoring democracy but of establishing it in the first place. These nations are capitalist, but different in political structure from the capitalist democracies. Their political systems are authoritarian, with little chance for political participation and few individual political or civil rights; formal guarantees may exist, but are ignored in practice. The military or other national security forces have a large part in maintaining the unequal social structure.

In some cases, these situations are associated with deeply polarized class structures, as in some countries in Central America like Guatemala and El Salvador (LaFeber, 1984; North, 1985). In wealthier countries, the "pie" is large enough that shifts to the left or right in elections are not fundamentally threatening; policies may change with administrations but a general level of prosperity, accommodation, and legitimacy (marxists might prefer the term hegemony) mean that electoral stakes are low. In poorer capitalist societies, large class cleavages mean that the outcomes of democratic elections can potentially lead to major transformations. The property-owning classes fear that democracy would lead to the victory of a socialist party or of strongly reformist positive liberals (such as the Arbenz government in Guatemala in the 1950s). Some members of these classes, especially large landowners involved in agro-export production, prefer military dictatorships to this possibility of left-wing electoral victories. When democratic political processes led to the victory of socialists or reformers, the military overthrew the elected government.

The history of Guatemala since the 1954 coup against the left reformist government of Jacobo Arbenz illustrates this sequence of events. Since 1954, Guatemala has had a sequence of military regimes and even the apparent restoration of formal democracy in the last few years has not completely halted murders by units of the military. The right to organize unions and pressure groups and freedom of speech and assembly are still tenuous; exercise of civil rights carries great risks. The direct or indirect role of the military or national security forces in maintaining a status quo creates extremely dangerous situations for activists. They are subjected to murders, disappearances, and torture by military or paramilitary death squads. Their mobilizations have to aim first at basic human rights before democratic rights can be established (Americas Watch Reports, 1987, 1988, 1990; Black, 1984; Handy, 1984; Manz, 1988; Schlesinger and Kinzer, 1983; Smith-Ayala, 1991).

In addition to military regimes, there are other forms of authoritarian states. Some have a single party or are one-party-dominant states. In the one-party-dominant states there is more than one legal party but only one party consistently wins elections and holds all or most important offices. The Institutional Revolutionary Party (PRI) in Mexico is an example of one-party dominance

(Laurell, 1992). The one-party-dominant condition presents special problems to movements seeking to enlarge democracy, since the outward forms of democracy are present—regular elections, legality of opposition parties, and so on—while the substance of democracy is lacking. Movements for democracy have a more difficult time framing their demands to potential supporters inside and outside the country in the case of these partially democratic regimes.

Transforming Communist Single-Party States into Liberal Democracies
Single-party Communist states sparked human rights and civil rights activism. Intellectuals and artists sought the freedom of expression that characterized the western democracies, and workers hoped to build an independent union movement. A substantial constituency existed to support a rebirth of civil society, with the opportunity to organize autonomous movements and political groups, discuss and criticize policies, and, in the long run, establish a multiparty system. Movements sporadically emerged in Eastern Europe in the 1950s and 1960s (East Germany in 1953, Hungary in 1956, Czechoslovakia in 1968; and repeatedly, albeit on a smaller scale, in Poland), but were suppressed, sometimes with subsequent attempts at co-optation through economic reforms, as in Hungary. The movements became large and difficult to repress with the emergence of Solidarity in Poland, a movement that unified industrial workers, intellectuals, activists in the Roman Catholic Church, and a wide spectrum of dissidents in the late 1970s. Though temporarily checked by a martial law government, the movement was not crushed (Ascherson, 1981; Karabel, 1993; MacDonald, 1983; Michnik, 1985; Potel, 1982; Walicki, 1991).

By the late 1980s, with the Soviet Union's own wave of reforms in the Gorbachev era, Solidarity, as well as similar movements in Czechoslovakia, Hungary, and East Germany, ousted the Communist parties from rule and established forms of liberal democracy in the region (Ash, 1989; Gwertzman and Kaufman, 1990; Kagarlitsky, 1992; Livingstone, 1992; Marks and Lemke, 1992).

Pro-Democracy Movements   The existence of many authoritarian and repressive regimes has relaunched liberalism as the movement of opposition, a challenge to the status quo in much of the world. While a couple of the largest blocs of repressive states has given way to more democratic forms (in the southern cone of Latin America and in eastern Europe and Russia), there are still many regions and nations that are far from liberal democracies. The struggles to restore, defend, or establish liberal democracy are under way not only as national movements within specific countries, but also as a transnational movement; there are many separate national human rights and pro-democracy movements as well as a unified transnational movement.

The ongoing challenge to the repressive status quo now takes the form of the human rights movement. In the broadest sense of the term, this movement seeks to limit violent and coercive action against any human being. Thus, it works for the end of slavery (still prevalent in many regions, sometimes in hidden forms) and the protection of children. But, most of its efforts are directed toward limiting the actions of states, which are typically the most powerful coercive institutions. In this way, the human rights movement is squarely within the liberal tradition.

More specifically, the human rights movement seeks to end genocide and ethnocide, torture, detention without trial, punishments imposed without due process, capital punishment, and imprisonment for beliefs or personal characteristics and private behaviors. It opposes state actions that have no legal or constitutional basis and arbitrary actions by the state and its agents. This outlook corresponds to the general liberal position on civil rights, civil liberties, individual freedom, and the rule of law. At the core of the ideology is the protection of individuals against states and other powerful organized groups.

International Organizations   One of the most important organizations within the human rights movement is **Amnesty International; Americas Watch** and **Helsinki Watch** are examples of more regionally oriented organizations with similar goals. The human rights movement generally uses strategies of drawing international attention to abuses and rallying the public in liberal democratic countries to put pressure on their own governments to place sanctions on states that commit violations.

One can make a distinction between human rights movements and civil rights movements: The latter include the goals of the former but add a more positive set of political goals—the rights of individuals and groups to express and freely circulate political opinions and form associations, unions, and political parties without fear of reprisals (including loss of employment).

National Human/Civil Rights Movements   These movements have had a powerful role in recent history, especially in Latin America, South Africa, and the former Soviet bloc. In these regions, they have had to work in conditions of illegality and sometimes severe repression. For example, **Solidarity** in Poland was one of the forces that began the disintegration of the Communist states in eastern Europe. Organizations like the **Civic Forum in Czechoslovakia** brought this process to its culmination. In Argentina, the **Madres of the Plaza de Mayo** (the relatives of people who have **disappeared** by action of the military regime) took great personal risks to bring the struggle for democracy into the open, to make Argentinians aware of the crimes of the dictatorship. The union and student movements in South Korea helped to accelerate the shift toward democratic institutions there. The **African National Congress (ANC)** has finally achieved a liberal democratic structure in South Africa, with full political and civil equality, based on the dismantling of apartheid, the signing of a new constitution, and multiracial, one-person–one-vote elections. In South Africa, as in many other regions that have entered into or returned to democracy, economic hardships and economic inequality remain major problems.

There are other cases where the struggle for human rights and civil rights still continues. In Guatemala, the **Mutual Support Group (GAM)** has drawn international attention to the tens of thousands of murders committed by the military, but the military still controls the political life of the country and has set narrow limits on the restoration of democracy. In China, the government attack on demonstrators in Tiananmen Square in 1989 has temporarily put a halt to the **pro-democracy movement** (Lin, 1992; Lu Yuan, 1989). But even in these embattled cases, the movements have initiated processes of democratization that may eventually be realized.

Movement Support Bases   The support base for many of these movements is among more educated strata—especially students and other intellectuals—because they tend to have the time and resources that allow them to engage in movements. They are more directly concerned with the right to circulate ideas. The relatives of the disappeared form the core of the movement in countries like Argentina and Guatemala.

In many circumstances, the concern with civil rights, civil liberties, and liberal democracy combines with economic and ethnic struggles. Civil rights and liberal democracy allow mobilization for more class and ethnic equity. When a subordinate class or ethnic group is numerically strong, a representative democracy can mean reforms that have deep-reaching social and economic consequences. Therefore, human rights and pro-democracy movements may involve poor people, the working class, the traditional constituencies of the left, as well as subordinate ethnic groups. Unions as organizations and union members have had important roles in civil rights movements in South Korea, Poland, South Africa, and many places in Latin America. Civil rights movements often emerge among ethnic groups seeking a greater political voice or new forms of the state, as in South Africa and Northern Ireland, and among the Palestinians.

Strategies

Transnational Conscience Constituencies   Most contemporary human rights movements pursue strategies of bringing repression and crimes of the state to public awareness—not only to conationals, but also to global communities. The audience is located in the liberal democratic nations, in those places where liberalism is already institutionalized. For many human rights and civil rights movements a **conscience constituency** located in liberal democracies is almost as important a component of the movement as in-country activists. In many cases, developed capitalist democracies impose **sanctions** against repressive states; for example, trade embargoes, divestment of capital, curtailment of arms sales, or loss of favored nation trading status. At a minimum, the movements call for the end of military support or foreign aid to these regimes.

These strategies have had varying degrees of success, depending on the economic weight of the nation; for example, the United States has been loathe to undertake sanctions against China, with its potential market of over a billion customers. Also, until recently, the U.S. government has been so afraid of "communist subversion" that it has tolerated or even supported authoritarian regimes that commit many human rights abuses, including disappearances and murders. The collapse of the Soviet bloc may reduce these fears and make it possible for the U.S. government to turn away from such regimes.

Hunger strike by pro-democracy demonstrators in Tiananmen Square, Beijing, China, May 16, 1989. The sign on the demonstrator in the foreground makes a reference to the words of Nathan Hale (1755–1776), an American revolutionary war hero executed as a spy by the British.

Armed Struggle   In some circumstances, democracy movements decided to engage in **armed struggle**; the ANC as well as some of the popular forces in Guatemala have used this strategy. After all, in its initial historical forms in the early nineteenth century, liberalism had included clandestine organizations and violent revolutions. Like most of the movements in this book, liberalism is prepared to undertake many different strategies, including violent ones, to bring into being its vision of society.

SUMMARY

While ideologies of liberalism and liberal democracy sustain the status quo in the prosperous capitalist societies, they remain revolutionary forces in many other regions. In the United States, we have such a long and pervasive history of liberal hegemony and the institutionalization of the liberal vision of society that we only occasionally recognize it as the ideology of a movement; most important, the Civil Rights Movement, which finally extended political and juridical equality to all citizens. We take liberal democracy and the liberal separation of spheres for granted; most U.S. citizens subscribe to one or another version of these viewpoints, seeing these variants as part of mainstream politics in a market democracy. Yet, liberalism was and is a totalizing vision of a good society, and in many parts of the world it still represents a revolutionary alternative to the status quo. Movements for human rights, civil rights, and democratic political institutions form a major current of contemporary transnational movements.

KEY TERMS AND CONCEPTS

classic liberalism
civil society
social contract
citizens
Rechtsstaat
civil rights
civil liberties

liberal democracy

negative liberalism
laissez-faire ideology
the night watchman state
neoliberalism

positive liberalism
the Progressive Era
the New Deal
welfare state
guided capitalist economy
countercyclical fiscal policy
integration of the working class

libertarians

the civil rights movement
Plessy v. Ferguson
Brown v. Topeka Board of Education
Montgomery bus boycott
sit-ins, freedom rides, and nonviolent
    civil disobedience
voter registration drives

1964 Civil Rights Act
1965 Voting Rights Act
de facto and de jure segregation
ethnonationalism; cultural
    nationalism
internal colony
black power
political and juridical equality
economic equality
cultural autonomy

**global liberal democratic
    movements and the human rights
    movement**
maintaining liberal democracies in
    nations with structural inequalities
Unidad Popular (Chile)
Amnesty International; Americas
    Watch; Helsinki Watch
Solidarity
Civic Forum in Czechoslovakia
Madres of the Plaza de Mayo
the "disappeared"
African National Congress (ANC)
Mutual Support Group in Guatemala
    (GAM)
pro-democracy movement in China
global conscience constituencies
sanctions
armed struggle

Ernesto Che Guevara, Argentinian physician and activist in Africa and Latin America, is associated with the strategy of the *foco*, the small insurgency that sparks a revolution in a society with large class inequality. 1964.

CHAPTER 8

The Old and New Left

The Varieties of Socialism

The bourgeoisie, historically, has played a most revolutionary part. . . .
    The bourgeoisie cannot exist without constantly revolutionizing the instruments of production, and thereby the relations of production, and with them the whole relations of society. . . . Constant revolutionizing of production, uninterrupted disturbance of all social conditions, everlasting uncertainty and agitation distinguish the bourgeois epoch from all earlier ones. All fixed, fast-frozen relations, with their train of ancient and venerable prejudices, are swept away, all new-formed ones become antiquated before they can ossify. All that is solid melts into air, all that is holy is profaned, and man is at last compelled to face with sober senses, his real conditions of life, and his relations with his kind.
    —Karl Marx and Friedrich Engels, *The Communist Manifesto,* 1848.

Imagine yourself an industrial worker in England, France, or the United States in the nineteenth century. You have to work long hours in a factory or mine; it is stifling hot, the machines are noisy and dangerous, and the air is filled with lint or coal dust. Your wages are only enough to buy bread, tea, sugar, and an occasional piece of fatty meat; you live in a tenement, crowded into a small apartment or a dank basement, with neither privacy nor indoor plumbing. There is little you can do to raise your wages, because there are so many people in the city who are desperate for a job; the job is yours on a "love it or leave it" basis—and there are plenty of unemployed workers who would gladly take it. The law permits your employer to replace you if you strike or "cause trouble" or for any reason whatsoever. If you are a woman or a child you are paid even less than a man; everyone in the family has to work to make survival possible. There are no health benefits or pensions or worker's compensation; if the male breadwinner dies or is disabled in one of the frequent industrial accidents, the family's standard of living will fall even further: Begging, prostitution, or scavenging may become your only options. The good old days?

    This vignette may seem like the vanished past to people in the United States or western Europe, but it is still a reality in many developing nations. During the week in which I wrote this paragraph, 250 women and girls died in a fire in a toy factory in Thailand. From the point of view of the millions of people who lived and continue to live in conditions like these, liberalism seems like empty promises. Even if workers enjoy formal equality as citizens in some of these nations, their economic circumstances make a mockery of their rights and freedoms.

These vignettes may seem like "long ago and far away" to many readers. Are there any similarities among these impoverished, exploited laborers and workers in the contemporary developed core nations? Consider the following situations: The steel mills close in Chicago, leaving behind unemployed workers and deteriorating neighborhoods; unemployment is hitting even the most prosperous and well-trained workers in western Europe, in countries like Germany and Sweden; when companies downsize in the United States, middle managers and professionals face either joblessness or expanded workloads; an increasing proportion of jobs in contemporary economies are part-time jobs or jobs in which wages are too low to support a family, like those in the fast-food industry. From the perspective of the left, these situations are not the result of individual bad luck, but the inevitable outcomes of the capitalist economy. And the employers who make the decisions to relocate, downsize, and reorganize the production process regardless of the social consequences are caught up in the relentless logic of capitalist competition on a global scale.

SOCIALISM: THE CHALLENGE TO CAPITALISM

Socialism is an ideology that challenges the basic premises of liberalism. Socialists have a fundamentally different view of how societies are put together. For socialists, inequality in the economic domain inevitably permeates every sphere of society. Liberalism is inextricably connected to capitalism: economic activities are left in private hands, the means of production are privately owned, and economic production and exchange are regulated by the mechanism of the market. Liberals see no contradiction between the private form of the economy and political freedom and formal equality of individuals—on the contrary, in the eyes of liberals, they lend strength to each other. Socialists view this arrangement in exactly the opposite way: The private and unequal structure of the economy creates a general situation of inequality that blocks the attainment of individuals' real potential, freedom, and political participation.

Yet, despite this clash between socialism and liberalism, the two ideologies have areas of overlap, and the associated movements have, at times, coexisted and even cooperated. They share roots in Enlightenment ideas about human rights and the possibility of changing human society through reason, critical analysis, and purposive action.

This chapter traces the origins of socialist movements and discusses two of their main forms—**revolutionary socialism** and **social democracy.** In the twentieth century, these two large currents were able to use state institutions to transform societies. **Left**-wing ideologies have also appeared in more fragmented movements, especially in the **New Left** of the 1960s and in the general thrust of the **new social movements.** The chapter concludes with a discussion of contrasts in socialism and populism.

Historical Development

Emergence   Early forms of socialism appeared in the age of revolutions (Abendroth, 1972). The French Revolution had a radical wing that hoped the Revolution would bring about extensive social leveling; that it would go beyond ending feudal privileges and giving peasants a chance to seize and divide feudal landhold-ings, and would end the division between rich and poor. These hopes were dis-appointed, except the division of feudal estates, and what came to be called "the social question" was not addressed in a practical way during the Revolution, and certainly not during the more conservative era that followed (Arendt, 1965).

Early socialist movements appeared in the first half of the nineteenth cen-tury. Some radicals continued to apply the strategies of the liberal revolution-ary movements, forming small conspiratorial groups, organizationally discon-nected from the growing numbers of wage workers. These groups were usually rooted out by the authorities (Hobsbawm, 1962).

Others, especially in England, engaged in mass agitation for democratic rights, especially the right to vote. In the United States, white male suffrage was granted within a few decades of the Revolution; in other countries, property re-strictions disenfranchised most working-class men well into the century. The **Chartists** (as the movement was called in England) and other campaigners for political rights believed that these political rights would eventually lead to bet-ter social and economic conditions. If the working majority of the population were enfranchised, a socialist program might become law by parliamentary means. These mass movements also succeeded in reducing the length of the le-gal working day to 10 hours. Chartism has been described as a "huge move-ment" in the numbers of people mobilized for demonstrations (Hobsbawm, 1962:153). It did not have a cohesive or well-organized structure. Indeed, dur-ing the first part of the nineteenth century there were no large, centralized, or bureaucratized mass parties of any political orientation.

Utopian socialists, who experimented with new ways of life, were another wing of socialist organization. They formed small communities in which prop-erty was held in common and all members contributed cooperatively to eco-nomic and social life. Utopian socialist thinkers abounded in western Europe, but a favored site for experiments was the United States, which was perceived as a vast, open laboratory for new social arrangements. Radical communes in the United States tested new ideas about food, sex, and work, from Fruitlands' avoidance of meat, root crops, and fertilizers to Oneida's organized promiscu-ity to the larger and more substantial effort to create a socialist community in New Harmony, Indiana (Garner, 1977). These experiments appealed especially to intellectuals and small numbers of skilled workers; the growing masses of factory workers and miners were less likely to get involved.

Structural Strains and Support Bases: The Proletariat   Socialism developed beyond these initial forms as the modern working class took shape in the later part of the nineteenth century and the first part of the twentieth century, not only in the industrializing world, but also in peripheral regions. In the core in-dustrial regions, like western Europe, the industrial centers of the United States, and Japan, the working class consisted of factory workers, construction work-ers, miners, and workers in home industries and sweatshops, such as garment assemblers. In addition to the industrial working class, many shop clerks and office workers experienced low wages and long working hours.

In the peripheral and semiperipheral regions, in southern and eastern Europe, Latin America, and the European colonies, the working class was, as yet, proportionately smaller and more heterogeneous. It included growing numbers of factory workers as well as wage workers engaged in the extraction and transportation of raw materials, the mineral wealth and tropical commodities that moved from the periphery to the core. Gold and diamond miners in South Africa; laborers on banana plantations in Guatemala, rubber plantations in Indochina, and sugar fields in the Dominican Republic; "coolies" dragging heavy loads in the cities of Asia; dockworkers in African seaports and railway hands in India: All these laborers formed part of a new, globalizing class of wage laborers—the proletariat—and many of them worked for far less pay and under much harsher conditions than the industrial workers in the developed nations.

Landless peasants formed a growing semiproletariat in the periphery. Once peasant and landlord had maintained a close but unequal relationship; in some regions, like China, they were even linked together in the same clans. In traditional agriculture, productivity was low and production was oriented toward subsistence, consumption, and local markets. Globalizing markets in foodstuffs changed these relationships. In countries like Italy, the entry of North American and Argentinian grains produced on more fertile soils with modern farm equipment led to a collapse of local production and the displacement of peasant farmers. In other regions, landowners increasingly used peasants as a wage labor force for short-term and seasonal needs, breaking traditional bonds of personal dependency (Wolf, 1969).

These economic strains created social dislocations and formed the social support base of union movements and socialist movements on a global scale.

Marxism: The Decisive Formulation   In the second half of the nineteenth century, socialism crystallized around the work of **Karl Marx** and **Friedrich Engels,** two German social theorists and revolutionaries (McClellan, 1977). They emphasized that their thinking was scientific, rather than utopian, in that they tried to understand the structure of capitalist society and the possibilities for change that were inherent in it. In some way most socialist ideology draws on their work.

Their revolutionary program began with an *analysis* of the capitalist system. Inequality in it is not just a division between rich and poor, but the qualitative difference between the class that owns the **means of production** and hires workers (the **bourgeoisie**) and the class that survives by **selling its labor power** (the **proletariat**). This relationship between capital and wage labor is inherently unequal. Profit is derived from the low level of wages relative to the market value of the goods that workers produce.

Furthermore, capitalism is a system of production for exchange value, not use value; needs and wants in capitalism are satisfied by **commodities**—things produced for profit, for exchange value. Their production is regulated by the **market mechanism,** by supply and effective demand, not by the existence of human needs. To use a contemporary example, milk cows are slaughtered in the United States to reduce excess capacity, while children in Ethiopia (and the United States) go hungry because their families cannot purchase the milk at prices that render a profit.

Decisions about production are made by *privately owned firms in response to market conditions.* Therefore, the class of owners, investors, and employers carries an enormous weight in the process of societal development. The movement of capital determines which regions will prosper and which will decline. For example, steel companies closed down the mills on the south side of Chicago. Owners and top management made these decisions, not the workers who were laid off or the communities that lost jobs. The constant search for lower labor costs and higher profits spurs technology and the global expansion of capitalism.

In Marx and Engels' theory of historical development, liberalism and capitalism present a set of promises that are inherently not possible to fulfill within the capitalist system: Capitalism and liberalism promise freedom, political rights, and the realization of each individual's unique talents and potentials. In this respect, the capitalist system (and its liberal ideology) is an advance over slavery and feudalism. But the class structure of capitalism makes these promises impossible to fulfill, because workers are reduced to instruments of production whose only function is to generate profits. The capitalist class itself is also diminished and dehumanized in this system.

For Marx and Engels, only **communism** can fulfill these possibilities in the long run. Communism is pictured as a society of high technology, preserving capitalism's inventiveness, but putting it directly to human uses rather than allowing it to be channeled through the market mechanism into the goal of maximizing profits. It is to be a society without a state, without coercive institutions. Everyone cooperates for the common good. Specialization that confines human beings into narrow, repetitive routines comes to an end. Each person is free to develop a wide range of talents and interests. Marx and Engels describe communism as ". . . an association, in which the free development of each is the condition of the free development of all" (*Communist Manifesto,* in McClellan, 1977).

Socialism is a necessary intermediate step between capitalism and communism. In socialism, the means of production are transferred from private to public ownership. A process of planning and democratic discussion replaces market mechanisms. Production begins to shift from the goal of exchange value—profit—to use value. Basic human needs are met first and foremost. Human beings are no longer exploited and then junked like depreciated machinery, nor are whole regions abandoned as capital shifts to areas of lower costs.

Marx and Engels believed that socialist revolutions would come about rather quickly and occur first in the most developed capitalist countries. Here, the process of industrialization and technological innovation had gone furthest; workers were already working in a collective and cooperative way in giant enterprises. Capital was becoming increasingly concentrated through mergers, bankruptcies, and buyouts. In this way, capital itself was laying the groundwork for an end to private property; a revolution would only have to expropriate a small number of giant firms. The socialist state formed in this revolutionary process would exercise coercive powers—that, after all, is what every state does—but it would do so as the representative of the vast majority, of all those who do not own capital.

What mechanism would bring about socialist revolution? Marxists point to the dialectical interconnection of two forces. On the one hand, the process involves a **determined structure** that is external to human intentionality: There can be no socialist revolution or a transition to socialism and communism without the prior existence of advanced capitalism. On the other hand, revolution requires an **agent** (or an **acting subject of history**), specifically the organized working class. Workers have to become aware that it is through their efforts as a class that they can bring about a transformation to a form of society that is superior to capitalism.

Thus, a socialist movement has a twofold mission: It must take steps to actually make this transformation take place and propagate new forms of consciousness. It has to organize the working class and draw in possible allied strata like intellectuals or displaced small business owners and form a bloc of social forces that have an interest in the end of capitalism.

Marx and Engels were faced with a conceptual problem that they recognized very clearly. The only models of successful revolutions in the modern world were the French and American Revolutions and other liberal and nationalist uprisings that followed the French pattern. They knew that this model was not appropriate for a socialist revolution, that a socialist revolution would somehow have to be different—but they were not sure how. They also saw that unions, which were gaining strength throughout the industrialized world, were an important ingredient in the organization of the working class but were not prepared to take state power. Unions could defend and expand the rights of workers in the workplace; they could contribute to the formation of working-class consciousness, but they were not organizations with either the structure or vision to lead the working class in the transformation of society from capitalism to socialism. What form of movement had to be developed that would coalesce the power of the working class and channel it toward capturing the state? Marx and Engels had difficulty developing a political project that matched the brilliance of their social and economic analysis; it was easier to understand the structure of capitalism than organize the movement to end it. As a first step toward forming such a movement, they brought European working-class organizations into an association known as the **International** (Abendroth, 1972).

Dilemmas of Organization and Strategy   By the end of the century, after the death of Marx and Engels, socialists came up with two divergent answers to the question of what form the movement should take. One led to revolutionary socialism and the vanguard party, and the other to social democracy and the mass party engaged primarily in electoral politics.

Decentralized Forms   Before we examine revolutionary socialism and social democracy, we should consider one form that has not survived—the idea of "one big union" and the related **anarcho-syndicalist** movements. The **Industrial Workers of the World (IWW)** is a particularly good example of a strategy and organization based on the premise that if enough workers could be brought into a militant unionlike structure, a series of mass strikes would eventually destabilize the capitalist system and provoke a collapse of the economy and the state. Into the breach opened up by this collapse would step the movement of workers—decentralized, militant, and democratic. Workers should organize at the point of production where their power is most concentrated. They should never get involved in electoral politics, which are just a trap to draw the working class into the liberal state in order to legitimate capitalism. And they have no need for the leadership of professional revolutionaries—they are all capable of revolutionary action, and only through universal involvement can they ensure that the postcapitalist state really represents the entire class (Hobsbawm, 1973:57–58).

By World War I, this movement structure had failed, leaving only two major variants for most of the century—mass parties with bureaucratized structure or vanguard parties. Nevertheless, for the New Left, new social movements, and diffused cultural resistances of the 1990s, the idea of decentralized, spontaneous, anarchic, and egalitarian mass action makes refreshingly postmodern sense (Dubofsky, 1969; Kornbluh, 1964).

Mass Party or Vanguard Party   The choice between a mass party and a vanguard party was shaped by at least three factors: the political opportunity structure, the nature of the mass support base, and the movement's own theoretical analysis.

The first factor was the political situation. A mass party was possible only in nations where civil rights were extensive enough to permit legal organization of socialist parties. In nations where all parties were illegal or socialist parties were specifically banned, mass organization was difficult to accomplish, as was also the case in nations that had no institutions of political democracy like elections or an effective parliament. The prior success of liberal, liberal democratic, and/or liberal nationalist movements was a precondition for the formation of mass social democratic movements. They created a political structure that made legal organizing possible, opened space for left-wing parties, and raised hopes among socialists and their support base that a peaceful, electoral transition to socialism was possible. There is a bit of a chicken-and-egg dynamic here, since liberal democratic institutions were most likely to appear where the working class was large, skilled, politically aware, well-organized, and able to form an alliance with progressive capitalists and middle-class forces to defeat the reactionary landed classes. In short, these conditions were most completely met in western Europe (Abendroth, 1972; Hobsbawm, 1962, 1979).

Second, was the relative size and political sophistication of the working class; a mass party was a more promising strategy where workers were skilled, politically aware, and a substantial part of the population. To organize an effective mass party in nations where many workers were illiterate and unskilled, and where peasants formed a majority, would be difficult. In the core capitalist countries that had industrialized by the later part of the nineteenth century, the condition of a large and politically sophisticated working class was generally met by the beginning of the twentieth century. In semiperipheral regions of southern and eastern Europe (Russia, Spain, southern Italy, the Balkans) and the periphery (the colonial regions and large parts of Latin America), the working-class base was still too small to support a mass party (Hobsbawm, 1989; Wolf, 1969).

Third, the movement developed a theoretical understanding of what the transition to socialism might look like, whether a gradual process that worked itself out through liberal democratic institutions or a revolution and a complete restructuring of the state. The theoretical analysis was influenced by actual social conditions; where liberal democratic political systems existed and the working class was large and politically aware, the idea of a gradual transition was more realistic. By the end of the nineteenth century, the alternative forms of the socialist movement began to take shape.

SOCIAL DEMOCRATS

In western and central Europe, where some liberal democratic institutions existed and a large skilled industrial working class formed, the initial action of socialists was to build mass parties involved in elections, parliamentary action, and legislation, as well as direct attention to building a working-class base and a socialist political culture. These parties fought to expand the rights of the working class, gaining victories such as health insurance systems, the 8-hour workday, pensions, and the right to unionize. The mass support base of these parties was the industrial working class, especially workers in the **union movement.** The rapid growth of the industrial labor force throughout western and central Europe led to the rapid expansion of the socialist parties in the period from the 1870s to World War I (1914–1918) (Abendroth, 1972; Fletcher, 1987). A new international network linking these parties, the **Second International,** was established.

Theoreticians of the Second International generally pictured the end of capitalism coming about through a series of crises and a collapse of the economy; they emphasized the "determined" nature of the transition to socialism. Parties were needed to protect workers' rights and, eventually, to step into the breach opened up by a growing economic crisis.

The First World War dealt a shock to many of these parties. Only a few of the European socialist parties resisted the tide of nationalism that drew them into supporting the war, and the Second International collapsed. After the war and the Bolshevik revolution in Russia, they split into communist and socialist movements. Hopes receded for a "crash" that would bring capitalism to an end, and many of the socialist parties focused increasingly on electoral successes.

The parties and movements of the Second International were the precursors of contemporary socialist and social-democratic parties, most strongly concentrated in western and central Europe, but also found in Canada, Japan, Australia, and New Zealand. Generally, these parties have names like Socialist Party, Social-Democratic Party, or Labor Party, although there is considerable variation in the terms from country to country (Elliot, 1993; Fletcher, 1987; Smith and Spear, 1992).

The socialist and social democratic parties gradually gave up the idea that economic crisis is inevitable and only the use of force makes a transition to socialism possible. They retained the emphasis on mass organization and the use of means defined as legitimate within the liberal democratic system.

Ideology

The ideology of contemporary social democrats rests on three premises. These premises are not necessarily incompatible with marxist ideas. In fact, some, but not all, social democrats see themselves as marxists, but they deemphasize the concept of revolution. The first premise is that socialism can come about gradually and peacefully, within the political framework of liberal democracy.

In the second premise, socialism is considered the outcome of a progression of stages from political democracy to social democracy to economic democracy. Political democracy was achieved in the first part of the twentieth century in most liberal democratic nations when universal suffrage and the right to form socialist parties were attained. Social democracy and its accompanying social equity is a current goal for these parties; this goal is closely tied to the idea of a welfare state that offers all citizens benefits like health care, quality education, child care, and so on. Economic democracy is a long-term goal to be attained by increasing public control over economic resources, the production process, and investment. The attainment of economic democracy is accomplished by a gradual shift of control over capital from private firms to public entities, including investment boards run by workers and citizens. Taxation is one of several instruments for expanding the public sector. This development is an evolutionary, not a revolutionary process. No violence need take place and the state does not have to be overthrown. Economic democracy and the attainment of socialism in the fullest sense is only in its initial stages, even in the most developed of the social democratic societies like Sweden.

The third premise of contemporary social democrats is that during this process, socialist parties can coexist peacefully with capitalism. Social democrats point to many nations where the transition from feudalism to capitalism was peaceful and evolutionary, for example, Denmark and Sweden; they believe that a transition to socialism could take a gradual and nonviolent form. As the number of people who own no means of production expands, elections are likely to be won by parties that represent these interests. More and more people in most societies are wage and salaried workers and have no particular interest in maintaining the power of capitalist property owners. As long as the expanding welfare state is run efficiently and fairly, working people will support the parties that stand for universal social rights and economic participation.

Historical Accomplishments

Social democratic parties have enjoyed a considerable level of success in the more developed capitalist countries, with the marked exception of the United States. Throughout the twentieth century, they have had a record of expanding rights and social services. In Scandinavia and northern Europe in particular, they have had a key role in building well-functioning welfare states. The very high standard of living of these regions is, in large part, due to the parties' ability to distribute resources equitably among the population.

Sweden Sweden illustrates the social democrats at their most effective and successful. The discussion of social democracy in Sweden is based on a number of sources (Esping-Andersen, 1985; Heclo and Madsen, 1987; Jenson and Mahon, 1993; Milner, 1989; Pontusson, 1987; Tilton, 1990).

By the 1920s, the social democratic party had a large electoral base that had grown as Sweden industrialized, in sectors such as iron ore mining, steel, wood

products, and shipbuilding. When the Great Depression in the 1930s left 30 percent of the Swedish workforce unemployed, the party became a major force in
the society. From the 1930s to 1976 and again in the 1980s, it was the governing
party in Sweden. It was closely allied with the LO (the wage workers' trade
union organization). A corporatist structure emerged in Sweden in which the
LO entered into nationwide collective bargaining with the employers' federation, under the auspices of a government that was supportive of workers' demands, yet prepared to accept the continuation of private ownership of firms.
Ninety percent of Swedish firms continued to be privately owned.

The socialist government, however, instituted many social services, in
health care, parental leaves, job retraining, and so on. The term **People's Home**
came into use to describe the feeling of security, collective responsibility, and
belonging in a society created by this structure. Taxes were high; the "social
wage"—the value of services and benefits—helped to equalize income distribution. Sweden became a society with a socialist governing party, an extensive
system of social benefits, and a capitalist economy. The other Nordic countries
have similar arrangements, although with a less continuous history of social
democratic governance, and by late twentieth century enjoy the highest living
standards in the world (Jenson and Mahon, 1993; Thurow, 1993: 204).

In other areas of Europe, socialist and labor parties have not been as uni-
formly successful, neither being elected as consistently nor appearing as efficient and uncorruptable as the Scandinavian parties. However, the Labour
Party in England established universal health care and improved access to education after World War II. Other parties with a social democratic orientation
became influential in post-World War II European politics by pushing states to
improve standards of living for working people.

The Support Base   The support base of these parties continued to include the
industrial working class, but the parties also succeeded in drawing support
from the "middle strata"—white-collar workers, employed professionals, government employees, and other salaried workers. Even some fractions of capital
supported their program because their administrations (in northern Europe)
were efficient, public-spirited, and a major cause of high living standards.

For most of the social democratic parties, the union movement formed a key
link or "transmission belt" between the party and the support base in the working class. Strong unions, generally united in a national union federation or umbrella group, brought individual workers into a larger political structure and
helped to organize electoral support for the social democratic party. The unions
and the parties together created a working-class culture that was politically sophisticated and unified around the idea of class solidarity. Although their formal education was often limited, industrial workers shared an understanding
of the political process and participated in organizations with an ideology and
strategy of social change; in marxist terms, workers who participated in socialist parties and unions developed a **counter-hegemonic consciousness** that systematically challenged capitalism and liberalism.

North Americans sometimes refer to European nations that have or had socialist governing parties as "socialist"; for example, many Americans believe erroneously that Sweden is a socialist country. It is true that Sweden has had a long history of a social democratic governing party and many socialist policies like public services and publicly owned utilities and infrastructure; but, even in Sweden, 90 percent of enterprises remain privately owned. It would be more accurate to describe these nations as **capitalist democracies with elements of socialism.**

In the United States, the absence of institutions like universal health care, child care, family leave, stipends for university education, and strong labor unions is probably largely a result of the absence of a social democratic party prepared to fight for public policies of this type. For complex historical reasons that include the ethnic and racial division of the working class, the pervasive strength of liberal ideology, and the two-party constitutional framework, socialist parties remained small in the United States (Davis, 1986).

Dilemmas

The Movement in Power: Structural Constraints   Social democracy originally defined itself as a process of transition from capitalism to socialism. But the realities of modern capitalist countries are such that this process promises to be very slow. Social democrats who hold political power have to accommodate themselves to the capitalist economy. Their programs are, in effect, transformed into policies of extending public services, developing public infrastructure (like rail systems, airlines, and utilities), and identifying optimal levels of taxation.

It became clearer in the 1970s and 1980s that an "excessive" amount of taxation, public sector expansion, and labor militancy would lead to capital flight, disinvestment, and a downturn in the economy. Such an economic downturn easily led to losses at the polls for social democratic parties. In other words, social democrats would not really move toward a transition to socialism without precipitating considerable opposition. The opposition from capital translated itself into less investment and a worsening economic climate, which resulted in many votes against the social democrats. It appeared as though capitalism in the liberal democracies had a built-in homeostatic device: Too much "creeping socialism" would lead to a loss of investor confidence, which would lead to an economic downturn, and eventually to voter disenchantment with social democrats.

Social democratic parties tend to deal with this problem by reducing their efforts to shift the balance of power toward labor and giving up on their expansion of the public sector. This retreat makes it difficult to sustain their claims to be socialists. It raises doubts whether they are really committed to a transition to socialism and whether such a transition could ever really be carried out by gradual means. They face a dilemma: Carry on with socialist policies but risk losing voter support or maintain voter support by backing down on policies that threaten to shrink profit margins and precipitate reduced investment (Miliband, 1969; Przeworski, 1987).

This dilemma is serious for social democratic parties in the developed and prosperous capitalist nations; it is overwhelming for mass socialist parties in the poorer capitalist nations. A victory by a socialist party (or even mildly reformist party) is likely to be "read" by capitalists as a step toward limitation on profit and property. Measures designed to redistribute income, expand social services, and strengthen the rights of labor in a society with a small economic "pie" are extremely threatening to capitalists and their allies in the middle class. In Sweden or Germany, the economy is strong and capitalists may accept certain policies of social democrats like high taxes or more regulation; in a nation like Chile or Guatemala, capitalists are not prepared to make concessions. In addition, international credit agencies like the World Bank and the International Monetary Fund have been very reluctant to extend loans to countries that are defined as limiting free markets or spending too much on social services.

Under these circumstances, capital flight takes place as investors shift their money abroad, inflation takes off, and the economic situation worsens—at first, for the middle class, but eventually for everyone. In this situation, the socialists in office in poorer countries run the risk not only of losing elections, but also of succumbing to a military coup. In addition to the economic risks of embarking on socialist policies in a poor nation, reformers during the cold war period faced the likelihood of U.S. intervention, as happened in Chile with the overthrow of Salvador Allende's democratically elected socialist government in 1973.

In short, while social democratic parties and reform movements appeared outside the most affluent core societies, their successes were far more limited there, their access to state power was sporadic and discontinuous, and their ability to implement social democratic policies highly constrained.

The Changing Support Base   In addition to these structural constraints on socialist movements as governing parties, social democrats are now facing a changing support base. The historical strength of the parties rested on the alliance between the political party and the union movement, with both based solidly in the industrial working class. The unions created a grass roots sustaining structure for a party. The party and the unions together contributed to a working-class political culture and were, in turn, deeply rooted in working-class culture as a whole.

As the working class in late twentieth-century societies becomes fragmented and scattered into different sectors, the parties lose their cohesive character. In England, for example, the Labour Party is facing a diversifying base and a weakened trade union support structure (Smith and Spear, 1992). In Sweden, the Social Democrats have lost some of their working-class base, while gaining middle-class voters. Despite the gains among middle-class voters, the net effect may be a decline in party strength as the party becomes less unified in its programs and disconnected from its trade union support structure.

Working-class culture, especially working-class political culture, has diminished throughout Europe and the United States (where it was weaker from the start). In part, popular culture and the media have displaced it from the hearts and imaginations of young people. Class lines may still exist in an objective sense, in terms of economic relationships, but they are no longer clearly reflected in a "them and us" mentality, let alone a sophisticated class consciousness expressed in working-class organizations. The subjective or cultural side of class divisions is blurred. Culture no longer comes in neatly distinct proletarian and bourgeois versions. Even new cultures of class and ethnic resistance, like punk, metal, and hip hop, are not integrally connected to unions or to socialist politics (Gaines, 1992; Willis, 1990).

The communities that nurtured the working-class culture have dispersed through gentrification, deindustrialization, economic restructuring, and even the rising affluence and suburbanization of the working class. At the level of the individual, in the process of forming one or more collective identities, sudden shifts in roles and uncertain labor markets have disrupted stable working-class identity. A young person may be a community college student, a fast-foods worker, a feminist or a fundamentalist (or even both—Stacey, 1991), a rock musician, a small entrepreneur in the informal economy—all positions and interests that may change quickly and unpredictably. They are not tied to stable class-identified organizations like unions, and many of them have a blurred or contradictory class location (Wright, 1994). Under these conditions, the support base for socialist movements presents formidable obstacles for organizers.

MARXISM-LENINISM AND REVOLUTIONARY SOCIALISM

Historical Origins: Socialism in Russia

As mass socialist parties expanded and enjoyed a certain measure of success in western Europe, socialists continued to look for alternative models in order to address the problems that mass parties faced in tsarist Russia and other authoritarian states. In these states, socialist parties were illegal and, indeed, little could be accomplished by any party since the powers of elected bodies were virtually nonexistent. Even if socialists had been allowed to organize freely, their hopes of success were limited by the fact that the majority of Russians were poor peasants. The peasants dreamed of taking over their landlord's estate and of freedom from the oppressive forces of the state that taxed them and forced them into military service. Their circumstances were vastly different from those of skilled craftspeople and industrial workers in western Europe. They were not literate, had not experienced interdependent and cooperative work in factories, and were often superstitious and fatalistic. They fit Marx's description of French peasants—"potatoes in a sack"—in other words, although they were all alike, they were not interdependent members of a more complex association that could form the basis of socialism.

Russian socialists debated whether it was possible to build a mass party in Russia and they pondered how a transition to socialism could come about at all. Some theorists thought that Russia would first have to attain a more developed stage of capitalism. In this process, wealth would gradually shift out of agriculture into industry, the middle classes would establish liberal democratic institutions, and the peasants would be transformed into an industrial proletariat. Only then would socialism be a feasible project (Gurley, 1975).

Leninism: Basic Ideas

Lenin became the leading theorist of the majority wing (Bolsheviks) of the Russian Social Democrats. He challenged the belief that a gradual process of capitalist development and political liberalization was a necessary condition for a transition to socialism in Russia. His challenge was formulated as a new analysis of Russia and of the revolutionary process in general.

State and Revolution   First, he dismissed the strategy of the mass party and involvement in electoral processes on the basis of the following analysis. All states are functionally adapted to preserve a specific type of class order. They are coercive apparatuses designed to keep one class in economic, political, and cultural power. A revolutionary class cannot just "use" the preexisting state apparatus; it is not designed for the revolutionary program. The revolutionary class must dismantle the existing state apparatus and construct a new one, adapted to the new condition of society and the purposes of the new ruling class; for instance, the French and American revolutionaries—the bourgeoisie—violently overthrew the monarchy and replaced it with a republic. The bourgeoisie could not use the absolutist monarchy for its own interests or to implement its overall vision of society.

Socialists can use liberal democratic institutions to get themselves elected into office but, once elected, they will never be able to carry out an expropriation of capitalist property or establish socialism. The capitalist state is designed to protect and serve capital; it cannot be gradually and peacefully converted into a socialist state. Trying to keep the existing apparatus and implement socialism through it will lead either to an inability to restructure society or to a violent counterrevolution. (The discussion about Sweden and Chile on pp. 163–166 suggests that Lenin's analysis may be accurate.) Therefore, Lenin was not disturbed by the fact that Russia had no democratic institutions for socialists to "work through" (Lenin, 1974).

The Vanguard Party   Lenin's second consideration was his concept of the **vanguard party.** His observations of working-class movements in Europe suggested to him that workers left to their own devices rarely develop a class consciousness and a level of organization beyond that of forming trade unions and engaging in "spontaneous" actions like mass strikes, demonstrations, and so on. Neither union organizing nor spontaneous actions involve the recognition that a socialist revolution is, above all, a capture and reorganization of the state. Only a political party with a theoretical overview of state and society can spearhead such a revolution. Lenin believed that a vanguard party was more suited to this task than a mass electoral party.

The concept of the vanguard party allowed the Bolsheviks to "do an end run" around the problem of the low level of consciousness of the Russian masses; the vanguard party would lead them and actively raise their con-

sciousness. Its formulation of political theory and its guidance in political practice would speed up the process of revolution. It would not be necessary to
"wait around" while determined economic processes gradually created new
forms of consciousness or opened up new political possibilities. Thus, Lenin's
concept of the vanguard party put weight on the "voluntaristic" side of marxist theory, the emphasis on human agency in history, in contrast to the theories
of the Second International, which emphasized the determined processes of
structural change (Lenin, "What is to be Done?" in Tucker, 1975:12–115).

Imperialism   The third element of Lenin's thought was the theory of **imperialism.** Lenin focused on the global expansion of capitalism. Capitalism remained
a single system, but its development was uneven; some regions remained "backward" not only because of their traditional cultures, but also because imperialism needed regions with low labor costs, low raw material costs, and opportunities for investment. A transition to socialism did not have to begin in the most
advanced regions of this global system; it could begin in a backward region,
since capitalism in the age of imperialism was really a single system.

A socialist revolution in a backward region would have to carry out certain
tasks that capitalism had already accomplished in the advanced regions. One
task was **primitive accumulation,** the extraction of a surplus from agriculture
that would provide resources for industrial development. A second task was
the spread of literacy and more enlightened attitudes among the mass of the
population. Lenin thought that a socialist revolution in a backward society like
Russia could speed up the development process, compressing two processes:
accomplishing the modernization that had elsewhere been associated with capitalism *and* building socialism. An attack on the capitalism of the advanced, imperial powers could begin by "subtracting" the backward superexploited regions from the global system.

The Revolutionary Socialist Model

The victory of the Bolsheviks in the Russian Revolution supported the leninist
model. Although the revolution did not succeed in any developed industrial
capitalist country, the example of Russia made a powerful impression in the
countries that were backward and exploited as colonies or as dependent regions
within the global capitalist system. Revolution and rapid industrialization
seemed possible, and the vanguard party seemed a feasible model of organization and strategy. There was no need to work through the liberal institutions
that were designed to thwart socialism or wait until a region was economically
and culturally like the developed capitalist nations. This was an unlikely
prospect since imperialism depended on the maintenance of backwardness,
poverty, and repression in its periphery.

This view of the transition to socialism was referred to as **marxism-leninism.** Since it emphasized revolution rather than evolution or gradual development as the mechanism of the transition, it is also referred to as **revolutionary
socialism.** The Bolsheviks in Russia called themselves **Communists,** referring
to the long-term goal of communism as Marx envisioned it; they understood

that they were still engaged in building socialism and that communism was not likely in the near future.

After the Russian Revolution, socialist parties throughout the world splintered into mass parliamentary parties and parties that followed the vanguard model; the latter usually called themselves **Communist parties** and it is from this choice of name that the common image of communism derives. Communists became the term for participants in many revolutionary socialist movements and movements with a marxist-leninist ideology. The most powerful parties and movements aligned themselves with the Communist Party of the Soviet Union (Abendroth, 1972; Gruber, 1974). Smaller parties, movements, and sectarian groups splintered off over specific points of ideology or stands toward the Soviet Union.

Problems of the Soviet Model   In the Soviet Union and other nations in which Communist parties came to power, single-party states were formed. The state apparatus became controlled by the party, which used it to carry out its conception of how to establish socialism. Until World War II, this situation prevailed only in the Soviet Union, which increasingly became a model for political and economic development for other revolutionary socialist states. This model had several key characteristics, most notably a repressive single-party political system and an economic development plan focused on the rapid buildup of heavy industry.

The Single-Party Political System   The vanguard party became increasingly detached from its potential constituents—workers and peasants. In the original leninist conception, it was to be organically linked to the masses, leading them by example, persuasion and dialogue, and gradual development of socialist consciousness. Instead, it became increasingly repressive, and in the Stalinist period (late 1920s to 1953), it became the vehicle of dictatorship. Afterward, especially during the Brezhnev era (1960s to early 1980s), it turned into an apparatus of careerists, the **nomenklatura** as it came to be called in Russia and eastern Europe; instead of leading the society by an example of commitment and vision, it became a stratum of managers dedicated to preserving their own power and privileges. Without a civil society in which problems and policies could be openly debated, there was no mechanism for revitalizing the party.

Current debates point in many different directions to explain this process: the problems inherent in the leninist conception of a single-party vanguard model, in which there are no public and organized opposition forces permitted in the society; the extreme conditions of civil war, economic hardship, and foreign support for counterrevolutionaries that beset the Soviet Union and almost all subsequent revolutionary socialist states; the "secrecy, hierarchy, and discipline" that were necessary for the revolutionary movements to come to power (Leys, 1994); the absence of liberal democratic traditions in practically all societies that had socialist revolutions, first and foremost of them tsarist Russia, in which an absence of a democratic political culture combined with mass illiteracy and popular mentalities of submissiveness, fatalism, ignorance, and apathy to permit autocratic rule (Brovkin, 1987; Farber, 1990; Marcuse, 1961; Medvedev, 1977; Moore, 1965).

Socialist Accumulation: Heavy Industry and Central Planning   A second feature of the model was the attempt to move rapidly from an agrarian society to heavy industry, with production in all sectors specified through central planning. In the Soviet Union this leap was executed in the late 1920s and 1930s. The foundation for primitive **socialist accumulation** was laid by the rapid and forced collectivization of agriculture during which millions of people died in executions, labor camps, and famines. The huge collective farms formed in this process had to contract to sell their output to the state, thus providing a resource base for industrial takeoff concentrated in coal, steel, capital goods, and military production (Carr, 1967; Gurley, 1975; Moore, 1965).

The consequences of these policies were persistent imbalances in the Soviet economy, with a lagging agricultural sector and an underdeveloped consumer goods sector. These initial and inflexible economic and technological directions also contributed to later difficulties in retooling for innovation in areas like electronics, which became the global cutting-edge technologies after the Second World War. The great leap of combined development—a model that was to compress capitalist and socialist development and enable the revolutionary socialist state to catch up to advanced capitalist societies—had serious costs, both in immediate human terms and in imbalanced, inflexible economic outcomes.

Later revolutionary socialist states, especially China and Vietnam, tried to remedy some of these problems by a stronger focus on agricultural development. Yugoslavia experimented with **market socialism,** a system that combined nonprivate ownership of firms with market mechanisms rather than consolidated production priorities and resource allocation through a central plan (Bertsh and Ganshow, 1976; Denitch, 1994).

These models tended to produce systems of health care and education that were good or even outstanding, considering their initial low level of development and productivity, but they lagged behind capitalist market economies in consumer goods production and ability to innovate (Kornai, 1989).

Geopolitics after the Russian Revolution

The relationship of the socialist parties, the Communist parties, and the spectrum of liberal parties has been stormy and volatile.

The Popular Front and the Fight against Fascism   At first, Communist parties aligned with the Soviet Union refused to cooperate with socialist or liberal parties. By the mid-1930s, the threat of fascism in Nazi Germany, Fascist Italy, and Japan became so strong that the Popular Front was developed to link socialist, Communist, and liberal parties against fascism, forming a precursor to the alliance between the Soviet Union and the western liberal states that won in World War II (Carr, 1982).

In this period (from the mid-1930s to the onset of the cold war in the late

1940s), Communist parties in many countries began to adapt their goals more to national problems and issues. For example, in the United States the Communists had an important role in organizing industrial unions and in the early stages of the Civil Rights Movement (Garner, 1977; Healey and Isserman, 1990; Richmond, 1972).

The Cold War   The alliance between Communists and liberals fell apart at the end of the war. The defeat of the Fascist Axis powers left the globe divided into two hostile spheres, the relatively small Soviet sphere, consisting of the Soviet Union and the eastern European countries where the Soviets enabled Communist parties to come to power, and the rest of the world, which was capitalist but otherwise highly heterogeneous in terms of economic development and political systems. The renewed hostility between the Soviet Union and the capitalist nations came to be called the **cold war;** it had an immediate effect on all movements and parties of the left.

In the East   In the Soviet sphere of influence, eastern Europe, non-Communist parties (liberal and social democratic parties) were suppressed, often in violent purges. Because of the dominance of the Communist Party in these nations, westerners called them Communist countries. The ruling parties used the term socialist, since they defined themselves as building a real socialism, in contrast to the merely envisioned socialism of the left in the west.

Western Europe   Communist parties were ousted from government in Italy and France in the late 1940s. In these countries (and several other western nations), they had made a decision to form aboveground mass parties that would engage in the same electoral process as the socialist and liberal parties, but they were barred from the governing coalition of parties. Employers attempted to fire and blacklist Communist activists. The parties remained legal, however, and attracted a large working-class base. They were associated with a large sector of the union movement and had a role in sustaining a working-class culture of opposition to capitalism (Hellman, 1988; Sassoon, 1981).

In this region, they began to converge with the socialist parties in strategy, organizational form, and even ideology. By the 1970s, this type of Communist Party was sometimes referred to as Euro-Communist; the term meant not only that the party was located in western Europe, but also that it had become similar to the social democratic parties in the region. The Euro-Communist parties renounced the concept of "dictatorship of the proletariat" and began to theorize a gradual transition from capitalism to socialism in the most developed nations (Blackmer and Tarrow, 1975; Hellman, 1988).

For example, in the late 1970s, the Italian Communists attempted to construct "the historic compromise"; that is, to work out a formula with the Christian Democratic ruling party for participating in the governing of Italy. Red Brigade terrorism was a major factor in closing off this opportunity, as the ultra-left brigades murdered politicians involved in the policy, most notably Aldo Moro, the head of the Christian Democrats (Hellman, 1988; Sassoon, 1981).

There was considerable variation in the extent to which Communist parties adopted the social democratic model. In Italy, the party shifted fairly successfully, distancing itself from the Soviet Union, democratizing its structure, and accepting the decline of traditional working-class political culture. By the 1990s, it had even changed its name to the Democratic Party of the Left. In France, the leadership tried to sustain the original model, and the party markedly lost electoral strength (Jenson and Ross, 1988).

The Suppression of Communist Parties   In some regions, Communist parties remained or became illegal and, therefore, were unable to form large parties with an involvement in electoral politics that characterized western Europe in the cold war period.

For example, a Communist movement with a revolutionary strategy persisted after Greece resisted the Nazis in World War II; but the Yalta accords defined Greece as in the western sphere of influence, so the Soviet Union did not intervene when the Communists were defeated and uprooted in a civil war with British intervention on the anti-Communist side. Similarly, Communist movements were suppressed in violent operations in postwar Philippines, Malaysia, and in 1964, Indonesia.

In the United States, individual Communists were driven out of major institutions—unions, the movie industry, universities, and so on—during the late 1940s and the 1950s. They were fired and blacklisted; that is, refused employment anywhere in the industry in which they had worked. This purge is usually referred to as McCarthyism after Senator Joe McCarthy who was its best-known proponent, but it was part of a larger and well-organized process. One of the most important phases of this process actually began before McCarthy's rise to national prominence, and that was the purge of Communists from labor unions (Aronowitz, 1973; Caute, 1978; Healey and Isserman, 1990).

Revolutionary Socialism in the Third World

In the nations that were still part of colonial empires, Communist parties became the core groups of many **national liberal movements,** both before and after the Second World War. In these regions, the leninist model seemed very promising; it spoke to all the problems that beset the struggles for independence and better economic and social conditions. The liberal model of politics and society seemed hypocritical as long as the liberal capitalist nations were colonial powers. Communist parties, usually organized along leninist vanguard lines, had an important role in independence movements in Vietnam, Indonesia, and the Philippines (Anderson, 1993).

The Chinese revolution, under the leadership of Mao Zedong and the Chinese Communist Party, also demonstrated the efficacy of this model with its seizure of the state in 1949 and its dramatic and violent restructuring of society, especially the expropriation of landowners, many of whom were killed. On the basis of the Chinese experience, some revolutionary socialist movements became **maoist**—that is, they revised their marxist-leninist model with an emphasis on the peasantry as a revolutionary class. Even postcolonial nations with a primarily nationalist ideology looked to the Soviet Union and China for a model of a single-party political system and a centrally planned economy (Chaliand, 1989).

Marxism-leninism also appealed to the subordinate classes in nations that had a long history of political independence but had remained economically dependent on the developed capitalist nations. These nations were primarily in Latin America and the Caribbean.

Here, two interrelated problems confronted movements. One was the uneven distribution of wealth. Wealth, land, and political power remained concentrated in the hands of a small oligarchy, while the masses of people lived in conditions of terrible poverty. The second problem was dependency within the global economy. Many of these nations produced a limited number of tropical foodstuffs (like coffee or sugar) or minerals (like copper in Chile or tin in Bolivia). Global markets for these products were controlled by transnational firms, and quotas were often set by the powerful developed capitalist buyer nations. External dependency was connected to internal inequality; the wealthy classes profited in this limited and unequal international trade as plantation owners, mine owners, or commercial brokers (Frank, 1972).

Marxism-leninism spoke directly to these problems, promising both a socialist redistribution of land and other productive resources *and* a path of development that would break out of imperialist exploitation. The Cuban revolutionary example inspired insurgents throughout the hemisphere (Castañeda, 1993; Wolf, 1969; Zeitlin, 1967).

In short, revolutionary socialism, usually in one form or another of marxism-leninism, came to have a powerful influence on movements in the regions of peripheral capitalism throughout the postwar period. The vanguard party, the idea of leaping over the stage of capitalist development, and the hopes that national autonomy could be combined with socialism were ideological themes central to insurgent movements in eastern and southeastern Asia, Latin America, and Africa (Walton, 1983).

Examples of these movements include the Huks and later the New People's Army in the Philippines; the movements of small revolutionary *focos* in Cuba, Guatemala, Bolivia, and Colombia, and (at a later date) the larger Guerrilla Army of the Poor in Guatemala, the maoist Shining Path in Peru, and the Sandinistas in Nicaragua; the New Jewel movement that came to power in Grenada; and the insurgencies against Portuguese colonialism in Angola, Mozambique, and Guinea-Bissau. These movements were by no means identical, nor did they mechanically apply earlier marxist-leninist models (Black, 1984; Fagen , Deere, Coraggio, 1986). They all made an effort to adapt the general model to the specific conditions of their own nations—the problems of the peasantry, the form of economic dependence in the global marketplace, the readiness of middle classes to become allies, and so on. They were keenly aware of changing conjunctural factors, including the willingness of the United States to get involved in counterinsurgency operations, which had waned during the post-Vietnam era of the 1970s and then reawakened in the Reagan period (Halliday, 1989).

Some of these revolutionary socialist movements in the Third World (especially in Latin America) broke with the Communist parties that existed in their nation or colonial region. They moved away from the strategy of the Communists, which was usually to build a base in a union movement, try to remain a legal party, and form alliances with nationalist-populist parties (Castañeda, 1993). In some cases, like Guatemala in the later 1950s and 1960s, the Communist strategy was not feasible because the regime repressed all forms of the left (Black, 1984). In other cases, like Cuba, young leftists felt impatient with the Communist strategy; the prospect of slowly building a support base in a relatively small class of wage workers seemed less attractive than other strategies such as the revolutionary *foco*—the band of armed insurgents—or the mass guerrilla army of poor peasants (Castañeda, 1993).

The major successes of revolutionary movements were not in Latin America but in the former colonial regions in Southeast Asia and Africa, where they combined with nationalist insurgencies against the French and later the United States, in Vietnam, Laos, and Cambodia; and against the Portuguese in Mozambique, Angola, and Guinea-Bissau. Other nations joined the ranks of socialist-oriented states through internal processes, including coups by military officers with marxist ideas, for instance, in Benin (Africa) and Suriname (South America).

Movements became embroiled in the cold war on a global basis, especially during the 1970s and 1980s (Halliday, 1989). The First World (the developed capitalist nations) battled against the Second World (the nations of "real socialism" under the leadership of Communist parties) in the Third World (regions that were only beginning their economic development and had not yet chosen one of the two leading models). States and movements in the Third World that opposed Communism looked to the United States; such forces had to claim to be democratic to legitimize themselves with the media and the public in the market democracies, even when the regimes they instituted were repressive and authoritarian. Revolutionary movements and the states they formed sought support from the Soviet Union, or, in fewer instances, China. These forces had to claim to be socialist, even when they could not or would not introduce many of the features of socialism specified in marxist-leninist theory, such as a more egalitarian distribution of resources, technological modernization, and the organization of a party that could reach, involve, and lead the masses. As noted in Chapter 4, "Movements, Societies, and States," breaking with the logic of global markets was nearly impossible for many of the smaller revolutionary states.

Whether they aligned themselves with the capitalist or the Communist nations or remained nonaligned, many Third World states faced problems in economic development and in building national institutions. The societies continued to be divided into a large poor majority and a small elite. The elites included large business owners, leading government officials, and top military officers; the exact composition varied, depending in part on the socialist or capitalist orientation of the regime. Ethnic divisions also presented obstacles to creating democratic institutions and organizing an effective public sector, as defined in either socialist or liberal ideology. Regardless of their geopolitical alignment, the states' divided social structures and unfavorable position in the global economy increased the probability of government corruption and authoritarian rule, ethnic conflicts, and military coups (Leys, 1994).

From one perspective, these movements and states were pawns in the cold war, promoted by the superpowers for strategic objectives. From another point of view, movements, parties, and states in the Third World played off the superpowers against each other to obtain aid, loans, military hardware, and other resources while their ideological allegiances remained ambiguous and in some cases (such as the Siad Barre regime in Somalia) changeable and opportunistic.

The number of **states of a socialist orientation** grew in successive waves of revolutions through the 1970s, until, by 1980, there were about two dozen such nations; the exact number varied according to observers' criteria of socialist orientation and the assessment of how far and decisively each nation had moved along the road to socialism (Halliday, 1989). Many of them were small and very poor, like Guinea-Bissau and Benin in western Africa. All of them, including the larger ones like Cuba and Vietnam, had made the transition to socialism under difficult circumstances, including civil wars, embargoes, and problems in transforming dependent economies. In the 1980s, the Reagan doctrine meant that the United States directly or indirectly supported armed counterinsurgencies as well as internal countermovements against the socialist-oriented Third World states, most notably the contra war against the Sandinistas in Nicaragua.

The Third World socialist states' need for economic and military support made them a burden on the Soviet Union. Faced with its own economic problems and the inability to keep up with the Reagan administration's escalation of the arms race, the Soviet Union began to withdraw its support from revolutionary movements and states and forced them into negotiations with counterinsurgent forces. By 1990, the marxist-leninist road to socialism appeared to be unsuccessful both in the semiperipheral areas (like the Soviet Union and eastern Europe) and in the contested Third World (Castañeda, 1993; Halliday, 1989).

The failure of the marxist-leninist model has reorganized our sense of geography. During the cold war, there was a First World/west (the capitalist democracies), a Second World/east (the Communist or "real" socialist states), and a Third World in which capitalism and revolutionary socialism contested each other. First, Second, and Third World are no longer coherent categories; the Second World is essentially gone, and the Third World turns out to be highly heterogeneous. Now all regions of the world are integrated into a global system of markets and states that has many gradations of prosperity and democracy. At the top there are still the core market democracies, the former First World where much of the well-off quarter of the globe's population is concentrated (Thurow, 1993). At the bottom of the structure are very poor nations that have growing levels of absolute poverty and are ruled by states that are both repressive and disorganized (Leys, 1994). In between is great diversity and instability. The middle levels include some post-Communist nations like Hungary and the Czech Republic that may join the prosperous market democracies. Other post-Communist states face troubled futures in both their economic and political systems, and they may end up like the former Third World in their quality of life (Przeworski, 1991). The growing economies of East Asia—the "little dragons" of South Korea, Taiwan, Singapore, and Malaysia—are rising rapidly, though some of these nations are still marked by inequalities and authoritarian political institutions. In the middle of the global spectrum are also developing nations like Egypt, Mexico, the Philippines, Brazil, and India that have to cope with high levels of poverty, growing populations, and enormous structural pressures on their political systems, so that democratic institutions exist only in fragile or partial forms. In short, the entire global system is no longer understandable in terms of a few clear categories, like First, Second, and Third World. It is in both economic and political flux, economic and political changes are not associated with each other in any simple way, and it is hard to predict changes in the system as a whole (Halliday, 1989; Przeworski, 1991; Thurow, 1993).

THE NEW LEFT

The New Left was a series of movements that emerged to challenge "the system" in most developed market democracies from the late 1950s to the early 1970s. It drew on the traditions of radical democracy and anarchist movements as well as socialism. In many ways, its emergence heralded the decline of the older forms of the left, the fragmentation of the working-class base, and the fragmentation of socialist ideology into a more diffuse left-wing orientation. Because it was not a single movement or an organized party, its ideology is difficult to sum up neatly, but a few major themes stand out. My discussion is based on several sources (primarily, Aronowitz, 1973; Barkan, 1984; Breines, 1982; Caute, 1988; Flacks, 1971; Georgakas and Surkin, 1975; Gitlin, 1980, 1987; Gitlin and Hollander, 1970; Gorz, 1982; Harris, 1983; Isserman, 1987; Katsiaficas, 1987; Katz, 1992; Mallet, 1975; McAdam and Rucht, 1993; Miller, 1987; Sale, 1973; Sayres, 1984).

Ideology

Radical Democracy   One major theme of the New Left was the right of people to make the decisions that determine their lives. This phrase included many interrelated ideas. One was **radical democracy:** People should participate in the political system, directly as well as through elected representatives, and the public or political sphere should be one of lively debate, not elitist top-down decision making.

Community Organizing   Another idea of the New Left was the empowerment of communities, especially communities of the oppressed. These communities should throw off the yoke of an "internal colonialism" that oppressed and exploited people of color, the working class, and poor people within the developed capitalist nations. The communities would then build political and economic institutions that served the community itself, not the enterprises and power structures external to it.

The Global View: Anticapitalist and Antiwar   Many in the New Left considered themselves socialists; they were strongly opposed to corporate capitalism, especially the giant multinational corporations. At the transnational level, the New Left was a major component of the movement against the arms race and the movement within the United States (with support in western Europe) to end the war in Vietnam.

Emergence

New Strains, New Support Bases   The New Left was born out of several older movements in the nurturing environment of the post-World War II booms—the economic boom as well as the baby boom. The "old left," especially activists close to the Communist parties in the west, contributed to it; after Khrushchev's "crimes of Stalin" speech in 1956, many persons in or close to the Communist parties moved away from the parties, but hoped to revive the spirit and the ideas of the left in the west where they had been suppressed and had become dormant during the cold war. Social democrats also wanted to revitalize the ideas of their movement, detaching the promise of socialism from parties that seemed bureaucratized in Europe and ineffective in the United States.

The **peace movement** was a second major component in the formation of the New Left. In the late 1950s, nuclear war seemed to be a real possibility, a terrible threat that haunted everyday life. The media were full of articles about the A bomb and the H bomb. Schoolchildren practiced "nuclear war drills." (In my school, they were identical to tornado drills; we sat in the hall and learned to shield our faces from flying glass and debris.) The nuclear powers still conducted aboveground tests with accompanying fallout. This situation sparked movements against nuclear weapons development, testing, and the general threat of nuclear war; they were especially strong in Western Europe and Japan (Parkin, 1968). Activists in the peace movement often became activists in the New Left.

In addition to these transnational beginnings of the New Left were national circumstances that accounted for the shape of the emerging movements in a variety of countries. For example, in the United States, the Civil Rights Movement was the immediate predecessor of the New Left; young white people who had seen the poverty and oppressed conditions of black people wanted to go beyond ending de jure segregation in order to create a society with economic as well as juridical equality. They transferred skills they had learned in voter registration drives in the south to community organizing in the cities of the north. In Italy, some of the energy of the New Left came from Catholicism; students at Catholic universities searched for a way of living Christian ideals of social justice.

The climate of the later 1950s and the 1960s was favorable for the growth of a revitalized, decentralized, youth-oriented left. The United States and western Europe were enjoying an economic boom. Employment rates were high and good jobs were growing; young people felt a sense of economic security. The large baby-boom age cohort felt powerful and unified; millions of young people were going through the same experiences of education and coming of age. For the first time in human history, sizable numbers of people entered higher education; a mass of literate, self-confident young men and women congregated on university campuses. They debated ideas, dreamed that they could become agents of change, and believed in their own youthful idealism. At the same time, they were disappointed by the **multiversities,** the large institutions that they saw as factories for producing professionals and managers to serve capital and for conducting research for the military-industrial complex and the corporations. From the University of California at Berkley to the suburban campuses of the University of Paris, these institutions were impersonal, cold, and alienating. Marx's vision of workers developing class consciousness as they labored in giant factories seemed to be coming true for students, massed in the tens of thousands in these new "knowledge factories."

New Forms of Consciousness   New forms of consciousness could not be class consciousness as socialists once understood it. The spirit of the times was a consciousness more of youth than of class; much of the discourse of the movement called on an identity based on age: "Youth will make the revolution." The youthfulness of the New Left was expressed in its everyday life, in its enjoyment of "sex, drugs, and rock 'n' roll"; it was not a movement that was only about the economy and the political system, but about changing life in general.

Insofar as the movement was about class consciousness, it was an effort to understand the terms working class or proletariat in a new and expanded sense. The terms had to include the white-collar workers, salaried professionals, middle managers, and administrators who were being prepared by the multiversities to serve capital and the capitalist state. At the same time, the old working class was also changing. A new generation of workers no longer rushed into teen marriages or dreamed of neat little bungalows; like college students, they smoked dope, uncoupled sex from marriage and procreation, read underground comics, and despised authority (Aronowitz, 1973; Gorz, 1982, 1985).

And finally, and almost paradoxically, the new forms of consciousness included a sense of privilege in both a negative and a positive sense: On the one hand, young intellectuals saw how different their lives were from those of the truly oppressed and they were moved to change conditions of poverty and exploitation; on the other hand, they believed that their theoretical understanding of capitalist society as a system placed them in a strategic position to bring about revolution.

New Forms of Organization and Resource Mobilization   The structure most organizers in the New Left were drawn to was not the vanguard party; they had little use for the idea of party discipline or the centralization of power. On the contrary, the traditions they preferred were those of left-wing movements that seemed to have been left behind in the historical development of socialism—radical democracy in the American and French Revolutions, utopian socialism, anarchism, some features of populism in the United States, and the anarcho-syndicalism of the IWW. From these movements and their direct experience as community organizers, they took the ideas of democratic participation, opposition to hierarchy and bureaucracy, and decentralization.

The typical organization, especially in the United States, was a national network of loosely linked local chapters, collectives, or communes; for example,

Students for a Democratic Society (SDS), the leading organization of the New Left in the United States, had this form. It represents a transition from movements formed into mass organizations with members and distinct boundaries to movements that are constantly shifting and growing national networks of locally engaged activists. The New Left sometimes used the term commune to refer to some of these small local groups, but its meaning was totally different from the huge collective farms that characterized Chinese socialism of the period; commune meant a group of politicized hippies, in a slum apartment or a cabin in the woods, experimenting with sex and ideas.

Decentralized structures, idealism, youthful energy, personal experimentation, and disillusionment with corporations and multiversities formed a volatile mixture. The movement was well-suited to fast, spontaneous, and unpredictable public demonstrations and protests against structures of authority. Sit-ins in university offices, corporate headquarters, or draft stations were examples of these tactics. Larger demonstrations—like the marches on Washington to protest the war in Vietnam—could also be organized effectively through national networks.

The New Left and the media lived in hostile symbiosis; each needed and used the other, and the tactic of the demonstration was perfect for gaining media coverage. But, in the final analysis, the media made it difficult for the movement to communicate its message intelligently to larger audiences or to build a more coherent internal structure because the media liked "stars," while the movement wanted to be democratic (Gitlin, 1980).

Worker-Student Alliance?

In Europe, the great fear of political and economic elites was that students would be able to form an alliance with young workers; in other words, that the movement would spread from campuses to factories. Such a movement would have the ability to halt production, challenge capitalism, and destabilize the entire existing structure. A loose coordination of worker and student activism did emerge in France in the spring of 1968, and in Italy, in 1968 and 1969; the student movement in no sense controlled or organized the activities of workers, but waves of strikes and occasional factory seizures spread through industry. In France, General de Gaulle was able to mobilize a mass counterdemonstration and signaled the government's hardening opposition to the worker-student challenge. In Italy, the strike wave continued longer, led to larger gains by workers, and only gradually ebbed away (Barkan, 1984; Tarrow, 1989, 1991).

Hippies   In most of the other countries of western Europe and in the United States, the New Left was less successful in reaching young people in factories and offices as a political movement; but its **antiauthoritarian** and antirepressive vision did have a considerable force in society. The "hippie" side of the ideology, more than its message of political revolution and socialism, continued to influence youth and the popular imagination.

The Antiauthoritarian Legacy and the New Social Movements   The stagflation of the 1970s brought relief to embattled elites; the shrinking job market forced workers and students to give more attention to their immediate economic prospects and abandon youthful dreams. In the United States, the "Vietnamization" of the war under President Nixon (i.e., the withdrawal of U.S. troops) produced a winding down of the New Left's antiwar activity. Contrary to media images, a "big chill" did not necessarily descend on the ideas of the New Left; but changing personal and historical circumstances reduced the level of movement activity or shifted it into new areas (Fendrich and Lovoy, 1988).

The New Left remains visible, though sometimes in mutated, hidden, or surprising forms. Several movements that are now active—the women's movement, the environmental movement, the gay and lesbian movement—are successors of the New Left. Segments of these movements, both in the United States and Europe, see themselves as left wing. They sometimes explicitly combine socialism with the new themes of the movements—gender and sexual orientation issues, environmental concerns, peace activism, antiracism, and so on. Some of them describe themselves as **left libertarian** and explicitly oppose state power as much as they oppose capitalism. These political movements as well as many cultural currents like punk, alternative rock, and, in important respects, metal, inherited from the New Left its opposition to authority, structurelessness, and disrespect for convention (Gaines, 1992; Weinstein, 1991).

The New Left made it easier for subterranean cultural traditions of the west—sexual experimentation, drug use, homosexuality, and "bohemia" (reborn as beats and hippies)—to surface beyond the confines of small marginalized communities. The New Left brought together concerns of personal life with political and economic issues; and it merged the lifestyles (if not the political activities) of many students and young workers throughout the affluent market economies. In many ways, it was a prototype for the postmodern movement—decentralized, loosely networked in form, media-oriented, self-aware with a touch of irony, eccletic in its choice of ideological models, antiauthoritarian, and both local and global in its concerns.

These organizational characteristics presented a number of problems, however. The movements seemed to lack a strategy for accomplishing their goals. Their commitment to radical democracy turned them away from use of the state. Their rejection of bureaucracy and internal structures of authority led to decision making by informal cliques, usually composed of the most active participants, a process that was really no more democratic than the hierarchies of the old left (Freeman, 1973). Their mobilization tended to be rather shallow, in that there was little mass involvement on an ongoing basis as there had been in the older forms of the left, in the unions and the social democratic and Communist parties. Commenting on left-wing feminists within the Italian labor movement, one writer comments: ". . . the process [of gaining autonomy for women within the unions] had taken place without mass involvement of working women. (In common with other 'new social movements,' this was essentially a mobilization of 'participants.')" (Beccalli, 1994:104).

The new social movements are even weaker than the New Right in building a deeply rooted mass movement with a general strategy. The New Right was not consistently rooted in a mass base, but it had an ideological core that was able to use patched-together constituencies to focus political pressure at the national level; the more scattered components of the new social movements lack a central guiding organization.

THE LEFT AT THE END OF THE CENTURY

The current contemporary wisdom is that socialism was a failure. This view is something of an oversimplification (Blackburn, 1991). We can point to several distinct successes of socialism, considering both its social democratic and revolutionary variants.

Socialist Successes

Antinazism and the Defeat of the Axis   The partnership between the Soviet Union and the western liberal democracies was essential to the defeat of the Axis powers and, specifically, Nazism in the Second World War (1939–1945). In the final analysis, despite the apparent antagonism of socialism and the market democracies, both forces recognized a common heritage of faith in human progress, a faith unalterably opposed to the Nazi glorification of violent racism. Whatever strategic interests may have motivated Stalin, Churchill, and Roosevelt, I believe these common ideals were a major factor in this partnership.

Socialists, Communists, and Developed Capitalism   In the advanced capitalist nations, mass socialist movements have forced a more even distribution of wealth and a pattern of development that has produced high living standards and widespread prosperity. This achievement was accomplished by the social democratic parties. Communist parties were major contributors to this outcome by their organizing activities during the Popular Front and the post-World War II periods, when they followed the social democratic model after being stranded in the capitalist sphere; this role is most evident in the case of the Euro-Communist parties, especially in Italy (Jäggi, Müller, and Schmid, 1977; Sassoon, 1981).

Without the pressure of these social democratic and mass-based Communist parties and their associated trade union movements, it is likely that western Europe and Japan would have ended up with far more unequal distributions of wealth and more authoritarian capitalist regimes. Socialist movements were successful not in bringing about socialism but in making capitalism more equitable and democratic. Capitalist democracies with high living standards and political rights came into being only thanks to pressure from socialist movements. Here, we can see a certain degree of convergence with positive liberalism.

Decolonization   Revolutionary socialism had a major role in decolonization. Without the leadership of Communist parties in the colonial regions, post-World War II decolonization would have moved far more slowly. Furthermore, the existence of the Soviet Union spurred the western colonial powers to move more quickly in granting independence for fear that Soviet-aligned revolutionary movements would grow. The cold war forced concessions on the west. Even desegregation in the United States in the later 1950s and the 1960s received a boost from fears in Washington that the image of a racist America would drive newly independent nations toward the Soviets.

Socialism and the Physical Quality of Life   Within the "real" socialist nations formed by revolutions, the quality of life in terms of education, health care, and the condition of women was higher than in capitalist nations at a comparable level of economic development, at least until the 1980s. The state gave priority to education and health. Socialist ideology led to some improvements in the condition of women, especially in terms of legal rights and access to education, even though occupational segregation persisted as did low standards in reproductive and sexual rights. Comparing the Soviet Union or Cuba to the United States is obviously unfavorable to the socialist systems, since they had been at a lower standard of living at the time of their revolutions; a more logical comparison matches "real socialist" states with capitalist states that have a similar GNP per capita. This comparison shows that the socialist states made considerable progress in the physical quality of life. In a few key areas, like longevity and infant mortality, the gap was narrowed even with the advanced capitalist countries. At any given level of development, the socialist nations had better physical quality of life than comparable market economies, except among the very poorest and most recent additions to the bloc of nations of socialist orientation. Among market democracies, those with powerful social democratic parties like Sweden have the highest living standards (Ceresota and Waitzkin, 1986; Garner and Garner, 1994; Navarro, 1993).

The Enlightenment Legacy   Socialism is an important ideology and movement because it challenges liberalism on the basis of a similar philosophy; that is, as an heir to Enlightenment thought. It shares liberalism's heritage of secular thought, faith in the possibility of human progress, and a belief in a critical, questioning stand toward institutions. Without socialist pressures, liberalism could stagnate into a system of formal political equality accompanied by escalating class inequality. Without socialism, the main challengers of liberalism would once again become conservative currents of thought, especially religious fundamentalism. Socialism (along with feminism) offers an alternative to liberalism that seeks to preserve and fulfill liberalism's values rather than reverse them.

The Challenge to Socialism

Having identified some positive features of socialist movements in the twentieth century, I have some doubts about their future, which arise from two sources: The unsuccessful outcome of the great experiment of the Communist (or "real" socialist) nations, specifically the Soviet Union; and the changing character of the major support base of socialism, the working class.

The former issue means that socialists have to reconsider what models of transition to socialism make sense, both for the developed core nations and in the periphery, with its mix of developing economies and extremely poor nations. Social democracy can improve living standards, but there is little evidence that it can actually produce a qualitative shift from capitalism to socialism. Revolutionary socialism can succeed in the periphery as a strategy of taking power, but its ability to create satisfactory alternatives within the global market system appears limited; by satisfactory alternatives, I mean societies that are democratic and prosperous, rather than impoverished and coercive. At this time, socialist revolution has little appeal in liberal democracies with strong market economies. The New Left and the new social movements promise **democratic socialism** adapted to the ideals of developed liberal democratic societies, but seem to lack a convincing strategy for bringing it about.

The transformation of the global market economy and its accompanying changes in the nature of the working class is another problem. The working class has not disappeared, but its activities, composition, location, and political consciousness are different from its condition and character in the later nineteenth and early twentieth centuries. In the core economies, the proportion of industrial workers in the labor force is shrinking. New technologies, the globalization of production processes, and new capital and labor markets have disconnected labor from factories, communities, industrial regions, and even from nation-states (Reich, 1992). The current varieties of socialism do not seem to have kept up with these transformations of the support base, and even union organizing has lagged behind changing flows of investment.

The implications for socialism as a movement may be that its ideology will fragment and distinct pieces will recombine with the ideologies of other movements such as environmental movements, the peace movement, women's movement, civil rights, human rights movements, and ethnonationalist movements. These pieces may be contradictory and even opposed to each other. For example, ethnonationalist movements might preserve socialism's goal of managing the economy, but lose socialism's universal and humanistic values; meanwhile, the left libertarian movements could preserve these values, but lose the ability to influence state policies and shape economies. Conservatism fragmented and recombined with other ideologies as its social base—the landed classes—declined. Socialism has not lost its base in this way, and structural strains within capitalism have not disappeared; yet, socialist movements at the moment seem unsure how to respond to the restructuring of the economy, the transformation of the working class, and the loss of a proletarian collective identity.

POPULISM AND THE LEFT

Populism is an ideology and a type of mobilization that is sometimes associated with left-wing movements, but it is an ambiguous activism and there is considerable disagreement about its place in the spectrum of movements. Populism means an ideology of or for "the people." It is a view and a movement that calls for a mobilization against the rich and powerful in the name of the people. Populist discourse is strongly **antielitist.** Populism differs from socialism in that it uses the categories "rich and poor" or "elites and the people" and, usually, does not have an elaborated analysis of capitalism as a system. The ambiguity of the term "the people" allows populist movements to take on many forms and goals.

These multiple forms of populism, as well as the ambiguity of its defining ideas, causes disagreements among theorists about the nature and position of populism. The term populism is used differently by activists and scholars, and there is disagreement about whether it is fundamentally an egalitarian and democratic movement or a mobilization in which a mass of people is manipulated by authoritarian leaders.

Populist movements are sometimes defined as a division of the left, but they tend to have much vaguer ideologies than socialism. There is also some overlap among populism, positive liberalism, and radical democratic movements. Populist themes appear in a number of movements that are not left wing in any meaningful sense of the term. For example, fascist, nazi, nationalist, and religious fundamentalist movements may use elements of populist thought.

Populism is not currently a movement with a coherent ideology like the varieties of liberalism, socialism, or Islamic integralism. It is an element within movement ideologies or a mode of operating *rather than* a definable movement. It is a way of combining some themes of liberalism—especially positive liberalism—with themes of socialism and packaging them in a way that appeals to a divided support base. Socialism and liberalism have clear ideas about the shape of the economy: Socialism calls for public ownership and overall planning; liberalism calls for private ownership and markets, at times with government intervention. Populism as a movement and movements that use themes from populist thought do not have a clear vision of the economic sphere of their "good society."

Populism promises a better life, less economic inequality, and more political involvement for the people, the ordinary person outside the elite. For some theorists and activists, it is associated with mass mobilization *and* democratic participation; for other observers, this mobilization is an enthusiastic public response to symbols and leaders with little or no real mass involvement in discussion and decision making.

Its supporters see it as a movement that can bring together a wide spectrum of social groups that would not agree on a more rigorous, sharply defined socialist ideology. In this way, it can generate a mass base for economic reforms and for a reduction in economic inequality (Boyte and Riessman, 1986). Its antielitist themes can be used to rally potential supporters who favor more democracy, more citizen participation in government, and less top-down decision making by corporations, technocrats, and government bureaucrats.

Its critics say that populist movements are often devoid of real participation or power at the base of the movement. They believe that the vagueness of populist ideas makes possible the manipulation of supporters of populist movements by leaders. They point to the demagogic uses of populist discourse; antielitism can be used for intellectual and cultural leveling to a low common denominator. Antielitism, without a coherent program for reform, can produce cynicism about politics and government, the sort of sniping at politicians that is the stock-in-trade of talk radio. These kinds of antielitist attitudes rarely contribute to more democratic participation.

Antielitism can foment conspiracy theories about secret cabals running the country. Conspiracy theories are not scientific theories, but primitive conceptions of politics associated with fear, suspicion, alienation, and simplistic explanations of complex processes. In conspiracy theories, all political and economic outcomes are believed to be the result of deliberate and secret machinations by one or another small group of superpowerful people, usually associated with banking, intelligence agencies, or a specific ethnic group (often Arabs or Jews). A conspiracy mentality is often associated with the worldview of the radical right (Adorno, 1993; Ridgeway, 1990). Currently, in the United States, the Populist Party is a small movement organization that holds conspiracy theories about government, expounds anti-semitic views, and is part of the radical right.

The critics of populism point to the historical association of populism with right-wing movements and ethnic bigotry. They use the term authoritarian populism to refer to a manipulative set of appeals that promise mass political participation and more equality, but only deliver a stronger state—virtually the opposite outcome from the promises of more democracy.

For example, authoritarian populism appeared in the mobilizations that Juan Perón used to support his authoritarian rule in Argentina in the 1940s (Adelman, 1994; James, 1988; Ranis, 1993). Workers and poor people—the descamisados (the "shirtless ones")—supported Perónism and received benefits such as social services and higher wages; but they did not participate in democratic processes. In many ways, Perónist populism was a preemptive move to integrate the working class and discourage it from joining socialist or communist unions and parties.

History

A brief overview of the history of populist mobilizations will give the reader a sense of how ambiguous the term is and how populism is more a theme that can appear within diverse ideologies than a movement ideology in its own right.

The Populists in Europe and North America   Populist themes (as distinct from identifiable movements that actually used the term) appeared as early as the economic radicalism of artisans and small tradespeople in the period of the French Revolution. These rebellious classes were not socialists, but they opposed the powerful and wealthy—the mercantile classes, the large landowners, and the emerging owners of industrial capital. They wanted to make sure that they would not be economically squeezed out in the evolving structure of a capitalist society. They also clearly called for an extension of democracy and an end to their exclusion from politics, since voting and other forms of political participation were still confined to the wealthy.

Populism has been on the political scene as an identifiable movement and viewpoint since the late nineteenth century. At that time, distinct populist movements emerged, especially in North America. In the United States, the term was used specifically for movements of farmers and small business owners against large capitalist interests like banks, utilities, and railroads; populists called for government regulation of these enterprises to alleviate the economic pressure on the "little guy" (Garner, 1977; Hofstadter, 1955). Populist mobilizations, sometimes in an uneasy convergence with the Progressive Movement and/or socialism, led to reforms such as the regulation of interstate commerce and utilities.

By the twentieth century, the populist movement in the United States ebbed for several reasons. Some reforms had been accomplished. Given the difficulties of sustaining third-party mobilization within the U.S. political system, movement activists eventually entered the Democratic Party and influenced its policies rather than maintain a separate organizational structure. Black and white farmers did not work well together; white racism weakened the southern branch of the movement. Some of the populist support base turned its attention increasingly to cultural status-politics issues like prohibition and fundamentalism and away from the economic issues that had sparked the populist movement.

Latin American Populism   After the decline of the populist movement in the United States, movements with populist discourses emerged throughout Latin America, most notably the Perónists in Argentina (Adelman, 1994). These movements formed coalitions of the urban poor and some parts of the organized working class and the middle class. They promised more economic equality, less power for the landed oligarchy, and less dependence on foreign capital. They varied in the extent to which they were able (or willing) to deliver on these promises.

Probably the most effective populist leader was Mexico's Lázaro Cárdenas, who carried out land reform and nationalized the petroleum industry in the 1930s. In Argentina, Juan Perón supported domestic industrialization and more benefits for Argentina's working class. Both leaders created a dominant party, a strong state, and a pattern of corporatist rule through the mobilization of sectors like the trade unions, small business associations, and farmers.

Populism on the Right   Populist appeals became part of fascist and nationalist movements in Europe after the First World War. These movements excoriated capitalism—particularly banking and Jewish enterprises—but once in power did not institute socialist policies, though the state intervened in the economy, unemployment diminished, and some welfare measures were instituted to benefit the working class. Organizations like independent trade unions and parties of the left and center were suppressed; thus, in the case of these right-wing regimes, populism was completely disconnected from the goal of democratic participation. The Nazis used the term "Volk" to mean both "the people" and the "ethnorace." In Nazi ideology, populism was closely tied to racism and anti-semitism.

The New Left and Neighborhood Movements   In the United States, the New Left used populist language and images such as calls for "power to the people" and an antielite and antiexpert vision of participatory democracy and decentralized decision making (Gitlin, 1987).

After the New Left faded in the mid-1970s some of its populist momentum passed to coalitions of citizens and neighborhood groups (Boyte and Riessman, 1986). The socialist, anticapitalist elements of New Left ideology were muted in the process, but a wide range of people who were not students became involved in movements, especially local organizations. For example, they mobilized in opposition to expressway construction, urban renewal, bank redlining (a practice of denying home mortgage loans in certain neighborhoods that bankers deemed to be in decline), and other decisions by urban developers, government agencies, and financial institutions that threatened neighborhoods (Boyte and Riessman, 1986; Mollenkopf, 1983; Squires, Bennett, McCourt, and Nyden,

1987). There was some overlap and convergence among these local neighbor-hood movements and the new social movements, especially in their grass roots character, the formation of networks rather than bureaucratic organizations at the national level, and their somewhat volatile histories (Castells, 1983).

Many of these neighborhood movements illustrate the incorporation of a conservative spirit into left-wing movements. The movements grew out of the wish to keep neighborhoods from changing, and this outlook could mean op-position to government agencies like urban renewal departments, real estate developers in the private sector, and/or in the case of some white ethnic com-munities, the influx of African American and/or Latino residents and desegre-gation policies like busing (Rieder, 1985). The structural strains that urban working-class communities faced could potentially be framed in three distinct ways: support conservative mobilizations against government intrusions and government bureaucrats; support left-wing or socialist mobilizations against market forces and, specifically, real estate developers, speculators, and the cap-italist state—rather than big government; or justify racist mobilizations against new neighbors of color and against school busing and other desegregation poli-cies. Fortunately, most community organizations did not opt for racist activism.

Populist ideology brought together and blurred two distinct patterns of op-position to the kinds of changes that were taking place in the 1970s. One of these patterns was a potentially conservative mobilization that opposed positive lib-eralism and the expansion of government functions. The other pattern of op-position was directed against private sector forces that threatened neighbor-hoods; this opposition was potentially anticapitalist. Neighborhood activists felt that the federal and local governments were helping private sector devel-opers, especially through urban renewal policies; therefore, populist activists could unite an anticapitalist and an anti-big government framing of the issues (Squires et al., 1987). From the perspective of the left, the problem was that pop-ulist antigovernment framing ended up easily as an ideological position that supports conservative mobilizations: "government off our backs."

Populist Themes in the New Right   At the same time that the New Left, new social movements, and community organizations used the term populism and some of the ideas of populism, the New Right did the same. Antielitism and op-position to big government and the welfare state were major elements in the framing of New Right ideology. These two opposed ways of framing populism contended with each other in the 1970s and 1980s.

Both sets of movements pointed to the same structural and cultural strains, one putting a leftward spin to the problems, the other a rightward spin. For the left, the problem was the impact of the market, aided and abetted by the capi-talist state; capitalists influenced political elites with whom they shared social origins and/or economic interests. In this view, the welfare system was de-signed to defuse the demands of poor and working people (Piven and Cloward, 1977). The outcome of government and private sector coordination was a falling standard of living for working people, the corrosive impact of the market on communities, and a declining quality of life.

For the right, the problem was too much government, an oppressive tax burden, government waste, government agencies controlled by special interests, a welfare system designed by government bureaucrats and abused by welfare cheats, and so on (Lo, 1982).

Either spin had a certain populist twist to it. Both criticized elites, focused on concerns of the common man, viewed some of the institutions of positive liberalism and the New Deal legacy with suspicion. In many ways, these discourses expressed the weakening of the New Deal coalition (organized labor, white ethnics, African Americans, the south, and left liberals) and the fragmentation of the working-class base of positive liberalism (Lowi, 1969). The new formulations were efforts to identify and frame the new structural strains that faced the United States at the end of the long economic boom (Phillips, 1970).

The rightward spin to populist discontents turned out to be more powerful in reaching the electorate, if not in mobilizing people for movement activism. The New Right appears to have been more successful in mobilizing diffuse populist sentiments into voting behavior than were left-leaning new social movements and grass roots community groups. The New Right may have been more successful because of its technological versatility, its better access to the media, and its greater opportunities for resource mobilization (see Chapter 6). In the Reagan era, the Republican Party seems to have been able to translate populism into electoral victories. However, the ensuing policies did not resolve the problems, as noted in Chapter 6, "Conservative Movements and Ideologies." By the late 1980s, populist framing momentarily spun leftward, probably contributing to Bill Clinton's victory in the 1992 presidential race, and then rightward in the 1994 congressional elections (Phillips, 1990).

Observers studying the New Right in England have also used the term populism—authoritarian populism—for some of the discourses and practices of Thatcherism (Hall and Jacques, 1983). For example, on the populist side of the ideology, the English right and the Thatcher wing of the Conservative Party emphasized nationalism, rallied popular sentiment against some practices of the welfare state, defined their own social origins as more plebian than those of the British establishment, and claimed to be challenging this established elite in the name of more vital new entrepreneurial interests. The authoritarian side of the Thatcher program was evident in the centralization of some government functions, secrecy in government operations, the hard line on Northern Ireland, the cutbacks in social services, and the intransigent stand on the miners strike in 1985. This analysis of the New Right in England was quite controversial (Jessop et al., 1984); one criticism was that it focused too strongly on the discursive appeals of Thatcherism without explaining them in terms of the underlying transformations of English society and economy—the structural strains that generated the upsurge of the right in both England and the United States.

These examples illustrate the ambiguous nature of the term populism, its association with antielitist mobilizations on the right as well as the left, its association with both the extension of democracy and authoritarian forms of rule, and the controversies and disagreements among scholars as to how to use the term.

A Global Phenomenon

Recently, the term populism has been applied to phenomena as diverse as the Islamic revolution in Iran, the candidacies of Ross Perot and Pat Robertson, and the persona of Russian politician Boris Yeltsin. These examples point to the association of populism with the strong leader, a characteristic that is less evident in recent populist movements and currents of opinion in the United States.

The Strong Leader: Mass Participation or Mass Manipulation?   To its supporters, populism is indeed the voice of the people. It stands for opposition to cultural, political, and economic elites. It is an effort to achieve greater economic equality while respecting private property and the free market. It confers the benefits of positive liberalism, but with genuine mass involvement, rather than through the decision making of a small circle of economic experts and technocrats.

To its detractors, populism is a manipulative, ambiguous appeal for a strong leader who seeks to present a facade of mass support. It uses rhetoric about the "little guy" to mask its unwillingness or inability to undertake a specific and coherent economic policy—whether positive liberalism, socialism, or a free-market capitalism.

Divided Support Bases: The Ambiguity of Populism   One explanation of this manipulative, elusive, and ultimately empty discourse (as its detractors see it) is that the support base of populism is deeply divided in many countries, especially in developing nations and peripheral economies. It includes both the urban poor (especially, but not exclusively, those outside the industrial working class) and small entrepreneurs (farm owners, shopkeepers, small business people). The former would like to see far more economic leveling and more social services. Since they are not organized into unions or parties of the left, they are mobilized into networks of support for an attractive leader, especially one with media appeal (Perlman, 1979; Wiarda and Kline, 1990). Meanwhile, the small business base has distinct economic interests centered on protection from both the organized working class (especially autonomous unions and Communist parties) and large capital. Populism holds these two elements of the social base together with antielitism as a slogan that appeals to both and a deliberate blurring of its economic policies. This view of populism is useful for some nations, although in others (like Argentina) populist mobilizations also included the industrial working class.

Populism and Nationalism

Nationalist movements are particularly attracted to populist appeals for two reasons. First, nationalist movements can use populism to blur awareness of class distinctions while still giving some attention to economic inequality; populism draws attention away from class divisions in the nation. Second, the radical anticapitalist side of populism is consistent with ultranationalist attacks on foreign capital and "foreigners," whether entrepreneurs of ethnic minority status (e.g., Jews in Europe, Chinese in Southeast Asia, Indians in East Africa) or transnational corporations. But, on occasion, socialists have also welcomed populist leaders as allies, convincing themselves that antielitism could be a step toward a genuinely socialist program.

Populism: A Summary

Abrahamian summarizes populism, especially in the nations of the former Third World, as follows:

> By [the term populism] I mean a predominantly middle-class movement that mobilizes the lower classes, especially the urban poor, with radical rhetoric against imperialism, foreign capitalism and the political establishment. In mobilizing the "common man," populist movements use charismatic figures as well as symbols, imagery and language that have potent value in their popular culture. They promise to raise drastically the standard of living and make their country fully independent of the West. Even more important, in attacking the status quo with radical rhetoric, they intentionally stop short of threatening the petty bourgeoisie and the whole principle of private property. Thus populist movements inevitably emphasize the importance not of economic-social revolution, but of cultural, national and political reconstruction. (1991:106)
>
> . . . These populisms [in Latin America and Iran] all use mass organizations and plebiscitary politics to mobilize the masses, but at the same time distrust any form of political pluralism, liberalism and grass-roots democracy. All have ambiguous attitudes toward the state. On the one hand, they do not want the government to threaten middle-class property. On the other hand, they want to strengthen their government by extending its reach throughout society and

Values of the left were incorporated into New Social Movement mobilizations for peace, the environment, and rights of women and gays and lesbians.
Campaign for Nuclear Disarmament march. London, October 24, 1981.

providing social benefits to the urban poor. What is more, these populisms elevate the leader to a demi-god who not only stands way above the people but also embodies their historical roots, future destiny, and revolutionary martyrs. Despite all the talk of the people, power emanates down from the leader, not up from the masses. (1991:118–119)

Populism is an indispensable concept for the analysis of several movements discussed in Chapters 9 to 11 because they use populist themes in their ideological positions. Liberalism clearly privileges the market and private enterprises (even if some variants call for regulation and expansion of the public sector); socialism calls for the public ownership of the means of production. Populism carefully blurs distinctions between these positions. Populism is therefore a useful position for movements like ethnonationalism, religious fundamentalism, and some forms of fascism that do not see the economic sphere as the most important issue in the reconstitution of society and do not want to become embroiled in class conflicts.

SUMMARY

Movements and ideologies of the left share a set of goals, but differ sharply in the means they consider necessary and desirable to attain these goals. They agree on two positions: belief in essential human equality (a position they share with liberal democracy) and in the need to socialize the means of production in order to ensure equality and cooperation in place of exploitation and conflict, which they see as inherent in market economies (a position that sets them apart from liberals).

Social democrats believe that socialism can come about by an evolutionary change within democratic, advanced capitalist societies. They were and continue to be a strong political force within many European democracies in the form of mass parties and are associated with effective welfare states in these regions. In contrast, revolutionary socialists emphasize the need for a break in political institutions, the establishment of a new form of the state, and the creation of vanguard organizations to lead this transformation. They formed Communist states (most notably, the Soviet Union) and a number of revolutionary socialist states in the Third World, many of which have gradually or suddenly returned to market systems. Left libertarians maintain a considerable distance from states and eschew disciplined party structures; they have been a consistent, but relatively small, current in the left, from anarcho-syndicalists like the Industrial Workers of the World, to the New Left and the new social movements in the second half of the twentieth century. So far, these three currents (social democrats, revolutionary socialists, and left libertarians) have not coalesced into a single democratic socialist ideology.

All currents of the left have to meet the challenges posed by the end of the Communist states and a decline in the coherence of the industrial working class, long assumed to be the agent or social basis of transformation. The working class continues to exist as a category within the global capitalist economy in the sense that a majority of people in the world are wage workers or peasants—but, at the moment, it has little collective identity as a class or effective organization on a global scale.

Populism is a vague set of antielitist ideas using terms like rich and poor and elites and the people. Some populist ideas overlap left-wing ideology, but they are considerably less precise. Therefore, populist notions appear in a wide range of movements, including those of the radical right.

KEY TERMS AND CONCEPTS

origins of the left
socialism
revolutionary socialism
social democracy
the left
the New Left
new social movements
Chartism
utopian socialists
landless peasants

marxist views of society
Karl Marx and Friedrich Engels
means of production
bourgeoisie
proletariat
buying/selling labor power
commodities
market mechanism
communism and socialism
determined structure
agent/acting subject of history
First International

anarcho-syndicalism
Industrial Workers of the World
   (IWW)

social democrats
union movement
Second International
the "People's Home" in Sweden
counter-hegemonic consciousness
capitalist democracies with elements
   of socialism

**marxism-leninism and
   revolutionary socialism**
state and revolution
the vanguard party
imperialism
primitive accumulation
marxism-leninism
revolutionary socialism
Communists
Communist parties
nomenklatura
socialist accumulation
market socialism
the Popular Front
cold war
national liberation movements
maoism
states of a socialist orientation

**the New Left and the new social
   movements**
radical democracy
community organizing
the peace movement
multiversities
Students for a Democratic Society
   (SDS)
antiauthoritarian
left libertarian
democratic socialism

populism
antielitism

Bishops in the progressive wing of the Roman Catholic Church lead a procession. The bishops promised to maintain their activism in the preferential option of the poor, despite opposition from Pope John Paul II. Goiania, Brazil, September 5, 1988.

CHAPTER 9

Movements of Faith

A Sampler

Then I saw a new heaven and a new earth; for the first heaven and the first earth had passed away, and the sea was no more.

—Revelation 21:1.

Do not think that I have come to bring peace on earth; I have not come to bring peace, but a sword. For I have come to set a man against his father, and a daughter against her mother, and a daughter-in-law against her mother-in-law; and a man's foes will be those of his own household. He who loves father or mother more than me is not worthy of me; and he who does not take his cross and follow me is not worthy of me. He who finds his life will lose it and he who loses his life for my sake will find it.

—Matthew 10:34–39.

Every day is 'Ashura and every place is Karbala.

—Shi'a saying.

Imagine yourself in one of the enormous cities of western Asia or northern Africa. The wonderful old city with its markets and mosques has been swallowed up by a bleak and drab new city, built to accommodate hundreds of thousands of migrants from the countryside. The landscape of your neighborhood is composed of shabby cement apartment blocks, dust, and the fumes of ceaseless traffic jams. The streets are filled with throngs of people desperate to survive by whatever means necessary. The promises of the nationalist movement have not been kept; once in power, the movement formed a government marked by corruption, mismanagement, bureaucracy, and the misrule of a single dominant party. The government has sold the resources of the nation to foreigners, and officials have pocketed the profits; nothing has trickled down to improve the life of your community.

In this landscape of despair, there is only one source of light and hope: Islam. The five pillars of Islam give meaning to your day, your year, your life: A professed belief in God and in the message of faith conveyed through the prophet Muhammad; prayer five times a day; observance of the fast of the month of Ramadan; pilgrimage to Mecca; and commitment of resources support all members of the community, your brothers and sisters in faith. Thus, time and space are ordered and made sacred; your solidarity with other believers is affirmed; the world reflects the will of its Creator. The sixth pillar of Islam also shapes your actions—jihad, struggle. You know that the western media carelessly translate this word as "holy war," calling up images of hordes of suicidal fanatics armed with scimitars and car bombs. But, you are aware of its true and deeper meaning, a struggle to bring the world into accord with the design of God. This struggle can take place in your own heart, in conversations with friends, in your choice of clothing, at the ballot box, in the organization of a movement, and if necessary, in armed conflict.

An important element of this struggle is the goal of establishing an Islamic republic in your nation. In it, state and religion would form a seamless whole, no longer ripped apart in a poor imitation of western liberalism. Law and government would reflect the Qur'an, the word of God. The social fabric of family and community would be restored, rewoven from the tattered condition left by the encounter with the west. Every day now you see boys turned into beggars and thieves, girls forced into prostitution, government officials bribed, peasants losing their land, workers exploited. . . . These abuses and injustices would end. Capitalism would not be abolished in an Islamic republic, but it would be limited by the teachings of Islam. The restoration of an Islamic society of justice and economic solidarity could begin if your movement came to power.

RELIGION AND THE MODERN WORLD

Religious movements have existed throughout the history of complex societies. Religion offers a vision of a more just world, one in which values are realized and the despair and exploitation of the existing society are brought to an end. Most of the great world religions feel deeply and express forcefully a bitterness about existing conditions and a hope for redemption. In some religions, this redemption is almost entirely put off to the afterlife or a messianic future time, but, in most, there is some effort to bring about a better world here and now, to bring the social order closer to an ideal that is referred to as God's will or the "mandate of heaven." Religious movements are organized responses to the widespread perception that there is a gap between what *is* and what *ought to be*.

The history of religious movements forms a large part of the history of complex societies. Our discussion begins with the revolutions that posed challenges to religion at the end of the eighteenth century. Religious communities responded to these challenges in a number of different ways. Some accepted modern society to a large extent while trying to reform it. Others responded by movements with fundamentalist and/or integralist views of faith and society. This chapter is a sampling of movements based on religious faith.

Liberalism separated church and state, making religious belief and practices a private, personal matter. This separation did not weaken religious belief; on the contrary, it strengthened individual commitment by making faith voluntary (de Tocqueville, 1990). It did seem to eliminate the ability of religions to influence the shape and structure of the social order through the state apparatus; it fragmented religious practice into individual practices. Nationalism, in part, supplanted religion as the basis of identity. Industrial capitalism produced rapid and unprecedented changes in communities, undermining the social basis of religion. Families fractured into wage-earning individuals. Millions of people left villages and migrated to cities or to faraway countries where they lost their ties to a religious community and a sacred landscape (Lerner, 1958). Finally, the Enlightenment and liberal secularism directly challenged religion as a system of belief and discourse; the discourse of science and the social sciences confronted and pushed aside the language of religion (Zeitlin, 1994).

The Challenge of the Modern

These challenges to religion took place on a global basis, but in different forms in different regions, shaped by both the nature of the prevailing religion and the uneven spread of industrial capitalism. The three major faiths of west Asian origin—Christianity, Islam, and Judaism—responded differently than communities with other spiritual traditions. Jews, Christians, and Muslims responded differently from each other, and within each of these faiths there was further differentiation; not all communities within these faiths produced social and political movements. Populations of European origin and in the global core regions responded differently than those in which liberal and western ideas were imposed from the outside. Both the character of the religions before modernization and the impact of modernization influence the social movements that emerged from religious communities.

Religions—more precisely, religious communities—responded to these new conditions in a complex variety of ways (Zald and McCarthy, 1987). Some accepted liberal ideas about the separation of state and religion virtually completely; these religious groups emphasized faith as a personal choice and a private matter. For example, by the twentieth century some of the mainline Protestant churches in Europe and North America had accepted these arrangements and were engaged in relatively little social activism.

Other religious communities participated in reform movements, seeking to make changes within the liberal framework; they were willing to coexist with liberalism, nationalism, and capitalism, but without accepting any of them uncritically. This position gave these religious groups a role in movements for change, both conservative movements and movements on the left. For example, at the turn of the century in the United States, the concept of the social gospel brought many Protestants into reform mobilizations associated with the Progressive Movement and its attempts to reduce poverty and ameliorate capitalist society. In Europe and Latin America after the Second World War, Christian Democratic parties and movements combined religious tenets with political activism, usually in centrist or moderately conservative positions. In the United States in the 1960s, many churches and synagogues supported the Civil Rights Movement by direct participation and by the commitment of financial resources; in the 1980s, churches and synagogues supported human rights mobilizations in Central America (Findlay, 1993; Morris, 1984; Parks, 1992). These examples suggest that religious faith can be the basis for social movement activism with goals of reform as well as revolution and transformation.

Other religious communities rejected one or both of the central premises of liberalism. They rejected the idea that religion is only one among many competing, and yet, basically compatible discourses, that religion should be in dialogue with other discourses, and that scientific discourse has displaced religious discourse in interpreting nature. This rejection of liberal premises is called *fundamentalism,* which insists on the primacy and literal truth of religious texts, as well as certain specific interpretations of these texts.

Some religious communities rejected the liberal principles that state and religion should be separate institutions and religious belief and practice are personal or private matters. This position is called *integralism,* which insists on the unity of state and society within a religious faith.

Fundamentalism and integralism encouraged totalizing movements of faith and were directed against the liberal view of society and belief systems. Fundamentalism and integralism reject the marketplace model of liberalism, the idea that discourses should engage in a sort of friendly competition with each other, with everyone "buying" the religion or secular belief system that is most appealing to individual preferences.

Finally, some religious activists are engaged in transformative movements that are allied with, or part of, socialist movements; in these cases, there is a convergence of religious commitment to social justice with secular socialist ideologies. This convergence has been most developed in liberation theology among Roman Catholics and similar perspectives among Protestant activists.

Judaism, Christianity, and Islam have shared origins and characteristics that dispose believers to high levels of movement activism. The chapter begins with a reflection on how the teachings of these faiths contribute to movement formation. The discussion of specific movements starts with a look at two movements within the Christian faith that have converged with liberal and socialist movements: Christian democracy and liberation theology. I then focus on fundamentalism and integralism within Christianity and Islam in order to illustrate the way some religious movements challenge modern cultural and political institutions. The chapter ends with a brief overview of the role of religion in communal conflict and the convergence of religious movements with ethnonationalist movements.

THE PEOPLE OF THE BOOK: JEWS, CHRISTIANS, AND MUSLIMS

These three west Asian faiths share a common origin and are integrally connected to each other historically and in their ideas. In addition to their distinctive monotheism, they share several characteristics that produce a high level of social and political activism. One is the embodiment of the faith in a **sacred text**—Torah, Bible, Qur'an—seen as God's revelation. The sacred text makes these three religious communities **people of the book** (an Islamic term) and opens up the question of what it means to guide human action by the text. The meaning and interpretation of the text become a source of contention. The focus on the book also embeds all three faiths in **history**; the present is always seen in reference to the past, to the moment of revelation, as well as to the future, the moment of **redemption** and the fulfillment of the text. Time is, therefore, not an

eternal cycle, like natural cycles of days, seasons, and life cycles, but a linear unfolding of human history.

Second, all three faiths share the tradition of **prophecy.** This word is commonly used to mean foretelling the future, but here I return to its religious
meaning, which refers to an individual judging the present state of society, calling for a renewal of moral conduct, and warning of the consequences if such a
renewal does not take place. Prophecy is a challenge to the status quo, an accu-
sation against *what is*, since it does not correspond to God's *should*. Prophecy is
closely connected to the sacred text, which allows us to see the failings of our
present conduct and measure it against the standard set by God. Prophecy challenges the actions of not only the individual, but also society as a whole.

All three faiths share what sociological theorist Max Weber called a moral
breakthrough—the constant judgment of human conduct and the existing social order by an immutable standard of morality, revealed in God's word in its
written form (Weber, 1963). One can see how sacred texts, historical time, and
prophecy lead to activism in social movements of all kinds, and provide special
impetus toward fundamentalism (concern with the text and its interpretation)
and integralism (the effort to build a society in accord with God's will).

Finally, Christianity and Islam (Judaism less so) became **universalizing**
faiths early in their history; God's message was intended for everyone, not just
one ethnic group with its distinct language and culture. This view had two consequences. On the one hand, it supported a radical egalitarianism, most fully
developed in Islam; it eliminated any notion of ethnic superiority and paved the
way for a complete rejection of modern racism. On the other hand, the universal message of Christianity and Islam supported use of the state and military
power to spread the faith and embraced an intolerance of other people's gods.
In some ways universalism justified integralism.

I emphasize here the strong similarity of Islam, Christianity, and Judaism
and the way in which these characteristics sustain the formation of social movements in cultures and communities that share these faiths. These characteristics
shaped social movement formation in the modern period.

In the nineteenth and twentieth centuries, Judaism, Catholicism, Protestantism, and Islam faced the challenges posed by modern, liberal societies. Each
major religion took a different course, depending on its own structure, existing
belief system, history, and organization. Within these religious faiths were further divisions among communities that looked differently on questions of
modernity; for example, liberal Protestants in contrast to fundamentalists, or
Reform Judaism in contrast to Conservative and Orthodox Judaism. (The following discussion is based on Capps, 1990; Cohen, 1990; Dekmejian, 1985;
Marty, 1984; Marty and Appleby, 1992; Munson, 1988; Nielsen, 1993; Riesebrodt, 1993; Watt, 1988; Weber, 1958, 1963; Wills, 1990.)

Fundamentalism

One widespread response of religions to the modern in the nineteenth and early
twentieth centuries was their tendency to split into a modernist/liberal and tra-

ditionalist, or fundamentalist, current. This was most marked among Christians, especially Protestants.

The focus was on interpretation of the sacred texts of the faith, how strictly to apply the codes of conduct specified in these texts, and whether or not to accept a larger role for scientific discourse. The "people of the book"—Jews, Christians, and Muslims—believe their book to be the word of God, which can mean inspired by God, inerrant, and/or literally true. Christian fundamentalists, especially, insisted not only on the inerrancy of the Scriptures, but also on their literal truth.

Clashes with Science   Fundamentalists do not accept the discourse of science on the creation of the world and the emergence of different species of animals and plants. They insist that the account of creation in the Bible is true in a literal sense and is not a metaphor, myth, or other nonliteral representation. Christian fundamentalists also give a literal reading to Revelation, the last book of the New Testament, which is an account of the end of the world and the Last Judgment. There is, however, considerable disagreement among fundamentalists on the interpretation of Revelation (Boyer, 1992; Wills, 1990). Both Christian and Islamic fundamentalists reject the idea that the sacred book might be questioned, revised, or only partly accepted; if the book in its present form is the word of God, such challenges are inherently blasphemous.

Issues of Personal Conduct, Gender, and the Family   Fundamentalists insist on a strict interpretation of the many prescriptions and prohibitions that appear in the sacred books. Yet, even here, there is ample room for differing views of what practices apply to the community of faith; for example, Christian fundamentalists hold the Old Testament to be literally true as an account of the creation, but do not believe that kosher laws or circumcision are practices binding on Christians.

Fundamentalism clashes with liberalism in its emphasis on those parts of the sacred texts that specify gender relations and personal behavior. Fundamentalists are reluctant to adapt practices of family life to the individualism fostered by liberal ideology, with its loosening of patriarchal authority. Thus, fundamentalists are less willing than religious modernists to change the sphere of gender and the family.

Yet, as with any conservative ideology, the exact historical point of reference, what was to be conserved and what could be changed, was not precise or self-evident in any of the three faiths. For example, in Islam, conservatives hearken back to some relatively narrow interpretations and codifications of the rights of women (especially those associated with the Abbassid caliphate), and not to others that encourage equality between men and women (Ahmed, 1992; Kabbani, 1992–1993). Christianity, from the very start, has discussed the elements of Jewish law that should be kept, dropped (e.g., circumcision and kosher laws), and altered; in actual practice, Christian fundamentalism draws on late nineteenth-century neotraditional ideals of family life far more than on the Bible.

Political and Territorial Issues   In some instances, literal readings of sacred texts had immediate political implications; for example, the Jewish fundamentalist interpretations of passages in which God gave Judea and Samaria (specific areas) to the Jews legitimated Jewish settlement in the territories occupied by Israel after the 1967 war, since they corresponded to the regions mentioned in the Bible (Nielsen, 1993).

Integralism

A second response to the modern was debate over the relationship between state and religion. Integralist thought emerged to insist on reversing the religion-state separation that had been imposed by the liberal state. For integralists, religious values should give form to all other institutional spheres of the society—the political system and the law, the family and gender systems, and, but a bit less, the economy. The apparatus of the state should be used to implement the religious orientation of all practices of civil society. Religious integralism aims toward theocracy. For example, family law should follow religious teachings; schooling should be religiously based.

Fundamentalism and integralism strongly overlap; many integralists are also fundamentalists and many (but not all) fundamentalists incorporate integralist social practices. They are not, however, identical viewpoints.

Fundamentalism and Integralism

Protestantism   Of all the faiths, Protestantism is closest to modern forms of ideology; indeed, in many ways, the Protestant Reformation in the early sixteenth century marked the onset of modern forms of society and, in the view of some theorists, even formed a precondition for the rise of capitalism (Weber, 1958).

Protestantism with its many denominations split into liberal/reformist and fundamentalist groups. For historical reasons, integralism played only a minor role in Protestant thought. The Protestant Reformation contributed to looser ties between church and state in western Europe, although this had not been intended by the leaders of the Reformation. Protestant thought places strong emphasis on the individual, which created a certain distance from societal, collective, and state-centered approaches to institutionalizing religion. Protestant denominations, therefore, had a shorter and less solid tradition of integralism to draw on than Catholics and Muslims.

On the other hand, the polarization of modernists/liberals and fundamentalists is particularly marked in the Protestant denominations, which disagreed about such issues as Darwinian evolution and the historical interpretation of the Bible (Wills, 1990). Some denominations and churches within Protestantism decided to reconcile religion with biological science and historical analysis of the Bible. Others—the fundamentalists—insisted on a more literal reading of the Bible that would preclude the teaching of evolution or research on "the historical Jesus." Protestants and churches historically linked to Protestantism (the

Church of the Latter Day Saints, Jehovah's Witnesses, Seventh Day Adventists) were more likely than other Christians to prepare for a literal fulfillment of the events described in Revelation (Boyer, 1992).

The Roman Catholic Church   The Roman Catholic Church did not divide over issues inherent in the challenge of modernism, but the issues were debated within the church. Integralism, more than fundamentalism, remained a major theme in Catholic social thought, because the church had been closely tied to states throughout the European Middle Ages. In the final analysis, the Catholic Church had always maintained some degree of critical distance from secular rulers, so its integralism was never total, even in the European Middle Ages.

Reform and convergence with secular movements and parties became an option for Catholics in the twentieth century; after an initial period of resisting the liberal state, the church explored a number of ways to coexist with it and gradually transform it. As a unitary organization, the church tended to have a cohesive official response to modern institutions at any given historical point, unlike the Protestant community with its many denominations. But, over time, the Roman Catholic Church made several changes in its stand on modern institutions. These shifts reflected the influence of different forces within the church—those that emphasized social justice and the radical egalitarianism of Jesus and those that emphasized conservative values of hierarchy and authority (Carlson and Ludwig, 1993).

The Catholic Church remained unified and moved slowly and reluctantly toward coexistence with scientific discourse. It remained deeply suspicious of the liberal state, a stand that was associated with the troubles of the papacy during Italian unification. Apart from this specific issue, the church was ambivalent about what its relationship should be to the liberal state. Historically, in the European Middle Ages, it had been integralist insofar as Catholicism was the dominant and established religion; yet, even then, there had been some distance between the church and secular political power holders—kings and emperors. By the later nineteenth century, the prospects for Catholic integralism were no longer strong in western Europe and the Americas. The church was prepared to modify its stand, "to render unto Caesar what is Caesar's," and accept a considerable degree of church-state separation, although still hoping to influence policy on issues like abortion. (The role of the Russian Orthodox Church, schisms within it, and its relationship to the state cannot be included for reasons of space.)

Islam   Islam had an even stronger history of integralism than the Catholic Church but, like Protestantism, it also had a flexible decentralized structure. There is no single organization, let alone individual, that formulates the position of Islam on any given topic or issue. Thus, Islamic response to modern society was diversified, including integralist movements, acceptance of religion as a private matter, and a variety of intermediate positions such as favoring the establishment of Islam as a national religion, but in a relatively liberal form. Many Muslims welcomed a more individualistic and private exercise of their faith, a convergence with the western model of religious practice. Others deplored the separation of religious faith from social and political institutions, seeing these patterns as a western imposition and a violation of basic Islamic ideas about the unity of faith and society.

In the Islamic world, the response of religious institutions was complicated by the fact that liberalism and secularization were imported from the west—often under conditions of military occupation. These ideologies were difficult to disconnect from imperialism. This dimension added complexity to splits between integralists and liberalizers, since the latter appeared to be acquiescing to the western model.

Historically, integralism had been a strong element of Islam. Unlike Christianity, Islam does not have a consistent history of discourse that valorizes the separation of state and religion, as does Jesus' remark, "Render unto Caesar what is Caesar's and unto God what is God's" (Matt. 22:21), and his rejection of earthly powers (Matt. 4; Luke 4). Islamic societies, from Muhammad's own community through the caliphate, had been constituted by a unity of religion and other institutions, such as law, the family, and the political system. Therefore integralism became a major feature of Islamic resurgence in the twentieth century.

Some scholars believe that fundamentalism is not an altogether accurate description of conservative Islamic movements; they argue that this term is a misnomer used by western writers who inappropriately transfer a concept from Christian discourse into the discussion of Islam (Hassan, in Cohen, 1990). Fundamentalism in Islam would be more accurately considered conservative interpretation and codification of the teachings of Muhammad. For some, it also includes the view that since the Qur'an is God's word, challenges to it are blasphemy (Cassel, 1994; Newberg, 1994).

Judaism   In Judaism, discussion primarily focuses on how strictly to interpret the Torah itself (the first five books of what Christians call the Old Testament) and the various commentaries on the Torah. As Jews began to participate more freely in the life of modern European and North American nations, Judaism split into various currents, ranging from Reform Judaism at the liberal end, through conservative, orthodox, and ultraorthodox interpretations. In Judaism, unlike Protestantism, these differences had more to do with the strictness with which specific commandments and practices were followed (like the kosher laws that proscribed certain foods), than with a position on the literal truth of the account of creation. Preparation for the Messiah and charismatic forms of leadership appeared in relatively small communities of the ultraorthodox.

The founding of the state of Israel in the 1940s revived integralist themes (Nielsen, 1993). Up until that point, there had been no connection between the religious community and a state for nearly 2000 years. The existence of Israel raised the question of whether the state should enforce religious teachings and whether the territorial boundaries of Israel were in some way specified in God's covenant with the Jewish people.

Religious Movements as Countermovements

Religious movements not only resist some or all of the institutional arrangements and discourses of liberalism, but also form in opposition to other movements that are contending to give shape to contemporary societies.

Socialism and Communism   For several reasons, religious movements are often at odds with socialism and communism as well as liberalism. First, many varieties of socialism and communism are explicitly opposed to religion and espouse atheism; they reject discourses that explain the world in terms of God or gods. This characteristic is particularly true of marxism and marxism-leninism. Second, socialism and communism place a strong emphasis on capitalism as a major source of exploitation and injustice. Religious movements are generally more willing to coexist with capitalism; their stand ranges from the hope that capitalism can be ameliorated by religious precepts (in the case of the Catholic Church and some Islamic movements) to strong support for capitalism (in the case of many communities within Protestant fundamentalism). Liberation theology, however, is closer to socialism.

During the period of the cold war, some Protestant fundamentalists connected anticommunism with apocalyptic interpretations of scripture. The Soviet Union was identified with anti-Christ or with the book of Ezekiel's mysterious "king of the north"; they anticipated nuclear war as a fulfillment of these prophecies (Boyer, 1992).

Finally, religious movements accuse socialism and communism of fomenting class conflict; they point to the unity of all believers, a view that precludes a discourse focused on class. Religious movements draw, reinforce, and/or bring about a collective identity that is an alternative to a class-based identity. They often merge supporters of more than one class origin. For example, Christian democracy had a base among peasants, factory workers, and the middle class in twentieth-century Italy. Contemporary Islamic movements bring together members of the lower middle class with the urban poor and peasants.

Socialism and communism, in turn, are inclined to label most religions and religious movements as "opiates of the people"—forms of discourse that seek to dull the awareness of class structure. There have been a few attempts to reconcile marxism and Islam as well as marxism and Christianity; after all, these forms of discourse share an emphasis on justice and a hope for universal redemption from misery and exploitation. But the relationships between the left and movements of faith remain uneasy.

Feminism   The relationship of religious movements to feminism has been particularly stormy. Most religious movements draw on sacred texts that came into being during a period of strong patriarchal institutions in the world's civilizations. The stamp of patriarchy is especially marked in the Bible and the Qur'an; Judaism, Christianity, and Islam share origins in patriarchal cultures of the west Asian and Mediterranean regions. The high degree of gender differentiation and gender inequality that appears in the sacred texts poses a problem for feminist approaches to these religious traditions. It is possible to read these texts as challenging the then-prevailing systems of gender stratification and as opening the way for radical gender equality. For example, Islam greatly expanded and enhanced the rights of women, eliminating female infanticide and ensuring women's inheritance and property rights (Ahmed, 1992). Both Jesus and Muhammad spoke to women as equals. Yet, present-day conservative interpretations of the texts seek to highlight, freeze, and institutionalize the elements of gender stratification that existed in west Asian societies; they reject alternative readings of the Bible and the Qur'an that challenge gender inequality (Kabbani, 1992–1993; Keller, in Carlson and Ludwig, 1994; Mernissi, 1991). These gender issues have become highly contested terrain for movements and countermovements.

The problem of gender equity is especially acute in feminism's relationship to fundamentalism and integralism. Fundamentalism makes a contemporary feminist reading of the texts difficult. Integralism carries conservative religious codes into the political and juridical system, using the force of the state to institutionalize and enforce traditional gender systems and family structure (Ahmed, 1992; Hatem, 1985; Kabbani, 1992–1993; Mernissi, 1991).

Racism and Ethnonationalism   Religious movements, in both the Christian and Islamic traditions, have been powerful sources of resistance to racism and racist movements and, to some degree, to ethnonationalism. Both of these religions are strongly universalizing. They emphasize that their message of faith is directed at all human beings. Insofar as they make distinctions among persons, the distinction is between believers and unbelievers, and not of language, physical appearance, national identity, or class. The distinction between the believer and the unbeliever can be overcome by conversion, by the choice to accept God's message of faith and redemption; all human beings are potentially—in essence—equal in the eyes of God.

Historically, Muslims have been more consistently antiracist than Christians, specifically Christians of European origin who have often followed ethnoracist ideologies and practices and, in some instances (for example, the Christian Identity movement or the Dutch Reformed Church in South Africa), even used religion to justify racism. Yet, as we will see in Chapter 11, "Fascists, Nazis, and Neo-Nazis," Christian faith was one of the ideological sources of resistance to Nazi rule in Europe.

Premodern or Postmodern?

New Features of Movements of Faith   Religious movements are sometimes seen as old-fashioned or traditional because they draw on texts and practices that are hundreds or even thousands of years old. But this viewpoint is misleading in several respects. Insofar as they are different from the world of liberalism, nationalism, and capitalism, it is because they claim to be postmodern and not because they are premodern.

Alternatives to the Modern World   Most contemporary religious movements are reactions to the modern world. They are reaffirmations of traditions in opposition to a social and cultural environment that has attacked and undermined traditions. They are formed around a highly self-conscious discourse of opposition to the modern; that is, opposition to liberalism, secularism, separation of state and religion, dismantling of traditional gender roles, and so on. One analyst even defines fundamentalism as a global opposition to the modern: "The argument that fundamentalism emerges out of the defensive interplay between orthodoxy and modernity can be crystallized through three simple propositions. Nearly everything else that distinguishes fundamentalism in its global contours derives from these, namely, *all fundamentalist sects share the deep and worrisome sense that history has gone awry. What 'went wrong' with history is modernity in its various guises. The calling of the fundamentalist, therefore, is to make history right again*" (Hunter, in Cohen, 1990:58–59).

Religious discourse speaks powerfully to millions of people who have become disillusioned by nationalism, liberalism, socialism, and the difficulties of economic development. Religious movements have a strong understanding of both economic desperation and social disintegration, two major problems of our era.

Contemporary movements of faith do not just look to the past for the shape of the future, although the past may indeed contain some models for the future, like Muhammad's religious community in Medina. On the contrary, they envision a future that is distinct from the past and the present. These movements are not only negative reactions to modernity, but also offer a positive vision of a society that is different from what is and what has been, a society in accord with God's design.

Organizational Sophistication   Contemporary religious movements are organizationally and strategically attuned to the contemporary situation. They are as adept at using contemporary media and military technologies as any other movement. They are sophisticated in their ability to mobilize resources. For example, televangelism in the United States made effective use of television as a medium for disseminating conservative, politicized fundamentalism (Hadden, 1993).

Awareness of Society and Social Change   Above all, contemporary religious movements are sophisticated in their analysis of states and societies, enabling them to build political influence and to evaluate and fine-tune their own effectiveness. Movements of the faith are by no means simple or unreflective. They have a high degree of awareness about the structure of contemporary societies and themselves as agents of change. Like all contemporary movements, they are self-conscious; alongside their religious discourse, they are also engaged in a sociopolitical analysis of themselves, society, and processes of societal change. In this respect, they are different from any traditional, unreflective adherence to faith that peasants or other isolated, illiterate populations might have had in the past.

Modern Support Bases   Another way in which religious movements are different from premodern or traditional religious communities is in their support bases. In many cases, these support bases are composed of people who are literate and active in modern occupations associated with the national economy and government. They are not (or are only in part) uneducated farmers, isolated peasants, or villagers in remote areas, although these demographic categories may form a reservoir of piety and passive support for religious movements. In the United States, many middle-class people with jobs or businesses in the national or regional economy are involved in fundamentalist churches and in politicized, conservative coalitions of Christians (Perry, 1994; Wilcox, 1992). In Iran, support for the Islamic revolution came not only from the peasantry, but also from the bazaaris or merchants. In much of the Islamic world, young military officers and students from lower-middle-class backgrounds support Islamic movements; their backgrounds in terms of class, education, and occupation are often similar to those of supporters of nationalist or left-wing movements. Christian Democrats in Europe include substantial numbers of people in middle-class positions—white-collar workers, farm owners, small business owners, and so on.

One of the most important characteristics of the support base of religious movements (with the partial exception of liberation theology) is that it sees its collective identity in cross-class or nonclass terms. A religious, rather than a class, identity is both a cause and a consequence of involvement in religious movements. In this respect, it may even be accurate to use the term postmodern for religiously based movements, since nonclass collective identities appear to have become stronger during the last few decades (Burnham, 1981; Jelen, 1993; Jelen and Wilcox, 1992).

The success of Ayatollah Khomeini and the Islamic revolution in Iran in 1979; the growing numbers of Mormons; the influence of evangelical Protestants in Latin America (Stoll, 1990); the role the Christian right has in the Republican Party in the United States; the electoral victories of Islamic organizations in Algeria, Turkey, Pakistan, and elsewhere attest to the ability of religious movements to be a force in shaping the global situation at the end of the twentieth century.

The next few pages are a sampling of different types of movements with a religious orientation. The first is Christian Democracy, which represents an attempt to reconcile Catholicism with the liberal state and find an active role for Catholics within market democracies. This movement played an important part in the cold war era in Europe and, to some extent, in Latin America. Second, is an examination of liberation theology, which attempts to reconcile Christianity—especially Catholicism—with socialism; it draws its analysis from marxism but grafts it onto core Christian values. Third, Christian—especially Protestant—fundamentalism and its interconnection with conservatism in the United States and other regions are discussed. Fourth, some of the ideas and practices of Islamic integralism, the struggle to create Islamic societies, are explored. Finally, we will discuss communal conflict and violence; religions not only create movements to influence state and society, but also clash with other religions in the process. As throughout the analysis, our emphasis is particularly on movements that have a vision of social transformation and not only individual redemption.

The discussion focuses on the "people of the book"—Jews, Christians, and Muslims. All three faiths have devoted considerable attention to the connection of belief and political power. These faiths have had a great global impact. Even peoples who are not converted have taken on some of their characteristics; modern Hindu belief and practice is a case in point. It is these three religions and the religions that have been influenced by them that are most likely to generate political movements.

CHRISTIAN DEMOCRACY

The origins of the ideology of Christian Democracy are in the social teachings of the Roman Catholic Church. The goals include fuller participation of the poor in social, economic, and political life. At the same time, Christian Democrats (like the Roman Catholic Church, generally) condemn an explicitly marxist ideology and reject the marxists' concept of class as a fundamental division between owners of capital and workers. Christian Democrats argue that this concept foments class hatred and division. They prefer to use terms like rich and poor to draw attention away from qualitative differences between owners of capital and workers; rich and poor suggests a gradation of wealth. It also implies that the rich can change their actions in accordance with Christian teachings. The poor can exert political pressure to bring about a better society, but stop short of revolution; empowerment is a term that is preferred to revolution.

Indeed, capitalism leads to exploitation and injustice, but these problems can be remedied without a transition to socialism, in the perspective of Catholic social teachings. For example, a just wage is one that allows a family to live in dignity. The right to organize unions contributes to greater economic equality. Market forces cannot be eliminated but they must be tempered by social justice. Several papal encyclicals embody many of these social and economic ideals. In addition, Christian Democrats generally share the views of Catholic Church hierarchy on issues like abortion and religious schooling.

Historically, Christian Democracy evolved from the papacy's decision to involve Catholics in the Italian political system after a long period of unmitigated opposition to it. By the beginning of the twentieth century, Catholics were permitted, and even encouraged, to form a party that would take a Catholic perspective in the party spectrum of the liberal state. Christian Democracy in western Europe was strengthened during World War II when it joined Communists and liberal democratic forces in the Resistance, a unified opposition to fascism and the Nazis.

After World War II, this coalition with Communist parties collapsed. Christian Democratic parties formed in West Germany, several Latin American countries, and Italy, and became a bulwark of opposition to Communist parties and movements during the cold war. Christian Democracy's spirit of critical support

for capitalism, its active appeal to the poor, its use of a Christian discourse of social justice, and its cross-class alliances made it ideologically attractive to the
more progressive anti-Communist forces in the U.S. government. For example,
John Kennedy saw Christian Democrats as a viable alternative in Latin America, as a "third way" between reaction and communism; Christian Democrats
promised to gradually redistribute the power and wealth of the entrenched oligarchy without, however, taking the path of socialist revolution. The Alliance
for Progress, Kennedy's program of aid to Latin American nations, placed considerable hope on the viability and growth of Christian Democratic parties in
the region. This strategy had worked well in Italy and (in a somewhat different
way) Germany, nations where the Marshall Plan (a postwar U.S. aid package)
and economic revival strengthened integration into the democratic capitalist
sphere. Its success in Latin America was far shakier; the differences between
rich and poor were too great to be mended into a coherent social fabric.

Wherever Christian Democratic parties emerged, their support base cut
across class lines. They appealed to urban and rural poor people, farmers, small
town residents, artisans, small business owners, older women, and middle-
class Catholics. Obviously, they appealed to those who shared their Catholic
views, but they also appealed to those who saw them as protection against the
growth of communism. They attracted industrial workers who were not influenced by left-wing forces. They organized unions that competed with the left-
wing unions associated with the Communists and Socialists. In recent decades,
especially in Germany, they have also appealed to a newer, better-educated
Protestant and nondenominational base.

The organization and strategy of the Christian Democrats is to form a political party and compete in electoral politics. Indeed, they have lost many of
their movement characteristics and have become a permanent institutionalized
element of the political scene. As a party, they are very open to forming alliances
and coalitions, especially with parties of the center right of the political spectrum. On occasion, they may also occupy a position of the center left, as they
did in Chile in the waning years of the Pinochet regime when they had a part
in the return to a limited democracy there.

Once in power, as they were in Italy throughout most of the post-World
War II era, Christian Democrats have succeeded in staying in office by skillful
use of clientelistic politics (Leonardi and Wertman, 1989). Clientelism, or patronage politics, plays an important role in securing the support of groups who
have no strong ideological stake in the party. Thus, the party has toned down
its Christian teachings and shifted to developing a powerful patronage machine
that provides jobs, favors, and government contracts for its supporters. In practice, it is neither fundamentalist nor strongly integralist; the issue of abortion is
a major concern for the party; yet, even here, it is prepared to accept some
pragamatic compromises with other parties on an interim basis.

Even within these largely institutionalized parties, there are several currents, reflecting different emphases in the ideology, and different support bases.
For example, the Christian Democrats in Italy encompassed secularized technocrats, clientelistic politicians, and the conservative Catholic integralists of

Communion and Liberation. Communion and Liberation was founded in 1969, and its political arm, the Popular Movement, was organized in 1975. This formation successfully reached out to young people and has organized student groups, radio stations, publications, community centers, and cooperative enterprises. It offers "an intense life in common" (Leonardi and Wertman, 1989:218), restoring movementlike enthusiasm to conservative and centrist Catholic life in contrast to the institutionalization of the mainstream of the Christian Democrats. After the disclosure of widespread corruption in the Christian Democratic Party in Italy and its electoral defeat in the early 1990s, some factions of the party are attempting to revitalize it by a moral reawakening and a strong anti-Mafia position.

In short, Christian Democrats represent an adaptation of a religious movement to life within the political system of market democracies. A convergence with the more conservative part of the spectrum of political parties has gradually taken place but, in our broad sense of the term liberal, Christian Democrats are players in the liberal state. In the process, compromise, pragmatism, and institutionalization have obscured much of its distinct ideology and muted its religious character.

LIBERATION THEOLOGY[1]

Just as the Christian Democrats represent a pragmatic adjustment of Catholicism to the liberal state, liberation theology is a movement that brings together Catholicism and socialism. Historically, Christians have noted convergence between religious values and socialist values. The Gospels are filled with a spirit of solidarity, hostility to worldly wealth, and "good news for the poor." The Christian churches throughout the Middle Ages and the early modern period gave rise to movements that preached and practiced an intense social leveling within the community of believers; segments of the Catholic Church and the radical wing of the Protestant Reformation were involved in these protosocialist movements (Hill, 1972). In the eighteenth and early nineteenth centuries, Protestant denominations outside the Church of England became a base for the formation of working-class identity and even radical politics (Thompson, 1963). In the twentieth century, the worker-priest movement turned to empowerment of the poor. The ideas of the worker-priest movement converged with some communist views, but as organizations the two movements were antithetical.

Vatican II (a council of the church to review doctrine and policy) in the 1960s freed the church to respond more vigorously to issues of poverty and injustice. This shift in the church coincided with left-wing insurgencies in Latin America. The ideas that came to be called liberation theology were a response to the same conditions that gave rise to revolutionary movements (Boff and Boff, 1987; Crahan, 1988; Lancaster, 1988; Lernoux, 1982, 1990; Scheper-Hughes, 1992; Smith, 1992).

[1]Based on research by Angel DeJuan, Jr.

Liberation theology was born in Latin America to end the oppression, exploitation, and misery of the majority of the population, especially in the countries that have a sharply unequal distribution of wealth. Brazil and Guatemala are two examples of countries with particularly unequal class structures where liberation theology has had an important role in the organization of popular movements for social justice. But, within Latin America, there is considerable variation in support from the hierarchy of the church (Crahan, 1988). In Brazil, liberation theology as a practice has had strong support, and extensive organization among the poor has taken place, especially among landless peasants. Its influence has been strong in Guatemala, El Salvador, and Chile, all nations with a history of severe government repression. Clergy have spoken out and organized against this repression and have been among its victims.

Liberation theology is an ideology that is based on the following ideas: Christians should be active in the **option of the poor,** that is, in the struggle for social and economic equality and justice. Liberation theology identifies capitalism as the major cause of poverty and injustice. Breaking with more conventional Catholic social teachings, it does not see much hope for ameliorating capitalism or kindling a spirit of charity and human solidarity among the wealthy. Christians should oppose capitalism in order to bring about a more just society. Liberation theologians are ready to accept a marxist analysis of capitalist society. They speak in a discourse of class, not just in terms of gradations of rich and poor. Only the social ownership of the means of production can create the conditions under which poverty can be alleviated.

Liberation theologists are quick to point out that they do not speak of class hatred; they do not intend to harm capitalists as human beings but, rather, to redistribute their property. In fact, capitalists are themselves victims of the system, since they are dehumanized by their power and their reliance on the exploitation of others. A class analysis is a means for understanding society, not the basis of hatred of individual human beings (and, indeed, this attitude is also true of marxism). A class analysis does not point to the elimination of the capitalist class as individual human beings but as a distinct group in society; the goal is the elimination of a system of relationships that is unjust and inhumane. In liberation theology, a marxist analysis of capitalism becomes the intellectual foundation for a Christian practice of solidarity and empowerment.

Another major element of liberation theology is its use of **dependency theory.** Dependency theory explains the poverty of developing nations (or the former Third World) in terms of the economic dominance of the developed capitalist nations; the poor nations are poor not because they are backward and underdeveloped but because they were systematically underdeveloped by the capitalist powers in Europe, North America, and Japan. Their economies are tied to export promotion, especially of tropical products like coffee, sugar, and bananas. They are sources of cheap labor for agriculture, mining, and manufacturing. They do not set the terms of trade for their products and are often forced into competition with one another.

This dependency is reinforced by military intervention and covert operations carried out by the armed forces and intelligence agencies of the developed

capitalist nations; for example, U.S. support for the coups against democratically elected socialists like Salvador Allende in Chile (1973), or reformers like
Jacobo Arbenz in Guatemala (1954) and João Goulart in Brazil (1964) (Kolko,
1988).These operations reinforce repression of reformers, socialists, union organizers, and movements that struggle to improve living conditions for the majority of the population. Dependency theory points to the interconnection between global inequality and domestic inequality.The landowning oligarchy, the
agro-export businesses, owners of manufacturing plants, and commercial brokers all profit from the continuing existence of poverty and low-wage labor.
Liberation theology calls for a recognition that capitalism and dependency are
the structural forces that cause misery and inequality.

Liberation theology is not only an ideology. Its adherents are active in organizing in the poorer nations of Latin America and in some communities in the
United States. While a small number of people have joined the armed struggle
of guerrilla movements, the large majority prefer nonviolent action, especially
the organization of villages and communities to claim human and civil rights,
improve their economic conditions, and merge into larger movements.

One of the most important forms of action is the formation of **Christian
base communities** in slums and shantytowns of large cities and among peasants and indigenous peoples. These base communities are dedicated to spiritual
needs and consciousness-raising, the development of critical thinking and
questioning, and increased assertiveness. For example, in Brazil, priests, nuns,
and lay intellectuals have begun literacy programs in poor rural areas; reading
and writing are steps toward gaining a larger view of the world and developing more self-confidence (Freire, 1970). Literacy classes and Bible reading help
oppressed people affirm their dignity and become active in the struggle for their
rights. As they change their feelings about themselves they become politically
involved. Eventually, the community does not have to continue to rely on out-
siders, clergy, and intellectuals for its leadership.

Priests, nuns, and educators involved in these programs emphasize that
learning is a two-way street; they, in turn, learn about everyday life from the
poor and come to understand priorities and realities. In this way, as the
movements become more political they will not lose sight of the people's immediate needs. The usual top-down hierarchical organization of the church is
reversed, paving the way for a new relationship between Catholic clergy and
lay people.

Community organizing often involves forming **producer and consumer cooperatives, credit unions,** and **labor unions**. In producer co-ops, members
manufacture and market agricultural goods or crafts (Jones, 1992). In consumer
co-ops, they sell goods at lower prices than they would have to pay to profit-
making retail establishments in their neighborhood or village. Credit unions
pool savings and make small amounts of capital available to people who would
not normally get bank loans or government credit for their farming operations
or for small enterprises. Labor unions pressure employers for better pay, benefits, and working conditions. These economic organizations have multiple functions; on the one hand, they improve daily life, and on the other hand, they

develop leadership skills and a wider awareness of social and economic structure.

The smaller community organizations may eventually form nationwide networks and movements, part of the **popular movement** that struggles for social change. Popular in this context means "of the people, of the majority that is poor." Increasingly, movements organized by progressive Catholics cooperate with more secular socialist and communist movements in some Latin American countries, like Guatemala.

Opposition to liberation theology has come from other elements in the Roman Catholic Church, especially from Pope John Paul II and the Congregation for the Doctrine of the Faith. These forces see its ideology as too close to marxism and have accused it of fomenting class hatred. In some nations, conservative bishops have also opposed it. They see it as a threat to the status quo, since the upper levels of the hierarchy often have social origins in the oligarchy and other ruling strata that make them wary of revolutionary and reformist thinking (Crahan, 1988). Archbishop Oscar Romero of El Salvador, who was murdered by a right-wing death squad when he spoke out for land reform and social change, is more the exception than the rule at the top of the hierarchy.

The military and the oligarchy oppose liberation theology, and priests, nuns, catechists, and members of Christian base communities have been murdered by the security forces and death squads in El Salvador and Guatemala (Keller, in Carlson and Ludwig, 1994; Menchu, 1984; Smith-Ayala, 1991).

A more subtle form of opposition comes from governments that have encouraged right-wing Protestant evangelical churches as a countermovement to liberation theology, especially in Guatemala. These churches preach acceptance of the political status quo. They are often strongly antiunion and see individual enterprise, not collective struggle, as a way to improve life.

In summary, liberation theology represents a convergence of Christian and socialist ideology, a way to actualize Christian ideals of love and justice while using an analysis and strategy shared with socialism.

CHRISTIAN FUNDAMENTALISTS AND THE RELIGIOUS RIGHT

This section discusses movements of politicized **Christian fundamentalists** in the United States, persons whose religious faith leads them to participate in movements of the **religious right.** Political scientists use the term religious right for movements that hold the following views: first, a conservative stand on social issues such as abortion, gay rights, and family structure; second, a call to narrow the gap between state and church in the United States, especially on issues like prayer in schools and public funding for religious education; third, strong opposition to communist and socialist movements or ideas, in the United States or elsewhere; and fourth, support for free enterprise and opposition to positive liberalism.

Support Base

To avoid stereotyping all religious conservatives as part of a political-religious right-wing movement it is important to qualify the support base of the Christian right. The potential support base of the religious right is primarily among evangelical Protestants; but not all evangelicals are fundamentalists, nor are all fundamentalists politically mobilized. Over 50 million Americans define themselves as **evangelical Christians** who recognize Jesus Christ as their personal savior, believe the Bible to be inerrant, and are prepared to propagate their faith. Only about a quarter of evangelical Christians define themselves as fundamentalists; and not all fundamentalists are politically mobilized in a consistent direction (Wilcox, 1992).

There are three very important exceptions to the connection between religious and political conservatism. First, much of the current movement activity takes place among Protestants; conservative Catholics may become coalition partners on some issues, especially abortion, homosexuality, and school curriculum, but are divided from the Protestant base organizationally and ideologically. (*New York Times*, 1993; Perry, 1994). Catholic religious teachings are rarely unreservedly pro-free enterprise, and this may be one reason why conservative Catholics are not a large proportion of the supporters of the religious right.

Second, not all evangelical Protestants are fundamentalists, nor are all fundamentalists politically mobilized toward the right, even in actions as limited as electoral choices (Wilcox, 1992). Many evangelical Protestants (as well as many observant Catholics) have been mobilized more toward a liberal political stand, especially on foreign policy issues where they oppose U.S. military action and give qualified support to Third World reform and revolutionary movements.

Third, although African American Protestants often have conservative stands on theological and social issues, they are generally not politically mobilized in these directions; issues of racial justice and economic opportunity evidently tend to take precedence, leading them into different kinds of political action and alliances (Perry, 1994; Wilcox, 1992).

In short, the connections between the support base of religiously conservative Christians and the explicitly right-wing political movement are complex; there is considerable slippage here, as between most movements and potential support bases.

In demographic terms, one study of supporters of the Moral Majority, an important network of the religious right that was active during the Reagan era, found that they were more likely to be white, less well-educated, and located in the south than other Americans; there were no marked differences in income between Moral Majority supporters and others. There was little evidence that they are any more irrational or psychologically troubled than anybody else (Wilcox, 1992). Although this study was confined to supporters of one specific network, the findings probably indicate general demographic characteristics of the religious right. The Christian Coalition, formed by Pentecostals rather than fundamentalists in a strict sense of the term, is probably somewhat more urban and less southern in its base than the Moral Majority (Perry, 1994).

Ideology

The most interesting and puzzling aspect of movements with a fundamentalist support base is why they are so decisively oriented toward an ideology of the right and enter coalitions with economic and political conservatives. How did a conservative religious position on the reading of the Scriptures become aligned with right-wing political activism? This alignment can be understood in terms of a historical process of response to changes in American society and culture.

As we noted above, Christian fundamentalism developed at the beginning of the twentieth century in reaction to the encroachment of science—specifically the Darwinian model of evolution. Darwinian evolution was incompatible with a literal reading of Genesis; it threatened the belief that the Bible is not merely inspired by God or inerrant in a spiritual sense, but that it is literally correct. Fundamentalism also arose in opposition to the interpretation of the Bible as a historical document, written and translated at different times and under varying conditions; historical research was an area of religious scholarship that had grown during the nineteenth century. Thus, one element of fundamentalism was an insistence on a literal reading of the Bible as the word of God; such a reading excluded evolution and analysis of the Bible as a historical document.

Fundamentalism and Social Conservatism   Christian fundamentalism came to oppose the social gospel. The social gospel was a discourse of many Protestant denominations at the end of the nineteenth century that emphasized Jesus' message of reaching out to the poor, charity in the most profound sense of the word, and social justice. While the social gospel was not nearly as radical as today's liberation theology, it did contain the theme that society itself needed to change to be in accord with Christian values; it was one of the forces that gave energy to the Progressive Movement in the United States with its many social reforms and to the establishment of settlement houses to minister to the needs of immigrants and the poor (Lasch, 1965).

Christian fundamentalists were more likely to be located in small towns in the "Bible belt," far from the problems of the large cities. In part, they were less educated than the members of the more liberal and socially reformist denominations and congregations. They rejected the **social gospel** of outreach and social change, preferring to emphasize two other themes: **individual salvation** and **premillenarian beliefs** based on the book of Revelation.

Revelation is a powerful and detailed vision of the end of the world as we know it and the division of humanity into the saved and the damned. It (and shorter passages in other books of the Bible, chiefly Daniel, Ezekiel, and Paul's first and second letters to the Thessalonians) caught the attention of the fundamentalists and became a central element for their understanding of what constitutes the essence of reality. Fundamentalists differed among themselves about the form in which these final events would unfold, but agreed that preparation for the future took precedence over social reform (Boyer, 1992; Wills, 1990).

Because of their conservative stand on cultural issues, Christians fundamentalists gradually became allies of sociopolitical conservatives, including some sectors of public opinion that favored laissez-faire policies and less government intervention in the economy. At first, this alliance was by no means a foregone conclusion since many small-town and rural Protestants were more active as populists than as conservatives. Free-market conservatism and **cultural conservatism** are not completely compatible in either theory or practice and, indeed, alliances among activists holding these positions came about gradually.

Some analysts in the 1950s and 1960s explained the emergence of culturally conservative Protestant movements earlier in the century as **status politics,** movements that grew out of cultural discontents rather than economic issues associated with class inequalities. Waves of immigrants threatened core values of Protestants of European origin, whose cultural primacy was no longer assured. The expanding role of science also threatened religious values. The result of this sense of cultural siege was a cycle of movements that were moralistic, puritanical, and nativist in character, aimed at curbing challenges to these core values. In short, the waves of cultural conservatism were responses to the cultural conflicts that arise in a changing multicultural society—conflicts that were as acute in 1900 as in the 1990s (Bell, 1964; Gusfield, 1963). Sociologists and political scientists were writing about the movements of the early decades of the century and a subsequent wave in the 1950s; but their analysis can also apply to the formation of a religious right in the last couple of decades, in which cultural values ("culture wars" and social issues), rather than class inequalities, seem to be the focus of collective identity formation and mobilization (Simpson, 1983). Shifts to status politics could be *caused* by structural economic strains, visible to the outside observer but not experienced in economic terms by the participants. For example, in the most recent wave of cultural conservatism, the decline of Fordism and the fragmentation of the working class may be shifting the focus of concern in mass constituencies from economic issues to cultural strains. The United States has had more waves of status politics than other countries because class identity has always been weak and diffuse.

The career of politician and presidential candidate William Jennings Bryan illustrates the shift away from populism to cultural conservatism among many Protestants in small towns and rural areas. At the end of the nineteenth century, Bryan stood for government intervention to protect farmers and small entrepreneurs from the railway and banking interests; though certainly no socialist, he was moved by the populist ideology of protecting the "little guy" from big business. By the 1920s, he became a symbol of fundamentalist opposition to Darwinian theory as he was a witness for the prosecution in the Scopes trial, in which a school teacher was tried for teaching evolution. A similar trajectory was traced by some currents in the Progressive Movement that shifted from participation in a broad-based reform movement to increasing concentration on prohibition, a goal that was fueled by fears that American values were being undermined by the habits and values of the wave of southern and eastern European immigrants. This shift from economic and structural reform to status politics and cultural issues was most marked among small town, lower-middle-class white Protestants (Gusfield, 1963).

In the first decades of the twentieth century, fundamentalists began to disengage themselves from economic reformers who championed some type of positive liberalism. They began to concentrate on what they saw as the overwhelming threat from cultural liberals and secularizers. They were also increasingly concerned about the rise of socialism and communism, which were perhaps even more directly threatening than liberalism. Liberalism had, after all, merely separated religion and government; Communists in the Soviet Union were trying to suppress religious institutions altogether. Already by the 1920s, a first wave of politicized fundamentalism was strongly anticommunist.

Meanwhile, some business interests sought the support of religious conservatives. By the 1920s and 1930s, the emphasis on individual salvation and the rejection of collective social action for economic change made fundamentalists more likely to cooperate with employers and less likely to become union members or socialists (Pope, 1965). These tendencies accelerated after World War II.

The 1950s: Anticommunism   In the 1950s fundamentalists developed political organizations whose main goal was anticommunism and joined in the general cold war spirit of opposing communism both domestically and globally. The Christian Anti-Communist Crusade was one example of this type of movement organization. Vis-à-vis communism, the fundamentalist stand was one of unquestioning support for capitalism and American foreign policy during the cold war. The fundamentalist right began to make effective use of television to promote the goals of cultural conservatism, patriotism, and opposition to communism (Hadden, 1993).

The Post-Vietnam Era   Even as they celebrated patriotism, fundamentalists and Pentecostals became increasingly ambivalent about much of American culture, an ambivalence that reflected the changing realities of American political life. Since its founding, America had been both secularized as a polity *and* predominantly Christian as a society. The overwhelming majority of the population after all were Christians; even if Christian symbols were officially barred from public life, private belief remained strong, stronger than in any other economically developed nation (Burnham, 1981; Wills, 1990). Fundamentalist Christians had largely accepted this state of affairs. They were not integralists; on the contrary, as Protestants they shared a tradition that emphasized the individual conscience and the congregation, not the state, as guarantors of faith. As long as government remained neutral and most institutions of civil society like the media accepted conservative Christian ideals of family life and personal behavior, religious conservatives felt at ease with American culture.

But, after the war in Vietnam, the religious and cultural atmosphere of the United States began to change. Fundamentalists were increasingly disturbed by what they saw as a shift away from the Christian foundation of the nation. This change was taking place on several levels: The federal government seemed to be undermining religion, rather than merely keeping it separate from the state; in civil society, a breakdown of values and behavior was taking place; the media were increasingly open and unapologetic about showing this breakdown (Robinson, 1981); and movements like feminism and gay rights that seemed to promote this breakdown were appearing.

Roe v. Wade (the 1973 decision of the Supreme Court supporting the right to abortion) marked a turning point for many fundamentalists, an indication that the federal government was opposed to religious teaching and not merely neutral. Court decisions that banned school prayers also underlined this rejection of religious values by government.

Meanwhile, in civil society, disturbing trends in behavior and values were taking place—increase in violence, teenage sex and pregnancy, divorce, child abuse, a rise in out-of-wedlock births, increasing production and sale of pornography, drug use and abuse, open sexual cohabitation and extramarital relations, and acceptance of homosexuality. Religious conservatives tended to place all these behaviors together and condemn all of them. They were dismayed with new social movements that actually promoted rather than opposed some of the behavior. The women's movement and movements of gays and lesbians threatened core values about gender and sexuality. These movements seemed to be promoting and supporting the breakdown in family structure and values in civil society. The media ceased condemnation of such behavior—instead they seemed to glorify it: With the end of the motion picture production code, the proliferation of cable channels and adult videos, the expansion of the pornography industry, and the parading of sexual activities on talk shows, the media were cashing in on a collapse in personal morality rather than trying to reverse it.

At the very moment that America and capitalism were winning the cold war, fundamentalists believed that a new challenge to faith was emerging. Like all movements, fundamentalists were under pressure to universalize their discourse to attract a larger base, to reach out to potential supporters who did not share an identical set of concerns and beliefs. Many Americans were disturbed by high divorce rates, changes in family structure, high rates of teen pregnancy, drug abuse, media violence, pornography, and rising crime rates. Substantial numbers of Americans were not comfortable with an expansion of gay rights (Michael et al., 1994). The phrase "family values" served to attract a larger base than any one of these issues (especially abortion) would have mobilized. Fundamentalists in the strict sense of the term were joined in their political activism by Pentecostals who shared many of their religious and cultural positions (Hadden, 1993). On the abortion issue itself, Protestant fundamentalists were able to form coalitions with conservative Catholics (Perry, 1994).

Organization and Strategy

The New Christian Right that emerged in the 1980s was organizationally diverse and sophisticated. It derived strength from a loose coalition with economic conservatives in the networks of the New Right, but this coalition was not always successful. A few examples of New Christian Right mobilizations follow.

Televangelism and Media Mobilization   One type of mobilization was the skillful use of the media, especially television. There had already been a number of conservative and even fascist-oriented Christian media personalities, like Father Coughlin and his anti-semitic, anti-New Deal, and anti-finance-capital radio program in the 1930s, as well as anti-Communist preachers in the 1950s (Hadden, 1993). In the 1980s, **televangelism** emerged as a powerful way to reach out to conservative Christians. One scholar suggests three reasons for the dominance of evangelical programs in television. Televangelists were less restrained about asking viewers for money to cover the expense of airtime than were mainline churches; a 1960 FCC ruling made it possible for stations to charge for public-service airtime, and many local stations preferred evangelical ministers who were prepared to pay to other types of public-service programming, including mainline religious programming; the mainline churches were not sure that "meaningful religious commitment" could be developed through television and were somewhat reluctant to use the medium (Hadden, 1993:116–119). Pat Robertson (a Pentecostal minister) pioneered his Christian Broadcasting Network in 1977 and was followed by many others, in fact, to the point of market saturation and declining viewers per station (Hadden, 1993:122).

Televangelism had limits as a movement mobilization strategy. These limits were similar to the problems encountered by the New Right in its direct-mail mobilizations and by the New Left and the new social movements in their reliance on demonstrations. Like these mobilizing strategies, televangelism created responses that had shallow roots and little organizational continuity. Viewers sent in money, voted for some Republican candidates, and perhaps felt moved by certain sentiments, but did not form lasting ties to each other or to national organizations.

In addition to the problems arising from the lack of regulation and the impact of several major scandals, televangelism as a vehicle for social conservatism declined when some viewers lost interest in the mixture of religion and politics (Hadden, 1993:121–125). For example, from 1985 to 1988, Robertson lost about half his audience (Hadden, 1993:126).

Electoral Politics   An important wing of the New Christian Right joined with more secular conservatives to form pressure groups within the Republican Party. Abortion was a key issue, though not the only one. Since many Republican activists were in this coalition of religious forces and conservatives, it was able to influence the party platform, congressional nominations in some districts, and the selection of federal judges, including nominees to the Supreme Court. The Moral Majority, an organization associated with Jerry Falwell, is an example of this kind of mobilization for electoral politics. It is important to keep in mind, however, that not all fundamentalists were mobilized for conservative politics (Wilcox, 1992).

Another foray of religious activists into electoral politics was represented by Pat Robertson's candidacy for the presidency, as a Republican hopeful. Robertson was not a fundamentalist, but closer to the charismatic or Pentecostal position that stresses speaking in tongues, prophecy, healing, and other ecstatic practices over the study of Scripture, although Pentecostals agree with fundamentalists that the Bible is God's revealed and inerrant word. Despite historical differences between fundamentalists and charismatics, there has been a growing ability to work together on issues in the political sphere (Hadden, 1993; Perry, 1994).

After the Republican defeat in 1992, the Christian right has focused more on maintaining and extending its power at the local level and state levels of the Republican Party, in some states. The United Republican Fund has served as a resource-mobilizing organization for cultural conservatives in the party.

Abortion   A wing of the movement concentrated direct action on the abortion issue. Movements like Operation Rescue demonstrated and picketed at abortion clinics. Persons at the fringe of the movement have bombed clinics and killed doctors who perform abortions. Direct action against abortion continues to be important to the religious right and has united Catholic conservatives, Protestant fundamentalists, and Pentecostals, not always in the same organizations, but in aligned strategies (Perry, 1994). Abortion was a key issue because it condensed feelings about respect for life, support for more traditional female roles defined by motherhood, and anger about the shifting position of the government (Luker, 1984).

Grass Roots Cultural Actions   A major set of organizations concentrated on grass roots action, especially around issues of education. Schools have always been a key terrain for contesting cultural issues. Schools contribute to molding the new generation and, at least symbolically, determine the values of the society in years to come. Many fundamentalists left the public school system and sent their children to private schools, often referred to as Christian academies. In the south, they joined other whites who pulled out of public education because of racial integration, but throughout the United States the unremitting secularization of the public system was the major factor in their withdrawal. By the 1980s and 1990s, this retreat from the challenge of changing the public education system seemed ill-advised: Fundamentalists joined a broader coalition in favor of school choice, government distribution of tuition vouchers that could be used in private schools; and Christian conservatives turned their attention to school prayer, curricula, and book selection.

Fundamentalists and their allies undertook to bring the value orientation of schools more in line with fundamentalist Christian thought. This strategy included pressure to remove from library shelves and curricula those books that expressed the values of secular humanism, undermined belief in God, encouraged nonmarital sex, and presented witchcraft in a light-hearted way.

Religious conservatives on school boards also opposed curricula that supported tolerance for homosexuality. The most notable success of this type of opposition was the firing in 1993 of Joseph Fernandez as superintendent of New York schools after his support for such a curriculum. The materials used in the curriculum included books depicting, in positive terms, the lives of children whose parents have same-sex partners (*New York Times*, 1993).

In these incidents, fundamentalists often found a wider support base among parents who felt that they did not have sufficient control over curricular decisions or were concerned about the condition of families in America, although not themselves fundamentalists. This wider support base was mobilized by populist appeals against an elite that supposedly made curricular decisions against the conservative values of parents without parental consultation. With the Clinton presidency and the loss of influence in the executive branch of the federal government, winning these local conflicts became an even more important strategy for the Christian right (Perry, 1994).

The Continuing Role of the Christian Right   The role that religion should have and will have in American life remains an area of conflict and movement activity; the lines between religion and state are in dispute. So, too, is the question of how a society should arrange personal life, sexual activity and orientation, the role of women, and the structure of the family. Politicized conservative Christian movements bring their own answers to these questions; they contest the answers of liberalism and feminism. All these forces struggle for influence in the state, particularly in the areas of family policy, family law, and education policy. These conflicts are not likely to disappear in the near future. The Christian right will probably concentrate more on local organization for the time being, perhaps reemphasizing national electoral mobilizations and media outreach when local bases are more widely and firmly established. It is also likely to develop coalitions with other movements, including free-market conservatives (as was the case in some of the New Right mobilizations) and, perhaps, populist activists who feel family and community values are threatened by liberal institutions.

ISLAMIC INTEGRALISM

A wave of movements is revitalizing the Islamic world. These highly politicized movements are seeking a new relationship between state and society in nations with large Muslim populations. Western observers often refer to these movements as "fundamentalist" but this term suggests too close an analogy to Protestantism (Hassan, in Cohen, 1990). It is true that Islam shares key features with Christianity: monotheism; a sacred text that is the inerrant word of God; the prophetic tradition; a universal mission that reaches out to all humanity; and historical origins in patriarchal societies of western Asia. Islam and Christianity have different and divergent histories, however, and these circumstances force us to avoid simply transposing terms from Christian discourse into Islamic belief. The following discussion of Islamic movements is based on several sources (Abrahamian, 1991; Ahmed, 1992; Arjomand, 1988a, 1988b; Dekmejian, 1985; Esposito, 1983; Geertz, 1971; Hassan, in Cohen, 1990; Hiro,

1989; Howe, 1992; Kabbani, 1992–1993; Mernissi, 1991; Moaddel, 1993; Mortimer, 1982; Munson, 1988; Riesebrodt, 1993; Watt, 1988).

Islam and Christianity

The text of the Qur'an differs from the Bible in that it is more unified and cohesive. Many Muslims know Arabic. In contrast, the Bible was compiled from texts written at many times and places; most readers know the Hebrew and Greek texts that constitute, respectively, the Hebrew Bible and New Testament only in translation; in the case of the New Testament, the Greek text already represented a translation from Aramaic, the language used by Jesus and his community. Thus, in Islam there is less room for dispute over what is meant by terms like inerrant or literal in the reading of the sacred book; although, as in all texts, there is room for different emphases and interpretations. Conservatives in Islam have probably put less energy into the rejection of scientific inquiry than Christian fundamentalists; but they have identified challenges to the Qur'an as blasphemy.

Integralism is more in accord with Islam than with Christianity, in which the church-state-society relationship has always been problematic. Christianity began in a colony of the Roman Empire and spent over 300 years in conditions of persecution; only with the reign of Constantine did it become a state religion. After the Protestant Reformation at the beginning of the sixteenth century, the ties of churches to the state were once again questioned and weakened. Even in between, in the period of Roman Catholic hegemony in the European Middle Ages, the church had a difficult and often distant relationship to secular rulers. In contrast, Islam began almost immediately as a unity of society and state. Muhammad fled from Mecca to Medina in year 1 of the Islamic calendar (622 Christian era) and established a community of believers there; this **umma** (Islamic community) lasted 10 years and gave form to Islamic ideas about an integrated society/polity in which life was in accord with the will of God and the practice of the prophet. Shortly thereafter, Islam as a unified state and society became hegemonic in a vast territory of western Asia and north Africa.

Although later historical developments created situations in which Muslim populations were ruled by states that were not Islamic, this condition of separation between state and religion was generally not recognized as in accordance with the design of God. Of course, as the liberal state was imposed on or adopted by nation-states in the Islamic world, some Muslims shifted to the liberal western model of separation of religion from the state and became content to define religion as a distinct institution and a private practice; but many did not. The current rise of Islamic movements, then, is not so much about interpretations of a sacred text (fundamentalism) as it is about the reconstitution of an integrated society/state that embodies the will of God (integralism).

Differences within Islam

Islam at one level is an integrated whole, a unity of discourse and practice. At another level, it includes many divergent beliefs and practices (Geertz, 1971).

Some of this differentiation arises out of its accommodation to pre-Islamic cultures. Islam in Nigeria is, of necessity, different from Islam in Bosnia or Indonesia, since these places had completely different pre-Islamic cultures. It may be useful in this context to remember that not all Muslims are Arabs, although Islam began among Arabs, and the Qur'an is written in Arabic.

Apart from the differentiation caused by different ethnic and cultural traditions, Islam itself has also developed in different directions. A major division in Islam is that between **Sunni** and **Shi'a**; Sunni represents a majority, constituting about 85 percent of Muslims, while Shi'a is in a majority in Iran and has some followers in Iraq, Bahrain, and Lebanon. The split took place early in the history of Islam, in conflict over the succession of leadership of the Islamic community. Shi'a recognizes the claims of Ali (a cousin and son-in-law of Muhammad) and his sons Hasan and Husayn. These claims were defeated in a large battle at **Karbala** (in present-day Iraq), where Husayn was killed. This incident marks the beginning of a tradition of struggle and martyrdom in Shi'a, a tradition that makes it more open to questioning the legitimacy of rulers and challenging those authorities that fall short: "Every day is 'Ashura (the tenth day of the month of Muharram, the day of the battle of Karbala) and every place is Karbala" (cited in Munson, 1988:23). A reader familiar with Christian thought will recognize a similarity here to Pascal's remark that Christ's suffering lasts to the end of time; in other words, Karbala or the Crucifixion are not only historical incidents, but continuing truths of suffering, struggle, and redemption that must be part of the believer's life at all times.

Shi'a includes stronger messianic beliefs than Sunni Islam. These beliefs are focused on the return of the **Hidden Twelfth Imam** (in general usage, an *imam* is a religious leader; here the term is used to mean one of Muhammad's descendents as well as a person who is pure and sinless). Like the martyrdom at Karbala, the belief in the Twelfth Imam infuses Shi'a with a sense that the everyday world of political action is inseparable from a messianic transformation that is unfolding within the apparently ordinary and visible process of history. The ordinary, visible surface of everyday life and politics as routine contains within itself a truer, but hidden process of redemption.

Shi'a awards more legitimacy to **charismatic leadership** than orthodox Sunni thought in which all believers are equal. In orthodox Sunni practice, leadership is exercised by the **ulama,** religious scholars who interpret the Qur'an and the tradition of the prophet; these interpreters do not, however, have any special powers or sacred status beyond their learning and piety.

In summary, politicized movements within the Shi'a tradition tend to be different from those in Sunni Islam. Both traditions give rise to integralist movements, but Shi'a gives more legitimacy to charismatic leadership and draws on its history of martyrdom, struggle, and the search for legitimate authority.

Historical Conditions

Recent decades have seen the rise and growth of integralist movements throughout the Islamic world. In Iran, in 1979, an Islamic revolution ousted the

Shah and established an Islamic republic. In Afghanistan, Islamic forces fighting the Soviet Union and Communists prevailed and are currently trying to establish a state. Sudan has become an Islamic republic. In Algeria, the Islamic party has won elections, although the ruling nationalist party has prevented it from taking office. In Egypt, a variety of Islamic organizations oppose the existing government. In countries like Saudi Arabia and Pakistan, where the state is already Islamic in nature, Islamic resurgence has reinforced this orientation. Islamic movements—most notably, Hamas—contend with the Palestine Liberation Organization for leadership of the Palestinians. In Turkey, Islamic parties have won local victories at the polls. Young people throughout the Islamic world show their faith by their dress and comportment; women wearing veils and head coverings take part in a practice that expresses opposition to westernization and secularization in universities and government offices. These are only examples of the many situations and forms in which Islamic integralists contend for hegemony. The western media have focused on terrorism, but this strategy only constitutes one small part of a much larger and more nuanced struggle. Observers vary in their emphasis on the causes of the emergence of Islamic integralism.

Imperialism   Some analysts point to the sense of strain caused by the west's repeated efforts to control the Islamic world: colonialism; the imposition of boundaries for western Asian nation-states by Britain after the breakup of the Ottoman Empire in the 1920s; the imposition of the state of Israel and the displacement of the Palestinians; conflict over petroleum development and prices, especially in Iran in the 1950s, as well as more recently; and the Gulf War. The west has consistently treated the Islamic world as a region of dependency, if not outright colonialism. Efforts to achieve autonomy from western control are portrayed by the western media and scholars as fanaticism! Along with this political, military, and economic intervention has come a great deal of unwanted cultural change: Liberalism has been imposed along with colonialism and economic exploitation. In this view, Islamic movements challenge the imposition of western culture and political institutions.

Growing Class Inequality   Other analysts point to internal strains as causes of Islamic movements. One of these is the growing class differentiation within Islamic countries as a result of their integration into the global capitalist economy. Islam (far more than some forms of Christianity) emphasizes the *equality of believers*; it does not contain a discourse of hierarchy in the same way that medieval Catholic thought did. Thus, although rich and poor have existed in all Islamic societies, classes remained fairly open and social mobility was possible. Recent decades have seen increasingly unequal distributions of wealth and income in many Islamic countries and, in some, there is an increasing proportion of the population in absolute poverty. Strata of capitalists have emerged whose wealth is tied to the international economy, to petroleum as well as trade and manufacturing; mobility into these strata is far more difficult than mobility into small entrepreneurship. The class structure appears to be closing up and rigidifying. There have been marxist responses to these conditions, calls for socialist revolution that would end injustice and growing inequality by a transformation of the economy. The Islamic response is very different: Marxist class consciousness and conflict is not the answer—the answer is a *reconstitution of the community of believers as a community of equals.* The state needs to be captured and transformed, not so much to end capitalism as to rebuild society in accordance with faith. In the process, many Islamic integralists are also populists, picturing a sort of modified capitalism with more opportunities, less concentration of wealth, and more social services (Abrahamian, 1991).

Disappointment with Nationalism   A second major internal strain is caused by the record of ruling parties in the region. Many of these states were formed by nationalist movements at the end of a period of colonial rule (as in Algeria in 1962) or indirect western control (as in the case of Egypt). The movements and the parties they established changed from being sources of hope for economic development and cultural revival to sources of disappointment. In large part, like many postcolonial and/or revolutionary states in the Third World, they had enormous problems in developing within the global economy. Some had no resources; others (like Iran and Algeria) had primarily energy resources whose prices in global markets they could not fully control. Rapidly growing populations added to the problem of attaining widespread prosperity and a good physical quality of life.

Furthermore, it must be said that many of the ruling parties fell into corruption and misuse of those resources that were available (Howe, 1992). There was little "trickle down" of wealth to the mass of the population. Strata of capitalists and high-level government officials enriched themselves. The condition of the urban and rural poor did not improve; and middle strata like shopkeepers, white-collar workers, employed professionals, and civil servants slipped into more desperate conditions. Inflation and unemployment created bleak prospects for the younger generation, even better-educated young people.

In summary, the rise of Islamic integralism might be said to be overdetermined—caused by an inextricable combination of factors: western domination, disintegration of social relationships, growing class division, economic problems in the global system, and elite misrule and mismanagement.

The factors that account for the Islamic movements' ability to come to power in some societies (Iran, Afghanistan), but not others (Egypt or Iraq, for example), require a detailed case-by-case analysis beyond the scope of an introductory treatment. In addition to differences in the level and intensity of structural strains in each society, one important source of difference is the political opportunity structure of the nations. Cultural variation and external intervention (for example, the Soviet involvement in Afghanistan) also account for some differences in outcomes.

Support Base and Organization

There is general agreement that the support base of Islamic integralism is young people, especially students and junior military officers. As in most movements, intellectuals have a large part in forming the discourse of the movement. In Iran, shopkeepers and merchants also supported the Islamic revolution, in part, because the Shah had undertaken policies that alienated them, like the closing of bazaars. In many countries, lower civil servants and other white-collar workers are among active supporters of movements. In short, the movements are particularly strong in the lower middle class.

The urban and rural poor might be thought of as a reservoir of support, currently more passive than active (Dekmejian, 1985). Their Islamic practices are often not sufficiently pure and austere to provide the basis for a movement as sophisticated and intellectually coherent as contemporary Islamic integralism. Their faith is not particularly self-aware, and as we have seen, self-awareness is an essential ingredient of contemporary political ideologies and movements.

There is a wide variety of organizational forms. Islamic movements, like most of the movements we are exploring, are quite flexible and ecclectic in their choice of organizational forms and strategies. Within Shi'a, there has been a tendency to form groups around the charismatic leaders. In Sunni, the **brotherhood,** a nationwide network of local groups organized around a mosque and its religious leaders has been a common pattern. When necessary, the movements may form smaller secretive organizations, the kind that engage in the terrorism so fascinating to the western media. In nations where Islamic parties are not illegal, the movements form parties and contend in elections.

Islamic Movements in Power

Once in power, Islamic integralists have to develop three distinct sets of policies. One is bringing law and the juridical system in line with **Islamic law;** this project includes the key areas of family and gender system practices, as well as the expression of religious beliefs. It results in practices that conserve gender differentiation, strong sanctions against certain kinds of behaviors (adultery, use of alcohol, immodest dress, etc.), restrictions on certain kinds of religious expression (for example, the exercise of non-Islamic faiths like Baha'i in Iran, as well as attempts by Muslims to question or revise the Qur'an), and a tendency toward corporal and capital punishment.

For complex historical reasons, many of these codes are based on interpretations of the Qur'an and Islamic practices that were formulated hundreds of years after the life of Muhammad; some Muslims believe that they are not true to the spirit of gender equality and revolutionary debate that prevailed in early Islam (Kabbani, 1992–1993; Mernissi, 1991). Westerners and liberals see these codes as cruel and intrusive into the sphere of private life and freedom of worship and speech. Islamic integralists see them as the first step toward creating a consensual and universal community of faith in which sanctions are no longer necessary.

A second and very difficult set of policies concerns the economy; here, Islamic states run into the same problems of disengaging from global capitalism that all revolutionary states have to confront. Establishing even a small measure of international independence and internal populist measures is difficult (Abrahamian, 1991).

The third project is forming the apparatus of the state; the new state must be both in accord with Islamic precepts and a viable entity in a world of nation-states. The fact that Ayatollah Khomeini modeled the Iranian Islamic republic on the French republic suggests that the constitutional structure of an Islamic state is not unambiguously defined within the Islamic faith (Abrahamian, 1991). Even more severe problems of establishing a legitimate government face the various contending Islamic movements in Afghanistan.

In summary, Islamic integralism is based on a *coherent, universalistic, and egalitarian* vision of society. It emphasizes religious identity realized within the community of believers; in this community, the distinction among state, religion, and other institutions of civil society comes to an end. Islamic integralism is also an effort to rebuild cultures and societies that have been severely damaged by contact with the west. Although it is true that it makes use of violence, specifically terrorism, this is neither unique to Islamic integralism nor its most important feature.

RELIGIOUS MOVEMENTS AND COMMUNAL CONFLICT

The basic ideas of religious movements are not easily described. Secular movements like liberalism and socialism emerged and diverged relatively recently, so their ideologies are still relatively unified, while the traditions from which movements of faith draw are hundreds of years old and have had time to develop into many different forms. Even considering only the people of the book (Jews; Catholics, Protestants, and other Christians; and Muslims), we can point to just a few major shared beliefs. Once we look at other traditions of faith and values (Buddhism, Hinduism, the Confucian ethic, Taoism, the Yoruba pantheon, the many religions of native Americans, etc.), the diversity is stunning. For this reason, the chapter offers a sampler of movements based on religion.

The selection is drawn from the faiths of the people of the book; this choice is not entirely arbitrary or a result of more personal experience with the religions of Europe and western Asia. These faiths have characteristics of monotheism, sacred texts, historical narratives of inspiration, universal missions, prophetic traditions, and codes of conduct that make them particularly likely to generate movements with societal visions and political goals. Other religions begin to generate sociopolitical movements as they come into contact with these west Asian faiths. For instance, the Sikh community and its vision of a Sikh state emerged from the impact of Islam on Hindu traditions in northern India. The Taiping Rebellion that swept nineteenth-century China was influenced by Christian ideals. Hinduism had been a set of widely divergent and mutually tolerant practices, not a single sharply defined religion. It is now becoming more like the west Asian faiths, after its contact with Islamic and Christian invaders of India; in this new, revitalized, unified, and self-redefining form it is coming into conflict with Islam in India (Vanaik, 1992).

Religious movements not only challenge existing states, but also clash with each other. Regions where different communities of faith live in close proximity and experience historical inequality tend to be regions of communal conflict. Each religion develops movements and organizations that contend for control over or influence on the state. The entire west and south Asian region is particularly volatile because of the overlap of **religious movements and ethnonationalism.**

South Asia contains not only established states with a religious orientation (most notably Islamic Pakistan), but also states with contending communities: India with its Hindus, Muslims, and Sikhs, among others; Sri Lanka with its Buddhist-Sinhala and Hindu-Tamil populations. In India, these conflicts take many forms: Islamic insurgency in Kashmir and Sikh separatism in the Punjab; conflicts over sacred sites between Hindus and Muslims; disputes over family law; and the formation of integralist Hindu political parties that call for a closer tie between the state and the faith (Singh, in McGarry and O'Leary, 1993). Conflicts expressed in religious discourse are superimposed on ethnic rivalries, economic inequalities, and a resentment of historical advantages (especially the Hindu perception that British rule favored the Muslim minority). The state in India has had difficulty in separating itself from religion; for example, family law is entirely organized on the basis of religion, with each religious community subject to a separate code. Thus, religious tensions are almost immediately translated from civil society into the sphere of the state (Vanaik, 1992).

Western Asia is also a region of conflicts expressed in religious terms and here, too, there is a superimposition of religion difference with ethnic and national rivalry, economic conflicts, and historical inequities in the formation of nation-states and the drawing of national boundaries. There is no space to review the many conflicts in this region at length. Examples include the conflict within Lebanon between Muslim and Christian Arabs; the Israeli-Palestinian conflict; the clash of Shi'a and Sunni, especially in Iraq; the role of Islamic integralists within the larger movement of Palestinians that had, until recently, been largely one of secular nationalism; and fighting between different Islamic factions in Afghanistan.

Mentioning southern and western Asia is not to imply that Europe and Africa are immune to ethnoreligious conflicts. In Northern Ireland, Protestants and Catholics seek distinct futures for the disputed region (O'Duffy, in McGarry and O'Leary, 1993). The Serb-Croat-Muslim conflicts in the former Yugoslavia are considered largely religious, since the three groups speak the same language (Denitch, 1994). In southern Sudan, non-Muslim separatists fight the Islamic state. The distinctly Islamic character of Eritrea contributed to the movement to separate from Ethiopia with its Christian society and marxist state party.

These intricate layerings of religion, ethnicity, political power, and economic circumstances provide ample opportunity for states and movements to support like-minded organizations in other nations. It is a little conspiratorial to believe that Iran is behind all Islamic integralist movements. Saudi Arabia

Women members of the Islamic Revolutionary Guard Corps at ceremonies honoring Palestinian martyrs. Tehran, Iran, October 15, 1990.

has supported Islamic movements and parties, although usually within nations that are predominantly Sunni. And the United States government was a major source of arms and other resources for the Islamic fighters in Afghanistan; U.S. anticommunism led to support for Islamic integralists, in disregard for their explicit hostility to the west.

The foreseeable future is not likely to diminish the activism of movements of faith. Their roots are deep in long-standing systems of beliefs; their contemporary forms are nurtured by economic inequity and societal strain.

SUMMARY

All religious movements are concerned with social justice and the restructuring of society in accordance with God's design as each faith understands it. They call on potential supporters in the name of an identity based on faith. There is a large variety of religious movements, and some of them have created coalitions or patterns of convergence with other movements. Christian Democrats have integrated their faith with the realities of party systems in the liberal democracies. Liberation theology draws on socialist ideology in its effort to mobilize the poor, especially in the Third World, to realize Christian teachings of social justice. The Christian right brings together conservative religious and political ideologies. In some regions, especially southern and western Asia, movements of faith overlap ethnonationalist movements.

In discussing religious movements, it is necessary to distinguish fundamentalism (the effort to preserve and live out a literal meaning for a sacred text) and integralism (the unity of state and society within a system of religious hegemony). Fundamentalism is more typically found in Protestantism, integralism in Islam and Roman Catholicism.

The Islamic and Christian faiths (emerging from a shared Jewish origin) are particularly likely to generate societal and political movements because of their universalism, their prophetic tradition with its challenge to the status quo, the role of the written text as God's word, the emphasis on morality, and the sense of history as a process that leads toward redemption. Other religions, like Hinduism, generate movements especially when they are influenced by the structure of these faiths.

Movements of faith, far from being traditional, are very much responses to the modern world, sophisticated in their strategies, their technologies, and their analysis of societies. They draw their support from mixed-class social bases that often include the urbanized and literate lower middle classes.

In addition to being movements with their own vision of a just society, many movements of faith are also powerful countermovements that direct their efforts toward limiting other movements, including liberalism with its individualism and its separation of religion and state, racist movements, feminism with its rejection of traditional gender arrangements, and socialism and communism. In the view of some observers, many movements of faith constitute a postmodern phenomenon, in the sense that they challenge liberalism and the Enlightenment.

KEY TERMS AND CONCEPTS

characteristics of Judaism, Christianity, and Islam
sacred text
people of the book
historical time and redemption
prophecy
universalizing faiths
fundamentalism
integralism

religious movements as countermovements

Christian democracy and liberal democracy

liberation theology and the left
Vatican II
the preferential option of the poor

dependency theory
Christian base communities
producer and consumer co-ops; credit unions; labor unions
the popular movement

Protestant fundamentalism and the religious right
issues in Protestant thought: the social gospel, individual salvation, premillenarian beliefs
evangelical Christians
cultural conservatism
status politics
Roe v. Wade
televangelism

Islamic integralism
Qur'an
umma
Sunni, Shi'a
Karbala
the Hidden Twelfth Imam
charismatic leadership

ulama
the Muslim brotherhoods
Islamic law

communal conflict
religious movements and
   ethnonationalism

A participant in demonstrations that precipitated the fall of the Communist party in Czechoslovakia. Prague, Czech Republic (formerly Czechoslovakia), November 23, 1989. The movement combined themes of national autonomy with liberal democratic goals.

CHAPTER 10

Nationalism

Thus the native discovers that his life, his breath, his beating heart are the same as those of the settler. He finds out that the settler's skin is not of any more value than a native's skin; and it must be said that this discovery shakes the world in a very necessary manner. All the new, revolutionary assurance of the native stems from it. For if, in fact, my life is worth as much as the settler's, his glance no longer shrivels me up nor freezes me, and his voice no longer turns me into stone. I am no longer on tenterhooks in his presence; in fact, I don't give a damn for him. Not only does his presence no longer trouble me, but I am already preparing such efficient ambushes for him that soon there will be no way out but that of flight.

—Frantz Fanon, *The Wretched of the Earth,*
Grove Press, New York, 1966, pp. 36–37.

You are sitting on a ledge, a hidden vantage point in a fold of the cliffs high over the road. Waiting, waiting. . . . Soon the convoy of trucks and armored cars will crawl along the road, little dots in the gray and brown landscape of desert and rock. You are ready. So are the other fighters, teenage boys like yourself. So is your bazooka, manufactured far away, in the arms factories of a friendly nation. Maybe you are guerrillas of a national liberation front; or perhaps you call yourselves freedom fighters . . . in any case, all you have to do now is sit still, scan the landscape, and wait for the invaders to ride into the valley. Never again will these men drive across the sacred soil of your fatherland.

NATIONALIST PROCESSES

Nationalist movements have been a major geopolitical force for at least 200 years. At the end of the twentieth century, they remain vigorous international actors, creating new countries and dismembering existing ones. Many of us view nationalism with ambivalence. We may feel that our own national identity is a source of pride and meaning. Even if we are not strongly nationalist in sentiment, we recognize that our own fate as individuals is inextricably bound up with the fortunes of our nation, with its economic and political future. Yet,

233

we also see many examples of the cruelty, violence, and hatreds fomented by nationalist movements.

This chapter emphasizes two processes associated with nationalist ideology and nationalist movements. The first operates at the level of societies; it is the process of **nation-state formation,** the organization of politically centralized territorial units associated with groups that believe they have a shared ethnic identity. This geopolitical process has been underway for over 200 years, and nationalist movements have been a major factor in it. The process has not been continuous but, rather, has taken place in distinct waves.

Nationalist movements often use elements of the ideology of other movements—liberalism, conservatism, socialism, and fascism or ethnoracism. These combined forms are especially important for guiding the nationalist movement once it has attained state power.

The second process is the formation of a collective identity—a **national identity.** It operates at the level of individuals and groups. It can precede the formation of nationalist movements; individuals develop a sense of national identity and then enter or organize nationalist movements. It can accompany nationalist movements; such movements voice the discourse of national identity and mobilize people in terms of this identity. Finally, it can follow the formation of nation-states; once the nationalist movement is in power it builds institutions that confirm national identities and exclude or limit other bases of self-definition and collective action like religion, class, and gender.

The chapter concludes with a variety of current situations that can generate nationalist movements. From the viewpoint of nationalist discourse, these situations are structural strains that are best resolved by nationalist mobilizations.

NATIONALIST IDEOLOGY

Nationalist ideology is a discourse about the boundaries of societies and states; it calls for an association of physical space, ethnic or cultural group, and state. In other words, ethnic-cultural groups are defined as nations with an inherent right to a territory and a corresponding nation-state. Nationalist ideology's basic premise is that people who have a shared cultural heritage and language should also have their own political institutions and territory.

Human beings have been divided into ethnic groups with distinct languages and/or cultures since prehistoric times. Yet, nationalism is a modern movement; what is new is its claim that these ethnic cultural groups should be the building blocks of human society, the primary basis of each individual's identity, and the defining element of territorial states. Nations and nationalism are such pervasive forces in our times that it is sometimes hard to remember that the nation is an imagined community, a socially constructed reality rather than one given by nature (Anderson, 1991).

Prior to the eighteenth century, the globe consisted of a large variety of political units. Generally, these political units were not nation-states with precise boundaries that corresponded to the settlement pattern of a single ethnic group.

Some of the units were large multiethnic empires: The Ottoman Empire that spanned western Asia, parts of North Africa, and the Balkans, and included Turks, Arabs, Greeks, South Slavs, Jews, Armenians, Kurds, and several smaller ethnic groups; the Habsburg domain in central and eastern Europe, comprised of German-speaking Austrians, a large number of Slavic peoples, Jews, and Hungarians; the tsarist Russian state that extended from Poland to the Pacific; and the vast lands of the Spanish crown in the Americas (Gellner, 1983; Hobsbawm, 1962).

Other regions were controlled by small kingdoms, chiefdoms, and city-states like those of western Africa and western Europe in the Middle Ages. In these regions, a single ethnic group was often divided into several distinct political units, like the city-states of the Yoruba in west Africa. Still other regions were inhabited by peoples without state institutions who lived in villages or loose confederations of tribes without a central authority. Only a few territories were organized into what we would recognize as a nation-state: France had been formed into one in the seventeenth century; Imperial China corresponded to a centrally ruled state dominated by the Han (ethnic Chinese). Now, at the end of the twentieth century, after 200 years of state formation, colonization, and decolonization, almost every inch of the globe is claimed by a nation-state.

Thus, in the intervening years, parallel processes took place to form nations out of these earlier units, sometimes carving empires into smaller states, sometimes grouping villages and clans together into larger units. Nationalist movements emerged to define **imagined communities,** build national identity, and make territorial claims. Nation-states themselves, once formed, took measures to strengthen this basis of identity. Individuals had once thought of themselves as members of extended families, clans, and local village communities. They were induced—sometimes forced—to begin to see themselves as members of a larger community, the nation. Institutions like central governments, armies, and school systems molded people into a nation. And people themselves banded together into nationalist movements in order to form such nations.

Even by looking at our own life course, we can recapture a little of the flavor of nation-building. When we were little children we thought of ourselves as members of a family; we probably had some notion of a neighborhood, a small territory for play and friendship. Once we started school we learned of a larger entity—the nation (let's say the United States, for the sake of an example). The Pledge of Allegiance, the Star-Spangled Banner, the map on the wall, the stories about presidents gradually planted in us the sense of our nation. The media, especially television, contributed to a sense of a shared way of life and destiny that united millions of individuals who would never meet (Anderson, 1991). Those who were able to travel experienced the vastness of the country and met fellow citizens; but, many who never left their neighborhoods or small towns had sufficient sense of country and, therefore, patriotism to join the armed forces and fight and die for the nation.

The process of forming an imagined community (Anderson, 1991) is at the heart of all movements, not just nationalism. We have already noted how liberalism defines a community of citizen-individuals and socialism calls for class consciousness. Religious movements call on supporters to think first of their faith. Nazism evokes a community of race. Feminism privileges gender identity and calls for the solidarity of women across all other lines of division.

Of all these possible imagined communities—class, religion, race, gender, and nation—*nation has been the most consistently realized in the last 200 years*. It is the basis of identity that has most consistently become the basis of states. Even states that have claimed to represent other forms of solidarity have been forced to define themselves, at least partly, in national terms. For example, the Soviet Union claimed to represent the proletariat as a historical force, and Iran after 1979 became an Islamic republic; yet, each had to represent and express class or religious interests as *national* interests. The fate of these nonnationalist movements became dependent on loyalty to a nation and national institutions.

We can best understand this primacy of nationalism in historical terms. It is not inherent in human nature, but the result of specific historical developments after 1500 and especially after the eighteenth century.

NATIONALISM AND THE "MODERN WORLD"

The Spread of Nationalism: Global Replication

Nationalism was linked to the spread of modern capitalism and to the dominance of European states in the nineteenth and twentieth centuries. In the early modern period (1500–1800), western European societies began to form into a pattern that included transnational markets and political entities—nations—that corresponded roughly to lines of ethnicity, language, religion, and culture. For example, Dutch Protestants formed the Netherlands; France was welded into a Catholic, French-speaking kingdom; the small states of the Iberian peninsula were consolidated into two states—Spain and Portugal. Britain was something of an exception to this process, since the English did not fully succeed in imposing their language and culture on the conquered Celtic areas (Cornwall, Wales, Scotland, Ireland); thus, Britain retained many of the features of a multiethnic empire rather than a unitary nation-state. In this first round of nation-state formation, the units were formed almost entirely by top-down processes, by the expansion and cultural hegemony of an **absolutist monarchy** or other type of strong central government. Nationalist movements from below played little part in forming these national states, with the exception of the revolt of Dutch Protestants against the Spanish crown in the sixteenth century.

These economic and political arrangements spread across the world and were institutionalized into the global system with which we are now all familiar: a combination of transnational markets and nation-based political and economic units (Wallerstein, 1974). Three characteristics of this system contributed to the formation of nationalist movements across the globe. **Colonialism** forced indigenous populations to form themselves into nationalist movements and eventually nation-states, as the only way out of colonial rule was to organize into political institutions like those of the colonial power. **Literacy** (and later, electronic media) created the sense of imagined community among readers of the same language. The **transnational market economy** created a situation in which only peoples organized into nation-states could have some control over their economic destiny.

Colonialism   Having formed nation-states in Europe by the early nineteenth century, Europeans imposed many of the associated institutions on their colonies, carving these regions into territories with precise boundaries and centralized administrations. In order to combat European colonialism, the indigenous peoples had to adopt institutions and movements that took the form of nationalism and the nation-state that corresponded to the territories and administrations created by the colonial regimes.

Movements that rose against the colonialists in the name of religion or the local clan, city-state, or tribe were suppressed. For example, in Sudan in the late nineteenth century, the British massacred the followers of the Mahdi, who rebelled against British rule in the name of Islam. Despite their fighting spirit, clans, tribes, and traditional kingdoms like those of the Zulu in southern Africa were overwhelmed by European armies and firepower.

Only movements that united the whole colony in the name of a modern new nation eventually succeeded in gaining independence. When anticolonial forces accepted the discourse of the nation and gave up the discourses of faith, clan, or traditional kingdom, they were able to contend for state power. By 1960, although European states had given up most of their colonies, they had succeeded in establishing capitalist economic institutions and nation-state political systems throughout these regions. Nationalist movements in Africa and Asia had succeeded in ousting the European colonial powers, but only by structuring their societies on the European nation-state model within the global market economy (Davidson, 1992; Leys, 1994).

Once connected to state power and national economic interests, nationalism as an ideology was promoted with more consistency and force than any other possible basis of identity. Those individuals and communities that preferred the discourses of faith, class, or gender had to form movements that lacked access to standing armies, government media, and public school systems.

Ethnic communities that had no nation-state or had become disconnected from one, like Jews, overseas Chinese in Southeast Asia, and South Asians in Africa, depended on their wits and the tolerance of their nationally rooted neighbors. The fate that these communities suffered in the twentieth century—expulsion, restrictive legislation, confiscation of property, local violence like lynchings or pogroms, and systematic genocide—were ample evidence that survival was difficult for deterritorialized populations who did not have control over national institutions.

Nationalism and Mass Literacy   Nationalism is linked not only to armies and other state institutions, but also to mass literacy. Literacy unites all users of a specific language into a large community (Anderson, 1991; Gellner, 1983).

Before the days of radio and television, an oral culture was only able to bind those people who were within earshot of each other. The connections that were formed were those of family and village life; at most, they were a confederacy bound together by orators. Literacy existed in the large civilizations, but it did not promote national identity. In the Islamic world, literacy was closely attached to religion, to reading the Qur'an. The identity it built was a religious identity; though frequently written in Arabic, Islamic religious texts promoted an Islamic rather than an Arab identity. In other parts of the world—especially China and Europe—literacy was confined to an elite and set this elite apart from the masses. The identity it built was one of class exclusiveness and privilege, the formation of priests and mandarins, rather than inclusion of all speakers of a language into a nation. In western Europe, literacy generally meant literacy in Latin, not the diverse vernaculars that people actually spoke.

The technological innovation of movable type, invented in the middle of the fifteenth century, and the religious upheaval of the Protestant Reformation in the early sixteenth century transformed the meaning of literacy in northern Europe. What began as a religious movement—the notion that each Protestant should read the Bible in his or her own language—became a movement both toward mass literacy and a change in identity. Local communities saw themselves as part of larger linguistic communities—for instance, Germans or Swedes. At the same time, the larger sense of a shared Catholic religious identity broke down with the formation of national Protestant churches (Febvre and Martin, 1976).

Thereafter, literacy quickly became secularized. New strata sprang up that had professional interests in promoting a national language. By the late eighteenth century, schoolteachers, writers, and lawyers promoted a linguistically based nationalism. These strata formed the key support base for nationalist movements; first, in Europe and among European settlers in the Americas and, later, throughout the world. They promoted the establishment of a national language that became the printed and, therefore, hegemonic form of the language, while most people continued to speak local variants, now defined as dialects. For example, in Italy, the form of Italian spoken in Tuscany became the basis of standard Italian.

In the twentieth century, the electronic media have played a similar role, but a more explosive one. Once, only literate strata formed the sense of a national community; the illiterate masses remained unconvinced, still immersed the local world of the small village or the slum neighborhood (Lerner, 1958). With radio, movies, and television, a sense of national identity could reach the illiterate poor as well as the literate middle strata. National governments as well as nationalist movements set to work with vigor to reach out and form these larger imagined communities; in many cases, they worked in competition and conflict with each other, trying to build different and distinct movements and states.

Global Markets and National States   A third structural factor that contributed to the formation of nationalist movements was pressure to survive in a global economy. The nation-state was a strong shell that could mitigate the impact of global markets on the ethnic community or communities that formed the state. The state could protect the people from exploitative practices in labor markets and unfavorable terms in global markets for raw materials, manufactured goods, and capital, whether the nation exported or imported these (Reich, 1992).

The single clearest example of the role of nationalism in economic development is the top-down reorganization of Japanese society in the **Meiji Restoration**, the creation of a modern nation-state in Japan in the 1860s. Japanese political elites understood that if the Japanese failed to form such a nation-state they would suffer the same fate as China, which remained politically independent, but had become economically dependent through the penetration of foreign enterprise. A nation-state could set tariffs or quotas on imports, manage its own patterns of class accommodation, make decisions about industrial development, and launch infrastructure projects ranging from railroads to universities. The state was the mechanism by which global capitalism could be harnessed and managed for the benefit of the ethnic group or people.

This conception of the nation-state as the mechanism for integrating a people into the global economy on favorable terms was necessarily first influential among elites—intellectuals and entrepreneurs. It required a more sophisticated understanding of economics than the nationalism of the imagined community based on sameness. For this reason, it tended to be a theme in nationalist mobilizations, but rarely their major focal point.

Waves of Nationalism

Nationalist movements and nation-state formation emerged in distinct waves. These waves were associated with the colonial expansion of the European powers; reactions against that expansion; the spread of literacy and, later, electronic media; and the formation of global markets.

Nationalist ideology also played a role in the timing of the waves, since each wave encouraged the organization of new nationalist movements. The process has accelerated over time, since the formation of new nation-states creates a sense of relative deprivation and even fear in ethnic communities that do not have their own state. As more and more ethnic communities succeed in constituting states for themselves, lacking such a state becomes a structural strain.

Nationalism in Western Europe and Latin America   The emergence of new ideologies centered on ethnic and linguistic identity coincided with the rise of capitalist classes and stronger central governments to create nation-states in western Europe by the eighteenth century. Nationalism was not yet a movement with a base among workers, peasants, and the urban poor. The adherents and activists were typically literate members of the upper and middle classes, and sometimes even young, rebellious aristocrats, who saw themselves as breaking away from conservative political institutions. Growing middle-class literacy spread these ideas quickly into the Spanish territories of the Americas and into central, southern, and eastern Europe. Nationalism became a strong wave throughout Europe and the regions controlled by European settlers—the modern movement was on its way (Anderson, 1991; Febvre and Martin, 1976; Hobsbawm, 1962; Wallerstein, 1974). The first wave of nation-building led to the formation of independent nation-states in the Americas (from 1776 into the 1820s). It led to the establishment of nationalist movements in central, southern, and eastern Europe—in places that were to become the modern states of Italy, Hungary, Poland, Greece, Czechoslovakia, Yugoslavia, and so on. The first wave of nationalism was often combined with some form of liberalism, since nationalist activists were also liberals who challenged the rule of monarchs and a landed nobility.

Nationalism from Above   The nineteenth century saw some successes among these movements, but also failures to break out of the Prussian, Austro-Hungarian, and tsarist-Russian empires. Nation-building from above rather than from below was more successful in the middle and latter part of the nineteenth century, with the consolidation of centralized states in Germany, Italy, and Japan. The landed aristocracy realized that their continued existence depended on the formation of centralized states with strong capitalist economies; they had to make common cause with the emerging manufacturers and the literate middle strata to build such nation-states. The old feudal structure in Japan and the fragmented political systems in the regions that were to become Italy and Germany were no longer viable economic and political units—as the Japanese elites, for example, realized very quickly when Admiral Perry sailed into Tokyo Bay in 1853. Regions that failed to form nation-states on the western European and U.S. model would end up as colonies or weak, dependent kingdoms like China.

   Therefore, in the latter part of the nineteenth century, nation-state formation was less the product of mass nationalist movements than of top-down restructuring, initiated by modernizing elites. The Meiji Restoration in Japan, the Risorgimento that unified Italy (with some mass movement involvement by Garibaldi and his Red Shirts), and the unification of Germany under the hegemony of Prussia were the three chief examples of this process (Clark, 1984; Hobsbawm, 1979; Mack Smith, 1968; Trimberger, 1978).

   In this phase of nationalism—nationalism from above—nationalist ideology often combined with conservatism. Elites restructured institutions in order to safeguard their position. They called for nation-state formation to preserve order and protect existing institutions and class structure, if necessary by making some changes. The resulting states were generally liberal states, but the liberal institutions were formed gradually, as envisioned by Burkean conservatism. In some cases—Prussia under Bismarck, for example—these changes could even include some concessions to the working class like pensions, health-care plans, or shorter working hours in order to unify the nation and ward off socialist mobilizations (Hobsbawm, 1989).

   In this top-down phase of nation-state formation, some of the movements of the first wave of nationalism (like Italian nationalism) achieved their goal of forming a nation, but they did not realize the goal of liberal democracy with mass participation in the political process, let alone socialism; nation-state formation became increasingly dissociated from the original democratic goals of first-wave activists.

Self-Determination in Eastern Europe and Western Asia   By the twentieth century, a second wave of mass nationalist movements contributed to the breakup of large multiethnic empires in eastern Europe and western Asia. In this period, nationalism was often formulated as the right of **self-determination**; that is, the right of people with a shared culture to control the territory in which they reside and build its political, economic, and social institutions. This right was invoked after World War I by nationalist movements and the victorious powers to divide the Ottoman, German, and Austro-Hungarian empires in eastern Europe and western Asia into nation-states like Czechoslovakia, Yugoslavia, Lebanon, Syria, Kuwait, and so on.

In eastern Europe, some of the new nations were, in fact, multiethnic states like Yugoslavia and Czechoslovakia, creating preconditions for further conflicts and divisions. France and England established control over many of the new states in the Arab world, so that nationalist movements there had to continue a struggle for real independence (Tibi, 1990). The tsarist Russian empire was kept largely intact, becoming the multiethnic Soviet state (Lieven and McGarry, in McGarry and O'Leary, 1993).

Decolonization   A third major wave of nationalism and nation-state formation took place in the 15 years after World War II, when the European colonial empires in Africa and Asia were divided into independent nation-states. World War II speeded the process by weakening the colonial powers and undermining or, in some cases, destroying the colonial administrations. Nationalist movements succeeded in guiding the struggle for independence; the transition could be peaceful, or accompanied by violence, if the colonial powers resisted the demands of the movements as in Vietnam and Algeria (against the French), Indonesia (against the Netherlands), and the Mau-Mau movement in Kenya against British rule (Walton, 1983).

In this wave of nationalism, nationalist ideology was often combined with socialist themes. National independence included economic autonomy, a break with the logic of global markets, which the movements saw as dominated by the former colonial powers and transnational companies located in the core regions (Chaliand, 1989).

Once in power, the nationalist movements had to confront the difficult task of building autonomous economies as well as state institutions. Few of them succeeded in escaping neocolonial economic dependency on the developed capitalist nations. A socialist break with the logic of global markets turned out to be very difficult to accomplish. The new elites also tended to turn away from the socialist restructuring of their own society (Chaliand, 1989; Fagen, Deere, and Coraggio, 1986; Halliday, 1989; Howe, 1992).

Eastern Europe and the Former Soviet Union   A fourth wave of nationalism and new nation-state formation is now underway, located mainly in the nations of the former Soviet bloc—in eastern Europe, in the successor states of the Soviet Union, and within Russia itself (Denitch, 1994; Lievan and McGarry, in McGarry and O'Leary, 1993; Schöpflin, in McGarry and O'Leary, 1993).

Lenin and the Bolshevik revolutionaries had believed in the right to self-determination and were sympathetic to cultural differences among Soviet peoples, but understood this right in terms of regional autonomy within the Soviet Union. Under Stalin, this limited autonomy was further reduced. The federal structure gave few real powers to the republics that formally constituted the Soviet Union, but generally permitted the development of indigenous party and state elites within the republics. For example, Armenians held elite positions in Armenia, Georgians in Georgia, and so on. Language diversity and the artistic side of indigenous traditions received considerable support from the Soviet state, as long as these cultural institutions were apolitical and not associated with any kind of separatist organizations or religious establishments. Some regions—especially the Baltic republics annexed in 1940 and Kazakhstan—experienced large influxes of ethnic Russian immigrants (Lievan and McGarry, in McGarry and O'Leary, 1993; Suny, 1990; Žižek, 1990).

In both the Soviet Union and eastern Europe, the Communist parties appeared to discourage strong national and ethnic identification, partly to discourage separatist and anti-Soviet movements and partly to combat racist and chauvinist forms of thought. One might conclude that their antinationalist stand included both pragmatic and idealistic motives.

I use the phrase "appeared to discourage," because some analysts believe that the Communist regimes actually produced nationalist sentiment, created a "compulsive attachment to the national Cause," and promoted the interests of the dominant ethnic group (Žižek, 1990). Which specific group was dominant varied from country to country; Communist parties had perpetuated ethnic dominance rather than created truly multicultural states with power sharing or consociational institutions. Denying the importance of ethnonationalist collective identities became a way to pretend that ethnic dominance was not a reality (Žižek, 1990; Farkas, 1994).

Communist regimes blocked out the global market and, thus, preserved nationalist sentiments and prevented the formation of newer and more complex identities to match the globalization of the capitalist economy. Centrally planned command economies preserved archaic attitudes, including ethnic and national hostility and a view of the state as all powerful. Elsewhere in the world, international markets created identities that cut across national lines and were based on economic interests and occupational specializations. Already noted is the pragmatic function of nationalism to support institutions and policies that cushion the effects of the global economy on a nation; for example, industrial policy, participation in trade negotiations, and health and safety regulations to protect workers (Reich, 1992). The socialist economies attempted to insulate the nation from the capitalist world economy; an ideological consequence of this insulation was that many people in the Soviet Union and other Communist nations failed to understand and develop the pragmatic side of nationalist senti-ment. Nationalism was often equated with passions—love, hatred, or other pri-mordial feelings—not with a rational calculation of how a nation could pursue a unified and coherent course of action in the global economy in order to bene-fit all its citizens.

Thus, we have three different interpretations of why nationalism exploded with such force after the collapse of Communism. Nationalism was a *backlash* to Communist efforts to suppress national feeling. Nationalism was a *continuation* of the Communist regimes' promotion of ethnic dominance and a national cause. Nationalism reflected the *preservation* of ethnic identities in a system that had not been exposed to the global forces of the market, so these more primor-dial forms of identity politics persisted in the region after they had been eroded in the capitalist world.

In any case, once the Communist system collapsed, national identities and nationalist parties emerged in large numbers in eastern Europe, in the former Soviet Union, and even within parts of Russia. Exile communities and other anti-Communist forces in the west gave material support to nationalist move-ments (Denitch, 1994). In eastern Europe, some of these movements aim to re-build states as capitalist democracies with viable market economies; Hungary and the Czech Republic are examples of states that may be able to accomplish these goals. Other movements put their energy into settling old scores with ri-val ethnic groups, expelling migrants who settled in their territories during the Communist period, and/or expanding their territories. The ethnic wars in Tadzhikistan, the Caucasus region of the former Soviet Union, and the former Yugoslavia are examples of worst-case scenarios (Denitch, 1994; Hockenos, 1994a; Kaldor, 1993; Laqueur, 1993; Magas, 1993; Schöpflin, in McGarry and O'Leary, 1993; Suny, 1990; Thompson, 1992; Yergin and Gustafson, 1993).

It will be many years before eastern Europe and the former Soviet Union have stable boundaries and peaceful states. Some observers believe that a con-tinuing process of fragmentation is likely. The region has already doubled its number of states in only a 4-year period; another doubling is not impossible be-fore the end of the century and would result in the formation of a large number of microstates, some with populations and economies smaller than that of a metro area like Chicago and its suburbs (Farkas, 1994).

Nationalism interferes with the ability of the new states to survive eco-nomically. The small new states can only be viable within a trading bloc that re-constitutes a rationalized version of the economic integration that had been im-posed by the Soviet Union. Let me use an example that I saw firsthand: One of the very largest industries in Latvia (one of the three Baltic states) manufactured parts for telephone systems and electronic appliances; the plant was entirely in-tegrated with suppliers and end users in other parts of the Soviet Union. When Latvia became an independent nation, trading ties were broken with Russia; this plant and similar enterprises lost their reason for being because the prod-ucts were not competitive in global markets. The workers have been put on un-paid vacations every other month.

These new microstates and ministates have not only economic problems, but also problems of ethnic tension. To use the example of Latvia again: About half the population is ethnic Russian, since Russians were encouraged by the Soviet government to settle in the Baltic republics during Soviet rule. Many Russians who live in Latvia do not speak Latvian. Their schools and their informal social life are entirely segregated from that of Latvians. The new government of Latvia is debating the future of Russians in Latvia, who now find themselves a political minority, though they constitute half the population and often have no ties to anyone or anywhere in Russia. Those associated with the Russian armed forces may be forced to leave; others will possibly be able to obtain citizenship, but only after a long waiting period during which they may be blocked from acquiring property, a key right of citizenship as the nation shifts to a system of private ownership; only a few may be allowed to become citizens more quickly. So far, Latvia has been a rather "good" case, enjoying a fair amount of western support and trying to resolve these problems without recourse to violence.

The situation is worse in states in more isolated regions, such as Moldova or the central Asian states (Lievan and McGarry, in McGarry and O'Leary, 1993). Will the 25 million Russians dispersed in the non-Russian states of the former Soviet Union form movements to preserve or reclaim rights, perhaps putting pressure on Moscow to support them? Will ethnic expulsion take place, in more or less violent forms? What will be the fate of minorities (political and/or numerical) in the new states (Gurr, 1993)? These questions point to the potential for continuing nationalist mobilization and conflict. We are not at the end of the fourth wave of nationalism.

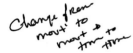

THE SUPPORT BASE OF NATIONALISM: FROM LITERATE MIDDLE STRATA TO ENTIRE POPULATIONS

Educated Middle Strata   Historically, nationalism was connected to the middle strata (Hobsbawm, 1989). As we noted, it was literate people who initiated nationalist movements and formulated nationalist ideologies, both in the first waves of nationalism in Europe and Latin America and in the anticolonial nationalist movements in Asia and Africa. The connection between national state formation and the establishment of governments and school systems drew in teachers and government functionaries.

The European and Latin American pattern was repeated in the nationalist movements in the colonized regions of Asia and Africa. Many nationalist leaders had obtained a western education, sometimes in the colony and sometimes in the colonial power (Anderson, 1991).

Military Officers   In later phases of decolonization, military officers had a significant role; military skill was important in some independence struggles and the army was often the first and most powerful national institution, one that welded young men from remote villages and small tribes into citizens of a modern nation.

The formation of nation-states in the region of the former Ottoman Empire illustrates the involvement of military officers; for example, the transformation headed by Kemal Ataturk that formed the modern state of Turkey after World War I (Trimberger, 1978). A generation later, in the same region, military leaders in the Arab states had a strong role in making their nations more independent from the European powers, like General Mohammad Naguib and Colonel Gamal Abdel Nasser who led a revolution in Egypt in 1952 against King Farouk and British intervention.

The Working Class: False Consciousness or Realistic Attachments?   Around the beginning of the twentieth century, workers in Europe and North America were somewhat more likely to be mobilized by socialism than by nationalism; but, as Hobsbawm points out, no class was immune to xenophobia and jingoism, and these forms of nationalist sentiment also appeared among peasants and the upper classes. Around the turn of the century, nationalism was promoted by political elites and the press in Europe as an antidote to the spread of socialism (Hobsbawm, 1989).

We have seen that, in a global system formed by nation-states and markets and characterized by large global differences in wealth, there is an economically rational or pragmatic component to national identity. Workers may have decided that identity as English citizens before World War II or, currently, as U.S., German, or Japanese citizens is worth more than international working-class solidarity across national lines. In part, national economic policy protects their advantages within the global structure. Working-class loyalty to the nation was not always motivated by jingoism; pragmatic considerations were also essential.

Mobilization after Nation-State Formation   Once nation-states were formed in a region, the entire population was, to some extent, mobilized along national lines; educational institutions, army experience, documents like passports that defined the individual in terms of a national identity are institutions that make national identity an official reality and a lived experience. In this way, classes and communities not part of the original support base of nationalist movements became mobilizable as ethnic or ethnic national identity overwhelmed all other possible forms of identity. For example, at the moment in Latvia, identity as Latvian or a Russian is a label on which is written each individual's future citizenship rights and economic opportunities. Under these conditions, claiming a collective identity along class or gender lines and downplaying the importance of ethnic national identity makes little sense in practice. The cases of Rwanda and the former Yugoslavia are even more extreme; ethnic identity is a matter of life or death—and no alternative self-definition is respected by those who carry arms. Political processes associated with the formation of nation-states have *reified* ethnonationalist identity—turned it from an imagined community that competed with other forms of solidarity into an inescapable reality backed up by institutions of coercion and violence (Denitch, 1994).

The Role of Elites in Nationalism   In discussing nationalist mobilization, we should keep in mind the complex mix of top-down nationalism and mass movements in the formation of nation-states. Several major periods of nation-state formation involved mostly **elite-initiated consolidation and mobilization,** especially the early modern formation of nation-states in western Europe and the late nineteenth-century unification and revitalization in Germany, Italy, and Japan. Even during the waves of nationalist movements, some movements did not have large mass bases. They were formed primarily by middle-class strata, by lawyers, teachers, and government functionaries.

In many cases of nation-state formation, especially during the third wave that formed new nations in western Africa after World War II, the nationalist movement succeeded more through top-level negotiation with former colonial powers than through any mass mobilization. For example, African scholar Basil Davidson thinks that "fewer than a thousand" persons formed the anticolonial leadership in the Gold Coast (now Ghana) (Vadney, 1987:235). The relatively small European settler population in west Africa was probably a major reason for this relatively easy transition to independence.

Mass Mobilizations   We should be aware that some nationalist movements were mass-based. Nationalism in India was initiated by the Indian National Congress, founded in Bombay in 1885; its founders were mostly intellectuals, journalists, businessmen, lawyers, and other professionals, generally university-educated, English-speaking, and of high-caste social origins. But, in the twentieth century, especially because of the leadership of Mohandas Gandhi, it greatly expanded its support base. His use of nonviolent means, like boycotts of English-made goods and large, peaceful demonstrations and marches, helped to bring hundreds of thousands of Indians into movement activism. When the Congress Party passed a "Quit India" resolution in 1942, the British unsuccessfully tried to suppress the movement by arresting 60,000 people, attesting to the dimensions of nationalist support (Vadney, 1987:108). Many peasants and artisans were attracted by Gandhi's criticism of industrialization, manufactured imports, and the erosion of village life. The condensation of Gandhi's goals into three terms furthered the building of an interclass nationalist support base: *Swaraj* (independence or self-government); *satyagraha* (nonviolent resistance); and *swadeshi* (the preservation of indigenous and local institutions, purged of their defects and inequalities—in short, autonomy or self-reliance) (Moore, 1965:372–378). These three abstract philosophical principles could bring together the village artisan worried about competition from British imports, the intellectual defending Indian culture, the lawyer seeking to build liberal democratic institutions in an independent nation, and the business owner looking for protection for Indian enterprise.

Mass Armed Struggles   In other regions, nationalist movements were equally large, but the authorities were more repressive and attempted to use massive force to prevent the end of colonial rule. National independence came only after mass struggles involving armed rebellion. Apart from the well-documented anticolonial wars in Vietnam and Algeria against the French in the 1950s and early 1960s; Indonesia against the Dutch in the late 1940s; and Angola, Mozambique, and Guinea-Bissau against the Portuguese in the 1970s; there were also scores of smaller wars. For example, a rebellion against the French took place in Madagascar in 1947; the state of siege was not lifted until 1956, tens of thousands of Malagasy died, and several thousand were held as political prisoners (Vadney, 1987:100). These nationalist mobilizations were very different from a smooth transfer of power by the colonial government to a small nationalist elite.

Complexity and Interclass Character of Support Bases   In this section, two characteristics of nationalist movements have been stressed: Smaller movements are usually centered in the *educated strata,* in literate groups involved in modern occupations like teachers, lawyers, journalists, and sometimes entrepreneurs. Larger movements have an *interclass support base.* They bring together the educated base with a larger supporting bloc that may include peasants, factory workers, the urban poor, and, in some cases, traditional landed elites, all united against an external enemy.

NATIONALIST MOVEMENTS IN POWER

States and Societies

Nationalism offers no formula for the social order. It does not spell out the form that political, economic, and social institutions should take as long as they further the interests of the nation. So, nationalist movements pursue different visions of the social order and implement them in different ways once they arrive at state power. Nationalist movements, once they are in power, establish two key institutions: institutions that define citizenship and membership in the nation and regulate ethnic conflict; and institutions that define the relationship of the state and the economy.

Exclusionary and Inclusionary Nationalism   Some forms of nationalism are inclusionary or **assimilationist.** They include within the nation any ethnic group living in the national territory, as long as it accepts the political system and culture of the dominant ethnic group. The nation is composed of citizens who share political and social values. Any person living within the national territory is potentially a citizen and should be induced to share these values. This assimilation usually implies fluency and literacy in the national language. France and the United States are examples of nations that have generally followed an assimilationist policy. Immigrants were encouraged to learn the national language, adopt the values and customs of the dominant group (Anglo-Europeans in the case of the United States), and become citizens (Horowitz, 1992). Inclusive nationalism also tended to extend citizenship rights to members of minority ethnic groups living in the national territory, accompanied by pressure to assimilate culturally by learning the national language and changing their customs. In France, for example, Jews, Basques, and Bretons were permitted and also pressured to become French in their speech habits, attendance in the national public school system, and general outlook.

When postcolonial nations formed in Africa and Asia in the middle of the twentieth century, they generally had to be somewhat inclusionary; since most of them formed along territorial lines set by the colonial powers, they included diverse ethnic groups that had to be brought together. However, many of them did not use a model of forced or voluntary assimilation to a dominant ethnic culture; instead, some effort was made to move toward **power-sharing** or **consociational** arrangements, sometimes involving elaborate rotation of public offices among ethnic groups; veto rights for minority groups; proportional division of resources like access to higher education; and ethnic control over religion, family law, and other cultural institutions (Lijphart, 1977; McGarry and O'Leary, 1993).

Other forms of nationalism are exclusionary. The nation is conceived of as a group into which one is born. Only those who are born into the dominant ethnic group, who can trace their ancestry within it, can really be part of the nation. This **essentialist view of the nation** is often associated with racism. The nation is formed by "blood," by ties that are both biological and mystical. The political entity of the nation-state is a reflection of the essential and organic unity of a people. Many German nationalists did not want to recognize Jews or Slavs living within German territory as "real Germans"; this racial definition of Germanness was amplified under Nazi rule. Establishing German citizenship is still difficult; many people of Turkish origin, for example, are not German citizens even if they are born in Germany, attend German schools, and use German as their first language. Similarly, Koreans whose families have lived in Japan for generations are not seen as members of the Japanese nation.

An exclusionary definition of a nation often implies that members of a core ethnic group have rights to citizenship in the nation regardless of where they live—rights that are different from the immigration opportunities of other groups. For example, Israel established the "law of return" that gave immigration rights to all Jews (defined by having a Jewish mother, or, rarely in practice, by religious conversion), while other people do not have these rights. Similarly, Italy gives immigration and citizenship rights to persons who can trace their descent from an Italian (until recently, only through the male line).

In some ways, this inclusionary/exclusionary distinction is oversimplified. There are many modes of managing ethnic diversity. For example, McGarry and O'Leary (1993:4–40) suggest eight such modes. They first define two broad categories—**eliminating or managing** differences. Within each of these categories they identify four normatively ranked modes. Ways of eliminating differences range from genocide to integration. Ways of managing differences range from hegemonic control to power sharing. The outcomes depend on a range of factors and are by no means fixed: The size, cultures, and class positions of the ethnic groups; the colonial policies; patterns of national development and the condition of the national economy; the training and ideology of nationalist leaders; and external pressures all have a part in shaping the outcome. Nationalist movements make decisions about **ethnic conflict regulation**

Ethnic Cleansing Serbia

once they are in power; they also arise as the result of problems in such regulation.

Nots turn on own

Political and Economic Institutions   Since nationalism as an ideology does not propose a clear vision of what society should be like, it is compatible with several other ideologies and forms of economic and political institutions, which have changed over history. Some of these combined forms—liberalism, ethnoracism, and socialism—are described in the following sections. Conservative ideology was one of the main elements of nationalism, especially from the later nineteenth century on; since it was most prominent in elite-initiated national consolidation, rather than in mass movements, I am not going to discuss it here.

Liberalism   Nationalism is associated not only with different definitions of who belongs to the nation, but also with different kinds of political and economic institutions. In the first wave of nationalist movements, nationalism was generally associated with liberalism. The two forces came together in the movements against empires and absolutist monarchies in Europe and the Americas in the late eighteenth and early nineteenth centuries. The liberal vision of a nation of citizens engaged in forming a government matched well with the nationalist vision of a unified people building its own institutions. Multiethnic empires were broken up in the name of both liberalism and nationalism. New states were formed that united people who spoke the same language and had a shared sense of history. Liberal democracy as well as liberalism continued to be compatible with nationalism (Hobsbawm, 1962).

The compatibility of liberal democracy and nationalism persisted as nationalism spread from Europe and the Americas to the colonized regions in the twentieth century. Ideals of the French and American Revolutions inspired nationalist leaders. The colonial powers were called to account for practicing liberal democracy at home, while subjecting the colonies to racial oppression and exploitation. They saw European (or North American) forms of society as offering viable models for nations they hoped to form, by violence if necessary. For example, the leaders of India's Congress Party, one of the main forces for independence, were influenced by the British political system. Although he was a Communist, Ho Chi Minh was inspired by the American Revolution.

But, in the meantime, two other kinds of movements began to influence nationalism: racism and fascism; and socialism, especially marxism-leninism.

Fascism/Ethnoracism   From the start, some forms of nationalism had expressed racist and essentialist ideas about the unity of a people and the nation. These ideas were often associated with a glorification of violence and a hatred of other nations. For example, a nineteenth-century German romantic nationalist wrote: "I call for hatred of the French, not just for this war. I want it to last for a long time, I want it to last for ever. . . . But, O German people, that this radiant hatred may be and continue, you must wage war, a hot, bloody and collective war of all Germans against the oppressors. Only their blood can wash away the shame which stains you; only their blood can restore the dignity which you have lost . . ." (Arndt, cited in Tibi, 1990:136–137). These sentiments pointed toward a strong state, organized around military ventures. Citizen representation was less important than an effective executive power to unite the nation and pursue its national interests abroad. In the twentieth century, these themes of nationalist ideology coincided with fascism, Nazism, and other forms of ethnoracism.

Mass support for a fascist or nazi version of nationalism often came from strata that felt threatened by the expansion of markets and the presence of ethnic groups whose economic activities affected local commerce and crafts. In eastern Europe, particularly Jews—but in some places also Germans—were identified with the disruptive effect of larger markets on local economies, because they were often merchants or small industrialists (Gellner, 1983). Peasants and artisans allowed their anger at new economic arrangements to be turned into anger at a "foreign" ethnic group. "Anti-semitism is the socialism of idiots," said Russian Jewish writer Isaac Babel.

Frantz Fanon, an anticolonial revolutionary, deplored similar tendencies in the postcolonial nations: "From nationalism we have crossed over to ultranationalism, to chauvinism and finally to racism. The foreigners are called to leave; their shops are burned, their street stalls are wrecked, they are being lynched . . ." (cited in Tibi, 1990: 56–57).

The contemporary wave of nationalism in the former Soviet Union and eastern Europe often builds on fascist models of state and society that incorporate the exclusion and expulsion of ethnic minorities, the formation of centralized, repressive states, and the belief that nations define themselves only in violent struggle against other peoples and nations (Denitch, 1994; Laqueur, 1993).

Socialism   In the twentieth century, especially during decolonization, nationalism was sometimes associated with socialism. Vietnam, the independence movements in Angola and Mozambique, and Cuba are good examples of situations in which these two ideologies were associated.

In some ways, the two ideologies appear incompatible: Identity and mobilization are either along class lines or along lines of the nation. But, from the socialist viewpoint, it was important that international relations be among free peoples as a first step toward building socialism as a global system. Thus, nationalism and national independence was a necessary condition for socialism; the globe had to be decolonized before socialism could appear on the agenda. It is not possible to skip the national period in the evolution of socialism (Fanon, 1967). Socialists, therefore, supported decolonization and nationalist movements.

Nationalist movements had several reasons for the association with socialism. One was that marxist-leninist-oriented parties had been able to bring about revolutions in the twentieth century; this type of movement seemed to be a good organizational model for nationalist movements that faced the armies of the colonial powers.

Another reason was to expand the appeal of the nationalist movement to a larger support base. Nationalist leaders used socialist appeals to mobilize the masses for a prolonged struggle against the colonial powers. If workers and peasants thought that they were about to trade foreign exploiters for a native capitalist and bureaucratic elite, there would have been less enthusiasm for taking the risks that the independence struggle required. Independence had to mean a better way of life, access to land, and more evenly distributed income and social services. Formal political independence had to be accompanied by a more equitable economic order. Some nationalist leaders like Ho Chi Minh in Vietnam believed in these socialist promises; there, the Communist Party spearheaded the nationalist struggle against the French. For others, socialism remained only a slogan. Nationalist and Communist organizations remained separate, and the former was prepared to oust and suppress the latter once national independence was accomplished (Chaliand, 1989; Walton, 1983).

The third reason nationalists adopted socialism was the sense of time pressure in economic development. Judging from the experience of the west, many nationalist leaders concluded that it might take centuries for the market to spread prosperity through the nation. The later a nation came to economic development, the more important the role of the state. It had been relatively limited in England, the first industrializing nation. In Germany, Japan, Sweden, even the United States—the successful later industrializers—governments had taken a more active part in the capitalist economy. After that, only the Soviet Union—a socialist state—seemed able to catch up as an industrial power; at least, so it seemed to some nationalist leaders in the 1950s and 1960s.

The development of infrastructure, the launching of new enterprises, the start-up of industries, and the distribution of services and income to the masses of people would require extensive state involvement in the new nations; hence, some form of centrally directed economy in view of the nationalist leadership. Many postcolonial nations like Algeria, Egypt, India, Guinea, and Zimbabwe began their economic development with states that owned and managed national resources and implemented development plans. This state guidance included many elements of socialism and was often referred to by this term (Chaliand, 1989).

Both U.S. and Soviet foreign policy analysts concluded erroneously that these elements of socialism in the economy and the role of the state represented a stable progression toward socialism; the Soviets were pleased, the Americans dismayed. Yet, in the long run, systems like Guinea, Zimbabwe, Tanzania, and Somalia (to name a few) did not really develop in a clear-cut socialist direction (Halliday, 1989).

A fourth reason for the association of nationalism and socialism was external, prompted by the weak position of the new nations in the global economy. Nationalist leaders in the decolonizing regions realized that formal political independence did not solve the problem of economic dependence. New nations like Nigeria and Ivory Coast continued to be dependent on the developed capitalist nations—and the former colonial powers—in global markets. Prices for their export commodities were not under their own control; foreign firms and foreign investments shaped their economies (Frank, 1981). Therefore, many nationalist leaders favored some form of break with capitalism as a global system. In their minds, socialism was connected with more **economic self-reliance**; the Chinese experiments in the 1950s suggested that this route to development might be feasible.

Finally, the association of nationalism and socialism had its opportunistic side. If a nation's leadership voiced elements of socialist ideology, formed parties modeled on the Communist parties of the Soviet Union and China, and instituted socialist economic planning, it could draw support from the Soviet Union and China (Chaliand, 1989; Halliday, 1989).

In the final analysis, the anticolonial marriage of socialism and nationalism was not a very happy one. Those elements of socialist planning that were introduced often led to the formation of privileged state bureaucracies, rather than the improvement of living standards and mass political participation (Howe, 1992). However, capitalism also failed to produce social equity, economic development, and democratic institutions in many postcolonial states.

Authoritarian States   The single most common outcome of nationalist movements, especially in the most recent waves, appears to have been an authoritarian state that is not liberal democratic, socialist, or fascist. These states are generally associated with market institutions, but they are rather different from the market democracies in the core regions. Some of these states have a default quality to them; they emerge as the nationalist movements in power fail to create states that are clearly market democracies, socialist, or fascist. The states that emerge in such a process of *not* choosing to become socialist, liberal, or fascist are authoritarian, and the economies are more or less capitalist. The nationalist movements often use populist discourses; actual practice leans more toward the authoritarian and manipulative side of populism than its egalitarian possibilities.

A large number of the world's states fall into this category. Many nations in Africa, the former Soviet bloc, and some in Latin America and Asia have authoritarian political systems with military dictatorships and/or single-party rule or single-party dominance. They have market economies and, usually, large state sectors. They lack the racism and mass mobilization that define fascism. They lack liberal democratic institutions that assure civil rights and some degree of representation (O'Donnell, 1973).

One type of authoritarian state often associated with nationalism is referred to as **Bonapartism** (after Louis Bonaparte, Napoleon's nephew, who came to power in France in the middle of the nineteenth century). The Bonapartist state is dominated by an individual, a dictator or strong man, who may have risen from the ranks of the military. He usually has some formal title like president but, in effect, has an unlimited stay in office and very strong executive power. Often the Bonapartist leader represents himself as the only force capable of guiding and unifying the nation in troubled times. He claims to be above the fray of the contending classes and parties. Populist rhetoric that refers to the people as an undifferentiated mass with a common will represented by the leader characterizes Bonapartist regimes.

Another type of authoritarian state associated with nationalism is the **military regime**; a circle of military officers rules the nation, suppressing representative bodies like parliaments and legislatures and generally ignoring constitutional rights. Alongside the military power structure, there is usually a civilian administrative apparatus that supports the military.

Another form of state associated with some nationalist movements is the the **dominant-party state.** In the single-party state, only one party is allowed to exist; there are no autonomous political parties or movements. The Nazi and Fascist states were single-party states, as were and are the historical Communist states like the former Soviet Union and China. In the dominant-party state, several parties are permitted to exist, but electoral laws—and, if needed, vote fraud—make it impossible for opposition parties to form a national government. There is no alternation in office of parties with different policies and programs. A good example of a dominant-party state is Mexico; since 1929, only one party has held the presidency and practically all the governorships; it has held a majority in the legislative bodies and has run the government bureaucracy. Only the Institutional Revolutionary Party (PRI) has effectively held power (Laurell, 1992).

These different forms of state may overlap somewhat. The single- or dominant-party state is sometimes formed by nationalist military officers. The Bonapartist leader may have been an officer. States that claim to be socialist may, upon close examination, really be authoritarian capitalist states with a large government sector and a powerful bureaucracy. States that claim to be part of the free world may have free markets, but little or no political freedom. One has to conclude that a large proportion—perhaps a majority—of the states formed by nationalist movements in the last 100 years are authoritarian states with weak market economies.

In short, nationalist ideology is primarily about the *boundaries* of nation-states and societies. It is therefore compatible with a variety of other movements and ideologies that specify more precisely what the form of the social order should be. It is also compatible with authoritarian political systems that lack clear-cut ideologies about the nature of society and simply claim to enhance the strength of the nation-state.

STRATEGIES OF NATIONALISM

The Formation of Collective Identities

All the movements we are examining in this book are ongoing processes, constantly redefining themselves. This open-ended character is probably strongest in nationalism, since it is least explicit about the substance of the social order it seeks to establish. Nationalism involves a constant renegotiation of ethnic identity, physical boundaries of states, and the match between ethnicity and the state. Nationalist movements are underway in scores of places. Some examples of these movements and the ways in which they renegotiate the social order are discussed. The strategy of nationalist movements highlights ethnic identity and links that identity to state formation and territorial claims.

Ethnic Identities   As we have already seen, nationalism is about identity. Nationalist movements appeal to ethnic identity and assert that such an identity exists and is valuable. They are engaged in the **social construction of national**

identity. Therefore, one of the activities of nationalist movements is the invention of histories, traditions, and identities. As Gellner points out, over 8000 languages and dialects are spoken in the world; which languages (not to mention, which ethnic groups without a distinct language) will form the basis of a nation-state (Gellner, 1983)? There is no set answer to this question; the formation of nationalist movements and the demand for self-determination are continuing processes.

Nationalism may end in genocide; it often begins in the writing of grammar books and history texts. A dialect, or the spoken language of an ethnic group, is standardized and transformed into a written language by the work of grammarians, often intellectuals with a political interest in this formalization of a language. This transformation gives it political substance and makes written communication easier. Novels and news begin to appear in the language; nationalist pamphlets begin to circulate. Literate people are drawn into the imagined community defined by the shared printed word (Anderson, 1991). In the twentieth century, electronic media contribute to this feeling; the radio, for example, played an important part in German and Arab nationalism. But, when nationalist movements find that their access to the electronic media is limited by states that oppose them and control the airwaves the movements have to fall back on print.

History and **traditions are invented** or reinvented and embodied in history books and rituals. The books relive the past triumphs of the people and nation and hark back to periods when (supposedly) the ethnonation had its own territorial state. Traditions like the coronation of royalty or military ceremonies recall a splendid past. That these histories and traditions are often pure invention is not fully recognized by the people who are mobilized; invented traditions can have an emotional impact. The English were particularly adept at inventing traditions, rituals, and uniforms in the nineteenth and early twentieth centuries that were supposed to unify the United Kingdom, create national feelings, and dazzle colonial peoples (Hobsbawm and Ranger, 1992).

Objects like royal crowns, scepters, military uniforms, flags, statues of military heroes, and anthems are designed to be **symbols of the nation** and to create feelings of national identity. These objects can be manufactured by political rulers to reaffirm existing states or by movements to make new claims. The controversy about whether flag burning is constitutionally protected free speech in the United States illustrates how important symbols can become; the symbol is inextricably linked to reality. Because people have died in warfare for their country, the symbol of the flag gains power and legitimacy. One of the first acts of revived national feeling in eastern Europe was to topple statues of Lenin to mark the end of Communism and Russian hegemony and restore old street names and revive pre-Communist flags.

In a more subtle process, historical maps may be redrawn by nationalist movements; regions claimed by a nationalist movement are shown to have been separate states once, and disputed boundaries are drawn in new ways. Archaeologists cease being scholars and become activists in nationalist movements, as their dusty digs are used to establish contested ethnic spheres. Did

Transylvania always have a mix of Romanian, Hungarian, and German populations, or was it once primarily Hungarian? Apparently academic questions
become focal points of disputes.

Limiting, Focusing, and Polarizing Identities   While nationalist intellectuals
establish or invent historical and linguistic claims, other movement activists
work on focusing ethnic identity. Most people have multiple identities and
could define themselves in several different ways. A South African could for instance think of herself as Zulu, Black African, or citizen of the republic (or for
that matter, woman or worker); which of these possible identities will she
choose as the basis of political action? A German-speaking citizen of the Italian
region of Alto Adige might think of himself as Tirolian, ethnic German, potential Austrian citizen, or Italian; how does he choose from among these options?
A person of Puerto Rican background living in Chicago might think of herself
as Puerto Rican, Hispanic or Latina (terms that have different connotations), or
citizen of the United States—perhaps all three at the same time—as well as
worker, woman, Catholic or Pentecostal, and so on. A major task for nationalist movements is to induce people to select the identity that corresponds to the
nationalist mobilization and end up feeling that this identity is the natural
choice.

To expedite this process, movement activists may form political parties or
pressure groups as well as carry out symbolic and propaganda activities. The
political parties and pressure groups try to tie concrete, local economic and political interests to the identity. The more the movement can merge feelings and
specific opportunities (like jobs) with the ethnic identity, the more effectively it
can mobilize people. These feelings may be positive—pride and self-esteem—
and negative—resentment and victimization.

The establishment and manipulation of concrete rewards and policies can
be used to polarize populations and set the stage for violent confrontations,
"ethnic cleansing," or other antiminority movements. For example, in the
spring of 1990, when the new post-Communist Croat leadership in Croatia began to purge the old Communist appointees they first fired those who were
members of the Serb minority; they also did little to respect symbols of Serb
culture like the Cyrillic alphabet; and finally, they used Croat police forces
in Serb minority regions of Croatia. These policies polarized the situation
and made the position of Serb moderates virtually untenable (Schöpflin, in
McGarry and O'Leary, 1993:201). Often, ethnic wars are not as inevitable as they
are later claimed to be, and in many cases, they do not arise from centuries-old
differences but from actions and policies deliberately undertaken by nationalist activists to polarize groups and heighten conflict (Denitch, 1994; Gottlieb,
1993).

In some circumstances, movements may undertake violent actions that polarize a population and force it to select an ethnic identity. For example, political separation followed by "ethnic cleansing" in Bosnia did not permit people
to retain a general Yugoslav identity or avoid defining themselves in ethnic
terms (Denitch, 1994). Violence divided communities along the ethnic lines se-

lected and imposed by the nationalist militias. In South Africa, the Zulu-based Inkatha movement has tried to force Zulus to identify as Zulus and not as members of the larger, more inclusive African National Congress (ANC). It has engaged in violent attacks on ANC members that make it more difficult for Zulus to function in the ANC. This strategy of Zulu separatism complicated the ANC's efforts to unify all potential opposition forces against the apartheid government.

In these cases, the strategic role of violence is to impose ethnic identity and speed the process of mobilization. The person who remains ambivalent about identity, tries to live with multiple identities, maintains interethnic friendships or family ties, or seeks an alternate nonethnic identity (like class or religion) is isolated and threatened (Denitch, 1994).

Parties and movements try to influence the existing state, pressuring for goals such as regional autonomy; separate or, at least bilingual school systems; ethnic TV and radio stations; the use of the ethnic language in courts and government offices; and so on. Success in these areas, in turn, enlarges the movement. As more institutions recognize the ethnic language and culture, more emotional and material gains induce individuals to identify with the movement. A nationalist movement organized as a party may then become the majority party in the region. Some movements are satisfied with increased regional autonomy. Others press on for a state of their own, sometimes by peaceful means and sometimes through armed struggle.

At a crucial point in many nationalist movements, as in many other contemporary movements, strategies of armed conflict and violence are used. Terrorism and guerrilla forces are often selected as nationalist strategies. A regular army, supplemented by paramilitary forces and militias, may also be used in nationalist movements, for instance, in Croat and Serb expansion into Bosnia (Denitch, 1994).

Once in power, nationalist movements may continue to mobilize the population to violent conflict and consolidate their hold by attacks on neighboring states. Military operations are not only a way of establishing an autonomous state, but also the basis for confirming the new ethnic national basis of identity. This identity becomes an inescapable reality when people are conscripted, everyone is asked to make sacrifices to defeat the enemy, and alternative forms of identity and allegiance are labeled as treason. Warfare is a way of building nationalist sentiment and imposing nationalist loyalties, for movements both in and out of state power (Goodwin and Skocpol, 1989; Skocpol, 1988).

EMERGENCE OF NATIONALIST MOVEMENTS

It is impossible to identify all the situations in which nationalist movements arise. I have already identified the historical circumstances of several major waves of nationalism, largely associated with the breakup of colonial and multiethnic empires. Nationalism continues to appear in many places where ethnicity and nation-state boundaries are imprecisely matched. Specific situations in which nationalist movements emerge are defined as instances of structural strain by nationalist movements.

The following illustrations are only meant to offer examples. Those examples should not be thought of as a typology, with rigid, exhaustive, and mutually exclusive categories. Quite the contrary—nationalist movements are extremely fluid and may pursue a combination of goals or shift as circumstances change. Readers will surely think of other circumstances and other illustrations. There are, however, some shared characteristics in these histories. Many of the movements are the result of three distinct phases of ethnic relations associated with the formation of multiethnic states (often formed in colonization or empire building) and their later breakdown into nation-states.

In the first, precolonial phase, distinct ethnic groups were present, but their settlement patterns did not correspond to nation-states with precise boundaries. The relations among ethnic groups were by no means always peaceful, egalitarian, and idyllic. Sometimes there were hostilities and warfare; in other cases, groups were stratified by relations of subordination and superordination. For example, in Rwanda and Burundi, two states in central Africa in which genocidal conflict is currently taking place, the pastoral Tutsi ruled over agricultural Hutu; the two groups had a castelike relationship but shared the same language (Lemarchand, in McGarry and O'Leary, 1993).

In the second phase, an external power intervened in the relationships among ethnic groups. This intervention took different forms; often, it was direct colonial rule; in other cases, it was indirect external pressure or the formation of a multiethnic state like the Soviet Union. The institutions associated with this intervention varied. At times, the colonial or hegemonic power favored one ethnic group over the others and opened government posts, military careers, or commercial opportunities to it. To return to the example of Rwanda and Burundi, the Belgian rulers favored the Tutsi, especially the elites within this group, and opened more political and educational opportunities for them than for the Hutu; in addition, they imposed taxes and compulsory labor and crop obligations on the Hutu peasantry (Lemarchand, in McGarry and O'Leary, 1993:155–156). The Belgians also allowed the Tutsi to become dominant in the emerging modern sectors of the economy, leading to much greater wealth differences than had existed in precolonial times. In some colonies, this type of favoritism was part of a deliberate divide-and-rule policy. In other cases, as with the Ibo in British-ruled Nigeria, one ethnic group simply seemed more able to benefit from such opportunities, perhaps because of a better match between their culture and the modern colonial institutions. In either case, ethnic groups began to differ markedly in their success in the new modern political and economic institutions that emerged in the colony or multiethnic state. These differences created the conditions for postcolonial conflict over scarce government jobs, university openings, and other resources.

The colonial or hegemonic powers also altered the older ethnic patterns by permitting or inducing immigration. For example, the British brought Indian laborers to Fiji in the Pacific, to Guyana and Trinidad in the Caribbean region, and to east Africa; they permitted European Jews to settle in Palestine. In the Soviet

Union, Russians were encouraged to move out of Russia and settle in other areas like the Baltic republics and Kazakhstan. These patterns of migration were to have profound effects on the new nations that later formed out of the empires.

In the third phase, the colonial or hegemonic powers withdrew or were ousted from the colonies. They left specific forms of political and economic institutions, each with its own pattern of ethnic relations. The colonial powers or intervening states had drawn the borders of most of the new nations, and these lines did not always match ethnic settlement. Sometimes multiethnic states were created, as in Nigeria; sometimes, one ethnic group was divided between two or more new nations. For example, after a period of unsettled boundaries in what had been the Austro-Hungarian Empire, fully one-third of Hungarians (Magyars) found themselves outside Hungary, in Romania, Czechoslovakia (now the Czech Republic and Slovakia), and Croatia.

In many cases, the colonial or hegemonic power created a new nation with fragile mechanisms for regulating ethnic conflicts, which broke down in the postcolonial period. Ethnic tensions escalated into **ethnic warfare.** One reason for breakdown was an uneven or rapidly changing demographic balance. One ethnic group increased more rapidly than the others, because of a higher birth rate or in-migration or, possibly, because it was larger in the first place. These differences in growth rates led to breakdowns in democratic institutions—one person, one vote sounded good to a large or growing group, but not to a group whose relative size was small or shrinking.

In the case of Burundi and Rwanda, the Hutu constituted about 85 percent of the population. Hutu electoral victories would have reversed the Tutsi dominance that had hardened during Belgian rule, and the Tutsi began to take steps outside the electoral process to prevent elections and the seating of elected Hutu officials. Although the patterns were not identical in Burundi and Rwanda, in both countries, a series of army coups, political assassinations, and ethnic insurgencies finally escalated into genocidal conflicts (Lemarchand, in McGarry and O'Leary, 1993).

Another cause of breakdown in some countries was concentration of some ethnic groups in sectors of the political system and an economy that seemed closed to certain groups. Disputes over language and cultural symbols also erupted. Other nation-states intervened in these breakdowns to protect their co-ethnics and, sometimes, to expand their own sphere of interest.

To understand the emergence of ethnic conflict and nationalist movements, we have to look at a sequence of causal factors: precolonial ethnic tensions and inequalities; colonial/hegemonic policies that intentionally or unintentionally amplified these tensions, and often added new ones associated with modern institutions such as the establishment of borders, access to economic and political resources, and/or resettlement and immigration policies; postcolonial processes that upset the shaky balance the colonial powers had left in place. Some accounts overemphasize one or another of these elements, blaming primordial hatreds and age-old rivalries, imperialism, or the inability of the new nations to govern themselves; a more objective analysis looks at the whole sequence of ethnic relations, ethnic policies, and **escalation of conflicts**.

Patterns of Structural Strain

Irredentism and Separatism   One of the most common types of nationalist movement is the irredentist or separatist movement that seeks to establish a new nation-state in a region of an existing state. The effort to establish the state of Biafra in the eastern region of Nigeria is an example; the Biafran war in the late 1960s was fought by the other regions of Nigeria to suppress this movement and force Biafra to remain in Nigeria (Levin, 1993). Eritrea successfully broke away from Ethiopia after years of fighting. Within the new state of Georgia (formerly part of the Soviet Union), Abkhazians and Ossetians are seeking to form separate states of their own. Irredentism usually means a movement to reestablish a preexisting state; separatism is a more general term that includes breaking away to form a new state or reestablish an old one.

Separation and Reunification   Sometimes nationalist movements seek to disengage a region, not to form a new state but to unite it with a neighboring state. For several decades, the Irish Republican Army has tried to reunite Northern Ireland with the Irish republic, detaching it from the United Kingdom and British rule (O'Duffy, in McGarry and O'Leary, 1993). Movements of Somalis living in the Ogaden province in Ethiopia tried to annex that province to Somalia during fighting in the 1970s.

Carving Out New Nation-States   Some movements attempt to establish a new nation-state within territory held by another group. The Zionist movement established the state of Israel after World War II in territory inhabited by Arabs and governed by the British. And the Palestine Liberation Organization, as well as other Palestinian nationalist movements, would like to establish a Palestinian state in territory currently held by Israel.

Nationalist movements may attempt to establish a new nation-state by detaching territory from existing nation-states in such a way that an ethnic group scattered in several states can have a state of its own. For decades, Kurds living in Iraq, Turkey, Iran, and the Soviet Union have tried to form a Kurdish state in that region (Malek, 1989). In the case of the Kurds, no core state as yet exists. In other cases of this type of nationalism, a core exists and the movement attempts to expand it as it brings more members of the ethnic group together; the formation of a "greater Serbia," now taking place in the former Yugoslavia is an example of such an enlargement of an existing core territory (Magas, 1993).

Decolonization and Opposition to External Hegemony   Nationalist movements have been major forces for decolonization; for example, the independence movement in India. Also, they have been forces in opposition to economic hegemony or political dominance by another nation. For example, much of the appeal of Solidarity in Poland rested on its opposition to Soviet influence.

Expulsion of "Foreigners" and "Ethnic Cleansing"   Nationalist movements may take on a racist and chauvinist character, aimed at expelling or even killing people who are labeled as foreign elements within an existing nation-state. For example, the National Front in France is an anti-immigrant party that encourages this type of labeling. Sometimes these mobilizations are launched by incumbent elites to drive "foreigners" out of the society, as in Idi Amin's expulsion of East Indians from Uganda or attacks on the Muslim minority fomented by the government of Myanmar (Burma). In some of the central Asian successor states of the Soviet Union, Russians are being expelled. The goal of this type of nationalist movement is to enhance the connection between an ethnic group and the territorial state by eliminating other groups from the territory. Such attacks make the businesses, homes, jobs, university places, and other resources of the expelled group available to members of the expelling group; in this way, such expulsions are a temporary substitute for economic development, a way of expanding resources for the dominant ethnic group.

Shifting the Balance of Ethnic Group Power   Nationalist movements may arise to shift the balance of power among groups in a multiethnic state or to preserve that balance if a dominant group feels threatened. The group that is in the numerical majority may favor representative government and a liberal democratic political system; the smaller group may feel forced to use violent or antidemocratic means to preserve its rule or expand its rights, since representative democracy and civil liberties threaten its position. The African National Congress and the white fascistlike AWB (Afrikanervolkswag) are examples in South Africa (Adam and Moodley, in McGarry and O'Leary, 1993; Saul, 1991).

The Pacific island nation of Fiji provides a good example of how movements can both emerge from and further polarize a situation of interethnic tension. The British colonial administration had imported laborers from India around the turn of the century; ironically—in hindsight—this policy had been undertaken to protect indigenous Fijians from exploitation as laborers. The Indian population grew rapidly and outnumbered the Fijians by 1945. For several decades, a delicate balance was worked out between the two communities; Fijians dominated the civil service and owned the land, while Indians were active in small-scale commerce and rented land from Fijians for commercial sugar production. In fact, Indians excelled in education, but part of the ethnic bargain involved limiting the Indian share of public sector jobs even if they were qualified for them in larger proportions than the Fijians. In each community, an ethnonationalist nucleus developed to challenge the negotiated accommodations that existed between Indian and Fijian leaders. Among Fijians, these mobilizations initially included a nationalist party with a "Fiji for the Fijians" slogan and, later, established the Taukei movement, which carried out road blocks and fire bombings against Indian political organizations. The movement was probably initiated or, in any case, amplified by a small group of members of a Fijian party distressed by defeat at the polls. These disturbances gave the Fijian-majority military an excuse to carry out a coup; it led to a new constitution that reserved the presidency and prime ministership, as well as a majority of seats in parliament, for Fijians and gave them preference in civil service appointments (Premdas, in McGarry and O'Leary, 1993).

This example illustrates the role of nationalist movements in upsetting fragile power-sharing arrangements. The nationalist movement was not only the result of underlying structural strains; it amplified these strains and speeded up a process of polarization. The normative issues are complex in this example, as in so many nationalist mobilizations. The indigenous Fijians have become a minority in their own country, and face the numerical dominance—hence, potentially also the political, cultural, and economic dominance—of an ethnic group that originates in a much larger and more powerful state (India). At the same time, it seems unfair that individual Indians—virtually all born in Fiji—should be denied citizen rights that are normally guaranteed in liberal democracies.

Revitalizing Weak States   Nationalist movements may seek to revitalize an existing nation-state they define as weak or dependent. This goal was one of the most important elements of Nazi ideology; Germany was not only to expand in order to gain new territory and bring in ethnic Germans scattered in other countries of Europe, but also to regain its power and military strength. Gaullism was a moment in France in the 1960s that heralded General de Gaulle as an individual who would revive French strength; the movement resulted not only in his presidency, but also in major changes in the constitution toward a republic with a strong presidency. Sometimes these types of **national revitalization** movements are launched by ruling elites and have a top-down structure and momentum.

Cultural Autonomy and Ethnonationalism   The term nationalism is often used for movements whose goal is **cultural autonomy** for an ethnic group within a multiethnic state, even when the ethnic group is territorially dispersed. For example, in the United States, one can speak of a black nationalist movement that called and continues to call for institutions like Afrocentric schools and more community-based media and economic development.

This usage makes sense as long as we remain aware that it is not identical to movements that call for a new nation or even for regional autonomy within the existing nation. Here, the term nation is almost a metaphor; African Americans in the United States certainly can form an imagined community—a collective identity as a people—and can develop and control institutions like churches, mosques, schools, and political pressure groups. In this respect, they are like ethnic groups with claims to nationhood, but their territorial claims are necessarily limited by their dispersion in the territory of the United States.

The nationalism of a dispersed group is different from the nationalism of groups like Native Canadians, Inuit in both Canada and the state of Alaska, and Welsh and Scots in Britain, who retained a distinct territory even if it was settled and exploited by other ethnic groups (Levin, 1993). The United States was formed as a multiethnic society largely by voluntary and involuntary migration, an assimilationist policy which encouraged mobility, and strong market forces; these conditions scattered ethnic groups across the national territory. It is difficult for many ethnic groups in the United States to make nationalist claims for distinct territories. Americans of African, European, Asian, and Latin American backgrounds live scattered in the national territory. Native Americans and Hawaiians, as well as Mexican Americans in the southwest, see themselves historically associated with distinct territories, territories that have been extensively encroached upon by other ethnic groups. In the absence of such distinct territories, nationalist movements are more about cultural autonomy; in this sense, such movements' goals overlap liberal notions about opening a large number of options in civil society.

EXTERNAL SUPPORT

Nationalist movements, particularly of the separatist or irredentist variety, present excellent opportunities for a state that is intent on destabilizing some other state. The hostile state provides money, arms, training, and, in some cases, secure bases for the nationalist-separatist movement. For example, South Africa supported the National Union for the Total Independence of Angola (UNITA) guerrillas against the revolutionary government of Angola, hoping to reduce Angola's role as an opponent of the apartheid regime and diminish Angola's capacity to serve as a revolutionary model for other African states and movements. In turn, Cuba sent troops to support the Angolan government. The government and the insurgents had distinct ethnic support bases, so there was a superimposition of several lines of conflict—ethnic, regional, ideological, and alignment with the cold war blocs.

As Eritreans tried to separate their region from Ethiopia, many large powers sent support, sometimes in surprising sub-rosa cooperation: Saudi Arabia and other Muslim states supported the Eritreans; the Soviets and Cubans supported the Ethiopian government because it was presumably marxist, and the Israelis probably supported it to oppose growing Arab influence in the region (Halliday and Molyneux, 1982).

Rumors of external support multiplied on both sides during the cold war; the superpowers and their allies charged that nationalist movements were pawns or proxies of the rival superpower, that they were funded and armed in order to destabilize members of the respective blocs. In the view of western governments and media, many nationalist movements (like the IRA and the PLO) were said to have been funded or supported by the Soviet Union, either directly or through shadowy intermediary states like Libya or Cuba. The Soviet Union, in turn, charged western powers with supporting nationalist and separatist movements against its allies. In many cases, these examples of external support are reasonably well documented. The Soviet Union and, initially, China, supported the communist-nationalist independence movement in Vietnam. The United States overtly supported the Islamic-nationalist mujahidin forces in Afghanistan in their resistance to the Soviet invasion in 1979. In other cases—such as the concept of a Soviet-backed transnational terror network—the evidence remained unconvincing, and the charges seemed to be manufactured for cold war propaganda purposes.

Sometimes, layers of proxies made it difficult to see the links between movements and external powers; intermediate countries and patrons made it more difficult to trace the roles of the superpower and other interested nations in arming and encouraging separatist and nationalist movements. Aid was covert and filtered through layers of intermediaries. "Enemies of my enemies are my friends" became an operating principle, leading to morally and even strategically questionable policies.

For example, the Khmer Rouge under the leadership of Pol Pot had come to power in Cambodia in 1975–1976. The Khmer Rouge was an insurgency influenced by the ideas of Stalin and Mao Zedong. This movement in power murdered hundreds of thousands of Cambodians in a vicious and unrealistic program of imposing peasant communism on the society (Chandler, 1994:96). Hundreds of thousands more died in a famine caused by the Khmer Rouge's ill-conceived agricultural plan. (This situation became familiar to many westerners through the movie *The Killing Fields*.) In January of 1979, the Vietnamese army entered Cambodia, ousted Pol Pot, and established a Vietnamese-backed government; though neither democratic nor autonomous, this new government was, at least, not genocidal and it restored more livable and humane conditions. Pol Pot reconstituted the Khmer Rouge guerrillas as a nationalist force and attacked Vietnam-aligned Cambodia from bases in Thailand. He "stressed his nationalist credentials, and posed as an authentic patriot" (Chandler, 1994:98). Because the Soviet Union and Vietnam opposed Pol Pot and the Khmer Rouge, some anti-Soviet powers, including the United States, China, and Thailand, supported him and, until recently, backed the Khmer Rouge as the legitimate candidate for Cambodia's UN seat (Chandler, 1992, 1994; Vadney, 1987:507–511)!

COUNTER MEASURES

A government under attack by a nationalist movement fights back with a variety of means.

Concessions and Co-optation

A government may try to co-opt the movement and especially its leadership, offering more economic opportunities, concessions about language rights like separate schooling or media systems, and even limited regional autonomy. For example, the federal government of Canada has allowed the French-speaking province of Quebec to make laws that preserve French culture and language, such as a ban on outdoor signs in English and compulsory French-language schooling for all children except Anglophones (children of non-English-speaking immigrants must attend French schools) (Tremblay, in Levin, 1993).

Repression

The central government can also undertake repressive measures, imprisoning leaders of the nationalist movement, especially if some members of the movement use violent means. Nationalist movements sometimes put severe strains on liberal governments, which may turn to practices that violate civil rights, like torture, prolonged detention without trial, and so on. Some of the measures taken by the British government against IRA nationalist forces in Northern Ireland are examples of these practices.

The same Anglo-dominated Canadian government that was prepared to make concessions to the French-speaking population tended to take repressive measures against mobilizations by the Native Canadian population; only after the 1960s did the aboriginal movements become more cohesive and more successful (Asch; Macklem; Tanner; in Levin, 1993).

Resettlement Policies

Another common countermeasure is to encourage migration of the dominant ethnic group into the contested region in order to dilute the strength of the potentially irredentist local ethnic group. The Romanian government encouraged ethnic Romanians to settle in Transylvania, reducing the percentage of Hungarians in the region and thereby making it more difficult to call for a transfer of the region to Hungary. China has pursued a similar settlement policy in Tibet by encouraging ethnic Chinese to move there. The Soviet government encouraged Russian settlement in the Baltic states after it annexed them in 1940. When settlers move in, an ethnic group may become a minority in its own region, as happened to native Hawaiians.

Under certain conditions, a central government resorts to the resettlement of the potentially nationalist group itself, often preemptively, before there is evidence of a real irredentist movement. This kind of preemptive countermeasure almost always involves violations of civil liberties and human rights, as an entire population is lumped together, labeled, and deported without evidence of any specific illegal acts. Stalin deported the Crimean Tartar and Volga German populations to central Asia, because he believed their nationalist aspirations might make them side with the Germans during the Second World War. These measures have also been undertaken in supposedly liberal democratic political systems. Fears that pro-Japan sentiment and activities might develop among Japanese Americans during World War II led to the federal government's decision to relocate all persons of Japanese ancestry living on the west coast to special camps, even though many of them were U.S. citizens.

BEYOND THE NATION-STATE?

In the last decades of the twentieth century, nationalist movements and nationalist conflicts are under way in many regions, especially in the former

Soviet bloc states. In that region, nations are fragmenting into smaller, supposedly more ethnically homogenous states. For example, Yugoslavia has splintered into many pieces, some of them still at war and fragmenting further. The Soviet Union has broken up, and several of its successor states continue to divide. Czechoslovakia has split into the Czech Republic and Slovakia.

But there are also signs of the opposite kind of process, especially in western Europe; European integration has brought many nations together into a larger economic union. Nationalism has become more flexible as ethnic groups and distinct regions find new ways of integrating into the unity of Europe, other than forming separate nation-states.

Two processes are involved in these new prospects for nationalism. One results from the end of the cold war and the other from the increasing integration and globalization of markets, which forces smaller economies to form larger trading blocs.

The End of the Cold War

The end of the cold war has affected nationalist movements in contradictory ways. On the one hand, they have lost their superpower sponsors. The flow of funds and arms has diminished. The stronger states no longer have much reason to back nationalist movements for their own geopolitical ends, and this lack of interest has weakened nationalist movements and forced some of them into negotiations. For example, the end of the cold war is probably one of the main reasons why the PLO and the Israelis are negotiating.

But, on the other hand, there is less interest among the stronger states in limiting regional wars, now that regional wars are not likely to spread into a nuclear confrontation between superpowers. Ethnic conflict and ethnic insurgencies, even to the point of genocide, receive little attention from states that are capable of intervening; fighting in southern Sudan, violence in Rwanda, and clan warfare in Afghanistan are examples of bloodshed in which major powers are reluctant to become directly involved.

Postnationalism in the Global Economy

The rapid restructuring of the global economy is having unpredictable effects on nationalism. Small states are not economically viable by themselves, but, their small size may confer a degree of autonomy and flexibility on economic development within trading blocs and global markets. The modern world was characterized by a global system in which a transnational economy of markets (capitalism) coexisted with a political system composed of nation-states (Wallerstein, 1974). Capitalism will continue as a transnational system, but its political units may no longer be only (or even primarily) nation-states, but other entities like **supranational** trading blocs (like the European Community), **subnational** zones of development (like Tuscany or the south of England), and culturally autonomous areas like the Basque region. We are only beginning to imagine this system (Camilleri and Falk, 1993).

At the same time that the fourth wave of nationalism is causing armed conflicts and dislocations, and fragmenting ministates, there are some signs that nationalist movements can also move toward more constructive outcomes within the new regional blocs and global markets. Nationalist movements will continue to influence the outcome of these processes, but it is possible that the outcome will not continue to be the formation of separate, distinct, and rigidly defined nation-states as in the nineteenth and twentieth centuries.

In the European Community, an effort is underway to integrate a more balanced structure of regional, national, and subnational units with more rationally designed rights and functions at each level. Nation-states will continue to be building blocks within the European Community, but more economic processes will operate at the level of Europe as a whole and at the level of subnational regions—for example, Tuscany within Italy (Leonardi and Nanetti, 1995). The nation-state is being dissolved into both supranational and subnational entities. Nationalist-separatist movements like those of the Basques are discovering that more regional autonomy is possible without a total break from the nation-state (Keating, in McGarry and O'Leary, 1993). The extreme power, centralization, and rigidity of the nation-states formed during the nineteenth century in Europe are being tempered by the integration of the European economy as a whole and better economic planning at subnational levels.

So far, these developments away from nationalism are most visible in Europe and, there, only in embryonic form. It remains to be seen whether they will be repeated elsewhere. Trading blocs in North America, Central America, and South America such as NAFTA are being formed. More regional cooperation in Africa would be a good development strategy. If and when such trading blocs emerge, nationalist movements will probably have a part in determining their form and the relative strengths of different nations and/or ethnic groups within them.

However, it might be useful to keep in mind that the softening of nationalism and the weakening of the nation-state can have some drawbacks. The nation had functioned in the more developed core countries to chart a course of economic policy and ensure some sharing of benefits among the citizens of the nation-state. For example, Germans and Swedes of all classes shared in the post-World War II economic miracles of these countries, and a large cross section of U.S. citizens enjoyed growing prosperity in this period as well. National policies to encourage growth and social equity, strong domestic markets, and the Fordist accumulation model had all been part of the long economic boom in the United States and Europe. If the nation no longer functions to channel investments, ensure job growth, and develop education and infrastructure, growing class gaps may appear in relatively wealthy and egalitarian countries.

At least one major U.S. economist calls for a "positive economic nationalism" that improves the citizens' standard of living, enhances their skills and productiv-

Insurgents in Afghanistan combined nationalist, Islamic, and anti-socialist themes. Conflicts among factions and movements slowed the formation of a viable new regime after Soviet withdrawal and the fall of the Soviet-backed government. Mujahidin with a captured tank, Gardez, Afghanistan. April 22, 1992.

ity, and ensures a relatively egalitarian society (Reich, 1992). In Reich's words: "It [positive economic nationalism] seeks to encourage new learning within the nation, to smooth the transition of the labor force from older industries, to educate and train the nation's workers, to improve the nation's infrastructure, and to create international rules of fair play for accomplishing all these things. The objectives of such investments are unambiguously public" (Reich 1992:312).

I will conclude this chapter on a cautiously positive note—nationalism has all too often meant hatred and conflict; perhaps, in the future, it can play a more constructive role in forming national communities that are responsible and public spirited.

SUMMARY

More than any other type of movement, nationalism is a constant process, a constant flux of defining and redefining ethnic identities and trying to match nation-states to these identities. In some ways, it is more accurate to speak of nationalisms, than nationalism, because each specific instance is different from the others. The movements have tended to come in major waves—first in western Europe and Latin America, later in eastern Europe and western Asia, then in Africa and southern Asia, and most recently, again in eastern Europe as well as in the former Soviet Union. The result of these waves is that most of the globe is organized into nation-states. Large multiethnic states are fewer than in the past, and colonial empires have virtually disappeared. At the same time, regions where nation-states were established in the past are still undergoing movements of ethnic conflict and formation of new states.

National identity and nationalism, like all forms of collective identity, are *socially constructed.* The nation is an imagined community, not a primordial or natural bond. Literacy, expanding markets, and colonialism have all contributed to the emergence of national identities and nationalist movements. Once formed, nationalist movements extend an ethnonationalist identity into mass constituencies, sometimes polarizing ethnic groups. Once in power, nationalist movements create states that strengthen these identities further, linking them into educational systems, national media, armed forces, and other institutions.

Nationalism is more about getting the boundaries of societies "right"—that is, finding a match of territory, state, and ethnicity—than it is about social, economic, and political institutions within this state. Nationalist movements do not have one single vision of a just social order, so the final form of the states and societies they bring into existence is not predetermined. Sometimes these states are capitalist democracies; sometimes they contain elements of socialism. Frequently, they end up with market economies and some form of authoritarian state.

Like all movements, nationalisms are in conflict with each other, with other types of movements, and with existing states. Despite the beginnings of subnational and supernational entities (autonomous regions, trading blocs, etc.) the process of nationalism is not likely to stop in our lifetimes, and the possibilities for movements and conflicts remain endless.

KEY TERMS AND CONCEPTS

nation-state formation
national identity
imagined communities
absolutist monarchy
colonialsim
literacy
transnational market economy
global markets and national states
Meiji Restoration (Japan)
self-determination
decolonization
elite-initiated nationalism

nationalist movements in power
exclusionary and inclusionary
   nationalism
assimilation

power sharing and consociationalism
essentialist views of the nation
eliminating or managing ethnic
   diversity; ethnic conflict regulation
ethnoracism
economic self-reliance
authoritarian states
Bonapartism
military regime
one-party dominant states

nationalist identity formation
ethnic identity
the social construction of national
   identity
the invention of tradition
symbols of the nation

ethnonationalist conflicts
ethnic warfare
the escalation of conflicts
irredentism and separatism
national revitalization

cultural autonomy
resettlement policies
supranational and subnational
   territorial units

Adolf Hitler (right) prepares to address a
rally in Nürnberg, Germany, 1938.

CHAPTER 11

Fascists, Nazis, and Neo-Nazis

Ethnoracism and Myths of Blood

. . . since true idealism is nothing but the subordination of the interests and life of the individual to the community, and this in turn is the precondition for the creation of organizational forms of all kinds, it corresponds in its innermost depths to the ultimate will of Nature. It alone leads men to voluntary recognition of the privilege of force and strength, and thus makes them into a dust particle of that order which shapes and forms the whole universe. . . . This self-sacrificing will to give one's personal labor and if necessary one's own life for others is most strongly developed in the Aryan.
—Adolf Hitler, *Mein Kampf,* Houghton Mifflin, Boston, 1962, pp. 297, 299.

A cold wind blows through the parking lot of a shabby minimall or the empty spaces of a drab European housing project . . . a group of youths stands huddled together, loading shadowy objects into a car. One of them walks over to two newcomers to draw them into the venture. He is a fair-complexioned lad with a shaven head and heavy boots. His eyes shine and his voice is hoarse with intensity as he tries to win over the two new men: "You know there's going to be race war. We have to make the first moves, to act and not just react. Soon we'll be a minority in our own country. The foreigners are taking our jobs. They breed like rabbits. The Jews control the banks, the stock market, and the media. A white man can't get credit anymore, we can't start businesses. And blacks have taken over the government, they can live high on welfare, ruin our schools and our neighborhoods, and get all those jobs they are not qualified for. Our government no longer represents us, the Aryan heart and soul of this nation. We built this country, we made it great with our sweat and blood and guts, and now we are strangers in our own land. We will not be a great nation again until we are a white Aryan nation again with real leaders. We can make this happen, but it's going to be violent, it's going to be race war. You know in the final showdown, it will all split apart along race lines—each will have to stick with his own. We're stockpiling weapons, because only the strong will survive. Are you for us or against us? You look white, soon you'll see there is no other choice. If you are with us, join us tonight as we make the flames leap high!"

Fascism and Nazism persist as movements and ideologies; in the last few years, in both western and eastern Europe, movements that had nearly been eliminated in World War II are experiencing growth and resurgence. In the period from World War I to World War II (from 1918 to 1945), fascism and Nazism were mass movements that came to state power. Their ability to present themselves as the solution to complex social and economic problems made them powerful in the interwar years and continues to make them appealing to a support base that is frustrated by economic stagnation and the challenge of living in multiethnic societies. This discussion concerns fascism and Nazism as movements that are similar in ideology and organization, although a few important distinctions have to be made between them. The focus is on Nazism, because it is the most distinct and extreme form of the movement; fascism has similar features but is generally less extreme. Nazism provides the clearest example of the types of states and societal policies that emerge when these movements come to power.

NAZI AND FASCIST IDEOLOGY

The major ideas of nazi and fascist ideology revolve around a conception of nature as a realm of *domination,* struggle, and violence among species, races, and individuals; the stronger forms dominate or destroy the weaker ones. Human society, as part of nature, must follow these same principles (Hitler, 1962).

Ethnoracism

At the core of nazi and fascist ideology is *racism,* a set of ideas about the superiority and inferiority of ethnic groups. Ethnicity is conceptualized as "race," as an immutable fact that binds together biological and cultural traits. Fascism and Nazism are *essentialist:* The characteristics of different ethnic groups and nations are not based on language and culture, which can change, but are inherent in the nature of these groups. This view is implicitly or explicitly influenced by the doctrine of **scientific racism** that was widespread among Europeans around 1900; scientific racists postulated consistent, all-encompassing, and genetically inherited differences among groups they called Caucasoids, Negroids, and Mongoloids, as well as many smaller groups like Alpines, Nordics, Semites, and so on. These differences were not confined to features of physical appearance like skin color or hair form, but were believed to be fundamental and all-inclusive and, thus, to produce variations in intelligence and modes of thought. Fascism and Nazism accept this view (which has since been thoroughly discredited by twentieth-century anthropology and biology) and insist on the natural superiority of some peoples over others. Because Nazism and fascism were largely a European phenomenon, they ascribed superiority to whites over other "races" and to Aryans over a variety of other peoples. **Racial essentialism** also postulates that "racially pure" groups exist and are superior to those believed to be mixed or hybrid.

Historically, although Nazism and fascism were, and generally continue to be, ideologies primarily of people of European origin, racial essentialism could become the ideology of any ethnic group. For example, the ideology of the Nation of Islam (not to be confused with Islam) in the United States contains racial essentialist ideas about innate and immutable differences between whites and people of color; in some versions of the movement's ideology, the former are represented as the creation of the devil, that is, fundamentally evil. The Pan-Africanist Congress in South Africa rejects the possibility of a multiracial and multicultural society, calling for the elimination of whites from the nation in terms that are ethnoracist. During the period of Japanese fascism and militarism in the first part of the twentieth century, Japanese elites used ethnoracist discourse, especially in relation to other Asian nations. Recently, the racial essentialist term *minzoku* has reentered Japanese politicians' discourse in preference over less organic terms for a people (Van Wolferen, 1990:268–269). In historical practice, though, Europeans and populations of European origin have been considerably more involved than other ethnic groups in propagating this ideology, because it justified institutions of slavery and colonial expansion from which they benefited for several centuries (Fields, 1990).

In racial essentialist ideology, nation is defined as a racial entity in struggle with other such nations. The Nazis used the German word "Volk" to refer to the ethnic group conceptualized as a race, the "ethnorace." The metaphor of "blood" was often used to express this racial ethnic identity.

In short, one key element of fascist and nazi ideology is concern about the boundaries of society. The society and nation-state should be composed only of the superior race. Other peoples are to be used as a coerced labor force in a colonial situation, expelled, driven into remote areas, or even exterminated. The strong nationalist themes in fascist and nazi thought are always exclusionary rather than assimilationist. Not all persons living in a national territory can be members of the nation, only those of the right blood. Blood as a mystical, essentialist, and biologically innate bond of an ethnic group is a key symbol in fascist and nazi discourse.

Nazism was particularly fixed on a racial definition of the nation and carried this doctrine to its extreme conclusion, genocide. The program of the Nazi Party, formulated in 1920, included the statement: "None but members of the nation may be citizens of the State. None but those of German blood, whatever their creed, may be members of the nation. No Jew, therefore, may be a member of the nation" (University of Colorado, 1952). As Nazi Germany expanded eastward during World War II, non-German groups were treated as subhuman: Jews and gypsies were systematically exterminated, Slavs were treated as slave labor.

Nazism made racism the central theme of the state and carried racist policies to the extreme of genocide on a mass scale; but racism and extermination of other "races" were not new phenomena in themselves. These practices of exclusion, enslavement, and extermination had already appeared in European colonial expansion in the Americas and Africa. What was new in Nazi practices was their application to other European populations, the scale and technological sophistication of the murders, and the openness with which the Nazis proclaimed these policies. The policy of ethnic expulsions (referred to as ethnic cleansing by the **ethnonationalist** forces) that has been applied in the former Yugoslavia is a contemporary example of the doctrine that a nation cannot contain more than one ethnic group as citizens (Denitch, 1994). However, in Italian Fascism, these racist ideas were much less prominent than they were in Nazism and most other European varieties of fascism.

Domination, Leadership, and Collective Will

The appeal to blood, to elemental and irrational forces of nature, also appears in discourse about the relationships *within* the ethnic racial nation and among all those who share a racial identity; though racially linked, they are not equals among themselves. Their essential superiority or inferiority should be expressed in the institutions of the society, in leadership or subordination (Adorno et al., 1993). *Leadership* expresses simultaneously the *natural superiority* of some individuals and the ability of these individuals to intuitively know and embody the collective will of the ethnic racial people as a whole.

Liberalism, socialism, and most forms of religious doctrine emphasize the equal worth of all human beings, although in somewhat different ways: Liberalism emphasizes political equality, socialism adds to this economic and social equality, and religious faith phrases the concept of human equality in terms of personhood or equality within the community of believers. Fascist and nazi discourse explicitly rejects the view that human beings are potentially equal or equal in their essence. Nature and, hence, human society as a part of nature, are inherently systems of domination in which the superior races destroy the inferior ones and strong individuals lead weak individuals. Human beings, even within the same ethnic group, are inherently divided into leaders and followers. Power in the state and in the party hierarchy must flow along these *natural* lines of **domination and obedience**.

There is a great ideological emphasis on charismatic leadership, on the extraordinary individual who makes and breaks the rules because of his superior nature. He embodies the will of the people and, therefore, no institutionalized mechanisms of voting or representation are needed to understand the collective will; the leader expresses this will in his own being and in his own decisions. The Nazi term for this principle of organization embodies the concept: the **Führer** principle, the principle of the leader (University of Colorado, 1952).

The Nazi conception of the Führer was expressed in many documents of the party and state, as in this treatise on law: "The Führer-Reich of the people is founded on the recognition that the true will of the people cannot be disclosed through parliamentary votes and plebiscites but that the will of the people in its pure and uncorrupted form can only be expressed through the Führer. . . . The Führer is no 'representative' of a particular group whose wishes he must carry out. He is no 'organ' of the state in the sense of a mere executive agent. He is rather himself the bearer of the collective will of the people. In his will the will of the people is realized . . . " (Huber, in University of Colorado, 1952:74). Thus, the leader (whether the Führer in Nazi discourse or the Duce in Italian Fascist ideology) embodied two key principles: the **organic unity** and cohesion of the people, which is never divided along lines of distinct interests; and the natural imperative of strong leadership.

The Strong State and Ethnoracial Unity   A third element of fascist and nazi ideology is the *glorification of a strong, repressive, and unified state* and contempt for the intricate mechanisms and legal forms of the liberal democratic state. The foundation of this contempt is, once again, a conception of nature as a realm of struggle and violence among racial entities. Nations and races are pitted against each other. In this struggle, legislatures, representative government, multiparty systems, and elaborate protection of individual rights interfere with the survival of the Volk. One-party rule is natural and necessary. Any opposition forces can, and must be, suppressed in the interests of racial ethnic unity and hegemony. Left-wing and centrist parties, unions, and minority ethnic groups have to be silenced, broken up as organizations, and, if necessary, eliminated by the killing of their individual members.

After Hitler was asked to form a government in 1933, the first action of the Nazi Party was "Gleichschaltung"—coordination—a euphemism for the transformation of Germany into a single-party state with the purge of possible opposition forces from all important government positions (Kershaw, 1987, 1989). The formation of a special coercive apparatus was a key element of this process. The SS—the Blackshirts—already existed as a paramilitary group and they became a part of the new coercive apparatus. The gestapo—the secret state police—was newly formed.

However, the repressive nature of the Fascist and Nazi states was not only an opportunistic way of grabbing power; it was integrally connected to any ideology of violence and domination. Violence and repression are not means to an end, as they are for many other social movements. After all, liberalism, socialism, nationalism, and militant religious faiths have also used these means, but justified their use as measures that contributed to some higher goal such as peace and social justice. But, for fascism and Nazism, violence and domination are part of an unending and immutable natural order.

Symbols and Discourses of Irrationality   Fascism and Nazism command attention by their extravagant use of symbols: Flags and banners, swastikas and salutes, slogans and mass rallies, uniforms and boots. Compared to these flamboyant displays, liberals and social democrats seem a bit dull—legislators making deals, functionaries administering programs, men in gray suits writing memos. . . . The symbolic displays associated with fascism and Nazism are a deliberate choice to draw public attention and "stir the blood" of potential followers. They are also an outward manifestation of an ideological commitment to action and an explicit rejection of reason, deliberation, and compromise. The displays call for a welling up of irrational feelings of racial and national loyalty, submission to a leader, unreasoning solidarity in a cause that is greater than individual self-interest. Anything that is connected to theory, to intellectualizing, to profit making—anything that is complex or calculated—is rejected (Hitler, 1962).

The symbols and displays may refer to an imagined racial past; for example, the swastika was a sun symbol of the Aryan people, a racialized conception of ethnic groups that speak Indo-European languages. The *fasces*, a bundle of rods from which fascism gets its name, was a symbol of the strength in unity of the ancient Roman state; the Italian Fascists adopted it as their symbol, thereby evoking the power of Rome. The SS used a lightening bolt insignia, a reference to the deadly power of natural forces; and this symbol is still used by neonazi groups in the United States, like the Aryan Nations (Ridgeway, 1990: 23, 161).

Hitler had a keen sense of the importance of these symbols. He devotes several pages of *Mein Kampf* to the creation of the Nazi flag: "I myself, after innumerable attempts, had laid down a final form: A flag with a red background, a white disk, and a black swastika in the middle" (1962:496). He describes how a variety of color combinations had to be rejected; for example, a predominantly white flag was not a good idea, because "white is not a stirring color. It is suitable for chaste virgins' clubs, but not for world-changing movements in a revolutionary epoch" (1962:495). The design of armbands and party insignia called for similar attention. Hitler was perceptive about the power of the spoken word, explaining that the orator, unlike the writer, can respond directly to the audience and, thus, ultimately impose his will on it. Even the time of day matters; people are more suggestible in the evening, more open to a bond with the speaker (1962:463–479). Like visual symbols, actions such as street fighting formed a bond, a supposedly more powerful emotional tie to the ideology than an attachment accomplished through study or discussion.

One scholar sums up these antirationalist and antidemocratic appeals of fascism as follows: "The conception of objective law vanished under fascism. Among its most significant features was a violent rejection of humanitarian ideals, including any notion of potential human equality. The fascist outlook stressed not only the inevitability of hierarchy, discipline, and obedience, but also pointed out that they were values in their own right. Romantic conceptions of comradeship qualify this outlook but slightly; it is comradeship in submission. Another feature was the stress on violence. This stress goes far beyond any cold, rational appreciation of the factual importance of violence in politics to a mystical worship of 'hardness' for its own sake. Blood and death often acquire overtones of erotic attraction, though in its less exalted moments, fascism was thoroughly 'healthy' and 'normal,' promising return to a cosy bourgeois, and even prebourgeois peasant, womb" (Moore, 1966:447).

Agrarian Nostalgia   Nazi and fascist ideology included nostalgia for agrarian life. The sturdy farmer was idealized and contrasted favorably to the city dweller who was exposed to the corrosive influences of Jews, the money economy, and cosmopolitan culture. In Nazi discourse, these ideas were summed up by the expression *Blut und Boden* ("blood and soil"). These appeals to traditional agrarian culture appear also in contemporary ethnoracist groups. For example, the Posse Comitatus in the United States has a social base among midwestern farmers who saw their way of life eroded in the 1970s and 1980s. Farmers facing bank foreclosures and feeling overwhelmed by taxes saw these problems as part of a Jewish conspiracy to destroy the white Christian farmer (Ridgeway, 1990).

The Dilemmas of Anticapitalism   Woven into these fairly direct appeals was a more ambiguous and contradictory discourse about the economy. On the one hand, fascism and Nazism had to appeal to a mass of people in a post-World War I Europe that was experiencing hard times. Inflation, bankruptcy, the loss of farms and savings, and, later, unemployment devastated the middle class. The market economy was not working well for them. So fascism and Nazism contained many attacks on capitalism. The word Nazi is an abbreviation of the German name of the party: the National Socialist German Workers Party—a name that implies a socialist orientation. In parts of Germany, Nazis led attacks on banks' attempts to foreclose on small farmers. On the other hand, nazi and fascist movements sought allies among large capitalists and conservative political elites close to industrial and landowning interests. These potential allies were likely to be put off by too much anticapitalist rhetoric.

The ideology attempted to reconcile these contradictory pressures in several ways. One of the functions of **anti-semitism** was to replace a critique of capitalism. The movements targeted socialist and communist groups for attacks to distinguish themselves from these challengers of capitalism and thereby gained support as countermovements against the left. Fascist and Nazi ideology called for a **corporatist state** that was supposed to reconcile capital and labor.

The Nazis distinguished capitalism from Jewish enterprise; they attacked the latter while toning down their attacks on capitalism as an economic system. This view of capitalism as a basically good system that has been distorted by finance capital, and especially by Jewish control of banks, is also prominent in the ideology of the racist movement in the contemporary United States. For example, the Federal Reserve System, as well as private banking are viewed as ways in which Jews have gained control of the monetary system (Posse Comitatus, in Ridgeway, 1990:118–119). In some of the new right-wing movements in eastern Europe and the former Soviet Union, anti-semitism has a similar function; Jews become scapegoats or folk devils to explain the dislocations and difficulties associated with the transition to capitalism (Hockenos, 1994a, 1994b; Laqueur, 1993). Anti-semitism functions ideologically to channel economic dissatisfaction away from business enterprise onto Jews. Through anti-semitic appeals, right-wing extremists connect modern issues like dissatisfaction with the market economy to old, persistent folk traditions of hostility to Jews; this framing aligns with the prejudices of some parts of their mass support base.

Both Nazism and fascism made every effort to distinguish their criticism of capitalism from marxism, socialism, and communism. They emphasized their hatred of the left and translated this hatred from discourse into attacks on all the organizations of the left, like the Socialist and Communist parties and trade unions. Nazism and fascism were able to expand when they emphasized their role as countermovements against the left (Mayer, 1971). For example, Fascist extralegal squads began to build support by helping large landowners in central Italy terrorize and suppress left-wing organizations among peasants (Cardoza, 1982). Thus, whatever misgivings their wealthy supporters might have had about anticapitalist *talk,* they were reassured by Fascist and Nazi *action* against left-wing organizations.

The **functions of anti-semitism and anticommunism** in the ideology of the extreme right are important. These functions include frame alignment with traditional prejudices in the support base, the effort to displace economic resentments from the impersonal workings of the market to identifiable groups, and direct appeal to wealthy conservative elites concerned about left-wing movements. Anti-semitism and anticommunism as discourses function together to permit movements to appeal to anticapitalist attitudes in the support base while remaining distinct from the left and acceptable to incumbent elites.

Fascist and nazi theorists generally supported a corporatist structure of society in which occupations and industries would form cross-class organizations that united workers and owners. Enterprises would be privately owned, but the state would coordinate them, supposedly for the good of the nation as a whole. In practice, this meant the end of autonomous unions; owners had to submit to some state intervention in the economy, but to many it seemed a small price to pay for the suppression of unions and anticapitalist parties. The way a corporatist system functioned in Fascist Italy probably reassured German business interests that the Nazis, once in power, would tone down their anticapitalist sentiments. Corporatism (and populism) were ideologies that allowed fascism and Nazism to criticize capitalism and intervene in the market, without threatening to put an end to private property.

FASCIST AND NAZI SUPPORT BASES

Considerable research has been devoted to examination of the social groups that supported Nazism and fascism. Extensive voting data and party membership data shed light on this topic.

Active Participation and Party Membership

In class terms, the lower middle class formed the largest part of the social base. Artisans, small business owners, farm owners, and white-collar employees were disproportionately likely to become party members; manual workers were underrepresented in the party (Gerth, 1940; Poulantzas, 1974).

The lower middle class had been particularly hard hit by the economic dislocations that rocked Europe in the interwar period. Unlike the industrial working class, the lower middle class found little that was appealing in communist and socialist ideology; even though many of them had been dashed into the wage-earning proletariat or the ranks of the unemployed, they were not ready to act on the basis of this new condition or define capitalism as the enemy. They continued to see themselves as the "little guy," caught between the militant left and the cunning schemes of finance capital. Small farm owners and small businesspeople felt especially exploited by banks, the "shadowy forces" of finance capital, and broker merchants.

These economic resentments translated into anti-semitism, since Jews were stereotyped as financiers, speculators, and merchants. The Nazis effectively manipulated this "little guy in the middle" feeling and its accompanying anti-semitism to gain the allegiance of small farm owners and artisans.

The Nazis also excoriated what they called the "bourgeois democratic press," the media that undermined respect for the nation, the army, and morality under the guise of objective reporting; these attacks on the press helped win the support of people who felt that the mainstream newspapers did not represent their interests and values (Hitler, 1962).

Voting Behavior: Class and Religion in Germany

A similar pattern of support appears when we look at the electoral strength of German parties in the 1920s and early 1930s. Three parties maintained relatively uniform strength through much of this period (the Weimar Republic): The Socialists (a social democratic party that formed the core of most German governments in this period); the Communists who distinctly distanced themselves from the Socialists; and a centrist Catholic party. On the right wing of the party spectrum, the Nazis gathered strength during the 1920s and became the dominant party of the right, gaining virtually all the votes that had gone to other parties of the extreme right and eventually drawing votes from the center right as well. In other words, the two parties of the organized working class (Communists and Socialists) maintained their electoral strength against Nazi appeals, as did the Catholic-oriented party. The Nazis were increasingly able to collect the votes of the other sectors of society—the non-working class and non-Catholics; in other words, they gained a disproportionate number of votes from middle-class Protestants. Of course, being a blue-collar worker or a Catholic was not a guarantee of not being a Nazi voter; these characteristics simply reduced the probability. To put it another way, the voting base that gave the Nazis a plurality (though not an absolute majority) by 1932 was disproportionately lower middle class, rural and small town, and Protestant (Kershaw, 1990).

Social Bases of Support in Interwar Europe

Similar, though somewhat less precise, data confirm the conclusions for other European countries in the interwar period. Fascist movements and parties drew their strength from the lower middle classes (Carsten, 1967:232). Individual large capitalists made important financial contributions to the parties and some individuals in the industrial proletariat joined them, but fascism depended on the lower middle class for mass mobilization and support. In the early 1920s, before Mussolini came to power, the Fascists in Italy were a cross-class movement, with a center of gravity in the lower middle class but a considerable number of supporters in other classes, even among poor farm owners, sharecroppers, and day laborers (Cardoza, 1982:320–321).

Specialists in Violence

One other social group should be mentioned as significant to the support base: former officers and noncommissioned officers. They formed a major part of many right-wing movements after World War I, including those movements that would eventually come to power. One historian characterizes them as those "for whom no jobs were waiting, who had got accustomed to the use of violence, and felt themselves deprived of their 'legitimate' rewards" (Carsten, 1967:232). They were frustrated by the outcome of the war, by the loss of territory that many nations—especially Germany—suffered, by the pointless sacrifices that even supposedly victorious powers like Italy endured; they were especially prone to the idea that the armed forces had been "stabbed in the back" by politicians and financiers. As noted in the opening chapters, specialists in violence make a useful contribution to movements that seek to capture and consolidate state power (Kershaw, 1989; Lasswell and Lerner, 1966; Müller, 1987).

The Social Base of Contemporary Ethnoracism

The distribution of support for racist groups in the contemporary United States and Europe indicates similar patterns in social bases of moderate income groups, rural people, Protestants more than Catholics, and (in the United States) southern whites and midwesterners. In the U.S. south, groups like the **Ku Klux Klan** draw on a long tradition of racist organizing.

The portrait of ethnoracism as a predominantly **lower-middle-class** movement has been complicated by economic recession in recent years; young white working-class people turned to racist groups in Europe and the United States to cope with unemployment, competition with "foreign workers" at home and in the global marketplace, affirmative action, and difficulties of living in multicultural societies where being white is not automatically a guarantee of high status and access to good jobs. For example, materials circulated by one ethnoracist group in the United States complain that being white is no longer "an honor and a privilege" (Ridgeway, 1990:16). The decline of average real wages of white men in the United States in the past two decades and double-digit unemployment rates in European countries like England contribute to a sense of resentment to which centrist and left parties have not responded effectively.

Youth was historically and continues to be a social category attracted to fascist and nazi ideology, especially the thrill of action and the rejection of slow deliberative processes. A sense of racial unity, street fighting, the discourse of strength, and colorful symbols and uniforms appeal to young people of both middle- and working-class background who feel left out of labor markets and alienated from school. They believe they have little to gain from individual competition in the market society. When and where socialist, communist, or other left-wing movements fail to reach out to and organize disaffected young people, ethnoracist movements (along with cultural currents like punk or metal) can fill the vacuum (Gaines, 1992; Denitch, 1994).

FASCIST AND NAZI ORGANIZATION

Fascist and Nazi organization was shaped by two factors: The ideological imperative toward **charismatic leadership;** and a realistic calculation of what measures had to be taken to capture and hold state power. These forces led to the formation of a party with a charismatic leader, a top-down structure of command, and a great concentration of resources and effort in **coercive apparatuses.** At the same time, many analysts emphasize the **formlessness** of these parties, perhaps a short-term advantage and a long-term liability. The characteristics that made it possible for them to come to power may have contributed to their defeat; instead of being able to sustain authoritarian rule for a prolonged period of time, they rapidly embarked on ventures of expansion, war, and genocide that weakened their control. Far from being rigid and orderly hierarchies, they contained conflicts and tensions; they were flexible and sophisticated as organizations designed to take power, but formless and undisciplined once they controlled the state (Kershaw, 1987, 1989, 1990).

Before accession to state power, the contradictory nature of the movement organizations was crucial to their success. They contained a wild, violent, action-packed street-fighting side and a more sober, conservative, and disciplined side. These two sides appealed to different elements of the support base, with the street fighters drawing in restless youths and displaced military officers, while the more conservative political leaders could appeal to business interests and the economically hard-pressed lower middle class.

This structural division had a direct strategic value, since street fighters helped create the disorder that "responsible leaders" in the movement could then promise to suppress. The street fighters (especially the **storm troopers,** or "Brownshirts," in the Nazi Party) engaged in street battles with Communists, creating the impression of disorder and an impending wave of violence; Hitler could promise that if he became chancellor he would rule with a firm hand, putting an end to the Communist threat and saving Germany from chaos.

Mussolini used a similar strategy of simultaneously threatening disorder with paramilitary units and promising order to incumbent elites. Throughout 1922, the Fascist squads were active in suppressing a left-wing strike, organizing mass rallies, murdering political opponents, and taking over provincial towns in northern Italy (Clark, 1984: 220). At the same time, Mussolini negotiated with elected government officials and the king in order to be asked to form a government. The king was swayed by both fear that the army might refuse to curb the Fascists in case of open hostilities and hope that the Fascists could be appeased and absorbed into the routines of Italian politics if they were allowed into the government. The March on Rome—on October 27 and 28—was a mass mobilization of **Blackshirts** from provincial towns, an incident that many historians describe as a rampage. It took place at the very moment that the king asked Mussolini to form a government. Once the regime was in power it proved impossible to dislodge. "Mussolini won by being 'brought into the system' by a king and a governing elite that could see no other way of containing organized violence" (Clark, 1984:221).

Once the movement was in power, the differences between the disorderly side and the conservative proponents of order and a firm hand had to be resolved, since the division no longer had value as a means of persuading incumbent elites to support the entry of the movement into government. In 1934

Germany, the storm troopers were murdered by another paramilitary forma-tion, the **SS,** on the **Night of the Long Knives.** But tension among different parts of the Nazi apparatus was never fully resolved. The heads of different police and military units, as well as other Nazi officials, competed with each other for power and formed fiefs of their own within the Nazi state.

Part of the formlessness of the Nazi and Fascist states came from the cen-trality of charismatic leadership. When the charismatic leader (Hitler or Mus-solini) did not give specific commands, sections of the state under different sub-leaders were left to contend with each other. Spheres of competence and chains of command were poorly defined.

Hitler's architect, Albert Speer, presents a picture of this competition within the Nazi hierarchy, including the situation in which Hitler signed orders for "in-compatible ideas and plans . . . creating a confusing and impenetrable thicket of contradictions" (Speer, 1970:321). In Nazi Germany, energy and resources were poured into areas that coincided with Hitler's "ideological predilections"—es-pecially the extermination of the Jews—and not into activities essential to the viability of the state (Kershaw, 1989:63).

Charismatic leadership led to unexpected and eventually ill-advised ven-tures. A single individual could make decisions without adequate planning and feedback from a staff of advisers. The imagination of the charismatic leader overwhelmed the process of military and budgetary planning. Some historians point to Operation Barbarossa—the invasion of the Soviet Union in the summer of 1941—as an example of a whimsical and ill-advised decision of Hitler's. In fact, the whole general pattern of extremely rapid and aggressive expansion in Europe was probably not the product of sound military planning but of indi-vidual decisions of the charismatic leader (Kershaw, 1989:64). Mussolini's join-ing the Axis with Hitler in 1938 is perhaps another example of a poorly con-ceived decision, since up to that point Mussolini had enjoyed a certain degree of popularity with Churchill and other conservative leaders, and had by no means burned his bridges with England, France, and the United States.

The exercise of charismatic authority combined with the growth of coercive apparatuses like the SS contributed to the vast dimensions and detailed plan-ning of the "final solution," as the Nazis referred to the genocide of European Jews. Other states and nations had murdered ethnic groups in wars and colo-nial occupations; but Nazi genocide was unprecedented in its thoroughness and commitment of resources to the murder of millions of people at the very moment that the nation was fighting a global war.

Contemporary U.S. racist movements have learned some organizational and strategic lessons from historical Nazi and Fascist movements: The need for multiple and even contradictory appeals, targeted to both an action base and more conservative incumbent elites; structural looseness; the construction of links and networks among different organizations of the racist movement; pen-etration of mainstream media through cable channels and recruitment among police officers, since both the media and coercive institutions are key targets needed to expand the movement. For example, Tom Metzger of the White Aryan Resistance remarks, ". . . there is no center. It's like associations or networking. No fancy headquarters, or store fronts, or even bookstores. Yet it's all over the place" (Ridgeway, 1990:172).

NAZISM AND FASCISM AS HISTORY

This section reviews theories that explain why Nazism and fascism emerged when and where they did. Many of these theories treat the movements as historical phenomena characteristic of specific places (Germany, Italy, Japan, and many smaller nations in eastern and southern Europe) and a specific time (the period from the end of World War I to the 1940s).

Conjunctural Theories

Conjunctural theories explain Nazism and fascism in terms of the characteristics of a time period, namely the economic and social problems of the post-World War I period. The devastation of the war, inflation, the impact of reparations on the German economy, and, by the 1930s, the Great Depression—all contributed to the destruction of liberal political systems, the uprooting of the middle classes, and the opening of a "space" in the political system for mass movements of the extreme right.

Conjunctural theories point to a long-term economic crisis in the global capitalist system during this entire period. Agricultural production stagnated, income was unevenly distributed, and growth was spasmodic (Heilbroner, 1989). Many governments experimented with protectionist policies—high tariffs—to help their struggling national industries, but these policies contributed to sluggishness in global trade. The Great Depression was merely the most dramatic and culminating form of this long-term crisis. Nazism and fascism were rather extreme political responses to the crisis. They appeared in many European states of the period, not just Germany and Italy. In this view, it is unlikely that this type of mass movement will again reemerge on a large scale or come to state power. The global capitalist economy continues to have cycles of expansion and recession but, at the end of the twentieth century, governments have many tools at their disposal to cope with these problems.

Structural Theories

A second set of theories are referred to as structural theories. These theories point to the social structure and political system of different societies to account for the rise of different kinds of movements. There are several overlapping structural explanations for the rise of fascism and Nazism.

Late Industrializers   The simplest of the structural theories explains the success of these movements in terms of the late industrialization of Germany, Japan, and Italy. Nations in which industrialization took place early—England and France—experienced a gradual process of development in which the liberal state allowed capital to take its own course in industrialization. Late industrializers were characterized by a strong central state and a propensity toward state intervention in the economy; nations that came late to industrialization could only "catch up" if their states were authoritarian and deeply involved in economic development. This feature of the state, in turn, opened up possibilities for fascist-type movements, because incumbent elites had little or no commitment to liberal institutions. In Germany and Italy, incumbent elites allowed the Nazis and Fascists to form the government. In Japan, there was no sharp break between the strong industrializing state that enabled Japan to catch up to European powers around the turn of the century and the later, fascist-like state that joined the Axis; the former evolved into the latter.

Late industrializing states were also latecomers to colonialism. The prime areas of Africa and southern Asia had already been seized by the western European powers: England, France, the Netherlands, Belgium, and Portugal. Therefore, Germany and Japan expanded their empires into areas already held by the early colonizing powers (the French and British colonies in Southeast Asia) or into regions where existing states resisted the new imperialists (China, the Soviet Union, and Europe itself). These late efforts at imperial expansion meant war with some very powerful states. Nationalism and ethnoracism took extreme forms to justify this expansion.

Late industrialization theories run into some problems. One is that they don't explain why a fascist mass movement came to power, since a strong, authoritarian conservative state with little or no mass-movement support could have carried out the necessary programs to attain industrial and colonial expansion. Also, these theories do not explain why some late industrializers like Sweden remained liberal democracies.

Class Blocs and Political Institutions   A more complete version of structural theory explains fascism by examining the timing of capitalist economic development, class formation, and political modernization (Abraham, 1986; Gramsci, 1971; Mayer, 1971; Moore, 1966).

Where the bourgeoisie (large and small business interests and allied professionals) and the working class formed a bloc to remove the landed class from state power before industrialization took off, the resulting modern political system remained stably liberal democratic. The formation of this bloc could come about in several ways: In France, it happened in the French Revolution; in the United States, it occurred as northern industrialists, artisans, and small farmers supported the Union against the southern planter class. It could happen peacefully too, as in Sweden and Denmark, where the landed class gradually ceded its political power to a broader spectrum of the society. In all these countries, a large bloc of capitalists, professionals, small entrepreneurs, wage workers, and farmers (and even some parts of the landed class itself, especially in Scandinavia) developed a consensus in support of liberal and liberal democratic political institutions. The political system restricted the power of one of the major antidemocratic forces in modern societies—the landed elite.

As a country modernized and an industrial proletariat developed (largely replacing artisans and other older parts of the working class), it too was drawn into this consensual political culture and the associated institutions of mass parties and representative government.

This pattern had three major consequences, all important for restricting the possibilities for fascist ascendancy. One result was that the bourgeoisie was closely tied to liberal democratic institutions; it was less likely to hold antidemocratic values. Second, the landed elite was relatively weak and/or well-integrated into the liberal system; in this subaltern position, it was not in a strategic position to invite a fascist movement into power. Third, the working class, including the industrial proletariat, was more inclined to accept the liberal democratic rules of the political game; it was less likely to turn to revolutionary movements and ideologies, even in the face of the economic strains of the first part of the twentieth century, like the Great Depression. The relative weakness of revolutionary socialist movements, in turn, made the bourgeoisie feel more secure; bourgeois political leaders did not see a pressing need to turn to fascist movements as a bulwark against socialism and communism.

In these societies (like the United States, Britain, and the Scandinavian countries), fascist ideologues and movements appeared during the depression; but their mass following remained relatively small. Fascist parties won few votes. They could not capture or penetrate the institutions of the state. They were not invited by incumbent elites to form a government.

A marxist theorist might use the term **bourgeois hegemony** to describe a social and political system in which the bourgeoisie became the culturally and politically leading class as well as the economically dominant class. A non-marxist social scientist would look at this process more in terms of value consensus and the formation of liberal political institutions. Despite the differences in terminology and spin, the two analyses are fairly similar: Where a large historical bloc of bourgeoisie and working class formed before industrialization, the society ended up with liberal democratic institutions, a bourgeoisie that felt secure, a working class that was not revolutionary, and a political structure that offered little opportunity to fascist movements.

A different outcome appeared in those societies in which no liberal democratic bloc was formed by the bourgeoisie and the working class before industrialization. Italy, Japan, and Germany were examples of such societies. In these societies, modernization was a top-down process initiated by parts of the landed class itself in cooperation with industrialists. Economic development took place on terms set by capitalists and large commercial landowners. It was a **conservative modernization** imposed from above. There was little involvement by workers or peasants in the formation of modern political institutions and no history of social revolution. Even where liberal state institutions existed (as in Italy), they enjoyed little mass support or involvement.

As a consequence of this development pattern, commitment to liberal democratic institutions was not widely diffused, either among elites or the rest of the population. As the industrial proletariat grew in size, it found few channels in the political system for achieving its interests; proletarian activism turned increasingly toward revolutionary movements. This, in turn, created an anxious and weak bourgeoisie, pushed into even closer alliance with with conservative landed classes, with which the bourgeoisie had never broken in the first place. The bourgeoisie did not feel able to lead on its own, nor did it have allies in the working class. Industrial capitalists were present in Italy, Germany, and Japan, but they did not have a vision of themselves as a class that exercised moral and political leadership for the whole society within liberal rules of the game. Instead, they pursued narrow economic self-interest. When presented with threats or problems—like militant unions, a communist or socialist movement, or economic downturns—they were prepared to compromise with the fascist movements. Because of their own cultural and political weakness, capitalist interests were constantly forced to look for allies among landed elites, which were fundamentally antidemocratic and open to an alliance with fascist movements.

Under stresses like the First World War, the depression, or the challenge of left-wing movements, the bloc of the bourgeoisie and the landed class quickly abandoned democratic institutions and invited the fascist movements into government. The sense of threat grew sharply after World War I and the emergence of communism. In this period the elites in these societies inclined to look for support from movements like fascism and Nazism that were explicitly anti-marxist and used violence to suppress unions and left-wing parties. Nazism and fascism were thus able to mobilize resources, such as financial support from middle and large business enterprises by their ability to function as counter-movements to communism and socialism (Guerin, 1973; Gillingham, 1985; Mayer, 1971; Sohn-Rethel, 1987).

In terms of political culture, conservative and authoritarian themes prevailed in the bourgeoisie and the landed class while the industrial proletariat leaned toward revolutionary socialism. In terms of political opportunity structures, the **persistence of representatives of the landed class in the ruling bloc**, in key positions of power, created a situation in which political figures were willing to invite leaders of fascist or nazi movements to form a government. In a parliamentary system, taking power could come about legally in this way, a route followed by both Hitler and Mussolini.

The final ingredient in the societies in which fascists came to power was a middle class that felt little allegiance to either liberal democracy or to shared interests with large capital. Artisans, independent farmers, shopkeepers, and white-collar workers saw themselves as squeezed between big business and a militant, communist working class. They saw their relationship to big business as antagonistic; its successes seemed to mean their decline as banks foreclosed on farms, small shops went out of business, and crafts work gave way to cheaper factory-made goods. In their view, large enterprises were not the locomotive of the economy, creating jobs and expanding opportunities for smaller businesses, but a threatening force. This dissociation from large capital opened up the middle classes for the anticapitalist side of fascist-nazi ideology, especially the attacks on finance capital. The middle strata were also frightened by militant working-class movements, especially the growth of Communist parties and various short-lived left-wing insurgencies that took place in Europe shortly after World War I. Factory occupations in Italy, Bela Kun's brief, ill-fated

Communist republic in Hungary, and the short-lived Munich Soviet republic in Germany were examples of the incidents that led the middle classes to look for countermovements to working-class mobilization (Carsten, 1967:170). The middle strata were not tied to either big business or workers by a shared history of struggle for a liberal democratic political system, since such a struggle had not taken place in these societies, or only in truncated form. As discussed above, it was especially the middle strata that provided the mass base of the fascist and nazi movements.

The weak hegemony of the capitalist class thus contributed to the expanding political role of fascist and nazi movements. It was this weak and anxious ruling bloc of capitalists and landed interests that supported these movements. At first, the incumbent elites financed the movements and used them as a violent force against the left; eventually, the elites actually invited them to form governments, both in Germany and Italy. Once invited to run the state apparatus, neither the Fascists nor the Nazis could be dislodged from it (Abraham, 1986; Clark, 1984; Gramsci, 1971; Mayer, 1971).

Structural theory takes care of some of the problems that late industrialization theory encountered. By going beyond a simple economic determinism (late industrialization) and bringing in class relationships and political and cultural processes, this theory helps us understand why an antidemocratic mass movement—and not merely an authoritarian elite—came to power in these societies. It explains the puzzle of Sweden; though Sweden industrialized late and did not have a revolution against the landed aristocracy, it did have a history of class integration and cooperation.

Fascism and Nazism as Capitalism's Last Resort   Another theory that examines class relations defines fascism and Nazism as capitalism's ace in the hole or last resort, that is, a form of state that capitalists encouraged when the liberal state failed to contain socialist and communist movements and perform other vital functions of the state in a capitalist society.

In one version of this view, popular among some theorists associated with Communist parties, capitalism turns to authoritarian and specifically fascist forms when the organized working class threatens its power within the "rules of the game" of the liberal democratic state. When the working class votes for Communist and Socialist parties and forms powerful trade unions, capitalists feel threatened. They worry that their profit margins will shrink as workers gain higher wages and benefits; and they fear that a government formed by parties of the left will shrink their control over the economy. Under these conditions, capitalists are willing to forget their enthusiasm for democracy and install a fascist-type movement that represses the left (Guerin, 1973; Trotsky, 1944).

The theory that fascism represents a last resort of capitalism in conflict with a powerful working class requires some qualification. It is still necessary to use the concepts of weak hegemony or conservative modernization to explain why, in some societies, the bourgeoisie can rule through liberal democratic states and, in others, it cannot. In some versions, the ace-in-the-hole view tends to underestimate the power and autonomy of the fascist and nazi movements. Once in power they were ruthless in suppressing any opposition, whether from workers or the bourgeoisie; and they undertook a war that destroyed the stable business climate that capital prefers, a war that eventually destroyed the economy as a whole. Perhaps sorcerer's apprentice is a better metaphor than ace in the hole; the helper (the fascist and nazi movements) turns out to be independent and unmanageable, once called upon by the apprentice (capital).

Yet, when in power, fascism and Nazism accomplished some of the functions that the liberal state in Italy and Germany had not accomplished, functions that were necessary for the success of large business enterprises. Especially in Italy, financial institutions were reorganized in a form that was much more efficient than during the period of the liberal state (Garner, 1974; Poulantzas, 1974). Despite the Fascist and Nazi promises to small businesses, the small business sector did not expand and monopolies were not broken up. This theoretical perspective points to the way in which the Nazi and Fascist states were constrained to function in support of large enterprises, regardless of the movements' ideology and their promises to middle-class constituencies, because of the logic of the economy they had to manage once they took over the state apparatus. Finally, the movements succeeded in suppressing the left and integrating the working class into capitalist society, through a combination of force, improved employment opportunities, and nationalist and corporatist appeals. Though the imperialist and militaristic projects of fascism and Nazism eventually led to a self-destruction of the movement-states, capitalism as a system did survive the war. Many of the major industrial enterprises revived after the war in all three Axis powers, except in the zone of eastern Germany under Soviet control. The three former Axis powers were very successful in the postwar global economy.

Cultural and Psychological Explanations

Following are some theories of fascism and Nazism that concern psychological and cultural factors. These theories identify personality patterns like the **authoritarian personality** as characteristic of societies in which fascist-type movements emerged. Some connect these psychological characteristics of individuals to family structure. For instance, Germany and other central European nations are said to have had authoritarian patriarchal families that generated a propensity to obey and command. All relationships are organized around domination and submission. The ideology of the Führer principle is a political projection of the relationship of the children to the father; the Führer commands; he demands obedience; he protects, but at the cost of total submission; and so on. Just as the father embodies the interests and identity of the whole family, so the Führer embodies the nation as a totality. A family exists only insofar as it does not fragment into individuals, and it is the father who expresses its collective will.

Social scientists carried out empirical studies of these psychological interpretations of fascism, ranging from a psychoanalytic reading of Hitler's autobiographical writing (Erikson, 1964) to the development of a personality inventory (the F scale) to measure predispositions to fascism and an authoritarian personality (Adorno et al., 1993; Bettelheim and Janowitz, 1964). The results suggest some connections, but more work is required to link psychological and structural theories. A number of questions remain to be answered: Did societies in which fascist-type movements came to power have more authoritarian families and individuals? Was the German or Italian lower middle class more authoritarian in its character structure than the working class?

Another line of analysis looked for the origins of Nazi ideology in German culture. After all, anti-semitism, nationalism, and a preoccupation with ancient Germanic traditions had been themes in German culture for over a century before the formation of the Nazi Party. In this view, there was considerable continuity between the movement ideology and German culture, in general, and German nationalism, in particular. The scattering of German speakers throughout eastern and central Europe, as early as the end of the Middle Ages, had already focused attention on the mismatch between national boundaries and the actual distribution of ethnic communities.

This cultural explanation highlights themes in European culture, not only German culture, although German movements perhaps expressed these themes in the most extreme and concentrated forms. Anti-semitism was prevalent throughout Europe; Jews had been not only targeted by Christian doctrine as responsible for the death of Christ, but also segregated into commercial occupations that brought them into conflict with peasants and artisans. In this view, Nazism played on and amplified these long-standing themes in German culture and European culture as a whole. Both Italian fascism and Nazism drew on other currents of European thought in the late nineteenth and early twentieth centuries: racism, a colonialist mentality, and a jingoistic nationalism. Support for these cultural explanations comes from the diffusion of fascist movements and ideologies throughout interwar Europe. While they did not come to power independently everywhere, such movements appeared in practically every European country in the interwar period (Carsten, 1967).

Here we can construct a value-added explanation of the type discussed in Chapter 3, "Social Movement Theories." It could go something like this: Early twentieth-century European culture permitted the framing of discontent into ethnoracist discourses. Movements espousing such ideology came to power where three additional conditions were met: Liberal democratic values and institutions failed to unite a broad spectrum of classes and offer an alternative ideology to ethnoracism and ultranationalism. The class structure was deeply divided and contained elites—especially landed interests—that shared political power without commitment to liberal democracy. The political opportunity structure facilitated the entry of Fascists and Nazis into control of the state by allowing a party to form a government on the basis of a request or agreement from incumbent elites.

Consequences of Nazism and Fascism

Theorists try to understand the consequences as well as the causes of the fascism and Nazism. Since the Nazi state in Germany lasted only 12 years, of which the last 6 years were committed to a global war, it is difficult to assess its impact on social structure. The focus of analysis has to be on its toll in human life, especially the **genocide** of about 6 million people who were deliberately targeted for destruction.

In Germany by the late 1930s and throughout the Nazi-occupied territories after 1939, racial laws barred Jews from all areas of social and economic life and, in some cities, segregated them in ghettos. Shortly thereafter, Jews as well as Romanies (gypsies), political prisoners, prisoners of war, and disabled people were transported to death camps built in various central European countries. A large bureaucracy and physical resources like the rail system were used to implement this policy of genocide (Arendt, 1977). The camps were factories of death; each day, in the largest of the camps, thousands of people were killed, usually in gas chambers. Many others died of diseases, starvation, and the effects of tortures. Within a few years, about 6 million human beings were systematically murdered in this way, as is extensively documented in trial testimony, the accounts of survivors, Nazi records, and the physical evidence collected in the camps. Nazism not only brought about these planned killings; it also set in motion a war that cost the lives of at least 14 million people in battle casualties, famines, epidemics, and shooting of prisoners.

The enormous destructiveness of Nazism is curiously disproportionate to its ability to transform German social structure, which actually appears to have been rather limited. Despite rhetoric about itself as a revolutionary force that would set a new course for Germany, the Nazi state did not change or reverse the fundamental pattern of German development as an industrial capitalist society.

A historian sums up this view: "Objective social reality, the measurable statistical consequences of National Socialism, was the very opposite of what Hitler had presumably promised and what the majority of his followers expected him to fulfill. In 1939 the cities were larger, not smaller; the concentration of capital greater than before; the rural population reduced, not increased; women not at the fireside but in the office and factory; the inequality of income and property distribution more, not less conspicuous; industry's share of the gross national product up and agriculture's down, while industrial labor had it relatively good and small business increasingly bad. The East Elbian estates continued to be run by the gentry, the civil service by doctors [i.e., university graduates], and the Army by generals whose names began with 'von' [i.e., aristocrats]" (Schoenbaum, 1966:285). In other words, neither the nostalgic agrarian side of fascist-nazi ideology nor the ambiguous discourse about social revolution were realized. In Japan, there was even more continuity in social structure between the parliamentary period and the fascist-militarist regime (Moore, 1966:299). Similarly, in Italy, class structure and economic development did not change dramatically after 1922 when the liberal state was replaced by a fascist dictatorship. Capital felt more secure in its conflicts with the working class, which had lost its ability to organize, and financial institutions were more efficient; but no fundamentally new course of development emerged.

In short, these movements produced an enormous loss of human life. They unintentionally produced major geopolitical changes, ushering in the cold war, the division of Europe and the globe into two spheres of interest, and the formation of Communist states in China and eastern Europe—hardly their goals. Yet, in some ways, they did not have a major or lasting transformative impact on the structure of the societies in which they came to power.

RELATED FORMS OF STATES AND MOVEMENTS

Nazism is characterized by an ideology organized around racism and ultranationalism, as well as charismatic leadership and the strong state; it is a mass movement, aimed at mobilizing a large support base. Fascism is a closely related movement, differing from Nazism primarily in being less virulently racist. The term fascism is often applied to a wide range of other parties, movements, and states that do not share all these characteristics. The reader should be aware of these inclusive applications without necessarily agreeing with them.

Right-Wing Authoritarian Regimes

One related form of state is the right-wing authoritarian regime, often led by military officers. Examples include Spain under Franco (from 1939 to the mid-1970s), the colonels' regime in Greece in the late 1960s, Argentina and Uruguay in the later 1970s and early 1980s, and Chile under Pinochet (from 1973 to the late 1980s). In many respects, fascist Japan was more similar to these right-wing military governments than to Nazi Germany.

Generally, these regimes lack a mass movement base. They enjoy a certain amount of support, especially from some large capitalists and some of the middle classes, but they do not mobilize these supporters into a movement or organization. They do not have a flamboyant and elaborated ideology; when they do put forth some ideas, they are usually a fragmentary replication of core fascist ideology, with the same appeals to strong leadership, ultranationalism, antisemitism, the need to crush communism, and so on. They are less inclined to use the term revolution or make reference to anticapitalist themes than the Nazis.

Like Nazis and Fascists in power, the authoritarian right-wing regimes suppress opposition parties and put an end to civil liberties. They use violent means to crush opponents and terrorize the population; the Pinochet regime in Chile, the dirty war conducted by the Argentinian military, and the persistent repression in Guatemala have cost tens of thousands of lives in murders and disappearances. Torture is routinely used to terrorize potential opponents of the regime into silence. Sometimes murders are targeted, sometimes they are random—in either case, they are designed to suppress organized opposition and keep the population passive.

Like fascism and Nazism, the right-wing regimes permit capitalist enterprise to continue, while suppressing movements and parties of the left; thus, their regimes may be seen by their supporters as a price capital pays to weaken labor as an antagonistic force.

Authoritarian Populist Movements

A second related phenomenon is the authoritarian populist movement. These movements include much of the ideology of fascism, have charismatic leaders, and also form repressive states once in power. They differ from the historical fascist movements in making a stronger effort to integrate the working class. They lack or tone down the racist ideology that is at the heart of Nazism and many European cases of fascism. The best example of such a movement is Perónism in Argentina, named after Juan Perón, who was dictator during the forties and fifties. Perónism had many elements of left-wing fascism in its systematic effort to include the working class in the party, ensure benefits for workers, and organize Perónista labor unions.

More distantly related are authoritarian regimes with less popular mobilization. The Mexican state has some authoritarian populist features; a single party (PRI) dominates the political system (although its monopoly of power has decreased in recent years) (Laurell, 1992). It rules through a corporatist structure in which peasant organizations, unions, and associations of business owners form sections of the dominant party and act as transmission belts between the government and key sectors of Mexican society. It would not be accurate, however, to refer to the Mexican regime as fascist despite some overlapping features with Fascist states.

Some of the governments that have emerged in eastern Europe and the former Soviet Union after the fall of the Communist states are also formed by authoritarian populist movements with strong leaders; Boris Yeltsin may turn out to be this type of leader.

Finally, as mentioned in Chapter 10, "Nationalism," a number of nationalist movements share features of fascism, especially the emphasis on the identity of the nation and a dominant ethnic group. There is considerable agreement among social scientists that phenomena like authoritarian military regimes or right-wing populism are in some ways similar to fascism, although that term is not directly applied to them because they miss certain key defining elements of fascism/Nazism in the strict sense of the term; key elements like a mass movement or a racist ideology.

Controversial Clusters

I would like to mention three bolder, larger, and more polemical assimilations of fascism/Nazism with other political forms. Each is politically charged and controversial and implicates some interesting issues in the analysis of movements and states.

Totalitarian Concept   The concept **totalitarian** became popular during the cold war; it combines Communism and fascism/Nazism into a category of states distinguished by single-party domination and the absence of civil society, autonomous political organizations, and civil liberties (Arendt, 1973; Lasswell and Lerner, 1966; Nolte, 1966). Such an association ignores the substantial

differences between Communism and fascism/Nazism in ideas and in economic practices. The former emphasized human equality as a goal, opposed
racism in theory (if not always in practice), and formed states with centrally
planned state economies. The latter rejected the notion of equality, embraced
racist ideology, and preserved capitalist economies based on private ownership
and market mechanisms.

Right-Wing Concept   The concept **right wing** incorporates fascism and
Nazism with varieties of conservative thought. Indeed, some conservatives
share fascism's contempt for equality and democracy; like Fascists and Nazis,
they believe that human society is inevitably characterized by dominance and
hierarchy. They may also be contemptuous of an open, secular and culturally
diverse society, preferring one held together by a single tradition and strict social order. They also share fascism and Nazism's implacable opposition to the
left. But the conservative reaction is suspicious of mass movements. In Nazi
Germany, aristocratic conservatives eventually turned against Hitler, though
too late to be effective.

And while laissez-faire conservatives may be on the right of the spectrum
in the United States, they are generally supportive of civil liberties. Libertarians
and free-market conservatives, especially, oppose rather than advocate a strong
state. Thus, the association of the fascist and nazi right with different forms of
the conservative right makes only a limited amount of sense; it is especially
questionable to combine free-market or laissez-faire advocates with Nazis and
Fascists.

Guided Capitalism Concept   A third bold association is the concept of a
guided capitalism that groups together phenomena like fascism, the New Deal,
and Swedish social democratic corporatism. This is probably the most interesting and theoretically sophisticated combination. It derives from both conjunctural and structural theories and is based on the following analysis.

In the decades after World War I, capitalism experienced a major, global crisis marked by stagnation and eventual depression. It became clear to economists and political leaders that policies of limited state intervention in the economy would not resolve the crisis; far from being a self-regulating mechanism,
the market economy seemed to have a tendency to plunge into ever deeper
troughs of falling investment, falling wages, and overproduction of goods that
could not be sold. This economic crisis carried with it the possibility of deepen-
ing class divisions and social revolution.

Under these conditions, stronger capitalist states had to be developed in
some form, either fascist or within a liberal democratic system. These strong
capitalist states had to manage the economy, take action to initiate an upswing,
and integrate the working class. Which of the political forms emerged was
partly determined by the nature of class relations in the society and the strength
of the different movements. At least three distinct models of the strong capitalist state emerged: The fascist form; and two distinct liberal democratic models—the New Deal in the United States, associated with the presidency of

Franklin Delano Roosevelt, and the Swedish model. All three models involved direct intervention by the state to solve economic problems, with the aim of reducing the troughs of economic downswings. They all contained some corporatist institutions for integrating the working class into the system.

Fascism boosted investment by curbing the left and working-class organizations and, thereby, improving the climate for capital. On the whole, its corporatism was coercive and presented a weak role for labor. It came into being where a fascist or Nazi mass movement existed, the working class and business had been historically divided with little history of common political action, and landed interests remained strong; in short, where capital's hegemony was weak.

The New Deal improved the demand side of the market by enabling labor to form unions, institute collective bargaining, and raise wages; this increased demand, in turn, helped stimulate investment. The New Deal was a guided capitalism that emerged in a society where capital was strongly hegemonic, the landed aristocracy had been defeated in a civil war, and a long history of liberal democratic institutions existed. It emerged in the context of a strong union movement, and the New Deal and labor developed a mutually supportive relationship (Geoghegan, 1991). The growth of organized labor became the main institution for integrating the working class.

In Sweden, a third model appeared. Like the United States, its form of guided capitalism remained within a liberal democratic political framework. In this model, the working class was relatively powerful. It not only organized into labor unions, but also formed a social democratic party. The national federation of labor unions was connected to the party and was much stronger than the CIO and the AFL (the leading U.S. labor union federations). The working class was not so much a junior partner of capital in the system (as in the United States), but more nearly an equal force in the corporatist structure. In Sweden, the outcome was a guided capitalism that tilted toward the working class, with ample benefits and governmental commitment to a near-full employment economy (Weir and Skocpol, 1983). (This model also appeared in other northern European countries, although nowhere else in as clear a form as in Sweden.)

All the models of guided capitalism, even the fascist and nazi forms, provided more social benefits than government had before. All experimented with *corporatist* organization, efforts to regulate price structures and labor-management relations within whole industrial sectors. In this view, the Swedish model is guided capitalism that combines liberal democracy and socialism, integrating the working class on particularly favorable terms. The New Deal is a liberal democratic version of the new interventionist state with labor as the junior partner of capital. Fascism is a repressive (and less successful) version of the same process of evolution toward guided capitalism, in which the corporatist formula gives the working class only a limited place and the entire system is held together by ethnoracism or ultranationalism rather than by liberal democratic ideology.

The three concepts—totalitarianism, the right, and guided capitalism—have to be used carefully. They point to some interesting continuities and similarities among Nazism/fascism and other forms of states and movements, but we need to keep in mind that each grouping has limitations.

RESISTANCE AND COUNTERMOVEMENTS

As fascism and Nazism spread through Europe and east Asia, they met with various movements of resistance. The most massive opposition came from the nations that were under attack and were defending their national sovereignty and global interests—liberal democratic capitalist nations like the United States and Britain, as well as the Soviet Union. But, within the regions occupied by the Axis powers, movements of **resistance** also formed. Three types of movements made important contributions to resistance: Movements within the Christian churches; Communist and other left-wing movements; and liberal democratic nationalism. In other words, the movements covered in the preceding four chapters—liberal democracy, nationalism, the left, and Christian movements— became countermovements to fascism and Nazism.

In many parts of Europe, Christians—especially Catholics—resisted what they saw as the illegitimate authority of the Nazi and Fascist states. Even though the leadership of the Catholic Church had compromised with Italian Fascism (in the Lateran pact of 1929) and even with Nazism, the compromises were not wholeheartedly or consistently supported by the church as an institution; and, certainly, not all Catholics were prepared to accept these compromises. They resisted the policies of genocide by helping Jews escape or hide, and they formed partisan groups that engaged in attacks and guerrilla warfare against the Nazis and Fascists. For example, in Italy, the Catholic resistance formed units of partisans called the Green Flames (Clark, 1984:313–314).

A second major force in the resistance were Communists; throughout Europe, China, and Southeast Asia, Communist parties took the initiative in fighting against the occupying armies of the Axis. Communists were probably the largest and best-organized of the resistance forces in Axis-occupied Europe. Other forces of the left also participated.

Nationalists also contributed to the resistance, especially once they grasped that the Axis had no intention of permitting independent states to form in the regions they occupied. In places in eastern Europe like the Ukraine, some nationalists shared Nazi anti-semitism and favored the Nazis as an anti-Communist force. In Southeast Asia, nationalists hoped that the Japanese would free them from British, French, or Dutch colonial rule. But these initial sympathies were usually reversed when the German and Japanese occupation forces acted with great brutality and showed little respect for indigenous nationalist aspirations.

In many places occupied by the Axis, two or more of these resistance movements cooperated. For example, in China, the Nationalists and the Communists coordinated their fighting against the Japanese, although they were locked in mortal combat both before and after the Japanese occupation. In France, nationalist forces and Communists participated in the resistance. And in Italy,

Communists and Catholics (as well as smaller movements of liberals and left-ists) became **partisans,** guerrilla fighters in the resistance against the Fascists and the German army of occupation (Clark, 1984).

It was rarer for citizens of occupied countries to engage in resistance when they were not already members of movements or organizations that had ideologies of opposition to fascism and Nazism. Unorganized citizens may well have been appalled at Nazi (or Fascist) brutality and in despair over the loss of liberties and national sovereignty; but they were not in a good position to undertake actions of resistance.

Danish, Bulgarian, and Italian resistance to Nazi genocide was a noteworthy exception to apathy and collaboration. Each country's style of resistance reflected its political culture and opportunities. In Italy, individuals evaded authorities' orders. In Bulgaria, the government and citizens together ignored or snarled German plans for deportation of Jews; for example, when German officials wanted Jews concentrated in the capital, Bulgarian officials ordered them dispersed into the countryside. The Danish government cooperated with the German occupation in some respects, but explicitly objected to racial laws, weakening German resolve to implement them. Meanwhile, Danish citizens hid Jews and eventually smuggled about 6000 of them to Sweden on fishing boats. Virtually all the rest survived the war in hiding. The proximity of neutral Sweden and the willingness of that nation to accept the Jewish refugees from Denmark were essential to the success of the operation. In the final analysis, however, it was the willingness of the Danes to accept responsibility for the fate of Jews (not all of whom were Danish citizens) that set the plan in motion (Arendt, 1977: 171–175, 185–188).

At the end of the twentieth century, neonazi movements and ethnoracism appear to be on the rise again, but so are movements of opposition. In Europe—especially in Germany, France, and England—thousands of marchers take part in periodic demonstrations against racism. Many of these marchers are young people; many are from white working-class or lower-middle-class backgrounds, not very different from those of the ethnoracists; many are people of color, Arabs and Africans in France, West Indians and south Asians in England, Turks in Germany. Sometimes their style is similar to that of the neo-Nazis: leather jackets, shaved heads, combat boots, an affinity for rock and metal. Their marches show that a revival of ethnoracism in Europe would meet spirited opposition, not only from more established antiracist forces like socialists, Euro-Communists, and religious groups, but also from youth and the new working classes.

THE RESURGENCE OF NAZI AND FASCIST MOVEMENTS?

If I had written this book a decade ago, the chapter on fascism and Nazism would probably have remained a short historical note. It turns out that this chapter may not yet be closed. Three distinct types of movement are emerging that suggest a resurgence.

Neo-Nazis

One movement involves the rise of violent neo-Nazi groups, especially in Germany, but also elsewhere in Europe; these groups have primarily targeted immigrants, sometimes in violent attacks like firebombings of residences for refugees or the homes of Turkish immigrants. Some analysts see them as a response to the economic dislocation that Germany is experiencing after unification. A global recession in the early 1990s and high levels of youth unemployment expand support for such movements in England and Australia.

The same type of group is visible in the United States, although on a smaller scale than in Germany. Groups like the White Aryan Resistance, the refurbished Ku Klux Klan, neo-Nazi skinheads, and right-wing survivalists and militias draw support, especially from alienated young whites who face unemployment, dead-end jobs, and declining real income. For example, in Chicago, high schools in economically depressed and culturally isolated south suburbs have disproportionately more Nazi skinhead activities than in the affluent northern suburbs (Sid Price, personal communication). In the midwest, the desperate situation of farmers in the 1980s faced with foreclosures and bankruptcies led to support for the Posse Comitatus and right-wing militias (McLemee, 1995; Ridgeway, 1990).

The Ethnoracist Mass Party

A second movement is the mass party in Europe that offers a platform of nativism, thinly veiled racism, and restrictive immigration and citizenship policies. Many of these parties are opposed to European unity, arguing against it on nationalist grounds. The National Front in France, the British National Party, the Republicans in Germany, and the Freedom Party in Austria are major examples of such parties. Although they remain small, they have won seats in the national parliaments. Their strength increased in the 1980s, and they received between 5 and 25 percent of the vote in national and state/local elections (Hockenos, 1994b:24).

The mid-1990s have seen further expansion of electoral support for some of these parties. Although the German Republicans lost support at the polls in local elections in 1994, the Freedom Party in Austria "captured more than 30 per cent of the vote in three states" (Hockenos, 1994b:24–25). In the spring 1994 elections in Italy, an electoral alliance that included the neofascist National Alliance, won a sufficiently large bloc of seats in parliament to form a government. The presence of the National Alliance in the coalition is the first time since World War II that a fascist party has been able to participate in governing a state in western Europe (Hockenos, 1994b:24). Even countries with a weak fascist past, like the Netherlands, the Scandinavian countries, and England have right-wing parties, though their levels of electoral support are still low. Virtually all these parties focus their appeal on antiforeign stands, with anti-European integration forming a second theme.

Ethnoracists are also participating in electoral politics in the United States. The Populist Party is an example of an organization that conducts campaigns;

it offers populist economic appeals and leans toward conspiracy theories to explain political processes. In some regions, its support base overlaps that of more action-oriented ethnoracist groups of the neonazi type. The party and front organizations formed by Lyndon Larouche, which were active in the 1980s, had an ideology that recalled fascist ideas, although they were not markedly racist; the movement combined attacks on finance capital, a fixation on monetary policy, conspiracy theories involving the CIA and the British royal family, extreme anticommunism, a strong antidrug platform, and vague appeals to working people (in its name—the American Labor Party).

The considerable electoral support that David Duke attained in Louisiana as a Republican candidate for senator and governor, as well as his election to the state legislature, suggests that the extreme, racist right has the capability to infiltrate the respectable right. Action strategies of groups like the KKK or WAR (White Aryan Resistance) can thus be linked to respectable strategies of expanding influence in right of center public opinion. Duke toned down his KKK past in favor of more populist appeals and used code words like welfare in place of outright attacks on blacks. The Republican Party was not able to dissociate itself from his campaign. The search for electoral support on the part of contemporary racist movements recalls the German Nazis' growing strength at the polls and their use of this strength as an entree into government.

Ultranationalism in the Post-Communist Nations

The third neofascist movement is composed of the ultranationalist parties and organizations that have emerged in eastern Europe and in the territory of the former Soviet Union after the fall of Communism. Entire small states like Croatia and Serbia have come under the control of these forces (Denitch, 1994). All these parties and states are characterized by extreme nationalism, ideologies of hatred toward other nations and ethnic groups, restricted civil liberties and control of the media, and (in many, but not all, cases), concentration of power in a single individual. These movements are undertaking policies of what they call ethnic cleansing, driving ethnic minorities out of what is defined as the national territory. The events in the former Yugoslavia are the most widely described and extreme examples of this process, but ethnic expulsions are under way in others nations as well. Murder, rape, seizure of homes and farms, intimidation, expulsions, and concentration camps are used to force other ethnic groups out of the territory claimed by the ethnoracist movement. These movements and the states they dominate refuse to accept the possibility of multiethnic societies.

Causal Factors in Ethnoracist Resurgence

The rise of all these movements can be attributed to a combination of factors: a sluggish, recessionary, and increasingly competitive global economy that creates conflicts over dwindling jobs and services in the core economies; the postmodern and post-Fordist breakdown of models of class integration that worked during the boom in the core economies, from 1945 to the 1970s; high levels of immigration from Third World countries and/or the former Communist regions into western Europe (and the United States) that creates a sense of ethnic competition; and in eastern Europe, a vacuum of power, ideology, and viable economic institutions left by the collapse of Communism.

The West   In the west, both the small violent movements of neo-Nazis and the larger right-wing parties with a claim to respectability can be understood as one response to the structural strains generated by the post-Fordist economy. Western Europe and North America had experienced high levels of prosperity and relatively low unemployment rates in the postwar period, but this structure of economic growth and class cooperation is now under stress. The Fordist forms of integrating society have broken down in many ways. Companies are moving their plants from these regions, automating, and downsizing their workforces; these decisions result in higher unemployment and poor prospects for youths about to enter the labor force. Even nations like Germany and Sweden, which had enjoyed excellent opportunities for workers, including ample benefits, participation in company decision making, very low unemployment, and well-designed job training programs, are now losing some of these advantages.

Resentment has built against groups who are believed to be taking jobs and using other scarce resources (like social services) and benefitting from affirmative action policies. The **economic dislocations associated with post-Fordism** cause resentments that are displaced onto immigrants and ethnic minorities. Economic insecurity is compounded by the strains of living in multiethnic and multicultural societies formed by immigration. There is also anger against the loss of jobs to lower-wage economies; since there is little that the average person can do to halt these movements of investments and jobs, the anger and frustration are easily displaced onto scapegoats and folk devils, especially immigrants who are identified by physical appearance or different cultures. Driving out foreigners and halting immigration are a cut-rate way of responding to complex economic issues.

Reconstituting a postindustrial version of Fordist policies of growth and national integration is a difficult project. It requires a thoroughly hegemonic understanding on the part of capital that it may be worth giving up some of the short-term savings and profits to be derived from workforce cutbacks in order to sustain longer-term national economic growth and social integration (Reich, 1992). This requires political vision and leadership on the part of the business community (Thurow, 1993).

Certainly these current structural strains are not the same conjunctural factors that contributed to the rise of fascism and Nazism in the interwar period, and there is some reason to believe that ethnoracist movements in the west will not come to power. Most of the developed capitalist democracies have many mechanisms in place to cushion the effect of recession. Furthermore, the fear of Communism that led conservative elites to invite Fascists and Nazis into governments in interwar Europe is no longer present; the collapse of Communism has eliminated a major focus and purpose of the extreme right. Even with post-Fordist strains, most of these societies are less divided than they were earlier in the twentieth century.

Finally, knowledge of history may prevent its reenactment; few people want a repeat of world war and genocide, even if they intensely dislike other ethnic groups. Or to put that into more theoretical terms: Movements that frame their vision in ethnoracist terms are likely to have difficulty in aligning their discourses with those of the majority of a population that rejects these frames. The contemporary media are generally not sympathetic to mobilizations that use ethnoracist framing.

For all these reasons, it is unlikely that the democratic capitalist nations will see fascist movements come to state power; but these movements may influence governments to pass more restrictive immigration laws, as has already been the case in Germany. The right-wing parties may influence a wide range of policies proposed and implemented by centrist and conservative parties (Hockenos, 1994b:24). The outcome may be less a dramatic reestablishment of ethnoracist states than a shift in discourse and policy that stretches liberal democratic forms further and further toward an ethnoracist right.

Post-Communism and Ethnonationalism   The outlook is more bleak in the former Communist regions undergoing a **transition from socialism to capitalism.** Here the constellation of factors points toward fascism and ultranationalism (Denitch, 1994; Farkas, 1994; Hockenos, 1994a; Laqueur, 1993; Yergin and Gustafson, 1993).

The economic situation is desperate, with both hyperinflation and unemployment destroying the constricted, but relatively predictable, living standards experienced under the socialist systems. The legal infrastructure of capitalism is not yet firmly in place; its imposition in property laws, as well as the establishment of capital markets and financial institutions, are experienced as oppressive and externally manipulated processes. The absence of experience with capitalism leads to confusion about its workings. It is easier to blame somebody—Jews, foreigners, and so on—than see these problems as systemic or understand why the problems are likely to be particularly acute during the transition from socialism to capitalism. Cuts in state subsidies, unemployment, high prices, the appearance of profit as a motivating force, increasing gaps in incomes and standards of living, the collapse of health-care systems and other social services, and a confusing welter of claims about property ownership contribute to fears of conspiracy and the impulse to blame specific groups.

The image of the Jewish financial mastermind exploiting the decent folk of the nation is easily resurrected by movements and elites, even in places where Jews no longer live. Jews can be conveniently blamed for the failures of Communism, since they (along with non-Jews) participated in Communist movements and regimes; at the same time, Jews can be held responsible for the disappointments involved in the rebuilding of capitalism, which they are depicted as masterminding from abroad. These images are convenient in the sense that they provide simplistic explanations for complex problems and draw attention away from the inability of the new power holders to build viable and democratic market societies.

Jews are not the only scapegoats of economic chaos and the failures of the transition to capitalism. Many ethnic and nationalist hatreds have been allowed to surface, and there is ample recall—both true and false—of past abuses (Denitch, 1994). "Every national group in East Europe has had episodes in its history when it was abused at the hands of a rival nationality and when it did the abusing. These latter epochs are often touted as 'moments in the sun' for the nation—when 'justice and reason' prevailed and the good guys were on top" (Farkas, 1994).

Neither the tradition of the liberal state nor its actual institutions are firmly in place; with the exception of the Czech Republic, almost no nation in the region has had a long period of liberal democracy. This constellation of economic, cultural, and political factors makes it highly likely that many states in the region will end up (in the foreseeable future) with **authoritarian nationalist** regimes. Whether the label fascist will be precisely correct can be debated; but certainly the forms will be similar to historical fascism in a combination of the following elements: the absence of representative democracy and civil liberties; state control of media; a capitalist economy with considerable government involvement; arbitrary personal exercise of power; a single or dominant party; and an ultranationalist and/or ethnoracist ideology that emphasizes historical resentments rather than a positive and inclusive sense of national identity (Denitch, 1994; Farkas, 1994).

Neo-Nazis at a rally in memory of Rudolf Hess (deputy leader of the Nazi Party). Wunsiedel, Germany, August 18, 1990.

SUMMARY

This chapter discussed the ideologies and the types of movements that can be referred to as right-wing extremist and ethnoracist. German Nazism and Italian Fascism were two major historical examples, but this type of movement has existed in many countries and is undergoing some degree of resurgence now. The ideologies emphasize domination as a positive value, the strong state, and ethnonationalism and ethnoracism based on an essentialist conception of ethnicity. The class base of ethnoracism as a mass movement has most commonly been the lower middle class in Europe. The structural strains of World War I, economic stagnation, and the Great Depression contributed to its historical rise. Fascist-type movements came to power in late industrializing countries with incomplete political modernization and divided class structures. The movements were organized to operate within the political opportunity structures of these nations and exert pressure on incumbent elites to invite them into the government. Once in power, they formed repressive state institutions with a large component of charismatic leadership.

Current economic and cultural strains associated with post-Fordist accumulation patterns, globalized markets, and cultural diversity may be leading to the appearance of new forms of such movements.

KEY TERMS AND CONCEPTS

ethnoracist ideology
scientific racism
racial essentialism
ethnonationalism
collective will
the leader (Führer)
domination and obedience
organic unity of the ethnorace
the strong state
the functions of anti-semitism and
    anticommunism
the corporatist state

**ethnoracist support bases and
    organization**
Ku Klux Klan
specialists in violence, lower middle
    classes, and youth
charismatic leadership
coercive apparatus of the party-state
formlessness of the party structure
storm troopers (Brownshirts)

Blackshirts (Italy)
the SS and the Night of the Long
    Knives

**historical causes, consequences, and
    countermovements**
weak bourgeois hegemony
conservative modernization
persistence of representatives of the
    landed class in the ruling bloc
authoritarian personality
genocide

related phenomena
right-wing authoritarian regimes
authoritarian populism
totalitarian concept
the right
guided capitalism and forms of
    corporatism

resistance; partisans

contemporary forms of ethnoracism
neo-Nazis
ethnoracist mass parties
ultranationalism
economic dislocations associated
   with post-Fordism

postcommunism and
   ethnonationalism
the transition from socialism to
   capitalism
authoritarian nationalism

| Women's suffrage march. New York, 1912.

CHAPTER 12

Sex, Gender, Reproduction

Challenges to the Status Quo

*The heart of the movement, as in all freedom movements, rests in women's
knowledge, whether articulated or still only an illness without a name, that they are
not inferior—not chicks, nor bunnies, nor quail, nor cows, nor bitches, nor ass, nor
meat. . . . Women know that male supremacy is a lie. They know they are not
animals or sexual objects or commodities. They know their lives are mutilated,
because they see within themselves a promise of creativity and personal integration.
Feeling the contradiction between the essentially creative and self-actualizing human
being within her, and the cruel and degrading less-than-human role she is compelled
to play, a woman begins to perceive the falseness of what her society has forced her to
be. And once she perceives this, she knows that she must fight.*
    —Marlene Dixon, "The Rise of Women's Liberation," *Ramparts*,
            December 1969, Vol. 6, No. 8, pp. 57–64.

Dr. X is a neurosurgeon at a university-affiliated hospital in the United States. Each
morning she has breakfast with her husband and two children in her beautiful home and
then spends her day performing surgery, seeing patients, and writing articles for medical journals. Her parents encouraged her to be the best in her field. When she entered
her teens, they stressed high achievement in math and science and paid for her education at the most demanding institutions. Both her work and her family life are fulfilling,
but she is often concerned about women's issues. Like all women in her city, she sometimes feels unsafe, especially at night, when she does not like to go out alone. She is
not happy with her child-care arrangement, which involves hiring a Central American
refugee as a baby-sitter; she is aware that her own professional life depends on the labor of another woman who has a much lower income. She is disturbed by the way
women's health issues are treated by the medical profession. And she would like to have
more women colleagues, to reduce the old boy atmosphere among the male surgeons.

Mrs. A lives in a cluster of huts on a dusty plain in the countryside of a "less developed country." Before dawn, she gets up to begin a day of working in the fields, pound-
ing millet, hauling water from a distant well, collecting and carrying firewood and dung
for fuel, and taking care of her eight children. Her parents expected her to do chores and
take care of the younger children. When she entered her teens, her clitoris was cut off
in a ceremony that women as well as men agreed is essential for forming an adult, mar-
riageable woman. Her relationship with her husband is not close—he has to work as a

laborer, far away in the city—and when he returns, he sometimes beats her. But she lives in a circle of kinswomen, children, and woman friends—an ever-present source of companionship and support. She wishes that the family had more land—one acre is not enough to even meet subsistence needs. She would like to have money to buy beads and yarns for crafts work and arrange a way of transporting her goods to market. But she knows that it is impossible for women to get credit from a bank or development agency to start a small business or buy land and farm implements.

Do these two women have anything in common besides the fact that they are women? Do the differences between them based on culture, economic class, and nation overwhelm any similarities based on gender? Is there any reason to bring these two women together into women's movements or a feminist movement? If Dr. X does anything to change the conditions of Mrs. A's life, is she being patronizing, ethnocentric, and a busybody? And what about the woman from Central America—the baby-sitter—is there any reason for her to feel solidarity with either Mrs. A or Dr. X?

CHALLENGING THE GENDER SYSTEM

A variety of movements that challenge existing arrangements in the sphere of gender, sexuality, and social reproduction are reviewed in this chapter. These movements seek to change the meaning of gender, the social construction of masculinity and femininity with all of its accompanying definitions of men's and women's roles and socially appropriate behaviors. They seek to end gender stratification. Movements that undertake this challenge directly are usually called feminist movements. Other movements challenge gender arrangements indirectly by seeking to improve the conditions under which women live, with less explicit attention to gender stratification. Since the support base of these reform movements is primarily composed of women and women are the most direct beneficiaries of these changes, the movements are generally termed women's movements. Also considered in this chapter is a movement that challenges existing ways of viewing sexual orientation (i.e., heterosexuality and homosexuality), the gay and lesbian movement. Directly or indirectly, all the movements in the chapter raise questions about the organization of the family as a social institution.

The chapter begins with an overview of feminist ideology. Feminism is not a unitary ideology. There are a number of different ways of viewing and challenging gender stratification. I explore the structural conditions that have given rise to feminism; it is largely a movement of the most economically developed societies. The varieties of feminism both overlap and challenge liberal and socialist visions of the good society.

Women's movements appear not only in the developed core societies, but also in the societies of the periphery. The structural strains that contribute to the emergence of women's movements and the organization and mobilization strategies of these movements are discussed. Movements that challenge compulsory heterosexuality have emerged fairly recently, mostly in the liberal democratic core societies where economic and political conditions are favorable.

A theme that runs through the chapter is the difficulty of sustaining mobilizations that challenge gender stratification and sexual arrangements. Two problems contribute to this condition. One is the problem of initial mobilization:

In most societies, the potential primary support bases (women and/or people with a homosexual orientation) do not live in fully separate communities. The lives of potential movement participants are intertwined with the lives of others who have a much lower stake in these mobilizations or who may actually be opposed to them. This intertwining reduces the likelihood of the formation of collective identities or forms of consciousness that lead to movement involvement. A second problem is that gender and family arrangements in many societies are connected to religious beliefs or other deeply rooted values; a challenge to these arrangements sets in motion powerful countermovements.

For these reasons and for reasons inherent in the ideology of the movements, there have not yet been societies in which the challenging movements have acquired enough power to reorganize institutions in a fundamental way. Thus, in this chapter—unlike all the preceding chapters about movements—I do not look at the record of the movement in power or the movement-state. To date, the outcome of the movements considered in this chapter has generally involved reform rather than decisive and rapid transformation of society. Many of these reforms are liberal reforms. They create leeway for personal choices about behavior and increase the political and juridical equality of men and women.

FEMINIST IDEOLOGY: WHAT DO WOMEN WANT?

At the beginning of the chapter, I posed some questions about the two women in the vignettes who live under strikingly different conditions: Do these women have the same interests because they are women? Is there a movement that joins them together? These kinds of questions confront movements that challenge existing gender systems. What these movements have in common is an analysis of societies that focuses on the sphere of sex, **gender**, and **social reproduction** in the largest sense of the term. Their ideology identifies this sphere as the root cause of inequality, domination, and injustice. Inequality and domination in this sphere necessarily spill over into all other institutions and activities in human society. Neither the liberal dream of equal citizenship nor the socialist vision of equality in economic cooperation are ever likely to be realized as long as gender inequality persists. Inasmuch as existing societies are characterized by male domination, social justice and human solidarity cannot be achieved by either political reforms or social revolutions that fail to address gender inequality.

A few definitions may help clarify what I will call feminist ideology. By feminism, I mean an ideology that demands the equality of men and women in economic and political participation and in the activities of civil society. Equality does not always mean an identity of interests or actions, however. Feminism is distinguished from women's movements, which can include feminism but, generally, involve the mobilization of women around narrower, more specific issues, or in forms that make less pointed reference to male domination (Chafetz and Dworkin, 1986:65–66). Feminism explicitly challenges existing gender systems and the way they form the core of societies. Women's movements do not always express this explicit challenge.

Feminists use the concept **male domination** as a shorthand for the many ways in which women are excluded and discriminated against in most institutions and societies, as well as for the ways in which this state of inequality is perpetuated, whether legally or by violence. Male domination does not mean that all men contribute to this system consciously, nor does it mean that men benefit more from domination than they would from greater equality. Sometimes the term **patriarchy** is used by feminists as a synonym for male domination, although its usage by social scientists is generally more limited; in its more precise meaning it refers to a system of control exercised by males through their roles as heads of households. A more scholarly and neutral term for male domination is **gender stratification**, but this phrase is used by academics rather than activists.

Feminist ideology is clearly a radical challenge to existing types of societies. In many ways, it is more radical than other ideologies because it calls for change in the sphere of private life focused on gender, sexuality, and family. Liberalism accepts the status quo in the sphere of reproduction, not out of any great conviction, but because it is reluctant to use the state to make changes in this private area of civil society. Religious movements are concerned with gender, sexuality, and the family, but most reaffirm or revitalize a traditional value system. Socialism begins its project of societal transformation with the economy and the state, often postponing change in the most private and intensely felt institutions—sexuality, sexual identity, the gender system, and the family. Because feminism challenges these private institutions and behaviors, it can be an extremely threatening movement for many people and societies. Feminists make a *public issue* of what liberals and others are willing to define as a private matter, "family business."

It is tempting in a chapter on feminism and women's movements to examine the nuances of different versions of women's movements and feminism. Like many movements that have not come to power, feminism spends much time examining its own discourses, rather than instituting practices or making changes. This situation leads to disagreement over fine points. The fact that women are a category of people dispersed in very different class, ethnic, and national settings contributes to ideological differences.

Instead of beginning with some very abstract ideological issues— which lead to rifts—I find it clearer and simpler to begin with a discussion of issues that concern women. Feminism sees these issues as part of a single system of gender stratification that the movement challenges; different varieties of feminism give priority to different issues, while still seeing all of them as evidence of male domination. Other types of women's movements are more inclined to treat the issues separately

Here, then, is a list of the kinds of problems and forms of inequality that women's movements address. Feminism points to these problems (and perhaps several additional ones) as evidence of a coherent system of gender stratification, male domination.

- Women in many societies are confined to the home, to the private sphere or that of physical and **social reproduction**. In some societies, they are literally not permitted to enter the public sphere.
- Women are discriminated against in the economy. They are occupationally segregated, often in lower-paid or less-valued work. In many nations, they

are paid lower wages, even if they do the same work as men. They are rarely promoted into managerial positions and, especially, positions that involve supervising the work of men. Their supervisors are often men. They are channeled into segmented labor markets formed by hiring practices that keep them out of many sectors of the economy. They have less access to credit than men. Their labor in the household economy remains **invisible**—that is, it is not officially recorded as productive labor and they do not receive an individual income from it. Even when they are able to enter professional and managerial jobs, they encounter a **glass ceiling** beyond which promotion is unlikely.

- When women enter the paid labor force, they are expected to continue performance of the bulk of household and child-care activities, resulting in a **double shift** of work.
- In many societies, laws discriminate against women. Laws often limit women's rights to own property, obtain divorces, and act in other ways that are available to men.
- **Violence**, as well as the law, is used to control the behavior of women. Rape and **domestic violence** (and the threat of these acts) is used to maintain male dominance. Although these acts are illegal in many countries, they are not prosecuted effectively; they are used to intimidate women, limit their sexual freedom, and keep them out of the public sphere.
- Women do not have equal access to education. In many societies, even where there are laws about compulsory school attendance, girls are less likely than boys to attend or complete primary and secondary schools and, especially, to obtain a postsecondary education.
- Women's health care and physical well-being are not priorities. In some societies, girls have higher mortality rates than boys because of neglect and malnutrition. Female health issues do not get the same level of funding as other needs.
- Women are denied **reproductive rights**, and participation in reproductive decision making. This complete or partial exclusion includes contraception, sterilization, abortion decisions, and access to child care.
- Women are treated according to a **sexual double standard** that defines men—but not women—as sexually autonomous and entitled to pleasure. Women's sexuality is consistently controlled and limited, either by men in their families or by the state. **Genital mutilation** is a particularly extreme case of such denial of pleasure to women. **Sexual harassment** of women by men who have economic power over them, a double standard of conduct, compulsory heterosexuality, and the stigmatization of "illegitimate" births are all examples of the way women are denied sexual autonomy.
- Women are disproportionately misrepresented in discourse; sexist language and misogynistic pornography are examples of **cultural representations** that devalue women.
- Women lack **political representation**. They are vastly underrepresented in the entire political system, in party organizations, in elected positions, in decision making in international agencies and nongovernmental organizations, in the judiciary, and in upper-level administrative posts in state bu-

reaucracies in practically every country in the world and in international organizations.

- Women are exploited as providers of intimate services, primarily prostitution but also surrogate mothering; these services are offered as commodities, but women have little or no control over these commercial exchanges (Grant, 1992).
- **Family leave** and child-care policies either do not exist in many societies or are organized on the assumption that only women should have this type of responsibility.

To look at this list and decide that it "adds up to" a situation of patriarchy or male domination is a step toward feminist ideology. Feminism asserts that these problems are manifestations of underlying inequality in the gender systems of all contemporary societies. Inequality is always to the disadvantage of women. From a feminist viewpoint, humanity is split in half, with one-half systematically devalued. Feminism seeks to end this **systematic devaluation**; the two genders must have equal value.

However, different types of feminism give priority to different types of problems. They disagree on the meaning of equal value and on what changes in society have to be made in order to achieve this goal. Different types of feminism are in dispute over the following kinds of questions: Should the movement build on the similarities between men and women or should it focus on differences? Should the movement strive for the integration of women into existing political and economic institutions or are these institutions irredeemably male-dominated? Are men, with a few exceptions, potential allies who can be included in a movement for gender equality? Or are men inevitably part of the problem and, hence, to be excluded from the movement, which must be autonomous, perhaps even separatist? What issues should be given priority in the allocation of scarce movement resources: Issues of violence against women or issues of unequal participation in social, economic, and political life? Is it necessary to combine feminism with another ideology, such as socialism, liberalism, or ethnonationalism?

Nonfeminist women's movements recognize the existence of the problems on the list, but choose to not use the ideological concepts of patriarchy or male domination as shorthand to link these problems into a system. For their movement, they do not use the term feminism to define an ideology and movement that opposes male domination. They do not explicitly state the idea that these problems are evidence of and results from a basic system of gender stratification.

VARIETIES OF FEMINISM AND WOMEN'S MOVEMENTS

Feminism is a modern, fully developed, radical movement with an analysis of society that emphasizes gender stratification; it is most strongly associated with the developed capitalist nations and with the educated, middle classes throughout the world (Chafetz and Dworkin, 1986).

First-Wave Feminism

In western Europe and North America, systematic and public concern with women's rights began with the Enlightenment and the "rights of man" doctrine of the American and French Revolutions. Prior to that time, women had rebelled in various ways, often risking persecution as witches; but there were few opportunities to form larger movements with a women's rights ideology (Chafetz and Dworkin, 1986).

Mary Wollstonecraft was among the first to formulate a claim for the rights of women, for the same civil liberties and human rights that men were obtaining in the revolutions; *A Vindication of the Rights of Women* was published in England in 1792. The demand for the extension of liberal democratic rights to women grew throughout the nineteenth century. 1848 was a particularly active year, and in many respects, it marked the beginning of **first-wave feminism**, a movement in the industrializing nations to bring women into full political and juridical equality. The Seneca Falls convention took place in the United States to bring together the leadership of several currents of the movement. Despite disagreements, the movement took shape around the issue of equal rights, since women were still excluded not only from voting, but also from rights that men had in family law and property ownership. However, such basic equality was only one step toward equal participation in society by men and women. Socialist feminist protests against the exclusion of women from suffrage occurred in France (DuBois, 1991:25). These movements united liberals, utopian socialists, and other kinds of socialists as well as feminists. From the beginning, feminism and socialism were intertwined because both believed that the promise of equality offered by liberalism could not be fulfilled without radical changes in social and economic institutions.

The first wave of feminism culminated in the successes of the **women's suffrage movement** in the later part of the nineteenth century and the first decades of the twentieth century. Suffragists were well aware that the vote would not solve all of women's problems; but, they also recognized that voting was a necessary first step in the framework of the liberal democracies, since only groups that could vote could introduce a larger range of issues into the political system. By 1920, this first wave of feminism had succeeded—often against powerful opposition—in winning the right to vote in northern Europe and English-speaking settler states in North America, Australia, and New Zealand. Even a right as basic as suffrage was not won elsewhere until considerably later (DuBois, 1991).

There were already two distinct currents of opinion in first-wave feminism. One called for women's rights, specifically suffrage, as an extension of their human rights. Women should have the same political and economic rights as men. A second current of opinion put more emphasis on the difference between men and women; women should participate in social and political life because they would bring their unique qualities to it—a more caring and nurturant outlook. In practice, both of these currents could agree on suffrage as a goal; but their theoretical differences were not resolved.

The "Woman Question" in Socialist States

At this point, I digress from a historical discussion of feminism in the market democracies in order to summarize the relationship between feminism and socialism as it developed from the early twentieth century to the present. Socialism and activism for women's rights were closely connected in most industrialized nations, in western Europe, North America, and Japan (Hane, 1988). Although they increasingly avoided the concept feminist, socialist movements gave attention to women's issues. As socialism moved from its utopian and radical origins to forming mass parties and organizations with a prospect of coming to state power, it developed an inconsistent record of support for gender equality. In some cases, socialists preferred to combine the entire list of women's issues with the kinds of changes they hoped to bring about in the economy and the state. They hoped that the end of capitalist class distinctions, the formation of a publicly planned and socially responsive economy, and the entry of women into productive work would resolve women's problems.

Communism and the "Woman Question" The record of the Communist states in women's emancipation was mixed (the discussion is based on Funk and Mueller, 1993; Molyneux 1986, 1990, 1991; Posadskaya, 1992; Robinson, 1985; Rowbotham, 1992; and Stacey, 1983). Women did attain formal legal equality with men. They did enter paid productive labor in large numbers. And they benefited from the development of social services, especially child care and improvements in education and health care. But, in other areas, little progress was made. The party leadership and the upper levels of state bureaucracies included few women. The state and party were timid about confronting traditional cultural practices and ideals that limited and marginalized women. For example, the Soviet state was restrained in imposing western socialist ideas about women's equality on the Islamic central Asian republics; when it attempted to do so by creating new laws, these laws were rarely enforced at the local level (Massell, 1968). Women's health needs were accorded low priority; for example, abortion rather than contraception was widely used in birth control in the Soviet Union and a number of eastern European countries. In other cases, abortion was criminalized (Romania) or forced on women as a population control measure (China). In all these instances, women were not able to make decisions about reproduction and their own bodies. The pressure of economic development was used as an excuse to leave occupational segregation and other kinds of economic discrimination in place. And, since no autonomous organizations were permitted, no movements of women could emerge to demand change (Molyneux, 1990).

The Transition to Capitalism: A Step Backward? Even with all these defects, socialism as practiced in the Communist states had brought about gains for women. The return of these states to capitalism in the 1990s has meant declines in women's opportunities, the reappearance of misogynist discourse in the media and in political deliberation, and massive unemployment among women. As many societies rush to overturn the legacy of socialism, socialist ideas about the emancipation of women are among the first values to be rejected (Bishop, 1990; Funk and Mueller, 1993; Molyneux, 1991; Watson, 1993).

Misogyny in Discourse   Freedom has resulted in the circulation of pornography and license to publicly demean women, but little sex education or constructive discussion of women's sexuality is taking place. From a feminist perspective, it appears that the post-Communist nations have now adopted only the worst side of freedom of speech—the right to produce and circulate materials that are degrading to women. The good side of free speech—the right to discuss sexual issues and organize an autonomous movement—seems to be lagging behind. Prudishness about women's sexuality and traditional notions about femininity persist in the post-Communist nations. The Communist states failed—often refused—to revise these old habits. In the west, these habits were worn away by social changes in the postwar period. In the east, they not only persisted, but are now being promoted again as part of a backlash against even the moderate and limited reforms that communism accomplished in the area of gender discourse and representations of women. These attitudes militate against the organizing of mass-based feminist movements; women are even more fearful than in the west that feminist activism will lead to labels of unfeminine or man hater (Posadskaya, 1992).

Unemployment   Unemployment is a new and upsetting experience throughout the region, but it has particularly affected women. Women have been deliberately made to bear the brunt of the sudden labor force cutbacks that affect virtually all sectors of the economy. Women have been fired and laid off in much larger proportions than men, sometimes with the explicit reason, "men are the breadwinners." Sectors of the economy like health care and education have been cut back and these cutbacks affect women employees more than men. In addition, cutbacks in child care and family allowances have left women without the support systems they need for labor force participation.

Reproductive Rights and Health Care   Access to abortions is being limited (for example, in Poland and in the areas of Germany that had been the German Democratic Republic), in many cases, with little or no compensating attention to contraception and women's health-care needs. Decisions about abortion access are being made by legislatures that are overwhelmingly male and often under pressure from the Roman Catholic Church.

The Beginnings of Autonomous Movements   It is now possible to organize autonomous feminist movements in Russia and the countries of eastern Europe; but these movements remain small and are generally limited to intellectuals associated with study groups or new research institutes (Cockburn, 1991; Molyneux, 1991; Posadskaya, 1992). In the long run, the formation of autonomous women's movements may produce improvements in the condition of women; but, in the short run, the concrete gains women made in Communist states are being lost.

The Social Democratic Record   A different and more positive picture is presented by the countries in western Europe with a history of social democratic governments. The social democratic states in Scandinavia have a strong record on gender issues, particularly in supporting women's labor force participation by providing social services (Jenson and Mahon, 1993). In recent years, these family policies have become increasingly gender-neutral; for example, both fathers and mothers have the right to parental leaves. Usually, mothers take advantage of the leaves, but the concept of a parental leave demonstrates the value of being a parent for both sexes (Sorrentino, 1990). Legal and social stigmatization of illegitimacy has disappeared.

In several of these countries, especially Norway, women have achieved a substantial level of representation in government and political parties. Political parties on the left took the lead in establishing quotas for women's representation on slates of candidates, and these measures eventually led to the entry of women into parliament and the cabinet (Skjeie, 1991). However, women are still sharply underrepresented in the private sector, in corporate management.

The mixed historical record of socialist countries has influenced contemporary socialist feminists and marxist feminists. They have recognized that gender and class issues cannot be easily separated and that socialist economic policy does not automatically take care of the woman's question (Rowbotham, 1992). Parties and movements of the left have to develop policies of gender equality and be prepared to implement them when they have access to state power. At the same time, socialist feminists continue to challenge liberal feminists to become aware that gender does not automatically unite women across class lines.

Second-Wave Feminism

While socialist movements in power in the Communist bloc and the Scandinavian social democratic nations attempted with varying degrees of success to reduce some elements of gender inequality, feminism as a movement seemed relatively dormant, or becalmed, in North America and much of western Europe (Rupp and Taylor, 1987; Whittier, 1995).

However, another wave of feminism was building power. Structural strains and political opportunities contributed to the emergence of second-wave feminism. The structural strains had to do with the gap between women's growing educational attainment and affluence, on the one hand, and their limited participation in the economy and political life, on the other hand. In the United States, the tensions experienced around this structural fact were popularized in books like Betty Friedan's *The Feminine Mystique* (1963), which gave voice and political substance to the malaise felt by many women at a time when suburban life and motherhood were seen as the definitive goals for educated women.

While women's labor force participation was still fairly low, those women who were in the workforce experienced considerable discrimination; for example, flight attendants were among the first to connect labor-management issues to problems of gender discrimination (Davis, 1991). Collective identity among women was also heightened by the successes of the Civil Rights Movement; the movement showed that there were expanding opportunities for marginalized segments of society to win juridical equality and participate more fully in the life of the nation.

Mobilization followed along the lines of networks established in earlier periods of activism by women who had a role in the New Deal. The networks were reactivated in the Kennedy administration (Davis, 1991; Freeman, 1983).

By the early 1960s in the United States and western Europe, a new genera-tion of women became determined to build on the success of the suffragists and learn from the limitations of first-wave feminism. For these women, feminism in the market democracies had to mean addressing a wide range of economic, cultural, and social issues, as well as changing laws and the political system.

The diverse backgrounds and interests of the women, as well as the size and complexity of the task they had set themselves, lead to a highly differentiated and fragmented movement. To some observers this fragmentation means that feminism is coming to an end as a coherent movement. To others, this frag-mentation is not necessarily a source of weakness; it permits a flexible and un-forced division of labor among movement organizations.

Equal Rights Feminism   Second-wave feminism began with the push for le-gal equality, equality in government regulations, and equity in educational and economic opportunities. This theme was most strongly developed in the move-ment in the United States, but the results were fairly similar in Canada and western Europe. Some women worked for changes in laws and government regulations like **Title IX** in the United States, which specified equal funding for the education of men and women, including high school and college sports. In the area of equal legal rights and equal treatment by government agencies, the movement made many changes, although, in the United States, the Equal Rights Amendment was never ratified by the states (Mansbridge, 1986).

Some activists focused on reproductive rights; access to abortion was one of the key issues in this area, and it was liberalized in the United States (in *Roe v. Wade*, a 1973 Supreme Court case) and most of western Europe. This issue brought women's movements into direct confrontation with some religiously oriented movements and organizations.

Women's employment expanded rapidly. More women entered the labor force and began to enter occupations previously monopolized by men or closed to women. Although women entered these jobs individually, movement activ-ity made a difference; **affirmative action** policies opened doors in the 1970s that would otherwise have remained shut. The movement for equity in education opened professional schools to women. Many women benefited from these policies, even though they did not consider themselves part of a feminist move-ment that was pressuring the federal government toward gender equality. The combination of movement pressures, a supportive climate of public opinion, and the "pull" of a relatively advantageous labor market in the 1960s created new opportunities. Of course, occupational segregation persisted, and many women in corporate management encountered a glass ceiling in the company beyond which they were not promoted.

In short, much of the early part of the second wave involved liberal ideals of equality and equal rights in all spheres of the society—laws, reproductive rights, educational and athletic opportunities, political office, and occupations (Davis, 1991; Freeman, 1983). This process took place in much of western Europe as well as North America (Backhouse and Flaherty, 1992; Katzenstein and Mueller, 1987).

Ideological Diversification

As women moved toward juridical equality in North America and western Europe and entered the paid labor force in increasing numbers, the ideology of feminism began to diversify. These divisions reflected the intellectual orientations of activists as well as diversity in the support base. As in the Civil Rights Movement, gains in juridical rights led to a focus on more intractable cultural and economic issues and to divisions in the movement.

The diversity in the circumstances of women's lives makes it difficult to sustain a single unified ideology (de Beauvoir, 1974). Women's other identities, like class and ethnicity, mold their identity as women and determine their view of feminist goals. Women generally live scattered among men, and their diverse experiences with men (even within the same class and cultural milieu) contribute to the formation of different emphases within feminism. Gender is socially constructed in many institutions and relationships, so it is difficult for activists to find strategic sites for mobilizations.

The pressures inherent in the diversified support base of feminism lead to the emergence of many currents within feminsim. Some of these currents emphasize the considerable differences among the experiences of women. These differences cause different views of what should be the priorities of the movement. Why should an immigrant working in a sweatshop or a cook paid below the minimum wage in the fast-food industry feel moved to protest when a corporate manager hits the glass ceiling or a network news broadcaster can't get into a private club?

New currents of the movement increasingly emphasized differences between men and women, a view that the founding activists of second-wave feminism had not shared. Rather than giving priority to helping women attain traditionally male political power, juridical rights, and career opportunities, they celebrated women's culture and women's distinct contributions to society.

Liberal Feminism   Liberal feminism continues to be an important current of the movement in North America and western Europe. Liberal feminists accept the social structure of the market democracies. Within this structure, they seek to open economic and political opportunities to women, integrate women into existing institutions on an equal basis with men, and eliminate legal and economic barriers to the equality of men and women as individuals. Women should have the same rights, privileges, and duties as men. Equal rights in all social institutions will further relations of equality between women and men in personal life. Women and men are seen as **essentially similar**. The starting point of feminist mobilization tends to be middle-class women and, in multiethnic societies, women of the dominant ethnic groups; women in these relatively privileged class and ethnic categories give priority to narrowing the gap in opportunities between themselves and men in the same strata.

Socialist Feminism   Socialist feminists agree with liberal feminists in the emphasis on the essential similarity of men and women, but believe that equality between women and men as human beings can be attained only in a society in which the mode of production is transformed. Public ownership of productive enterprises, a more cooperative organization of production and reproduction, and public discussion of economic priorities are needed to create institutions in which women and men can participate as equals. The economy and gender relations have to be transformed together to realize equality. Socialist feminists give more attention to the intertwining of class and gender inequality than liberal feminists.

Radical Feminism   Like liberal feminists and socialist feminists, **radical feminists** had a support base among well-educated women, for the most part in western Europe and among women of European background in North America. Many radical feminists were influenced by their experiences in male-dominated organizations of the New Left in which they felt marginalized. Although most considered themselves socialists, they saw the disappointing record of revolutionary regimes on gender issues, which made them think that many socialist feminists underestimated the barriers to attaining equal rights for women in socialist systems. They questioned liberal feminists' goal of integrating into institutions that are both capitalist and patriarchal: What was the point of women becoming corporate CEO's, professional basketball players, and fighter pilots, when institutions like corporations, commercial sports, and the military were hopelessly inhuman? What was needed was a completely restructured society that broke away from all the oppressive hierarchies, including male domination, of existing societies (Echols, 1989; Willis, 1993a and b).

These radical challenges to both liberal feminism and the male-dominated left swept through women's movements in Europe and North America. Groups like the Redstockings in the United States, as well as women's centers, bookstores, and health and media collectives exemplified the beginning of this trend in the 1970s. The movement organizations that formed among radical feminists were quite different from those of liberal feminism. Instead of national organizations with professional staffs and lobbying expertise, radical feminists formed collectives, sometimes linking local groups with larger but very loosely connected national networks. Radical feminism was one element of the European new social movements and shared the antiauthoritarian values of the larger current (Beccalli, 1994; Echols, 1989; Willis, 1993a and b).

Working Mothers and Social Feminism   Social feminists began to formulate a discourse of differences between women and men, focused on women's involvement in motherhood. Social feminist ideas had already been present in the current of the suffrage movement that believed that women would bring more civility and caring to public life. Social feminism had also appeared in European countries where it had contributed to the expansion of social services. Especially in Europe, unions had supported some social feminist policies like on-site day care and maternity leaves in order to meet the needs of their members, working women who balanced jobs and family responsibilities (Black, 1989; Hewlett, 1986).

A premise of social feminism is that within the market economy, individuals who take care of children cannot compete on equal terms with individuals who do not have this responsibility. A discourse of equal rights that is not backed up by social support for mothers leads to the segregation of women in pink-collar occupations, part-time jobs, and mommy tracks. Women end up with lower incomes, few promotions, and a much higher probability of sinking into poverty.

Beyond these specific social service policies, **social feminism demands a valorization of the whole sphere of social reproduction**. Some currents of social feminism go beyond seeking support for women as mothers and call for more parental involvement in family life, including policies like parental leaves (Black, 1989). Others, like the largely symbolic wages-for-housework movement in Italy argued that tasks like housework have to be recognized as a societal necessity rather than a private service provided by wives for husbands.

There is an overlap between social feminism and socialist feminism, which is clearly discernible in the policies implemented by social democratic governments in Europe, which combined ideas from both currents. There can also be an overlap between social feminist ideology and conservatism, since both highlight the value of family life and tend to identify women with the role of motherhood.

Women of Color: Womanism and Black Feminism   African American feminism and womanism emerged in the United States to address the overlap of gender and ethnic stratification; the analysis of the multiple jeopardies of gender, class, and ethnicity is vital to understanding how diversity among women complicates the goals of feminism (King, 1990). The African American experience provides the framework for understanding issues faced by feminism in all multicultural and ethnically stratified societies.

African American women in the United States used their experiences to build a movement that overlapped but also diverged from other varieties of feminism. Some writers and activists prefer to use the term womanist to summarize the history, struggles, and strategies of this movement (hooks, 1981, 1989; Walker, 1984). At least three circumstances led them to challenge the trends they saw in the predominantly white feminist movements.

One condition faced by African American women was that white middle-class women's growing equality was often based on the exploitation of women of color in reproductive labor, both as domestics and as low-paid workers in service industries like fast foods, child care, and health care (Glenn, 1992).

A second condition was that women of color faced a different class situation than European American women. They were already in the labor force, but disproportionately in the worst kinds of jobs; and they were most likely to live in poverty, lack health care and access to housing, and be subjected to sexual violations and deprived of reproductive choices. Class exploitation and racism complicated gender inequality in ways that white middle-class women often failed to grasp and sometimes perpetuated (King, 1990). Issues like the corporate glass ceiling were irrelevant to many African American women who saw this concern as a way in which white middle-class women attained equity with white middle-class men, leaving women of other classes and ethnic groups in a marginalized situation.

Finally, slavery and racial oppression had produced different gender relations among African Americans than among European Americans. On the one hand, African American women have always been more active in the community and the economy than white women, and have shared equally with men in struggles to end racism. On the other hand, African American men are oppressed in a way that middle-class white men are not. "Black women were saying to black men, 'we are not one another's enemy,' 'we must resist the socialization that teaches us to hate ourselves and one another' "(hooks, 1984). Some degree of unity between African American men and women was necessary, given the massive racism of U.S. society; African Americans had to work out the terms of this unity for themselves. The "broken patriarchy" of the African American experience called for a different kind of movement than the forms of patriarchy experienced by white Americans. Similar themes were taken up by movements of Latinas and Asian Americans. In a society as culturally diverse as the United States, different types of women's movements were necessary to address these different experiences.

This diversity within U.S. feminism along class and ethnic lines pointed to the need for a more differentiated feminist analysis in any society with ethnic stratification and class inequality.

Beyond Patriarchy: Difference Feminism   One part of the feminist movement (sometimes referred to as **cultural feminism**) in both the United States and western Europe began to emphasize issues of difference between men and women and to do so in a more radical way than the social feminists. This part of the movement focused on three challenges: the problem of violence against women; the persistence of male domination in discourse, images, and representations of women; and a global vision of feminism based on a positive assessment of women's culture.

Violence against Women   Violence against women became a focus for this part of the movement by the late 1970s. Issues of violence, sexuality, and women's bodies are unambiguously women's issues; they necessarily unite all women. No woman, of any class or ethnic background, is immune to rape and other forms of sexual violation. Date rape and sexual harassment are included as instances of men's violent and aggressive sexual practices. Domestic violence is part of a general system of control of women by men, systematically carried out and legitimated informally—and in some societies, even formally—and generally ignored by law enforcement agencies; it is not just a deviant act committed by a few disturbed men.

The issue of violence against women generated many movement organizations and activities, including groups such as COAR (Campus Organized Against Rape) in the United States. University campuses were a major organizing site, since they brought together many young people in a situation that highlighted gender. Women's shelters and rape victim advocacy programs appeared across the United States and in many other countries. Some changes in sexual assault laws, police handling of domestic violence cases, and institutional codes of conduct were gradually accomplished. The Senate hearings on Clarence Thomas's nomination to the Supreme Court and Anita Hill's sexual

harassment charges against him brought national (and international) attention
to these issues and helped spark changes in institutional regulations.

Discourse   Cultural and difference feminism also placed strong emphasis on
challenging and changing discourse. Men's violent behavior toward women is
supported by misogynistic discourse in everyday speech, science, the media, religion, pornography, and so on. These discourses legitimate rape, domestic violence, and other forms of social control and institutionalized inequality. Patriarchy
is perpetuated in discourse, in interaction, in culture. Changes in the economy or
the legal system have to be accompanied by changes in discourse and culture.

If Women Ran the World . . .   There was also a longer-term and more visionary goal for difference feminists, beyond defending women from violence
in all its forms. This global vision expanded ideas that had already appeared in
the radical critiques of liberal feminism. The world would be a better place if
women's values were the guiding principles rather than male values of violence
and domination. The capitalist patriarchal economy shattered families and destroyed human ties in the name of production, rationalization, and profit; the
military-industrial state made war and destroyed human life. Women must
have a leading part in building a more humane society that is organized around
a different value system. A few difference feminists are essentialists, seeing care
as based on woman's nature; most are not, but emphasize that women have in-
ternalized these human values more fully in the course of their lives than men
typically do (Black, 1989; Bunch, 1987; Gilligan, 1993).

Fragmentation: Weakness or Flexibility?

Divisions like these took place in second-wave feminism in most of the developed market democracies, not only the United States (Beccalli, 1994). The
women's movement appeared to fragment along lines of culture and ethnicity,
social class, sexual orientation, and fundamental ideological principles. Equal
rights feminists disagreed with difference feminists. Women of color built
movements that were separate from those of women of European origin. Lesbians united with heterosexual women on many issues, but maintained distinct
perspectives on sexuality and political organization.

Does this fragmentation leave these movements weak and divided? Does it
mean that energy and intelligence are poured into struggles between and
within the movements rather than into a unified challenge to oppressive gender arrangements? Or does fragmentation also mean flexibility and outreach to
a larger share of the potential support base?

STRATEGY AND ORGANIZATIONS

As the previous discussion has made clear, women's movements in the market
democracies are characterized by diversity and fragmentation, and a resultant

large number of organizations, some localized and short-lived. Earlier in the century, the observer might have labeled such formlessness and fragmentation as weakness; the model of the mass bureaucratized party or the tightly disciplined vanguard party still dominated ideas about effective movement organization. Now, at the end of the century, we are revising these models to fit the realities of contemporary societies, which include electronic information technologies and fragmented support bases rather than clearly defined communities of potential movement members. The segmented, acephalous type of movement may be more flexible than the tightly organized movement. Movements that are formed by loose networks or computer-linked local groups may be very effective in mobilizing people, especially when a movement is trying to reach a large, diversified support base.

Such looser, informal networklike movements may be useful for overcoming problems that women's movements face: the scattering of women among men and the rarity of separate communities of women. As French philosopher and feminist, Simone de Beauvoir, noted: "They live dispersed among males, attached through residence, housework, economic condition, and social standing to certain men—fathers or husbands—more firmly than they are to other women" (de Beauvoir, 1974:xxii).

There are several forms of women's movements in the developed market democracies (Ferree and Martin, 1995). One is the large, nationwide organization that enjoys some degree of stability and focuses especially on political reform. Many of these tend to be liberal feminist– and equal rights–oriented. They serve as umbrella groups that bring smaller organizations together; above all, they are pressure groups and lobbying organizations that seek to improve the conditions of women within existing economic and political structures. A good example is NOW (National Organization for Women) in the United States. Some of the larger organizations of women of color, like National Institute for Women of Color, have a basically similar format. Movement organizations that support women in politics, like National Women's Political Caucus, have a nationwide structure and some professional staffers (Davis, 1991).

A second major organizational form is the women's collective or women's center, now often associated with a college or university, as well as the older health and media collectives. These groups tend to be smaller, less bureaucratized, often more short-lived, and more open to radical interpretations of feminism. They form national networks through ties among individuals or academic programs like women's studies. Some observers (Beccalli, 1994) see this form of politics as withdrawal, a kind of self-marginalization. The movement exists, but devotes most of its energy to internal matters and the elaboration of discourses. Since the public sphere has been defined as male-dominated, the movement develops a distance and indifference toward it, which leads to almost no concrete mobilizations or reform projects other than some local mobilizations against violence. In Europe, a dialogue can persist between this movement and movements of the left; in the United States, given only a fragmentary left, cultural feminism may become rather isolated, perhaps once again dormant or becalmed.

A third organizational form is the women's caucus within other organizations such as unions or professional associations. This type of organization rarely defines the large, radical goals of the movement, but works for an expansion of women's participation in specific institutions and occupations. These caucuses and occupational associations have an important part in extending women's participation in economic and educational institutions. In many countries, these caucuses may also exist within parties, especially parties of the left (Beccalli, 1994).

At this point, the strategy of women's movements and feminism in the market democracies is not to take power. Rather, one important goal is to become an ongoing part of the political process, in electoral politics and legislation, the judiciary, and the formation of public opinion; expanded political power can then be used to protect reforms in other areas, such as reproductive rights or more effective protection from violence (Davis, 1991). Another goal is to change gender discourse, creating more positive representations of women. A third strategic goal is protection and expansion of the gains women have made in education and occupations. Feminists realize that any form of gender equality, even the limited goal of integration into existing institutions, is a long-term prospect.

WOMEN'S MOVEMENTS IN GLOBAL PERSPECTIVE

Mobilization to alter the gender system is taking place globally. Many of these movements have not adopted the vision of western feminism. They are more focused on specific issues, and some have deliberately avoided the term feminism. These women's movements are responses to the conditions of life in countries that are not developed market democracies.

Problems and Issues

The most important of these conditions is the presence of a large number of people who live in very constricted material circumstances, in some cases in absolute poverty. It is closely associated with a class structure in which the middle class is relatively small, while the percentage of the population that are peasants, low-wage workers, and underemployed is large. Many of these nations have a constricted political sphere as well; some of them have repressive governments, while others can sustain few independent political organizations because of poverty, rural isolation, and limited media access.

These conditions form barriers to organizing women: Women, as well as men, may feel that poverty or economic underdevelopment, not gender oppression, is the leading problem; middle-class women find it difficult to reach and mobilize poor women, especially the rural poor; and building mass movements of any kind encounters the problems of access and resources.

Poverty and Invisible Labor: Class Divisions   In many of these societies, the majority of women are integrated into the economy on unfavorable terms, as low-wage workers in export industries, peasants or crafts workers performing *invisible* work in the rural household economy, servants, street vendors, and sometimes beggars or prostitutes. The term invisible applied to the work of women in a household means that the work is not recorded in official statistics on economic participation, is not adequately compensated, and is dismissed as unimportant and assumed to be part of the "natural" family chores of women. The general economic situation creates a sense of solidarity with men in their own social class and a sense of distance from middle-class women, who may be viewed not as sisters but as exploiters.

Gender Stratification in Households and Communities   Yet, women in the working classes also suffer oppression as women; they receive a smaller share of household income and wealth—even food in some regions—than men even when their contribution in work is large (Afshar, 1993; Pryer, 1987). They are excluded from access to credit, land ownership, government technical training programs, and other kinds of economic resources. They are subject to violence both within the household and in the public sphere. Patriarchal cultural definitions restrict their mobility and autonomy, especially their right to make sexual and reproductive choices. When women's relationships with men break down, women are at great risk of sliding into absolute poverty; two-thirds of the world's poorest households are headed by females. Women's movements in many countries face the challenge of organizing women to overcome these multiple disadvantages without a direct confrontation with individual men or with patriarchal institutions.

Women's movements have identified a few of the most pressing issues as their priorities. The number one priority in many countries is improving women's economic situation by expanding access to credit, organizing cooperatives of farmers and crafts workers, bringing women producers into markets, and unionizing women wage workers. A second major priority is reducing violence against women. The issues of rape and wife beating are made public; silence is broken as a first step to changing behavior. In some societies, confrontation with men over these issues of gender violence is avoided as appeals are made to men as fathers and brothers to help create more respect for women. (Kabeer, 1988). A third issue is reproductive rights, especially expanding access to contraception and, in some cases, abortion. These efforts often run into powerful opposition from religious institutions and from nationalist forces who define birth control as an imperialist strategy employed by the west to curb the power of the Third World. Women's movements also challenge programs of sterilization or forced abortions.

Reinterpreting Tradition   Finally, in the realm of culture, women's movements seek to renegotiate religious and cultural traditions in such a way as to end the devaluation of women while respecting the tradition as a whole. In societies that have been disrupted by the impact of the west, efforts to change the gender system, question religious teachings concerning gender, or alter the structure of the family may be seen as a further imperialist onslaught against national culture and religious values. For example, within Islamic societies there are many ongoing debates about the roles of women (Ahmed, 1992;

Mernissi, 1991). Islam is compatible with a wide range of gender policies, from the restrictive interpretations in Saudi Arabia and Iran to the more egalitarian ones in a secularized state like Turkey and in some Palestinian communities. Islam (like any religious tradition) is not a static set of rules, but a set of practices that is discussed and reinterpreted.

The case for expanded roles for women can be argued on religious grounds within both Islamic and Christian traditions. The elevation of women within the society can lead to a purer and more orthodox religious practice, unalloyed by local superstitions that women fall into when they remain uneducated and isolated. Women's movements also argue that more complete adherence to the religion dictates more respect for women, not in order to make them more similar to men, but to treat them with more dignity as persons (Hatem, 1985; Kabeer, 1988).

Forms of Organization

The issues suggest that women's movements must develop in cooperation with other kinds of movements and organizations—socialist movements and unions; governmental and nongovernmental economic development agencies; rural cooperatives and credit unions, including those with a religious affiliation; political parties; and religious institutions. In this cooperative work, the enhancement of the status of women may be only one of several goals or, perhaps, only a by-product of other goals, such as national economic development. Both strategically and in terms of organizational structure, women's movements in many countries cannot operate alone or focus explicitly on feminist goals of women's emancipation, autonomy, and equality. A few examples will illustrate women's movements that form in these limited opportunity structures.

Government-affiliated Women's Organizations   The governments or ruling parties of many nations have established commissions or councils focused on women's issues. These organizations are not movements, but they can become starting points for the formation of movements. By mobilizing women and stimulating their participation in institutions, government organizations may unintentionally create conditions for more autonomous activism. They contribute to what Smelser called structural conduciveness (1963).

For example, in China, the All-China Women's Federation reflects the concerns of the state and Communist Party that women be involved in the development of China. This federation is an example of an organization with a relatively low degree of autonomy and a high level of control by male leadership in the party. It includes many women who are committed to more gender equality in Chinese society, but see few options other than working through the federation. In Brazil, the Council for Women's Rights is also a governmentally supported organization, but has independence from any one party. In Nicaragua, during the Sandinista period, the AMNLAE represented the interests of women as part of the Sandinista organizational structure; it was challenged by autonomous feminist groups and eventually had to contend with the overwhelming problems of the contra war and economic crisis (Molyneux, 1986). Even within these constraints, it was able to accomplish some reforms and raise the level of awareness of women's issues. Sometimes a government committed to priorities of economic development can create a better climate for women's movements; the left-leaning military regime in Peru in the 1970s (the Velasco government) stimulated the participation of more women in Peru's public life (Miller, 1991).

The Role of the United Nations   The connection between established organizations and women's movements has become stronger as the United Nations has given more attention to gender discrimination. The annoucement of a UN Decade of the Woman (1975–1985), and the UN-sponsored conferences in Mexico City and Nairobi gave legitimacy to women's concerns as an area governments should support and recognize. United Nations documents and statements also provide autonomous women's organizations with a basis of legitimacy (Bunch, 1987). For example, the first independent women's forum in the Soviet Union, in March of 1991, appealed to the 1981 UN Convention on the elimination of all forms of discrimination against women.

Support from Socialist Movements   Left-wing parties and movements have been attentive to women's issues, and women's movements have often been associated with them. For instance, in Bangladesh, the women's group associated with the Communist Party has gone beyond a limited range of class issues to address issues like violence against women (Kabeer, 1988). The association of socialist movements with women's movements is evident throughout Latin America. For example, in Mexico, it is the left-wing parties that have taken up the issue of reproductive rights (Miller, 1991).

The organization of women workers into unions is an important focus, especially as more and more women are drawn into the most exploited levels of wage work, often as assembly workers in electronics and textile export-sector industries in countries such as Mexico, Guatemala, El Salvador, the Philippines, and the United States (Davis, 1990; Fernandez-Kelly, 1984; Smith-Ayala, 1991).

Small-scale Organizing   Women have mobilized through a variety of nongovernmental organizations and agencies oriented toward rural development, the formation of credit unions and co-ops, and similar types of development projects. Many of these are small-scale projects—in fact, deliberately so—as a challenge to the tendency of the World Bank and many governments to fund megaprojects like dams and highways. The logic is that the large projects often disrupt the contribution of women to the local economy (not to mention the environment), depriving them of their stake in development. Small-scale projects expand women's control over resources without massive dislocations. They may alter gender relations within villages and families, but at a pace and scale small enough to allow for gradual renegotiation of roles and identities.

For example, in India, a group of women with leprosy produce handicrafts for export with help from social service agencies of the Catholic Church (Pushpika Freitas, personal communication). In Sri Lanka, village women obtained credit for processing cashew nuts with support from Christian and Buddhist clergy (Casinader, Fernando, and Gamage, 1987). Credit unions have been established in Bangladesh and India to extend credit to rural women. In El Salvador, women in refugee communities have formed handicrafts cooperatives. Many of these projects would not be possible without the involvement of traditional religious organizations.

Movements of Survival   Women form movements of survival. Often the social base of these movements are women in the poorest sections of metropolitan areas, settlements of underemployed people on the peripheries of cities. Many women are heads of families and/or the major earners in their households. They work as street vendors, scavengers, and domestics. The settlements often lack water, sewers, adequate housing, paved streets, clinics, and schools. Women who live under these desperate conditions, as well as women factory workers and poor women in rural areas, form community organizations and survival-oriented institutions, like the people's kitchens that prepare and share food in the poorest neighborhoods in Lima, Peru (Andreas, 1989).

Sometimes women engage in short-lived and spontaneous uprisings over the cost of food, housing, and public transportation. In some of these demonstrations in Latin America, women throng the streets beating empty pots and pans to symbolize the conditions of scarcity in which they live (a tactic that was also used by right-wing women against the socialist Allende government in Chile in the early 1970s). These movements and demonstrations speak to the most basic economic needs: food, shelter, clean water, public transportation. They are powerful because they are spontaneous, unpredictable, driven by pressing problems, and difficult for parties and governments to co-opt. On the other hand, they run the risk of remaining isolated. One writer comments: "Women's movements for survival are like firestorms, changing and dissolving, resistant to political definition" (Snitow, 1989:211).

Autonomous Feminist Organizations   Western-type autonomous feminist organizations exist in many peripheral capitalist nations. They tend to be based in the middle and upper classes. They are prepared to push certain issues further than the movements just described: gender discourse, sexual politics, and violence against women as a pervasive problem rather than an occasional aberration. In societies like China that allow no autonomous parties or movements, students and other intellectuals form small study groups at universities. In other societies, they may form larger organizations, develop their own media and research institutes, and work as pressure groups within parties. Feminists in countries as diverse as Bangladesh, Brazil, and Russia are carrying out this type of organizing. Their relations to government, socialist, religious, and other women's associations and movements range from mutually supportive to stormy (Cockburn, 1991; Miller, 1991; Molyneux, 1990).

Peace, Human Rights, and the Environment   The discussion of women's movements as a global phenomenon closes with the involvement of women in movements that extend and politicize women's familial commitments and the ethic of care. These movements expand the definition of women's issues to human rights, peace, and the preservation of the natural environment for future generations. The most powerful instance of this type of mobilization is in the human rights movement, especially in Latin America. It is exemplified by the Madres of the Plaza de Mayo, the women who silently appeared day after day in the square in front of Argentina's presidential palace to draw the world's attention to the disappearance and murder of their children by the military regime from 1976 to 1982. They were able to confront the military regime in this way because they could draw on the respect and legitimacy of motherhood (Bouvard, 1994). Similarly, women in Guatemala have formed the Mutual Support Group (GAM) for the relatives of the disappeared and a widows' association to publicize the crimes of the military dictatorship (Smith-Ayala, 1991).

In Japan, women have mobilized around issues of peace and environmental quality (Mackie, 1988). Activists in these movements believe that women have the opportunity and obligation to confront problems about which men are pressured to remain silent because of their job obligations or masculine role definitions. This pattern is also discernible in western Europe and North America. Peace or harmony with the environment are not only women's values, but also issues about which women have historically been outspoken. Men are often under pressure to focus on profit or war, conventional male roles from which they have difficulty breaking away; women are freer to question a system that they see as exploitive and militaristic. During the years of the cold war, a specifically women's peace movement was a point of cooperation between women in the United States and the Soviet Union.

In many countries, feminism as a movement that totalizes gender issues is not as fully developed as in the west or the developed market democracies. Women are more likely to be mobilized into organizations that *link* women's issues with issues of economic development, human rights, and/or socialism. These organizations vary in the degree of their autonomy and the extent to which the **linkage among women's issues and other concerns** subordinates women's emancipation to other goals.

As one observer says: "It is not the *linkage* itself that constitutes the problem—principles such as social equality and women's emancipation can be realized only within determinate conditions of existence. So linking the program for women's emancipation to these wider goals need not necessarily be a cause for concern because these wider goals may constitute the preconditions for realizing the principles. The question is rather the nature of the links: are gender interests *articulated into* a wider strategy of economic development, for example, or are they irretrievably *subordinated to it?* . . . In the latter case, the specificity of gender interests is likely to be denied or its overall importance minimized. The issues are trivialized or buried, the program for women's emancipation remains one conceived in terms of how functional it is for achieving the wider goals of the state" (Molyneux, 1986:300).

FEMINISM AND WOMEN'S MOVEMENTS

Structural Theory

This section begins with a summary of a structural study that tries to answer the question: In what types of societies do women's movements, and specifically feminist movements, emerge? This comparative and historical study suggests that women's movements first emerge as a society urbanizes and industrializes (Chafetz and Dworkin, 1986). The higher the average educational level of women and the larger the size of the middle class, the larger the size of the women's movement. Specifically *feminist* movements are somewhat more likely to appear in societies with larger proportions of women labor-force participants working in male-dominated occupations. The authors of this study conclude that the existence and size of women's movements in general, and feminist movements specifically, can be explained in terms of the society's economic structure, that is, its level of industrialization, the size of its middle class, and its occupational structure including women's educational attainment, labor-force participation, and entry into a wider range of occupations (Chafetz and Dworkin, 1986:221).

Support Base

At a more individual, within-society level of explanation, women tend to participate more in feminist movements when they are well educated and/or involved in middle-class occupations. Women in other circumstances may be participants in a women's movement that lacks a distinct feminist ideology. As noted in other chapters, any mobilization calls on the formation of a specific identity. Every individual can look in the mirror and see an ethnic identity, a racial identity, a class identity, or a gender identity. Why should anyone see herself as a woman when she can see herself in terms of a competing identity? Women as a category present some difficult problems for mobilization.

The more separated a segment of the population geographically and socially, the easier it is organized. Isolated communities of the working class have historically been easier to organize than working-class individuals scattered throughout a large city. For example, when many workers lived in mining towns or industrial zones, they were more easily mobilized by union organizers and socialist movements; now that workers live in dispersed patterns with consumption habits that are very similar to those of managers or lower-level professionals, they are harder to reach. To convince them that their class or occupational identity is their most salient identity for political action is especially difficult (Geoghegan, 1991; Kerr and Siegel, 1954). Ethnic groups are often easily mobilized by ethnic nationalist movements because they live in a separate territory; and they can sometimes be appealed to in a distinct language.

In contrast, women are anchored to families and communities that include men. They are usually in daily contact with men and belong to the same class and ethnic group as the men in their families and households. A discourse that asks women to think of themselves as separate and, to some degree, opposed to their fathers, brothers, sons, and husbands may not make much sense in the circumstances of many women's lives. Apart from a few expressions or verbal mannerisms, there is no separate women's language. Women, for the most part, do not live separately from men; therefore, it is difficult for a feminist movement to make gender a salient identity for political mobilization (de Beauvoir,

1974). For this reason, lesbians play an important role as a vanguard group in feminist movements, since they are less continuously integrated into households with men and are more likely to sustain a distinct women's discourse and political perspective.

Are men part of the support base for women's movements? Our discussion would point to two circumstances in which they can be mobilized: One is the involvement of men in women's movements that do not seek to transform the entire gender order but only to reform part of it, especially in conjunction with economic development, democratization and human rights, and/or socialism. Men participate in such mixed movements and, on occasion, may even lead or control them. The second circumstance in which men support movements for greater gender equality is under conditions of economic development where there is a comfortable margin in the system; when men are not threatened by an expansion of women's rights because there is enough to go around, they may support fairly extensive changes.

The clearest societal example of a willingness to reduce patriarchal control is in northern Europe, where social democratic parties have participated in creating a general climate of equality. Under these conditions, the gender system is seen as less of a zero-sum game. The expansion of women's rights and women's participation in the economy and the political system are less threatening to men because the society is prosperous enough to sustain such participation. Greater gender equality, in turn, creates a unified, more skilled and educated, less violent, and more politically aware society, which also benefits men.

The immediate cause of this relatively high level of gender equality in Scandinavia is undoubtedly the strength of socialist movements and parties in the region; they have had a direct effect in reducing gender stratification, as well as an indirect effect of contributing to the general high level of equality and prosperity; the gender equalizing impact of socialism in Scandinavia was perhaps reinforced by pre-Christian cultural traditions of relatively more gender equality than in southern Europe and west Asia.

COUNTERMOVEMENTS

Cultural Conservatives

The main countermovements to women's movements and, especially, to feminism are culturally conservative movements and fundamentalist religious movements. Countermovements have been particularly active in the United States (Faludi, 1991). Some observers in the United States link them into a movement they call the religious right. The conservative and fundamentalist movements actually agree with feminists about the importance of the sphere of the family, gender, and social reproduction. Unlike liberals or socialists, they are likely to see this sphere as the most important element of society. For feminists, if it does not become a sphere of equality, all of society will remain oppressive; for cultural conservatives, if it does not retain its traditional gender-differentiated nature, all of society will fall apart (Erwin, 1993).

For both feminists and antifeminists, this sphere is far too important to be left to the vagaries of individuals' private choices or to the impact of market forces in the economy, as liberals are inclined to do. Feminists and conservatives agree that society, and especially the state as the guiding institution of society, should do something about current forms and trends in the gender system, the family, and the whole sphere of private life; but they have opposing visions of what changes should take place. Both the feminist movement and the countermovements look to public policy and government actions (in legislation, judicial decisions, regulations, decisions by school boards or public libraries, and so on) as the terrain on which these issues are fought.

The clash of movement and countermovement has focused on a number of issues, above all the issue of abortion (Luker, 1984). Far from being the concern of a single-issue movement, the abortion issue condenses a host of gender-related issues: The meaning of being a woman; the centrality of motherhood in a woman's life; the relationship among self, body, and society; the meaning of sexuality; and the nature of life itself. If men and women are, above all, similar to each other, then women should have the same rights to make decisions about their bodies as men and should not be forced to bear children against their will. If women are different from men, and if this difference is defined by their ability to bear children, then the notion of an equal right may make little sense and has to be weighed against the sanctity of human life in all its forms. On this issue, some churches—especially the Catholic Church—have been very active in support of antiabortion groups.

Forms of the family and personal life are another area of conflict. Feminists tend to suggest that women (and men) should have the right to form many kinds of families; for instance, single-parent households, matrifocal households, and domestic partnership arrangements between people of the same sex. Singlehood, gay and lesbian relations, or a wider range of heterosexual sex partners should be acceptable alternatives to monogamous marriage and the nuclear family. Cultural conservatives vehemently disagree; they insist on the validity of religious traditions, but often update or reread these to make them more suited to the economic and cultural climate of contemporary societies (Stacey, 1991). Usually, what the countermovements mean by traditional family is the ideal of the middle-class family that developed in the later part of the nineteenth century (Coontz, 1988).

Groups like the Eagle Forum, Women for America, and the Pro-Family movement in the United States have taken the lead in calling for an updated and revitalized version of traditional family structure and family values. They suggest that many social problems like crime are rooted in the disintegration of the traditional family. These countermovements have been very active in the right wing of the Republican Party. In some localities, they have tried to overturn laws that prohibit discrimination against gays and lesbians. Another focus of activity is the choice of books for public libraries and school systems. Efforts to increase the level of tolerance for gay and lesbian households in school curricular materials, for example, have met with strong opposition by parents' groups in New York City (where a school superintendant was forced to resign after supporting such a curriculum) and elsewhere (*New York Times*, February 11, 1993).

Pornography: Unexpected Alliances

The pornography debate is a particularly interesting arena for movements and countermovements in that it has divided feminists and led one segment to side with cultural conservatives in a rather unexpected alliance. To some feminists, pornography creates a climate for violence against women; it degrades women and appears to legitimate acts like rape, mutilation, and torture. Women are exploited in the production of pornographic movies and videos, a growing industry. Feminists have formed movement organizations to limit consumption of pornographic materials; Women Against Pornography is an example of such a group.

From the point of view of anticensorship feminists, censorship of pornography not only violates free speech rights; it also plays into a conservative program of suppressing discussion of sex, making sex seem sinful, and denying women's sexuality. From the point of view of the anticensorship feminist perspective, emphasizing women's vulnerability reinforces the idea that women are helpless and in need of protection above and beyond the general protection afforded to all citizens in laws against assault, child sexual abuse, and so on. After all, sexual assault and child abuse are already illegal; it should not be necessary to censor or criminalize verbal or visual representations as long as specific acts are illegal (Gardiner, 1993; Kahn in Matteo, 1993).

One interesting element of this debate is the convergence of the activities of some antipornography feminists with those of some cultural conservatives. It suggests that, taken to their logical extreme, some varieties of difference feminism may overlap the conservative view that women are fundamentally or essentially different from men, that they are defined by biological functions like sex and motherhood, and that they are vulnerable to the predatory instincts of men and, hence, in need of special protection above and beyond the general protection of all citizens against violence.

GAY AND LESBIAN MOVEMENTS

Gay and lesbian movements, like feminism, challenge the prevailing organization of the private sphere of sexuality, gender, and societal reproduction; and by challenging the organization of that sphere they challenge the social order as a whole. Yet, at the same time, gay and lesbian movements are liberal movements with the goal of civil rights and liberties for a previously excluded segment of society and libertarian movements with the aim of reduced state regulation of personal behavior (Bawer, 1994). Gay and lesbian movements share a number of historical characteristics with feminism, as well as some key elements of ideology. They began largely as vindications for the rights of an oppressed group, but in the process of defining and asserting these rights, they question the organization of modern societies (Taylor and Rupp, 1993).

Like feminism, gay and lesbian movements are a product of industrialized, urbanized, capitalist societies. Like feminism, their analysis of modern capitalist societies explores multiple contradictions: Modern societies contain the possibility for disconnecting sex from procreation more completely than any previous society. Declining fertility and improved contraception enable heterosexuals to think about sex as play or as an expression of personal feelings; these discourses and practices, in turn, valorize other forms of sexual experience, including homosexual acts and identities. Also, capitalism and the institution of wage labor and individual income make possible individual survival without either an extended or even a nuclear family. Adults do not have to live in families and households focused on heterosexual couples and children in order to survive economically (D'Emilio, 1992). According to one writer, "In divesting the household of its economic independence and fostering the separation of sexuality from procreation, capitalism created conditions that allow some men and women to organize a personal life around their erotic/emotional attraction to their own sex. It has made possible the formation of urban communities of lesbians and gay men and, more recently, of a politics based on sexual identity" (D'Emilio, 1992:7).

D'Emilio and others point out that at the same time that capitalism eroded the economic importance of the heterosexual family and household, modern capitalist societies also produced an "enshrinement" of the nuclear family and its privatized "home as haven" ideology. The nuclear family lost its economic importance, but retained a great ideological weight. It became defined as the proper way to organize sexuality, socialization of children, and the sphere of societal reproduction (D'Emilio, 1992:11). These contradictions are now given political voice and brought out in the conflicts of movements and countermovements over these institutions.

The liberal political system that sometimes accompanies capitalism permits more individual choices about identity and personal life. The enlarged concept of privacy rights made the choice of identity more acceptable; individuals could formulate gay and lesbian identities (Herdt, 1992). The liberal model of society created an atmosphere conducive to the emergence of movements centered on these issues. Out of these contradictions between possibilities and prevailing discourses, between freedoms and restrictions, gay and lesbian movements gradually emerged in western Europe and North America. This emergence involved three stages.

Formation of Communities and Subcultures

The first step was the formation of homosexual communities and cultures, found, to some extent, in most industrialized and urbanized nations by the late nineteenth century. Previously, individuals had engaged in homosexual acts but, generally, did not develop a distinct homosexual identity, let alone form distinct communities of persons with a gay/lesbian identity. In large part, this absence of **gay and lesbian culture, community, and identity** was the result of extremely punitive codes of behavior, especially in the Christian world. It was also the result of the economic difficulties people encountered in living outside family households. In some societies, religious communities may have provided a partial exception to the prevalence of family households and compulsory heterosexuality. There were also some explicitly homosexual communities, such as the lesbian communities of silk weavers in China, women who had an independent source of income and were not tied into the prevailing practices of patrilocal and patriarchal marriages (Stacey, 1983). In the west, however, such communities remained prohibited until the onset of industrialization and urbanization.

Civil Rights Mobilizations

The second stage involved public and political demands for civil rights for homosexuals, specifically for the decriminalization of sexual acts between consenting adults, the end to police harassment, and an end to purges of homosexuals from public employment. Gay and lesbian communities and culture had expanded and become more visible in many western societies by mid-twentieth century. Newspapers, bars, and sections of cities supported homosexual identity and solidarity. In the United States, by the early 1950s, cautious associations like the Mattachine Society helped create nationwide connections, building on a sense of identity that developed during the Second World War (Adam, 1987). Small groups emerged in the United States to protest against the purges of homosexuals and the climate of sexual repression that accompanied the anticommunist activities of Joe McCarthy and his allies in the 1950s.

In the late 1960s in the United States, these communities formed the basis for movements for civil rights of gays and lesbians. "A massive, grass-roots liberation movement could form almost overnight precisely because communities of lesbians and gay men existed" (D'Emilio, 1992:10). The climate of the 1960s, with its mixture of civil rights organizing and generalized rebellion, also contributed to the movement. In the United States, the precipitating incident was the Stonewall riot in 1969, a mass demonstration in the streets which began as a protest against police harassment in New York City. After that, the small number of political organizations exploded: "By 1973, there were more than eight hundred lesbian and gay male groups scattered across the country" (D'Emilio, 1992:86).

Even in the most liberal societies in western Europe and North America, the civil rights emphasis of this movement continues, since many of the demands have not been won, as the issue of gays in the military in the United States makes clear. The effort by cultural conservatives to prohibit the passing of local or state-level antidiscrimination laws indicates that the civil rights phase of the movement has not been completed in the United States. Gays and lesbians have struggled for custody rights to their children or recognition for familial or guardianship rights in the case of disability (Lewin, 1991). Groups like the Gay and Lesbian Task Force (which works on both a national and local level) and the Gay Media Coalition have a role in supporting changes in laws through court cases and legislative change and in fostering more tolerance in mass public opinion.

In much of western Europe, homosexual acts have been decriminalized and gays can form political organizations (Adam, 1987). For example, in Italy, gay civil rights groups work to change public perceptions and social restrictions. The greatest public acceptance is in Bologna and the "red" central regions of Italy while, in the more traditionally Catholic northeast and south, homosexuality is still stigmatized.

In the post-Communist nations in eastern Europe, Russia, and the rest of the former Soviet Union, conditions for political organizing are still very difficult. Informal stigma makes coming out and entering the political sphere as a gay or lesbian daunting and dangerous. A gay demonstration did take place in Moscow, and within the feminist movement in Russia, there is a lesbian group called SAFO (after Sappho, a lesbian poet in ancient Greece) (Molyneux, 1991).

Cuba is moving toward a more open atmosphere than the post-Communist nations. The Cuban government pursued an antigay policy for many years that involved labor camps in the 1960s and purges of the ministry of culture in the 1970s and universities in the early 1980s; but homosexuality is now decriminalized and a cultural opening is taking place, signaled, for example, by the showing of a movie with a frank and sympathetic portrait of a gay man (Levinson, in *Cuba Update*, 1993). Young people now "consider it 'uneducated' to have prejudice against people for their sexual preference" (de Vries, in *Cuba Update*, 1993). The mandatory quarantining of people with AIDS or an HIV-positive diagnosis into segregated residential facilities suggests both serious attention to their health-care needs and a paternalistic and restrictive attitude. This policy is now being discussed and reconsidered (*Cuba Update*, 1993). As civil rights for gays and lesbians are achieved in many societies, some activists are satisfied with this level of change and see the movement as a reform movement (Bawer, 1994).

Challenging Sexual Institutions

A third stage of the movement involves going beyond civil rights and antidiscrimination goals to a larger questioning of a social order that is based on multiple forms of repression: the channeling of sexuality into **compulsory heterosexuality** and procreation; narrow and stereotyped definitions of gender that had once forced gay people into gender inversion and restricted roles like butch or drag queen (Herdt, 1992:46); shame and secretiveness associated with the private sphere; and discourse defining "normal" and "deviant." Raising these questions is dangerous for a movement that still has to contend with homophobic violence and a large array of conservative countermovements. Only the outlines of radical themes in homosexual movements are currently visible. One very concrete goal that is at the boundary between limited reform and transformative vision is the call for the recognition of domestic partners in health insurance, pensions, tax policy, campus life, and so on, a policy that a few universities and corporations have agreed to extend to their employees.

This phase of the movement currently centers on academic programs and media groups producing newspapers, journals, movies, and gay/lesbian history projects; in general, groups and networks engaged in changing discourse and the cultural climate at the frontier rather than in the mass media. As in the feminist movement, these relatively small groups and networks are freer to try out radical ideas. Others work with young people, supporting them in coming out (Herdt, 1992). This activity is sometimes a focus of countermovement concern. The more radical parts of the movement also challenge prejudice and stigma with humor and defiance; Queer Nation, for example, turns a derogatory term into a celebration of identity. Some parts of the movement disagree with the more confrontational discourses and practices, and would prefer to keep the movement oriented around liberal reforms that emphasize the similarities between gays and everyone else, rather than the celebration of their differences (Bawer, 1994; Herrell, in Herdt, 1992).

Coming Out and Collective Identity

The shift from potential identity to actual movement commitment is a crucial process, but no more automatic one for persons building a gay and lesbian movement than in any other movement. The question of whether **sexual orientation** is biologically determined, socially constructed, or some combination of both is involved in the definition of gay and lesbian identity. The ideology of the movement leans toward the first, more essentialist view, which sociologists (including gays) tend to question, since they prefer to look for a combination of causal factors (D'Emilio, 1992). In any case, before movement activism can take place, there has to be a process of identity formation and social negotiation that moves from individual self-acceptance to a more public coming out to, finally, political mobilization and action. As with all movements, other identities make competing claims. On the one hand, the centrality of sex to the sense of self impels people into movements of sexual orientation. But, on the other hand, the possibility of remaining closeted (in a way that women or racial ethnic groups cannot remain invisible) works against unity and political action among gays and lesbians. The persecution and stigma attached to homosexuality can affect the individual in contradictory ways, leading him or her to conceal sexual orientation or make it a first priority in a struggle for rights.

The absence of ethnic or class determinants of sexual orientation complicates the picture. Gays and lesbians may be of any economic or ethnic background. Movements of sexual orientation, like feminism, have to unify people who may have divergent economic or ethnic group interests or, in this instance, also divergent gender interests (Cochran, Langston, and Woodward, 1991; Moraga and Anzaldua, 1983; Smith, 1983). Again, Horizons in Chicago provides a vivid example of how a community tries to bridge these possible divisions: "The code of solidarity extends to a value never to judge other youths in the group. In Chicago, with its pronounced ethnic traditions, continuing racism, and intergroup tensions, this cohesion among multicultural adolescents is remarkable" (Herdt, 1992:41). At the time Herdt observed Horizons, the interview sample was 43 percent white, 30 percent black, 12 percent Hispanic, 2 percent Asian, and 13 percent of mixed ethic background (Herdt, 1992:36).

Gay and lesbian march on Washington, April 25, 1993.

Many women have preferred to organize as feminists or as lesbians within women's movements rather than join into movements of sexual orientation formed by gay men; gender can divide, producing different meanings for sexual experiences and orientation and different patterns of building movements. Lesbians are challenged by the situation of being "gay within the women's movement and women within the gay movement" (Stanton, 1993).

This short section can only begin to introduce the reader to movements of sexual orientation. My sense is that, despite the strength of countermovements associated with cultural and religious conservatives, modern societies will continue to produce movements that challenge—and perhaps ultimately radically restructure—the present form of the private sphere.

SUMMARY

This chapter is about movements that challenge existing discourses and institutions of gender and sexuality. Three major types of movements were identified: Feminist movements that challenge gender stratification; women's movements that concern themselves with one or more problems that affect women, but are less explicit about gender stratification as a system of inequality; and movements of sexual orientation. Feminist movements and movements of sexual orientation are characteristic of economically developed market democracies in which sufficient resources and an open political opportunity structure make the organization of such movements possible. Women's movements that have less of a totalizing vision and promote a less explicit challenge to the sex/gender status quo, are found in many societies, often in conjunction with other movements, parties, institutions, and even government agencies. Gay and lesbian movements include liberal currents as well as more radically transformative perspectives.

All movements oriented toward sex and gender face the problem of mobilizing a support base that is dispersed across ethnic and class lines. These movements also face strong and organized opposition from groups and counter-movements that find challenges in this sphere to be threatening to cultural and personal identity.

KEY TERMS AND CONCEPTS

feminist ideology
gender
social reproduction
male domination and patriarchy
gender stratification
invisible labor
glass ceiling
double shift
violence against women; domestic
    violence
reproductive rights
sexual double standard
genital mutilation
sexual harassment
issues of cultural and political
    representation
family leave policies
the systematic devaluation of women

feminism and women's movements
first-wave feminism
women's suffrage movement
women in the Communist states
women in social democratic states

second-wave feminism
equal rights feminism
Title IX
affirmative action
the essential similarity of women and
    men versus the politics of
    difference
socialist feminism
radical feminism
social feminism and the valorization
    of the sphere of reproduction
womanism and black feminism
cultural feminism and difference
    feminism
the linkage of women's issues and
    other concerns

gay and lesbian movements
gay and lesbian culture, community,
    and identity

compulsory heterosexuality
coming out and collective identity
sexual orientation

Anti-nuclear power demonstration at
Seabrook, New Hampshire, nuclear power
station construction site. April 30, 1977.

CHAPTER 13

Green Warriors, Green Lobbyists

My young men shall never work. Men who work cannot dream, and wisdom comes in dreams.

You ask me to plow the ground. Shall I take a knife and tear my mother's breast? Then when I die she will not take me to her bosom to rest.

You ask me to dig for stone. Shall I dig under her skin for bones? Then when I die I cannot enter her body to be born again.

You ask me to cut grass and make hay and sell it, and be rich like white men. But how dare I cut off my mother's hair?

—Smohalla, Nez Perce, 1877, in Jerome Rothenberg (ed.),
Technicians of the Sacred, Anchor, Garden City, NY, 1969, p. 361.

I tell thee that those living things,
To whom the fragile blade of grass,
That springeth in the morn
And perisheth ere noon,
Is an unbounded world;
I tell thee that those view-less beings,
Whose mansion is the smallest particle
Of the impassive atmosphere,
[t]hink, feel and live like Man.

Percy Bysshe Shelley, *Queen Mab*, f. II 444–445, lines 226–234.

The landscape at the southern edge of Chicago is a large dismal plain, crossed by polluted canals and expressways. The suburbs here are not communities of beautiful houses and elegant malls; they are suburbs of ramshackle frame houses, dingy malls with boarded-up stores, and convenience stores fortified with locks and window bars. Unkempt scrub woods and small lakes are dotted across the open spaces; there are fish in the lakes, but no one eats the strange creatures that have infected tumors and two heads. This is a landscape of abandoned mills, toxic pools, and landfills that hold all of Chicago's growing mounds of trash. The smell of decay mingles with the sweet, heavy, nauseating stench of a paint factory; to live here means *always* to breathe in these smells. In the middle of this plain, Chicago meets its poorest suburbs, communities that are jobless and bankrupt. There, at the borderline of city and suburb, is your home—a low-rise public housing project where poor African Americans are segregated from the gleaming office towers and exciting nightlife of the downtown lakefront. All this you have endured, but you have just heard an announcement that jolts you into action: Desperate for jobs and revenue, the suburban government has agreed to build a giant incinerator that will burn the garbage of Chicagoland—within a half mile of your home. You start talking to your neighbors, organizing a grass roots movement to stop the incinerator: "Fight environmental racism!"

ENVIRONMENTAL MOVEMENTS—A NEW FORCE

Environmental movements seek to open the boundaries of human society into a larger system; they ask us to see humanity as part of nature and nature as a whole as harmonious and interconnected. Like racist movements, they demand action in accordance with nature; but they are quite different from—and to some extent, diametrically opposed to—racist movements in their conceptualization of nature and the conclusions they draw from this image. Racism asserts that nature is inherently violent and based on the domination of the weak by the strong; therefore, racist ideology narrows the circle of unity and respect for life to a race. Environmental ideology opens the circle of unity to all of nature, beyond the human race. In its view, nature is not an inert entity to be used and dominated, nor is it a system of domination; rather, nature is an intricate, interconnected web of which we form a small part.

Environmental movements have many new features, characteristics that set them apart from movements with a longer history. A new kind of structural strain produces the movement; the movement calls for new forms of collective identity and experiments with new patterns of organization. Like feminism, women's movements, and the gay and lesbian movement, environmental movements have not formed a state or become a major force in a government; the distance between these movements and states is not necessarily seen as a failing by activists since they question coercive power and hierarchy. This skepticism about power may be a new characteristic or perhaps an extension of liberal ideology's call for the expansion of civil society and the shrinkage of the state.

The following discussion covers the varieties of environmental ideology, points to the rapid expansion of the movement and the diversification of its support bases, and explores some of the novel features of its organization and strategy. Many examples are drawn from the antinuclear movement, which is one of the most carefully studied environmental movements.

IDEOLOGY

Like all the movements under discussion, environmentalism is differentiated into many currents and distinct movement organizations, with a few basic themes that appear in many of these different forms of environmentalism (Commoner, 1990; Merchant, 1992; Sale, 1993; *Worldwatch Paper Series*).

Agreement

The Web of Nature   The most important and widely shared of these positions is that life on the planet is *interconnected* and relatively fragile. The changes associated with industrialization and population growth necessarily have an impact on the environment—there is no free lunch. Human beings are currently altering the environment in ways that are destructive of other species, may be damaging to human life, and are rapidly becoming irreversible. For example, species diversity is already being lost as we exterminate many forms of plants and animals.

Environmental Impact—No Free Lunch   A second point of agreement is that human beings must become more *responsible* for the environmental impact of our actions. The true costs of economic production and development must be calculated; nature is neither an inexhaustible treasure house nor a giant garbage can; we have to recognize the problems of resource depletion and waste material. We also have to recognize that environmentally sound policies have costs; for instance, if a society takes steps to protect a forest and its plant and animal species, timber workers might lose their jobs. These costs have to be dealt with equitably; for example, in the case of the forest, everyone in the society must share in the costs of retraining workers for new jobs. Furthermore, everyone in the society must share the burden of reducing waste by recycling, cutting consumption, and making an effort to restore resources.

Democracy and Decision Making: Beyond the Nation-State   Third, many environmental movements place an emphasis on *grass roots democracy*. They like to see themselves as less hierarchical than other organizations and call for more citizen participation in decision making. They are often deeply mistrustful of "experts" for several reasons (Gorz, 1993; Hagen, 1993). Experts block the capacity of ordinary citizens to explore and understand technical matters and participate in decision making at a time when it is vital that all human beings understand environmental issues. Experts have had a very poor record: Many have been either mistaken in their conclusions or used by political and economic interests to disseminate inaccurate information. For example, scientists in nuclear, chemical, and biological weapons development in the United States and the Soviet Union failed to alert the public about risks of weapons testing and nuclear waste—on the contrary, scientists were even used by government to allay fears that later turned out to be justified (Davis, 1993; Fradkin, 1989; Fuller, 1984; Gallagher, 1993; House Subcommittee, 1980; Medvedev, 1979). Scientists played a similar role in nuclear power development; from the viewpoint of the environmental movements, scientists often participated in supporting such development without sufficient consideration of the risks (Adato et al., 1987; Flavin, 1987; Hertsgaard, 1983; Price, 1990; Yearly, 1992).

Respect for Life   Fourth, most environmental movements are *nonviolent*. A small number are prepared to undertake ecosabotage or even risk human life in order to prevent environmental destruction, but these are exceptional rather than typical viewpoints. Respect for life is closely tied to the ideology of the interconnection of life on earth and, therefore, includes empathy and compassion for nonhuman life; this theme is reflected, for example, in the animal rights movement that opposes the instrumentalization of animals by human beings in such ways as killing animals for fur and subjecting animals to experiments and cosmetics testing (Jasper and Nelkin, 1993).

Nonviolence and respect for life are associated with a distance from states and suspicion about the uses of state power. Many environmental movements would like to see a long-term reduction in the power of states, because states are inherently coercive. They would like to see more cooperation among human beings across the barriers created by nation-states to protect national interests.

Their concerns about state power place many environmental movements among the left-libertarian new social movements. Unlike the older currents of the left, they (like gender/sexuality movements) are cautious about becoming major players in institutional politics. But they recognize that their position includes some contradictions because, in the short run, one of the most important ways of protecting the environment is through increased government regulation.

Sustainable Development   Environmental movements criticize capitalist economic development as well as industrial growth in any economic system. For several decades now, it has seemed clear to most of them that capitalism with its system of private profit and public costs encouraged practices that damaged the environment. The entire value system of capitalism with its emphasis on growth and material production is inherently antienvironmental (Benton, 1992; Bookchin, 1990).

The poor environmental record of the Second World (the former Communist nations) has become apparent. Finally, there is public awareness of accidents in Soviet nuclear weapons development as well as nuclear power plants like Chernobyl, the poisoning of Lake Baikal, and pollution in industrial zones throughout eastern Europe (Flavin, 1987; Matthiessen, 1991; Medvedev, 1979; Peterson, 1993). The environmental movement recognizes that industrialization and the priority of accumulation, not merely capitalism, constitute the problem. When socialism imitates capitalism's misuses of technology and the capitalist mystique of growth, socialism results in the same environmental problems as capitalism.

This revised view has not put an end to many environmentalists' interest in finding alternatives to capitalism; but it suggests that socialism cannot be defined only in terms of public ownership and central planning. Socialism (or whatever else one might choose to call alternatives to capitalism) has to be a different system from capitalism in its use of technology and its conceptualization of nature, not only in its patterns of ownership and economic decision making. Environmental activists point to the need for a thoroughly *new model of economic development*, one that utilizes renewable resources, deemphasizes growth, and reduces large-scale interventions in the natural environment.

Disagreement

While there is substantial agreement on many of the preceding elements of ideology, there are also disagreements within the environmental movement. It is

not a single unified movement, but a set of movements, movement organizations, mobilizations, networks, and currents of opinion; it even includes the
programs of institutionalized actors like government regulatory agencies that
may come under the influence of movement activists. The high tolerance among
movement activists for this fragmented, networklike structure is one of the *new*
movement characteristics of environmentalism (Price, 1990).

I do not want to overemphasize the disagreements within the movement.
Some of the disagreements may be false choices, false either/or's that most
movement activists reject; they can see the truth on both sides of the disagreement. The disagreements do make a difference, however, in the choice of strategies and the allocation of resources.

Overpopulation or Overconsumption?   One of the most important areas of
disagreement is the relative importance of overconsumption and overpopulation as problems. Environmentalists in the north—the developed core capitalist nations—usually include population growth as a major cause of environmental destruction. They point to problems such as encroachment on the rain
forest and the lands of Amazonian Indians by landless Brazilians or the strip-
ping of forest cover to meet fuel needs in Nepal as examples of places where
population growth has created crisis conditions. In addition to these actual
crises, they point to the longer-term pressures caused by population growth.
After all, at current rates, the world's population will double from 6 billion in
2000 to 12 billion in 2040 (Brown, 1994; Merchant, 1992: 31).

Other environmentalists, more likely to be located in the south, (the developing nations) point the finger at the rate at which developed nations deplete
resources and produce wastes. For example, the United States, with less than 6
percent of the world's population, uses as much as 40 percent of the world's
nonrenewable fuel resources. The developed nations as a whole, with about a
quarter of the world's population, use about three-quarters of the world's resources and generate much of its waste. In the view of southern observers, both
depletion and pollution are currently problems of the north, because the populations in the north have much higher standards of living—also known as overconsumption and overproduction—than the south. If current levels of resources and development were more equitably distributed, the south's living
standards would rise, population growth would level off, and the total amount
of environmental damage would, at least, not increase.

From the south's point of view, the north is hypocritical: It was northern
populations that burgeoned in the nineteenth century and it is the north that enjoys the products of a developed industrial economy—and now the north appeals to humanity's future and the environment in an effort to block the south
from embarking on a similar course of development.

Both sides are partially right, but their confrontation and their intransigent
viewpoints make it more difficult to plan and implement policy on an international basis (Mellor, 1988). This basic difference is compounded by the role of
governments in both the north and the south in protecting national interests, including national population growth, business interests, regional development
projects, and so on.

Reformist Pragmatism or Transformative Vision?   A second set of disagreements focuses on the scope of movement goals. As a whole, the movement is
divided between submovements and movement organizations that see themselves as primarily reformist and those that have extensive and explicit goals of
transformation. Indeed, the German Greens, one of the most organizationally
developed forces in the environmental movement, split into a realo and a fundi
wing over these kinds of differences (Bookchin, 1990; Hulsberg, 1988).

Liberal Pragmatists and Limited Reforms   One cluster of environmental
movements could be described as liberal and pragmatic. This position is found in
mass movements and lobbies in many developed nations and even within some
governmental and international development agencies. The position could be
summed as up as a form of positive liberalism: Governments should undertake
some intervention in the capitalist economy in order to prevent or repair damage
to the environment. For example, some antinuclear activists focus on stopping the
construction of nuclear power plants (Price, 1990). This position does not mean
that pragmatic movement activists (in the antinuclear movement or other movements) have no larger vision of sustainable development; it just means that they
are focusing on some feasible and immediate changes as a necessary first step.

This pragmatic position is probably the oldest within the environmental
movement, having begun with the *conservation movement* around the turn of the
century. As part of the Progressive Movement in the United States, pressure
groups succeeded in inducing government to protect land, resources, and scenic
areas from development. Because a "robber baron" type of capitalist development
in the later part of the nineteenth century led to the destruction of forests and the
decimation of animal species like the buffalo, citizen's groups called on government to regulate industrial processes and land use. National parks and wilderness
areas were established. This movement, like the larger Progressive Movement,
had a base in the middle class, especially among white, educated Protestants. The
Progressive Movement as a whole was a step toward positive liberalism. Private
ownership and the market were not attacked as institutions, but the movement
emphasized regulation to protect the public interest and the nation's resources.

This pragmatic and liberal viewpoint continues to be important in the environmental movement, especially in the United States. Large lobbying and political pressure groups like the Environmental Defense Fund in the United
States exemplify this viewpoint. This part of the movement is prepared to work
with government agencies and may even seek to become institutionalized
within regulatory agencies like the Environmental Protection Agency. Similar
forms of environmentalism are also starting to have a role in the European
Community (Dalton, in *Annals*, 1993).

Even market enthusiasts are finding a home within the environmental
movement. There is increasing interest among policy makers, businesses, and
some environmentalists in using market mechanisms rather than extensive
government regulation to reduce pollution. In these plans, government is envisioned as intervening primarily to set maximum levels of pollution, but within
this overall limit, companies could buy and sell pollution rights; companies that

have installed new equipment to reduce pollution below specified limits could sell pollution credits or pollution rights to other companies in excess of the limit. Thus, the market—with a push from government—rewards low-pollution companies with lower costs and additional revenues while raising the costs of high-pollution companies. This system uses market mechanisms to incentivize pollution reduction. Similarly, tax incentives can be used to encourage conservation and reduce pollution. (See *The Economist*, September 2, 1989, for extensive discussions of such mechanisms.)

Other forces within the larger environmental movement disagree with these limited and pragmatic measures. They see environmentalism as a vision that points to a fundamentally transformed society, not as a set of policies that promotes environmentally sound practices in industrial market societies. They believe that, unless activists hold to the larger vision, the pragmatic reforms will add up to little real change.

Ecosocialists   Ecosocialists form one current that takes a different view from the liberal reformers. They are more likely to believe that capitalism and good environmental practice are inherently incompatible. Capitalism emphasizes growth, especially growth in manufactured products and the expansion of productive capacity. No one has yet been able to describe a steady capitalism, a capitalism without growth in the production of physical objects. The lack of such models—both in the real world and in computer simulations—makes ecosocialists believe that a profit-driven system cannot be steady state or committed to sustainable development. Capitalism means private profits, mostly calculated on a short-run basis. The environmental costs of profitable business practices are "dumped" onto society, the public, and the taxpayer, who have to pay for waste cleanup and increased health-care problems. Furthermore, capitalism has created such an extensive ideology of consumer wants through advertising, that many people cannot envision environmentally responsible ways of enjoying a high quality of life. Healthy habits of life, clean air and water, extensive parks and green belts, more time for family or community life—these are not the goods that capitalism offers, nor are they products that render a profit. Capitalism is based on profits that are realized in the following process: People's time and energy are harnessed to the goal of earning money so that, as consumers, they can buy more of the goods that they produce as workers. If a lot of people decided that this behavior is a stupid rat race and went off to hike in the woods or produce amateur theatricals, the capitalist economy would be in serious trouble (Gorz, 1985, 1993).

Ecosocialists do not believe that economic development, science, and technology must come to a halt; but they do have to be redefined and applied to new goals, to a sustainable economy. Capitalism stands in the way of a more rational and beneficial model of economic and technological development (Benton, 1992).

Radical Ecologists: Questioning the Uses of Science and Technology
Groups like ecofeminists, radical ecologists, deep ecologists, and some ecoanarchists question many of the foundations of both liberal and socialist environmentalism. They believe that science and technology, as they developed in the

west, were construed from the start as forces for dominating or mastering nature. The attitude of western societies (and their clones elsewhere in the industrialized world) is that nature is external to human life, that nature is to be used and exploited to enhance human existence, and that nature is an object to be transformed. From the point of view of radical ecology, as long as this ideology of domination prevails, little real change is likely to take place on environmental issues (Davis and Foreman, 1991; Merchant, 1992).

Ecofeminists   Ecofeminists point to a parallel between the exploitation and domination of nature in patriarchal societies and the exploitation and domination of women. For some ecofeminists, women are indeed more part of nature than men, defined by the natural processes of monthly cycles and childbirth; for most ecofeminists, the mapping woman = nature, is a part of patriarchal ideology, a justification for exploiting both. In either case, the emancipation of women from male domination is closely linked to the reconstitution of the relationship between human beings and the rest of nature (Adams, 1993; Biehl, 1991; Diamond and Orenstein, 1990).

Spiritual Ecology   Some ecofeminists, as well as **spiritual ecologists**, turn to a broad range of religious and spiritual traditions to justify their view of nature. In some cases, they may believe that an environmental consciousness is compatible with the Judaeo-Christian tradition, reading in Genesis that God gave human beings stewardship over the earth; the term "stewardship" is replacing the older usage "dominion" with its connotations of domination and control. In this view, human beings must take care of God's handiwork, not destroy it. For example, the new Roman Catholic catechism now takes this position, emphasizing environmental responsibility and referring to the sinfulness of environmental destruction.

For some spiritual ecologists, the Jewish and Christian religious are too anthropocentric: To say that human beings are the stewards of God's creation is to imply a great separation between humanity and nature. Furthermore, the western religions conceptualize God as transcendent; that is, separate and distinct from the created world. Therefore, some spiritual ecologists prefer to turn to religions that are pantheistic, with a concept of the sacred as *immanent*, diffused throughout the world. In Japanese Shinto belief, rocks, as well as plants and animals, have a spiritual being. For Native Australians and Native Americans, all forms of landscapes and nature are sacred; the sacredness may also be concentrated in some special regions, for example, the great Ayers rock in Australia or the Black Hills in the United States. In Polynesian belief, **mana** is power that is diffused throughout the world. Ecofeminists revive (or invent) spiritual traditions centered on a goddess or earth mother, religions that existed in southern Europe and western Asia before being displaced by patriarchal religions. Some scientists have used the name **Gaia** (mother earth in ancient Greek thought) to represent the sum total of all natural processes conceived as a vital force (Adams, 1993; Lovelock, 1988; Merchant, 1992).

In all of these views, nature cannot be treated exploitively or carelessly. Plowing, mining, dumping, deforesting are like raping or mutilating one's mother or desecrating a sacred place. In their opposition to Hawaiian Electric Company's plans to undertake drilling operations to release geothermal energy from Kilauea Volcano, Native Hawaiians appealed to respect for their goddess Pele whose sanctuary is in the mountain: "Drilling is a sacrilege, . . . no different than trashing a Christian cathedral" (Merchant, 1992:226).

Ecoanarchism   Other forms of radical ecology are less spiritual and closer to political anarchist forms of thought. The domination that man has exercised over nature is closely associated with domination, coercion, and hierarchy within human societies. Nature is an interconnected web; human beings can also form themselves into communities of mutual support and economic cooperation. Ecoanarchists question some of the mystical and antirational themes in ecofeminism and spiritual ecology; most ecoanarchists see themselves as continuing and extending the rational, universalist, and humanistic goals of the Enlightenment, but freeing these values from their association with corporate and state structures in the capitalist west and the (now defunct) state-bureaucratic east. Ecoanarchists with this position are close to the more libertarian wing of ecosocialists (Bookchin, 1990:160–171).

Other ecoanarchists give more attention to "primitive" and "tribal" peoples, whom they see as providing a model of viable societies and small-scale economies that exist without centralized institutions of coercion. The cultural survival of indigenous populations in fragile envirnoments like the rain forest and the Arctic is not a matter of protecting these cultures like endangered species by creating reserves for primitive people and animals. On the contrary, indigenous peoples' way of life has to expand and become a model for other cultures in order to replace the destructive and coercive forms of society that "civilized" people have formed. Central governments, standing armies, and transnational corporations are all institutions of domination as well as forces of environmental destruction.

Deep Ecology and Earth First   Deep ecology and the Earth First movement take some of these ideas further (Devall and Sessions, 1985). For them, human beings are a species that is out of control, destroying and overrunning the earth. They make an effort to end **anthropocentric** ways of thought. The preservation of nature as a whole, not the expansion or even survival of the human species, has to be the goal of the movement. This premise often leads to an emphasis on reducing human populations as a priority, to a **neo-Malthusian** position (the belief that population growth inevitably outstrips resources and, hence, must be curbed at all costs). From the vantage point of nature, epidemics or famines are not necessarily bad, since they are a way of restoring balance when more benign and planned methods fail. Furthermore, viruses and other microorganisms that are seen as harmful in a human-centered ideology are seen as part of nature in a biocentered or ecocentered worldview (Ehrenfeld, 1978).

This non-human-centered ideological position can lead to a vanguard mentality, since most human beings defend their own interests and only a small core of people look beyond anthropocentrism. With a vanguard mentality comes a taste for direct action, for **monkey wrenching** to halt environmental destruction (Abbey, 1975; Foreman and Haywood, 1987). Some movement organizations are prepared to undertake actions that destroy property or even put human life at risk: Sinking ships engaged in whaling and drift netting and "spiking" trees with metal rods that break saws are examples of **ecosabotage**.

Such actions create tensions within the movement. Tensions arise between environmental radicals and pragmatists who worry that direct action and ecosabotage may undermine movement legitimacy with government agencies, media, and potential mass constituencies. Tensions exist between neo-Malthusian radicals and some environmentalists of the global south who find this position insensitive to the condition of poor people, people of color, and people in developing regions; to them it appears to be an arrogant viewpoint of privileged classes and peoples. There are also disagreements between activists whose views stem from a rational and humanistic core set of values and biocentric and/or spiritual radicals who reject these values (Bookchin, 1990; Jackson, 1995).

Environmentalism and Ethnoracism?   The more imaginative and anarchistic white racists see possible connections between their movement and *some* versions of radical ecology (Metzger, interview cited in Ridgeway, 1990:169–170, 174). The **survivalist** and ethnoracist far right claims to share with radical ecology an interest in preserving wilderness and halting the surge of population in the global south. The biocentric and neo-Malthusian discourse of some ecologists overlaps some of the survivalist and social Darwinist discourse of the far right that voices a belief in survival of the fittest and elimination of the weak through a ruthless natural process. Whether any connections—especially organizational links—between the two movements can be brought into being, or are just wishful thinking on the part of the white Aryan movement, is hard to say.

Ultranationalist themes can also be found among some Russian environmentalist activists who see themselves defending their lakes and soils against communists, capitalists, Jews (who are portrayed as too urban, materialistic, and denatured to care about the environment), the west, and so on. In these mobilizations, there is some resonance between environmentalism and what I called the agrarian nostalgia of the far right, its position of claiming to defend a rural way of life (Matthiessen, 1991). I must emphasize that these racist or ultranationalist views are not at all typical of the environmental movement.

Splits

Like all movements in this book, when looked at under a microscope the apparent cohesion of an environmental/ecological ideology splits into many positions, some of them in tension with one another. But, these splits may not be detrimental to the movement in the long run. They may reflect a division of labor within the movement that has come about in a spontaneous fashion and permits the movement to reach diverse constituencies and confront a broad range of issues. What one observer says of the antinuclear movement may be true of the environmental movement as a whole: "It is unusual that each of the antinuclear movement's various organizations seems to fulfill a specific function for the movement as a whole. This is a primary advantage of a loosely structured movement with many organizations that do not compete with one another either for ideological leadership or for power over the movement. Division over ideological leadership has always fragmented the socialist movement, preventing the cooperation of competing factions or a consensus on the goals of the movement. The synthesis of varied organization goals in the antinuclear movement is one of its most distinctive features" (Price, 1990:79).

SUPPORT BASE: HISTORICAL DEVELOPMENT

The history of the environmental movement is largely one of growth and diversification. As environmental problems have become both more widespread and more acute over the course of the last three decades, the movement has drawn in more supporters and has mobilized people in an ever-larger range of communities. It started with limited **conservation** goals among well-educated Europeans and European Americans at the turn of the century. It has become a diversified surge that spans nations and classes, including mainstream, pragmatic organizations and anarchist and socialist combined movements among educated people in developed nations, as well as movements of survival among the globe's most marginalized populations.

Beginnings

The modern environmental movement had its historical origins in the conservation movement associated with the Progressive Era around the turn of the century. Before the modern conservation movement, there were centuries of resistance to the imposition of development based on a capitalist, industrial, and Eurocentric model. Native Americans defended their land and way of life from white settlers. The Black Hills became a focal point of conflict in the United States, as whites took away one of Native Americans' most sacred sites to use for gold mining and, later, tourism and commercial development. English settlers took from Native Australians their landscapes of rock formations and ponds, each imbued with sacred meaning associated with spiritual beings, ancestors, and a mythic origin in the Dreamtime. Initial resistance on the part of indigenous peoples was generally crushed, so that by the beginning of the twentieth century it *appeared* to be a hopeless cause. Economic development of what had been sacred landscapes seemed to be an inexorable modern trend. Since these forms of resistance appeared to be premodern and doomed, conventional social movement history identifies the beginnings of the *modern* environmental movement with the conservation movement. It was only in a postmodern phase of environmentalism that indigenous resistance reemerged to become a major current in the larger movement; we can now see that it had not really been eliminated, only reduced to a dormant form for a century or so.

Second-Wave Environmentalism Confronts New Problems

Like feminism after suffrage was won, the modern environmental movement became becalmed, or dormant, during the period from 1920 to the 1950s; perhaps, the rise of fascism and Communism, the depression, and the Second

World War drew energy into other issues. Second-wave environmentalism began in the 1950s, especially among scientists in the United States, who became aware of the effects of DDT and other pesticides that were widely used during and after the war (Carson, 1962). The effects of nuclear weapons testing and nuclear power plant development were also a cause for concern and united peace activists in the United States, western Europe, and Japan in the beginnings of an environmental movement (Price, 1990; Rochon, 1988).

In the early phase of the movement, both activists and larger constituencies were primarily educated and middle class. Scientists had a major role in starting movement organizations and in framing the issues for a larger public. For example, in the United States, the Union of Concerned Scientists drew attention to both the problems of the nuclear arms race and the failings of the Nuclear Regulatory Commission in protecting the public from the risks of nuclear technologies (Price, 1990:30).

Another major component of the environmental movement was, and continues to be, a **conscience constituency** of persons who are activists on a broad range of issues; they coincide with part of the left and/or mainline church support base. The term conscience constituency implies that the mobilization is based on a set of moral or ethical values rather than on immediate interests. For this reason, environmental issues may be only part of a larger set of concerns held by activists. For example, a study of supporters of the Campaign for Nuclear Disarmament in England found that they were generally middle class and held attitudes to the left of center on a range of issues (Parkin, 1968). As noted in Chapter 9, "Movements of Faith," not all religious activism in the United States is on the right side of the political spectrum; and indeed, some mainline church groups have been active in peace and environmental issues.

In short, the environmental movement began to grow because the world itself had changed; the new objective conditions or structural strains included the arms race; the manufacture, use, and waste disposal of substances that had not been in use before; and an accelerated pace of industrial development.

Green Parties

In the 1950s and early 1960s, the environmental movement remained fairly small and mostly confined to educated people in the United States and a few other developed nations. But, by the late 1960s, the forerunners of green parties were formed in Europe, most notably in Germany and Italy. These movements pulled together activists from the New Left and the peace movement, the social activist sections of the Catholic Church and the Christian Democrats, and local citizens' groups engaged in a variety of protests (Hulsberg, 1988; Rensenbrink, 1992).

That Europe was one of the first points of mass party organizing was logical, because high population densities and a long history of industrial development created especially acute environmental problems; for instance, in the Rhine Valley and the industrial triangle of northern Italy. Environmental groups also formed in Japan, which confronted similar "side effects" of massive industrial development, such as the mercury poisoning of 400 people in the community of Minimata.

Expanding Organizations

By the 1970s, the effects of pollution and resource depletion were becoming much more visible in many more places. As the war in Vietnam came to an end and student movements in Europe shrank, some of the energy of the New Left went into the growing environmental movements. The green parties began to run for office in Germany, Italy, and Australia. Within multiparty parliamentary systems, relatively small parties like the Greens could win enough seats to become powerful swing members of coalitions (Papadikis, 1984).

In the United States, with its two-party structure, environmentalists formed lobbies and pressure groups that included organizations like the Sierra Club, which had been in the original conservation movement. The structure of pragmatic, or mainstream, environmental groups emerged to focus on the legislative process, government regulation, and key court cases. Meanwhile, alongside the development of the large national movement organizations, **local mobilizations** and citizens' action groups continued to take place, for example, against the siting of nuclear power plants and toxic waste dumps. These demostrations and local protests were a significant factor in slowing down the growth of the nuclear industry in the United States and some western European countries (Campbell, 1988).

The support base of larger national organizations and the activist core of the local demonstrations and mobilizations still tended to be well educated and hold attitudes on the left side of the political spectrum. For example, a 1979 survey of antinuclear demonstrators found that "participants in both demonstrations tend to be young, well-educated, politically liberal, and evenly split between the sexes" (Scaminaci and Dunlap, cited in Price, 1990:99). "No more than 4 percent identified themselves as Republicans" (Price, 1990:99).

It was during this period that the environmental movement was identified as one of the main components of the **new social movements**. Since the United States had a long history of decentralized movement activity across the whole political spectrum, these types of movements did not seem all that new there; however, in western Europe, they marked a change in the nature of the left, from coherent national parties to more decentralized overlapping mobilizations (Mayer, 1991).

New Support Bases: The Globalization of the Movement

By the late 1980s, these local movements had taken a significant turn; in increasing numbers, they were led by working-class people, people of color, indigenous populations, and communities in the Third World. The devastation of the lands of indigenous peoples in the Amazon, the United States and Canada, and Southeast Asia reawakened resistance against encroachment by settlers, loggers, and road builders (Hecht, 1989; Hecht and Cockburn, 1989). Megaprojects of governments and international development agencies like the World Bank, which funded highway systems and dams, came under attack by coalitions of First World environmentalists and the communities that would be displaced and destroyed by such projects. Environmental issues like toxic waste in the rivers and the sea of the Baltic region, acid rain damage to forests in East Germany and Czechoslovakia, and the degradation of Lake Baikal and the Aral

Sea became the focal points of movements in the Soviet Union and the Communist states in eastern Europe. People who had been forced to accept political repression and/or poverty in the Second and Third Worlds finally exploded when they saw their land and sea poisoned and when they grasped the consequences for their own health (Peterson, 1993).

Ghettoized communities in the United States began to take the lead in combating **environmental racism** (Bullard, 1990). For example, African American residents of a public housing project in a low-income area on the south side of Chicago organized against the siting of a waste-processing incinerator near their community. The environmentalists lost this particular struggle because the promise of jobs swayed local politicians to accept the plant; but the energy of the protest is so great that the environmental issues continue to surface in the area (*Chicago Tribune*, 1991, 1992, 1993).

Environmental mobilizations in eastern Europe and the Baltic region (at that time still annexed to the Soviet Union) shared some characteristics with western European activism. In some ways these movements were like the European new social movements in both their spontaneous, decentralized organizational forms and their support base of young, educated people with a generally questioning attitude toward social institutions.

In other regions, the new activists were often distinctly different from the young, educated, left-libertarian base of the environmental movement; the new mobilizations acted in rage, in the struggle to survive, and in defense of their sacred landscapes. Communities of industrial workers, isolated rural populations, populations of Third World countries that contracted to accept First World waste, people of color within Europe and North America, and indigenous groups were all vulnerable. In their view, corporations and governments were particularly inclined to dump toxic wastes, construct landfills, or locate nuclear test sites in "backyards" where costs were lower because protest was calculated to be less likely. The environment was no longer just an issue for the educated middle class of European origin. "Environmentalist" no longer called up only the image of a European American graduate student or German hippy. He or she might be a working-class housewife in an industrial town in Latvia, a rubber tapper in the Amazon, a Cajun or African American resident of Louisiana's chemically polluted "cancer alley," a Mormon farmer and a Native American rancher concerned about nuclear testing and nuclear waste sites in the Great Basin region of Utah, or a mother in a Chicago housing project (Bullard, 1990; Davis, 1993; Hecht, 1989; Hecht and Cockburn, 1989; Levin, 1993; Mitchell, 1981; Schwab, 1993; Walsh, Warland, and Smith, 1993).

Problems of Collective Identity   The environmental movement has a twofold potential for mobilization. On the one hand, environmental destruction is a class issue that can unite marginalized communities on a global scale; the most oppressed and exploited peoples turn out to be the ones most at risk for environmental damage. On the other hand, it is an issue that could be universalized to all human beings. This twofold potential can lead to a more powerful movement if the various constituencies can be brought together; but it can also be used to divide the movement.

The formation of collective identities to undergird environmental mobilizations is a complicated process. It calls for a combination of the most universalized appeals, the future of humanity, and the most particularized ones, not in my backyard! Somehow the local problems that mobilize people have to be combined with a global rethinking of development strategies; all the **NIMBY's (not in my backyard** mobilizations) have to coalesce into pressure on very large national and transnational institutions like corporations, governments, and international credit agencies to make radical changes in their behavior. Otherwise, the local mobilizations unintentionally tend to shift problems like incinerator sitings, forest depletion, or nuclear waste-processing facilities into more vulnerable communities.

Increasingly, this shift is taking place on a global scale; for example, in Europe, Soviet-built nuclear power plants in eastern Europe may be rehabbed to provide power for western Europe, where antinuclear movements have succeeded in halting further construction in some countries. Strong local resistance to a project often moves the project to a new site rather than eliminating it. One activist's comments about the timber industry could be applied to many institutions that impact the environment: "[The industry] looks at the US as one province of the world. They have an integrated strategy, way out in front of the environmentalists, who tend to organize regionally. And the industry tends to move where the people and activists aren't around . . ." (Mark Winstein of Save America's Forests, quoted in Cockburn, 1993:53). These problems point to a need in the environmental movement to overcome its new social movement attitude of preferring local resistance; it has to form larger structures and plan long-term efforts to influence or exercise political power.

Problems of Sustaining Activism   Environmental mobilizations present problems to organizers because the adherents' commitments are somewhat detached from lifetime socialization in ethnic, religious, and/or class communities; environmental mobilization depends less on collective identities than on perceptions of problems that either immediately affect a community or are concerns of a conscience constituency. Commitment to the environmental movement can wane if a community is no longer directly affected by a specific environmental problem, if the problem has been moved out of its backyard. The conscience constituencies, on the other hand, are not bound to the movement by immediate self-interest, so they, too, may turn out to be a volatile support base.

The relatively shallow basis of environmental commitment explains a curious phenomenon: About 75 percent of the U.S. public identifies itself as environmentalist, yet concrete changes in environmental practices—even in so simple a matter as more stringent government regulation—come about very slowly; and when voters are faced with elections or referenda that are framed in terms of choices between jobs and environmental quality, many of them opt for jobs.

ORGANIZATION AND STRATEGIES

The outcomes of environmental movements are shaped by the movements' framing of structural strains, their ability to mobilize the support base, and the opportunity structures in which they operate. **Political opportunity structures** and national political cultures are a major determinant of movement organization and strategies. Since political opportunity structures and political cultures vary from one nation to another, transnational environmental movements have to adapt to national political systems. I will focus on the antinuclear movement for some of my examples, since it has been extensively studied.

Political Opportunity Structure and the Antinuclear Movement

In a landmark study of political opportunity structure and the antinuclear movement, Herbert Kitschelt compared the movement in four countries: the United States, Sweden, France, and West Germany (1986). Although all four countries are liberal democracies, the political system is more open in the United States and Sweden, permitting more local initiatives, referenda, participation in licensing proceedings, and so on. In these two countries the movements adopted **assimilative strategies** that used these mechanisms. In France and West Germany, with more centralized, closed, and unresponsive systems, the movement was more **confrontational**, using civil disobedience and mass demonstrations.

One might amend Kitschelt, however, by suggesting that the U.S. political system is more closed in terms of party formation; in contrast to Germany, it would be difficult and pointless to try to form a green party and turn it into a major electoral force in a two-party system like that of the United States. Furthermore, in decentralized political systems like that of the United States, the environmental movement can rarely win absolute victory. Both it and its opponents (the nuclear industry, the timber industry, and so on) may face off over and over again in state and local courts, in legislative processes at the state level, and in hearings before local and state-level regulatory commissions. The outcome is a patchwork of decisions and regulations with no clear victories.

National political culture also plays a part in environmental activism. It is quite striking, for example, that there is far more support for nuclear power in France than in the rest of western Europe. Although about half the French population opposed the expansion of nuclear power generation in 1986, "this is the lowest such figure in Europe" (Flavin, 1987:26). One observer suggests that this situation is the result of different attitudes toward elite decision making in France than in the rest of western Europe and North America: "At base, the French trust their elite" (Flavin, 1987:26). They seem to accept a rather closed, technocratic decision-making process, perhaps seeing this uncritical posture as a price that must be paid for French preeminence in technology. The French media are described as "less aggressive in pursuing nuclear stories than in most Western countries" (Flavin, 1987:26). This mentality in the mass public creates problems for the movement and is, perhaps, an additional force that propels the movement into more direct action strategies. French political culture contributes to the closed nature of the French political system along with political structure in a more precise sense, such as centralized decision making. In short, political culture, media framing, and attitudes toward technology and expertise play a part in the formation of movements.

Finally, political structures and cultures now have to be viewed in international perspective. Especially after the nuclear disaster at Chernobyl, **cross-border disputes** have become a major focus of movements in Europe. There has been tension between nonnuclear Austria and pronuclear Bavaria (Flavin, 1987:31). German and Luxembourg antinuclear groups challenge the French reactor sited on the Moselle, and Danish antinuclear forces oppose the Swedish nuclear plant sited across the narrow Oresund Strait between the two countries. Ireland and Britain clash over the dumping of Britain's radioactive wastes from the Sellafield processing plant into the Irish Sea (Flavin, 1987:30–32). The siting of nuclear plants is potentially a point of conflict between the Baltic Republics and Russia; while it may just be part of his ultranationalist bluster and, perhaps, only a joke, it is not funny to hear Russian politician Zhirinovsky threaten to build nuclear plants on the Russian-Estonian border and use giant fans to blow fallout into Estonia. These nuclear cross-border disputes and similar disputes over acid rain have the potential to link environmental movements with nationalist mobilizations.

Parties and Pressure Groups

Parts of the movement form national parties and pressure groups. The choice between these two options (party or pressure group) is conditioned by the political system. In nations with multiparty parliamentary systems, small parties can survive and exercise some weight; in two-party systems, there are few advantages to forming a party, so pressure groups, lobbying organizations, and legal defense funds are more effective. The Greens in Germany and Italy are a good example of party formation. The mainstream environmental groups in the United States–the Environmental Defense Fund, the Sierra Club, the World Wildlife Fund—are examples of pressure groups.

Both the parties and the pressure groups may be divided along ideological lines. For instance, the German Greens include both *fundis* (more radical, less inclined to compromise) and *realos* (more pragmatic). As a whole, the pressure groups include both conservative alliances with corporate support (World Wildlife Fund, for example) and groups with a stronger and less compromising grass roots base (e.g., the Sierra Club) (Cockburn, 1993; Price, 1990). The individual organizations may include different ideological positions among their membership. Whether party or pressure group, these organizational forms include some **professional staff**. In fact, some of them are rather large and bureaucratized.

Direct Action and Public Outreach

A second organizational style is to operate outside the established political system. The movement organization is a pressure group, but one that directs more of its attention to mobilizing public opinion than to lobbying governmental elites or engaging in negotiations with corporations. More energy is put into direct action, possibly including illegal actions or civil disobedience. The aim may be to influence a government decision (for example, to obtain a regulatory decision against a nuclear power plant), but the methods are to mobilize constituencies through public action rather than influence elites through largely institutionalized channels.

Direct action—including civil disobedience—and mass organizing are to be found in local and regional environmental groups. Protests against nuclear power plant development in the 1970s by the Clamshell Alliance in New England and at Diablo Canyon in California and the mass demonstrations and protests against water pollution in the Baltic states in the late 1980s are examples. In local and regional antinuclear mobilizations, a fairly small core of activists coordinates a larger support base (Price, 1990). Greenpeace USA is another example of this more direct style in a national organization (Shaiko, 1993).

Local direct-action groups overlap what might be called **movements of survival**, parallel to women's movements of survival mentioned in the preceding chapter. Like the women's movements, they may form, dissolve, and regroup; they are sometimes limited in resources and have difficulty in arranging media access to get their message out to a larger public. Sometimes, they are more effectively integrated into movements with a nationalist or ethnorights orientation than by the established environmental movement. For example, the protests in the Baltic region were part of the movement to restore the independence of Latvia, Estonia, and Lithuania from the Soviet Union. The environmental concerns of indigenous peoples in the Americas are linked to issues of cultural survival (in the Amazon) and increased regional autonomy (within Canada) (Levin, 1993).

Alternative Technology and Community Development

Finally, some environmentalists put their energy into developing alternative technologies and forming communities based on such technologies. They experiment with wind and sun as energy sources to replace nuclear power and fossil fuels; they try their hand at organic farming. They encourage similar types of small-scale sustainable development in the Third World and in the former Second World as farming is privatized and reduced in scale. They form local groups to help city communities support small environmentally sound industries in zones where the large industrial enterprises like steel mills left, leaving behind polluted facilities and no jobs. These efforts are quiet, often invisible to the media, and require a long-term commitment and vision, but they form a vital part of the movement.

COUNTERMOVEMENTS

Nuclear Power, Safer Than Sex
                    —Pronuclear T-shirt slogan (quoted in Useem and Zald,
                                            in Zald and McCarthy, 1987:278).

This chapter would not be complete without a mention of countermovements (Mottl, 1980; Useem and Zald, in Zald and McCarthy, 1987). It seems fair to state that countermovements are formed by people and organizations that have very different ideas about economic development than do environmentalists. More specifically, they see economic growth as an unalloyed positive value and they tend to believe that technological problems can have technological solutions. Not surprisingly, the countermovements have often been launched and funded by an industry that is under attack by an environmental movement. Industry-supported mobilizations create **problems for establishing the legitimacy of the countermovement**. Countermovements have been studied most extensively in the case of the pronuclear and antinuclear mobilizations (Price, 1990; Useem and Zald, in Zald and McCarthy, 1987).

Organization and Strategy

The pronuclear movement began with the formation of local and national groups and forums composed of, and brought together by, companies involved in the nuclear industry (Price, 1990:34–35). Originally, the industry acted as a pressure group that utilized institutionalized channels like lobbying, but as the antinuclear movement expanded and succeeded in halting plant construction, the industry-initiated organizations began to take on more movementlike characteristics (Useem and Zald, in Zald and McCarthy, 1987). Organizations formed by firms, trade associations, and employees of firms remained at the core of the new, increasingly movementlike mobilization. Among the most important national organizations in these mobilizations were the Atomic Industrial Forum and the American Nuclear Society. But a new wing of the movement was formed, a community wing composed of consumers concerned about energy costs and engineers and scientists who were not directly involved with the firms challenged by the antinuclear forces (Useem and Zald, in Zald and McCarthy, 1987). As antinuclear mobilizations developed at a local level, local countermovement groups were formed from both industry and the community wing, such as Save the Maine Yankee (a name that referred to a Maine nuclear power project).

As a whole, the movement remained decentralized, with the industry wing and the community wing somewhat disconnected. This decentralization permitted a division of labor in which the community wing could carry out activities like representing citizens at utility regulatory hearings, which the industry was not legally allowed to do (Useem and Zald, in Zald and McCarthy, 1987:286).

The countermovements were able to mobilize monetary resources far more effectively than the environmentalists. For example, one observer of the pronuclear and antinuclear mobilizations in Maine estimates that the antinuclear forces in the Maine Nuclear Referendum Committee raised only $127,000 compared to the pronuclear Save the Maine Yankee's $750,000, mostly from corporate donors. Since this particular mobilization centered on a referendum, the greater funding of the pronuclear side was an important factor in reaching the electorate; the pronuclear side did, in fact, win with about 60 percent voting against a shutdown (Price, 1990:1, 35).

Although the countermovements in the nuclear mobilizations were more able than the antinuclear forces to mobilize resources such as funds and professional staffs, they were less able to define themselves as a legitimate movement. The sociologists who studied the pronuclear movement found that it used three strategies to establish its legitimacy. One, as mentioned above, was to accept a decentralized structure in which the community wing was more readily seen by the public as a social movement and could be framed as a legitimate voice of the citizenry. More specific strategies to establish legitimacy involved expanding the support base and the goals of the movement. Activists made an effort to recruit women and African Americans into the movement, since persons with these characteristics were living symbols of support from the grass roots (Useem and Zald, in Zald and McCarthy, 1987:283). The pronuclear activists expanded the goals from the defense of a specific power plant to larger, more universalistic values such as independence from foreign oil, economic growth, free enterprise and the "American way of life" (Useem and Zald, in Zald and McCarthy, 1987:283).

In some cases of environmental countermovements, only the initial organization existed and its apparent mobilization of a larger constituency was merely on paper. For example, a group called Citizens for Sensible Control of Acid Rain emerged in the United States in the 1980s to demand that no special legislation be directed at acid rain; this organization claimed that the Clean Air Act would solve the problem of acid rain. It launched what appeared to be a huge direct-mail campaign involving the distribution and mailing of 600,000 packets to congressional representatives, in order to convince Congress that there was a mass public that wanted no additional legislation passed. Investigation by an environmental group (the Audubon Society) showed that no mass support base existed, and that various companies involved in coal mining and power generation had used millions of dollars and hired a public relations firm to create the appearance of a citizen mobilization (Luoma, 1987).

Other countermovements are more genuine. The original movement nucleus formed by the industry is balanced by a larger community constituency that is worried about jobs and regional development if the environmentalists succeed in blocking a proposed project, such as a nuclear power plant, an incinerator, a fossil fuel plant, a new mine, a timber operation, and so on. At the national level, concerns about dependency on foreign oil may be be used to win support for various kinds of projects. In Third World countries, the imperatives of reducing poverty and launching economic growth are powerful incentives for stepping up large-scale development projects and accepting international funding for such projects.

A more recent countermovement to environmentalism is the growing property rights movement in the United States. Landowners who feel that environmental regulation impinges on their right to use their property are forming local and state associations that seek to change or terminate environmental regulations. For example, landowners in Minnesota are contesting wetlands protection laws that limit, or put special conditions on, any development of private land that might damage wetlands. Property rights advocates, property rights associations, and landowners associations (as they are variously called) are networking nationally and have met recently in a summit conference in Utah. They are formulating a property owners' "bill of rights" as well as calling for changes in legislation and regulations, generally at the state level, but perhaps also increasingly at the federal level (National Public Radio, January 31, 1995).

Though in some respects these associations can be understood in terms of institutionalized interest group politics, their appeals refer to a larger vision centered on property rights, an important theme in conservative and negative liberal thought; in this respect, they seem to share the ideological universalization characteristic of social movements. The expansion of this countermovement among landowners in the mid-1990s reflects both the structural strain created by environmental legislation in recent decades and the belief that the political opportunity structure may change with Republican congressional and state-level victories in the 1994 elections.

Divisions in Key Constituencies

A factor in countermovement growth is the presence of divisions within organized groups that are key actors on environmental issues. These divisions make it more difficult for either the movement or the countermovement to diffuse an unambiguous framing of the issues.

Scientists and Engineers   Scientists and engineers are divided on many environmental issues. This division has important implications for the issues and how they are framed for the larger public and for elites that are the focus of pressure group tactics. Scientists are a major constituency of both movements and countermovements, and their publicly expressed views are key resources that both sides try to mobilize. Some scientists believe that the environmental movement has been alarmist on matters like global warming and that the data do not support a panicky attitude. On the issue of nuclear power, some scientists believe that nuclear power plants can be constructed to operate safely (Cohen, 1983; Ott and Spinrad, 1985; Weinberg and Manning, 1985). They also point to the environmental pollution caused by fossil fuel plants—the most realistic and feasible current nonnuclear method of power generation; fossil fuel plants are responsible for air pollution and acid rain and contribute to the problem of strip mining of coal. For example, Useem and Zald found that scientists and engineers were active in the pronuclear as well as the antinuclear movements and appeared in both the industry and the community wing of the pronuclear movement.

In other words there are differences of opinion among scientists on practically any specific environmental issue. Many scientists have the more general belief that new problems caused by technology can have technological solutions. This division of opinion means that some scientists support the countermovements rather than the environmental movement. Their voice makes it more difficult for the environmental movement to frame issues in a decisive way. Since the media follow conventions of objectivity that are defined by presenting both sides of an argument, media framing of these issues almost always ends up conveying inconclusiveness to the public (Schudson, 1978).

Organized Labor   Organized labor is also divided in many cases. Unions are concerned about the employment prospects of their members. While the ideology of the environmental movement stresses public responsibility for the displacement of workers involved in industries that have to be eliminated or scaled down, in actual practice, retraining and new employment do not always take place. Protection of forests has created tensions between timber workers and environmentalists. Unions may also favor large construction projects (dams, power plants, roads) and job-generating regional development. At the same time, union activists are concerned about safety issues; for example, the Oil, Chemical and Atomic Workers Union has an interest in stricter regulation of nuclear facilities (Price, 1990:95–97, 173). Organized labor, like scientists and engineers as professional groups, is not

Chico Mendes, head of the rubber tappers' union in Acre, Brazil, called for curbs on deforestation in order to preserve the livelihood of forest workers and indigenous peoples. Assassinated by landowners in 1988, he remains a symbol of the expansion and diversification of environmental movements.

unified on these issues. In turn, these divisions in key constituencies permit countermovements to expand their support bases and transform themselves from industry-organized pressure groups into social movements.

SUMMARY

The environmental movement is the newest of the movements in this book, so this is the shortest chapter–because the story is only beginning. The movement is concerned with changing conditions; the globe itself has changed with topsoil and water depletion, pollution, and the extermination of plant and animal species. These problems are growing with industrial development and population growth. Cross-border effects and the tendency to move problems like waste siting from developed regions into marginalized ones give global dimensions to the movement.

The movement takes many forms, including party formation, pressure group and lobbying tactics, direct action, and local protests and community organizing. In both ideology and organizational structure, environmentalism is not so much a single movement as a large array of movements and mobilizations; some are pragmatic and institutionalized with reform goals and lobbying or pressure group strategies; some are ideologically radical and utopian; and

some are movements of survival directed against local disasters like nuclear accidents, nuclear waste sites, and toxic waste disposal.

One of the most striking characteristics of the movement is the rapid expansion and diversification of its support base between the 1950s and the 1990s
from a primarily middle-class movement in the developed nations to a movement that encompasses a varied global array of communities, among them the
most marginalized ones.

The environmental movement has also set in motion countermovements.
Some of these are little more than industry pressure groups, others include a community wing in their mobilizations. Countermovements may increasingly draw
on conservative property rights discourses. Movements and countermovements
contend for support from strategic constituencies like scientists and organized labor; media framing of environmental issues is an important terrain of conflict.

KEY TERMS AND CONCEPTS

environmental ideologies
sustainable development
overpopulation/overconsumption
pragmatic environmentalism
ecosocialism
radical ecology
ecofeminism
spiritual ecology
mana
Gaia
ecoanarchism
deep ecology
Earth First
anthropocentrism vs. biocentrism
neo-Malthusian
monkey wrenching
ecosabotage
survivalism

**the growth of environmental
    movements**
conservation movement

second-wave environmentalism
conscience constituency
green parties and pressure groups
local mobilization
new social movements
environmental racism
NIMBY (not in my backyard)
assimilative and confrontational
    strategies and political opportunity
    structures
cross-border issues
fundis and *realos*
professional staff
direct action
movements of survival
alternative technology
countermovements; problems of
    establishing the legitimacy of the
    countermovement

PART THREE

Conclusions

Television heightens global awareness and
cross-border concerns; television images are
a strategic resource for movements. Millions
of viewers saw the damaged nuclear power
plant at Chernobyl (former USSR, now
Ukraine) in images like this one on French
television. *Antenne* 2, April 30, 1986.

CHAPTER 14

Making History

If you can look into the seeds of time,
And say which grain will grow and which will not. . . .
William Shakespeare,
Macbeth, Act I, Scene III, 58–59.

On the first weekend in June of 1994 in Chicago, two events condensed and expressed movement history. The fiftieth anniversary of D day, the Allied invasion of German-occupied Europe, was commemorated on a Chicago beach by a reenactment of the historic landing in Normandy. A day later, the Gay and Lesbian Pride Parade wound its way for 2 hours through the heart of Chicago's gay community; the annual event was a little special that year because 1994 was the twenty-fifth anniversary of the Stonewall riot. Two events, two anniversaries, two generations, two pieces of movement history: The first event was solemn and somber, a reminder of how the military alliance of liberal democracy and Soviet communism put an end to the dreams of the Nazis and fascists, a confrontation of movement-states that cost millions of lives. Most of the twentieth century had been taken up by this clash of modern movements and the states they formed—liberalism, nationalism, communism, fascism. The movements transformed the world by attaining state power and using the military power that goes with state power. The second event was happy—gay in the old as well as the new sense of the word, celebrating nonviolent change, with no unified message, little central organization. Death on the beaches . . . dancing in the streets.

The Gay and Lesbian Pride Parade illustrates, in capsule form, many of the characteristics of postmodern movements. The floats and marchers represent a movement that is refracted across the whole spectrum of U.S. communities and institutions. Earnest churchgoers mingle with drag queens in feather boas, lesbians on Harley-Davidsons, and boogieing body builders in leather harnesses. Socialists, civil libertarians, contingents from corporations like AT&T, and gay-bar floats stream by in a cross section of cultural and political identities; and each of these groups is usually multiethnic. Politicians courting the gay vote share the street with Act Up, radical AIDS activists carrying a sign that reads: "Red ribbons [a symbol of AIDS awareness] distributed in Illinois: 823,567; condoms distributed in Illinois prisons: 0. You can't put a red ribbon on your cock." Candies, confetti, discount beer coupons, and condoms rain down from the floats. The desire to be outrageous competes with what one observer calls "everyday sameness." "We are Methodists and lawyers and doctors and athletes and sing in choruses and bowl in sports leagues" (Herrell, 1992:245). The crowd lining the sidewalks is young, physically fit, casually dressed, good-natured, boisterous, and beer drinking; apart from clustering into demonstrative same-sex couples and groups, the viewers look like any young crowd of the 1990s.

Is this movement really a movement to extend civil liberties to a minority and, therefore, solidly within the liberal tradition (Bawer, 1994)? Or is it a radical challenge to fundamental institutions like the family? Is it a reform movement, changing a few ordinances and government regulations, or is it transforming the basis of our ideas about sexuality and personal identity and, hence, the very basis of society? Is it a movement that is fragmented to the point of incoherence, or is its fragmentation its strength? How is collective identity different in a movement that is formed by "adult participation in a network of institutions" rather than based on childhood socialization into class and ethnic identities (Herrell, 1992); and is this pattern not also found in other new and postmodern movements, like the environmental movement? Is there a gay and lesbian movement at all? Is the parade a sign of institutionalization, an expression of community, a gesture of defiance—or all of these (Herrell, 1992)? The "unsettled and conflicting definitions" (Herrell, 1992:249) and contradictory possibilities vividly illustrate changes in movement characteristics of many postmodern movements, not just the gay and lesbian movement; these questions point to some themes discussed in this chapter.

This chapter pulls together material from the preceding chapters in three ways. First, some common themes are identified, some *similarities* in the movements discussed in the preceding pages. In many ways these movements are very different from one another, but they all have to operate in the same environment; therefore, certain similarities arise from the constraints imposed by that environment. Looking at all of them together helps us understand how change takes place in the contemporary world.

The nature of the postmodern and its impact on movements is the second element of the chapter. In order to understand the nature of the environment in which all contemporary movements must operate, I return to the concept of the *postmodern*, which I introduced in Chapter 5. The postmodern is a convenient term for related economic, cultural, and political changes involving globalizing markets, the decline of the Fordist accumulation model, and a sense that states are limited in their ability to implement social and economic change. These changes influence movement ideologies and organization; they are associated with identity politics, network structures, and more attention to cultural issues. It is difficult to tell whether the postmodern era will last as long as the modern one or will turn out to be a short-lived period at the end of the twentieth century.

Third, the chapter ends by defining history as a process in which movements, countermovements, and states transform each other. Movements connect to each other in cooperation and conflict; movements challenge existing states and form new ones, which in turn are reformed or destroyed by movements. While the postmodern period may end within a few years, the dynamic of movements, states, movement-states, and countermovements is likely to continue for the foreseeable future.

FINDING SIMILARITIES

In this section, four major similarities among apparently totally different move-ments are identified and briefly discussed. These similarities arise from the fact that the movements try to pursue their distinct visions within the same global economic, political, and cultural structures; the visions may be different, but the historical circumstances are the same. A vision that is counter to the "way things are" is the basic characteristic common to all the movements; they must all contend with the challenge that they are committed to a social order that does not exist and may turn out to be impossible to realize. This quality imposes similarities on movements. The perspective I take in discussing similarities among movements is that of an outside observer who sees all the movements at the same time; this stand is necessarily distinct from the points of view of the movements.

1. *All these movements began as the products of modern societies; that is, societies that have been formed as a result of capitalism, industrialization, the global ex-pansion of markets, and the division of the world into nation-states.*

I will not go into the question of which of these elements of modernity is the master process, the determining element; perhaps the process is overdeter-mined, with all of these changes taking place together. Certainly capitalism has played a crucial role in this transformation. Before modern societies existed, there were social movements, especially peasant rebellions and cultlike reli-gious movements, but they were different in form and content from the ones that are now the major political actors. All contemporary movements share the modern idea that social institutions and societies can be changed by purposive action. Contemporary movements are acts of faith in the possibility of chang-ing society (Berman, 1982; Zeitlin, 1994).

The movements discussed in this book assert that there are problems in modern society, the discontents and alienation that people experience in their everyday life are the result of specific characteristics of modern society, and *their* movement can solve problems by changing society. The movements first and foremost identify societal problems. By **societal problems** I mean structural defects, not just social problems that can be resolved by small changes within the framework of the existing society. The idea that societal problems exist and can be remedied is, itself, a modern conception; suffering is seen as the result of societal strains, not as inevitable in the human condition (Zeitlin, 1994).

The societal strains to which the movements point may overlap those that the outside observer sees: class and gender inequality; the impact of capitalism on tradition; ethnic stratification; the difficulties of living in multicultural states and societies; the poverty and dependency of many regions of the globe; the breakup of communities and families; damage and depletion of the environ-ment; and so on.

To agree that these are real problems does not mean, however, that one has to agree that the solutions offered by movements are either realistic or desirable. For example, I consider marxist theories extremely powerful as explanations of social change in modern/capitalist societies. To say that marxist theory provides an excellent analysis of societal problems does not necessarily mean that I believe socialist movements have correctly applied theory to political practice in order to bring about change. Other movements, especially ethnoracism, are based on premises that are not only morally reprehensible, but also scientifically invalid. In the case of racist ideology, both identification of the societal problems and their solutions are false.

All the movements in this book are modern; but many of them take *different forms in different global regions*. For example, marxism-leninism was an attempt to adapt socialist theory and practice to the backward conditions that prevailed in Russia and other regions where the proletariat was small and there was a high level of foreign investment. In our own times, women's movements, human rights movements, and environmental movements vary with the region. Movements in economically developed market democracies have more resources and more opportunity in the political structure. In some cases, the forms of the movement are so different in various regions and types of society, that they are hard to recognize as variants of one movement.

All the movements in the book are modern, but they emerged at different times from the end of the eighteenth century to the end of the twentieth century, the modern era. They did not appear all at once, but in waves. A first wave of movements emerged in the age of revolution (Hobsbawm, 1962). These movements gave rise to the political revolutions of the late eighteenth century or were reactions against these revolutions. They were also associated with the industrial revolution and the end of the ascendancy of landed classes. Liberalism, nationalism, and conservatism were the major movements formed in this period.

By the later part of the nineteenth century, socialism in its modern form joined the list of transnational movements as a response to the spread and consolidation of capitalist forms of industrialization. At the end of the nineteenth century and the beginning of the twentieth century, first-wave feminism, Protestant fundamentalism, and racism/fascism were taking shape as movements and ideologies, and the conservation movement (a rather distant forerunner of environmental movements) appeared. These movements were mainly operating in the industrialized western nations, in the dominant nations of the age of empire (Hobsbawm, 1989). The extension of empires carried these movement ideologies—above all, nationalist ideology—across the globe.

In short, all of the movements in this book appeared during the modern age, but not all at the same time. The earlier emerging movements (conservatism, liberalism, nationalism, and socialism) changed in response to new economic, social, and political conditions; they also had to respond to the challenges posed by the later emerging movements. These movements have persisted in some form up to the end of the twentieth century, suggesting that the structural strains they initially addressed have not been settled.

2. *All the movements have powerful splitting tendencies in their ideologies; because they are about ideas, they face inherent barriers to building unity within the movement.* Because they are visions of a better society, they tend toward perfec-

tion or purity in their thought. Fine shades of meaning make a difference, and these differences in discourse produce splits in the movement and the movement organizations.

It would be easy to write a book about movements that does nothing but detail differences within movement ideologies, for example, tracing all interpretations of marxism-leninism, all distinctions within feminism, all varieties of Christian fundamentalism, and so on. I have resisted this temptation, but I am well aware that some readers will think I have dealt very insensitively with differences within movement ideologies. The closer a person is to a movement, the more she or he is likely to feel that these distinctions are very important. Few people who are not marxist-leninists really care how the Spartacists are different from the Revolutionary Communist Party, and the disputes over dispensationalism or the Rapture are of little concern to non-evangelicals. But movements are about ideas and, so, struggles over words and ideas are central to movements. Ideological differences frequently cause organizational divisions. This inherent tendency toward splitting is accelerated by three circumstances.

Purity and Powerlessness   Splitting is accelerated when a movement is out of power. A movement in power has to make compromises and take action. Purity and perfection have to be abandoned if the movement wants to effect change. A movement out of power has the luxury of making fine distinctions, of refining theory and discourse without having to match them to practice. It is under less pressure to test itself against reality, the whole set of circumstances inherited from the past.

For example, once the Islamic movement of Ayatollah Khomeini came to power in Iran it had to deal with issues like selling Iranian oil in global markets, rivalry with Iraq in the Gulf region, and managing a multiethnic and class-stratified society. Islamic integralism had to make compromises with external and internal forces within these conditions. Similarly, all forms of socialism that have been in state power—whether social democratic or marxist-leninist—have had to cope with a global market economy and with the persistence of capitalist class structure within the society the movement governs.

This connection between purity and powerlessness works the other way too: Once in power, a movement that is too attuned to ideological purity will be less likely to engage in the negotiation and compromise needed to stay in power. Unless it moves to extremely repressive methods, it will find that it can stay ideologically pure only at the cost of losing some of the support base that joined it for concrete advantages. To stay in power, ideological purity has to be given up to retain crucial support bases that have other options, that have "somewhere else to go" politically.

For example, the socialist and nationalist independence movement in Zimbabwe could not make good on some of its promises about socialism because distributing the property of white property owners (especially commercial farmers) to a large number of poor black subsistence farmers would have led to lower agricultural productivity and a drop in Zimbabwe's export trade; such redistribution might also have triggered a loss of external political support from major western powers. So, although the white property owners were a small numerical minority, they could force compromises in the movement's socialist ideology.

Complex and Detailed Ideologies Splinter More Easily A second factor in **ideological splitting** is the intensity, scope, and detailedness of the movement's vision: The more detailed, precise, and all-encompassing the vision, the more likely the movement is to split into small pieces.

Both liberalism and nationalism have relatively limited visions; there are large areas of social life about which neither liberal nor nationalist ideology makes promises. Remember that liberalism specifically limits the state's role in the private economy and that it also calls for limits on state involvement in the private, personal lives of citizens. Nationalism is not so much a purposeful limitation of state power as it is an ideology that is silent on these matters; by default, nationalist movements in power often follow liberal models of a private sector economy and a limited role of the state. This relatively limited vision has led to less splitting, more cohesion, and a greater likelihood of satisfaction among the support bases once the nationalist or liberal movement is in power. A limited and, therefore, more easily implementable vision is one of the reasons why liberalism and nationalism have been so successful in the formation of movement-states throughout the world. They are now more likely to be institutionalized forms of states, rather than movements pursuing new visions.

By the same logic, an intellectually more primitive movement like fascism and ethnoracism is less likely to split; it is easier to hold the pieces together when racial exclusion and the exercise of power are the main goals, than when the goals are a highly complex vision of a more just society, as in feminism, socialism, and most religious movements. *Detailed visions and complex ideas lead to splits.*

Movement Base Diversity and Splitting A third factor in splitting is the nature of the movement base. The more diverse it is, the stronger will be the tendencies toward splitting, all other things being equal. Feminism, for instance, reaches out to all women; therefore it has inherent problems of reconciling the diverse concrete interests and experiences of women who live in very different conditions.

A movement can cope with diversity of the social base in various ways. One is to generate a large number of distinct movement organizations that address different parts of the support base. Another strategy is to condense the issues to those of concern to everyone in the support base, while remaining silent on issues that are potentially divisive. For example, violence against women is a good issue for women's movements, since all women are at risk for rape and other forms of violence. Sometimes this type of condensation of issues takes the form of simplifying an issue to a lowest common denominator of shared prejudices, as in the Nazi's use of anti-semitic slogans. The Nazis were well aware that anti-semitism could unify strata of German society that had different economic interests and sharply contrasting attitudes toward capitalism. Small farmers, artisans, some big industrialists, and many white-collar employees could come together as anti-semites more easily than they could coalesce around an economic program.

The Usefulness of Fragmentation   Are splits always damaging to movements? Not at all. In some movements, they lead to a good division of labor within the movement. A movement may become more flexible if it can offer different ideologies and movement organizations to distinct sections of its support base.

Fascism and Nazism gained from its internal division between action-seeking, anticapitalist, paramilitary groups and more sober and conventionally conservative members. This division in ideology and actions actually had a strategic value, allowing the movement leadership to play a game of threats and promises with incumbent elites; they could threaten disorder at the same time that they could promise order. In the Civil Rights Movement and the environmental movement a similar advantage is derived from the existence of both radical and pragmatic wings. It is quite likely the case that, although the Palestinian nationalist movement is divided between the PLO and the Islamic forces of Hamas (among several divisions), there are benefits as well as drawbacks to its division; the threat that Hamas might grow to uncontrollable strength may have forced Israel to agree to negotiations with the PLO. We also saw that countermovements like the pronuclear mobilizations benefited from decentralization and fragmentation, which permitted a more complex **division of labor within the movement.** Fragmentation increased the legitimacy of the countermovement, since some sections of it were perceived as a real movement and not just a pressure group or a counterorganization formed by elites or social control agents (Gamson, 1975; Price, 1990; Useem and Zald, 1987).

3. *All these movements have multiple and changeable strategies.* They are all protean. (Proteus was a Greek river god who could never be caught because he was so good at changing his shape.) There is no simple mapping between the ideology of a movement and its strategy and organization.

Reform and Revolution: A False Distinction?   For a long time in sociology and political science, it had seemed useful to distinguish reform movements from revolutionary movements. The former were defined as having limited goals and operating within legitimate political structures; the latter were defined as having large goals and using nonlegitimate means, like terrorism and armed struggle. This distinction often breaks down. Movements operate at the boundary between the legitimate and the outlawed, the institutionalized and the noninstitutionalized. Movements challenge these boundaries, often in innovative ways. These challenges force social scientists themselves to reexamine the distinction between reform and revolution. We see that our neat distinctions between legitimate and nonlegitimate, institutionalized and noninstitutionalized, limited and large-scale, reformative and transformative are not so clear.

There are many examples to indicate the limited value of the distinction. Transformative movements can use *reform strategies.* Movements with very big

goals—western feminism, socialism, Christian fundamentalism—may use lobbying and the ballot box, strategies that appear to be limited and reformist.
Movements *shift rapidly back and forth from violent to nonviolent means and use both
simultaneously,* depending on their assessment of limits and opportunities; we
saw how fascism and Nazism used both legitimate and illegal means to come
to power. Movements may create **single-issue mobilizations** or single-issue
movement organizations as a **strategy** of **transformation.** Limited, or single-issue, movements like the antiabortion movement or Women Against Pornography are guided by complex, large, and elaborate visions of the social order. The
single issue is a condensation of the larger vision. Their apparently limited goals
and strategy are easily misread as single-issue initiatives. The single-issue form
of many mobilizations is really a small part of larger strategy of transformation.

The single issue functions in three ways as part of a larger process. It is a
condensation issue that stands for a larger vision. For example, to the participants
in antiabortion mobilizations, the unborn child is the focal point of an ethic of
care for all human life and is the most vulnerable point of the "seamless garment of life." Also, the movement hopes the single issue will produce an initial
reform that can serve as the first step in a series of changes that add up to a transformation; in other words, the reform is not seen as an endpoint of movement
activity but the first in a series of **transitional reforms.** Finally, the single issue
is selected because activists believe this issue will mobilize a maximum number
of new supporters.

*Revolutionary movements may settle for reforms; reform movements may plant the
seeds of revolution. Therefore, at any given moment it may be difficult to distinguish
movements engaged in transformations from movements aimed at more limited
changes.*

Movement members and activists are well aware that they are doing both
"little" reform work and "big" visionary work within the same set of practices—organizing a demonstration, sending a mailing to members, lobbying to
reform a law. The apparently innocuous reform or single-issue self-definition is
often part of a deliberate strategy of seeming to have reasonable, or limited,
goals. The little reform effort or single-issue activity brings new members into
the movement, who might still be hesitant to identify themselves with the larger
vision; it may also make changes in the climate for the movement, changes that
are imperceptible at first, but are likely to grow steadily. A small change in the
wording of a law or a government regulation can have large consequences for
movement strategies and goals. For example, in 1932, Congress passed the Nor-
ris-La Guardia Act, which took from federal judges the power to issue injunc-
tions and hear cases involving strikes. This act appeared to be a rather technical piece of legislation concerning federal jurisdiction in labor disputes; but in
practice, the act made possible the wave of industrial union organizing of the
late 1930s by keeping federal courts from ending strikes (Geoghegan, 1991:
43–44). The act dramatically altered the political opportunity structure. This situation was reversed by subsequent legislation; the specific provisions of the
1947 Taft-Hartley Act made union organizing more difficult and purged the
unions of some of their most political members, those in or close to the Com-

munist Party. Once again, a rather technical and precise piece of legislation had long-term consequences for unions, for left-wing movement organizations that saw unions as the building blocks of political action, and for the balance of class forces in the United States. "[It] led to the 'union busting' that started in the late 1960's and continues today" (Geoghegan, 1991:52).

Since both movement and countermovement activists tend to think in terms of large visions and long-run strategies, they are willing to work on small reforms, such as legislation that deals with procedural technicalities, in order to create conditions for mass mobilization and sweeping institutional changes. Small changes can make a big difference in the long run. This statement may sound like a cliché, but it is a consideration in the planning of movement strategies. Reform is often a first step in a revolutionary strategy.

Matching Strategies to Tasks   Movements use different strategies for different kinds of tasks, which explains the wide range of strategies used by any one movement. The strategies that are used to construct identity and mobilize potential members are often different from the ones used to bring about the proposed changes in institutions and society. A few movements are explicitly nonviolent; some (especially women's movements) have difficulty in undertaking armed struggle. Apart from these exceptions, most movements have a "by any means necessary" view of strategy and will use whatever combinations of strategy they believe will accomplish their tasks most efficiently under a given set of conditions.

Sometimes, these choices of specific strategies to match specific tasks confuse the public, which fails to understand the purpose of a particular strategy. For example, in conventional wisdom, it is often held that **terrorism** is pointless or counterproductive as a movement strategy. Terrorism is usually not effective in forcing political elites to make concessions—but that is not its purpose. Its target is the support base, and its purpose is forcing individuals in the potential support base to accept a certain collective identity and then **polarizing** them from others in the society. It can be used by ethnonationalist movements to split populations into two or more groups in conflict with each other, as happened at the onset of ethnic wars in Yugoslavia (Denitch, 1994). Acts of terrorism create fear and open breaches among groups that can no longer be healed by those who are opposed to the conflict. Terrorism isolates would-be peacemakers and preempts nonviolent means of conflict resolution.

Terrorism can be used to turn a support base against an unpopular regime. In this case, the strategy works by actually increasing regime repression; acts of terrorism harden the resolve of incumbent elites to suppress the movement and they begin to use more and more repressive methods in an increasingly indiscriminate way—to employ counterterrorism. People in the potential support base of the movement are left with no choice but to join the insurgent movement. For the purpose of polarizing populations and mobilizing potential adherents, terrorism may be quite useful. It requires great discipline on the part of the incumbent elites to not turn to repressive measures in the face of terrorism; the Italian state in the late 1970s, for example, was able to combat the Red Brigades with relatively little use of illegal repression.

Strategies of Violence   As global arms markets flood the world with small arms, violent strategies become increasingly easy and attractive. External supporters of movements find the overt or covert distribution of weapons one of the easiest ways to promote the insurgency they believe is in their own interest. Arms manufacture and sales have become one of the few growth industries of several of the former Communist countries, and these sources amplify the existing government, private, and black market flows of weapons. The United States continues to be a major supplier of weapons as well (Klare, 1994; Proxmire, 1994). The result is an increase in prolonged small-scale wars and insurgencies, like the massacres in Rwanda, the fighting in Angola and Afghanistan, the war between northern and southern Yemen, the wars in the former Yugoslavia, and bloodshed between factions in Somalia. Many of these are ethnic conflicts, although there may also be religious, class, and/or ideological differences among the opposing forces. These many prolonged small-scale wars have added up to millions of casualties on a global scale—homeless, disabled, traumatized, or dead.

4. *All these movements have to focus resources on at least two tasks: identity formation and mobilization of potential support bases, and working through the state to change society.*

Making Identities   Every human being has potentially many identities. In large, complex societies, these potential identities multiply: class, nation, gender, race, ethnicity, sexual orientation, language, lifestyle, region, religion, occupation, and the idea of the individual all summon human beings: "Listen to me, I am your true identity, your essential identity—the others are false!" Each of these **identities is socially constructed.** They are not given by nature to human beings. Of course, every movement tries to claim that its base of identity is the most important, most meaningful, most salient one—and often, the most natural or essential one, as well. A movement is, in part, a discourse about identity, a call to human beings to constitute their self around a particular identity which is constructed or highlighted by the movement (Althusser, 1971; Gamson, 1992)

Movements **mobilize** people who have been successfully summoned; that is, the movement encourages them to engage in actions and practices. It is not enough for persons to think of themselves as working people if they do not participate in unions or working-class parties or movements. A lesbian identity is of little value to movements of sexual orientation if women with this identity remain in the closet or come out to only a small circle of friends and family. Thus, movements not only summon one of many possible identities, but also demand to have this identity become public and connected to practices, to actions as well as ideas (Friedman and McAdam, 1992; Taylor and Whittier, 1992).

Identity formation and mobilization are not always sequential, with identity formation strictly preceding participation in mobilizations. Often, participation in a mobilization confirms and heightens the formation of a specific collective identity. An activist suggests that a wavering friend tag along for a demonstration, and the experience of activism confirms the identity. For this reason, demonstrations, rallies, and other public events have as one of their most important functions the confirmation or gelling of the identities of participants.

Crosscutting and Invisible Identities   Contemporary societies present distinct problems to movements in establishing identities and encouraging mobilization. Not only do possible identities multiply, but they also tend to **crosscut** (Lipset, 1960). Distinct castes and castelike communities in which class, ethnicity, religion, and occupation are **superimposed** are much rarer now than in the past, at least in the more developed economies. Identities are more freely assumed, yet also more hidden.

This situation has presented special problems to socialist movements: Class remains a pervasive dimension of stratification in society, but isolated communities of workers have become less common, especially in the economically developed countries. Thus, class has become an invisible identity that is hard to make salient. To some extent, this problem also besets religious movements. For example, in the United States, evangelical Christians form a potential support base for fundamentalist movements but do not live in separate communities where they are easy to identify and mobilize. On the other hand, ethnonationalist and racist movements can sometimes identify potential supporters more easily since they are marked by their language or appearance.

In some measure, many contemporary movements face the problem of identifying and mobilizing potential adherents who live scattered among "others" and bear no identifying marks. Organizers can no longer go to an isolated mining town or a religious community and find "their" people waiting to be mobilized. Potential supporters and activists are hidden in modern corporations and suburban developments, among people who dress like them and talk like them, even if they do not think like them. The salient identity for the movement has to be teased out from multiple, crosscutting identities. What outward signs distinguish the union activist from the "replacement worker" in the airline industry? Can we spot the pro-choice student and the pro-life student in a campus classroom?

The process of creating a society in which identities are multiple, crosscutting, and invisible began with the modern revolutions and the formation of liberal states. The juridical and political equality of citizens, which replaced membership in distinct estates and legally segregated ethnic communities, started the formation of an outward uniformity and equality that can veil large differences in worldviews. The economic transformations of advanced capitalist society have accelerated the process, dissolving many distinct class and occupational communities like mining towns and neighborhoods of industrial workers, although ethnic ghettoes persist. Part of what is meant by the postmodern condition is this accelerated decline in distinct, visible communities of identity, especially class identity. Movements have had to turn to new technologies—computer networks, direct mail—to seek out their constituencies.

Making Changes The other major task of movements is to create organizations that can make changes. This task may call for quite different skills and practices than identity definition and mobilization. Therefore, movements have to develop different sets of strategies. They include different specialists: lawyers and guerrilla fighters, writers and office managers. They can also address this problem by a division of labor within the movement: Some organizations summon identity, others work to change institutions. Of course, they mutually reinforce each other. For example, when NOW or the Gay and Lesbian Task Force win a court case, potential supporters are more likely to come forward; and if the circle of supporters and activists grows, the movements are in a better position to influence the legislative process.

Power Ultimately, in modern societies, movements have to connect to states in some ways in order to have an impact. They can **influence policy.** For example, the environmental movement has brought about government regulation of toxic waste disposal and the establishment of government agencies to monitor it. Policy can be formed in the legislative process, in executive decisions, through the courts, and in informal changes in practice. Movements can **exercise state power**, either through the ballot box, invitations from incumbents, or a seizure of power. In some cases, they can build new states from scratch, as many nationalist movements try to do.

Some movements explicitly reject all these ways of exercising power; because they oppose all forms of domination and coercion, they do not want to use the apparatus of the state to bring about their vision. This rejection leaves the movement without a concrete plan for bringing about change. New social movements that encompass parts of the New Left, the environmental movement, the gay and lesbian movement, feminism, and the women's movement have emerged in the most economically developed regions and have been reluctant to become part of the state or to influence it through institutionalized channels. Instead, these movements picture a transformation coming about by a seepage of new identities and practices into all relationships of the society. It remains to be seen whether this type of transformation is possible (Handler, 1992).

Hegemony The process of using the state to accomplish goals forces movements to undertake a new task, that of changing its discourse to appeal to a wider range of the members of society. This task—which some social scientists refer to as establishing **legitimacy** or **hegemony**—is in many ways the inverse of the identity-formation and mobilization process. It involves **universalizing** the message and vision of the movement to as many people as possible. Otherwise, the movement lacks the legitimacy needed to rule the society.

Let's look at a couple of examples. When middle-class commoners—lawyers, businessmen, and so on—seized power from the king and the nobles in the French Revolution, the ideologues of the Revolution formulated "The Rights of *Man*"—not a document about the rights of the middle class alone. It was important to convince everyone (including themselves) that this Revolution had a *universal, human* significance. It had to be more than a power grab by one social group. When the Bolsheviks came to power in Russia they could not rule with the support of the proletariat (industrial wage workers) alone; in a society in which a majority of the population were peasants, the vision of socialism had to expand to include some goals that would appeal to peasants—for example, access to land. The Bolsheviks even had to sacrifice some of the short-term interests of their working-class base—like low food prices—to attract support from peasants (Garner and Garner, 1981; Gramsci, 1971). Feminist movements have to indicate advantages that would accrue to men as well as women in a world in which there is more equality between the sexes (Bunch, 1987).

Therefore, establishing hegemony (or legitimacy) involves a discourse that universalizes the goals of the movement (or at least expands them to more groups), sometimes, even at the cost of asking the movement's original support base to sacrifice some of its interests. If this discourse and its associated practices are established successfully, the movement is accorded a right to rule or implement policy. If it is seen as serving only the interests of one class, ethnic group, or so on, its rule is more likely to be contested (Garner and Garner, 1981; Gramsci, 1971).

FROM MODERN TO POSTMODERN

The Impact on Movements

The four similarities discussed in the previous section held true of the movements from their beginning to the present. This section takes a look at the global changes taking place at the end of the twentieth century and asks what their impact is on movement goals, processes of identity formation and mobilization, and organization and strategies. This discussion will recap some of my remarks about postmodern societies in Chapter 5, but at this point we can keep in mind examples of movements from previous chapters and can focus on how the characteristics of postmodern societies affect movements.

Postmodern is a controversial concept. Some theorists *deny* that any major changes are taking place in contemporary societies. They insist that existing categories are adequate to discuss societies at the end of the twentieth century. Some marxists believe that the forms of class struggle and imperialism that were observed earlier in the century persist fundamentally unchanged (Callinicos, 1990). There are also mainstream sociologists who do not like the term postmodern and continue to use concepts such as technological innovation, industrialization, stratification, culture, and values without making major adjustments in their theoretical position. An opposed camp of theorists asserts that we are at the brink of a new age, an epoch that is dramatically different from the modern; this new era will force western social scientists to give up their Enlightenment faith in scientific inquiry and the possibility of historical progress.

I use the term postmodern to refer to concrete economic, political, and cultural changes, not to a philosophical watershed. Major changes *are* taking place, but we are not at the end of an epoch. Much of this change is best conceptualized as an acceleration of two processes that already characterized the modern age. One is the expansion of capitalism as a **global system of markets**. It is currently associated with the **decline of the Fordist accumulation model**. The other is the expansion of the private sector and the limitation of state functions. In my perspective, the postmodern means that these two processes have accelerated and taken on some new forms; the changes are concrete and notable and, therefore, require some new developments in theory, but fall short of an epochal shift. (This view is based on the following theoretical discussions: Appadurai, 1990; Aronowitz, 1988; Davis, 1986, 1990; Fukuyama, 1992; Jameson, 1984, 1988; Przeworski, 1991; Reich, 1992; Willis, 1990.)

It is useful to keep in mind that capitalism has involved global markets from the start, from its emergence about 500 years ago (Heilbroner, 1989; Wolf, 1982). But, in recent decades, this globalization has accelerated, especially in markets for labor, technology, capital, and ideas (i.e., media, information, and cultural products). This process has social and political consequences, most notably the fragmentation of working-class politics in the developed core economies; this shift, in turn, has an impact on collective identity and movements. Associated with the globalization of markets are new technologies, especially new communication and information technologies.

At the end of the twentieth century, the liberal and liberal democratic model of states and societies has, once again, become the leading model globally. The collapse of the Communist states, the return to democracy of many former military dictatorships in Latin America, and the end of the ethnoracist apartheid regime in South Africa mark the collapse of competing models (Castañeda, 1993; Przeworski, 1991). Of course, many authoritarian states persist, but they are default states, which have little ideological vision to back up their institutions. China (with about a quarter of the planet's population), Cuba and Vietnam, and a relatively small number of Islamic states are more or less the only ideological competitors to the liberal model. In global terms, this political shift means an expansion of the function of civil societies that continue to be divided by class and are becoming increasingly multicultural. The state is relatively limited in its functions, while a large and often heterogeneous civil society is the site of *private* economic, cultural, and personal practices. The state takes only a moderately active role in managing potential conflicts.

The limitation of state functions is closely tied to the globalization of markets. As markets in capital, labor, and ideas globalize, it is harder for the state to control its national economy. People, capital, ideas, technology, and production processes spill over national boundaries. Efforts to regulate these markets become futile and, in turn, are increasingly resisted and undone by those companies and individuals that benefit from globalization. As we saw in the debate on the North American Free Trade Agreement in 1993, opposition social forces like labor and companies that favored protectionist policies lost out in the decision. The European Community illustrates a similar loss of control by states over markets. With internationalization goes increased privatization in many markets, illustrated by the expansion of private electronic media in much of western Europe.

Globalization is likely to increase rather than lessen the disappointments that are faced by movements in power. We have already seen that movement-states must make many compromises with external and internal social forces; economic pressures interfere with their ability to realize their goals. These disappointments become even more likely as the economy continues to globalize.

Is postmodernism a long-term prospect? I don't know, but it seems to me that the two processes I have focused on here are likely to persist well into the twenty-first century. The major alternative to expanding markets and liberal states in the foreseeable future seems to be disintegration of one kind or another—as in Yugoslavia or Somalia—rather than new structures.

Several changes are visible when we observe movements in the postmodern age: more identity politics and a blurring of class support bases; more **structural fragmentation**; a reduced emphasis on the state as the mechanism of change; and greater emphasis on interactional and cultural resistance. In the following pages, how these changes in movements follow from the larger trends toward the postmodern is discussed, but clarification of some of the component trends of the postmodern and their implications for movements is essential before the changes in movements are considered.

Toward the Postmodern: A Historical Overview   The postmodern is a change in the global configuration of social relationships, the economy, states, technology, and culture. It is the most recent in a series of shifts in the relationships among global markets, societies, and states. Since 1500 or so, a world system of markets, nations, and ethnic groups has existed, a system that is dynamic and constantly changing (Heilbroner, 1989; Wallerstein, 1974, 1980; Wolf, 1982). One major shift in this global system took place around 1800, with the industrial revolution, the formation of liberal nation-states, and the transition from mercantilism to a more laissez-faire relationship between states and economies; these are the changes that are referred to in this book as the beginning of the modern era (Hobsbawm, 1962).

A long period of western expansion and global conflict followed, a period in which the industrial capitalist nations formed empires and fought with each other for global power and economic preeminence. After World War II, decolonization took place, and the developed nations enjoyed a period of relative stability for several decades. The system appeared to have acquired some permanent features. One of these was a global three-part division into a developed core, a Communist sphere, and a peripheral Third World. Another apparently stable feature was the Fordist accumulation model in the core economies, marked by mass production, mass consumption, strong internal markets, and some degree of accommodation between labor and capital. The breakdowns and changes marking the end of this short-lived period of apparent stability are a major part of the shift into a postmodern era (Appadurai, 1990; Jameson, 1984).

The apparently stable features of the postwar period are dissolving. Even much longer-standing features of the global economy, dating from the nineteenth century and the age of empire, are in flux, such as the distinction of the industrial, imperialist west from the largely nonindustrial and dependent "rest" (variously referred to as the Third World or the south). We are no longer in a global economy in which a developed core is distinguished by a Fordist model of growth and societal integration, while a periphery serves as a source of raw materials and low-wage labor. Some of this structure still exists, but it is rapidly changing. The Third World is rapidly differentiating, as parts of it become formidable competitors to the older core and parts of it sink into absolute poverty. The Second World is gone.

The political coalitions that accompanied Fordism in the developed core are weaker now—for instance, the New Deal coalition in the United States or the Swedish corporatist model. The distinct industrial working-class communities and political cultures associated with Fordist industrialization have disintegrated, allowing or imposing more complex choices of identity.

Let's look at some of the component processes of these global shifts in more detail.

The Globalization of Markets and Production Processes   One element of the postmodern is a new wave of globalization of labor markets, capital markets, and media markets. A glance at history shows us that labor markets and migrations have operated on a global scale for a long time—witness the trans-Atlantic slave trade, the massive migration of Europeans to the Americas, or the formation of overseas Chinese communities (Wolf, 1982). What is new here is perhaps more the scale and the variety of ethnic groups involved in current migrations. The globalization of capital markets and media markets are probably genuinely new phenomena. They accompany the globalization of production processes, for example, cars, clothes, and computer programs that are assembled in more than one country. The globalization of production rests on the globalization of scientific knowledge, information, and technology (Reich, 1992). With these flows of people, money, products, and technologies go flows of images and ideas. One author sums up these processes of globalization as ethnoscapes (migrations of people), mediascapes, technoscapes, finanscapes (flows of capital), and ideoscapes (Appadurai, 1990).

The Decline of the Fordist Accumulation Model and Its Political Consequences   As described in Chapter 5, the Fordist accumulation model that functioned in the core economies in the twentieth century and most successfully in the post-World War II period has declined, though certainly not completely disintegrated. This model worked for both capital and labor by the formation of domestic markets in which the workers of a nation were also the consumers of its companies' products. Industries that produced capital goods (machinery, plant equipment), consumer durables (cars, home appliances), and lighter consumer goods all benefited from this model of strong internal demand.

Fordism had a political as well as an economic side. After a period of considerable labor unrest early in the century, the working class was integrated into the system through political structures that contributed to widespread prosperity. In some countries like the United States, labor unions assured this integration and gave an organizational foundation to the development of the internal market, with the support of a positive liberal government. In other core countries, like Sweden, integration was more politically complex and sophisticated, involving labor parties or social democratic parties and national-level corporatist accommodation. In practically all the core societies, social movements like the labor movement and socialism became institutionalized political actors. (We saw earlier that the fascist version of this corporatist model was defeated and eliminated.) The government in most of the core countries served as arbiter or mediator in this system of class relations.

The shift to postmodernity involves a partial or complete breakdown of the Fordist model (Geoghegan, 1994; Harrison and Bluestone, 1988; Reich, 1992). Labor as an organized force has weakened. Production processes have shifted out of the core economies to other regions and have been more extensively automated. Large parts of the working class are no longer in relatively well-paid and secure jobs; instability and insecurity have even reached to middle management in the corporate restructuring of the 1990s.

The decline of the Fordist model was not just an economic process, a response by companies to the stagflation of the 1970s. The process also had a political component, involving a shift in governments' definition of their role away from balancing business and labor interests toward increasing the relative power of business by deregulating markets and intervening against strikes. This shift was most clearly visible in the Reagan and Thatcher governments of the 1980s, though repeated in a smaller way in other shifts toward the right in Europe. The influence of the New Right on governments in the 1980s, especially the Reagan and Thatcher administrations, may be one factor in the decline of the Fordist model. The role of movements of the right was to shift the state from a balancing or mediating position to supporting companies that had transnational interests and, at the same time, reducing support for organized labor.

Political culture also changed. Media framing increasingly shifted toward a definition of labor as a special interest that interfered with economic growth (Edsall, 1984; Geoghegan, 1991). The New Right reduced the role of positive liberal ideology in the political system. The working class had partially suburbanized and redefined its own values and interests, sometimes along ethnic lines or along status lines as homeowners and taxpayers. These shifts were most noticeable in the United States and Great Britain but also appeared in other developed market societies (Harrison and Bluestone, 1988; Davis, 1986; Edsall, 1984; Geoghegan, 1991, 1994; Levitas, 1986; Lo, 1990; Piven and Cloward, 1982).

The End of the Three-Part Global System   A major element of the postmodern is the collapse of a three-part geopolitical system, based on the developed and industrialized market economies (the First World), industrialized Communist societies (the Second World), and a markedly poorer, nonindustrial periphery (the Third World). The Second World, which claimed to represent the hegemony of the working class, declined and collapsed. The sharp distinctions between an industrialized core and a nonindustrialized, underdeveloped periphery are blurring, but this is likely to be a long, slow process.

Several component processes are involved in this growing lack of distinction between former First World and former Third World: One is the slippage of some First World populations into Third World standards of living seen, for example, in increasing unemployment rates and homelessness in the core economies. A second is the movement of people from the former Third World into the core economies and from poorer economies into the more economically powerful ones. For example, 25 percent of the population of inner London is now ethnic minority and this type of composition is also true of other world cities like Los Angeles (Davis, 1990; Sassen, 1994:103; Soja, 1993). Some nations' populations are composed of nearly 10 percent immigrants, as in Canada, Australia, South Africa, and Ivory Coast (the United States is at about 8.6 percent), whether as prospective citizens or long-term "guest workers." It might be useful to keep in mind, however, that 98 percent of the world's population lives in the country of its birth; and that high percentages of the foreign born have been a feature of many world cities and a number of countries since the nineteenth century (*National Public Radio*, June 11, 1994). A third process is the differentiation of the former Communist countries along a spectrum of integration into the global market economy that ranges from the fairly successful to the disastrous. A fourth trend is the formation of transnational elites comprised of both owners of capital and holders of advanced symbolic skills, such that class structure has become increasingly detached from nation-states and ethnicity (Appadurai, 1990; Reich, 1992).

And, finally, we need to include the emergence of some very successful nations in the former periphery along with the slide of other former Third World nations into absolute poverty. The Third World was always really a heterogeneous category, and is becoming even more so; South Korea and Mexico are now hardly in the same boat as Benin and Bangladesh, if they were ever really there at any time. Nevertheless, we need to remember that, in the past couple of decades, the most developed countries experienced increases in their incomes, the middle-range countries remained, at best, stationary, and the poorer countries lost ground (Castañeda, 1993:255–266). Uneven development and large inequalities among regions are still very much a part of the global structures, even if these inequalities are no longer so neatly visible in distinct categories.

All these changes involve a large number of complex interrelated subchanges. What they add up to is the persistence of a basically capitalist world system with a new configuration characterized by far more transnational integration, new forms of communities and culture contact, and a weakening of the control of nation-states over their economic and cultural destinies (Reich, 1992). This new configuration has a number of major implications for social movements.

Postmodern Movements

X   *Identity Politics and the Fragmentation of Social Class*   One shift is toward **identity politics.** What this phrase means is that movements are less clearly class-based. Religion, ethnicity, gender, sexual orientation, as well as issues and concerns like the environment or animal rights, rather than class, seem to form the basis of a larger number of movements than in the past. Whatever the basis of mobilization, the movements devote more attention to identity formation; it seems to take more effort for the movement to summon the right identity in the potential support base.

Fewer movements are based on a straightforward correspondence between social class and movement participation, in the way that socialism in most developed nations was based in the industrial working class. In the 1920s and 1930s, fascism, despite its nonclass rhetoric, had a definable core class base in the lower middle class. Class bases of movements have not disappeared entirely at the end of the twentieth century, but many movements like the environmental movement, Christian fundamentalism, gay and lesbian movements, Islamic integralism, and ethnonationalism have indistinct or unpredictable class bases; the identities summoned by the movements cut across class lines.

X   *Fragmentation of Movement Structure*   Under way is a major shift in movement strategy and organization toward a more fragmented, localized form; the totalizing visions remain, but the specific struggles and movement organizations are less unified into large mass parties, disciplined vanguard formations, and so on. If, by postmodern, we mean the end of totalizing visions, movements resist postmodernity; if the term means the end of rigidly structured organizations, then, indeed, movements are becoming postmodern.

There is more division of labor between multiple fragments of movements. These fragments may include organizations with professional staffs, grass roots organizations, impermanent ad hoc mobilizations, single-issue movements, parties, and pressure groups, depending on political opportunities afforded by each host nation. The fragmented or segmented character allows a complicated division of labor and high degree of adaptation to each separate national or local environment in which the transnational movement operates.

For example, Islamic integralism might take the form of a legal political party in one country, a network of local brotherhoods involved in cultural work in another country, and clandestine terrorist cells in yet a third national environment. In a similar way, the environmental movement includes professionally staffed national organizations, local citizen mobilizations, single-issue constituencies, elite direct-action groups, green parties, and many other fragments that give the movement, as a whole, flexibility and adaptability both within and across national boundaries (Price, 1990; Zald and McCarthy, 1987).

X *A Reduced Emphasis on the State as a Mechanism of Social Transformation*   Closely related to this fragmentation of structures is a shift away from the state as the lever of social change. The state and political processes are still important, but two changes have taken place. One is a change in movement activists' assessment of the state as mechanism of transformation. From the Old Left and its hopes for revolutionary socialist states to the New Right and its hopes for the Reagan and Thatcher governments, movement activists learned that states are inherently limited in their ability to transform society. This assessment is reinforced by postmodern trends; states seem less powerful and less activist in a period of accelerated globalization than they did before. The global economy and local cultural processes seem more vital in transforming societies than does control of the state.

This consideration brings me to another shift in movement activity—the increased focus on interactionist resistance, cultural practices, discourses, and organizing at a local level (Weinstein and Weinstein, 1993; Willis, 1990). Movements have not given up on their transformative visions, but they appear to be spending more time on cultural processes and microprocesses. This shift is visible in the activities of the new social movements in Europe, in grassroots mobilizations of the Christian right in the United States, and in the political correctness disputes in the United States.

At the risk of considerable oversimplification, let me contrast the old and new forms of movements, pulling together the themes of identity politics, structural fragmentation, reduced emphasis on the state, and more cultural and micropolitical practices.

In the old way, an organizer comes to (or emerges from) a community of angry and oppressed people who are similar to each other in class, ethnicity, religion, language, and occupation—let's say a community of landless laborers in Italy or miners in Chile. Their identity and their goals are not problematic; it is clear to them as well as the organizer who they are. Since their oppression is multiple and superimposed, class identity meshes with other bases of identity. The organizer rallies them to resist those who oppress and exploit them. This process takes place simultaneously in many similar communities. The organizers are linked into a cohesive national organization. On a national level, parties form that are either large and bureaucratic and designed to win elections or small and tightly disciplined to spearhead revolutions. It is important for the movement to be coherent and unified, both ideologically and organizationally.

Revolutions take place if and when order in the armed forces and police apparatus collapses and revolutionaries seize key government functions. Our image here is often derived from the Bolshevik capture of the Winter Palace in the October Revolution.

Repression by the state or social control agents takes the form of arrests, torture, exile, and executions; paralleling the movement's call for action against the state, the social control agents favor repression through frontal assaults of the coercive apparatus of the state against the movement.

The extent to which the old forms of movements still influence people can be seen from the uprising against the Yeltsin government in the fall of 1993; insurgents thought that seizing the TV studios and the parliament building might rally supporters nationwide and split the security forces. It did not happen.

new

New forms of movements are decentralized, fluid, and networklike. They are technologically sophisticated. They are both local and global, with levels linked by contact rather than command. The units are collectives, study groups, local citizens groups, as well as movement organizations with a professionalized staff. The movements are comfortable with internal differentiation, with both ideological splits and multiple movement organizations. This differentiation is not seen as a betrayal of a line, but as an advanced form of the division of labor. The movement contains radicals and moderates, amateurs and professionals, organizations with full-time staff people and supporters who drop in for an occasional demonstration or letter-writing campaign. These different types of activists and different kinds of organizations accept the diversity within the movement (Price, 1990).

This fragmented and complicated division of labor within the movement is useful in summoning the identity the movement emphasizes in its potential support base. Potential supporters are scattered socially and geographically. The movement has to tease out the right identity for its goals from the multiple crosscutting identities that most people have, particularly in the market democracies.

The new movements do not engage in frontal assaults on states but in the erosion of power. They seep into all institutional structures, transforming their practices and mentalities. They mutate effortlessly, adapting to circumstances. The most innocuous activities may become subversive: Forming a Bible or Qur'an reading group can be as powerful as training guerrillas—especially when it is formed among military officers.

In turn, the agents of social control do not limit their tactics to direct physical repression. They launch countermovements, calling up competing identities that have the potential to nullify the movement's mobilizations.

The differences between the old and the new should not be exaggerated. Identity formation was always an issue for movements. The old movements also had their discourse about boring from within—that is, penetrating institutions rather than attacking them from the outside. The front structure of the Communist parties was already a sophisticated way of mobilizing highly differentiated support bases. Nazis and Fascists worked out complex divisions of labor within their movements that allowed them to come to power with the support of incumbent elites.

Furthermore, the old and the new are not clearly distinct; there are many movements that fall somewhere in between on the spectrum. Yet, some shift does seem to be underway, and I will argue that it is a response to changing social conditions; the structure of societies and states is different at the end of the twentieth century than it was during the first half of the century; therefore, movements must adapt their organizations and strategies to the change.

Postmodern Societies and Postmodern Movements: Underlying Social Processes

At the beginning of this section of the chapter I discussed two changes, an economic one and a political one—the globalization of markets and the limitation of state functions. Here I want to pursue related changes in social relationships that connect the economic and political changes to changes in identity formation and mobilization.

Identity Politics and New Forms of Organizing   One change I already mentioned is that identity formation is becoming more complex; possible identities are multiplying, crosscutting, and, at the same time, becoming invisible or more hidden. Many communities of identity are being stretched out across the globe, disrupting old links between identity and spatial location. More and more ethnic groups are partially deterritorialized, like Turks in Germany and El Salvadorans in the United States (Appadurai, 1990). These changes present formidable obstacles to old styles of organizing which were addressed to communities of superimposed identities in an identifiable spatial location.

The results of these shifts can be seen in the decline of large national movements with a coherent class base and their replacement by movements that are fragmented and have a diffuse or crossclass base. Among these, we might list the new social movements in Europe in the 1970s and, by the 1990s, the phenomenon of identity politics in the developed core societies; that is, movements organized around ethnicity, gender, and/or sexual orientation. The surge of religious fundamentalism and nationalism also appear to be related to these shifts, and some authors include these movements under identity politics (Appadurai, 1990; Beyer, 1990).

The meaning of identity politics is complex. The term has been used to describe different types of situations. Mobilizations based on identity politics have a wide range of causes; they are responses to many different types of structural strain. Identity politics functions in different ways to alleviate strains experienced by the support bases. Sometimes identity politics is associated with an effort to revive premodern cultures or propagate antimodern ideologies, as in the case of religious fundamentalism; in situations like these, identity politics is a term that refers to the rejection of two major bases of modern allegiances—citizenship in a liberal nation-state and social class. In other cases, identity politics means the exact opposite, namely, an effort to integrate a group into the mainstream of the liberal political system, for example, in some currents of the gay and lesbian movement. In this case, identity politics is associated with citizenship claims, civil rights, and inclusion in the liberal democratic nation. (Bawer, 1994; Zald, 1994). Movements that pursue this type of identity politics are extensions of liberalism and continue the pattern of establishing political and juridical equality of formerly excluded groups. Identity politics has yet a third function. Within national and global market economies, identity politics can provide a shelter against gales of economic change; mobilizations of ethnic groups, women, the disabled, and so on, can work for policies that provide the specific group with opportunity and security in a volatile, competitive economic climate (Garner, 1994). European political scientists refer to this function of identity politics as corporatism. Corporatist mobilizations can provide immediate benefits to the group such as preferential hiring, job security, government contracts, and access to higher education. The group is partially protected from effects of the market. Identity politics can combine appeals based on corporatist interests with themes of defending and revitalizing cultural traditions.

All these forms of identity politics are associated with competing and cross-cutting identity claims. The proliferation of possible identities gives importance to the framing of movement ideologies for mass constituencies; movement activists compete to mobilize potential supporters by techniques of framing. The media have a role in this process, since their framing is often the first point of contact of the audience with a movement (Snow and Benford, 1988).

Identity Politics and the Left   Marxists tend to regret the transformation from class struggle to identity politics, and some of them argue that this shift should not occur, since capitalism still prevails (Callinicos, 1990; Wood, 1994). If marxism is to be a systematic and scientific understanding of human societies, marxists need to analyze the reasons for this shift in terms of the characteristics of advanced capitalism. Global markets in labor, capital, and culture have created a situation in which identity politics is displacing class politics; we cannot say whether this is a permanent or temporary shift, but in any case it has to be understood rather than merely deplored.

The left is faced with a paradoxical situation: At the very moment when Marx's *economic and social* analysis is fully realized, the subjective, political dimension of class conflict is at its lowest ebb since the 1890s. All markets are globalizing; markets in ideas, culture, and capital have become transnational. In virtually every country, peasants have become or are becoming wage laborers in manufacturing, agriculture, and services, so that a larger percentage of the world's population are proletarians (in a broad sense) than ever before; many of them live in unfavorable and even worsening conditions and are subjected to chronic unemployment and underemployment. With the collapse of the Communist states, all nations are (in Marx's words) "compelled to adopt the bourgeois mode of production," that is, to adopt a market economy and enter into global markets. The blurring lines between the First World and the Third World, the expansion of free trade, and the creation of webs of transnational high-tech production processes suggest that marxist predictions about capitalist development were accurate.

All the objective conditions for a powerful left are present; the puzzle is that this advanced form of capitalism is at present associated with relatively weak class consciousness and spotty left-wing organizing. To some people, the logic of the market seems overwhelming and irresistible; they choose to cope with it on an individual basis. To others, identity politics offers immediate benefits and more satisfying forms of solidarity.

Certainly there is a wide range of movements on the left, including populist mobilizations, religious communities, and sectarian insurgencies like Peru's Shining Path. There are intellectuals with a coherent critique of capitalism. Union activism is present in practically every country and region, from paperworkers in Decatur, Illinois, to miners in South Africa. There is substantial satisfaction with social democracy in those countries in which it has been implemented effectively, especially in northern Europe. There are left-wing parties, usually social democratic or left populist, that have won sizable numbers of votes in Latin America and Europe. The new social movements persist, and there is a leftward tilt to many feminist, environmental, peace, gay and lesbian, and human rights mobilizations. But these movements, ideologies, and dispositions do not add up to a left that is prepared to contest capitalist hegemony on a regional, let alone global, basis. At the moment, the left does not offer a cohesive, attractive, viable, and democratic alternative; though fragmentation can be an advantage in the postmodern era, the left may be in a phase of excessive divisions.

In the view of some left observers (Castañeda, 1993; Moberg, 1994; Przeworski, 1991) an alternative vision and program might include an extension of successful social democratic policies to poorer countries; an emphasis on strengthening democracy at the grassroots as well as in national political institutions; a better mix of public sector planning and the market to mend the defects of both the pure market and the command economy, especially with regard to the environment; some degree of income redistribution downward, especially in view of its redistribution upward during the past 15 years; more attention to full employment and shorter working hours; a revitalized and democratic labor movement; and a revived and updated social contract between capital and labor so that both parties can benefit from economic development. Much of this is little different from positive liberalism or the most cautious side of social democracy; but given the success of conservative countermovements over the past couple of decades, the expansion of markets at the expense of other institutions, the divided nature of the left, and the collapse of Communist states, this rather limited program may be the only possible starting point.

The first question to be answered during the next 25 years will be whether the market can deliver on its promises of prosperity and inclusion—growth and equity. If it fails to deliver these goods to millions or billions of human beings, a second question becomes whether identity politics can offer solutions and visions that people are more ready to follow than the vision of the left. If religious fundamentalism, nationalist and ethnonationalist movements, and other forms of identity politics offer more satisfying communities and more immediate benefits, they—and not the left—will be the mass-based alternative to the expansion of the market. The outcomes could vary among global regions. For example, the market may function well in eastern Asia, religious movements might become hegemonic in the Islamic world, and the left could successfully rebuild itself in a new social democratic or left populist form in Latin America.

At the moment, there is even the possibility that socialist ideology will become fragmented and survive primarily in recombined forms, like conservative ideology after the decline of the landed classes. Its themes of egalitarianism and social justice may recombine with ideologies of the peace movement, environmental movements, the women's movement, and liberation theology; the theme of using the state to control and limit the effects of global markets could be recombined with nationalism and ethnonationalism. The comparison to the ideology of the landed gentry is a little far-fetched; the working class has cer-

tainly not disappeared from the world scene as an economic category, even if
its level of political consciousness and organization is low.

The Global Web of Economic Structures, Political Systems, and Cultures
Movements have to deal with complex new patterns of local, subnational, national, regional, and global integration (Reich, 1992). Economies are integrated
at all of these levels and political forms are slowly shifting in these multiple directions. Movements had previously thought largely in terms of reforms won
at the national level and/or revolutions carried out against nation-states. These
patterns have become more complicated. For example, it is not enough to build
a national industrial union because some companies can easily move to a different country. Halting nuclear power plant construction in one community or
country does not solve the problem of cross-border fallout. Increasing numbers
of deterritorialized peoples (like Palestinians; Sikhs in the United States, England, and Canada; or Russians in Kazakhstan) multiply the potential for ethnonationalist and religious/nationalist mobilizations (Appadurai, 1990:302).
Global organization of movements is made more complicated by cultural differences among nations and regions and by the marked differences in political
opportunity structures.

These are not totally new developments. The modern world from the start
was composed of a complicated web of global markets, national states, and local cultures (Wallerstein, 1974). Lenin's concept of *imperialism* was an early effort to understand this global structure and apply the theory to the practice of
forming a socialist movement. We saw how the movement practice did not—
inherently, could not—keep up with the complexity of the global economic and
political structure, and the attempt led to all the problems of socialism in one
country. But the web has since become more complicated. The loose networklike form of postmodern movements is one effort to match the complex patterns
of global economic and political integration. Large, nationally based movement
organizations have to be supplemented, if not outright replaced, by more flexible and diversified forms.

The Power of Civil Society and the Limitations of the State   In many ways,
states and societies have become resistant to change; the apparent paradox is
that, as the state proves to be limited in what it can accomplish, it turns out to
be more powerful to resist movements. At first glance, it appears that states
have become more powerful at the end of the twentieth century because they
command more sophisticated technologies of surveillance and repression, from
computerized dossiers on dissidents to state-of-the-art police equipment. There
is some truth to this view, but the coercive apparatus of the state is only part of
a modern state's means of social control and by no means a sufficient condition
for suppressing social movements. In recent history, states with a large police
and/or military apparatus collapsed quickly when faced with internal dissent,
like the Argentine military regime after the Malvinas-Falklands defeat and the
eastern European Communist states after perestroika. Other well-armed states
turned out to be vulnerable to protracted insurgencies, fueled by external sup-

port and a flow of small arms (Halliday, 1989; Klare, 1994). A sophisticated coercive apparatus alone does not guarantee that the state will be able to suppress movements.

On the contrary, the major source of a state's power to resist movements lies in the state's connection to **civil society**. At the end of the twentieth century, social control is lodged in the flexibility of the state's responses to movements and mobilizations, which is enhanced by the adoption of some liberal democratic forms. By the last decade of the twentieth century, many states have a liberal political system or, at least, the facade of one. They permit some organizing of parties and movements and have some degree of civil liberties. The advantage to movements is that there exists a space for organizing. But the disadvantage, from the point of view of movements, is that the system has become far more flexible in absorbing dissent. In rigid states like the Soviet Union or the military regime in Argentina, elites lived in fear of dissent and subversion. In the liberal and partially liberal states that have replaced them, dissent appears not to make much difference. Some reforms may get instituted, but they often don't produce any major change. Systemic change remains unlikely because a great many changes can be absorbed and co-opted in the liberal democratic states.

The system does not rely on one line of defense—the coercive power of the state, with its military and police apparatus; it is defended by the vitality and diversity of civil society itself. For every movement, a countermovement can develop, either spontaneously or with a little help from elites who feel under threat. Any kind of identity can become the basis of a movement, an interest group, or a network. No one movement can easily become hegemonic. Ideas and ideologies compete among themselves and with scores of less dour and more entertaining identities and associations—why be a socialist if you can shop, surf, go to rock concerts, or pump iron at the health club?

Since the liberal states are generally also market economies, crucial economic decisions appear to be largely out of the control of the state anyway and not very directly amenable to movement pressures. With both economic and cultural decisions made privately and, in large part, outside the direct control of states, the systems are stronger, even if the states are weaker. The irony of the liberal state is that the less it does, the better it functions; it contributes most to stability when it leaves a large realm of decision making to the private processes of civil society. So, this type of state and society seems unlikely to fall to a frontal assault by a disciplined revolutionary movement.

As early as the 1930s, Antonio Gramsci (an Italian Communist imprisoned by the Fascists) contrasted the Bolsheviks' successful assault on the Russian state to the much longer war of position that he believed necessary for a socialist movement to come to power in western societies where the state was backed up by the rich associational life of civil society. "In Russia the State was everything. Civil society was primordial and gelatinous: in the West, there was a proper relation between State and civil society, and when the State trembled, a sturdy structure of civil society was at once revealed. The State was only an outer ditch, behind which there stood a powerful system of fortresses and earthworks . . ." (Gramsci, 1971:238).

His formulation already contains a sense of what socialism would face after the Second World War. By the end of the twentieth century, we can see that his analysis predicted the need for postmodern types of socialist movements that would be flexible and patient.

Later, in the 1960s and 1970s, the German New Left spoke of the need for a **long march through institutions**, a reference to the Chinese Communists' long march, in which they retreated to a remote area in order to rebuild their movement. In the image of the German New Left, it means that transformation has to begin by the slow work of changing existing institutions from within. But, socialism has learned these lessons more slowly than new movements of ecologists, women, and sexual minorities, as well as Islamic integralists and the Christian right. In order to realize their vision of society, movements must work through the institutions of civil society—engaging in grass roots political action, changing cultural discourses, reshaping families and communities, building cultures. This analysis can be found among both progressive and conservative movements, on the left and the right (Stacey, 1991). In the near future, there will not be any state-based quick-fix transformations.

Yet, the war of position and the long march through institutions may lead nowhere for many movements. An ecoanarchist comments wryly on the long march through institutions; he says it "amounted to little more than adapting to the institutions that exist without troubling to create new ones [and] led to the loss of thousands within the institutions. They went in—and never came out" (Bookchin, 1990:158).

Discourse Rather than Structure as a Focus   More recently than Gramsci, the French philosopher Michel Foucault (1976) visualized a resistance to power that is completely decentralized, ongoing, and not in direct confrontation with the state as a coercive apparatus. He pictures resistance as challenging practices and discourses, rather than organized structures of power. Although not a marxist, Foucault, in many ways, converges with Gramsci in pointing to the way in which the liberal state shifts conflict in civil society and diffuses it into a myriad of practices and discourses. Foucault argues that this shift became noticeable with the French Revolution. He describes the gruesome corporal punishments inflicted by the old regime and devotes several pages to the torture-execution of a man named Robert Damiens who attempted to kill the French king. He contrasts this public dismemberment with the postrevolutionary forms of social control, the development of self-surveillance, self-monitoring, and self-discipline, a regime of self-control furthered by new scientific fields such as medicine and psychology (Foucault, 1979). These changes are also related to the invention of childhood as a time for the molding of character—that is, the internalization of discipline—carried out in the nuclear family (Aries, 1965). As the point of social control shifts from coercive, physical repression and punishment meted out by states to self-control and interactive controls diffused throughout society, resistance to the exercise of power necessarily shifts as well. If the postmodern represents a further extension of the liberal model of a small state and a large civil society, then we can expect to find an extension of discursive and self-administered social control and the consequent shift in the focus of movements from confronting state power to changing micropractices (Foucault, 1976; Handler, 1992; Sawicki, 1991; Weinstein and Weinstein, 1993; Willis, 1990).

This model of resistance is closely connected to postmodern philosophy and deconstructionism. It tends to deny that the problem lies in specific forms of economy, political system, or social structures; it is discourses and practices at all levels, in all institutions, that must be changed, and not structures and organizations conceived as building blocks of reality. This interactionist resistance is never completed by an outcome such as a reform or a revolution because these outcomes would simply shift the sites and forms of power and resistance (Weinstein and Weinstein, 1993). **Interactionist and cultural resistance** is an ongoing process and may take the form of play, performance, and style rather than political organizing (Willis, 1990).

While even the new social movements do not go quite so far in replacing structure with discourse as their key concept, these postmodern views have influenced movements to some extent, leading to reflection on discourses, culture, and interactional micropractices, as well as—or even instead of—efforts to reform or transform structures and institutions. For example, parts of the feminist movement have focused on changing cultural representations of women in speech, television, and writing, emphasizing how gender stratification is embedded in these discursive practices. While hardly sharing Foucault's vision, the New Christian Right has also given attention to cultural matters, seeing the cultural sphere as more important and fundamental in many ways than economic or political structure.

I would argue here that it is postmodern reality (and not just postmodern philosophy) that causes movements to focus on cultural issues; advanced capitalism, new technologies, the global market, the explosion of the electronic media and information systems, and the expansion of the liberal state (where control is not centered in a single coercive apparatus) are the forces that shift attention to culture. Globalization, automation, new media systems, and the expansion of liberal democracy cause the profusion of discourses and identities that, in turn, dictates new forms for movement organization and strategy. The heightened emphasis on the cultural sphere—on discourses—is a product of other changes, but quickly takes on a force of its own and shifts movement practices into the terrain of cultural conflicts.

As the modern mutates into the postmodern (or is it just a more modern modern?), movements have to change their own practices. A high degree of reflection on society and on themselves is, therefore, a characteristic of contemporary movement activists across the ideological spectrum. In turn, this reorientation of movements toward discourses and identity politics is seen as one of the signs of postmodernism.

Changes in Movement Structure: Reality or Image?   A word of caution: We should not mistake appearance for reality. We may tend to see movements—both old and new—in terms of prevailing images and metaphors, as well as false recall on the part of movement activists. Many new characteristics were already present in old movements, since transnational movements have always adapted themselves to a variety of potential support bases, national political cultures, and opportunity structures. For example, the structure of the front already had many of the characteristics of the flexible networks of postmodern movements.

It is possible that the apparent organizational discipline and firm structure of the early twentieth-century movements was an illusion, an image or reconstruction circulated by the movements themselves (and sometimes by their enemies). We know now that the Fascists and Nazis were a great deal more disorganized than they pretended to be (Kershaw, 1989; Speer, 1970). Our belief in the disciplined marxist-leninist party is based on the writing of Joseph Stalin as well as that of anti-Communists; these two sets of antagonists may have engaged in a mutually useful misrepresentation of the party as an effective, totally cohesive victorious/menacing organizational weapon.

The description of early twentieth-century parties and movements as strong, disciplined, unified, and rigid was perhaps not just a deliberate misrepresentation, but also a view influenced by the prevailing imagery, discourse, and even aesthetics of the early twentieth century: Images of powerful machines fascinated artists and intellectuals of the period, because it was a period of industrialization based on internal combustion engines, electrical power, and metal-working technologies. Stalin picked the metaphor of steel for his name (first used in 1913)—hard, powerful, indestructible, useful for smashing and building.

Movements of our own day appear flexible, formed of loosely linked nodes, networking, mutating, penetrating silently, like worms or viruses or plastic fibers. The state is not smashed by an external machine; instead, society is transformed by a mutation in each of its cells, in the interactions and cultural practices that constitute civil society. These organic images are perhaps no more or less true than the steel images of the old movements, but are simply derived from our current fascination with computers and biotechnology. Is the shift in movement organization from hard structures like bureaucracies and vanguard parties to soft, flexible, nodular, mutating organic forms a reality—or a projection of our technological fantasies?

TRACING CONNECTIONS, SEEING OUTCOMES

An introduction to movements has to devote some attention to each type of movement, explaining its basic ideas, its growth and organization, and its impact as a distinct movement. But history is really a process formed by the impact of movements on each other, of states and institutions on movements, and of movements on states and institutions. So we have to look not only at the causes and consequences of each movement separately, but also at their interconnections and their relationships to states (Garner and Zald, 1985; Klandermans, 1992; Mottl, 1980). In an introductory interpretation of movements, it is impossible to cover all possible instances of interconnections and mutual influence; therefore, discussion of a few major patterns follows.

Interconnections

Combined Movements   One intentional type of interconnection is the combined movement, the movement (or ideology) formed by the overlap and recombination of two movements (or ideologies). As movement activists develop and refine their ideas, they may discover that some of their goals, values, or analyses have already been put forth by another movement. Or, they may discover that their ideology fails to cover some important issues or viewpoints and, therefore, needs to be supplemented by another ideology. In the combined movement, they deliberately unite two ideologies.

In some cases, the combined movement appears when one movement has lost its support base; the narrower, self-interested elements of ideology that function to mobilize constituencies decline, while the more universalized features persist. These universalized ideas are then picked up by intellectuals of other movements and worked into their ideologies. We observed this process taking place with conservative ideology. The base of conservatism in the landed gentry declined; but the ideas that had expressed the interests of the gentry in universalized form were combined with newer movement ideologies, ranging from laissez-faire liberalism to the New Christian Right to fascism. An originally coherent ideology was fragmented into themes that were combined with the ideas of movements whose aims are actually somewhat contradictory to each other and to the original ideology. As the industrial working class diminished in relative size and political strength in late twentieth-century Europe, many of the themes of socialism seemed to detach from this support base and float toward recombination with the ideologies of the new social movements.

A few examples will illustrate this type of connection. Socialist feminists see themselves as contending against both a mode of production (specifically capitalism) and the system of patriarchy or male domination. In the discourse of socialist feminists, to emancipate women (and men) requires examination of these two structures of inequality and control simultaneously. Ecofeminists combine environmental concerns with feminism; in their perspective, the historical tendency to dominate and destroy nature is closely associated with male domination of women. A new relationship between human beings and the natural environment can come into being only as men and women change their relationship from one of inequality and control to one of harmony, cooperation, and mutual respect. And, of course, there are also socialist ecofeminists, who highlight the importance of finding alternatives to capitalism as a necessary part of this transformation.

Combined movements are, in some degree, an inverse process to the splitting of movements. They represent a complementarity between two movements, sometimes bringing two parts of different movements closer together than ideologically distinct parts of the same movement. The combination exists especially in discourse, ideas, ideology, and goals. For example, the African Na-

tional Congress is an ethnonationalist movement, concerned with the oppressed condition of Black Africans; it is a civil rights movement, dedicated to
achieving political rights and juridical equality; and, historically, it has been a
socialist movement with the goal of restructuring the South African economy.

The combination can also exist in the person and actions of individuals;
people are members, activists, or leaders in more than one movement, and their
presence in each links the movements together. Martin Luther King began his
activism in the Civil Rights Movement but, by the late 1960s, he also spoke out
against the war in Vietnam and turned his attention to the rights of African
Americans as workers; as an individual, he helped link these movements.

The combination can exist in the practices of the movement, in the support
base it tries to mobilize or the way it organizes members; for example, an
ecofeminist might organize a local *women's* group to monitor pollution levels or
protest against the dumping of toxic waste. A priest committed to liberation
theology would choose to link Christian and socialist practices by organizing
workers or peasants.

Hegemonizing Relationships   Movements can instrumentalize each other
and use other movements' issues to expand their own support base and resources. This process is more opportunistic and unequal than the formation of
combined movements and ideologies. It is a process in which a movement uses
the resources or draws on the support base of another movement to strengthen
itself and pursue its own goals.

The movement that engages in this practice attempts to become *hegemonic*
within the array of movements it works to unify. Its ideology absorbs the other
ideologies, and its activists establish (or take over) leading decision-making positions. The *front* is often the organizational mechanism for carrying out this
type of expansion of a movement's support base. Nationalist and socialist
movements in the decolonizing world attempted to absorb each other in order
to expand their own support base and resources. In Vietnam, the movement
centered on the Communist Party succeeded in unifying a large spectrum of nationalist and anticolonial forces, while establishing and retaining a hegemonic
position within the National Liberation Front. In other cases, like Zimbabwe,
socialist forces were subordinated to nationalist or nation-building forces after
independence.

Alliances and Coalitions   Another kind of movement interconnection is the
alliance or coalition. It is looser than the combined movement and more equal
than the front structure. Two movements can remain distinct in their ideology,
but work together on common goals, share resources, and/or form coalitions of
political parties. For example, in many European countries, the Greens have
been willing to become coalition partners of socialist parties within a broad left
coalition. Sometimes, such alliances or coalitions are formed by the creation of
an umbrella group, an organization that unites representatives from the movement organizations that participate in the coalition. At other times, the coalition
may be looser, perhaps not even formally acknowledged.

If a movement comes to power, the coalition or alliance can become an effective basis for rule; or it may gradually turn into an unequal situation, with one movement absorbing, marginalizing, or even outlawing a weaker partner. The Nazis were able to absorb the organizations of the conservative right in Germany, and eventually eliminate them as independent groups. The right as a whole moved from a situation of loose alliance in the mid 1920s to one of Nazi hegemony by the early 1930s to, finally, one in which the Nazis became the only organized force in the society as they consolidated their power. Strange bedfellows may appear in the process of building issue-oriented coalitions or alliances, especially when the alliance remains organizationally loose, perhaps even tacit, rather than openly acknowledged. I have already mentioned the example of Women Against Pornography and antipornography forces in the Christian right as an example of convergent movement actions on the part of two very different movements. The antiabortion movement has united Catholics with parts of the New Christian Right, although they actually have opposed views on many other issues. For many Catholics in the movement, an antiabortion position involves respect for the seamless web of life, which includes opposition to war, militarism, authoritarian regimes in the Third World, and capital punishment; these other positions are generally not shared by the New Christian Right.

Convergence   Finally, there may be long-term convergences among movements that had different historical origins. This process is quite different from the short-term and sometimes unstable formation of coalitions among different movements. It is not the same process as forming a combined movement out of the conviction that the two ideologies complement each other. The long-term convergence tends to appear when movements operate with somewhat similar goals for a long time in the same environment. For example, such a long-term convergence has taken place between positive liberals and social democrats. They have gradually become more similar in ideology and, together, they have supported the formation of many of the institutions of the European welfare states.

Countermovements

A rather different type of interconnection is the movement/countermovement relationship. The movements are hostile to each other, their goals in general and on specific issues are diametrically opposed, and they devote resources to constricting or destroying the enemy. The preceding chapters have presented a number of examples.

Movements, Countermovements, and States

Much of what we call twentieth-century history is the story of movement-states locked into mortal combat with each other. The liberal capitalist states, formed by liberal and nationalist movements in the eighteenth and nineteenth centuries, were challenged by the Soviet Union and other states formed by movements with a marxist-leninist ideology. For a brief period in the Second World War, these two forces joined to destroy a third type of movement-state, the Nazi-Fascist states that formed the Axis. Then, they once again took up their own struggle in the cold war, which appears to have ended with the collapse of the historic Communist states in Europe and the Soviet Union. The cold war also involved a struggle by movement-states to hegemonize nationalist movements and gain influence over the decolonization process in the Third World. Nationalist movements succeeded in forming new states and tried to find independent routes to development. This history is an example of movement and countermovement on a grand scale, since each movement (liberal, Communist, Nazi-Fascist, and nationalist) came to form and dominate a set of states with military capabilities.

Movement and countermovement also exist on a smaller scale, for instance in the clash of women's movements and conservative religious movements, nationalist movements with each other, or neo-Nazi groups with socialist and human rights groups. The outcome of these clashes is complicated by the interaction of movements and states. Movements seek state power and, when they obtain it, they become formidable opponents to hostile movements. Once in state power, a movement has many resources, ranging from TV stations to prisons, to limit or suppress competing and opposing movements. For example, the Islamic revolution in Iran was in a good position to defeat socialist movements (like the communist Tudeh movement) or feminist movements once it came to power.

States can launch countermovements or tacitly enable them to come into existence and grow in order to curb or harass movements that challenge state power. For example, many observers think that the Zulu ethnonationalist Inkatha movement was permitted—perhaps even encouraged (through covert funding from the Ministry of Law and Order)—by the white government of South Africa in order to limit the actions of the African National Congress; by attacking ANC supporters, Inkatha tried to divide the black majority and divert ANC energy into defensive operations (Saul, 1991).

In short, movements, countermovements, and states are engaged in many complex relationships that change over time, but do not come to a halt. Movements can turn into states (come to state power) or influence state policy (implement reforms) as well as challenge states. States can launch movements as well as try to suppress them. History unfolds through a dynamic of conflict among movements, countermovements, and states; and the states themselves are often formed by movements.

This brings me to my final reflection: Far from being odd or extreme phenomena, movements are the essential "stuff" from which existing political systems are built. Perhaps the metaphor of a volcano is helpful: Movements are hot, fluid, dangerous, and unpredictable streams of lava. The current landscape of stable and predictable features like rocks and mountains—institutions and states—was formed by earlier eruptions that congealed and hardened. This process may occasionally slow down or halt, but it does not end. Many estab-

The Mothers of the Plaza de Mayo call for continuation of inquiries into thousands of disappearances during the military regime's "dirty war" in the 1970s. Buenos Aires, August 18, 1983. "Our children were tortured and killed, but their ideas remain" (quoted in Bouvard, 1994: 254).

lished states were formed in explosive bursts of movement activity, especially the varieties of liberalism and the successive surges of nationalism that have been shaping the geopolitical landscape for 200 years. In the twentieth century, socialist, Communist, and Nazi-Fascist movements formed states, as did new forms of nationalism. In recent decades, Islamic movements have begun the same process.

The crystallization of movements into established forces occurs not only in political systems, but also in ideologies. Yesterday's bizarre doctrine easily becomes today's conventional wisdom. This crystallization is an ongoing process; but it sometimes does not become evident until several generations after the first eruption of an ideology.

A belief in market democracy and nationalism is part of today's mainstream in the United States and many other nations. Support for the nation, the market, the rights of individuals, and a representative government have a taken-for-granted or commonsensical quality for many people in the United States. Many citizens of the United States believe that they have no ideology, only a vague commitment to the American way of life; we should remember that these commonsense notions are products of liberal and nationalist movements and ideologies that once seemed dangerous and revolutionary.

The particular movements in this book may succeed or fail; they may come to power, they may influence states and reshape institutions, they may be suppressed only to mutate into new forms, and they may eventually fade away—

before or after they have accomplished their goals. What is certain to persist, however, is the interplay of movements, states, and countermovements; this process will continue into the twenty-first century and beyond, because it is history—and no end to history is in sight.

KEY TERMS AND CONCEPTS

movement ideologies and strategies
societal problems
ideological splitting
movement base diversity
division of labor in the movement
transformative strategies and single-
   issue mobilizations
transitional reforms
terrorism and polarization
identity formation; the social
   construction of identity
mobilization of the support base
crosscutting or superimposed
   identities
influencing policy
exercising state power
legitimacy, hegemony, and the
   universalizing of movement
   visions

postmodern movements
global markets
decline of the Fordist accumulation
   model
identity politics
structural fragmentation
cross-boundary issues
civil society
the privatization of economic and
   cultural functions
the long march through institutions

interactionist and cultural resistance

relationships among movements
combined movement ideologies
hegemonizing relationships among
   movements
alliances and coalitions
convergence among movements
countermovements

Bibliography

I have concentrated on books and collections of articles, although individual articles are included primarily if they are cited in the text. I have placed together books that express a movement's ideas with books that analyze the movement from the viewpoint of an outside observer. The books are generally written at the level of the college-educated person with an interest in political science and sociology. Some are closer to good journalism, others to scholarly research.

The bibliography is organized into categories corresponding to the parts of the book. Chapters 1, 2, and 3, which cover basic concepts and theories, are grouped together in the section entitled "Social Movement Theory"; Chapters 4 and 5, which give an overview of movements and states in modern history are placed together in the section entitled "Movements in History." Each movement chapter has its own bibliographic section. In general, complete information is provided in the initial entry for each book with subsequent cross references, since some books are cited more than once.

SOCIAL MOVEMENT THEORY

Abendroth, Wolfgang. (1972). *A Short History of the European Working Class*. London: New Left Books.

Aberle, David. (1966). *The Peyote Religion among the Navaho*. Chicago: Aldine.

Adorno, Theodor W., E. Frenkel-Brunswick, D. Levinson, and R. Sanford. (1993). *The Authoritarian Personality*. New York: Norton.

Anderson, Benedict. (1991). *Imagined Communities*. London: Verso.

Anderson, Perry. (1984, March/April). "Modernity and Revolution." *New Left Review, 144*, 96–113.

Annals of the American Academy of Political and Social Science. (1993, July). *Symposium on Citizens, Protest, and Democracy*. Russell Dalton (ed.), Vol. 528. In this volume:

> Berry, Jeffrey. "Citizen Groups and the Changing Nature of Interest Group Politics in America," pp. 30–41.

> Gamson, William, and G. Wolfsfeld. "Movements and Media as Interacting Systems," pp. 114–125.

> Hagen, Carol. "Citizen Movements and Technological Policymaking in Germany," pp. 42–55.

> Hershey, Marjorie. "Citizens' Groups and Political Parties in the U.S.," pp. 142–156.

> Kitschelt, Herbert. "Social Movements, Political Parties, and Democratic Theory," pp. 13–29.

> Maguire, Diarmuid. "Protesters, Counterprotesters, and the Authorities," pp. 101–113.

McAdam, Doug, and Dieter Rucht. "The Cross-National Diffusion of Movement Ideas," pp. 56–74.

Rochon, Thomas, and Daniel Mazmanian. "Social Movements and the Policy Process," pp. 75–87.

Shaiko, Ronald. "Greenpeace USA: Something Old, New, Borrowed," pp. 85–100.

Arendt, Hannah. (1965). *On Revolution*. New York: Viking.

Aronowitz, Stanley. (1988). "Postmodernism and Politics," in Andrew Ross (ed.), *Universal Abandon: The Politics of Postmodernism*. Minneapolis: University of Minnesota Press.

———. (1973). *False Promises*. New York: McGraw-Hill.

Barkan, Steven, Steven Cohn, and William Whitaker. (1993, August). "Commitment across the Miles: Ideological and Microstructural Sources of Membership Support in a National Anti-hunger Organization." *Social Problems, 40,* 362–373.

Bell, Daniel. (1973). *The Coming of Post-Industrial Society*. New York: Basic Books.

Berman, Marshall. (1982). *All That Is Solid Melts into Air*. London: Verso.

Berry, Jeffrey. (1993, July). "Citizen Groups and the Changing Nature of Interest Group Politics in America." *Annals of the American Academy of Political and Social Science," 528,* 30–41.

Black, George, with Milton Jamail and Norma Stoltz Chinchilla. (1984). *Garrison Guatemala*. New York: Monthly Review Press.

Blackmer, Donald, and Sidney Tarrow. (eds.). (1975). *Communism in Italy and France*. Princeton, NJ: Princeton University Press.

Blumer, Herber. (1951). "Collective Behavior," in Alfred McClung Lee (ed.), *New Outline of the Principles of Sociology*. New York: Barnes & Noble.

Boggs, Carl. (1986). *Social Movements and Political Power: Emerging Forms of Radicalism in the West*. Philadelphia: Temple University Press.

Boyer, Paul. (1992). *When Time Shall Be No More*. Cambridge, MA: Harvard University Press.

Brown, Elaine. (1994). *A Taste of Power: A Black Woman's Story*. New York: Anchor/Doubleday.

Buechler, Steven. (1993, May). "Beyond Resource Mobilization? Emerging Trends in Social Movement Theory." *The Sociological Quarterly, 34,* 217–235.

Cardoza, Anthony L. (1982). *Agrarian Elites and Italian Fascism: The Province of Bologna 1901–1926*. Princeton, NJ: Princeton University Press.

Carr, E. H. (1972). *The Bolshevik Revolution 1917–1923*. London: Macmillan.

Chaliand, Gerard. (1989). *Revolution in the Third World*, rev. ed. New York: Penguin.

Cohen, Stanley. (1973). *Folk Devils and Moral Panics: The Creation of the Mods and Rockers*. St. Albans, England: Paladin.

Curtis, Russell L., and Benigno Aguirre. (eds.). (1993). *Collective Behavior and Social Movements*. Boston: Allyn and Bacon.

———, and Louis A. Zurcher. (1974). "Social Movements: An Analytical Exploration of Organizational Forms," in Russell Curtis and Benigno Aguirre (eds.), *Collective Behavior and Social Movements* (pp. 231–241). Boston: Allyn and Bacon.

Davies, James. (1962, February). "Toward a Theory of Revolution." *American Sociological Review, 27* (1), 5–19.

Deutscher, Isaac. (1966). *Stalin: A Political Biography*. New York: Oxford University Press.

Donald, J., and Stuart Hall. (eds.). (1986). *Politics and Ideology*. Philadelphia: Milton Keynes/Open University Press.

Eyerman, Ron, and Andrew Jamison. (1991). *Social Movements*. University Park, PA: Pennsylvania State University Press.

Fendrich, James Max, and Kenneth Lovoy. (1988, October). "Back to the Future: Adult Political Behavior of Former Student Activists." *American Sociological Review, 53,* 780–784.

Fernandez, R., and Doug McAdam. (1989). "Multiorganizational Fields and Recruitment to Social Movements," in P. G. Klandermans (ed.), *Organizing for Change: Social Movement Organizations across Cultures*. Greenwich, CT: JAI Press.

Flacks, Richard. (1988). *Making History: The Radical Tradition in American Life*. New York: Colombia University Press.

Foucault, Michel. (1982). *The Archeology of Knowledge*. New York: Pantheon.

——. (1979). *Discipline and Punish*. New York: Random House.

Freeman, Jo. (1983). "A Model for Analyzing the Strategic Options of Social Movement Organizations," in Jo Freeman (ed.), *Social Movements of the Sixties and Seventies* (pp. 193–210). New York: Longman.

——. (1979). "Resource Mobilization and Strategy: A Model for Analyzing Social Movement Organization Actions," in Mayer Zald and John McCarthy, (eds.) *The Dynamics of Social Movements* (pp. 167–179). Cambridge, MA: Winthrop.

——. (1975). *The Politics of Women's Liberation: A Case Study of an Emerging Social Movement and Its Relation to the Policy Process*. New York: McKay.

——. (1973). "The Tyranny of Structurelessness," in Ann Koedt, Ellen Levine, and Anita Rapone (eds.), *Radical Feminism* (pp. 285–299). New York: Quadrangle.

Gaines, Donna. (1992). *Teenage Wasteland*. New York: HarperCollins.

Gamson, William. (1992). "The Social Psychology of Collective Action," in Aldon D. Morris and Carol Mueller (eds.), *Frontiers in Social Movement Theory* (pp. 53–76). New Haven, CT: Yale University Press.

——, and G. Wolfsfeld. (1993, July). "Movements and Media as Interacting Systems." *Annals of the American Academy of Political and Social Science, 528,* 114–125.

Garner, Larry, and Roberta Garner. (1981, Fall). "Problems of the Hegemonic Party: The PCI and the Structural Limits of Reform." *Science and Society, 45* (3), 257–273.

Garner, Roberta, and Mayer Zald. (1985). "The Political Economy of Social Movement Sectors," in Gerald Suttles and Mayer Zald (eds.), *The Challenge of Social Control: Citizenship and Institution Building in Modern Society* (pp. 119–145). Norwood, NJ: Ablex.

Garrow, David. (1987). *Bearing the Cross: Martin Luther King, Jr., and the Southern Christian Leadership Conference 1955–1968*. New York: Random House.

Gerlach, Luther. (1983). "Movements of Revolutionary Change: Some Structural Characteristics," in Jo Freeman (ed.), *Social Movements of the Sixties and Seventies* (pp. 133–147). New York: Longman.

Gitlin, Todd. (1980). *The Whole World Is Watching*. Berkeley: University of California Press.

Gorz, Andre. (1985). *Paths to Paradise: On the Liberation from Work*. Boston: South End Press.

——. (1982). *Farewell to the Working Class*. Boston: South End Press.

Gramsci, Antonio. (1971). *Selections from the Prison Notebooks*. New York: International Publishers.

Greene, Thomas. (1990). *Comparative Revolutionary Movements: Search for Theory and Justice*. Englewood Cliffs, NJ: Prentice-Hall.

Gurley, John. (1975). *Challengers to Capitalism: Marx, Lenin, Stalin and Mao*, 2d ed. New York: Norton.

Hadden, Jeffrey K. (1993, May). "The Rise and Fall of American Televangelism." *Annals of the American Academy of Political and Social Science: Vol. 527, Religion in the Nineties,* Wade Clark Roof (ed.) pp. 113–130.

Handler, Joel. (1992). "Postmodernism, Protest and the New Social Movements." *Law and Society Review, 26* (4), 697–731. In the same volume, replies to Handler, including Steven Winter. "For What It's Worth," pp. 789–818.

Healey, Dorothy, and Maurice Isserman. (1990). *Dorothy Healey Remembers*. New York: Oxford University Press.

Hebdige, Dick. (1982). *Subculture*. London: Methuen.

Hershey, Marjorie. (1993). "Citizens' Groups and Political Parties in the U.S." *Annals of the Academy of Political and Social Science, 528,* 142–156.

Hobsbawm, Eric. (1989). *The Age of Empire*. New York: Random House.

Jasper, James, and Dorothy Nelkin. (1993). *Animal Crusades*. New York: Free Press.

Jenkins, J. Craig, and Charles Perrow. (1973). "Insurgency of the Powerless: Farm Worker Movements (1946–1972)," in Russell L. Curtis and Benigno Aguirre (eds.), *Collective Behavior and Social Movements* (pp. 343–355). Boston: Allyn and Bacon.

Johnson, Chalmers. (1964). *Revolution and the Social System*. Stanford, CA: Stanford University Press.

Katz, Donald. (1992). *Home Fires: An Intimate Portrait of One Middle-Class Family in Postwar America*. New York: HarperCollins.

Kitschelt, Herbert. (1991). "Resource Mobilization Theory: A Critique," in Dieter Rucht (ed.), *Research on Social Movements* (pp. 323–347). Boulder, CO: Westview Press.

———. (1990). "New Social Movements and the Decline of Party Organizations," in Russell Dalton and Manfred Kuechler (eds.), *Challenging the Political Order* (pp. 179–208). New York: Oxford University Press.

Klandermans, Bert (1992). "The Social Construction of Protest and Multiorganizational Fields," in Aldon D. Morris and Carol McClurg Mueller (eds.), *Frontiers in Social Movement Theory* (77–103). New Haven, CT, and London: Yale University Press.

———. (1991). "New Social Movements and Resource Mobilization: The European and the American Approach Revisited," in Dieter Rucht (ed.), *Research on Social Movements* (pp. 17–46). Boulder, CO: Westview Press.

Koopmans, Ruud. (1993, October). "The Dynamics of Protest Waves: West Germany, 1965–1989." *American Sociological Review, 58,* 637–658.

Kornhauser, William. (1959). *The Politics of Mass Society.* New York: Free Press.

Kuhn, Thomas. (1962). *The Structure of Scientific Revolutions.* Chicago: University of Chicago Press.

Lasswell, Harold, and Daniel Lerner. (1966). *World Revolutionary Elites: Studies in Coercive Ideological Movements.* Boston: M.I.T. Press.

Leonardi, Robert. (1994, March 31). "Le due anime della destra italiana." Interviewed by Marco Niada in *Il Sole-24 Ore,* No. 86, p. 5.

Lerner, Daniel. (1958). *The Passing of Traditional Society.* New York: Free Press.

Lo, Clarence. (1982). "Countermovements and Conservative Movements in the Contemporary U.S.," in Ralph Turner and J. F. Short (eds.), *Annual Review of Sociology* (pp. 107–134). Palo Alto, CA: Annual Reviews.

Luker, Kristin. (1984). *Abortion and the Politics of Motherhood.* Berkeley: University of California Press.

Mandel, Ernst. (1975). *Late Capitalism.* London: New Left Books.

Mayer, Margit. (1991). "Social Movement Research and Social Movement Practice: The U.S. Pattern," in Dieter Rucht (ed.), *Research on Social Movements* (pp. 47–120). Boulder, CO: Westview Press.

McAdam, Doug. (1982). *Political Process and the Development of Black Insurgency.* Chicago: University of Chicago Press.

———, John McCarthy, and Mayer Zald. (1988). "Social Movements," in Neil Smelser (ed.), *Handbook of Sociology.* Beverly Hills, CA: Sage.

McCarthy, John. (1987). "Pro-Life and Pro-Choice Mobilization: Infrastructure Deficits and New Technologies," in Mayer Zald and John McCarthy (eds.), *Social Movements in an Organizational Society* (pp. 49–66). New Brunswick, NJ: Transaction Books.

———, and Mark Wolfson. (1992). "Consensus Movements, Conflict Movements, and the Co-optation of Civic and State Infrastructures," in Aldon D. Morris and Carol McClurg Mueller (eds.), *Frontiers in Social Movement Theory* (pp. 273–298). New Haven, CT, and London: Yale University Press.

Melucci, Alberto. (1989). *Nomads of the Present: Social Movements and Individual Needs in Contemporary Society.* London: Hutchinson Radius.

Miliband, Ralph. (1969). *The State in Capitalist Society.* London: Weidenfeld and Nicolson.

Morris, Aldon D. (1984). *The Origins of the Civil Rights Movement.* New York: Free Press.

———. (1981, December). "Black Southern Student Sit-in Movement: An Analysis of Internal Organization." *American Sociological Review, 46,* 744–767.

———, and Carol McClurg Mueller. (eds.). (1992). *Frontiers in Social Movement Theory.* New Haven, CT, and London: Yale University Press. In this volume:

Ferree, Myra Marx. "The Political Context of Rationality: Rational Choice Theory and Resource Mobilization," pp. 29–52.

Friedman, Debra, and Doug McAdam. "Collective Identity and Activism: Networks, Choices, and the Life of a Social Movement," pp. 156–173.

Gamson, William. "The Social Psychology of Collective Action," pp. 53–76.

Klandermans, Bert. "The Social Construction of Protest and Multiorganizational Fields," pp. 77–103.

Morris, Aldon D., and Carol McClurg Mueller (*cont.*):

Lo, Clarence. "Communities of Challengers in Social Movement Theory," pp. 224–248.

McCarthy, John D., and Mark Wolfson. "Consensus Movements, Conflict Movements and the Co-optation of Civic and State Infrastructures," pp. 273–298.

Morris, Aldon. "Political Consciousness and Collective Action," pp. 351–374.

Mueller, Carol McClurg. "Building Social Movement Theory," pp. 3–26.

Oliver, Pamela, and Gerald Marwell. "Mobilizing Technologies for Collective Action," pp. 251–273.

Piven, Frances Fox, and Richard Cloward. "Normalizing Collective Protest," pp. 301–325.

Schwartz, Michael, and Shuva Paul. "Resource Mobilization versus the Mobilization of People: Why Consensus Movements Cannot Be Instruments of Social Change," pp. 205–223.

Snow, David, and Robert Benford. "Master Frames and Cycles of Protest," pp. 133–155.

Tarrow, Sidney. "Mentalities, Political Cultures, and Collective Action Frames: Constructing Meanings through Action," pp. 174–202.

Taylor, Verta, and Nancy Whittier. "Collective Identity in Social Movement Communities," pp. 104–130.

Zald, Mayer. "Looking Backward to Look Forward: Reflections on the Past and Future of the Resource Mobilization Research Program," pp. 326–348.

Mottl, Tahi. (1980, June). "The Analysis of Countermovements." *Social Problems, 27,* 620–635.

Muwakkil, Salim. (1994, April 18–May 1). "The NAACP Edges Closer to Nationalism." *In These Times,* pp. 18–19.

Neidhardt, Friedhelm, and Dieter Rucht. (1991). "The Analysis of Social Movements: The State of the Art and Some Perspectives for Further Research," in Dieter Rucht (ed.), *Research on Social Movements* (pp. 421–464). Boulder, CO: Westview Press.

Oberschall, Anthony. (1973). *Social Conflict and Social Movements.* Englewood Cliffs, NJ: Prentice-Hall.

Opp, K. (1986, January). "Soft Incentives and Collective Action: Participation in the Anti-Nuclear Movement." *British Journal of Political Science, 16,* 87–112.

Parks, Rosa. (1992). *Rosa Parks—My Story.* New York: Penguin/Dial.

Polanyi, Karl. (1957). *The Great Transformation.* Boston: Beacon Press.

Reich, Robert. (1992). *The Work of Nations.* New York: Vintage Books.

Riding, Alan. (1984). *Distant Neighbors.* New York: Vintage Books.

Riesebrodt, Martin. (1993). *Pious Passion: The Emergence of Modern Fundamentalism in the United States and Iran.* Los Angeles and Berkeley: University of California Press.

Rucht, Dieter. (ed.). (1991). *Research on Social Movements.* Boulder, CO: Westview Press.

Ryan, Charlotte. (1991). *Prime Time Activism.* Boston: South End Press.

Sawicki, Jana. (1991). *Disciplining Foucault: Feminism, Power and the Body.* New York: Routledge.

Scott, Alan. (1990). *Ideology and the New Social Movements.* London: Unwin Hyman.

Skocpol, Theda. (1979). *States and Social Revolution: A Comparative Analysis of France, Russia, and China.* London and New York: Cambridge University Press.

Smelser, Neil. (1963). *Theory of Collective Behavior.* New York: Free Press of Glencoe.

Smith-Ayala, Emilie. (1991). *The Granddaughters of Ixmucané.* Toronto: Women's Press.

Snow, David, and Robert Benford. (1988). "Ideology, Frame Resonance and Participant Mobilization," in Bert Klandermans, Hanspeter Kriesi, and Sidney Tarrow (eds.), *From Structure to Action: Comparing Social Movements across Cultures* (pp. 197–218). Greenwich, CT: JAI Press.

———, E. B. Rochford, Steven Worden, and Robert Benford. (1986, August). "Frame Alignment Process, Micromobilization, and Movement Participation." *American Sociological Review, 51,* 464–481.

Tarrow, Sidney. (1994). *Power in Movement: Social Movements, Collective Action and Politics.* New York: Cambridge University Press.

———. (1992). "Mentalities, Political Cultures, and Collective Action Frames: Constructing Meanings through Action," in Aldon D. Morris and Carol McClurg Mueller (eds.) *Frontiers in Social Movement Theory* (pp. 174–202). Boulder, CO: Westview Press.

———. (1991). *Struggles, Politics, and Reform: Collective Action, Social Movements and Cycles of Protest.* Ithaca, NY: Cornell University.

———. (1989). *Democracy and Disorder: Protest and Politics in Italy, 1965–1975.* New York: Oxford University Press.

Taylor, Verta. (1989, October). "Social Movement Continuity: The Women's Movement in Abeyance." *American Sociological Review, 54* (5), 761–775.

Tilly, Charles. (1978). *From Mobilization to Revolution.* Reading, MA: Addison-Wesley.

Touraine, Alain. (1981). *The Voice and the Eye: An Analysis of Social Movements.* New York: Cambridge University Press.

———. (1971). *The Post-Industrial Society: Tomorrow's Social History: Classes, Conflicts and Culture in the Programmed Society.* New York: Random House.

Trotsky, Leon. (1959). *The Russian Revolution.* Translated by Max Eastman. Selected and edited by F.W. Dupee. Garden City, NY: Anchor Books.

Turner, Ralph H., and Lewis Killian. (1987). *Collective Behavior,* 3d ed. Englewood Cliffs, NJ: Prentice-Hall.

Wallerstein, Immanuel. (1990). "Culture as the Ideological Battleground of the Modern World System," in Mike Featherstone (ed.), *Global Culture* (pp. 31–55). London, Newbury Park, CA, and New Delhi: Sage.

Weber, Max. (1958). *From Max Weber* [Hans Gerth and C. Mills. (eds.)] New York: Oxford University Press.

Weinstein, Deena, and Michael Weinstein. (1993). *Postmodern(ized) Simmel.* New York: Routledge.

Willis, Paul. (1990). *Common Culture.* San Francisco and Boulder, CO: Westview Press.

Wolf, Eric. (1969). *Peasant Wars of the Twentieth Century.* New York: Harper & Row.

Zald, Mayer. (1991). "The Continuing Vitality of Resource Mobilization Theory: Response to Herbert Kitschelt's Critique," in Dieter Rucht (ed.), *Research on Social Movements* (pp. 348–354). Boulder, CO: Westview Press.

———, and Roberta Ash. (1966, March). "Social Movement Organizations." *Social Forces, 44,* 327–341.

———, and John McCarthy. (eds.). (1987). *Social Movements in an Organizational Society.* New Brunswick, NJ: Transaction Books. In this volume:

Useem, Bert, and Mayer Zald. "From Pressure Group to Social Movement: Organizational Dilemmas of the Effort to Promote Nuclear Power," pp. 273–288.

Zald, Mayer, and John McCarthy. "Religious Groups as Crucibles of Social Movements," pp. 67–95.

———, and ———. (eds.). (1979). *The Dynamics of Social Movements: Resource Mobilization, Social Control and Tactics.* Cambridge, MA: Winthrop.

Zeitlin, Irving. (1994). *Ideology and the Development of Sociological Theory.* Englewood Cliffs, NJ: Prentice-Hall.

Zeitlin, Maurice. (1967). *Revolutionary Politics and the Cuban Working Class.* Princeton, NJ: Princeton University Press.

MOVEMENTS IN HISTORY

Abrahamian, Ervand. (1991, March/April). "Khomeini: Fundamentalist or Populist?" *New Left Review, 186,* 102–119.

Althusser, Louis. (1969). *For Marx.* London: Allen Lane.

Anderson, Benedict. (1991). *Imagined Communities.* London: Verso.

———. (1988, May/June). "Cacique Democracy and the Philippines: Origins and Dreams." *New Left Review, 169,* 3–31.

Appadurai, Arjun. (1990). "Disjuncture and Difference in the Global Cultural Economy," in Mike Featherstone (ed.), *Global Culture* (pp. 245–310). London, Newbury Park, CA, and New Delhi: Sage.

Arendt, Hannah. (1965). *On Revolution.* New York: Viking Press.

Aronowitz, Stanley. (1973). Cited under "Social Movement Theory."

Beccalli, Bianca. (1994, March/April). "The Modern Women's Movement in Italy." *New Left Review, 204,* 86–112.

Berman, Marshall. (1982). *All That Is Solid Melts into Air.* London: Verso.

Bluestone, Barry, and Bennett Harrison. (1982). *The De-Industrialization of America.* New York: Harper & Row.

Burke, Edmund. (1961). *Reflections on the Revolution in France.* Garden City, NY: Doubleday.

Castells, Manuel. (1983). *The City and the Grassroots.* Berkeley: University of California Press.

Davis, Mike. (1990). *City of Quartz.* London: Verso.

Denitch, Bogdan. (1994). *Ethnic Nationalism: The Tragic Death of Yugoslavia.* Minneapolis: University of Minnesota Press.

de Tocqueville, Alexis. (1990). *Democracy in America.* New York: Random House.

Deutscher, Isaac, (1966). *Stalin: A Political Biography.* New York: Oxford University Press.

Donald, J., and Stuart Hall. (eds.). (1986). Cited under "Social Movement Theory."

Durning, Alan. (1990, March/April). "Life on the Brink." *Worldwatch,* pp. 22–30.

Fagen, Richard, Carmen Deere, and J. L. Coraggio. (eds.). (1986). *Transition and Development.* New York: Monthly Review Press. In this volume:

Baumeister, Eduardo, and Oscar Neira Cuadra. "The Making of the Mixed Economy," pp. 171–191.

Burbach, Roger. "The Conflict at Home and Abroad," pp. 79–96.

Marchetti, Peter S. J. "War, Popular Participation, and the Transition to Socialism: The Case of Nicaragua," pp. 303–330.

Fairchilds, Cissie. (1984). "Women and Family," in Samia Spencer (ed.), *French Women and the Age of Enlightenment.* Bloomington: Indiana University Press.

Flacks, Richard. (1988). Cited under "Social Movement Theory."

Foucault, Michel. (1976). *The Archaeology of Knowledge.* New York: Harper & Row.

Frank, Andre Gunder. (1981). *Crisis in the Third World.* New York: Monthly Review Press.

Freeman, Jo. (ed.). (1983). *Social Movements of the Sixties and Seventies.* New York: Longman.

Fukuyama, Francis. (1992). *The End of History and the Last Man.* New York: Free Press.

Gamson, William. (1975). *The Strategy of Social Protest.* Homewood, IL: Dorsey Press.

Garner, Roberta. (1977). *Social Movements in America.* Chicago: Rand-McNally.

Geoghegan, Thomas. (1994, May 23). "West of Eden." *The New Republic, 218,* 30–31.

———. (1991). *Which Side Are You On?* New York: Farrar, Straus & Giroux.

Gerlach, Luther. (1983). "Movements of Revolutionary Change: Some Structural Characteristics," in Jo Freeman (ed.), *Social Movements of the Sixties and Seventies* (pp. 133–147). New York: Longman.

Gide, André. (1994). *Travels in the Congo.* Hopewell, NJ: Ecco Press.

Gitlin, Todd. (1987). *The Sixties: Years of Hope, Days of Rage.* Toronto: Bantam Books.

Goodwin, Jeff, and Theda Skocpol. (1989, December). "Explaining Revolutions in the Contemporary Third World." *Politics and Society, 17,* 489–509.

Gorz, Andre. (1982). Cited under "Social Movement Theory."

Gould, James A., and William H. Truitt. (1973). *Political Ideologies.* New York: Macmillan.

Greene, Thomas. (1990). *Comparative Revolutionary Movements: Search for Theory and Justice.* Englewood Cliffs, NJ: Prentice-Hall.

Gurley, John. (1975). *Challengers to Capitalism: Marx, Lenin, Stalin and Mao,* 2d ed. New York: Norton.

Habermas, Jurgen, (1987). *Knowledge and Human Interests.* Cambridge, England: Polity Press.

Halliday, Fred. (1989). *From Kabul to Managua.* New York: Pantheon.

———, and Maxine Molyneux. (1982). *The Ethiopian Revolution.* London: Verso.

Hamilton, et al. (1988). Cited under "Socialism, the New Left, and Populism."

Handler, Joel. (1992). "Postmodernism, Protest, and the New Social Movements." *Law and Society Review, 26* (4), 733–824.

Hanlon, Joseph. (1990). *Mozambique: The Revolution under Fire.* London: Zed Books.

Harrison, Bennett, and Barry Bluestone. (1988). *The Great U-Turn.* New York: Basic Books.

Hebdige, Dick. (1982). *Subculture*. London: Methuen.

Heilbroner, Robert. (1989). *The Making of Economic Society*. Englewood Cliffs, NJ: Prentice-Hall.

Hobsbawm, Eric. (1989). *The Age of Empire*. New York: Random House.

———. (1981). *Bandits*. New York: Pantheon.

———. (1979). *The Age of Capital*. New York: NAL Books.

———. (1962). *The Age of Revolution*. New York: NAL Books.

———. (1959). *Primitive Rebels: Studies in Archaic Forms of Social Movements*. New York: Norton.

Hounshell, David. (1984). *From the American System to Mass Production, 1800–1932*. Baltimore: Johns Hopkins University Press.

Howe, John. (1992, November/December). "The Crisis of Algerian Nationalism and the Rise of Islamic Integralism." *New Left Review, 196*, 85–100.

Hyden, Goran, (1980). *Beyond Ujamaa in Tanzania*. Berkeley: University of California Press.

Jameson, Fredric. (1984, July/August). "Postmodernism or the Cultural Logic of Late Capitalism." *New Left Review, 146*, 53–92.

Kandiyoti, Deniz. (1994). "Identity and Its Discontents: Women and the Nation," in Patrick Williams and Laura Chrisman (eds.), *Colonial Discourse and Post-Colonial Theory* (pp. 376–391). New York: Colombia University Press.

Kaplan, Robert. (1994, February). "The Coming Anarchy." *Atlantic Monthly*, pp. 44–76.

Laslett, Peter. (1984). *The World We Have Lost: England before the Industrial Age*. New York: Macmillan.

Lasswell, Harold D., and Daniel Lerner. (1966). *World Revolutionary Elites: Studies in Coercive Ideological Movements*. Boston: M.I.T. Press.

Lipset, Seymour Martin. (1960). *Political Man*. New York: Anchor/Doubleday.

Mandel, Ernest. (1975). *Late Capitalism*. London: New Left Books.

Marty, Martin, and R. Scott Appleby. (1992). *The Glory and the Power: The Fundamentalist Challenge to the Modern World*. Boston: Beacon Press.

Mayer, Margit. (1991). Cited under "Social Movement Theory."

McCoy, Charles Allan. (1982). *Contemporary Isms: A Political Economy Perspective*. New York: Franklin Watts.

Moore, Barrington. (1965). *Social Origins of Dictatorship and Democracy*. Boston: Beacon Press.

Parsons, Talcott, and Neil Smelser. (1956). *Economy and Society*. New York: Free Press.

Patterson, Orlando. (1991). *Freedom: Vol. I. Freedom in the Making of Western Culture*. New York: Basic Books.

Payer, Cheryl. (1982). *The World Bank: A Critical Analysis*. New York: Monthly Review Press.

Petras, James, and Morris Morley. (1975). *The United States and Chile*. New York: Monthly Review Press.

Polanyi, Karl. (1957). *The Great Transformation: The Political and Economic Origins of Our Time*. Boston: Beacon Press.

Przeworski, Adam. (1991). *Democracy and the Market*. New York: Cambridge University Press.

Reich, Robert. (1992). *The Work of Nations*. New York: Vintage Books.

Rhodes, Robert. (1970). *Imperialism and Underdevelopment*. New York: Monthly Review Press.

Riesebrodt, Martin. (1993). *Pious Passion: The Emergence of Modern Fundamentalism in the United States and Iran*. Berkeley: University of California Press.

Scheper-Hughes, Nancy. (1992). *Death without Weeping*. Berkeley: University of California Press.

Schlesinger, Stephen, and Stephen Kinzer. (1983). *Bitter Fruit*. Garden City, NY: Anchor/Doubleday.

Schoenbaum, David. (1966). *Hitler's Social Revolution*. Garden City, NY: Anchor/Doubleday.

Scott, Alan. (1990). *Ideology and the New Social Movements*. London: Unwin Hyman.

Sharpe, Kenneth. (1977). *Peasant Politics: Struggle in a Dominican Village*. Baltimore and London: Johns Hopkins University Press.

Skocpol, Theda. (1989, Spring). "Reconsidering the French Revolution in World-Historical Perspective." *Social Research, 56*, 53–70.

———. (1988, January). "Social Revolutions and Mass Military Mobilization." *World Politics, 40*, 147–168.

———. (1979). *States and Social Revolutions: A Comparative Analysis of France, Russia, and China*. London and New York: Cambridge University Press.

Soja, Edward. (1993). *Los Angeles 1965–1992: The Six Geographies of Urban Restructuring.* Unpublished paper, De Paul University, Chicago.

Spalding, Rose. (1994). *Capitalists and Revolution in Nicaragua: Opposition and Accommodation, 1979–1993.* Chapel Hill: University of North Carolina Press.

Tarrow, Sidney. (1993, March). "Modular Collective Action and the Rise of the Social Movement: Why the French Revolution Was Not Enough." *Politics and Society, 21,* 69–90.

Therborn, Goran. (1977, May/June). "The Rule of Capital and the Rise of Democracy." *New Left Review, 103,* 3–42.

Thurow, Lester. (1993). *Head to Head.* New York: Warner Books.

Tilly, Charles (1978). *From Mobilization to Revolution.* Reading, MA: Addison-Wesley.

Touraine, Alain. (1981). *The Voice and the Eye: An Analysis of Social Movements.* New York: Cambridge University Press.

Van Wolferen, Karel. (1990). *The Enigma of Japanese Power.* New York: Vintage Books.

Wallerstein, Immanuel. (1990). "Culture as the Ideological Battleground of the Modern World System," in Mike Featherstone (ed.), *Global Culture* (pp. 31–55). London, Newbury Park, CA, and New Delhi: Sage.

———. (1980). *The Modern World System II.* New York: Academic Press.

———. (1974). *The Modern World System.* New York: Academic Press.

Walton, John. (1983). *Reluctant Rebels.* New York: Columbia University Press.

Weber, Max. (1958). Cited under "Social Movement Theory."

Willis, Paul. (1990). Cited under "Social Movement Theory."

Wilson, William J. (1987). *The Truly Disadvantaged.* Chicago: University of Chicago Press.

Wolf, Eric. (1982). *Europe and the People without History.* Berkeley and Los Angeles: University of California Press.

———. (1969). *Peasant Wars of the Twentieth Century.* New York: Harper & Row.

Wood, James, and Maurice Jackson. (1982). *Social Movements: Development, Participation and Dynamics.* Belmont, CA: Wadsworth.

Zald, Mayer, and Roberta Ash. (1966, March). "Social Movement Organizations: Growth, Decay, and Change." *Social Forces, 44,* 327–341.

———, and John McCarthy. (1987). Cited in Mayer Zald and John McCarthy under "Social Movement Theory."

Zeitlin, Irving. (1994). *Ideology and the Development of Sociological Theory,* 5th ed. Englewood Cliffs, NJ: Prentice-Hall.

CONSERVATIVE MOVEMENTS AND IDEOLOGIES

Abraham, David. (1986). *The Collapse of the Weimar Republic.* New York: Holmes and Meier.

Bell, Daniel. (ed.). (1964). *The Radical Right.* New York: Doubleday. In this volume:

>   Hofstadter, Richard. "The Pseudo-Conservative Revolt," pp. 75–104.

>   Lipset, Seymour Martin. "The Sources of the Radical Right," pp. 307–372.

Blumenthal, Sidney. (1986). *The Rise of the Counter-Establishment: From Conservative Ideology to Political Power.* New York: Times Books.

Burke, Edmund. (1961). *Reflections on the Revolution in France.* Garden City, NY: Doubleday.

Capps, Walter. (1990). *The New Religious Right.* Columbia: University of South Carolina Press.

Carsten, F. (1967). *The Rise of Fascism.* Berkeley and Los Angeles: University of California Press.

Chalmers, Douglas, Maria do Carmo Campello de Souza, and Atilio Boron. (eds.). (1992). *The Right and Democracy in Latin America.* New York: Praeger.

Clark, Martin. (1984). *Modern Italy, 1871–1982.* New York: Longman.

Cohen, Norman. (ed.). (1990). *The Fundamentalist Phenomenon: A View from Within.* Grand Rapids, MI: Eerdmans.

Conover, P. J., and V. Gray. (1983). *Feminism and the New Right: Conflict over the American Family.* New York: Praeger.

Converse, Philip E. (1964). "Ideology in Mass Publics," in David Apter (ed.), *Ideology and Discontent.* New York: Free Press.

Coontz, Stephanie. (1993). *The Way We Never Were*. New York: Basic Books.

———. (1988). *The Social Origins of Private Life: A History of American Families 1600–1900*. New York: Routledge.

Crahan, Margaret. (1988). "A Multitude of Voices: Religion and the Central American Crisis," in Nora Hamilton, Jeffrey Frieden, Linda Fuller, and Manuel Pastor (eds.), *Crisis in Central America: Regional Dynamics and U.S. Policy in the 1980s* (pp. 227–250). Boulder, CO: Westview Press.

David, Miriam. (1986). "The New Right, Social Order, and Civil Liberties," in Ruth Levitas (ed.), *The Ideology of the New Right* (pp. 167–197). Cambridge, England: Polity Press.

Davis, Flora. (1991). *Moving the Mountain*. New York: Simon & Schuster.

Davis, Mike. (1981, July/August). "The New Right's Road to Power." *New Left Review, 128,* 28–49.

Desai, Radhika. (1994, January/February). "Second Hand Dealers in Ideas: Think Tanks and Thatcherite Hegemony." *New Left Review, 203,* 27–64.

Dorrien, Gary. (1993). *The Neo-Conservative Mind*. Philadelphia: Temple University Press.

Edgar, David. (1986). "The Free or the Good," in Ruth Levitas (ed.), *The Ideology of the New Right*, (pp. 55–79). Cambridge, England: Polity Press.

Edsall, Thomas. (1984). *The New Politics of Inequality*. New York: Norton.

Erwin, Lorna. (1993, August). "Neoconservatism and the Canadian Pro-Family Movement." *The Canadian Review of Sociology and Anthropology, 30,* 401–420.

Friedman, Milton, and Rose Friedman. (1980). *Free to Choose: A Personal Statement*. New York: Harcourt, Brace, Jovanovich.

Gaines, Donna. (1992). *Teenage Wasteland*. New York: HarperCollins.

Garreau, Joel. (1992). *Edge City: Life on the New Frontier*. New York: Anchor Books.

Genovese, Eugene. (1969). *The World the Slaveholders Made*. New York: Pantheon.

Geoghegan, Thomas. (1991). Cited under "Movements in History."

Gerth, Hans. (1940, January). "The Nazi Party: Its Leadership and Composition." *American Journal of Sociology, 45,* 517–541.

Gilder, George. (1981). *Wealth and Poverty*. New York: Basic Books.

Goldwater, Barry. (1960). *The Conscience of a Conservative*. Shepardsville, KY: Victor.

Gottfried, Paul. (1992). *The Conservative Movement*, rev. ed. New York: Twayne.

Gusfield, Joseph. (1963). *Symbolic Crusade: Status Politics and the American Temperance Movement*. Urbana, IL: University of Illinois Press.

Hadden, Jeffrey K. (1993). Cited under "Social Movement Theory."

Hall, Stuart, and Martin Jacques. (eds.). (1983). *The Politics of Thatcherism*. London: Lawrence and Wishart.

Harrison, Bennett, and Barry Bluestone. (1988). *The Great U-Turn*. New York: Basic Books.

Hayek, F. A. von. (1944). *The Road to Serfdom*. London: Routledge.

Hertsgaard, Mark. (1989). *On Bended Knee*. New York: Schocken.

Jessop, Bob, Kevin Bonnett, Simon Bromley, and Tom Ling. (1984, September/October). "Authoritarian Populism, Two Nations and Thatcherism." *New Left Review, 147,* 32–60.

Kirk, Russell. (1953). *The Conservative Mind*. Chicago: Regnery.

Klatsch, R. (1987). *Women of the New Right*. Philadelphia: Temple University Press.

Ladd, Helen F., and Julia B. Wilson. (1983). "Who Supports Tax Limitations: Evidence from Massachusetts Proposition 2 1/2." *Journal of Policy Analysis and Management, 2,* 256–279.

Lasch, Christopher. (1991). *The True and Only Heaven: Progress and Its Critics*. New York: Norton.

———. (1979). *Haven in a Heartless World*. New York: Basic Books.

Leonardi, Robert. (1994, March 31). "Le due anime della destra italiana." Interviewed by Marco Niada in *Il Sole-24 Ore*, No. 86, p. 5.

Levitas, Ruth. (ed.). (1986). *The Ideology of the New Right*. Cambridge, England: Polity Press.

Liebman, Robert C., and R. Wuthnow. (1983). *The New Christian Right: Mobilization and Legitimation*. New York: Aldine.

Lipset, Seymour Martin, and Earl Raab. (1978). *The Politics of Unreason: Right-Wing Extremism in America, 1790–1977*. Chicago: University of Chicago Press.

Lo, Clarence. (1990). *Small Property vs. Big Government: Social Origins of the Property Tax Revolt*. Berkeley and Los Angeles: University of California.

———. (1982). "Countermovements and Conservative Movements in the Contemporary United States." *Annual Review of Sociology, 8,* 107–134.

Mack Smith, Dennis. (1969). *Italy: A Modern History.* Ann Arbor: University of Michigan Press.

Macpherson, C. B. (1962). *The Political Theory of Possessive Individualism: Hobbes to Locke.* London: Oxford University Press.

Mansbridge, Jane. (1986). *Why We Lost the ERA.* Chicago: University of Chicago Press.

Mayer, Arno. (1971). *Dynamics of Counterrevolution in Europe, 1870–1956.* New York: Harper & Row.

McRobbie, Angela. (1994, January/February). "Folk Devils Fight Back." *New Left Review, 203,* 107–116.

Michael, Robert, John Gagnon, Edward Laumann, and Gina Kolata. (1994). *Sex in America: The Definitive Survey.* Boston: Little, Brown.

Moberg, David. (1993, February). "All in the Family." *In These Times,* pp. 18–20.

Moore, Barrington. (1965). *Social Origins of Dictatorship and Democracy.* Boston: Beacon Press.

Müller, Klaus-Jürgen. (1987). Cited under "Fascists, Nazis, Neo-Nazis."

Murray, Charles. (1984). *Losing Ground.* New York: Basic Books.

Nell, E. J. (1984). *Free Market Conservatism.* Oxford, England: Basil Blackwell.

Newman, Katherine. (1988). *Falling from Grace.* New York: Vintage Books.

Phillips, Kevin P. (1990). *The Politics of Rich and Poor: Wealth and the American Electorate in the Reagan Aftermath.* New York: Random House.

———. (1983). *Post-Conservative America.* New York: Random House.

———. (1970). *The Emerging Republican Majority.* New York: Anchor Books.

Piven, Frances Fox, and Richard Cloward. (1982). *The New Class War: Reagan's Attack on the Welfare State and Its Consequences.* New York: Pantheon.

Rieder, Jonathan. (1985). *Canarsie: The Jews and Italians of Brooklyn against Liberalism.* Cambridge, MA: Harvard University Press.

Riesman, David. (1961). *The Lonely Crowd.* New Haven, CT: Yale University Press.

Roberts, Paul Craig. (1984). *The Supply Side Revolution: An Insider's Account of Policymaking in Washington.* Cambridge, MA: Harvard University Press.

Robinson, Michael. (1981). "Television and American Politics 1956–1976," in Morris Janowitz and Paul Hirsch (eds.), *Reader in Public Opinion and Mass Communication* (pp. 98–116). New York: Free Press.

Rossiter, Clinton. (1955). *Conservatism in America: The Thankless Persuasion.* New York: Random House.

Scheper-Hughes, Nancy. (1992). *Death without Weeping.* Berkeley: University of California.

Schlesinger, Arthur, J. (1988). *The Age of Jackson.* Boston: Little, Brown.

Schumpeter, Joseph. (1983). *Capitalism, Socialism and Democracy.* Magnolia, MA: Peter Smith Press. (Originally published in 1942.)

Seidel, Gill. (1986). "Culture, Nation and 'Race' in the British and French New Right," in Ruth Levitas (ed.), *The Ideology of the New Right* (pp. 107–135). Cambridge, England: Polity Press.

Sibley, Mulford Q. (1970). *Political Ideas and Ideologies: A History of Political Thought.* New York: Harper & Row.

Sohn-Rethel, Alfred. (1987). Cited under "Fascists, Nazis, Neo-Nazis."

Stacey, Judith. (1991). *Brave New Families.* New York: Basic Books.

Stockman, David. (1986). *The Triumph of Politics: How the Reagan Revolution Failed.* New York: Harper & Row.

Trimberger, Ellen K. (1978). *Revolution from Above: Military Bureaucrats in Japan, Turkey, Egypt and Peru.* New Brunswick, NJ: Transaction Books.

Viereck, Peter. (1956). *Conservatism from John Adams to Churchill.* Princeton, NJ: Van Nostrand.

von Hayek, F. A. (1944). *The Road to Serfdom.* London: Routledge.

Whyte, William. (1956). *The Organization Man.* New York: Simon & Schuster.

Wilcox, Clyde. (1992). *God's Warriors: The Christian Right in the Twentieth Century.* Baltimore: Johns Hopkins University Press.

Wills, Gary. (1990). *Under God: Religion and American Politics.* New York: Simon & Schuster.

Wolf, Eric. (1982). *Europe and the People without History.* Berkeley and Los Angeles: University of California Press.

———. (1969). *Peasant Wars of the Twentieth Century.* New York: Harper & Row.

Wolfe, Alan. (1981, July/August). "Sociology, Liberalism and the Radical Right." *New Left Review, 128*, 3–25.

Womack, John. (1971). *Zapata and the Mexican Revolution.* New York: Knopf.

Zeitlin, Irving. (1994). Cited under "Social Movement Theory."

VARIETIES OF LIBERALISM AND THE
CIVIL RIGHTS MOVEMENT

Americas Watch Reports. (1987, 1988, 1990). *Guatemala.*

Ascherson, Neal. (1981). *The Polish August.* Harmondsworth, England: Penguin.

Ash, Timothy. (1989). *The Uses of Adversity: Essays on the Fate of Central Europe.* New York: Vintage Books.

Berlin, Isaiah. (1969). *Four Essays on Liberty.* New York: Oxford University Press.

———. (1958, October 31). "Two Concepts of Liberty." Lecture at Oxford University, Oxford, England.

Black, George, with Milton Jamail and Norma Stoltz Chinchilla. (1984). Cited under "Social Movement Theory."

Brown, Elaine. (1994). *A Taste of Power: A Black Woman's Story.* New York: Anchor/Doubleday.

Carson, Clayborne. (1991). *The Eyes on the Prize Civil Rights Reader.* New York: Viking/Penguin.

———. (1981). *In Struggle: SNCC and the Black Awakening of the 1960s.* Cambridge, MA: Harvard University Press.

Coser, Lewis. (1965). *Men of Ideas.* New York: Free Press.

Cruse, Harold. (1984). *The Crisis of the Negro Intellectual: A Historical Analysis of the Failure of Black Leadership.* New York: Morrow.

Dahl, Robert. (1990). *After the Revolution: Authority in a Good Society,* rev. ed. New Haven, CT: Yale University Press.

———. (1983). *Dilemmas of Pluralist Democracy.* New Haven, CT: Yale University Press.

———. (1963). *Preface to Democratic Theory.* Chicago: University of Chicago Press.

Davis, Mike. (1986). "Labor and American Politics," *Prisoners of the American Dream.* London: Verso.

de Tocqueville, Alexis. (1990). Cited under "Movements in History."

DuBois, Ellen. (1991, March/April). "How Women Won the Vote." *New Left Review, 186*, 20–45.

Eagles, Charles W. (ed.). (1986). *The Civil Rights Movement in America.* Jackson: University Press of Mississippi.

Findlay, James F., Jr. (1993). *Church People in the Struggle: The National Council of Churches and the Black Freedom Movement 1950–1970.* New York: Oxford University Press.

Friedman, Milton. (1962). *Capitalism and Freedom.* Chicago: University of Chicago Press.

———, and Rose Friedman. (1980). Cited under "Conservative Movements and Ideologies."

Fukuyama, Francis. (1992). *The End of History and the Last Man.* New York: Free Press.

Garrow, David. (1987). *Bearing the Cross: Martin Luther King, Jr., and the Southern Leadership Conference 1955–1968.* New York: Random House.

Graham, Hugh Davis. (1990). *The Civil Rights Era: Origins and Development of National Policy 1960–1972.* New York: Oxford University Press.

Goldwater, Barry. (1960). Cited under "Conservative Movements and Ideologies."

Gwertzman, Bernard, and Michael T. Kaufman. (eds.). (1990). *The Collapse of Communism.* New York: Times Books/Random House.

Handy, Jim. (1984). *Gift of the Devil.* Boston: South End Press.

Harris, David. (1983). *Dreams Die Hard.* New York: St. Martin's.

Hartz, Louis. (1955). *The Liberal Tradition in America.* New York: Harcourt, Brace & World.

Heilbroner, Robert. (1989). *The Making of Economic Society.* Englewood Cliffs, NJ: Prentice-Hall.

Hofstadter, Richard. (1955). *The Age of Reform.* New York: Knopf.

———. (1948). *The American Political Tradition.* New York: Random House.

hooks, bell, and Cornell West. (1991). *Breaking Bread: Insurgent Black Intellectual Life.* Boston: South End Press.

Kagarlitsky, Boris. (1992, March/April). "Russia on the Brink of New Battles." *New Left Review, 192,* 85–97.

Karabel, Jerome. (1993, March). "Polish Intellectuals and the Origins of Solidarity: The Making of an Oppositional Alliance." *Communist and Post-Communist Studies, 26,* 25–46.

Kelliher, Daniel. (1993, July). "Keeping Democracy Safe from the Masses: Intellectuals and Elitism in the Chinese Protest Movement." *Comparative Politics, 25,* 379–396.

LaFeber, Walter. (1984). *Inevitable Revolutions.* New York: Norton.

Laski, Harold. (1936). *The Rise of European Liberalism.* London: Allen & Unwin.

Laslett, John, and Seymour Martin Lipset. (1974). *End of a Dream: Essays in the History of American Socialism.* Garden City, NY: Anchor Books.

Laurell, Ana Cristina. (1992, July/August). "Democracy in Mexico." *New Left Review, 194,* 33–54.

Lin, Nan. (1992). *The Struggle for Tiananmen: Anatomy of the 1989 Mass Movement.* Westport, CT: Praeger.

Lincoln, C. Eric. (ed.). (1984). *Martin Luther King: A Profile.* New York: Harper & Row.

Lipset, Seymour Martin. (1960). Cited under "Movements in History."

Livingstone, Ken. (1992, March/April). "Can Democracy Survive in Russia?" *New Left Review, 192,* 98–104.

Lowi, Theodore. (1969). *The End of Liberalism.* New York: Norton.

Lu Yuan. (1989, September/October). "Beijing Diary." *New Left Review, 177,* 3–26.

MacDonald, Oliver. (1983, May/June). "The Polish Vortex." *New Left Review, 139,* 5–48.

Macpherson, C. B. (1973). *Democratic Theory.* Oxford, England: Oxford University Press.

———. (1965). *The Political Theory of Possessive Individualism.* London: Oxford University Press.

Malcolm X. (1965). *The Autobiography of Malcolm X.* New York: Penguin.

Manz, Beatrice. (1988). *Refugees of a Hidden War: The Aftermath of Counterinsurgency in Guatemala.* Albany: State University of New York Press.

Marable, Manning. (1991). *Race, Reform and Rebellion: The Second Reconstruction, 1945–1960.* Jackson: University Press of Mississippi.

———. (1985). *Black American Politics: From the Washington Marches to Jesse Jackson.* London: Verso.

Marks, Gary, and Christiane Lemke. (1992). *The Crisis of Socialism in Europe.* Durham, NC: Duke University Press.

McAdam, Doug. (1990). *Freedom Summer.* New York: Oxford University Press.

———. (1982). *Political Process and the Development of Black Insurgency.* Chicago: University of Chicago Press.

McCoy, Charles Allan. (1982). Cited under "Movements in History."

McMillen, Neil. (1991). *The Citizen's Council: Organized Resistance to the Second Reconstruction.* Urbana: University of Illinois Press.

Michnik, Adam. (1985). *Letters from Prison and Other Essays.* Berkeley: University of California Press.

Mill, John Stuart. (1978). *The Collected Works of John Stuart Mill* [J. M. Robson (ed.)]. Toronto: University of Toronto Press. (Originally published in 1859).

Morris, Aldon D. (1984). *The Origins of the Civil Rights Movement: Black Communities Organizing for Change.* New York: Free Press.

Morrison, Minion K. C. (1987). *Black Political Mobilization: Leadership, Power and Mass Behavior.* Albany: State University of New York Press.

North, Liisa. (1985). *Bitter Grounds.* Toronto: Between the Lines Press.

Parks, Rosa. (1992). *Rosa Parks—My Story.* New York: Penguin/Dial.

Petras, James, and Morris Morley. (1975). Cited under "Movements in History."

Phillips, Kevin P. (1970). Cited under "Conservative Movements and Ideologies."

Potel, Jean-Yves. (1982). *The Summer before the Frost.* London: Pluto Press.

Przeworski, Adam. (1991). *Democracy and the Market.* New York: Cambridge University Press.

Robinson, James, and Patricia Sullivan. (eds.). (1991). *New Directions in Civil Rights Studies.* Charlottesville: University of Virginia Press.

Rossiter, Clinton. (1955). *Conservatism in America: The Thankless Persuasion.* New York: Random House.

Rueschemeyer, Dietrich, Evelyne Huber Stevens, and John D. Stephen. (1992). *Capitalist Development and Democracy.* Chicago: University of Chicago Press.

Schlesinger, Stephen, and Stephen Kinzer. (1983). Cited under "Movements in History."

Singer, Daniel. (1990, November 26). "Poland Chooses—What's at Stake." *The Nation, 251,* 635–638.

Smith-Ayala, Emilie. (1991). Cited under "Social Movement Theory."

Therborn, Goran. (1977, May/June). Cited under "Movements in History."

Thompson, Edward. (1963). *The Making of the English Working Class.* New York: Random House.

Walicki, Andrzej. (1991, January/February). "From Stalinism to Post-Communist Pluralism: The Case of Poland." *New Left Review, 185,* 92–121.

Wiarda, Howard, and Harvey F. Kline. (eds.). (1990). *Latin American Politics and Development,* rev. ed. Boulder, CO: Westview Press.

Wills, Garry. (1981). *Explaining America: The Federalist.* New York: Doubleday.

Zinn, Howard. (1964). *SNCC: The New Abolitionists.* Boston: Beacon Press.

SOCIALISM, THE NEW LEFT, AND POPULISM

Abendroth, Wolfgang. (1972). *A Short History of the European Working Class.* London: New Left Books.

Abrahamian, Ervand. (1991, March/April). "Khomeini: Fundamentalist or Populist?" *New Left Review, 186,* 102–119.

Adelman, Jeremy. (1994, January/February). "Post-Populist Argentina." *New Left Review, 203,* 65–91.

Adorno, Theodor, et al. (1993). Cited under "Social Movement Theory."

Anderson, Benedict. (1993, November/December). "Radicalism after Communism in Thailand and Indonesia." *New Left Review, 202,* 3–14.

Arendt, Hannah. (1965). Cited under "Social Movement Theory."

Aronowitz, Stanley. (1988). "Postmodernism and Politics," in Andrew Ross (ed.), *Universal Abandon: The Politics of Postmodernism.* Minneapolis: University of Minnesota Press.

———. (1973). *False Promises.* New York: McGraw-Hill.

Bahro, Rudolf. (1981). *The Alternative in Eastern Europe.* London: Verso.

Barkan, Joanne. (1984). *Visions of Emancipation.* New York: Praeger.

Beccalli, Bianca. (1994, March/April). "The Modern Women's Movement in Italy." *New Left Review, 204,* 86–112.

Berman, Paul. (1993, Winter). "The Future of the American Left." *Dissent, 40,* 97–104.

Bertsh, Gary, and Thomas Ganshow. (1976). *Comparative Communism.* San Francisco: Freeman.

Black, George, with Milton Jamail and Norma Stoltz Chinchilla. (1984). *Garrison Guatemala.* New York: Monthly Review Press.

Blackburn, Robin. (1991). *After the Fall: The Failure of Communism and the Future of Socialism.* London: Verso.

Blackmer, Donald, and Sidney Tarrow. (eds.). (1975). *Communism in Italy and France.* Princeton, NJ: Princeton University Press.

Boggs, Carl. (1995). *The Socialist Tradition: From Crisis to Decline.* New York: Routledge.

———. (1986). *Social Movements and Political Power: Emerging Forms of Radicalism in the West.* Philadelphia: Temple University Press.

Boggs, James. (1963). *The American Revolution: Pages from a Negro Worker's Notebook.* New York: Monthly Review Press.

Boyte, H. C., and F. Riessman. (eds.). (1986). *The New Populism.* Philadelphia: Temple University Press.

Brecher, Jeremy. (1974). *Strike!* New York: Fawcett.

Breines, Wini. (1982). *The Great Refusal: Community and Organization in the New Left: 1962–1968.* New York: Praeger.

Brovkin, Vladimir. (1987). *The Mensheviks after October: Socialist Opposition and the Rise of the Bolshevik Dictatorship.* Ithaca, NY: Cornell University Press.

Carr, E. H. (1982). *Twilight of the Comintern 1930–1935.* New York: Pantheon.

———. (1972). *The Bolshevik Revolution 1917–1923.* London: Macmillan.

———. (1967). "Revolution from Above: Some Notes on the Decision to Collectivize Soviet Agriculture," in Kurt Wolff and Barrington Moore, Jr. (eds.), *The Critical Spirit* (pp. 312–327). Boston: Beacon Press.

Castañeda, Jorge. (1993). *Utopia Unarmed: The Latin American Left after the Cold War.* New York: Knopf.

Castells, Manuel. (1983). *The City and the Grassroots.* Berkeley: University of California Press.

Caute, David. (1988). *Year of the Barricades.* New York: Harper & Row.

———. (1978). *The Great Fear.* New York: Simon & Schuster.

Ceresota, Shirley, and Howard Waitzkin. (1986, June). "Economic Development, Political-Economic System, and Physical Quality of Life." *American Journal of Public Health, 76,* 661–666.

Chaliand, Gerard. (1989). *Revolution in the Third World: Currents and Conflicts in Asia, Africa, and Latin America,* rev. ed. New York: Viking/Penguin.

Clanton, Gene. (1991). *Populism: The Human Preference in America, 1890–1900.* New York: Twayne.

Cohen, Stephen F. (1975). *Bukharin and the Bolshevik Revolution: A Political Biography, 1888–1938.* New York: Random House.

Collier, Ruth Berins, and David Collier. (1991). *Shaping the Political Arena: Critical Junctures, the Labor Movement, and Regime Dynamics in Latin America.* Princeton, NJ: Princeton University Press.

Denitch, Bogdan. (1994). *Ethnic Nationalism: The Tragic Death of Yugoslavia.* Minneapolis: University of Minnesota Press.

Dubofsky, Melvin. (1969). *We Shall Be All: A History of the Industrial Workers of the World.* Chicago: Quadrangle Books.

Dunkerley, James. (1990, July/August). "Reflections on the Nicaraguan Election." *New Left Review, 182,* 33–52.

Dunn, John. (1972). *Modern Revolutions.* Cambridge, England: Cambridge University Press.

Eckstein, Susan. (ed.). (1989). *Power and Popular Protest: Latin American Social Movements.* Berkeley: University of California Press.

Elliot, Gregory. (1993). *Labourism and the English Genius: The Strange Death of Labour England?* London: Verso.

Esping-Andersen, Gøsta. (1985). *Politics against Markets: The Social Democratic Road to Power.* Princeton, NJ: Princeton University Press.

Fagen, Richard, Carmen Diana Deere, and Jose Luis Coraggio. (eds.). (1986). *Transition and Development: Problems of Third World Socialism.* New York: Monthly Review Press. Cited from this collection:

Baumeister, Eduardo, and Oscar Neira Cuadra. "The Making of a Mixed Economy," pp. 171–191.

Bengelsdorf, Carollee. "State and Society in the Transition to Socialism," pp. 192–211.

Burbach, Roger. "The Conflict at Home and Abroad," pp. 79–96.

FitzGerald, E. V. K. "Notes on the Analysis of the Small Underdeveloped Economy in Transition," pp. 28–53.

Marchetti, Peter, S. J. "War, Popular Participation and the Transition to Socialism: The Case of Nicaragua," pp. 303–330.

Farber, Samuel. (1990). *Before Stalinism: The Rise and Fall of Soviet Democracy.* London: Verso.

Fendrich, James Max and Kenneth Lovoy. (1988, October). Cited under "Social Movement Theory."

Fisher, R. (1984). *Let the People Decide: Neighborhood Organizing in America.* Boston: Twayne.

Flacks, Richard. (1971). *Youth and Social Change.* Chicago: Markham.

Fletcher, Roger. (ed.). (1987). *Bernstein to Brandt: A Short History of German Social Democracy.* London: Edward Arnold.

Frank, Andre Gunder. (1972). *Lumpen Bourgeoisie, Lumpen Development.* New York: Monthly Review Press.

Freeman, Jo. (1973). Cited under "Social Movement Theory."

Friedgut, Theodore, and Lewis Siegelbaum. (1990, May/June). "Perestroika from Below: The Soviet Miners' Strike and Its Aftermath." *New Left Review, 181,* 5–32.

Gaines, Donna. (1992). *Teenage Wasteland: Suburbia's Deadend Kids.* New York: HarperCollins.

Garner, Roberta. (1977). *Social Movements in America.* Chicago: Rand-McNally.

———, and Larry Garner. (1994, Spring). "Socialism, Capitalism and Health: A Comment." *Science and Society*, *58*(1), 79–83.

Georgakas, Dan, and Marvin Surkin. (1975). *Detroit: I Do Mind Dying*. New York: St. Martin's.

Gitlin, Todd. (1987). *The Sixties*. Toronto: Bantam.

———. (1980). *The Whole World Is Watching: Mass Media in the Making and Unmaking of the New Left*. Berkeley and Los Angeles: University of California Press.

———, and Hollander, Nanci. (1970). *Uptown: Poor Whites in Chicago*. New York: Harper & Row.

Gorz, Andre. (1985). *Paths to Paradise: On the Liberation from Work*. Boston: South End Press.

———. (1982). Cited under "Social Movement Theory."

Gottlieb, Roger S. (1992). *Marxism 1844–1990: Origins, Betrayal, Rebirth*. New York: Routledge.

Gramsci, Antonio. (1971). *Selections from the Prison Notebooks*. New York: International Publishers.

Gruber, Helmut. (1974). *Soviet Russia Masters the Comintern*. New York: Doubleday.

Gurley, John G. (1975). *Challengers to Capitalism: Marx, Lenin, Stalin and Mao*, 2d ed. New York: Norton.

Hall, Stuart, and Martin Jacques. (1983). *The Politics of Thatcherism*. London: Lawrence and Wishart.

Halliday, Fred. (1989). *From Kabul to Managua*. New York: Pantheon.

———, and Maxine Molyneux. (1982). *The Ethiopian Revolution*. London: Verso.

Hamilton, Nora, Jeffrey Frieden, Linda Fuller, and Manuel Pastor. (eds.). (1988). *Crisis in Central America: Regional Dynamics and U.S. Policy in the 1980s*. Boulder, CO: Westview Press. Note especially:

> Barry, Deborah, Raul Vergara, and Jose Rodolfo Castro. "Low Intensity Warfare: The Counterinsurgency Strategy for Central America," pp. 77–96.

> Crahan, Margaret. "A Multitude of Voices: Religion and the Central American Crisis," pp. 227–250.

Hane, Mikiso. (1988). *Reflections on the Way to the Gallows: Rebel Women in Prewar Japan*. Berkeley and New York: University of California Press and Pantheon.

Harris, David. (1983). *Dreams Die Hard*. New York: St. Martin's.

Healey, Dorothy, and Maurice Isserman. (1990). *Dorothy Healey Remembers*. New York: Oxford University Press.

Heclo, Hugh, and Henrik Madsen. (1987). *Policy and Politics in Sweden*. Philadelphia: Temple University Press.

Hellman, Stephen. (1988). *Italian Communism in Transition: The Rise and Fall of the Historic Compromise in Turin 1975–1980*. New York: Oxford University Press.

Hill, Christopher. (1971). *Lenin and the Russian Revolution*. Harmondsworth, England: Penguin.

Hobsbawm, Eric. (1989). Cited under "Social Movement Theory."

———. (1979). Cited under "Movements in History."

———. (1973). *Revolutionaries*. New York: NAL Books.

———. (1962). Cited under "Movements in History."

Hofstadter, Richard. (1955). Cited under "Varieties of Liberalism and the Civil Rights Movement."

Howard, Dick, and Karl Klare. (1972). *The Unknown Dimension: European Marxism since Lenin*. New York: Basic Books.

Isserman, Maurice. (1987). *If I Had a Hammer: The Death of the Old Left and the Birth of the New Left*. New York: Basic Books.

Jacobs, Harold. (1970). *Weatherman*. Berkeley, CA: Ramparts Press.

Jäggi, Max, Roger Müller, and Sil Schmid. (1977). *Red Bologna*. London: Writers and Readers Publishing Cooperative.

James, Daniel. (1988). *Resistance and Integration: Perónism and the Argentine Working Class, 1946–1976*. New York: Cambridge University Press.

Janoski, Thomas, and Alexander Hicks. (1994). *The Comparative Political Economy of the Welfare State*. New York: Cambridge University Press.

Jenson, Jane, and Rianne Mahon. (1993, September/October). "Representing Solidarity: Class, Gender and the Crisis in Social Democratic Sweden." *New Left Review*, *201*, 76–100.

———, and George Ross. (1988, September/October). "The Tragedy of the French Left: 1945–1988." *New Left Review*, *171*, 5–44.

Jessop, Bob, Kevin Bonnett, Simon Bromley, and Tom Ling. (1989). *Thatcherism: A Tale of Two Nations.* London: Blackwell.
———, et al. (1984). Cited under "Conservative Movements and Ideologies."
Katsiaficas, George. (1987). *The Imagination of the New Left.* Boston: South End Press.
Katz, Donald. (1992). *Home Fires.* New York: HarperCollins.
Klehr, Harvey, and John Earl Haynes. (1992). *The American Communist Movement: Storming Heaven Itself.* New York: Twayne.
Kornai, Janos. (1989). *The Economics of Shortage.* New York: Elsevier–North Holland.
Kornbluh, Joyce. (1964). *Rebel Voices: An IWW Anthology.* Ann Arbor: University of Michigan Press.
LaFeber, Walter. (1984). *Inevitable Revolutions.* New York: Norton.
Lenin, V. I. (1975). "What is to Be Done?" in Robert Tucker (ed.), *The Lenin Anthology.* (pp. 12–114). New York: Norton.
———. (1974). *State and Revolution.* New York: International Publishers.
———. (1960). *Imperialism: The Highest Stage of Capitalism.* Moscow: Progress Publishers.
Lens, Sidney. (1969). *Radicalism in America.* New York: Thomas Y. Crowell.
Leys, Colin. (1994, March/April). "Confronting the African Tragedy." *New Left Review, 204,* 33–47.
Lo, Clarence. (1990). *Small Property versus Big Government: Social Origins of the Property Tax Revolt.* Berkeley and Los Angeles: University of California Press.
———. (1982). Cited under "Social Movement Theory."
Lowi, Theodore. (1969). Cited under "Varieties of Liberalism and the Civil Rights Movement."
Mallet, Serge. (1975). *Essays on the New Working Class.* St. Louis: Telos Press.
Marcuse, Herbert. (1961). *Soviet Marxism: A Critical Analysis.* New York: Vintage Books/Random House.
McAdam, Doug, and Dieter Rucht. (1993, July). "The Cross-National Diffusion of Movement Ideas." *Annals of the American Academy of Political and Social Science, 528,* 56–74.
McClellan, David. (ed.). (1977). *Karl Marx: Selected Writings.* Oxford: Oxford University Press.
———. (1971). *The Thought of Karl Marx.* New York: Harper & Row.
Medvedev, Roy. (1977). *On Socialist Democracy.* New York: Norton.
Miliband, Ralph. (1969). *The State in Capitalist Society.* London: Weidenfeld and Nicolson.
Miller, James. (1987). *Democracy Is in the Streets: From Port Huron to the Siege of Chicago.* New York: Simon & Schuster.
Milner, Henry. (1989). *Sweden: Social Democracy in Practice.* New York: Oxford University Press.
Mollenkopf, John. (1983). *The Contested City.* Princeton, NJ: Princeton University Press.
Moore, Barrington. (1965). Cited under "Movements in History."
Navarro, Vicente. (1993, Spring). "Has Socialism Failed? Health Indicators under Capitalism and Socialism." *Science and Society, 57*(1), 6–30.
Padgett, Stephen, and William Paterson. (1991, March/April). "The Rise and Fall of the West German Left." *New Left Review, 186,* 46–77.
Parkin, Francis. (1968). *Middle-Class Radicalism: The Social Bases of the British Campaign for Nuclear Disarmament.* Manchester, England: University of Manchester Press.
Payer, Cheryl. (1982). Cited under "Movements in History."
Perlman, Janice. (1979). *The Myth of Marginality: Urban Poverty and Politics in Rio de Janeiro.* Berkeley: University of California Press.
———. (1976). "Grassrooting the System." *Social Policy, 7* (2), 4–20.
Petras, James, and Morris Morley. (1975). *The United States and Chile.* New York: Monthly Review Press.
Phillips, Kevin P. (1990). Cited under "Conservative Movements and Ideologies."
———. (1970). Cited under "Varieties of Liberalism and the Civil Rights Movement."
Piven, Frances Fox, and Richard Cloward. (1977). *Poor People's Movements: Why They Succeed, How They Fail.* New York: Pantheon.
Pontusson, J. (1987, September/October). "Radicalization and Retreat in Swedish Social Democracy." *New Left Review, 165,* 5–33.
Przeworski, Adam. (1991). Cited under "Movements in History."
———. (1987). *Capitalism and Social Democracy.* New York: Cambridge University Press.

Ranis, Peter. (1993). *Argentine Workers: Perónism and Contemporary Class Consciousness*. Pittsburgh, PA: University of Pittsburgh Press.

Reich, Robert. (1992). Cited under "Social Movement Theory."

Richmond, Al. (1972). *A Long View from the Left*. New York: Delta Books.

Ridgeway, James. (1990). *Blood in the Face*. New York: Thunder's Mouth Press.

Rieder, Jonathan. (1985). Cited under "Conservative Movements and Ideologies."

Robinson, Cedric. (1983). *Black Marxism: The Making of the Black Radical Tradition*. London: Zed Books.

Sader, Emir, and Ken Silverstein. (1991). *Without Fear of Being Happy: Lula, the Workers Party and Brazil*. London: Verso.

Sale, Kirkpatrick. (1973). *SDS*. New York: Random House.

Sassoon, Donald. (1981). *The Strategy of the Italian Communist Party: From the Resistance to the Historic Compromise*. New York: St. Martin's.

Sayres, Sohnya. (ed.). (1984). *The Sixties, without Apology*. Minneapolis: University of Minnesota Press.

Singer, Daniel. (1988). *Is Socialism Doomed? The Meaning of Mitterand*. New York: Oxford University Press.

Smith, Martin, and Joanna Spear. (1992). *The Changing Labour Party*. London and New York: Routledge.

Squires, Gregory, Larry Bennett, Kathleen McCourt, and Philip Nyden. (1987). *Chicago: Race, Class, and the Response to Urban Decline*. Philadelphia: Temple University Press.

Stacey, Judith. (1991). *Brave New Families*. New York: Basic Books.

———. (1983). *Patriarchy and Socialist Revolution in China*. Berkeley: University of California Press.

Tarrow, Sidney. (1991). Cited under "Social Movement Theory."

———. (1989). Cited under "Social Movement Theory."

Taylor, J. M. (1979). *Eva Perón: The Myths of a Woman*. Chicago: University of Chicago Press.

Thompson, E. P. (1963). *The Making of the English Working Class*. New York: Random House.

Thurow, Lester. (1993). *Head to Head*. New York: Times-Warner.

Tilton, Tim. (1990). *The Political Theory of Swedish Social Democracy*. New York: Oxford University Press.

Tucker, Robert. (ed.). (1975). *The Lenin Anthology*. New York: Norton.

———. (1973). *Stalin as Revolutionary*. New York: Norton.

Vilas, Carlos. (1986). *The Sandinisata Revolution*. New York: Monthly Review Press.

Walton, John. (1983). Cited under "Movements in History."

Weinstein, Deena. (1991). *Heavy Metal*. New York: Free Press.

West, Cornell. (1991). *The Ethical Dimensions of Marxist Thought*. New York: Monthly Review Press.

Wiarda, Howard, and Harvey Kline. (eds.). (1990). Cited under "Varieties of Liberalism and the Civil Rights Movement."

Wickham-Crowley, Timothy. (1992). *Guerrillas and Revolution in Latin America*. Princeton, NJ: Princeton University Press.

Willis, Paul. (1990). Cited under "Social Movement Theory."

Wohlforth, Tim. (1989, November/December). "The Sixties in America." *New Left Review, 178*, 105–123.

Wolf, Eric. (1969). *Peasant Wars of the Twentieth Century*. New York: Harper & Row.

Wright, Erik Olin. (1994). *Interrogating Inequality: Essays on Class Analysis, Socialism and Marxism*. London: Verso.

Zeitlin, Maurice. (1967). *Revolutionary Politics and the Cuban Working Class*. Princeton, NJ: Princeton University Press.

MOVEMENTS OF RELIGIOUS ORIENTATION

Abrahamian, Ervand. (1991, March/April). Cited under "Movements in History."

Ahmed, Leila. (1992). *Women and Gender in Islam*. New Haven, CT: Yale University Press.

Arjomand, Said A. (1988a). *The Turban for the Crown*. New York: Oxford University Press.

———. (1988b). *Authority and Political Culture in Shi'ism.* Albany: State University of New York Press.

Bell, Daniel. (ed.). (1964). *The Radical Right.* New York: Doubleday.

Boff, Leonardo, and Clodovis Boff. (1987). *Introducing Liberation Theology.* Maryknoll, NY: Orbis Books.

Boyer, Paul. (1992). *When Time Shall Be No More.* Cambridge, MA: Harvard University Press.

Bruce, S. (1990, December). "Modernity and Fundamentalism: The New, Christian Right in America." *The British Journal of Sociology, 41,* 477–496.

———. (1984). *One Nation under God? Observations on the New Christian Right in America.* Belfast, Ireland: Queens University, Department of Social Studies.

Burnham, Walter Dean. (1981). "The 1980 Earthquake: Realignment, Reaction, or What?" in Thomas Ferguson and Joel Rogers (eds.), *The Hidden Election* (pp. 98–140). New York: Random House; especially Appendix A, "Social Stress and Political Response: Religion and the 1980 Election," pp. 132–139.

Campo, Juan. (1991). *The Other Side of Paradise.* Columbia: University of South Carolina Press.

Capps, Walter. (1990). *The New Religious Right.* Columbia: University of South Carolina Press.

Carlson, Jeffrey, and Robert Ludwig. (eds.). (1993). *Jesus and Faith.* Maryknoll, NY: Orbis Books.

Cassel, Douglass. (1994, August 12). "Three 'Heretics' and the Cultures that Shape Their Lives." *Chicago Tribune,* sec. 1, p. 21, col. 1.

Cohen, Norman J. (1990). *The Fundamentalist Phenomenon: A View from Within, A Response from Without.* Grand Rapids, MI: Eerdmans. Note:

Hassan, Riffat. "The Burgeoning of Islamic Fundamentalism: Toward the Understanding of the Phenomenon," pp. 151–171.

Hunter, James Davison. "Fundamentalism in Its Global Contours," pp. 56–73. [Quotations on pp. 58–59.]

Crahan, Margaret. (1988). Cited under "Conservative Movements and Ideologies."

Dekmejian, R. Hrair. (1985). *Islam in Revolution.* Syracuse, NY: Syracuse University Press.

Denitch, Bogdan. (1994). Cited under "Nationalism."

de Tocqueville, Alexis. (1990). Cited under "Movements in History."

Embree, Ainslie. (1990). *Utopias in Conflict: Religion and Nationalism in Modern India.* Berkeley: University of California Press.

Esposito, John. (ed.). (1983). *Voices of Resurgent Islam.* New York: Oxford University Press.

Eve, Raymond, and Francis Harrold. (1990). *The Creationist Movement in America.* New York: Twayne.

Fern, D. W. (ed.). (1987). *Third World Liberation Theologies.* Maryknoll, NY: Orbis Books.

Fichter, Joseph. (ed.). (1983). *Alternatives to American Mainline Churches.* Barrytown, NY: Unification Theological Seminary.

Fields, Karen. (1985). *Revival and Rebellion in Colonial Central Africa.* Princeton, NJ: Princeton University Press.

Findlay, James F. (1993). Cited under "Varieties of Liberalism and the Civil Rights Movement."

Fleet, Michael. (1985). *The Rise and Fall of Chilean Christian Democracy.* Princeton, NJ: Princeton University Press.

Freire, Paolo. (1970). *Pedagogy of the Oppressed.* New York: Seabury.

Galanter, Marc. (1989). *Cults, Faith, Healing and Coercion.* New York: Oxford University Press.

Geertz, Clifford. (1971). *Islam Observed: Religious Development in Morocco and Indonesia.* Chicago: University of Chicago Press.

Green, John, James Guth, and Kevin Hill. (1993, February). "Faith and Election: The Christian Right in Congressional Campaigns 1978–1988." *The Journal of Politics, 55,* 80–91.

Gusfield, Joseph. (1963). *Symbolic Crusade: Status Politics and the American Temperance Movement.* Urbana: University of Illinois Press.

Gutierrez, Gustavo. (1988). *A Theology of Liberation.* Maryknoll, NY: Orbis Books.

Hadden, Jeffrey K. (1993, May). "The Rise and Fall of American Televangelism." *Annals of the American Academy of Political and Social Science: Vol. 527. Religion in the Nineties,* Wade Clark Roof (ed.), pp. 113–130.

Hatem, Mervat. (1985, Fall). "Conservative Patriarchal Modernization in the Arabian Gulf." *Contemporary Marxism, 11,* 96–109.

Hill, Christopher. (1972). *The World Turned Upside Down: Radical Ideas during the English Revolution.* New York: Penguin.

Hill, Samuel, and Dennis Owen. (1982). *The New Political Right in America.* Nashville, TN: Parthenon Press.

Hiro, Dilip. (1989). *Holy Wars.* New York: Routledge.

Howe, John. (1992, November/December). "The Crisis of Algerian Nationalism and the Rise of Islamic Integralism. *New Left Review, 196,* 85–100.

Jelen, Ted. (1993, February). "The Political Consequences of Religious Group Attitudes." *The Journal of Politics, 55,* 178–190.

———. (1992, August). "Political Christianity: A Contextual Analysis." *American Journal of Political Science, 36,* 692–714.

———, and Clyde Wilcox. (1992). "The Effects of Religious Self-Identification on Support for the New Christian Right: An Analysis of Political Activists." *The Social Science Journal, 29* (2), 199–210.

Jones, Rick. (1992). Communication on community organizing in El Salvador, DePaul University, Chicago.

Jorstad, Erling. (1990). *Holding Fast/Pressing On: Religion in America in the 1980s.* New York: Praeger.

Kabbani, Rana. (December 1992/January 1993). "Gender Jihad." *Spare Rib, 239,* 35–41.

Keller, Catherine. (1994). "The Jesus of History and the Feminism of Theology," in Jeffrey Carlson and Robert Ludwig (eds.), *Jesus and Faith.* Maryknoll, NY: Orbis Books.

Kolko, Gabriel. (1988). Cited under "Nationalism."

Lancaster, Roger Nelson. (1988). *Thanks to God and the Revolution: Popular Religion and Class Consciousness in the New Nicaragua.* New York: Columbia University Press.

Lasch, Christoper. (1965). "Jane Addams: The College Woman and the Family Claim," *The New Radicalism in America.* New York: Random House/Vintage Books.

Leonardi, Robert, and Douglas A. Wertman. (1989). *Italian Christian Democracy: The Politics of Dominance.* New York: St. Martin's.

Lerner, Daniel. (1958). Cited under "Social Movement Theory."

Lernoux, Penny. (1990). *People of God: The Struggle for World Catholicism.* New York: Viking/Penguin.

———. (1982). *Cry of the People: The Struggle for Human Rights in Central America—The Catholic Church in Conflict with U.S. Policy.* New York: Viking/Penguin.

Levine, Daniel. (1992). *Popular Voices in Latin American Catholicism.* Princeton, NJ: Princeton University Press.

Luker, Kristin, (1984). Cited under "Social Movement Theory."

Mainwaring, Scott, and Alexander Wilde. (1989). *The Progressive Church in Latin America.* South Bend, IN: University of Notre Dame Press.

Marty, Martin. (1984). *Pilgrims in Their Own Land.* Boston: Little, Brown.

———, and R. Scott Appleby. (1992). *The Glory and the Power: The Fundamentalist Challenge to the Modern World.* Boston: Beacon Press.

Menchu, Rigoberta. (1984). *I, Rigoberta Menchu: An Indian Woman in Guatemala* [Elizabeth Burgos-Debray (ed.)]. London: Verso.

Mernissi, Fatima. (1991). *The Veil and the Male Elite: A Feminist Interpretation of Women's Rights in Islam.* New York: Addison-Wesley.

Michael, Robert, et al. (1994). Cited under "Conservative Movements and Ideologies."

Moaddel, Mansoor. (1993). *Class, Politics and Ideology in the Iranian Revolution.* New York: Columbia University Press.

Mortimer, Edward. (1982). *Faith and Power: The Politics of Islam.* New York: Random House.

Munson, Henry, Jr. (1988). *Islam and Revolution in the Middle East.* New Haven, CT: Yale University Press.

New York Times. (1993, April 16). "Christian Coalition and New York Schools," p. A1:4.

——— (1993, February 11). "Non-renewal of Fernandez Contract," p. A1:5.

Newberg, Paula. (1994, August 7). "A Novel Forces Bangladesh to Weight Its Future as a Secular State." *Los Angeles Times,* sec. M, p. 2, col. 1.

Nielsen, Niels. (1993). *Fundamentalism, Mythos, and World Religions*. Albany: State University of New York Press.

O'Duffy, Brendan. (1993). In John McGarry and Brendan O'Leary. Cited under "Nationalism."

Parks, Rosa. (1992). Cited under "Social Movement Theory."

Perry, James. (1994, July 19). "The Christian Coalition Crusades to Broaden Its Rightist Political Base." *Wall Street Journal*, 75 (194), sec. A1, p. 1, col. 1.

Poloma, Margaret. (1982). *The Charismatic Movement: Is There a New Pentecost?* New York: Twayne.

Pope, Liston. (1965). *Millhands and Preachers*. New Haven, CT: Yale University Press.

Riesebrodt, Martin. (1993). *Pious Passion: The Emergence of Modern Fundamentalism in the U.S. and Iran*. Berkeley: University of California Press.

Robinson, Michael. (1981). Cited under "Conservative Movements and Ideologies."

Scheper-Hughes, Nancy. (1992). *Death without Weeping*. Berkeley: University of California Press.

Simpson, John. (1983). "Moral Issues and Status Politics," in Robert Liebman and Robert Wuthnow (eds.), *The New Christian Right*. New York: Aldine.

Singh, Gurharpal. (1993). Cited in John McGarry and Brendan O'Leary under "Nationalism."

Skocpol, Theda. (1982, May). "Rentier State and Shi'a Islam in the Iranian Revolution." *Theory and Society*, 11 (3), 265–283.

Smith, Christian. (1992). *The Emergence of Liberation Theology: Radical Religion and Social Movement Theory*. Chicago: University of Chicago Press.

Smith-Ayala, Emilie. (1991). Cited under "Social Movement Theory."

Stacey, Judith. (1991). *Brave New Families*. New York: Basic Books.

Stoll, David. (1990). *Is Latin America Turning Protestant? The Politics of Evangelical Growth*. Berkeley: University of California Press.

Thompson, E. P. (1963). Cited under "Socialism, the New Left, and Populism."

Vanaik, Achin. (1992, November/December). "Reflections on Communalism and Nationalism in India." *New Left Review*, 196, 43–63.

Watt, William. (1988). *Islamic Fundamentalism and Modernity*. London: Routledge.

Weber, Max. (1963). *Sociology of Religion*. Boston: Beacon Press.

———. (1958). *The Protestant Ethic and the Spirit of Capitalism*. New York: Scribner.

Wilcox, Clyde. (1992). *God's Warriors: The Christian Right in the Twentieth Century*. Baltimore: Johns Hopkins University Press.

Wills, Garry. (1990). *Under God: Religion and American Politics*. New York: Simon & Schuster.

Zald, Mayer, and John McCarthy. (1987). Cited in Mayer Zald and John McCarthy under "Social Movement Theory."

Zeitlin, Irving. (1994). Cited under "Social Movement Theory."

NATIONALISM

Anderson, Benedict. (1992, May/June). "The Last Empires: New World Disorder." *New Left Review*, 193, 3–13.

———. (1991). *Imagined Communities: Reflections on the Origin and Spread of Nationalism*. London: Verso.

Balibar, Etienne, and Immanuel Wallerstein. (1991). *Race, Nation, Class: Ambiguous Identities*. London: Routledge, Chapman and Hall.

Birch, Anthony. (1989). *Nationalism and National Integration*. London: Unwin Hyman.

Camilleri, Joseph, and Jim Falk. (1993). *The End of Sovereignty: The Politics of a Shrinking and Fragmenting World*. Brookfield, UT: Edward Elgar.

Chaliand, Gerard. (1989). Cited under "Social Movement Theory."

Chandler, David. (1994, May/June). "Epitaph for the Khmer Rouge?" *New Left Review*, 205, 87–99.

———. (1992). *Brother Number One: A Political Biography of Pol Pot*. Boulder, CO: Westview Press.

Clark, Martin. (1984). Cited under "Conservative Movements and Ideologies."

Coakley, John. (ed.). (1992). *The Social Origins of Nationalist Movements*. London: Sage.

Davidson, Basil. (1992). *The Black Man's Burden: Africa and the Curse of the Nation State.* New York: Random House.

Denitch, Bogdan. (1994). *Ethnic Nationalism: The Tragic Death of Yugoslavia.* Minneapolis: University of Minnesota Press.

Fagen, Richard, Carmen Diana Deere, and Jose Luis Coraggio. (1986). *Transition and Development.* New York: Monthly Review Press.

Fanon, Frantz. (1967). *The Wretched of the Earth.* Harmondsworth, England: Penguin.

Farkas, Richard. (1994). "The Nineties: Post-Communist Challenges," in Lawrence Graham, Richard Farkas, Robert Grady, Jorgen Rasmussen, and Taketsugu Tsurutani (eds.), *Politics and Government,* 3d ed. Chatham, NJ: Chatham House.

Febvre, Lucien, and Henri-Jean Martin. (1976). *The Coming of the Book: The Impact of Printing, 1450–1800.* London: New Left Editions.

Frank, Andre Gunder. (1981). Cited under "Movements in History."

Gellner, Ernst. (1983). *Nations and Nationalism.* Ithaca, NY: Cornell University Press.

Goodwin, Jeff, and Theda Skocpol. (1989). Cited under "Movements in History."

Gottlieb, Gidon. (1993). *Nation against State.* New York: Council on Foreign Relations Press.

Greenfeld, Liah. (1992). *Nationalism: Five Roads to Modernity.* Cambridge, MA: Harvard University Press.

Gurr, Ted Robert. (1993). *Minorities at Risk.* Washington, DC: United States Institute of Peace Press.

Haim, Sylvia. (ed). (1976). *Arab Nationalism, an Anthology,* 2d ed. Berkeley and Los Angeles: University of California Press.

Halliday, Fred. (1989). *From Kabul to Managua.* New York: Pantheon.

———, and Maxine Molyneux. (1982). Cited under "Movements in History."

Harris, Nigel. (1990). *National Liberation.* New York: St. Martin's.

Hobsbawn, Eric. (1992). *Nations and Nationalism since 1780,* 2d ed. New York: Cambridge University Press.

———. (1989). *The Age of Empire.* New York: Random House.

———. (1979). *The Age of Capital 1848–1875.* New York: NAL Books.

———. (1962). *The Age of Revolution 1789–1848.* New York: NAL Books.

———, and Terence Ranger. (eds). (1992). *The Invention of Tradition.* New York: Cambridge University Press.

Hockenos, Paul. (1994a). *Free to Hate: The Rise of the Right in Postcommunist Eastern Europe.* New York: Routledge.

———. (1994b, May 2). "Danube Blues." *In These Times,* 18 (2), 27–28.

Horowitz, Donald. (1992). *Immigration and Group Relations in France and America.* New York: New York University Press.

Howe, John. (1992, November/December). "The Crisis of Algerian Nationalism and the Rise of Islamic Integralism." *New Left Review,* 196, 85–100.

Kaldor, Mary. (1993, January/February). "Yugoslavia and the New Nationalism." *New Left Review,* 197, 96–112.

Kolko, Gabriel. (1988). *Confronting the Third World.* New York: Pantheon.

Laqueur, Walter. (1993). *Black Hundred: The Rise of the Extreme Right in Russia.* New York: HarperCollins.

Laurell, Ana Cristina. (1992, July/August). "Democracy in Mexico." *New Left Review,* 194, 33–54.

Leonardi, Robert, and R. Nanetti. (1994). *Tuscany in Europe.* London: Pinter.

Lerner, Daniel. (1958). Cited under "Social Movement Theory."

Levin, Michael. (ed). (1993). *Ethnicity and Aboriginality: Case Studies in Ethnonationalism.* Toronto: University of Toronto Press. In this volume:

Asch, Michael. "Aboriginal Self-Government and Canadian Constitutional Identity," pp. 29–52.

Levin, Michael. "Biafra and Bette: Ethnonationalism and Self-Determination in Nigeria," pp. 154–167.

Macklem, Patrick. "Ethnonationalism, Aboriginal Identities, and the Law," pp. 9–28.

Levin, Michael (*cont.*):

Tanner, Adrian. "History and Culture in the Generation of Ethnic Nationalism," pp. 75–96.

Tremblay, Marc-Adelard. "Ethnic Profile, Historical Processes, and the Cultural Identity Crisis among Quebeckers of French Descent," pp. 111–126.

Leys, Colin. (1994, March/April). "Confronting the African Tragedy." *New Left Review, 204,* 33–47.

Lijphart, A. (1977). *Democracy in Plural Societies: A Comparative Exploration.* New Haven, CT: Yale University Press.

Mack Smith, Dennis. (1969). Cited under "Conservative Movements and Ideologies."

Magas, Branka. (1993). *The Destruction of Yugoslavia.* London: Verso.

Malek, Mohammed. (1989, May/June). "Kurdistan in the Middle East Conflict." *New Left Review, 175,* 79–94.

McGarry, John, and Brendan O'Leary. (eds.). (1993). *The Politics of Ethnic Conflict Regulation: Case Studies of Protracted Ethnic Conflicts.* London and New York: Routledge. In this volume:

Adam, Herbert, and Kogila Moodley. "South Africa: The Opening of the Apartheid Mind," pp. 226–250.

Keating, Michael. "Spain: Peripheral Nationalism and State Response," pp. 204–225.

Lemarchand, René. "Burundi in Comparative Perspective: Dimensions of Ethnic Strife," pp. 151–171.

Lievan, Dominic, and John McGarry. "Ethnic Conflict in the Soviet Union and Its Successor States," pp. 62–83.

Mauzy, Diane. "Malaysia: Malay Political Hegemony and 'Coercive Consociationalism,' " pp. 106–127.

McGarry, John, and Brendan O'Leary. "Introduction: The Macropolitical Regulation of Ethnic Conflict," pp. 1–40.

O'Duffy, Brendan. "Containment or Regulation? The British Approach to Ethnic Conflict in Northern Ireland," pp. 128–150.

Premdas, Ralph R. "Balance and Ethnic Conflict in Fiji," pp. 251–274.

Schöpflin, George. "The Rise and Fall of Yugoslavia," pp. 172–203.

Singh, Gurharpal. "Ethnic Conflict in India: A Case Study of the Punjab," pp. 84–105.

Moore, Barrington. (1965). Cited under "Movements in History."

Nairn, Tom. (1988). *The Enchanted Glass: Britain and Its Monarchy.* London: Radius.

O'Donnell, Guillermo. (1979). *Modernization and Bureaucratic Authoritarianism.* Berkeley: University of California Press.

Reich, Robert. (1992). *The Work of Nations.* New York: Vintage Books.

Rock, David. (1993). *Authoritarian Argentina: The Nationalist Movement, Its History and Its Impact.* Berkeley: University of California Press.

Saul, John. (1991, July/August). "South Africa: Between 'Barbarism' and 'Structural Reform.' " *New Left Review, 188,* 3–44.

Skocpol, Theda. (1988, January). Cited under "Movements in History."

Smith, Anthony D. (1986). *The Ethnic Origins of Nations.* Oxford, England: Basil Blackwell.

Suny, Ronald. (1990, November/December). "The Revenge of the Past: Socialism and Ethnic Conflict in Transcaucasia." *New Left Review, 184,* 5–34.

Thompson, Mark. (1992). *A Paper House: The End of Yugoslavia.* New York: Vintage Books.

Tibi, Bassam. (1990). *Arab Nationalism: A Critical Enquiry,* 2d ed. New York: St. Martin's. (Ernst Moritz Arndt quotation on pp. 136–137.)

Townson, Michael. (1992). *Mother Tongue and Fatherland: Language and Politics in German.* Manchester, England: Manchester University Press.

Trimberger, Ellen K. (1978). Cited under "Conservative Movements and Ideologies."

Vadney, T. E. (1987). *The World since 1945.* New York: Penguin.

Wallerstein, Immanuel. (1974). Cited under "Movements in History."

Walton, John. (1983). Cited under "Socialism, the New Left and Populism."

Yergin, Daniel, and Thane Gustafson. (1993). *Russia 2010*. New York: Random House.

Žižek Slavoy. (1990, September/October). "Eastern Europe's Republic of Gilead." *New Left Review*, *183*, 50–62.

FASCISTS, NAZIS, NEO-NAZIS

Abraham, David. (1986). *The Collapse of the Weimar Republic*, rev. 2d ed. New York: Holmes and Meier.

Adorno, Theodor W., et al. (1993). Cited under "Social Movement Theory."

Arendt, Hannah. (1977). *Eichmann in Jerusalem: The Banality of Evil*. New York: Viking/Penguin.

———. (1973). *The Origins of Totalitarianism*. New York: Harvest Books.

Bettelheim, Bruno, and Morris Janowitz. (1964). *Social Change and Prejudice*. New York: Free Press.

Cardoza, Anthony L. (1982). *Agrarian Elites and Italian Fascism: The Province of Bologna 1901–1926*. Princeton, NJ: Princeton University Press.

Carsten, F. L. (1967). *The Rise of Fascism*. Berkeley and Los Angeles: University of California Press.

Clark, Martin. (1984). Cited under "Conservative Movements and Ideologies."

Coates, James. (1987). *Armed and Dangerous: The Rise of the Survivalist Right*. New York: Hill and Wang.

Corcoran, James. (1990). *Bitter Harvest: Gordon Kahl and the Posse Comitatus: Murder in the Heartland*. New York: Viking/Penguin.

Denitch, Bogdan. (1994). Cited under "Socialism, the New Left, and Populism."

Erikson, Erik. (1964). *Childhood and Society*, 2d ed. New York: Norton.

Farkas, Richard. (1994). Cited under "Nationalism."

Fields, Barbara. (1990, May/June). "Slavery, Race, and Ideology in the United States of America." *New Left Review, 181*, 95–118.

Fischer, Conan. (1982). *Stormtroopers*. London: Allen & Unwin.

Flynn, Kevin, and Gary Gerhardt. (1989). *The Silent Brotherhood: Inside America's Racist Underground*. New York: Free Press.

Gaines, Donna. (1992). Cited under "Social Movement Theory."

Garner, Larry B. (1974). *Marxism and Idealism in the Political Thought of Antonio Gramsci*. Unpublished doctoral dissertation, Columbia University, New York.

Geoghegan, Thomas. (1991). Cited under "Movements in History."

Gerth, Hans. (1940, January). "The Nazi Party: Its Leadership and Composition." *American Journal of Sociology, 45*, 517–541.

Gillingham, John. (1985). *Industry and Politics in the Third Reich: Ruhr Coal, Hitler, and Europe*. London: Methuen.

Gramsci, Antonio. (1971). Cited under "Social Movement Theory."

Gregor, A. James. (1974). *Interpretations of Fascism*. Morristown, NJ: General Learning Press.

Guerin, Daniel. (1973). *Fascism and Big Business*, 2d ed. Garden City, NY: Anchor Books.

Hamm, Mark S. (1993). *American Skinheads*. Westport, CT: Praeger.

Hitler, Adolf. (1962 edition). *Mein Kampf*. Translated by Ralph Manheim. Boston: Houghton Mifflin.

Hockenos, Paul. (1994a). *Free to Hate*. New York: Routledge.

———. (1994b). "Danube Blues." *In These Times, 18* (2), pp. 27–28.

Kershaw, Ian. (1993). *The Nazi Dictatorship: Problems and Perspectives of Interpretation*. New York: Routledge.

———. (ed.). (1990). *Weimar: Why Did German Democracy Fail?* London: Weidenfeld and Nicolson.

———. (1989, July/August). "The Nazi State: An Exceptional State?" *New Left Review, 176*, 47–67.

———. (1987). *The "Hitler Myth": Image and Reality in the Third Reich*. Oxford: Oxford University Press.

Laqueur, Walter. (1993). *Black Hundred*. New York: HarperCollins.

Lasswell, Harold, and Daniel Lerner. (1966). Cited under "Social Movement Theory."

Laurell, Ana Cristina. (1992, July/August). Cited under "Nationalism."

Mayer, Arno. (1971). *Dynamics of Counterrevolution in Europe, 1870–1956*. New York: Harper & Row.

McLemee, Scott. (1955, May 15). "Public Enemy." *In These Times, 19* (13), pp. 14–19.

Moore, Barrington. (1966). *Social Origins of Dictatorship and Democracy.* Boston: Beacon Press.

Müller, Klaus-Jürgen. (1987). *The Army, Politics and Society in Germany, 1933–1945.* Manchester, England: University of Manchester Press.

Neumann, Franz. (1972). *Behemoth.* New York: Octagon Books. (Originally published in 1942.)

Noakes, Jeremy, and Geoffrey Pridham. (eds). (1990). *Nazism 1919–1945: A History in Documents and Eyewitness Accounts.* New York: Schocken Books.

Nolte, Ernst. (1966). *Three Faces of Fascism.* New York: Holt.

Parliamentary Affairs. (1992, July). *Symposium on the Extreme Right, 45.* Includes Geoffrey Roberts. "Right-wing Radicalism in the New Germany," pp. 327–344.

Posse Comitatus. (1990). "Posse Noose Report," in James Ridgeway, *Blood in the Face.* New York: Thunder's Mouth Press.

Poulantzas, Nicos. (1974). *Fascism and Dictatorship,* French ed. Paris, France: Maspero.

Price, Sid. (1991). Personal communication.

Reich, Robert. (1992). Cited under "Nationalism."

Ridgeway, James. (1990). *Blood in the Face: The Ku Klux Klan, Aryan Nations, Nazi Skinheads, and the Rise of a New White Culture.* New York: Thunder's Mouth Press.

Schoenbaum, David. (1966). *Hitler's Social Revolution.* Garden City, NY: Anchor/Doubleday.

Singer, Daniel. (1991, July). "The Resistible Rise of Jean-Marie Le Pen." *Ethnic and Racial Studies,* [Special issue on migration and migrants in France] *14,* 368–381.

Sohn-Rethel, Alfred. (1987). *The Economy and Class Structure of German Fascism.* London: Free Associates.

Southern Poverty Law Center. (1989). *Hate, Violence and White Supremacy: A Decade Review.* Montgomery, AL: Southern Poverty Law Center.

Speer, Albert. (1970). *Inside the Third Reich.* New York: Macmillan.

Sternhell, Zeev, with Mario Sznajder and Maia Asheri. (1994). *The Birth of Fascist Ideology: From Cultural Rebellion to Political Revolution.* Princeton, NJ: Princeton University Press.

Thurow, Lester. (1993). Cited under "Movements in History."

Togliatti, Palmiro. (1976). *Lectures on Fascism.* New York: International Publishers.

Trimberger, Ellen K. (1978). *Revolution from Above: Military Bureaucrats in Japan, Turkey, Egypt and Peru.* New Brunswick, NJ: Transaction Books.

Trotsky, Leon. (1944). *Fascism: What It Is and How to Fight It.* New York: Pathfinder Press.

University of Colorado, Department of Philosophy. (1952). *Readings on Fascism and National Socialism.* Chicago: Swallow Press. In this volume:

> Huber, Ernst Rudolf. "Constitutional Law of the Greater German Reich," p. 74.

Van Wolferen, Karel. (1990). Cited under "Movements in History."

Weir, Margaret, and Theda Skocpol. (1983, January–April). "State Structure and Social Keynesianism: Responses to the Great Depression in Sweden and the United States." *International Journal of Comparative Sociology, 24* (1–2), 4–29.

Yergin, Daniel, and Gustafson, Thane. (1993). *Russia 2010.* New York: Random House.

Zellner, William W. (1995). *Counter Cultures: Skinhead, Satanism, The Unification Church, KKK, The Church of Scientology, Survivalists.* New York: St. Martin's.

FEMINISM, WOMEN'S MOVEMENTS, MOVEMENTS OF SEXUAL ORIENTATION

I have not attempted to provide a bibliography on feminism as theory or gender studies as a scholarly field, since that would have been an impossibly enormous task. The bibliography concentrates on movements and movement organizations.

Adam, Barry. (1987). *The Rise of a Gay and Lesbian Movement.* Boston: Twayne.

Afshar, Haleh. (ed). (1993). *Women in the Middle East: Perceptions, Realities and Struggles for Liberation.* New York: St. Martin's.

Ahmed, Leila. (1992). Cited under "Movements of Religious Orientation."

Andreas, Carol. (1989, November). "People's Kitchens and Radical Organizing in Lima, Peru." *Monthly Review, 41* (6), 12–21.

———. (1986). *When Women Rebel: The Rise of Popular Feminism in Peru.* Westport, CT: L. Hill Books.

Backhouse, Constance, and David Flaherty. (eds). (1992). *Challenging Times: The Women's Movement in Canada and the United States.* Montreal: McGill-Queen's University Press.

Balser, Diane. (1987). *Sisterhood and Solidarity: Feminism and Labor in Modern Times.* Boston: South End Press.

Bawer, Bruce. (1994, June 13). "Notes on Stonewall." *New Republic, 210,* 24–27.

———. (1993). *A Place at the Table.* New York: Simon & Schuster.

Beccalli, Bianca. (1994, March/April). Cited under "Socialism, the New Left, and Populism."

Berger, Iris. (1992). *Threads of Solidarity: Women in South African Industry, 1900–1980.* Bloomington: Indiana University Press.

Bishop, Brenda S. (1990, November). "From Women's Rights to Feminist Politics: The Developing Struggle for Women's Liberation in Poland." *Monthly Review, 42* (6), 15–34.

Black, Naomi. (1989). *Social Feminism.* Ithaca, NY: Cornell University Press.

Bonepath, Ellen. (ed.). (1982). *Women, Power and Policy.* New York: Pergamon.

Bouchier, David. (1984). *The Feminist Challenge.* New York: Schocken Books.

Bouvard, Marguerite Guzman. (1994). *Revolutionizing Motherhood: The Mothers of the Plaza de Mayo.* Wilmington, DE: Scholarly Resources, Inc.

Brenner, Johanna. (1993, July/August). "The Best of Times, The Worst of Times: U.S. Feminism Today." *New Left Review, 200,* 101–159.

Bridenthal, Renate, Claudia Koonz, and Susan Stuard. (eds.). (1987). *Becoming Visible: Women in European History.* Boston: Houghton Mifflin.

Bunch, Charlotte. (1987). *Passionate Politics: Feminist Theory in Action.* New York: St. Martin's.

Bystydzienski, Jill. (1992). *Women Transforming Politics.* Bloomington: Indiana University Press.

Casinader, Rex, Sepalika Fernando, and Karuna Gamage. (1987). "Women's Issues and Men's Roles: Sri Lankan Village Experience," in Janet Henshall Momsen and Janet G. Townsend (eds.), *Geography of Gender in the Third World.* Victoria, Australia: Hutchinson and State University of New York Press.

Chafetz, Janet Saltzman, and Gary Dworkin. (1986). *Female Revolt: Women's Movements in World and Historical Perspective.* Totowa, NJ: Rowman and Allanheld.

Charlton, Sue Ellen. (1984). *Women in Third World Development.* Boulder, CO: Westview Press.

Cochran, Jo Whitehorse, Donna Langston, and Carolyn Woodward. (eds.). (1991). *Changing Our Power.* Dubuque, IA: Kendall/Hunt.

Cockburn, Cynthia. (1991, Winter). "'Democracy without Women is no Democracy': Soviet Women Hold Their First Autonomous National Conference." *Feminist Review, 39,* 141–148.

Collins, Patricia Hill. (1990). *Black Feminist Thought.* New York and London: Routledge.

Collison, Helen. (1990). *Women and Revolution in Nicaragua.* London: Zed Books.

Coontz, Stephanie. (1988). Cited under "Conservative Movements and Ideologies."

Cruikshank, Margaret. (1992). *The Gay and Lesbian Liberation Movement.* New York and London: Routledge.

Cuba Update

   Cagan, Leslie. (1993, February/March). "AIDS Conference," p. 18.

   Levinson, Sandra. (1994, February). "New Cuban Film Breaks Taboo," p. 23.

   de la Concepcion, Juan Carlos, M.D., Raul Llara, and Sonja de Vries. (1994, February). "Thoughts in Flight," pp. 19–20. (Reprint of letter in February 16, *New York Times.*).

   Reed, Gail. (1993, Summer). "AIDS Update," p. 28.

Davis, Flora. (1991). *Moving the Mountain: The Women's Movement in America since 1960.* New York: Simon & Schuster.

Davis, Mike. (1990). *City of Quartz.* London: Verso.

de Beauvoir, Simone. (1974). *The Second Sex.* New York: Random House.

D'Emilio, John. (1992). *Making Trouble.* New York and London: Routledge.

Duberman, Martin. (1994). *Stonewall.* New York: Plume.

DuBois, Ellen Carol. (1991, March/April). "Woman Suffrage and the Left." *New Left Review, 186*, 20–45.

Echols, Alice. (1989). *Daring to Be Bad: Radical Feminism in America, 1967–1975.* Minneapolis: University of Minnesota Press.

Erwin, Lorna. (1993, August). Cited under "Conservative Movements and Ideologies."

Faludi, Susan. (1991). *Backlash: The Undeclared War against American Women.* New York: Crown.

Fernandez-Kelly, Maria P. (1984). *For We Are Sold: I and My People: Women and Industry in Mexico's Frontier.* Albany: State University of New York Press.

Ferree, Myra Marx, and Beth B. Hess. (1985). *Controversy and Coalition: The New Feminist Movement.* Boston: Twayne.

———, and Patricia Yancey Martin. (eds.). (1995). *Feminist Organizations.* Philadelpia: Temple University Press.

Fisher, Jo. (1994). *Out of the Shadows: Women, Resistance and Politics in South America.* New York: Monthly Review Press.

Freeman, Jo. (1983). Cited under "Social Movement Theory."

———. (1975). *The Politics of Women's Liberation.* New York: McKay.

Friedan, Betty. (1984). *The Feminine Mystique.* New York: Dell. (Originally published in 1963).

Fox-Genovese, Elizabeth. (1991). *Feminism without Illusions: A Critique of Individualism.* Chapel Hill: University of North Carolina Press.

Funk, Nanette, and Magda Mueller. (eds.). (1993). *Gender Politics and Post-Communism.* New York: Routledge.

Gardiner, Judy. (1993). "Women and Pornography." Unpublished paper, University of Illinois, Chicago.

Gelb, Joyce. (1989). *Feminism and Politics: A Comparative Perspective.* Berkeley: University of California Press.

Geoghegan, Thomas. (1991). Cited under "Movements in History."

Gilligan, Carol. (1993). *In a Different Voice: Psychological Theory and Women's Development.* Cambridge, MA: Harvard University Press.

Glenn, Evelyn Nakano. (1992, Autumn). "From Servitude to Service Work: Historical Continuities in the Racial Division of Paid Reproductive Labor." *Signs, 18*, 1–30.

Grant, Judith (1992). "Intimate Work: The Regulation of Female Sexuality and Reproduction." Unpublished paper, American Political Science Association, Los Angeles.

Gray, Francine du Plessix. (1991). *Soviet Women: Walking the Tightrope.* New York: Doubleday.

Hane, Mikiso (1988). Cited under "Socialism, the New Left, and Populism."

Harriss, Barbara, and Elizabeth Watson. (1987). "The Sex Ratio in South Asia," in Janet Henshall Momsen and Janet G. Townsend (eds.), *Geography of Gender in the Third World.* Victoria, Australia: Hutchinson and State University of New York Press.

Hatem, Mervat. (1985, Fall). "Conservative Patriarchal Modernization in the Arabian Gulf." *Contemporary Marxism, 11*, 96–109.

Herdt, Gilbert. (1992). *Gay Culture in America.* Boston: Beacon Press. In this volume:

Herdt, Gilbert. "'Coming Out' as a Rite of Passage: A Chicago Study," pp. 29–67.

Herrell, Richard. "The Symbolic Strategies of Chicago's Gay and Lesbian Pride Day Parade," pp. 225–252.

Hewlett, Sylvia. (1986). *A Lesser Life.* New York: Warner Books.

hooks, bell. (1989). *Talking Back: Thinking Feminist, Thinking Black.* Boston: South End Press.

———. (1984). *Feminist Theory from Margin to Center.* Boston: South End Press.

———. (1981). *Ain't I a Woman: Black Women and Feminism.* Boston: South End Press.

Jay, Karla, and Allen Young. (1972). *Out of the Closets: Voices of Gay Liberation.* New York: Douglas/Links.

Jenson, Jane, and Rianne Mahon. (1993, September/October). Cited under "Socialism, the New Left, and Populism."

Johnson-Odim, Cheryl, and Margaret Strobel. (1992). *Expanding the Boundaries of Women's History: Essays on Women in the Third World.* Bloomington: Indiana University Press.

Kabbani, Rana. (December 1992/January 1993). Cited under "Movements of Religious Orientation."

Kabeer, Naila. (1988, March/April). "Subordination and Struggle: Women in Bangladesh." *New Left Review, 168*, 95–121.

Katzenstein, Mary Fainsod, and Carol McClurg Mueller. (1987). *The Women's Movements of the United States and Western Europe*. Philadelphia: Temple University Press.

Kerr, Clark, and A. Siegel. (1954). "Inter-Industry Propensity to Strike," in Robert Dubin, Arthur Kornhauser, and Arthur Ross (eds.), *Industrial Conflict*. New York: McGraw-Hill.

Kimmel, Michael S. (1993, Fall). "Sexual Balkanization: Gender and Sexuality as the New Ethnicities." *Social Research: Vol. 60. Symposium on What's Left, What's Right*, pp. 571–587.

King, Deborah. (1990). "Multiple Jeopardy, Multiple Consciousness: The Context of a Black Feminist Ideology," in Micheline Malson, Elisabeth Mudimbe-Boyi, Jean O'Barr, and Mary Wyer (eds.), *Black Women in America*, (pp. 265–295). Chicago: University of Chicago Press.

Kuppers, Gaby. (1994). *Compañeras: Voices from the Latin American Women's Movement*. New York: Monthly Review Press.

Lewin, Tamara. (1991, December 18). "Disabled Woman's Care Is Given to Lesbian Partner." *New York Times*, sec. A, p. 26.

Liebman, Marvin. (1992). *Coming Out Conservative: A Founder of the Modern Conservative Movement Speaks Out on Personal Freedom, Homophobia and Hate Politics*. San Francisco: Chronicle Books.

Luker, Kristin. (1984). *Abortion and the Politics of Motherhood*. Berkeley: University of California Press.

Mackie, Vera. (1988, January/February). "Feminist Politics in Japan." *New Left Review, 167*, 53–76.

Mansbridge, Jane. (1986). *Why We Lost the ERA*. Chicago: University of Chicago Press.

Marcus, Eric. (1992). *Making History: An Oral History of the Struggle for Gay and Lesbian Civil Rights 1945–1990*. New York: HarperCollins.

Massell, Gregory. (1968). "Law as an Instrument of Revolutionary Change in a Traditional Milieu: The Case of Soviet Central Asia." *Law and Society Review, 2*, 179–228.

Matteo, Shirley. (ed.). (1993). *American Women in the Nineties: Today's Critical Issues*. Boston: Northeastern University Press. In this volume:

   Kahn, Madeleine. "The Politics of Pornography." pp. 235–252.

Melzer, Sara, and Leslie Rabine. (eds.). (1992). *Rebel Daughters: Women and the French Revolution*. New York: Oxford University Press.

Mernissi, Fatima. (1991). *The Veil and the Male Elite: A Feminist Interpretation of Women's Rights in Islam*. Cambridge, MA: Addison-Wesley.

Miller, Francesca. (1991). *Latin American Women and the Search for Social Justice*. Hanover, NH, and London: University Press of New England.

Molyneux, Maxine. (1991, Winter). "Interview with Anastasia Posadskaya." *Feminist Review, 39*, 133–140.

———. (1990, September/October). "The 'Woman Question' in the Age of Perestroika." *New Left Review, 183*, 23–49.

———. (1986). "Mobilization without Emancipation: Women's Interests, State and Revolution," in Richard Fagen, Carmen Deere, J. L. Coraggio (eds.), *Transition and Development* (pp. 280–302). New York: Monthly Review Press.

Moraga, Cherrie, and Gloria Anzaldua. (eds.). (1983). *This Bridge Called My Back: Writings by Radical Women of Color*. New York: Kitchen Table Press.

Morgan, Robin. (1992). *The Word of a Woman: Feminist Dispatches, 1968–1992*. New York and London: Norton.

———. (ed.). (1984). *Sisterhood Is Global: The International Women's Movement Anthology*. New York: Anchor/Doubleday.

Nash, June, and Maria P. Fernandez-Kelly. (eds.). (1984). *Women, Men and the International Division of Labor*. Albany: State University of New York Press.

New York Times. (1993, February 11). "Non-renewal of Joseph Fernandez Contract," p. A1:5.

Peters, J. S., and Andrea Wolper. (eds.). (1995). *Women's Rights, Human Rights*. New York: Routledge.

Posadskaya, Anastasia. (1992, September/October). "Self-Portrait of a Russian Feminist." *New Left Review, 195*, 3–19.

Pryer, Jane. (1987). "Production and Reproduction of Malnutrition in an Urban Slum in Khulna, Bangladesh," in Janet Henshall Momsen and Janet G. Townsend (eds.), *Geography of Gender in the Third World*. Victoria, Australia: Hutchinson and State University of New York Press.

Radcliffe, Sarah, and Sallie Westwood. (1993). *"Viva": Women and Popular Protest in Latin America*. New York and London: Routledge.

Robinson, Jean C. (1985, March). "Of Women and Washing Machines: Employment, Housework and the Reproduction of Motherhood in Socialist China." *China Quarterly, 101*, 32–57.

Rowbotham, Sheila. (1992). *Women in Movement*. New York and London: Routledge.

———. (1974). *Women, Resistance and Revolution*. New York: Vintage Books.

Rupp, Leila, and Verta Taylor. (1987). *Survival in the Doldrums: The American Women's Rights Movement, 1945 to the 1960s*. New York: Oxford University Press.

Sarti, Cythia. (1989, January/February). "The Panorama of Brazilian Feminism." *New Left Review, 173*. 75–90.

Sawicki, Jana. (1991). *Disciplining Foucault: Feminism, Power, and the Body*. New York: Routledge.

Shilts, Randy. (1982). *The Mayor of Castro Street: The Life and Times of Harvey Milk*. New York: St. Martin's.

Skjeie, Hege. (1991, May/June). "The Uneven Advance of Norwegian Women." *New Left Review, 187*, 79–102.

Smelser, Neil. (1963). Cited under "Social Movement Theory."

Smith, Barbara. (ed.). (1983). *Home Girls: A Black Feminist Anthology*. New York: Kitchen Table Press.

Smith-Ayala, Emilie. (1991). *The Granddaughters of Ixmucané*. Toronto: Women's Press.

Snitow, Ann. (1989, Spring). "Pages from a Gender Diary." *Dissent*, pp. 205–224.

Sorrentino, Constance. (1990, March). "The Changing Family in International Perspective." *Monthly Labor Review* [Special issue on the family], *113* (3), 41–58.

Stacey, Judith. (1991). Cited under "Conservative Movements and Ideologies."

———. (1983). Cited under "Socialism, the New Left, and Populism."

Stamiris, Eleni. (1986, July/August). "The Women's Movement in Greece." *New Left Review, 158*, 98–112.

Stanton, Suzy. (1993). Personal communication.

Stevens, Beth. (1988, September). "Women in Nicaragua." *Monthly Review, 40*(4), 1–18.

Taylor, Verta, and Leila Rupp. (1993, Autumn). "Women's Culture and Lesbian Feminist Activism: A Reconsideration of Cultural Feminism." *Signs, 19*(1), 32–61.

———, and Nancy Whittier. (1992). Cited in Aldon D. Morris and Carol McClurg Mueller under "Social Movement Theory."

Walker, Alice. (1984). *In Search of Our Mothers' Gardens: Womanist Prose*. New York: Harcourt, Brace.

Watson, Peggy. (1993, March/April). "The Rise of Masculinism in Eastern Europe." *New Left Review, 198*, 71–82.

Whittier, Nancy. (1995). *Feminist Generations*. Philadelphia: Temple University Press.

Willis, Ellen. (1993a). *Beginning to See the Light: Sex, Hope and Rock and Roll*. Middletown, CT: Wesleyan University Press.

———. (1993b). *No More Nice Girls: Countercultural Essays*. Hanover, NH: University Press of New England.

Wollstonecraft, Mary. (1975). *A Vindication of the Rights of Women*. New York: Norton. (Originally published in 1792).

Yee, Shirley. (1992). *Black Women Abolitionists: A Study in Activism, 1828–1860*. Knoxville: University of Tennessee Press.

ENVIRONMENTAL MOVEMENTS

Abbey, Edward. (1975). *The Monkeywrench Gang*. New York: Avon.

Adams, Carol. (ed.). (1993). *Ecofeminism and the Sacred*. New York: Continuum.

Adato, Michael, and the Union of Concerned Scientists. (1987). *Safety Second: The NRC and America's Power Plants*. Bloomington: Indiana University Press.

Benton, Ted. (1992, July/August). "Ecology, Socialism and the Mastery of Nature." *New Left Review, 194*, 55–74.

Biehl, Janet. (1991). *Rethinking Eco-Feminist Politics*. Boston: South End Press.

Bookchin, Murray. (1990). *Remaking Society: Pathways to a Green Future.* Boston: South End Press.

Brown, Lester. (1994). *Full House: Reassessing the Earth's Carrying Capacity.* New York: Norton.

Brown, Michael, and John May. (1991). *The Greenpeace Story.* New York: Dorling Kindirsly.

Bullard, Robert. (1990). *Dumping in Dixie: Race, Class, and Environmental Quality.* Boulder CO: Westview Press.

Campbell, John. (1988). *Collapse of an Industry.* Ithaca, NY: Cornell University Press.

Carson, Rachel. (1962). *Silent Spring.* Boston: Houghton Mifflin.

Chicago Tribune

> Goering, Laurie. (1991, April 24). "Foes of Robbins Incinerator United in Opposition and Fears," sec. 2S, p. 3. col. 1.
>
> ———, and Mary Sue Penn. (1992, December 23). "Southern Cook County Environmental Action Coalition and Counter-Demonstrators for Jobs," sec. 2S, p. 3, col. 5.
>
> Rubin, Bonnie Miller. (1993, October 24). "Incinerator Fight in Factory Belt (Summit, IL)," sec. 2C, p. 3, col. 4.

Cockburn, Alexander. (1993, September/October). "'Win-Win' with Bruce Babbit The Clinton Administration Meets the Environment." *New Left Review, 201,* 46–59.

———. (1989, January/February). "Trees, Cows and Cocaine: An Interview with Susanna Hecht." *New Left Review, 173,* 34–45.

Cohen, Bernard. (1983). *Before It's Too Late: A Scientist's Case for Nuclear Power.* New York: Plenum.

Commoner, Barry. (1990). *Making Peace with the Planet.* New York: Pantheon.

Dalton, Russell. (1993). Cited in *Annals* under "Social Movement Theory."

Davis, John, and David Foreman. (1991). *The Earth First Reader: Ten Years of Radical Environmentalism.* Salt Lake City, UT: Peregrine Smith Books.

Davis, Mike. (1993, July/August). "The Dead West: Ecocide in Marlboro County." *New Left Review, 200,* 49–73.

Devall, Bill, and George Sessions. (1985). *Deep Ecology.* Salt Lake City, UT: Peregrine Smith Books.

Diamond, Irene, and Gloria Orenstein. (eds.). (1990). *Reweaving the World: The Emergence of Eco-Feminism.* San Francisco: Sierra Club Books.

Druce, Nell. (1990). *Green Globalism: Perspectives on Environment and Development.* Oxford, England: Third World First.

The Economist. (1989, September 2). [Special issue on the environment and the market].

Ehrenfeld, David. (1978). *The Arrogance of Humanism.* New York: Oxford University Press.

Faber, Daniel. (1993). *Environment under Fire: Imperialism and the Ecological Crisis in Central America.* New York: Monthly Review Press.

Flavin, Christopher. (1987). *Reassessing Nuclear Power: The Fallout from Chernobyl.* Washington, DC: Worldwatch Institute.

Foreman, Dave. (1991). *Confessions of an Eco-Warrior.* New York: New Harmony Books.

———, and Bill Haywood. (eds.). (1987). *Ecodefense: A Field Guide to Monkeywrenching,* 2d ed. Tucson, AZ: Ned Ludd Books.

Fradkin, Philip. (1989). *Fallout: An American Nuclear Tragedy.* Tucson: University of Arizona Press.

Freudenberg, N. (1984). *"Not in Our Backyards!" Community Action for Health and the Environment.* New York: Monthly Review Press.

Fuller, John. (1984). *The Day We Bombed Utah: America's Most Lethal Secret.* New York: NAL Books.

Gallagher, Carole. (1993). *American Ground Zero: The Secret Nuclear War.* Boston: M.I.T. Press.

Gorz, Andre. (1993, November/December). "Political Ecology: Expertocracy versus Self-Limitation." *New Left Review, 202,* 55–67.

———. (1985). *Paths to Paradise.* Boston: South End Press.

Hagen, Carol. (1993). Cited in *Annals* under "Social Movement Theory."

Hecht, Susanna. (1989, January/February). "Chico Mendes: Chronicle of a Death Foretold." *New Left Review, 173,* 47–55.

———, and Alexander Cockburn. (1989). *The Fate of the Forest: Developers, Destroyers and Defenders of the Amazon.* London and New York: Verso.

Hertsgaard, Mark. (1983). *Nuclear Inc: The Men and Money behind Nuclear Power.* New York: Pantheon.

House Subcommittee on Oversight and Investigation. (1980, August). *The Forgotten Guinea Pigs.* 96th Congress, 2d session.

Hulsberg, Werner. (1988). *The German Greens: A Social and Political Profile.* New York: Verso.

Jackson, Cecile. (1995, March/April). "Radical Environmental Myths: A Gender Perspective." *New Left Review, 210,* pp. 124–140.

Jasper, James, and Dorothy Nelkin. (1993). *Animal Crusades.* New York: Free Press.

Kitschelt, Herbert. (1986). "Political Opportunity Structures and Political Protest: Anti-Nuclear Movements in Four Democracies." *British Journal of Political Science, 16,* 57–85.

Levin, Michael. (1993). Cited under "Nationalism."

Lovelock, James. (1988). *The Ages of Gaia: A Biography of Our Living Earth.* New York: Norton.

Luoma, Jon R. (1987, March). "Forests Are Dying but Is Acid Rain Really to Blame?" *Audubon,* pp. 37–51.

Matthiessen, Peter. (1991, February 14). "The Blue Pearl of Siberia." *The New York Review of Books, 38,* 37–47.

Mayer, Margit. (1991). Cited under "Social Movement Theory."

McDermott, Jeanne. (1987). *The Killing Winds: The Menace of Biological Warfare.* New York: Morrow.

Medvedev, Zhores. (1990). *The Legacy of Chernobyl.* New York: Norton.

———. (1979). *Nuclear Disaster in the Urals.* New York: Norton.

Mellor, John. (1988, November 8–13). "The Intertwining of Environmental Problems and Poverty." *Environment, 30* (9), 28–30.

Merchant, Carol. (1992). *Radical Ecology: The Search for a Livable World.* New York: Routledge.

Mitchell, R. C. (1981). "From Elite Quarrel to Mass Movement." *Society, 18*(5), 76–84.

Mottl, Tahi. (1980, June). Cited under "Social Movement Theory."

National Public Radio. (1995, January 31). "Property Rights Associations."

Nelkin, Dorothy. (1971). *Nuclear Power and Its Critics: The Cayuga Lake Controversy.* Ithaca, NY: Cornell University Press.

Ott, Karl O., and Bernard Spinrad. (1985). *Nuclear Energy: A Sensible Alternative.* New York: Plenum.

Paehlke, Robert C. (1989). *Environmentalism and the Future of Progressive Politics.* New Haven, CT: Yale University Press.

Papadikis, Elim. (1984). *The Green Movement in West Germany.* London: Croom Helm.

Parkin, Francis. (1968). *Middle-Class Radicalism: The Social Bases of the British Campaign for Nuclear Disarmament.* Manchester, England: University of Manchester Press.

Parsons, Howard. (1977). *Marx and Engels on Ecology.* Westport, CT: Greenwood.

Peterson, D. J. (1993). *Troubled Lands: The Legacy of Soviet Environmental Destruction.* Boulder, CO: RAND.

Price, Jerome. (1990). *The Antinuclear Movement,* rev. ed. Boston: Twayne/G. K. Hall.

Rensenbrink, John. (1992). *The Greens and the Politics of Transformation.* San Pedro, CA: R. & E. Miles.

Ridgeway, James. (1990). Cited under "Fascists, Nazis, Neo-Nazis."

Robbins, John. (1987). *Diet for a New America.* New Haven, CT: Stillpoint.

Rochon, Thomas. (1988). *Mobilizing for Peace: The Antinuclear Movement in Western Europe.* Princeton, NJ: Princeton University Press.

Sale, Kirkpatrick. (1993). *The Green Revolution: The Environmental Movement since 1962.* New York: Hill and Wang.

Scheffer, Victor. (1991). *The Shaping of Environmentalism in America.* Seattle: University of Washington Press.

Schudson, Michael. (1978). *Discovering the News.* New York: Basic Books.

Schwab, Jim. (1993). *Deeper Shades of Green: The Rise of Blue Collar and Minority Environmentalism in America.* San Francisco: Sierra Club Books.

Shabecoff, Philip. (1993). *A Fierce Green Fire: The American Environmental Movement.* New York: Hill and Wang.

Touraine. Alain, Zsuzska Hegedus, Francois Dubet, and Michael Weviorka. (1982). *Anti-Nuclear Protest: The Opposition to Nuclear Energy in France.* Cambridge, England: Cambridge University Press.

Useem, Bert, and Mayer Zald. (1982). "From Pressure Group to Social Movement: Organizational Dilemmas of the Effort to Promote Nuclear Power." *Social Problems, 30*(2), 144–156. Reprinted in Mayer Zald and John McCarthy. (eds.). (1987). *Social Movements in an Organizational Society* (pp. 273–288). New Brunswick, NJ: Transaction Books. (In-text page numbers refer to the 1987 reprinted article.)

Walsh, Edward. (1988). "New Dimensions of Social Movements: The High-Level Waste-Siting Controversy." *Sociological Forum, 3,* 586–605.

———, Rex Warland, and Clayton Smith. (1993, February). "Backyards, NIMBYs, and Incinerator Sitings: Implications for Social Movement Theory." *Social Problems* [Special issue on environmental justice], *40,* 25–38.

Weinberg, Alvin, and Russ Manning. (1985). *The Second Nuclear Era: A New Start for Nuclear Power.* New York: Praeger.

Worldwatch Paper Series. Miscellaneous, varied dates. Washington, DC: Worldwatch Institute.

Yearly, Steven. (1992, December). "Green Ambivalence about Science: Legal-Rational Authority and the Scientific Legitimation of a Social Movement." *British Journal of Sociology, 43,* 511–532.

CONCLUSIONS

Althusser, Louis. (1971). *Lenin and Philosophy.* London: New Left Books.

Appadurai, Arjun. (1990). "Disjuncture and Difference in the Global Cultural Economy," in Mike Featherstone (ed.), *Global Culture* (pp. 295–310). London, Newbury Park, CA, and New Delhi: Sage.

Aries, Philippe. (1965). *Centuries of Childhood.* New York: Random House.

Aronowitz, Stanley. (1988). Cited under "Social Movement Theory."

Bawer, Bruce. (1994, June 13). Cited under "Feminism, Women's Movements, Movements of Sexual Orientation."

Berman, Marshall. (1982). Cited under "Social Movement Theory."

Beyer, Peter. (1990). "Privatization and the Public Influence of Religion in Global Society," in Mike Featherstone (ed.), *Global Culture* (pp. 373–396). London, Newbury Park, CA, and New Delhi: Sage.

Bluestone, Barry, and Bennett Harrison. (1982). Cited under "Movements in History."

Bookchin, Murray. (1990). Cited under "Environmental Movements."

Bunch, Charlotte, (1987). Cited under "Feminism, Women's Movements, Movements of Sexual Orientation."

Callinicos, Alex. (1990). *Against Post-Modernism: A Marxist Critique.* New York: St. Martin's.

Castañeda, Jorge. (1993). Cited under "Socialism, the New Left, and Populism."

Davis, Mike. (1990). Cited under "Movements in History."

———. (1986). Cited under "Varieties of Liberalism and the Civil Rights Movement."

Denitch, Bogdan. (1994). Cited under "Nationalism."

Edsall, Thomas. (1984). Cited under "Conservative Movements and Ideologies."

Foucault, Michel. (1982). *The Archaeology of Knowledge.* New York: Pantheon.

———. (1979). *Discipline and Punish.* New York: Random House.

———. (1976). Cited under "Movements in History."

Friedman, Debra, and Doug McAdam. (1992). Cited in Aldon D. Morris and Carol McClurg Mueller under "Social Movement Theory."

Fukuyama, Francis. (1992). Cited under "Movements in History."

Gamson, William. (1992). Cited in Aldon D. Morris and Carol McClurg Mueller under "Social Movement Theory."

———. (1975). *The Strategy of Social Protest.* Homewood IL: Dorsey.

Garner, Larry, and Roberta Garner. (1981, Fall). "Problems of the Hegemonic Party: The PCI and the Structural Limits of Reform." *Science and Society, 45*(3), 257–273.

Garner, Roberta. (1994, Winter). "Transnational Movements in Postmodern Societies." *Peace Review, 6*(4), 427–433.

——— and Mayer Zald. (1985). Cited under "Social Movement Theory."

Geoghegan, Thomas. (1994, May 23) and (1991). Cited under "Movements in History."

Gramsci, Antonio. (1971). *Selections from the Prison Notebooks.* New York: International Publishers.

Halliday, Fred. (1989). Cited under "Movements in History."

Handler, Joel. (1992). Cited under "Social Movement Theory."

Harrison, Bennett, and Barry Bluestone. (1988). *The Great U-Turn.* New York: Basic Books.

Heilbroner, Robert. (1989). Cited under "Movements in History."

Herrell, Richard. (1992). Cited in Gilbert Herdt under "Feminism, Women's Movements, and Movements of Sexual Orientation."

Hobsbawm, Eric. (1962) and (1989). Cited under "Movements in History."

Jameson, Fredric. (1988). "Interview with Fredric Jameson," in Andrew Ross (ed.), *Universal Abandon: The Politics of Postmodernism.* Minneapolis: University of Minnesota Press.

———. (1984). Cited under "Movements in History."

Kershaw, Ian. (1989, July/August). Cited under "Fascists, Nazis, Neo-Nazis."

Klandermans, Bert. (1992). Cited under "Social Movement Theory."

Klare, Michael. (1994, June 13). "Armed and Dangerous." *In These Times, 18* (15) 14–19.

Levitas, Ruth. (ed.). (1986). Cited under "Conservative Movements and Ideologies."

Lipset, Seymour M. (1960). *Political Man.* New York: Anchor/Doubleday.

Lo, Clarence. (1990). Cited under "Conservative Movements and Ideologies."

Moberg, David. (1994, April 18–May 1). "In Praise of Taxes." *In These Times, 18* (11), 14–17.

Mottl, Tahi. (1980, June). Cited under "Social Movement Theory."

National Public Radio. (1995, January 31).

———. (1994, June 11).

Opp, Karl Dieter, and Christiane Gern. (1993, October). "Dissident Groups, Personal Networks and Spontaneous Cooperation: The East German Revolution of 1989." *American Sociological Review, 58,* 659–680.

———, and Wolfgang Roehl. (1990, December). "Repression, Micromobilization, and Political Protest." *Social Forces, 69,* 521–547.

Piven, Frances Fox, and Richard Cloward. (1982). Cited under "Conservative Movements and Ideologies."

———, and ———. (1977). Cited under "Socialism, the New Left, and Populism."

Price, Jerome. (1990). Cited under "Environmental Movements."

Proxmire, William. (1994, July 22). Interview on Wisconsin Public Radio.

Przeworski, Adam. (1991). Cited under "Movements in History."

Reich, Robert. (1992). Cited under "Movements in History."

Ross, Andrew. (1988). *Universal Abandon: The Politics of Postmodernism.* Minneapolis: University of Minnesota Press.

Sassen, Saskia. (1994). *Cities in a World Economy.* Thousand Oaks, CA: Pine Forge Press/Sage.

———. (1991). *The Global City.* Princeton, NJ: Princeton University Press.

Saul, John. (1991, July/August). "South Africa: Between 'Barbarism' and Structural Reform." *New Left Review, 188,* 3–44.

Sawicki, Jana. (1991). Cited under "Social Movement Theory."

Smith, Anthony D. (1993). "Ethnic Election and Cultural Identity." *Ethnic Groups* [Special issue on pre-modern and modern national identity in Russia and Eastern Europe], *10* (1–3), 9–25.

Snow, David, and Robert Benford. (1988). Cited under "Social Movement Theory."

Speer, Albert. (1970). Cited under "Fascists, Nazis, Neo-Nazis."

Stacey, Judith. (1991). Cited under "Conservative Movements and Ideologies."

Taylor, Verta, and Nancy Whittier. (1992). Cited in Aldon D. Morris and Carol McClurg Mueller under "Social Movement Theory."

Useem, Bert, and Mayer Zald. (1987). Cited in Mayer Zald and John McCarthy under "Social Movement Theory."

Wallerstein, Immanuel. (1990). Cited under "Movements in History."

———. (1980). Cited under "Movements in History."

———. (1974). Cited under "Movements in History."

Weinstein, Deena, and Michael Weinstein. (1993). *Postmodern(ized) Simmel.* New York: Routledge.

Willis, Paul. (1990). Cited under "Social Movement Theory."

Wolf, Eric R. (1982). *Europe and the People without History*. Berkeley and Los Angeles: University of California Press.

Wood, Ellen Meiksins. (1994, June 13). "Identity Crisis." *In These Times, 18* (15), 28–29.

Zald, Mayer. (1994). Personal communication.

———, and John McCarthy. (eds.). (1987). Cited under "Social Movement Theory."

Zeitlin, Irving. (1994). Cited under "Social Movement Theory."

Name Index

Subject Index